Local Public Finance and Economics

"This two volume project on the financing and governance of public spending, taxation, and borrowing in federal economies is sure to become the "go-to" reference for practitioners and policy-makers for implementing small changes or major reforms for the efficient and fair financing of national, provincial and local public goods. The authors bring their academic expertise and the wisdom earned through years of experience to the task. Highly recommended."

—Robert Inman, Richard K. Mellon *Professor, Wharton School, University of Pennsylvania*

Harry Kitchen • Melville McMillan
Anwar Shah

Local Public Finance and Economics

An International Perspective

palgrave
macmillan

Harry Kitchen
Department of Economics
Trent University
Peterborough, ON, Canada

Melville McMillan
University of Alberta
Edmonton, AB, Canada

Anwar Shah
Governance Studies
Brookings Institution
Washington, DC, USA

ISBN 978-3-030-21985-7 ISBN 978-3-030-21986-4 (eBook)
https://doi.org/10.1007/978-3-030-21986-4

This Palgrave Macmillan imprint is published by the registered company Springer Nature Switzerland AG
The registered company address is: Gewerbestrasse 11, 6330 Cham, Switzerland

Preface

This book is a part of a two-volume series on local governance: "Local Public Finance and Economics: An International Perspective" as volume 1 and "Local Public, Fiscal and Financial Governance: An International Perspective" as volume 2. This series is intended to serve as a comprehensive guide/reference for policymakers, practitioners, policy analysts and interested researchers, scholars, and students in local public governance and local public finance and economics worldwide. The series would also be of interest to government officials, policymakers, and public policy students internationally as it provides a comprehensive coverage of issues and presents a synthesis of lessons from worldwide experiences in local economic and fiscal governance. The series would also serve as useful reference books for undergraduate and graduate courses in public economics. The existing literature on local public finance and economics has typically a country-specific focus mostly of an industrial country, for example, *State and Local Public Finance* by Ronald Fisher, published by Routledge in 2016, has a US focus. Also, the literature does not give special attention to local public governance issues. This series attempts to fill this void by providing a state-of-the-art synthesis of the academic literature and supplementing it with lessons of experience from both industrial and developing countries. The series further presents one of the most comprehensive treatments of local economic and fiscal governance issues. Some of the newer topics covered include neo-institutional perspectives on the role of local government; tax instruments for environmental protection; performance-based budgeting; output-based intergovernmental transfers; fiscal rules and fiscal discipline; combating corruption; measuring, monitoring, and evaluating local government performance; and worldwide indicators on localization and closeness of the government to its people. In view of this, we hope that this series would be of interest to a wider range of audiences in both industrial and developing countries.

Peterborough, ON, Canada — Harry Kitchen
Edmonton, AB, Canada — Melville McMillan
Washington, DC, USA — Anwar Shah

Acknowledgments

This book represents the knowledge gained from several decades of research and teaching local public economics to graduate and undergraduate students in North America. In addition, it captures the practical experiences of policymakers and practitioners from industrial and developing countries gained through policy advice, senior policymakers, and high-level executives' retreats, conferences, workshops, seminar, and short courses. The authors are grateful to students, practitioners, and policymakers around the globe for enriching their knowledge with the insights gained from these interactions.

The authors are also grateful to their families and the editors of Palgrave Macmillan for their support and encouragement for completion of this volume.

Contents

About the Authors

Harry Kitchen is Professor Emeritus in the Economics Department at Trent University, Canada. Over the past 20 years, he has completed more than 100 articles, reports, studies, and books on issues relating to local government expenditures, finance, structure, and governance in Canada. In addition, he has served as a consultant or advisor for a number of municipal and provincial governments in Canada and the federal government, and has worked on projects in Russia and China. In 2013, he was awarded a Queens Diamond Jubilee medal for policy analysis and research contributions to municipal finance, structure, and governance in Canada. In 2017, he was appointed visiting scholar at the Institute of Municipal Finance and Governance, Munk School of Global Affairs, University of Toronto.

Melville McMillan is Professor Emeritus in the Department of Economics and a fellow of the Institute of Public Economics at the University of Alberta, Canada. McMillan's research and teaching interests are in public economics, particularly urban and local economics, fiscal federalism, and the demand/supply of public goods and services. He has written in these areas and has advised governments and organizations nationally and internationally (e.g., the World Bank). Although "retired," McMillan remains actively involved in academic and policy matters.

Anwar Shah is a senior fellow (non-resident) at the Brookings Institution, Washington, DC, USA; advisor/consultant to the World Bank; and Distinguished Visiting Professor of Economics, Southwestern University of Finance and Economics, Chengdu/Wenjiang, China. He has previously served the Government of Canada (Ministry of Finance), the Government of Alberta, and the UN Intergovernmental Panel on Climate Change. He has written more than two dozen books in English, subsequently translated in Spanish, Chinese, Vietnamese, and Russian languages and numerous articles in leading economic journals on governance, public management reforms, budget reform, federalism, local governance, fiscal reforms, and global climate change issues.

List of Figures

List of Tables

CHAPTER 1

Local Public Finance and Economics: Theory and the Practice—Introduction and Overview

"We will strive increasingly to quicken the public sense of civic duty. Thus in all these ways, we will transmit this city not only not less, but greater and more beautiful than it was transmitted to us."

—Oath of office required of council members in the ancient city of Athens
Source: National League of Cities Website https://www.nlc.org/the-athenian-oath

Introduction

Globalization and the information revolution during the past several decades have motivated a large and growing number of countries around the globe to reexamine the roles of various orders of government and their partnership with the private sector and civil society. These reforms typically involve shifting higher-order government responsibilities to local governments and beyond government providers, with the objectives of strengthening local governance. This movement has generated a large interest in learning from the history of nations as well as from current conceptual views and practices across countries on local government organization and finance.

A large body of conceptual and empirical evidence has also emerged during the past several decades that shows that external aid and technocratic solutions are of little help in alleviating poverty and misery and combat corruption in the developing world. Instead, the key to peace, order, good government, prosperity, growth, and a world free of poverty, hunger,

H. Kitchen et al., *Local Public Finance and Economics*,
https://doi.org/10.1007/978-3-030-21986-4_1

deprivation, and oppression lies in decentralized local governance with home rule that empowers citizens to hold governments to account for ensuring FAIR (fair, accountable, incorruptible, and responsive) governance. Empowered local governments hold the promise of good jobs, good homes, a good life, a good time for the young and the young at heart, and sweet dreams of a prosperous future for all. In an information age with a borderless world economy, where economic success is more closely tied to the competitive advantage garnered by skills and information base, local governments are at the core of the future growth and prosperity of any nation. In an age of mistrust in governments, local governments serve as a tool to overcome a lack of trust and restore confidence in governments through their commitment to improve social and economic outcomes. To meet these great expectations, local governments must be empowered to act as the primary agents of citizens exercising oversight on the shared rule by higher-order governments and beyond government entities in the local area. They must have the authority to act as facilitators of network governance at the local level supervising and coordinating the activities of higher-order governments and beyond government stakeholders such as hope, faith, and interest-based networks, private for profit and non-profit providers, and good Samaritans.

As noted earlier, a silent revolution has swept the globe during the past several decades to bring public decision-making closer to the people. Regrettably though in most parts of the developing world, people empowerment through local self-rule remains an unrealized dream due to path dependency and state capture by political, bureaucratic, and military elites. Formidable political and institutional hurdles stand in the way especially those that impede the poor to shape their own destiny. Reform is eternal; we never fully succeed but we owe it to billions of disempowered citizens of this world to keep trying to usher in a better future for all. This book takes a small step in this regard by bringing the international knowledge on the theory and practice of good local governance to the attention of a wider set of stakeholders and students. This introductory chapter provides foundation material for local governance and introduces the reader to the contents of this volume.[1]

[1] This chapter is a revised version of the introductory chapter in Shah, ed. (2006), "A Comparative Institutional Framework for Responsive, Responsible and Accountable Local Governance" Chapter 1: 1–38.

The chapter begins with an overview of basic concepts. It then provides a synthesis of conceptual perspectives on local government and central-local relations. A comparative analysis of local government organization and finance is also presented. Contrasting experiences of local governance in industrial and developing countries are highlighted. Conclusions of empirical evidence on the impact of localization/decentralization on good governance and growth are summarized. A final section introduces the two-volume series on local public governance and presents an overview of the contents of rest of this volume.

Basic Concepts in Local Government, Local Governance, and Local Public Economics and Finance

Local government refers to specific institutions or entities created by national constitutions (Brazil, Denmark, France, Italy, Japan, Sweden); by state constitutions (Australia, the United States); by ordinary legislation of a higher level of central government (New Zealand, the United Kingdom, most countries); by provincial or state legislation (Canada, India, Pakistan); or by executive order of the central government (China) to deliver a range of specified services to a relatively small geographically delineated area. Local governments are distinct administrative units from intermediate order governments, that is, states and provinces, in most countries. The overall objective of local governments is to maximize economic and social outcomes for residents and provide an enabling environment for private-sector development through efficient provision of local public services in a small geographical area.

Local governance is a broader concept and is defined as the formulation and execution of collective action at the local level to serve public interest. Thus, it encompasses the direct and indirect roles of formal institutions of local government and government hierarchies, as well as the roles of informal norms, networks, community organizations, and neighborhood associations in pursuing collective action by defining the framework for citizen-citizen and citizen-state interactions, collective decision-making, and delivery of local public services. Local governance, therefore, includes the diverse objectives of vibrant, living, working, and environmentally preserved self-governing communities. Good local governance is not just about providing a range of local services but also about preserving the life and liberty of residents, creating space for democratic participation and civic dialogue, supporting market-led and environmentally sustainable local development, and facilitating outcomes that enrich the quality of life of residents.

Local public economics and finance is primarily concerned with the subset of issues in local governance that have a direct bearing on the quantity and quality of local public services and their matching with local preferences and their impact on the economic and social outcomes for local residents and advancing local economic development. Thus it is more focused on local jurisdictional design, local autonomy in provision and finance of local public services, and facilitating network governance and regulating local production of public and private goods. Note that local government's primary role is in the provision of local services, that is, ascertaining local resident's preferences for public services and financing choices and articulating and aggregating local preferences for local public goods and public regulation of private activities. Production of local public services, that is, combining of diverse inputs to produce outputs efficiently and organize methods of delivery to final consumers in the least-cost manner, is a task that can be better done by public and private actors working in partnerships or in competition with each other. Separation of provision and production decisions has important implications for jurisdictional design. Jurisdictional design for provision would focus on ensuring responsiveness to local preferences, whereas technical efficiency considerations such as economies of scale and scope will determine production choices. These choices, however, can be harmonized by networking, contracting, franchising, and vouchering (Oakerson 1999; Ostrom et al. 1962).

Globalization and information revolution have recently created a heightened interest in public economics and finance in view of the growing role of local governments in advancing international competitiveness and growth. Globalization and the information revolution are forcing a reexamination of citizen-state relations and roles and the relationships of various orders of government with entities beyond government—and thereby an enhanced focus on local government and local governance. The concept, however, has yet to be embraced fully by the literature on development economics, because of the longstanding tradition in the development assistance community of focusing on national governments while neglecting the role of local governments or community organizations and the overall local institutional environment that facilitates or retards interconnectivity, cooperation, or competition among organizations, groups, norms, and networks that serve public interest at the local level.

Several writers (Dollery and Wallis 2001; Bailey 1999; Rhodes 1997; Stoker 1999) have recently argued that the presence of a vast network of entities beyond government that are engaged in local services delivery or quality of life issues makes it unrealistic to treat local government as a single entity (see also Goss 2001). Analytical recognition of this broader concept of local governance is critical to developing a framework for local governance. The principle of FAIR local governance requires adherence to that a local government is *fair* (is concerned with inclusiveness of all its residents), *accountable* (to citizens, through a rights-based approach), *incorruptible* (ensures openness and integrity of its operations), *responsive* (doing the right thing—delivering services that are consistent with citizens' preferences or are citizen focused), and *responsible* (doing the right thing the right way—working better but costing less and benchmarking with the best). Such analysis is important because the role of local government in such a setting contrasts sharply with its traditional role.

This chapter traces the evolution and analytical underpinnings of local government and governance as background to a better understanding of local public economics and finance in this book. The next section outlines analytical approaches to local governance that can be helpful in understanding the role of governments and comparing and contrasting institutional arrangements. It further develops a model of local governance that integrates various strands of this literature. This model has important implications for evaluating and reforming local governance in both industrial and developing countries.

The Theory: Conceptual Perspectives on Local Government and Central-Local Relations

Several accepted theories provide a strong rationale for decentralized decision-making and a strong role for local governments, on the grounds of efficiency, accountability, manageability, and autonomy.

- *Stigler's menu.* Stigler (1957) identifies two principles of jurisdictional design:
  - The closer a representative government is to the people, the better it works.
  - People should have the right to vote for the kind and amount of public services they want.

- These principles suggest that decision-making should occur at the lowest level of government consistent with the goal of allocative efficiency. Thus, the optimal size of jurisdiction varies with specific instances of economies of scale and benefit-cost spillovers.
- *The principle of fiscal equivalency.* A related idea on the design of jurisdictions has emerged from the public choice literature. Olson (1969) argues that if a political jurisdiction and benefit area overlap, the free-rider problem is overcome and the marginal benefit equals the marginal cost of production, thereby ensuring optimal provision of public services. Equating the political jurisdiction with the benefit area is called the *principle of fiscal equivalency* and requires a separate jurisdiction for each public service.
- *The correspondence principle.* A related concept is proposed by Oates (1972): the jurisdiction that determines the level of provision of each public good should include precisely the set of individuals who consume the good. This principle generally requires a large number of overlapping jurisdictions. Frey and Eichenberger (1995, 1996, 1999) have extended this idea to define the concept of *functional, overlapping, and competing jurisdictions* (FOCJ). They argue that jurisdictions could be organized along functional lines while overlapping geographically and that individuals and communities could be free to choose among competing jurisdictions. Individuals and communities express their preferences directly through initiatives and referenda. The jurisdictions have authority over their members and the power to raise taxes to fulfill their tasks. The school communities of the Swiss canton of Zurich and special districts in North America follow the FOCJ concept.
- *The decentralization theorem.* According to this theorem, advanced by Oates (1972, p. 55), "each public service should be provided by the jurisdiction having control over the minimum geographic area that would internalize benefits and costs of such provision," because
  - Local governments understand the concerns of local residents.
  - Local decision-making is responsive to the people for whom the services are intended, thus encouraging fiscal responsibility and efficiency, especially if financing of services is also decentralized.
  - Unnecessary layers of jurisdiction are eliminated.
  - Interjurisdictional competition and innovation is enhanced.

An ideal decentralized system ensures a level and combination of public services consistent with voters' preferences while providing incentives for the efficient provision of such services. Some degree of central control or compensatory grants may be warranted in the provision of services when spatial externalities, economies of scale, and administrative and compliance costs are taken into consideration. The practical implications of this theorem, again, require a large number of overlapping jurisdictions.

- *The subsidiarity principle.* According to this principle, taxing, spending, and regulatory functions should be exercised by lower levels of government unless a convincing case can be made for assigning them to higher levels of government. This principle evolved from the social teaching of the Roman Catholic Church and was first proposed by Pope Leo XIII in 1891. Subsequently, Pope Pius XI highlighted the principle of subsidiarity as a third way between dictatorship and a laissez-faire approach to governance. The Maastricht Treaty adopted it as a guiding principle for the assignment of responsibilities among members of the European Union (EU). This principle is the polar opposite of the *residuality principle*, where local governments are assigned functions that the central government is unwilling or thinks it is unable to perform. It also negates the principle of ultra vires where local governments can only undertake tasks defined in law by higher-order government.

Implementation Mechanisms

Achieving the optimal number and size of local jurisdictions requires the operation of community formation processes and the redrawing of jurisdictional boundaries.

- *Voting with feet.* According to Tiebout (1956), people consider tax costs and the public services menu offered by a jurisdiction in deciding where to live. Thus, voting with feet leads to the formation of jurisdictions, creating a market analog for public service provision. Oates (1969) argued that if people vote with their feet, fiscal differentials across communities are capitalized into residential property values. This conclusion has been refuted by formal tests of allocative efficiency proposed by Brueckner (1982) and Shah (1988, 1989, 1992). Both tests suggest that optimal provision of public services is not ensured by voting with feet alone but depends also on rational voting behavior.

- *Voting by ballot.* This line of research suggests that collective decision-making may not ensure maximization of the electorate's welfare, because citizens and their governmental agents can have different goals.
- *Voluntary associations.* Buchanan (1965) postulates that the provision of public services through voluntary associations of people (clubs) ensures the formation of jurisdictions consistent with the optimal provision of public services.
- *Jurisdictional redesign.* An important process for community formation in modern societies is redrawing the boundaries of existing jurisdictions to create consolidated, special, or multi-purpose jurisdictions.

Roles and Responsibilities of Local Governments: Analytical Underpinnings

There are five perspectives on models of government and the roles and responsibilities of local government: (a) traditional fiscal federalism, (b) new public management (NPM), (c) public choice, (d) new institutional economics (NIE), and (e) network forms of local governance. The federalism and the NPM perspectives are concerned primarily with market failures and how to deliver public goods efficiently and equitably. The public choice and NIE perspectives are concerned with government failures. The network forms of governance perspective are concerned with institutional arrangements to overcome both market and government failures.

Local Government as a Handmaiden of a Higher Government Order: Traditional Fiscal Federalism Perspectives

The fiscal federalism approach treats local government as a subordinate tier in a multi-tiered system and outlines principles for defining the roles and responsibilities of orders of government (see Shah 1994, 2004, 2014 for such a framework for the design of fiscal constitutions). Hence, one sees that in most federations, as in Canada and the United States, local governments are extensions of state governments (*dual federalism*). In a few isolated instances, as in Brazil, they are equal partners with higher-level governments (*cooperative federalism*), and in an exceptional case, Switzerland, they (cantons) are the main source of sovereignty and have greater constitutional significance than the federal government (see Switzerland 2003). Thus, depending on the constitutional and legal status of local governments, state governments in federal countries assume varying degrees of oversight of the provision of local public services. Note that this view of federalism contrasts with Kincaid's (1967) idea of a federal state comprising civic republics where civic republics were intended to be autonomous local governments and the federal government discharged responsibilities entrusted to them by civic republics. In a unitary state, subnational governments act on behalf of the central government. Therefore, a useful set of guidelines for the assignment of responsibilities for local public services in a unitary state would be that

- Policy development and standards of service and performance are determined at the national level.
- Implementation oversight is carried out at the state or provincial level.
- Provision and finance of local services by the local governments or by the metropolitan or regional governments.

In all countries, the *production* of services can be public or private or both, at the discretion of local or regional governments. Responsibilities for public services other than such purely local ones as fire protection could be shared, using these guidelines.

The assignment of public services to local governments or to metropolitan or regional governments can be based on considerations such as economies of scale, economies of scope (appropriate bundling of local public services to improve efficiency through information and coordination economies and enhanced accountability through voter participation and cost recovery) and cost-benefit spillovers, proximity to beneficiaries, consumer preferences, and budgetary choices about the composition of spending. The particular level of government to which a service is assigned determines the public or private production of the service in accordance with considerations of efficiency and equity. Large metropolitan areas with populations in excess of one million could be considered for subdivision into a first tier of municipal governments of smaller size responsible for neighborhood-type services and a second tier of metropolitan-wide government providing area-wide services. The first-tier governments could be directly elected, and elected mayors of these governments could form the metropolitan council at the second tier. Two-tier structures for metropolitan governance have been practiced in Melbourne, Australia; Vancouver, Canada; Allegheny county, Pennsylvania, United States; and Stockholm, Sweden.

In industrial countries, special-purpose agencies or bodies deliver a wide range of metropolitan and regional public services, including education, health, planning, recreation, and environmental protection. Such bodies can include library boards, transit and police commissions, and utilities providing water, gas, and electricity. These agencies deal with public services whose delivery areas transcend political jurisdictions and are better financed by loans, user charges, and earmarked benefit taxes, such as a supplementary mill rate on a property tax base to finance a local school board. If kept to a minimum, such agencies help fully exploit economies of scale in the delivery of services where political boundaries are not consistent with service areas. A proliferation of these agencies can undermine accountability and budgetary flexibility at local levels. Accountability and responsiveness to voters are weakened if members of special-purpose bodies are appointed rather than elected. Budgetary flexibility is diminished if a majority of local expenditures fall outside the control of local councils.

Private-sector participation can also take a variety of forms, including contracting through competitive biddings, franchise operations (local government acting as a regulatory agency), grants (usually for recreational and cultural activities), vouchers (redeemable by local government with private providers), volunteers (mostly in fire stations and hospitals), community self-help activities (for crime prevention), and private non-profit organizations (for social services). Thus, a mix of production and delivery systems is appropriate for local public services. In most developing countries, the financial capacities of local governments are quite limited. Fostering private-sector participation in the delivery of local public services thus assumes greater significance. Such participation enhances accountability and choice in the local public sector. However, assigning responsibility for the provision of service to a specific level of government does not imply that government should be directly engaged in its production. Limited empirical evidence suggests that private production and delivery of some services promotes efficiency and equity.

Fiscal federalism literature also provides guidance on financing choices for local governments. Four general principles require consideration in assigning taxing powers to various governments. First, the *economic efficiency* criterion dictates that taxes on mobile factors and tradable goods that have a bearing on the efficiency of the internal common market should be assigned to the center. Subnational assignment of taxes on mobile factors may facilitate the use of socially wasteful "beggar thy neighbor" policies to attract resources to own areas by regional and local governments. In a globalized world, even central assignment of taxes on mobile capital may not be very effective in the presence of tax havens and the difficulty of tracing and attributing incomes from virtual transactions to various physical spaces. Second, *national equity* considerations warrant that progressive redistributive taxes should be assigned to the center, which limits the possibility of regional and local governments following perverse redistribution policies using both taxes and transfers to attract high-income people and repel low-income ones. Doing so, however, leaves open the possibility of supplementary, flat-rate, local charges on residence-based national income taxes. Third, the *administrative feasibility* criterion (lowering compliance and administration costs) suggests that taxes should be assigned to the jurisdiction with the best ability to monitor relevant assessments. This criterion minimizes administrative costs as well as the potential for tax evasion. For example, property, land, and betterment taxes are good candidates for local assignment because local governments are in a better position to assess the market values of such assets. Fourth, the *fiscal need* or *revenue adequacy* criterion suggests that to ensure accountability, revenue means (the ability to raise revenues from own sources) should be matched as closely as possible with expenditure needs. The literature also argues that long-lived assets should primarily be financed by raising debt, so as to ensure equitable burden sharing across generations (Inman 2005). Furthermore, such large and lumpy investments typically cannot be financed by current revenues and reserves alone (see Table 1.1).

These four principles suggest that user charges are suitable for use by all orders of government, but the case for decentralizing taxing powers is not as compelling as that for decentralizing public service delivery. This is because lower-level taxes can introduce inefficiencies in the allocation of resources across the federation and cause inequities among people in different jurisdictions. In addition, collection and compliance costs can increase significantly. These problems are more severe for some taxes than others; so the selection of which taxes to decentralize must be made with care, balancing the need to achieve fiscal and political accountability at the lower levels of government against the disadvantages of having a fragmented tax system. The trade-off between increased accountability and increased economic costs from decentralizing taxing responsibilities can be mitigated by fiscal arrangements that permit joint occupation and harmonization of taxes to overcome fragmentation and by fiscal equalization transfers that will reduce the fiscal inefficiencies and inequities that arise from different fiscal capacities across regional and local governments.

The fiscal federalism perspectives presented above are helpful, but in practice they have resulted in some major difficulties—especially in developing countries—because the practice seems to emphasize fiscal federalism's structures and processes as ends rather than as means to an end. These structures and processes were designed as a response to market failures and

Table 1.1 Key considerations and tools for local government finances

Key considerations

The overall objective of local governments is to maximize social outcomes for residents and provide an enabling environment for private-sector development through efficient provision of public services. This requires that local financing should take into account the following considerations:

- Local government should limit self-financing of redistributive services
- Business should be taxed only for services to businesses and not for redistributive purposes
- Current period services should be financed out of current year operating revenues and future period services should be financed by future period taxes, user charges/fees, and borrowing
- Residential services should be financed by taxes and fees on residents
- Business services should be financed on site/land value taxes and user charges. Profit, output, sales, and moveable asset taxes may drive business out of the jurisdiction

Tools for local finance

- *Local taxes* for services with public goods or public bads characteristics—streets, roads, street lighting (public goods), traffic congestion, water and air pollution (public bads)
- *User charges* for services with private goods characteristics—water, sewerage, solid waste
- *Conditional, nonmatching, output-based grants* from national/state-order governments for merit goods or redistributive public services: education and health
- *Conditional matching grants* for spillovers in some services
- *Unconditional grants* for fiscal gap and equalization purposes
- *Capital grants* for infrastructure if local fiscal capacity is low
- *Capital market finance* for infrastructure if local fiscal capacity is high
- *Development charges* for financing growth with higher charges for developing land on local government boundaries
- *Public-private partnerships* for infrastructure finance but keeping public ownership and control of strategic assets
- *Tax increment financing districts* to deal with urban blight. For this purpose, the area should be designated for redevelopment and annual property tax revenues frozen at pre-vitalization levels. For a specified period, say 15–35 years, all tax revenues above base are used for redevelopment. Capacity improvements are undertaken through municipal borrowing/bonds against expected tax increments

Source: Inman (2005) and Boadway and Shah (2009)

heterogeneous preferences with little recognition of government failures or the role of entities beyond government. The new public management (NPM) and the new institutional economics (NIE) literature (synthesized in the following paragraphs) sheds further light on the origins of these difficulties. This literature highlights the sources of government failures and their implications for the role of local government.

Local Government as an Independent Facilitator of Creating Public Value: New Public Management Perspectives

Two interrelated criteria have emerged from the NPM literature in recent years determining, first, what local governments should do and, second, how they should do it better.

In discussing the first criterion, the literature assumes that citizens are the principals but have multiple roles as governors (owner-authorizers, voters, taxpayers, community members), activist-producers (providers of services, co-producers, self-helpers obliging others to act), and consumers (clients and beneficiaries) (see Moore 1996). In this context, significant emphasis is placed on the government as an agent of the people to serve public interest and create public value. Moore (1996) defines *public value* as measurable improvements in social outcomes or quality of life. This concept is directly relevant to local and municipal services, for which it is feasible to measure such improvements and have some sense of attribution. The concept is useful in evaluating conflicting and perplexing choices in the use of local resources. The concept is also helpful in defining the role of government, especially local governments. It frames the debate between those who argue that the public sector crowds out private-sector investments and those who argue that the public sector creates an enabling environment for the private sector to succeed, in addition to providing basic municipal and social services.

Moore (1996) has argued that, rather than diverting resources from the private sector, local governments use some of the resources that come as free goods—namely, resources of consent, goodwill, good Samaritan values, community spirit, compliance, and collective public action. This argument suggests that the role of public managers in local governments is to tap these free resources and push the frontiers of improved social outcomes beyond what may be possible with meager local revenues. Thus, public managers create value by mobilizing and facilitating a network of providers beyond local government. Democratic accountability ensures that managerial choices about creating public value are based on broader consensus by local residents (see Goss 2001). Thus, the local public sector continuously strives to respect citizen preferences and to be accountable to them. This environment, focused on creating public value, encourages innovation and experimentation, bounded by the risk tolerance of the median voter in each community.

The main current of the NPM literature is concerned not with what to do but with how to do it better. It argues for an incentive environment in which managers are given flexibility in the use of resources but held accountable for results. Top-down controls are thus replaced by a bottom-up focus on results. Two NPM models have been implemented in recent years. The first model is focused on *making managers manage*. In New Zealand, this goal is accomplished through *new contractualism*, whereby public managers are bound by formal contracts for service delivery but have flexibility in resource allocation and choice of public or private providers. Malaysia attempts to achieve the same through client charters, under which public managers are evaluated for their attainment of specified service standards (Shah 2005a).

The second model creates incentives to *let managers manage*. It applies the new managerialism approach, as used in Australia and the United States, whereby government performance in service delivery and social outcomes is monitored, but there are no formal contracts, and accountability is guided by informal agreements. In China and the United Kingdom, autonomous agency models are used for performance accountability. Canada uses an alternative service delivery framework: public managers are encouraged to facilitate a network of service providers and to use benchmarking to achieve the most effective use of public monies. The emerging focus on client orientation and results-based accountability is encouraging local governments to innovate in many parts of the world (Caulfield 2003).

Local Government as an Institution to Advance Self-Interest: The Public Choice Approach

Bailey (1999) has conceptualized four models of local government:

- A local government that assumes it knows best and acts to maximize the welfare of its residents conforms to the *benevolent despot* model.
- A local government that provides services consistent with local residents' willingness to pay conforms to the *fiscal exchange* model.
- A local government that focuses on public service provision to advance social objectives conforms to the *fiscal transfer* model.
- A local government that is captured by self-interested bureaucrats and politicians conforms to the *Leviathan* model, which is consistent with the public choice perspectives.

In the same tradition, Breton (1995) provides a comprehensive typology of models of government. He distinguishes two broad types of government. The first embodies the doctrine of the common good, and the second acts to preserve the self-interest of the governing elites. The second type can assume either a monolithic or a composite structure. In a monolithic structure, local government is subject to capture by bureaucrats or interest groups. Also, local government may maximize economic rents for dominant interest groups (as in the Leviathan model) or may advance compulsion or coercion. If the self-interest model assumes a composite structure, it may encourage Tiebout-type competition among local governments.

The public choice literature endorses the self-interest doctrine of government and argues that various stakeholders involved in policy formulation and implementation are expected to use opportunities and resources to advance their self-interest. This view has important implications for the design of local government institutions. For local governments to serve the interests of people, they must have complete local autonomy in taxing and spending and they must be subject to competition within and beyond government. In the absence of these prerequisites, local governments will be inefficient and unresponsive to citizen preferences (Boyne 1998). Bailey (1999) advocates strengthening exit and voice mechanisms in local governance to overcome government failures associated with the self-interest doctrine of public choice. He suggests that easing supply side constraints for public services through wider competition will enhance choice and promote exit options and that direct democracy provisions will strengthen voice (see also Dollery and Wallis 2001). The NIE approach discussed below draws on the implications of opportunistic behavior by government agents for the transaction costs to citizens as principals.

The Government as a Runaway Train: NIE Concerns with the Institutions of Public Governance

The NIE provides a framework for analyzing fiscal systems and local empowerment and for comparing mechanisms for local governance. This framework is helpful in designing multiple orders of government and in clarifying local government responsibilities in a broader framework of local governance. According to the NIE framework, various orders of governments (as agents) are created to serve the interests of the citizens as principals. The jurisdictional design should ensure that these agents serve the public interest while minimizing transaction costs for the principals.

The existing institutional framework does not permit such optimization, because the principals have bounded rationality, that is, they make the best choices on the basis of the information at hand but are ill informed about government operations. Enlarging the sphere of their knowledge entails high transaction costs, which citizens are not willing to incur. Those costs include participation and monitoring costs, legislative costs, executive decision-making costs, agency costs or costs incurred to induce compliance by agents with the compact, and uncertainty costs associated with unstable political regimes (Horn 1997; Shah 2005b). Agents (various orders of governments) are better informed about government operations than principals are, but they have an incentive to withhold information and to indulge in opportunistic behaviors or "self-interest seeking with guile" (Williamson 1985, p. 7). Thus, the principals have only incomplete contracts with their agents. Such an environment fosters commitment problems because the agents may not follow the compact.

The situation is further complicated by three factors—weak or extant countervailing institutions, path dependency, and the interdependency of various actions. Countervailing institutions such as the judiciary, police, parliament, and citizen activist groups are usually weak and unable to restrain rent-seeking by politicians and bureaucrats. Historical and cultural factors and mental models by which people see little benefits to and high costs of activism prevent corrective action. Further empowering local councils to take action on behalf of citizens often leads to loss of agency between voters and councils, because council members may interfere in executive decision-making or may get co-opted in such operations while shirking their legislative responsibilities. The NIE framework stresses the need to use various elements of transaction costs in designing jurisdictions for various services and in evaluating choices between competing governance mechanisms.

Local Government as a Facilitator of Network Forms of Local Governance

The NIE approach provides an evaluation framework for alternative forms and mechanisms of local governance. It specifically provides guidance in dealing with government failures in a hierarchical form of public governance. The framework is also suitable for examining local government involvement in a partnership of multiple organizations. Dollery and Wallis (2001) extend the NIE approach to these issues. They argue that a structure of resource dependency vitiates against collective action in the interest of the common good because of the tragedy of commons associated with common pool resources. This scenario results in failures in horizontal coordination in a multiorganization partnership.

One possible solution is to introduce a market mechanism of governance, whereby a contract management agency enters into binding contracts with all partners. However, this solution is unworkable because the potential number of contingencies may simply be too large to be covered by such contracts. A second approach to overcome horizontal coordination, the so-called hierarchical mechanism of governance, relies on institutional arrangements to clarify roles and responsibilities and to establish mechanisms for consultation, cooperation, and coordination, as is done in some federal systems. Such institutional arrangements entail high transaction costs and are subject to a high degree of failure attributable to the conflicting interests of partners.

Given the high transaction costs and perceived infeasibility of market and hierarchical mechanisms of governance for partnerships of multiple organizations, a network mechanism of governance has been advanced as a possible mode of governance for such partnerships—the kind to be managed by local governments. The network form of governance relies on trust, loyalty, and reciprocity between partners with no formal institutional safeguards. Networks formed on the basis of shared interests (interest-based networks) can provide a stable form of governance if membership is limited to partners that can make significant resource contributions and if there is a balance of powers among members. Members of such networks interact frequently and see cooperation in one area as contingent on cooperation in other areas. Repeated interaction among members builds trust. Hope-based networks are built on the shared sentiments and emotions of members. Members have shared beliefs in the worth and philosophy of the network goals and have the passion and commitment to achieve those goals. The stability of such networks is highly dependent on the commitment and style of their leadership (Dollery and Wallis 2001).

Local government has an opportunity to play a catalytic role in facilitating the roles of both interest-based and hope-based networks in improving social outcomes for local residents. To play such a role, local government must develop a strategic vision of how such partnerships can be formed and sustained. But then the local government requires a new local public management paradigm. Such a paradigm demands local government to separate policy advice from program implementation, assuming a role as a purchaser of public services but not necessarily as a provider of them. Local government may have to outsource services with higher production costs and subject in-house providers to competitive pressures from outside providers to lower transaction costs for citizens. It also must actively seek the engagement of both interest-based and hope-based networks to supplant local services. It needs to develop the capacity to play a mediating role among various groups.

A Synthesis: Toward a Framework for Responsive, Responsible, and Accountable Local Governance

We have reviewed ideas emerging from the literature on political science, economics, public administration, law, federalism, and the NIE with a view to developing an integrated analytical framework for the comparative analysis of local government and local governance institutions.

The dominant concern in this literature is that the incentives and accountability framework faced by various orders of government is not conducive to a focus on service delivery consistent with citizen preferences. As a result, corruption, waste, and inefficiencies permeate public governance. Top-down hierarchical controls are ineffective; there is little accountability because citizens are not empowered to hold governments accountable.

Fiscal federalism practices around the world are focused on structures and processes, with little regard for outputs and outcomes. These practices support top-down structures with preeminent federal legislation (i.e., federal legislation overrides any subnational legislation). The central government is at the apex, exercising direct control and micromanaging the system. Hierarchical controls exercised by various layers of government have an internal rule-based focus with little concern for their mandates. Government competencies are determined on the basis of technical and administrative capacity, with almost no regard for client orientation, bottom-up accountability, and lowering of transaction costs for citizens. Various orders of government indulge in uncooperative zero-sum games for control.

This tug of war leads to large swings in the balance of powers. Shared rule is a source of much confusion and conflict, especially in federal systems. Local governments are typically handmaidens of states or provinces and given straitjacket mandates. They are given only limited home rule in their competencies. In short, local governments in this system of "federalism for the governments, by the governments, and of the governments" get crushed under a regime of intrusive controls by higher levels of governments. Citizens also have limited voice and exit options.

The governance implications of such a system are quite obvious. Various orders of government suffer from agency problems associated with incomplete contracts and undefined property rights, as the assignment of taxing, spending, and regulatory powers remains to be clarified—especially in areas of shared rule. Intergovernmental bargaining leads to high transaction costs for citizens. Universalism and pork-barrel politics result in a tragedy of commons, as various orders of government compete to claim a higher share of common pool resources. Under this system of governance, citizens are treated as agents rather than as principals.

On how to reverse this trend and make governments responsive and accountable to citizens, the dominant themes emphasized in the literature are the subsidiarity principle, the principle of fiscal equivalency, the creation of public value, results-based accountability, and the minimization of transaction costs for citizens, as discussed earlier. These themes are useful but should be integrated into a broader framework of citizen-centered governance, to create an incentive environment in the public sector that is compatible with a public sector focus on service delivery and bottom-up accountability. Such integration is expected to deal with the commitment problem in various levels of government by empowering citizens and by limiting their agents' ability to indulge in opportunistic behavior.

Citizen-centric local governance. Reforming the institutions of local governance requires agreement on basic principles. Four basic principles of FAIR (fair, accountable, incorruptible, and responsive) governance are advanced to initiate such a discussion:

- *Fair governance.* This principle aims for inclusive and equitable local governance.
- *Accountable governance.* A local government should be accountable to its electorate. It should adhere to appropriate safeguards to ensure that it serves the public interest with integrity. Legal and institutional reforms may be needed to enable local governments to deal with accountability between elections—reforms such as a citizen's charter and a provision for recall of public officials.
- *Incorruptible governance.* A local government should ensure transparency and integrity of its operations.
- *Responsive and responsible governance.* This principle aims for governments to do the right things—that is, to deliver services consistent with citizen preferences. The government should also do it right—that is, manage its fiscal resources prudently. It should earn the trust of residents by working better and costing less and by managing fiscal and social risks for the community. It should strive to improve the quality and quantity of and access to public services. To do so, it needs to benchmark its performance with the best-performing local government (see Table 1.2).

Table 1.2 Salient features of citizen-centric FAIR local governance

Fair governance	
Specifies and meets standards for access to local services Improves economic and social outcomes Offers security of life and property	Offers shelter and food for all Has clean air, safe water, and sanitation Honest and fair tax administration
Accountable governance	
Lets the sunshine in: • Local government bylaw on citizens' right to know • Budgetary proposals and annual performance reports posted on the internet • All decisions, including the costs of concessions, posted on the internet • Value for money performance audits by independent think tanks • Open information and public assessment	Is fiscally prudent: • Operating budget in balance • Golden rule for borrowing • New capital projects that specify upkeep costs and how debt is to be repaid • Conservative fiscal rules to ensure sustainable debt levels • Major capital projects that are subject to referenda Maintenance of positive net worth
Incorruptible governance	
• Professionalism and integrity of staff • Safeguards against malfeasance • Streamlined processes and e-governance	• General administration costs subjected to public scrutiny • Commercially audited financial statements • Complaints and feedback acted on
Responsive and responsible governance	
Responsive governance: Has subsidiarity and home rule Has direct democracy provisions Has budget priorities consistent with citizens' preferences Has a noise-free and preserved environment Offers ease of commute and pothole-free roads Has primary school at a walking distance Has acceptable fire and ambulance response times Has libraries and internet access Has park and recreation programs and facilities *Responsible governance*: Follows due process: • The principle of ultra vires or general competence or community governance • The procedure bylaw • Local master plans and budgets • Zoning bylaws and regulations • Funded mandates Earns trust: • Strict compliance with service standards • Citizen-friendly output budgets and service delivery performance reports • Participatory budgeting and planning	Works better and costs less: • All tasks subjected to alternative service delivery test—that is, competitive provision involving government providers and entities beyond government • Financing that creates incentives for competition and innovation • Comparative evaluation of service providers • Public sector as a purchaser through performance contracts but not necessarily a provider of services • Managerial flexibility, but accountability for results • No lifelong or rotating appointments • Task specialization • Budgetary allocation and output-based performance contracts • Activity-based costing • Charges for capital use • Accrual accounting • Benchmarking with the best • Boundaries that balance benefits and costs of scale and scope economies, externalities, and decision-making • Boundaries consistent with fiscal sustainability

Source: Shah (2006) and Boadway and Shah (2009)

A framework of local governance that embodies these principles is called *citizen-centric FAIR governance* (Andrews and Shah 2005). The distinguishing features of citizen-centered governance are

- Citizen empowerment through a rights-based approach (direct democracy provisions, citizens' charter)
- Bottom-up accountability for results
- Evaluation of government performance as the facilitator of a network of providers by citizens as governors, taxpayers, and consumers of public services

The framework emphasizes reforms that strengthen the role of citizens as the principals and create incentives for government agents to comply with their mandates.

The commitment problem may be mitigated by creating citizen-centric local governance—by having direct democracy provisions, introducing governing for results in government operations, and reforming the structure of governance, thus shifting decision-making closer to the people. Direct democracy provisions require referenda on major issues and large projects and require that citizens have the right to veto any legislation or government program. A "governing for results" framework requires government accountability to citizens for service delivery performance. Hence, citizens have a charter defining their basic rights as well as their rights of access to specific standards of public services. Output-based intergovernmental transfers strengthen compliance with such standards and strengthen accountability and citizen empowerment (Shah 2006).

Implications for Division of Powers Within Nations: Role Reversals for Central and Local Governments

The framework described above has important implications for reforming the structure of government. Top-down mandates on local governance will need to be replaced by bottom-up compacts. Furthermore, the role of local government must be expanded to serve as a catalyst for the formulation, development, and operation of a network of both government providers and entities beyond government. Local government's traditionally acknowledged technical capacity becomes less relevant in this framework. More important are its institutional strengths as a purchaser of services and as a facilitator of alliances, partnerships, associations, clubs, and networks for developing social capital and improving social outcomes. Two distinct options are possible in this regard, and both imply a pivotal role for local governments in the intergovernmental system. The options are (a) local government as the primary agent, subcontracting to local providers, state, and federal or central government authorities and engaging networks and entities beyond government, and (b) local, state, and national governments as independent agents.

Option A: Local governments as primary agents of citizens. In this role, a local government serves as (a) a purchaser of local services, (b) a facilitator of networks of government providers and entities beyond government, and (c) a gatekeeper and overseer of state and national governments for the shared rule or responsibilities delegated to them. This role represents a fundamental shift in the division of powers from higher to local governments. It has important constitutional implications. Residual functions reside with local governments. State governments perform intermunicipal services. The national government is assigned redistributive, security, foreign relations, and interstate functions such as harmonization and consensus on a common framework. The Swiss system bears close affinity to this model.

Option B: Various orders of government as independent agents. An alternative framework for establishing the supremacy of the principals is to clarify the responsibilities and functions of various orders as independent agents. This framework limits shared rule. Finance follows function strictly, and fiscal arrangements are periodically reviewed for fine-tuning. Local governments enjoy home rule, with complete tax and expenditure autonomy. The Brazilian fiscal constitution incorporates some features of this model, albeit with significant deviations.

Feasibility of options. Option A is well grounded in the history of modern governments and is most suited for countries with no history of internal or external conflict in recent times. It is already practiced in Switzerland. War, conquest, and security concerns have led to a reversal of the roles of various orders of governments and to a reduction in local government functions in more recent history. Globalization and the information revolution have already brought pressures for much larger and stronger roles for local governments (see Shah 2001). Although a majority of governments have done some tinkering with their fiscal systems, the radical change recommended here is not in the cards anywhere. This is because the unlikelihood of overcoming path dependency—a tall order for existing institutions and vested interests—makes such reform infeasible. Under such circumstances, option B may be more workable, but here the clarity of responsibilities may not be politically feasible. In general, there is unlikely to be political will to undertake such bold reforms. Piecemeal adaptation of this model will nevertheless be forced on most countries by the effects of globalization and by citizen empowerment, facilitated by the information revolution.

A Comparative Analysis of Local Government Organization and Finance in the World

The following paragraphs highlight a few comparative features of local governments drawn from a comprehensive data-set for 182 countries developed by Ivanyna and Shah (2014).

Administrative Structure and Size

The number of local-government tiers varies from one to four in various countries. Having two tiers is the most common practice. Countries in the South and East Asia region have higher than average tiers. The number of local-government tiers varies inversely with the average per capita income of the country (see Table 1.3).

Table 1.3 Local government administrative tiers, population size, and area: a world view

	# Tiers		*Average population (thousand)*		*Av. area (thousand square kilometers (tsk)*	
	Mean	*Standard deviation*	*Mean*	*Standard deviation*	*Mean*	*Standard deviation*
Total	2.03	0.8	101.06	175.47	2.13	6.95
By region						
Southern Asia	2.43	0.98	79.76	75.5	0.32	0.58
Europe and Central Asia	2	0.74	29.49	56.28	0.29	0.4
Middle East and North Africa	2	0.86	111.79	116.41	5.14	15.68
Sub-Saharan Africa	2.02	0.76	171.64	178.56	4.09	8
Latin America and Caribbean	1.74	0.63	63.16	51.88	1.12	1.73
East Asia and Pacific	2.5	1	171.4	379.83	1.22	2.53
North America	2	0	11.6	6.79	1.32	1.72
By income						
High income	1.69	0.67	72.51	119.35	1.13	2.71
Middle upper income	1.76	0.72	67.3	78.76	4.09	13.25
Middle lower income	2.35	0.76	93.92	246.42	1.12	2.32
Low income	2.26	0.82	162.25	178.02	2.58	5.45

Source: Ivanyna and Shah (2014, p. 8)

Average population size of a local government is 101,000 with East Asia, Sub-Sahara, and Middle East and North Africa region having above average population size. Local governments in Europe (29,000) and North America (12,000) have relatively smaller average population sizes than the rest of the world. Lower-income countries have typically larger population size local governments.

Average area of local government is 2.1,000 square kilometers (tsk) with local governments in higher-income countries having much lower than average size.

Relative Importance

Local government relative importance is typically assessed either by local government share of national public expenditures or by national public employment. Both indicators show that relative importance of local government in most countries is quite weak. Notable exceptions are Scandinavian countries, China, Japan, and South Korea.

On average local expenditures account for 15 percent of national expenditures, with a minimum of 0 percent in several countries and a maximum of 67 percent in China. In 39 countries local governments account for less than 2 percent of national expenditures. In Scandinavian countries and in South Korea and Japan, local governments account for close to 50 percent or higher of national expenditures.

Local government share of national public employment has a world average of 23 percent with a minimum of 0 percent in seven countries and a maximum of 90 percent in China. In five countries (China, Albania, Finland, Norway, and Sweden), local governments account for more than three-fourth of public employment.

Security of Existence

Constitutional-legal status of local government does not necessarily insure against arbitrarily dismissal of local governments. Ivanyna and Shah (2014) note that only 6 out of 182 countries in their sample had any significant de-jure safeguards against arbitrary dismissal by higher-order governments. In practice though, historically, local governments in Europe, North America, and Brazil have had secure existence, whereas their counterparts in Africa and Middle East did not fare well in this regard.

Autonomy of Local Governments

Local governments work best when they enjoy home rule in a designated small geographic area, characterized by political, fiscal, and administrative autonomy from higher-order governments.

Political autonomy. Key indicators of political autonomy are that members of local legislature and the head of local executive are directly elected by local residents and are accountable to them for the security of their tenure. Local citizen-based accountability is typically asserted through direct democracy provisions. These are legislative provisions for obligatory local referenda for major spending, taxing and regulatory decisions, recall of public officials, and requirement for direct citizen participation in local decision-making processes.

Elected local councils permeate the scene with only one-third of the countries placing some restraint on direct elections. Direct elections of local executive heads are relatively less common with some restrictions of direct elections in three-fourth countries. Direct democracy provisions are even less frequently observed and about 40 percent of countries do not empower direct participation of citizens in local decision-making. Sub-Sahara Africa and the Middle East regions score poorly on all three indicators of local empowerment.

Fiscal autonomy. Local governments enjoy fiscal autonomy when their revenue means are consistent with their expenditure needs, that is, either having little or no *vertical fiscal gap*, that is, fiscal deficiency or such a gap/deficiency is filled by unconditional higher-order transfers; they have reasonable access to self-finance without recourse to higher-order governments (*tax autonomy*); they have access to credit market finance for infrastructure based upon their creditworthiness; and they have the ability to decide on the menu of public services and spending priorities consistent with local preferences (*expenditure autonomy*). In practice, local government fiscal autonomy is quite weak as large vertical fiscal gaps exist in local financing with a world average of 66 percent. In most countries local governments have limited access and control over local taxes and charges. Typically, they have control over only a third of their finances. They enjoy autonomy over about two-thirds of their spending. While infrastructure deficiencies are large, local governments have either no access to capital market finance or such access is highly constrained by higher-order government regulations.

Administrative autonomy. Administrative autonomy refers to a local government having the ability to hire, fire, and set terms of reference of local employment as well as having regulatory control over own functions. In practice, local government administrative autonomy is highly constrained in most countries. Only in about one-fourth of countries, local governments enjoy administrative autonomy. These countries are mostly in Europe, the Americas, and the Australia regions. In about half of the countries, central government retains control over HR policies for local government.

Contrasting Experience with Local Governance in Industrial and Developing Countries

Local Governance in Industrial Countries

Historical evolution and the current practice of local governance are instructive in drawing lessons for reform of local governance, especially in developing countries. There is great diversity in practice in local governance in industrial countries, but there are also some common strands. The diversity is in the institutional arrangements, which have evolved incrementally over a long period. This evolution has resulted in diverse roles for local governments and diverse relations with central governments across countries. In Nordic countries, local government serves as the primary agent of the people, whereas in Australia, that role is entrusted to state governments, and local government has a minimal role in local affairs (McMillan 2008).

There is no uniform model for local government size, structure, tiers, and functions across Organisation for Economic Co-operation and Development (OECD) countries. There are nevertheless a number of interesting common features. First, most countries recognize that finance must follow function to ensure that local governments are able to meet their responsibilities efficiently and equitably. Second, home rule is considered critical to meeting local expectations and being responsive to local residents. Therefore, local governments must have significant taxing, spending, and regulatory autonomy, and they must have the ability to hire, fire, and set terms of reference for employees without having to defer to higher levels of governments. Only then can local governments innovate in management by introducing performance-based accountability and innovate in service delivery by forging alternative service delivery arrangements through competitive provision, contracting, and outsourcing wherever deemed appropriate. They can also facilitate a broader network of local governance and harness the energies of the whole community to foster better social outcomes. Third and most important, accountability to local residents has been the factor most critical to the success of local governance in industrial countries. This accountability is strengthened through democratic choice, participation, transparency, performance budgeting, citizens' charters of rights, and various legal and financing provisions that support wider voice, choice, and exit options to residents.

Local Governance in Developing Countries

In the past local governance was the most neglected aspect of national governance in developing countries but recent years have seen some positive developments. With the silent revolutions of past three decades, local governments are increasingly assuming a larger role in public services delivery. However, with the exception of a handful of countries such as Brazil, China, and Poland, local governments continue to play a very small role in people's lives. They typically are bounded by the principle of ultra vires and allowed to discharge only a small number of functions, which are mandated from above. They have limited autonomy in expenditure decisions and hardly any in revenue-raising decisions. Their access to own-source revenues is constrained to a few nonproductive bases. Political and bureaucratic leaders at the local level show little interest in lobbying for more taxing powers and instead devote all their energies to seeking higher levels of fiscal transfers.

As a result, tax decentralization has not kept pace with political and expenditure decentralization. Hence, one does not find many examples of tax-base sharing, and even the limited existing bases available to local governments are typically underexploited. Fiscal transfers typically finance 60 percent of revenues in developing countries as opposed to only 33 percent in OECD countries. This distinct separation of taxing and spending decisions undermines accountability to local citizens because local leaders do not have to justify local spending decisions to their electorates.

Local self-financing is important for strengthening governance, efficiency, and accountability. Although most countries have opted for formula-driven fiscal transfers, the design of these transfers remains flawed. They do not create any incentive for setting national minimum standards or accountability for results and typically do not serve regional fiscal equity objectives either.

Local governments also typically have very limited autonomy in hiring and firing local government employees. In a number of countries with decentralization, such as Indonesia and Pakistan, higher government employees are simply transferred to local levels; financing is then provided to cover their wage costs. This approach limits budgetary flexibility and opportunities for efficient resource allocation at the local level.

Overall, local governments in developing countries typically follow the old model of local governance and simply provide directly a narrow range of local services. The new vision, with the local governments assuming a network facilitator role to enrich the quality of life of local residents, as discussed earlier in this chapter, is yet to be realized in any developing country.

Strength of Local Governments and Its Impact on Good Governance and Growth

Decentralization whereby local governments are empowered to make all policy and program decisions on behalf of their resident-voters represents a complex system of political, administrative, and fiscal autonomy and associated accountability mechanisms to ensure responsiveness and accountability to voters. In theory, such a system is expected to have positive impacts on the efficiency and equity of public service provision and provide an enabling environment to foster economic growth. In practice, these outcomes depend upon the existing institutional arrangements (including power relations) and coherence of decentralization policies to create the proper incentive environment for bottom-up accountability. This explains the myriad of outcomes that we see in practice. Nevertheless, a survey of empirical evidence presented by Boadway and Shah (2009) is broadly supportive of a positive influence of localization/decentralization policies on service delivery, macro management, integrity of governance (combating corruption), and economic growth. Shah (2010, 2014) further shows that countries with stronger local governments and with leaner intermediate order (provincial/state) governments do better than countries with stronger provinces and weaker local governments on all indicators of good governance and growth.

Recent empirical work by Ivanyna and Shah (2014) shows that strength of local governance as measured by closeness of public decision-making to the people is positively associated with higher human development index, lower incidence of corruption, and higher gross domestic product (GDP) per capita growth. They further demonstrate that comparative indexes on the strength of local governance

> could have predicted well in advance with a fair degree of accuracy, the countries that were ripe for popular people revolt such as the one experiences through the Arab Spring or similar movements across the globe that seek revolutionary changes in the political and economic systems to empower voiceless people. (Such indexes) further explain occasional popular revolts even in decentralized countries such as recent protests against government priorities that favored sports complexes over social services in public spending in Brazil. In this latter group of countries, citizen empowerment stimulates greater citizen activism to hold the government to account by delivering services consistent with local preferences. The indexes also provide useful barometers of the enabling environment for doing business or promoting growth and economic development and good governance (p. 33).

Conclusions of Conceptual and Comparative Analysis

We have presented a brief overview of the conceptual and institutional literature on local governance. A synthesis of the conceptual literature suggests that the modern role of a local government is to deal with market failures as well as government failures. This role requires a local government to operate as a purchaser of local services, a facilitator of networks of government providers and entities beyond government, and a gatekeeper and overseer of state and national governments in areas of shared rule. Local government also needs to play a mediator's role among various entities and networks to foster greater synergy and harness the untapped energies of the broader community for improving the quality of life of residents. Globalization and the information revolution are reinforcing those conceptual perspectives on a catalytic role for local governments.

This view is also grounded in the history of industrial nations and ancient civilizations in China and India. Local government was the primary form of government until wars and conquest led to the transfer of local government responsibilities to central and regional governments. This trend continued unabated until globalization and the information revolution highlighted the weaknesses of centralized rule for improving the quality of life and social outcomes. The new vision of local governance (Table 1.4) presented here argues for a leadership role by local governments in a multicentered, multi-order, or multilevel system. This view is critical to creating and sustaining citizen-centered governance, in which citizens are the ultimate sovereigns and various orders of governments serve as agents in the supply of public governance. In developing countries, such citizen empowerment may be the only way to reform public sector governance when governments are either unwilling or unable to reform themselves.

Table 1.4 The role of a local government under the new vision of local governance

Old view: twentieth century	*New view: twenty-first century*
Is based on residuality and local governments as wards of the state	Is based on subsidiarity and home rule
Is based on principle of ultra vires	Is based on community governance
Is focused on government	Is focused on citizen-centered local governance
Is agent of the central government	Is the primary agent for the citizens and leader and gatekeeper for shared rule
Is responsive and accountable to higher-level governments	Is responsive and accountable to local voters; assumes leadership role in improving local governance
Is direct provider of local services	Is purchaser of local services
Is focused on in-house provision	Is facilitator of network mechanisms of local governance, coordinator of government providers and entities beyond government, mediator of conflicts, and developer of social capital
Is focused on secrecy	Is focused on letting the sunshine in; practices transparent governance
Has input controls	Recognizes that results matter
Is internally dependent	Is externally focused and competitive; is ardent practitioner of alternative service delivery framework
Is closed and slow	Is open, quick, and flexible
Has intolerance for risk	Is innovative; is risk taker within limits
Depends on central directives	Is autonomous in taxing, spending, regulatory, and administrative decisions
Is rules driven	Has managerial flexibility and accountability for results
Is bureaucratic and technocratic	Is participatory; works to strengthen citizen voice and exit options through direct democracy provisions, citizens' charters, and performance budgeting
Is coercive	Is focused on earning trust, creating space for civic dialogue, serving the citizens, and improving social outcomes
Is fiscally irresponsible	Is fiscally prudent; works better and costs less
Is exclusive with elite capture	Is inclusive and participatory
Overcomes market failures	Overcomes market and government failures
Is boxed in a centralized system	Is connected in a globalized and localized world

Source: Shah (2006, p. 37)

Overview of This Volume

This volume is part of a two-volume series on local fiscal and economic governance issues.

Volume one (this volume) is focused on local public economics and finance and covers local government organization and assignment of expenditure and revenue raising, service delivery and regulatory responsibilities, and higher-order fiscal transfers and methods of capital and financing.

Volume two (forthcoming) presents an international perspective on local public, fiscal, and financial governance. It covers review of newer approaches in local public, fiscal, and financial management, local government integrity and financial accountability, political economy of local government reform imperatives and measurement approaches to local autonomy, and closeness of public decision-making to the people. Topics covered include alternate service delivery framework, local revenue administration, administration of property taxes, municipal budgeting and accounting, local performance budgeting, local fiscal discipline, decentralized provision and corruption, measuring and monitoring local government performance, municipal mergers, intermunicipal cooperation, and worldwide indicators on decentralization and localization.

The following paragraphs provide a brief overview of various chapters in this volume.

Chapter 2 provides a conceptual overview of the principles of expenditure and revenue assignment to local governments. Local government is seen to be more aware of local preferences and conditions and more accountable to local residents than senior governments providing local services. Hence, in many cases, decentralization to local governments is expected to be welfare improving but that requires an appropriate allocation of responsibilities and revenues. Core and noncore responsibilities are distinguished (e.g., local streets versus schooling). Financing follows function. Financing first follows the benefit criterion, that is, local residents pay for the local services from which they benefit—with user charges and local taxes although grants may be needed. Various (especially) noncore services involve interjurisdictional spillovers and/or redistributive considerations and so, if assigned to local governments, require intergovernmental transfers to achieve efficiency and equity objectives. Financing alternatives and appropriate uses are reviewed.

Chapter 3 surveys the fiscal structure of local government across the major industrial countries and to draw lessons from their practices and experience. The approach uses broad comparisons of local governments' expenditures and revenues to illustrate the diversity of practices across countries and to provide insight into how and why quite different arrangements can be workable fiscal arrangements. In contrast to core services, local government responsibility for social programs and the funding of those programs are the major determinants of differences among countries.

Chapter 4 is concerned with the size, structure, and responsibilities of local governments and local government jurisdictional design options. The recent trend where the municipal sector has attempted to increase its reliance on own-source funding and reduce its dependence on grants has been accompanied by a renewed interest in municipal structure and organization. This includes interest in municipal consolidations, amalgamations, and reliance on voluntary arrangements including intermunicipal agreements and/or service boards to improve the overall efficiency of the municipal sector. Municipal amalgamations, consolidations, and restructuring generally occur in response to the rapid increase in urbanization, a need to provide additional services passed down from senior levels of government, the desire of senior levels of government to deal with fewer municipalities, and the necessity of getting access to a local tax base that encompasses a wide geographical area.

Chapter 5 is focused on core local services and regulations. There are a set of services that local governments conventionally provide—that is core services. Those typically include services benefiting property (e.g., streets and roads), recreational and cultural services, and regulation of local activities (e.g., land use). The range of core services is examined and regulatory activities are reviewed in this chapter. Core services contrast with social services (e.g., schooling) for which responsibility assignments vary widely among countries.

Chapter 6 reviews expenditure and service delivery arrangements for social services. Responsibilities of local governments for social services—specifically schooling, health care, and social protection programs—vary substantially across countries. That variation accounts for the considerable differences found in the magnitudes of their budgets and in local governments' relative roles in the countries' public sectors. This chapter examines the roles of local government in the three areas in an effort to better understand the differences among those services, the differences across countries in the responsibility assignments among governments, and the implications for local public finance.

Chapter 7 provides an in-depth review of issues in local public infrastructure provision and finance. Local governments provide a notably large share of government infrastructure. Growing concern over the state of local government infrastructure in both developing and developed countries has highlighted the importance of capital expenditures and the way in which they are financed. Infrastructure funds may be drawn from a variety of internal sources including operating revenues (local taxes and user fees), earmarked taxes, reserves, special charges consisting of specific assessments, development charges, and other exactions made up of value capture levies, density bonusing, linkage fees, and parkland dedication. External capital funding may come from tax incremental financing, grants, long-term borrowing in the form of general obligation bonds, revenue bonds, tax-exempt bonds, and public-private partnerships. Each of these instruments is evaluated within the benefits received model of public finance.

Chapter 8 describes patterns of local taxation and issues in local self-finance through taxing local residents. Municipal governments rely on a variety of local taxes—mainly property, income, and sales taxes. International experience tells us that local governments are more efficient, responsible, accountable, and transparent when they raise the revenue that they spend. The best taxes are those based on benefits received with an immobile tax base; that do not create problems with harmonization or harmful competition between governments; and are easy to administer. This leads to a strong case for property taxation, but personal income and sales taxes may also be defended at the local level, although they are generally less effective at satisfying the criteria for a good local tax.

Chapter 9 provides an in-depth analysis of local land and property taxes. There are two components to the property tax—the base and the rate. In most countries, it is based on property value, but in some countries it is based on area. Regardless, the success of any assessment system depends on a number of critical components—property identification, uniformity in assessment, responsibility for assessment and its frequency, having an effective appeals mechanism, and making use of ever-improving mass assessment techniques. The tax rate is the second component. Local governments should be responsible for setting the local tax rate. Major issues include variable versus uniform tax rates, over taxation of business properties, use of tax limits, property tax incentives, regressivity and tax relief, and treatment of special properties.

Chapter 10 deals with local income, sales, and environmental taxes. Personal income and sales taxes are major local taxes in only a handful of countries; where they are used, they often (but not always) supplement local property taxes. Their attractiveness often depends on the services to be funded and alternative sources of tax revenue. While not as solid as the property tax in meeting the criteria for a solid local tax, they have enough positive features to meet some of the criteria. Some issues that must be considered include local administration versus piggybacking; setting local rates versus tax sharing; limits or no limits on tax rates; cross-border effects; harmonization with senior governments; and capacity to generate revenue. Although comparatively small but of potential importance, environmental taxes are also reviewed.

Chapter 11 discusses relative merits/demerits of fees in comparison to taxes. It provides guidance on how user fees should be set and for what services. User fees or charges should be based on usage of local public services. They are fair, efficient, and accountable where individual beneficiaries are identified, where non-users can be excluded and where per unit costs can be estimated. Unfortunately, their application seldom meets these criteria and, instead, is often designed to generate revenue. In particular, they should finance water, sewage, wastewater, solid waste, public transit, roads, and so on. Rates should be determined by municipal councils without regulatory restrictions unless, of course, the regulations are necessary to enhance local efficiency and accountability. Revenues should not be used to subsidize other local services. They are fair as long as they are based on benefits received.

Chapter 12 presents conceptual guidance on the design of fiscal transfers. This chapter reviews the principles of intergovernmental finance, with a view to drawing some general lessons of relevance to policymakers and practitioners. It provides a taxonomy of grants, their possible impacts on local fiscal behavior, and the accountability of grant recipients to donor governments and citizens. It also discusses performance-oriented, or output-based, transfers, an important tool for bottom-up (citizens enforced) results-based accountability.

Chapter 13 presents an overview of worldwide practices in higher-order fiscal transfers to local governments with a view to deriving lessons of interest to countries contemplating fiscal system reforms. The chapter presents an overview of the international practice in central/state fiscal transfers to local governments. It draws both positive and negative lessons from the international practice and provides pathways to design of such transfers for state governments contemplating reform of their fiscal transfers to local governments.

Chapter 14 provides a brief overview of grant financing practices across the world based upon a review of 41 metropolitan areas. It provides a typology of grant instruments and discusses their rationale and relevance for metro areas. It outlines stylized models of metropolitan governance existing institutional arrangements for developing a grant strategy for metropolitan financing. It also provides a review of worldwide practices in grant financing of metro areas. This is done (a) by type of metropolitan governance and (b) by type of country. The chapter highlights the divergence of the practice in grant financing from theory and draws lessons from grant financing of metropolitan areas and develops an agenda for reform.

References

Andrews, Matthew, and Anwar Shah. 2005. Citizen-Centered Governance: A New Approach to Public Sector Reform. In *Public Expenditure Analysis*, ed. Anwar Shah, 153–182. Washington, DC: World Bank.

Bailey, Stephen. 1999. *Local Government Economics: Theory, Policy, and Practice.* Basingstoke: Macmillan.

Boadway, Robin, and Anwar Shah. 2009. *Fiscal Federalism: Principles and the Practice of Multiorder Governance.* London and New York: Cambridge University Press.

Boyne, George. 1998. *Public Choice Theory and Local Government.* Basingstoke: Macmillan.

Breton, Albert. 1995. *Competitive Governments.* Cambridge: Cambridge University Press.

Brueckner, Jan. 1982. A Test for Allocative Efficiency in the Local Public Sector. *Journal of Public Economics* 19: 311–331.

Buchanan, James. 1965. An Economic Theory of Clubs. *Economica* 32: 1–14.

Caulfield, Janice. 2003. Local Government Reform in Comparative Perspective. In *Reshaping Australian Local Government*, ed. Brian Dollery, Neil Marshall, and Andrew Worthington, 11–34. Sydney: University of New South Wales Press.

Dollery, Brian, and Joe Wallis. 2001. *The Political Economy of Local Government.* Cheltenham: Edward Elgar.

Frey, Bruno, and Reiner Eichenberger. 1995. Competition Among Jurisdictions: The Idea of FOCJ. In *Competition Among Jurisdictions*, ed. Lüder Gerken, 209–229. London: Macmillan.

———. 1996. FOCJ: Competitive Governments for Europe. *International Review of Law and Economics* 16: 315–327.

———. 1999. *The New Democratic Federalism for Europe: Functional Overlapping and Competing Jurisdictions.* Cheltenham and Northampton, MA: Edward Elgar.

Goss, Sue. 2001. *Making Local Governance Work.* New York: Palgrave.

Government of Switzerland. 2003. *The Swiss Confederation—A Brief Guide.* Bern: Bundeskanzlei.

Horn, Murray. 1997. *The Political Economy of Public Administration*. Cambridge: Cambridge University Press.
Inman, Robert. 2005. *Financing Cities*. NBER Working Paper 11203, National Bureau of Economic Research, Cambridge, MA.
Ivanyna, Maksym, and Anwar Shah. 2014. How Close Is Your Government to Its People? Worldwide Indicators on Localization and Decentralization. *Economics: The Open-Access, Open-Assessment E-Journal*, 8 (2014–3): 1–61. http://dx.doi.org/10.5018/economics-ejournal.ja.2014-3.
Kincaid, John. 1967. *Municipal Perspectives in Federalism*. Unpublished Paper, Cited in Bowman and Kearney (1990).
McMillan, Melville. 2008. A Local Perspective on Fiscal Federalism: Practices, Experiences, and Lessons from Developed Countries. Chap. 7 in *Macrofederalism and Local Finances*, ed. Anwar Shah, 245–290. Washington, DC: World Bank.
Moore, Mark. 1996. *Creating Public Value*. Cambridge, MA: Harvard University Press.
Oakerson, Ronald J. 1999. *Governance Structures and Problem Solving in Metropolitan Areas: Responding to (Downsian) Growth-Related Problems*. Paper for the Workshop in Political Theory and Policy Analysis, India University, Bloomington.
Oates, Wallace. 1969. The Effects of Property Taxes and Local Public Spending on Property Values: An Empirical Study of Tax Capitalization and Tiebout Hypothesis. *Journal of Political Economy* 77: 957–971.
———. 1972. *Fiscal Federalism*. New York: Harcourt Brace Jovanovich.
Olson, Mancur. 1969. The Principle of Fiscal Equivalence: The Division of Responsibilities among Different Levels of Government. *American Economic Review* 59 (2): 479–487.
Ostrom, Vincent, Charles M. Tiebout, and Robert Warren. 1962. The Organization of Government in Metropolitan Areas: A Theoretical Inquiry. *American Political Science Review* 55 (December): 831–842.
Rhodes, R.A.W. 1997. *Understanding Governance: Policy Networks, Governance, Reflexivity, and Accountability*. Buckingham: Open University Press.
Shah, Anwar. 1988. Capitalization and the Theory of Local Public Finance: An Interpretive Essay. *Journal of Economic Surveys* 2 (3): 209–243.
———. 1989. A Capitalization Approach to Fiscal Incidence at the Local Level. *Land Economics* 65 (4): 359–375.
———. 1992. Empirical Tests for Allocative Efficiency in the Local Public Sector. *Public Finance Quarterly* 20 (3): 359–377.
———. 1994. *The Reform of Intergovernmental Fiscal Relations in Developing and Emerging Market Economies*. Washington, DC: World Bank.
———. 2001. *Interregional Competition and Federal Cooperation—To Compete or to Cooperate? That's Not the Question*. Paper Presented at the International Forum on Federalism in Mexico, Veracruz, Mexico, November 14–17.

———. 2004. *Fiscal Decentralization in Developing and Transition Economies: Progress, Problems, and the Promise*. Policy Research Working Paper 3282, World Bank, Washington, DC.

———. 2005a. On Getting the Giant to Kneel: Approaches to a Change in the Bureaucratic Culture. Chap. 9 in *Fiscal Management*, ed. Anwar Shah, 211–228. Washington, DC: World Bank.

———. 2005b. *A Framework for Evaluating Alternate Institutional Arrangements for Fiscal Equalization Transfers*. Policy Research Working Paper 3785, World Bank, Washington, DC. http://ssrn.com/abstract=873893.

———, ed. 2006. *Local Governance in Industrial Countries*. Washington, DC: World Bank.

———. 2010. Empowering States and Provinces or Unshackling Local Governments: Does It Matter for Peace, Good Government and Growth. *Pakistan Development Review* 49 (4 Part I Winter): 333–362.

———. 2014. *The Architecture of Multi-order Governance for the Information Age*. Keynote address on the 25th Anniversary of Fiscal and Financial Commission, Republic of South Africa, Cape Town, August.

Stigler, George. 1957. The Tenable Range of Functions of Local Government. In *Federal Expenditure Policy for Economic Growth and Stability*, ed. Joint Economic Committee, Subcommittee on Fiscal Policy, U.S. Congress, 213–219. Washington, DC: U.S. Government Printing Office.

Stoker, Gerry, ed. 1999. *The New Management of British Local Governance*. London: Macmillan.

Tiebout, Charles. 1956. A Pure Theory of Local Expenditures. *Journal of Political Economy* 64 (5): 416–424.

Williamson, Oliver. 1985. *The Economic Institutions of Capitalism*. New York: Free Press.

CHAPTER 2

Expenditure and Revenue Assignment: Principles

Introduction

Local governments exist in practically all countries. In many countries, they are not only a significant part but also a large part of the public sector. What determines what it is that local governments do and how they are financed? This is the assignment problem. That is, what responsibilities and what revenue sources should or might logically be assigned to local governments. This chapter provides insights into this question from the conceptual perspective; that is, the principles. The following chapter provides a perspective from an empirical survey; that is, the principles. The principles addressed in the section "Multi-tiered Government and the Rationale for Decentralization" provide the rationale for a multi-tiered system of government and the motivations for decentralizing some responsibilities from central government to local governments. In the section "The Role of Local Government in a Multi-tiered Structure," we outline those factors influencing what responsibilities should or might be assigned to local governments and extend that to identify what can be considered core and noncore local government services. How are local governments to fund those services? The revenue assignment issue is addressed in the section "Revenue Assignment." The main sources of revenues are charges for services and taxes (those two combine to be the major own-source revenues) and transfers from other governments. What is an appropriate revenue assignment depends very much upon the assignment of expenditure responsibilities. The last section is a brief conclusion.

H. Kitchen et al., *Local Public Finance and Economics*,
https://doi.org/10.1007/978-3-030-21986-4_2

Multi-tiered Government and the Rationale for Decentralization

Most of the public finance literature addresses problems from the perspective of "the" government. In fact, as we are well aware, very few countries have only one government. Almost all have many governments organized in two or more tiers—for example, unitary governments with an underlying tier of local governments, unitary governments with a regional tier between the central and the local levels, and federal governments with states or provinces each having local authorities. Of course, many structures are more complex. The prevalence of multi-tiered government indicates that there is a logic underlying such arrangements. Yet, it is only relatively recently, notably since the publication of Wallace Oates' *Fiscal Federalism* (Oates 1972), that multi-tiered government has been fully recognized and thoroughly analyzed by economists. That literature is known as the economics of fiscal federalism; that is, the study of the fiscal arrangements that exist among governments in a multi-tiered system. The fiscal federalism literature has grown immensely over the past 50 years and the topic now regularly garners treatment in most public finance textbooks.[1]

Economic and Political Motivations

Multi-tiered government and fiscal federalism are based on the decentralization of some government activities. Decentralization, here as is typical, refers to the devolving of political, fiscal, and administrative powers to subnational units of government (e.g., Burki et al. 1999). The basic, primarily economic, rationale for decentralization is presented in Oates' "decentralization theorem." It contends that, for public outputs that can be provided locally/regionally for equal cost, responsibility for provision should devolve to local/regional governments (Oates 1972, p. 35). The European Union's adaption of the decentralization theorem is its "subsidiarity principle" that states that functions should be assigned to the lowest level of government consistent with their efficient performance (Council of Europe 1985). These two perspectives emphasize the economics of the arrangement—if

[1] The vast number of references found in Bahl and Bird (2018) and Boadway and Shah (2009), two books providing comprehensive examinations of fiscal federalism and decentralization, illustrate the growth and extent of the literature. Earlier valuable contributions include those by Bahl and Linn (1992), Bird et al. (1995), Litvack et al. (1998), Manor (1999), McLure (1983, 1999), OECD (1987, 1997, 1999), Owens and Norregaard (1991), Shah (1991, 1994), and Ter-Minassian (1997).

costs are lower, or at least no higher, decentralize. These depictions of the arguments are, however, incomplete as their rationale is actually somewhat more complicated and incorporates political considerations.

The arguments of Oates (and others) for decentralization are also largely based on enhanced responsiveness and accountability. Local governments are expected to have a greater awareness of and sensitivity to local tastes and conditions and so be more responsive to local preferences and circumstances. Local government responsibility to local citizens and the accessibility of local politicians are believed to make local units more accountable for local benefits and costs than central politicians and bureaucrats. Although often implicit, an important assumption underlying the decentralization case based on responsiveness and accountability is that all levels of government are democratic.[2] These political conditions are vital to achieving the economic advantages of decentralization to be realized. The existence of numerous decentralized local governments serving their citizens is seen as improving the efficiency of local services, providing choice and offering competition among alternative local units, stimulating innovation, and controlling costs. As such, Oates' case embraces the insights of the earlier contributions of Stigler (1957) and Tiebout (1956). Stigler argued that local communities were entitled to consume the local public goods that they preferred and that local government was more effective because it was closer to the people its actions effected. Tiebout saw the multiplicity of local governments as affording opportunity for choice in local public services and competition in their delivery. Decentralization in this context reflects Bird's "bottom up" perspective (e.g., see Bird and Vaillancourt 1998, Ch 1) from which the effectiveness of decentralization is determined by the extent to which it enhances citizens' well-being because they make the decisions about the local public services that they receive.[3]

[2] A resulting additional argument for decentralization is that it enhances political participation. Greater responsiveness, accountability, and enhanced participation have long been seen as advantages of decentralization in the political literature. Other widely noted potential positive features of local government are greater transparency of government to local residents and, of course, greater autonomy. Shah (2014) advocates for movements toward FAIR (fair, accountable, incorruptible, and responsive) local governance and outlines a framework for evaluation. Blending these desirable characteristics with the economics of fiscal federalism has created a powerful case for decentralization and a more valuable tool for the analysis of decentralized government.

[3] Besley and Coate (2003) have extended the theory underlying the conventional arguments for decentralization. Their more general model assumes cost sharing of centrally provided outputs under a nationally uniform tax system, allows for non-uniform central provision

As Bird and Vaillancourt note, there may also be "top down" political motivations for decentralization. That is, the central government may promote decentralization for various reasons. Improved democratization is probably one of the more attractive reasons. That is, decentralization is promoted in order to expand and strengthen democratic institutions within a country. Latin America is often seen as providing examples of decentralization having this as an objective. Central governments may look to decentralization to shift political or fiscal burdens from it to lower tiers of government. For example, it may also be a way by which to ease regional or ethnic tensions by affording subnational groups greater say in local affairs. On the other hand, shifting responsibilities or taxes may be more to make life easier for the central authorities than to improve fiscal and political performance. In judging top-down changes, one would expect citizen welfare to be the ultimate criterion for most but the central authorities themselves may have different standards.[4]

across localities, locally elected representation to the central government, cooperative and non-cooperative legislative decision-making, varying degrees of heterogeneity in local tastes, and varying interjurisdictional spillovers. Heterogeneity of tastes and the degree of spillovers are central to the centralization-decentralization choice with less heterogeneity and more spillover favoring centralization. However, the case for decentralization is surprisingly strong and prevails even when tastes are uniform and spillovers significant. Also see Ingram and Hong (2008, 17–108).

[4] Critical assessments of fiscal federalism and, particularly, decentralization have emerged—motivated in part by difficulties experienced within some countries. Oates (2005) characterized those as an emerging second-generation of fiscal federalism. He categorized the second-generation literature (notably in Oates 2008) as having two strands. The first strand applies a broader range of economic modeling (i.e., beyond the more conventional public finance) to the questions of fiscal federalism while the second strand evolved from public choice with a focus on political institutions. Both address problems with decentralization that have or might occur. A dominant concern is the problems that emerge with soft (rather than hard) budget constraints on decentralized governments. Essentially, the second-generation literature focuses on problems that can arise when there are flaws in the decentralization design. Surveys of the impacts of decentralization generate mixed results but do point to the importance of good design and implementation (e.g., see Bahl and Bird 2018, Chapter 2). Also, there is some evidence that better-quality government enhances personal well-being (Helliwell and Huang 2008; Helliwell et al. 2018) and, though somewhat mixed and deserving of more detailed analysis, that decentralization can also increase well-being/life satisfaction (e.g., Bjornskov et al. 2008; Diaz-Serrano and Rodriguez-Pose 2012; Gao et al. 2014; Tomaney et al. 2011). Closely related is a literature on measuring the decentralization of government (e.g., Ivanyna and Shah 2014; Hooghe et al. 2010, 2016; Hooghe and Marks 2016). The OECD provides valuable recent overviews of fiscal federalism and decentralization (e.g., OECD 2013, 2016, 2018).

Administrative Motives for Decentralization

Decentralization may be motivated also by administrative factors. That is, central authorities may find it attractive to shift some of the decision-making and/or financing responsibilities away from the center primarily for administrative reasons. Three major forms of decentralization are most distinct here (e.g., Bird and Vaillancourt 1998; Burki et al. 1999). First, deconcentration is the passing along of greater decision-making authority and financial management responsibility from centrally located officials to (typically) lower and more geographically dispersed ranks of the central government's bureaucracy such as regional or local units. Because all the decisions continue to be made by employees of the central government, deconcentration is the most limited form of decentralization. The second form is delegation. Under delegation, subnational governments (or, e.g., special-purpose authorities such as housing or health authorities) undertake specific functions for the central government as agents of the central government. The local authorities are not controlled by the central government but they are accountable to it for the designated responsibilities. Devolution is the third form of decentralization. It occurs when the local authorities to which a responsibility has been devolved determine what is done to meet that responsibility and how it will be done. Normally, and certainly in the context of decentralization as considered here, the local authorities are elected by and accountable to their citizens.

Decision-making from the center can have its disadvantages. Even when centralized provision is attractive in order to provide nationally uniform services or for funding reasons, it can be difficult for a central administration to recognize and address local situations that impede successful delivery of services or that cause cost variations hampering efficient delivery. Having decision makers at the local level capable of recognizing and addressing such matters will result in more economical and satisfactory service. What degree of decentralization, if any, best suits the circumstances will depend on many factors yet to be addressed. Deconcentration, delegation, and devolution are all widely used and the choice and mix often varies considerably among countries.

Types of Decentralization and Their Interdependence

The motivations for decentralization suggest different types of decentralization in the sense of what is decentralized and how decentralization may occur. Three main types of decentralization are noted—fiscal, political, and administrative (Rondinelli 1999; Shah and Thompson 2004). A fourth type of decentralization, economic or market decentralization, is not always noted but can be important. These types are reviewed and then the importance of their interdependence noted.

Fiscal Decentralization

In discussions of decentralization and fiscal federalism, fiscal decentralization is normally the central issue. If responsibilities are to be devolved to local governments, they must have the resources with which to undertake those activities and the authority to make the related expenditure decisions. At the core of fiscal decentralization is the assignment question. That is, what responsibilities and what revenue sources are appropriately assigned to local governments? The assignment problem will be addressed in detail in later chapters, but for now we note that finance normally follows function. That is, the best assignment of revenues is normally determined by the assignment of responsibilities, so a logical approach is to first assign responsibilities and then assign revenues. Hence, if responsibilities are different, very likely revenue sources will be different.

A major decision has to do with the balance between own-source revenues and transfers from senior governments. In some cases, own-source revenues (local taxes and user charges) will be adequate but, in other cases, transfers will be necessary or appropriate. When transfers are involved, the issue is whether they will be unconditional or conditional. Unconditional grants afford local governments more autonomy in spending than conditional transfers which have "strings attached." How much autonomy local authorities have in raising their own-source revenues is also an issue. Here, the ability to set their own tax rates and charges is considered fundamental. In undertaking responsibilities that require large capital investments (and especially if irregular), borrowing is a logical means of financing.[5] When this is the situation, how much independent authority, if any, a local government has to borrow becomes an issue.

Fiscal decentralization involves many critical decisions. The choices made will depend upon many factors and circumstances. There is no single best combination—that is, no one size fits all. The challenge is to find a combination that is successful for the particular situation.

[5] It is important to recognize that borrowing is not a substitute for adequate funding. Debt must be repaid and debt-servicing costs met from the borrowing government's revenues. Borrowing only facilitates financing long-term capital investments, particularly when they are large and irregular.

Political Decentralization

Political decentralization refers to granting those affected by decisions about local public services a greater voice in making those decisions. In the terms of Burki et al. (1999), it involves a "deepening of democracy." Ultimately, political decentralization is seen as providing local citizens and their elected representatives on local councils more decision-making powers over local matters. The logic, of course, is that better decisions are made when made by those who must live with the consequences. Implementing political decentralization will certainly require expanding the authority and autonomy of local councils and ensuring that elected representatives are accountable to their constituents. Local decision makers accountable to local citizens have better knowledge of local preferences and conditions and, so, are more likely to be responsive and make efficient choices. One might believe as well that there is inherent merit in having decisions on local matters decided locally by those affected. It is not unreasonable to believe that people are happier if they make their own decisions as opposed to having them made by others even if the ultimate decision were the same (as if central decision makers had perfect information and respected local preferences).

Effective political decentralization requires more than local elections and councils. Local decisions must reflect the broad public interest. To do so requires active participation across civil society to reveal and advocate positions and to monitor performance on an ongoing basis. For example, political participation must extend beyond the elected and the electing of representatives. Citizens must be actively involved in the political process. Voting is definitely important and, for some, active participation will mean involvement in political parties or other forms of political organizations. Critical, however, is the participation in formal and informal interest groups that provide input to decision makers as their voices express opinions and help define preferences and, in turn, assess performance. Effective political participation requires information. Governments should provide much of this by making its finances, activities, and processes transparent to the public. The public is then able to monitor their government and will be assisted by the media, community organizations, and public interest groups. In these ways, citizens will be able to assess how well their needs and preferences are being met, how effectively public funds are being utilized and whether power is being abused. Political decentralization requires that the involvement of civil society in the local political process be promoted or, at least, not restricted.

Administrative Decentralization

The administrative decentralization as considered here must be distinguished from administrative decentralization as discussed in section "Administrative Motives for Decentralization" above. There, three forms of decentralization were noted—deconcentration, delegation, and devolution. Here decentralization, as elsewhere in section "Types of Decentralization and Their Interdependence," and administrative decentralization, in particular, are considered only in the context of devolution. That is, what is administrative decentralization when responsibilities are devolved to local governments?

Authority over local government's employees is the main issue in administrative decentralization. Administrative decentralization requires that the local government controls the recruitment, dismissal, and terms of employment of its staff. Without the ability to manage its own civil service, local governments' control over service delivery and performance will be eroded because their staff will have other allegiances and not be (as) accountable to local decision makers. For example, if the local bureaucracy is effectively part of the state civil service and relies on a state organization for placement and promotion (as in India and many other countries), their concern for satisfying their local "employers" is expected to be a lower priority. Central determination of local employees' salaries and benefits presents another concern (e.g., Dethier 2000). The centrally set conditions may or may not be right for the local circumstances (the rewards too generous or too little) and, in addition, they undermine local governments' control over their budgets.

Other aspects of administrative decentralization have to do with regulatory powers and contracting. Permitting local governments to regulate on purely local issues (e.g., parking) as opposed to common central regulations is consistent with administrative decentralization. Also, restrictions on local governments' ability to contract for the provision of services with private firms or with other governments may be unnecessary and prevent utilization of cost-effective alternatives. That is, constraining local governments to provide services through local public operations (e.g., garbage collection, road repair) or requiring them to acquire services from specific other governments or their enterprises (e.g., electricity or natural gas) may impose inefficiencies. Opening government production to competition with potential suppliers from the private and government sectors is part of the market-based decentralization.[6] Market-based decentralization is intended to expose governments or units within government to service and efficiency improving pressures where it is possible for that competition to have those positive effects. Introducing market-based decentralization also makes explicit the potential for public sector or government failure. Public sector intervention is based upon the existence of market failures and the potential for government to correct those and so enhance well-being. Governments, however, are themselves not immune to failure. The public sector creates incentives for the various actors (e.g., citizens, firms, politicians, bureaucrats) which may be contrary to the broad public interest and may lead political action astray (Dollery and Wallis 2001, Ch 3). Market-based decentralization is a controlling force in that it may penalize failing jurisdictions and motivate reform.

The Interdependence of Fiscal, Political, and Administrative Decentralization

Successful local government and successful decentralization requires a blend of good fiscal, political, and administrative decentralization. One, or even two, alone will not work well. For example, fiscal decentralization, even if internally well designed, will not be particularly effective if the local political system does not enforce responsiveness to local preferences and accountability to the local voters. Similarly, political decentralization will quickly lose its appeal and wither if it has no real function or authority. That is, if local government has no significant responsibilities, little effort will be invested in political action in that direction. Political activists soon ignore figurehead authorities to focus their energies on those with power. On the other hand, citizens will be poorly served if a weak political structure enables a local government with real responsibilities to be captured by a local elite or interest group. Similarly, service will suffer and citizens and local decision makers will be frustrated if the local bureaucracy answers to a different master despite reasonable fiscal responsibilities and political powers existing at the local level. Effective local government and decentralization requires a combination of fiscal, political, and administrative decentralization.

[6] For example, see Wiesner (2003) for a discussion of the role of market-based decentralization in Latin America and Dollery and Wallis (2001) for a more general discussion of competition in the delivery of public services. Oates (1999) includes a discussion of market-preserving federalism.

This volume is focused on the fiscal aspects of local government. It is based on the theory of fiscal federalism and its implications for decentralization. Despite the emphasis on the fiscal dimensions, the importance of the political and administrative aspects must not be forgotten. Administrative matters are addressed here to some extent, but the political perspective gets little explicit mention. These topics, especially the administrative aspects, are the focus of Volume II. Here, as in much of the fiscal federalism literature, it will typically be assumed that a relatively vibrant local political force is present and is effective in holding local government accountable and in making it responsive. Clearly, this is not always the case and perhaps not even usually the case especially in developing and transitional countries. The reader should keep in mind the importance of all three dimensions of decentralization.

The Role of Local Government in a Multi-tiered Structure: Service Responsibilities

The assignment problem is a fundamental issue in multilevel public finance. Both revenue sources and expenditure responsibilities must be allocated. It is widely recommended that responsibilities be determined first and that is the order followed here. Pursuit of guidance leads to examination of the three main branches of government (i.e., stabilization, distribution, and allocation). Not surprisingly given the earlier discussion, allocation—that is, the provision of goods and services—is the prevailing rationale for local government. The purpose and design of local government is more complicated than implied by the previous analysis. Those complications are addressed under three topics; economies of scale, problems with spillovers, and the implications of decision-making and transaction costs. Alternative approaches to coping with the complications introduced by these factors result in the identification of core and noncore local government responsibilities.

Musgrave's Three Functions of Government

Richard Musgrave identified three branches or economic functions of government—stabilization, distribution, and allocation (Musgrave 1959). How should these responsibilities of government be allocated in a multi-tiered system? The widely accepted argument is that central government should be assigned responsibility for macroeconomic stabilization and income distribution. Local governments lack important macroeconomic management tools (e.g., monetary and exchange rate instruments) and the impacts of fiscal policies (tax and expenditure efforts that might be aimed at macroeconomic problems) typically are weak because their effects spill beyond the local jurisdiction due to the interjurisdictional flow of products and the mobility of factors. Local governments' efforts at redistribution are also fraught with externalities as enhanced benefits for the poor induce in-migration, while the taxes to provide those benefits encourage the out-migration of capital and labor. While these recommendations hold quite well for local governments, in the variability and complexity of actual environments, there can be some flexibility in their application. For example, in federal countries with geographically large states or provinces (e.g., Canada), regional governments' fiscal and redistribution policies may be of some consequence. Also, even when local governments have no redistributive responsibilities, they are not unaware of the distributive implications of their actions to their own citizens; that is, especially through the distribution of services and the allocation of costs. In addition, they often choose to engage in some programs with clear and specific redistributional objectives, but the effects are usually marginal compared to those of programs operated by upper-level governments.[7]

Allocation, or the provision of goods and services, is where the scope for local government becomes clear. Many public sector outputs provide only, or almost only, local benefits. While there is still ample room for central (and provincial or state) governments to provide services when the benefits correspond most closely to their geographic boundaries, the prevalence and significance of local public outputs provides the rationale for local government. The case for decentralization that was outlined above was made on the basis of allocation. That is, representative local governments making decisions on local publicly provided outputs to local residents make choices that more closely satisfy local residents than when those services are determined by central decision makers. Usually, the main reason for the welfare gain from decentralization is that tastes and preferences vary among localities and local decision makers are better able to recognize and respond to those differences. Central governments are more likely to provide (more) uniform services despite the variations in local demands. This is the basic

[7] See Tresch (2015, Chapters 26 and 27) for a discussion of a redistributional role for local government.

argument for decentralization of many allocative decisions to local authorities, but optimal decentralization must take other factors into account. Discussing those is the role of the following section.

Assigning Responsibilities to Local Governments: Complicating Factors[8]

In making the case for decentralization and local government, implicit assumptions have conveniently set aside a number of potential complications. Tastes for local public outputs have been assumed to vary but, fortunately, those with different tastes are, or can be grouped geographically, into ideal, or at least reasonable, local government jurisdictions. Furthermore, the jurisdictions that determine the level of local public output encompass exactly those individuals that benefit from that public output. Thus, there is a perfect matching of citizens and beneficiaries or a perfect mapping of the decision-making jurisdiction and its service area. The boundaries of the local government include all the beneficiaries of its output and they all have a voice in the output decision. This situation is often also referred to as a perfect correspondence. In addition, beneficiaries pay the costs of the benefits received through an ideal system of taxes and/or charges.[9] Hence, local residents decide upon their preferred level of public output and, using an ideal tax system, make efficient choices.

Obviously, the assumptions underlying the ideal case can, at best, only be approximated in practice. Various factors intervene. In the simple model, economies of scale have not been an impediment to the local production of public outputs. Nor have interjurisdictional spillovers of the benefits of local government services posed problems. Also, the implication for high decision-making costs of having many overlapping local governments, each ideally sized but geographically different, being needed to provide the full range of local public services has not been a consideration. These issues complicate decentralization and the design of local jurisdictions and it is now time to consider the implications.

[8] For further discussion of the topics addressed in this section, see, for example, Dollery and Wallis (2001, Ch 2), Fisher (1996, Ch 6), and Oates (1972).

[9] See a public finance text (e.g., Fisher 1996) for details of the ideal allocation of the cost of public goods. The basic idea is that each individual is charged a personal marginal cost equal to that person's marginal benefit and the ideal level of output exists when, in the case of a pure public good, the sum of all individual marginal benefits equals the marginal cost of the output.

Economies of Scale

Adding members to the community can result in more people sharing the cost of the public output and making residents better off. Especially in the case of a pure public good (i.e., where cost does not change with the number of beneficiaries and an additional beneficiary does not reduce the benefits to existing beneficiaries; e.g., air pollution abatement), the costs to all beneficiaries will be reduced. This case, where cost savings result from larger numbers sharing fixed costs, arises from jointness in consumption and is best referred to as the economies of jointness or the economies of sharing. However, cost savings from this source are often called (rather misleadingly) economies of scale in the public economics literature. Economies of scale actually arise when unit costs decline when additional units of output are produced. For example, unit costs are less when 100 units per month are produced than when the output is 50 units. Similar scale economies can arise in the production of publicly provided goods (e.g., when operating a water treatment facility designed for 50,000 homes is less expensive than operating two each designed for 25,000 homes).[10] Naturally, communities will want to take advantage of economies of scale and economies of sharing when it is attractive to do so.[11]

Community population is a factor when economies of sharing is under consideration and is very likely a factor when it comes to achieving economies of scale. However, as population expands, individual influence on public decisions becomes smaller and community preferences may become more heterogeneous. Therefore, the community's choice may diverge from an individual's preference further as numbers increase (although if conditions are amenable to Tiebout sorting—that is, those with similar preferences congregate in the same communities—the preference divergence problem will be moderated). As a result, citizens considering the best size for their jurisdiction are likely to face a trade-off between cost savings resulting from sharing and scale economies and declining satisfaction from

[10]The problem of distinguishing between economics of sharing and economies of scale is that it is often difficult to distinguish between units of output when many individuals benefit from the same unit of output. For example, there could be economies of scale in the operation of an air pollution abatement system (e.g., cost per unit of particulate matter removed decline to some point) but the benefits of the improvement in air quality resulting from some additional abatement (change in output) could be enjoyed by many or few people (economies of sharing).

[11]For insight into and a brief review of empirical economies of scale analyses, see Byrnes and Dollery (2002).

the choice of local public output. The ideal size is when the difference in per person benefits and costs from these two sources that arise as population increases is at a maximum (or the marginal benefits from adding an additional person equals the marginal costs). Thus, where advantages from larger populations are available, local governments may try to attract in-migrants or to expand jurisdictional boundaries to increase numbers.

Communities may be able to secure the advantages of scale in public provision without expanding community size by engaging in intergovernmental agreements. For example, a local government may find that, through agreement with another local government, it can satisfactorily obtain certain services at a lower cost than it can provide those services itself. Such arrangements can be particularly appealing when there is little or no difference in local preferences for services or the product (e.g., utility services like electricity, sewerage treatment, or water supply) but can also be effective in those cases where differences in community preferences for services can be readily defined and monitored. A variety of agreements are possible. For example, they may be straightforward contracts with another community to deliver a service at a certain price or they may be joint ventures by two or more communities to supply services from a mutual operation to the partners. Especially when public service production is examined in areas encompassing smaller communities, a surprising number and variety of intergovernmental agreements are found.

This discussion of scale has ignored congestion. A large amount of empirical literature finds that per capita expenditures on local public outputs grow about in proportion to population for most jurisdictions. These results suggest that economies of scale and sharing are, if available at all, modest. This result occurs because for many locally publicly provided services, once a relatively modest population is reached, facilities need to be duplicated (e.g., fire stations, police precincts, libraries, recreational facilities, and streets). That is, many services are horizontally integrated through a network of similar facilities that expand with population.[12] Not only may sharing and scale economies be less advantageous than sometimes thought, but congestion may impose increasing cost with population that, itself, may disadvantage larger centers. That is, to remain appealing, larger jurisdictions may require other factors such as agglomeration economies to offset the pressures of congestion on public (and even private) services. When the costs of providing services to a community rises in the private sector as

[12] For discussion and empirical insights, see McMillan et al. (1981) and McMillan (1989).

in the case of (e.g., golf) clubs, the club's members can raise entrance fees or limit membership to maintain the numbers at the level ideal for its members. Local governments are more constrained in their responses to congestion. Because local governments cannot tax or charge new and old residents differently, in-migrants are faced with the same average cost of the local services as all other residents and not the higher marginal costs resulting from them adding to the population. Hence, there is an incentive for overpopulation in jurisdictions experiencing congestion. One means of addressing that available to local government is zoning. This is, imposing minimum standards on land use to control population size. Zoning also can indirectly control for other characteristics (e.g., income) as to maintain a group having more homogeneous demands for local government services. Also, if congestion (or other factors) is increasing local costs and taxes, mobile households and firms may, in multi-jurisdictional environments, be able to turn to more appealing alternatives. Thus, interjurisdictional competition will also serve to temper the growth of high-cost communities.

Interjurisdictional Spillovers

Contrary to the discussion so far, the benefits (and costs) of local government output are not always confined to the local jurisdiction. Some benefits may benefit nonresidents of the providing community because the outputs themselves spill beyond its boundaries (e.g., improved air or water quality due to local pollution abatement) or because those benefiting from local services migrate elsewhere (e.g., people schooled at local expense move to live, work, and pay taxes elsewhere) or because outsiders come to the providing jurisdiction to obtain services intended for local residents (e.g., use of recreational and cultural facilities). The problem here is that while citizens of the providing government pay all, or at least a disproportionate share of, the costs, they enjoy less than the full (or proportional) benefits. Hence, in the absence of offsetting forces, the service will be underprovided. Those enjoying the benefits of interjurisdictional spillovers tend to free-ride on the paying residents of the providing community.

The inefficiencies resulting from externalities of local public services might be corrected in various ways. An upper-level government might design grants to local governments to compensate for the spillover losses and so induce local authorities to produce the socially optimal level of service. This possibility will be discussed further when addressing intergovernmental grants. Local authorities may take some action on their own. One possibility is that they negotiate agreements with the neighbors benefiting from the spillovers for them to pay for the benefits received. Negotiations, however, are costly and the benefiting neighbors may have little incentive to cooperate. Expanding the area of the providing jurisdiction might internalize the benefits. However, it is more likely to internalize only a larger portion of the spillover and so only succeed in reducing the relative magnitude of the problem. Also, extending the boundaries of a local government often meets resistance and is not costless.

Cost spillovers are also a potential source of local government inefficiency. Tax exporting is a prime candidate. That is, local governments may be able to levy taxes exceeding the cost of local services on enterprises that shift a substantial part of that tax burden to nonresident buyers. An example is high property taxes levied on businesses or industries exporting most of their output beyond the local jurisdiction. Where tax exporting occurs, local services are subsidized and the expected result is that they will be oversupplied. Solving this problem is largely a matter of the appropriate assignment of local revenue sources and is discussed in that section. To be noted, however, is that the discussion of decentralization and local government has assumed that the cost of local public outputs are a local burden; that is, that the beneficiaries pay for the services that they select and receive. Underlying this assumption is that the income distribution is socially acceptable (or that any redistribution has already occurred).

Decision-Making and Transactions Costs

If decision-making and transactions costs were zero or low, the theory of decentralization implies that there would be many local governments each providing a public service to somewhat different but ideally sized communities of citizens and beneficiaries. Thus, there would be a multiplicity of overlapping and tiered local governments and individuals would be citizens of a large number of local jurisdictions. In this way, local government outputs would be most closely matched to local preferences. Decision-making and transactions costs, however, are not zero and often not small. A multiplicity of local governments would necessitate citizens being fully informed on the activities of each and participating in many elections and other public input and monitoring activities to make the system work well. Information and political participation have costs. In addition, there are certain unavoidable costs in the operation of any individual government. These realities create the possibility of trading-off some satisfaction on the output side for cost savings by reducing the number of local governments to a more manageable size.

When decision-making and transactions costs matter, a smaller number of local governments can mean that individual preferences are less well met but that the costs of political participation and government operations are lowered. (In addition, if jurisdictions are not ideally designed, there may be opportunities for further economies of sharing and scale and reduced externalities to be realized.) People will need to weigh the benefits and costs from the alternatives in making their choices. Theory and evidence suggests that there will be some clustering or bundling of local government activities (those conceptually ideal local governments of the simple decentralization model) with those having similar service areas and serving people with similar tastes being combined into a single multi-purpose local authority that, while not providing perfect correspondence, provides an acceptable accommodation. Hence, there may emerge a tier of multi-purpose local governments, a regional authority to address geographically broader issues and, in special cases, specific or special-function authorities. Various operational structures may emerge. For example, besides the local plus regional authorities mentioned, some may opt for a single large jurisdiction (e.g., a uni-city) and others may choose to have no regional tier but rely upon interjurisdictional agreements among the local governments to meet trans-boundary problems. Also, the disagreement and animosity that often accompanies local government restructuring demonstrates the range of opinions on these matters. The same rationale can be extended to the assignment of functions to the central government or, in a federal system, the assignment of responsibilities to state/provincial and federal governments. Thus, in making an assignment to consolidate activities among fewer governments, some activities might best be passed upward to state and/or central governments rather than left at a "local" level. These arrangements are effectively taking advantage of realizing economies of scope in government; that is, realizing savings by reducing the number of governments and having those remaining provide a wider range of services.

Geographic service areas and citizen preferences are not the only criteria to use when pursuing optimal jurisdictions. Intensity of preferences also matter. Multi-purpose local governments function best in a democratic system when preferences for the services for which the local authority is responsible are not too diverse. Under majority rule, each vote has an equal weight. If the preferences underlying those votes are quite different (some very strong and other quite weak), winning positions may actually reduce community welfare. In the absence of or as an alternative to other mechanisms that reflect intensity of preference (lobbying, coalition building, political parties, vote-trading, etc. that may be less well developed at the local government level), an option is to separate issues for which preferences are strong and have those decided by an alternative (possibly special-) purpose authority (McMillan 1976). A good example of where this may have emerged is found in the existence of school boards as local governments separate from the local general-purpose governments as in the United States.

What Do Local Governments Typically Do?

The preceding parts of this section outlined guidelines for the assignment of responsibilities to local government. To summarize, they are not expected to play a role in macroeconomic stabilization, they should have only a small role in distribution, but they have an important role to play in the provision of goods and services (i.e., allocation). The responsibilities of local governments should be limited to the provision of those goods and services for which the benefits are local and their service areas should closely match their geographic boundaries, in part, to facilitate local beneficiaries paying for the benefits that they receive and having similar stakes in the local services and decisions. The services that they provide, or at least are independently responsible for, should not involve significant spillovers (in the absence of other accommodation). Also, one expects that, for the activities undertaken, economies of sharing, scale, and scope are exploited.

Do the responsibilities of local governments correspond to these guidelines? To get some sense of this issue, it is necessary to outline the activities of local governments. Here, only an initial insight is offered into this matter as more detailed analysis and discussion is deferred to the next chapter. As demonstrated there, the responsibilities of local governments can be quite diverse and so considerable diversity can be found among countries. That diversity largely results from the varying treatment of the assignments of social services such as schooling and health care so those are discussed separately. The central point is that there are core and noncore local responsibilities.

Core Responsibilities

The tasks performed by local governments vary widely among countries. One can, however, distinguish between core functions and other, noncore, activities. Core functions refer to those activities for which local governments are responsible in almost all countries. This group typically includes responsibility for local roads and walkways, fire protection, parks and playgrounds, recreational and cultural activities and facilities, garbage collection and disposal, bylaw enforcement, business licensing, planning and land use control, drainage and probably water supply and sanitation services.[13]

The benefits from these functions are very localized in that the residents of the providing government (citizens and firms) are the beneficiaries. Interjurisdictional spillovers are minimal. The only services that might display notable economies of scale as population and volume of services increase beyond small communities are water and sewerage services and garbage disposal. Even for them, smaller communities in populous areas are likely to realize scale economies through intermunicipal agreements (or second-tier area-wide local authorities). While knowledge and good management are essential for effective delivery, these services, for the most part, are not difficult to provide and are within the capacity of local authorities. Where greater expertise is necessary, such as in water and sewerage systems, that can be contracted for from private firms or other government operators. Also, senior governments often provide expertise, advice, guidelines and, in cases, may impose regulations and scrutinize certain activities.[14] Citizens can readily monitor government performance in the delivery of most aspects of these services. Hence, there is a relatively high standard of accountability.

Noncore Responsibilities

Differences in the assignment of local government responsibilities become more pronounced when it comes to policing and to utilities such as electricity and natural gas. Intercountry variation is most pronounced when one turns to schooling, health, and social assistance. These social programs involve major costs and, although often having been a local government, non-profit or private responsibility initially, they have tended, in many countries, to be assumed in all or part by senior governments because of significant benefit spillovers beyond the community creating a national interest and/or there are social insurance and redistributive benefits. The

[13] For illustrations of the assignment of responsibilities among multi-tiered governments, see Table 4.1 of Chap. 4 and Shah (2006, Chapter 1).

[14] Even when services are purely local, citizens may prefer having an upper-level government to review certain activities (e.g., water quality, sewerage treatment, refuse disposal) to provide an informed and independent assessment of performance and especially of the less observable aspects.

patterns which emerge depend on history, geography, politics, and cultural factors as much as economic considerations (Shah 2006). When local governments are responsible for schooling, health, and/or social assistance, they are typically assisted by senior governments through intergovernmental grants or shared revenues or have significant local tax bases relating well to ability to pay.

These noncore activities are characterized by a blend of local and national interest and relative advantages. School serves as an excellent example. Schools serve local communities and those communities have a very strong interest in the education provided to their children. Also, even at a relatively small scale, schools can be efficiently and effectively operated. Hence, local governments are expected to be the most effective at delivering the service and at responding to local preferences. However, for productivity and citizenship reasons, people are also interested in the schooling of children elsewhere in the country. Thus, there is a national interest in schooling. That interest is reflected in concerns about curriculum, teacher qualifications, attendance, grading standards, and equality of opportunity. Uneven local tax bases and the implications for large differences in school funding and educational opportunities is often an important concern. Such broad-based interests legitimately call for the involvement of senior governments in schooling and, as noted, in various other public services (e.g., health services, transportation).

Central involvement can come in varying degrees and forms. At the basic level, the central government may simply define the responsibilities and set the ground rules for the operation of local government and let it proceed with its own activities and decisions. Usually, there are regulations covering those activities and monitoring by the central government. In many cases, such as major transportation projects with important spillover benefits, the central government will agree to cover or to share specific costs provided that the facility or program meets certain criteria or standards. For yet other functions for which a local government may be responsible, for example, schooling, basic health services, the central role may include some financing, policy setting, regulations, criteria, and so on. It is not uncommon that, in the case of schooling, the broader interests are deemed to be so great that the responsibility for the function is formally with a senior government although the actual delivery of the service may be delegated to local authorities. In some cases, the central role is so pervasive that there is minimal or no room for local discretion. The central government may define the program, its operations, and fund almost all of the costs. Social assistance programs undertaken by local governments in conjunction with central governments are occasionally of this sort. In such instances, the local governments are essentially agents of the center effectively contracting with the central government to provide central services. Although not exclusively so, central intervention is typically greatest in the case of those functions which go beyond the core local responsibilities; that is, largely social services such as schooling, health care, and social assistance. In some instances, the central government assumes full responsibility for the program and local authorities will have no role whatsoever.

Central involvement results in a more complicated set of principal-agent relations. Local governments must not only be accountable to local residents but also be accountable to the central authorities exercising some control over certain local activities. That is, local authorities need to be accountable to those above as well as those below. Because the interests and the arrangements can be complex, the intergovernmental relations can also be complex. To function effectively requires an appropriate assignment of responsibilities, clarity as to who is responsible for what, and coordination. Meeting these conditions enables governments to understand their respective accountabilities. Citizens, however, are sometimes confused and frustrated by shared responsibilities. As a result, if unhappy, they may blame "the government" and punish all those involved. Though crude, that response does put pressure on all the players to improve.

Noncore activities are not uniquely local responsibilities because there are broader (e.g., national) interests in those services. While those activities may be undertaken solely by local or central governments, more often those responsibilities will be shared. Responsibility sharing offers advantages but adds complexity and introduces complications. There is a wide range of workable responsibility sharing arrangements. Hence, the way that responsibilities are bundled varies considerably among countries. That variation, often resulting in large differences between the size of local expenditures and of own revenues, often makes it difficult to distinguish exactly the role and magnitude of local government in an economy.

Summary

The assignment of expenditure or service responsibilities is central to understanding and to determining the role of local governments. Of Musgrave's three functional areas of government (stabilization, distribution, and allocation), it is the allocative role that best suits local government. That is, local governments have little or no role in (re)distribution and stabilization but should be providing the goods and services that provide local benefits. While that is valuable guidance, the expenditure assignment problem is still complex. Ideal benefit areas differ for many local services and those often fail to match relatively inflexible jurisdictional boundaries. Hence, there are regular trade-offs to be made, involving scale economies, interjurisdictional spillovers, and decision-making and transactions costs. For a broad range of services, core services, local governments are well suited to provide these services in that they are able to internalize benefits and costs or resolve the issues arising from these complicating factors. Thus, one finds a relatively consistent set of (core) services provided by local governments in almost all countries. For certain services (notably the social services of schooling, health, social welfare but also policing criminal activity), the spillovers are normally so great or the distribution implications so large that national interests as well as local interests must be represented. To address this problem, responsibilities may be shared between local and upper-tier governments or responsibilities may be assigned to upper-tier (central or provincial/state) governments. Furthermore, responsibilities for such noncore services may be and are bundled in many different ways in different countries. Thus, it is not surprising that there is little uniformity in how noncore services are handled across countries. The important issue for the workability of noncore activities is that, whatever the arrangements, they be well designed.

Revenue Assignment

How revenues should be assigned to local governments depends upon the expenditure assignment. Local governments need to have the funds necessary to meet their responsibilities. There are two sources—local sources (i.e., own-source revenues; primarily user charges and taxes) and intergovernmental transfers. Local sources should relate closely to the benefits from local government services so that beneficiaries see a close link between the benefits and costs of services. The case for transfers depends primarily upon the relative efficiency in tax collection by the different levels of government and on the national interest or benefits from local governments' activities.

Own-Source Revenue

Considerable attention has been paid to how revenue sources and notably taxes should be assigned among levels of governments. Opinions differ to some extent. The conventional view focuses on the efficiency of tax collection in aggregate and can be criticized for neglecting the problems associated with the need for large intergovernmental transfers when expenditures are decentralized. More recent work puts greater emphasis on the potential costs of large transfers and also emphasizes the importance, particularly at the local level, of linking taxes to benefits.

The Conventional Criteria

The standard reference on the matter of tax assignment among multi-tiered governments is McLure (1983). Richard Musgrave's paper in that volume receives particular attention (Musgrave 1983). Musgrave recommended that taxes suited for stabilization and redistribution (such as corporate and personal income taxes) are best central government taxes and that the central government also tax mobile factors and tax bases that are quite unevenly distributed among jurisdictions. Immobile tax bases are typically better suited for taxation by local authorities. Taxes closely related to the benefits that they finance and user charges are advisable for all levels of government, but especially so for local and, if any, the intermediate level. Based on these criteria, Musgrave recommends the following assignment of major taxes:

central level: integrated income tax, expenditure tax, natural resource tax, user charges;
middle level: income tax, destination based product tax, natural resource taxes, user charges;
local level: property tax, payroll tax, user charges.

Interjurisdictional mobility of tax bases and concern for possible tax exporting feature large in these and subsequent tax assignment discussions, and especially so when addressing the assignment to local governments. The intent is to avoid taxes that distort the location of factors and those that enable governments to shift the burden of the taxes that they impose on to nonresidents. The result, in part, has been to narrow further the already limited tax bases recommended for local governments to property taxes (immobile base) and user charges (benefit levies).[15,16]

[15] See Dahlby (2001) for a "consensus view" of tax assignments. The shift of the payroll tax to the upper tier(s) of government has been prompted as well by its widespread utilization by senior governments to finance earmarked social benefit programs such as unemployment insurance and social security/pensions.

[16] This treatment reflects the usual top-down perspective on tax assignment in that the matter is decided at the center. In some cases, however, tax assignment is a bottom-up decision where federating states decide upon what tax powers the new central authority should have. See Dahlby (2001).

The conventional tax assignment recommendations imply a highly centralized tax system. Concerns about macro stabilization, redistribution, predatory tax competition, economic distortions, uneven bases, and administration and compliance costs lean toward assigning most (and notably the most productive) taxes to the central government. Hence, recommended assignments typically allocate personal and corporate income taxes, payroll taxes, value-added taxes, wealth/inheritance taxes, natural resource taxes, and tariffs to the central government.[17] While highly centralized tax systems are not uncommon, especially among developing and transition countries,[18] such highly centralized revenue structures contrast with the widespread recommendations for decentralization of responsibilities and expenditures, the decentralizing movements in many countries, and the fact that many other countries are already much more decentralized in both expenditure and tax terms than the recommended revenue assignment suggests.

If a country has a revenue structure that is more centralized than expenditure responsibilities, central to subnational transfers are required to fill the fiscal gap. Local governments, for example, must rely upon intergovernmental grants to fund their expenditures. A vertical fiscal imbalance exists in that the central government has the fiscal capacity to generate revenues beyond what is required to meet central expenditures while subnational governments lack the fiscal capacity to enable them to finance their assigned responsibilities. Fiscal gap-reducing transfers may come in a variety of forms. Some may be aimed explicitly at closing the gap by determining the expenditure needs less the revenue capacity of each potential recipient government and making a transfer of that, or some part of that, difference. Others may involve a formula-determined sharing of some predetermined central government revenue pool or the sharing of specific central government tax revenues either to jurisdiction of origin or by formula. Then again, others may be more ad hoc with the sharing of some amount of funding as determined in the central government's annual budget. In addition, central governments may rationalize a variety of other sorts of transfers as effectively gap closing.[19]

[17] In the interests of maintaining the advantages of an internal common market (i.e., free trade within the country) the only taxes, if any, on cross-border movements of goods and services should be national levies on foreign trade.

[18] Bird (1999) argues that the international adoption of national value-added taxes and their revenue importance have contributed to this centralization.

[19] A broader discussion of transfers—beyond the gap-closing role—appears in the latter part of this chapter.

Problems arise when subnational governments rely heavily upon transfers for financing. Very important is whether the transfers are adequate to enable recipient governments to actually meet the responsibility and associate expenditure expectations placed upon them. Also, although fiscal gap-closing transfers should normally be unconditional, granting governments are fond of conditional funding when making transfers. That is, the funds are often earmarked for specific uses or have other requirements attached to them. These conditions may distort priorities and resource allocation. As Bird (1999) points out in his "rethinking" of tax assignment, the excessive reliance on transfers sometimes "facilitates irresponsible behaviour" and has resulted in expanding efforts to design (relatively unsuccessful and probably unnecessary) "grand and convoluted transfer systems." Furthermore, a heavy reliance on transfers rather than own revenues interferes with the connection between taxes and benefits and distorts perceptions of the cost of government services. These problems have emphasized the need to adopt broader criteria for making the tax assignment decision.

Broadening the Tax Assignment Criteria

Foremost among the problems with the conventional view of tax assignment is its failure to recognize the importance of the link between expenditure decisions and tax decisions; that is, the benefit model of subnational, and especially local, government finance.[20] The benefit model of local finance is "perhaps the main practical guidance emerging from the theoretical literature" on decentralization (Bird 1993, pp. 210–211). A major implication of the benefit model is that "the essential economic role of local government is to provide to local residents those public services for which they are willing to pay" (Bird 1993, p. 210). This position is endorsed by Oates (1993) and Walsh (1992, p. 31) summarizes his support for the benefit model by the statement "no representation without taxation." Walsh continues, as an initial objective, "governments which are responsible for expenditure decisions should be responsible for raising the revenue to fund them and should have control over, and responsibility

[20] Dahlby (2001) notes several problems with the "consensus" view. Those are (a) the need to link expenditure and tax decisions, (b) a need to consider expenditure assignment and grant systems, (c) neglect of distributional impacts of subnational government policies, (d) overlooking certain problems of joint occupancy of tax fields, (e) ignoring that some economic shocks calling for stabilization are region specific, and (f) putting little emphasis on administration and compliance costs of alternative tax assignment regimes.

for, revenue sources adequate to enable them to do so." Decentralized local governments are to be responsive and accountable to their citizens. The starting point for realizing these objectives is to internalize both costs and benefits to the decision-making community. Only when the true costs of a service to local residents are recognized by them will they be able to reveal their true preferences and, when paying for those services, residents will demand accountability of their local governments.

Enhanced recognition of the benefit model for local government and of the importance of self-finance has added flexibility to the tax assignment analysis. For example, local governments may legitimately tax mobile units if they provide benefits to them. As Oates (1999) emphasizes, local governments should avoid nonbenefit taxes on mobile units but should, for efficiency reasons, levy benefit taxes on them. This perspective broadens the range of taxes that local governments might impose on products, factors, and households, provided that they reflect benefits received and/or are borne by residents of the jurisdiction. In some cases, taxes on sales or products, capital, labor, or households may be justified. Also, while benefit charges and taxes are usually expected to reflect the cost of services, some taxes may be designed to reflect willingness to pay as, for example, a local personal income tax. The success of such ability to pay levies, however, will depend upon the extent to which competing jurisdictions are willing to provide services to higher-income households through a tax system that is less redistributive.[21] An implication of decentralized responsibilities and expanded own-revenue sources is that those sources must be productive. There is little gained by assigning revenue sources to local governments if they fail to generate significant revenue.

Bird (1999) offers an additional perspective for rethinking tax assignment. He points out that there is a strong propensity for all (central and subnational) governments to tax business. Various incentives underlie this tendency. Naturally, governments want revenues from business at least sufficient to meet the costs of providing services to them.[22] Beyond that, however, tax exporting possibilities, the potential to obscure the cost of local services, the incentive to reduce the burden on local residents, and a vague understanding of the incidence of business taxes all make business taxes

[21] It is important to remember that property taxes, and especially those taxing improvements as well as land, also may not match benefits exactly and, like a local personal income tax, involve some redistribution. On the other hand, a local personal income tax may match better benefits and costs for a local service such as schooling.

[22] Kitchen and Slack (1993) found that about 40 percent of municipal government (i.e., nonschooling) expenditure benefited nonresidential property.

politically appealing. Often this situation results in a complex and distorting multiplicity, a "mish-mash," of subnational business taxes. Bird argues that it is logical to recognize the political and the benefit rationales for subnational business taxation and to seek better alternatives. For large regional (e.g., state) governments, he recommends extension of the national value-added tax (VAT) system to allow regional authorities access to this tax base using regionally determined rates. Bird argues that experience in Canada suggests that such a system is workable. For local governments, Bird recommends a variation on the conventional consumption-oriented VAT (i.e., production and income origin oriented rather than consumption and destination oriented) that he calls the BVT (business value tax).[23] Again, the base would be nationally determined but local authorities would have rate flexibility within limits. In both cases, these relatively neutral and nondistorting alternatives would replace a host of less attractive alternatives. The intention is that they would afford access to a source of significant revenue to better match expenditure requirements and increase the efficiency of the subnational and local tax systems.

There has been some evolution in the thinking on the tax assignment problem. Many recognize problems with and see less merit in the highly centralized system initially suggested. There is greater willingness to see the need for trade-offs in a functioning multi-tiered government structure. In assigning taxes to local governments, it is useful to look beyond predominately efficiency considerations in a somewhat ideal but abstract tax and transfer system to take account of the expenditure-revenue linkage, the existing system of taxation, the functioning of existing and likely any new intergovernmental transfers, and political forces. Careful analysis may lead to a more decentralized tax system. Some have even suggested a tax parallel to expenditure subsidiarity; that is, assign taxes to the lowest level of government able to implement them effectively and without significant negative side effects.

Merging Revenues with Expenditure Responsibilities

The major revenue options for local governments are user charges, local taxes, and intergovernmental transfers. While these alternatives are relatively few, they are diverse and there is an array of alternatives within each. Those are briefly reviewed below and important features noted. The selection of

[23] Also see Bahl and Bird (2018, pp. 208–211).

revenue sources depends critically upon the expenditure responsibilities assigned to local governments. That is, given some expenditure assignment, the preferred revenue assignments follow (i.e., finance follow function). Hence, when considering revenue assignment, one must do so in the context merging or coordinating it with the expenditure responsibilities. The revenue package selected, and there may be numerous options, should be consistent with the expenditure responsibilities of the local government. Thus, the revenue options are much like a tool kit to be used to design a functional revenue system for the specific expenditure situation. In undertaking the complete exercise, it is essential to remember that there is no single best system that fits all or even most situations. As Shah (2006, Chapter 1) indicates, it is important when designing assignments to recognize and consider the culture and evolution of the existing local government systems as those condition what is likely to be (at least initially) acceptable.

Own-Source Revenues

User Charges

If the fundamental role of local governments is to provide those services for which their residents are willing to pay, charging the users of those services the cost of their supply is a natural policy. Appropriately designed, user charges are the equivalent of private-sector prices. Charges convey information to the user as to the cost of the services and they indicate to the supplier consumers' willingness to pay. Proper pricing of public services promotes efficient provision and accountability of suppliers to customers. Bird (1993) identifies three types of user charges: (a) public prices such as charges for water and electricity, (b) service fees (notably for licenses) imposed on specific individuals for particular services, and (c) specific benefit taxes imposed on a specific group, often at their request, to finance services (e.g., local improvements like lane paving, street lighting, sidewalks) providing benefits particular to that group. A common complaint of user charges is that they disadvantage low-income consumers in comparison to subsidized supply or tax financing. However, studies have shown that the low-income people often benefit most from user fees because of service improvements and the reduced reliance on high-cost alternatives (World Bank 1994). Also, rate provisions aimed specifically at the poor are more effective than subsidized service to all. While a valuable means of financing local government, user charges are limited to services benefiting specific individuals who can be excluded from the service if unwilling to pay. Many local government services do not meet these criteria.

Taxes

Much of local government expenditure is to finance services that provide general or community benefits for which user charges are impractical if not impossible. Some form of taxation is required. Benefits realized from the expenditures financed are still an important consideration to taxpayers as they will compare benefits obtained with taxes paid and those comparisons are likely facilitated by reference to neighboring local governments. Benefits are important to the sense of fairness but the distribution of the tax burden among those of different means within the community is also a consideration even at the local level. Hence, both benefits received and ability to pay will have a bearing on the general satisfaction with the local finance system.

What Is a Local Tax?

Various questions can be asked in efforts to determine how local is a local tax. Common among those questions are: who determines the tax options available?, who defines the tax base?, who sets the tax rate?, who administers the tax?, and who receives the revenues? It is widely agreed that the dominating consideration is who sets the rate. Without the ability to set the rate, a local government is unlikely to have much influence over its revenues and revenue autonomy is central to the authority of a local government. Reasonable arguments can be made for a central authority restricting local governments' tax choices (e.g., not allowing a local corporate income tax) and for central determination of the tax bases (e.g., to avoid exploitation of unique resources or factors). Who administers the tax may be more of a convenience and cost issue than a matter of control subject to local authorities having options should the administrating government be lax or ineffective. Administration, or at least the choice of administration, should be by the government with the most at stake. Presumably, the local government imposing the tax receives all or, at least, the bulk of the revenue generated.

Typical Local Taxes

Major types of local taxes are noted here. The intention is only to provide a quick overview as the most important local taxes receive further treatment in later chapters.

Property taxes. Taxes on immobile property are widely recommended for and, not surprisingly, used by local governments. The tax base can vary in terms of the degree of distinction, if any, between land and improvements and in terms of whether the tax is based on capital or rental value. Rates too may vary among types of real property; for example, farm, residential, nonresidential. In particular, nonresidential property is often subject to higher tax rates. Higher or lower effective tax rates may be, fully or partly, realized through the assessment ratio; that is, the ratio of the assessed value for tax purposes and the actual market value. Tax bases and assessment practices are often regulated by upper-level governments.

Local personal income-related taxes. Personal income taxes are normally considered the domain of central (and state/provincial) governments but are also a tax base for local governments in a number of countries. As a local tax, the personal income tax works best if it can be "piggybacked" on or integrated with the personal income tax of the upper-tier government to minimize administration and compliance costs. Low flat rates are commonly recommended and observed. This form of local personal income tax covers all tax-filing local residents. If the central income tax covers few residents or raises little revenue, the effectiveness of a local income tax is constrained. Payroll taxation is a variant of a local income tax. Payroll taxes, however, tax only a portion of incomes (i.e., payrolls and so only those working for wages and salaries), for cost reasons focuses on large employers, and tax nonresidents employed in the local jurisdiction and so payroll taxes often confront issues of equity and efficiency.

Taxes on sales. General taxes on the sales of products and services, such as the VAT or general retail sales taxes, are typically the purview of upper-tier governments. Supplementary local sales taxes "piggybacked" onto state or central sales taxes are appealing for local governments where available but local sales taxes can be separately administered. In contrast to general sales taxes, local governments sometimes levy taxes on the sales of specific products. Taxes on alcohol and tobacco products, restaurant meals, entertainment, hotel services, utility bills, and motor fuels are examples.[24] In many cases, these too offer opportunities for coordination with parallel taxes imposed by central governments. Taxes on consumption can be attractive to local authorities. Those taxes reach a broad base, are imposed when money is spent and on those spending, might be related to benefits, and may generate significant revenues. Part of the appeal may

[24] When prices for the services of local government enterprises are above the levels consistent with user charges (e.g., utility charges exceed full costs), the difference is effectively a special sales tax on those services.

be that nonresidents bear a portion of the tax burden (via tax exporting). However, because consumers are more mobile than property or residence, there can be room for tax avoidance in a multi-jurisdictional tax-competitive environment. Both of the latter considerations are unattractive on efficiency and accountability grounds.

Taxes on business. As already noted, local property taxes on business may be levied at a higher effective rate than those on residential and agricultural properties. When, as typically the case, the cost of services to business is not correspondingly greater, this is an extra tax on business. In addition to any relatively uniform tax, there may be a variety of special business taxes based on enterprise characteristics such as floor area, storage capacity, type of business (e.g., profession, financial, industrial, utilities, etc.), sales, total assets, and the like. In many cases, business licenses and permits may fit into the business tax category. Taxes on the movement of goods across local borders (e.g., the octroi) can also be regarded as a form of business taxation. Because who bears the burden of business taxes (i.e., their incidence) is relatively obscure, business taxes are politically popular. Business taxes are also an effective way to raise a significant amount of local tax revenue. However, because (beyond property taxes) upper-level governments exploit the main sources of taxes collected on or through business (i.e., sales or value-added and income taxes), local business taxes appear in a multitude of forms and variations reflecting local opportunities and circumstances. As a result, they can be complex, economically distorting, and involve relatively large administration and compliance costs.[25]

Intergovernmental Transfers[26]

When the own-source revenues of local governments are insufficient to finance the expenditures necessitated by the assignment of local responsibilities, intergovernmental transfers (grants) will be required. Transfers may also be called for to correct for interjurisdictional spillovers. Here, a brief overview of transfers is provided of the forms and purposes of transfers.

[25] For those reasons, Bird (1999) has recommended a more uniform local business value-added tax.

[26] Besides the references cited below, the following provide valuable insights into intergovernmental transfers: Bird (2000), Bird and Smart (2002), Ebel and Yilmaz (2001), Martinez-Vazquez and Searle (2007), Shah (1999, 2004), and Shah and Thompson (2004).

Fiscal Gap-Filling Transfers

There is no assurance that independent and objective revenue and expenditure assignments, even after allowing for some practical flexibility, will result in local governments' revenue capacities matching their expenditure needs. If a fiscal imbalance exists (presumed, as is typical, to the disadvantage of local government), intergovernmental transfers will be needed to close the fiscal gap so that local responsibilities can be adequately performed. Gap-closing transfers should be unconditional and, so, available to be used according to local priorities. Such transfers can be made as unconditional lumpsum grants, but tax or revenue sharing is often used as a gap-closing mechanism. Tax (revenue) sharing exists when a specific share(s) of the revenue from a particular upper-level government's tax(es) is assigned to local government. Shared revenues are allocated by formula or returned to the jurisdiction of origin. Local revenues from sharing arrangements are sometimes categorized as local taxes but, because local governments can almost never determine their share and so cannot influence the amount of revenue derived, they are treated here (more appropriately) as intergovernmental transfers. Addressing fiscal imbalances is an important reason for intergovernmental grants. Fiscal imbalance, however, is a macro problem but it has an important micro parallel, fiscal disparities.

Fiscal Equalization

Individual local governments are not alike in their fiscal capabilities. Some are better able to meet their responsibilities than others. Indeed, some are fiscally disadvantaged to the point that they find it difficult or impossible to meet expenditure requirements with their own resources. Hence, even if there were no overall fiscal imbalance at the local level, fiscal disparities among localities can be expected to call for equalizing transfers to ensure that at least the poorest localities are not unduly disadvantaged. While most widely seen as an equity issue, there is also an efficiency argument for equalization because differences in net fiscal benefits and the resulting fiscally induced migration can distort resource allocation (Boadway and Flatters 1982).[27]

Equalization programs vary in form and objective. They may be intended to ensure that each municipality can provide at least some minimum standard of service; that is, raising the bottom. Another criterion is

[27] At the local government level, however, fiscal disadvantages may be offset in part through capitalization into property values.

that governments be able to provide comparable services while imposing comparable tax rates. Equalizing all to the capacity of the richest municipalities may also be an objective. This latter objective relates closely to Bird's recommendation that, for reasons of the accountability arising from a close tax-expenditure link, revenue and expenditure assignments be determined such that (at least) the richest municipalities have sufficient own resources to meet their expenditure requirements (Bird 1993). That is, there would be no fiscal gap for the most well-off municipalities. In such a case, equalizing transfers must be made by the upper-tier government (i.e., be paternalistic) because the richest localities do not have the surpluses to enable transfers from the rich to the poor. Such fraternal transfers require that a large number of municipalities have fiscal capacities beyond their requirements (e.g., a rich half and a poor half) that can afford the equalizing transfers needed by the less fortunate municipalities. The fact that most equalization is financed by upper-level governments need not imply that the assignment problem leaves only the rich municipalities without a fiscal gap. Fraternal transfers necessarily involve some stress between rich and poor jurisdictions that there are advantages in avoiding.

Ideally, equalization grants would offset differences in revenue-generating ability and expenditure requirements among individual governments. Neither of these, but certainly expenditure requirements, is necessarily easily determined. Hence, approximations are normally made. One relatively simple form is to offset differences in per capita tax base(s). A refinement is to incorporate better measures of expenditure requirements than the per capita criterion; for example, the number of students in schools. Sometimes, an allowance for cost of service differentials is added as well although the economic grounds for this factor are debatable. A more general approach toward equalization is found when tax- and revenue-sharing funds are allocated by formula. Such formulae encompass various factors reflecting tax capacity, need, and/or cost. As such, the available funds are distributed in a somewhat equalizing fashion and so combine, with more or less success, gap-closing, and equalization transfers. As with gap-closing transfers, equalization grants should also be unconditional and are typically so in practice. However, because equalization may be incomplete, equalization objectives may be pursued through other transfers as well.

Correcting for Externalities

Interjurisdictional spillovers of locally provided services will result in underprovision if there is no compensation for the external benefits. Otherwise, the local jurisdiction experiences all of the costs but realizes only a portion of the benefits. Services characterized by spillovers could include schooling, transportation facilities used by nonresidents (especially for through traffic as opposed to that for the use of local shops or workplaces), some police services, and certain health-care programs. Conditional grants with appropriate matching requirements are suited to the correction of spillover problems. The transfers are directed to support the spillover-generating activity. Open-ended matching grants should be used when the spillover exists for all, even the last, units produced. If the spillover benefits of the marginal units are zero, then closed-ended matching (where only inframarginal units are subsidized and the grant becomes zero once the spillover benefit becomes zero) is appropriate. Conditional block grants supporting selected programs (e.g. to some minimum standard) are an extreme case of closed-ended support. Externality correcting conditional funding are very much about "getting the prices right" in the public sector and improving efficiency.[28] In practice, too often conditional funding is overused as a substitute for gap-closing grants and, sometimes, equalization grants. However, because the use of conditional funding often depends upon the fiscal circumstances of the granting government, the economic impact can favor the better-off local governments which can afford to take advantage of matching grant programs. Because conditional funding is often directed toward infrastructure finance and stimulates local outlays more than unconditional transfers, changes in conditional transfers are occasionally used by central (or state) governments to promote or retard (local) government spending for stabilization purposes.

[28] Bird (1993) offers an additional rationale for conditional matching grants. Conditional matching funding can induce local governments to spend some of their own funds on the grantor's priorities (e.g., achieving minimum standards or greater uniformity of local services) thus stretching the grantor's budget. While a legitimate perspective, the basis for the mutual interest is in some shared or spillover benefits. Gramlich (1977) classifies conditional transfers aimed at such grantor policy objectives as also blending the advantages of centralized finance and decentralized supply as having a political-institutional justification. However, because those grants have an efficiency basis, they are distinguished here from the politically motivated grants below.

Political Reasons

In any system, transfers will exist that do not improve the economics of public provision or result in a better reflection of citizens' preferences. Rather, they will serve very narrow and perhaps unattractive political interests. While sometimes an important if not dominant basis for allocating transfers, such grants are not analyzed further here and get little attention in this volume other than to discourage their use and to recommend methods to minimize their role and any damage that they might impose.

Transfer Design

The economic motivations for intergovernmental transfers provide a sound guide to grant design. Theory and experience, however, suggest that there are a variety of other criteria to keep in mind, although many are implicit in the forgoing discussion. Providing adequate resources from transfers, both in aggregate and to meet specific functions, is fundamental if own resources are insufficient to enable local governments to do their job. Also, transfers should be fixed (with clear rules and well-defined limits) so that recipients face a hard budget constraint. That is, transfers are not to be determined by deficits and are not to be negotiable; rather, any additional spending comes from the recipient's own funds. A version of this criterion is that marginal expenditures are to be financed fully by the local authorities. The expectation is that while transfers may affect the average price of local public services, local decision makers will face and recognize the full cost at the margin and so constrain spending to where marginal benefits equal marginal cost. The objective is responsible and accountable local government despite the (even potentially heavy) reliance on transfers. This criterion reflects the efficiency objective and the desire to make the prices right.

How transfers are allocated and knowing how they are allocated is important. The distribution of funds needs to be determined by objective criteria consistent with the efficiency and equity objectives. Those rules or formulae should be transparent to the recipients so that they can understand how their allocation and that of others was determined and be confident that they are fairly treated. Relative simplicity encourages transparency. Also, any conditions on the use of grants should be explicit and readily understood so that the local authorities can be accountable to the donor and their residents. Transfers should also be predictable. Otherwise, budgeting and the effective use of funds will be difficult. Explicit criteria for how the pool of funds for gap reducing or for equalization is determined will help.

Final Observations on Merging Expenditure Responsibilities and Revenue Authority

Previous discussions have indicated that expenditure responsibilities will often not correspond perfectly to local jurisdictional boundaries. In addition, it is also unusual that the own-revenue assignment will match expenditure requirements. Both cases call for some flexibility and typically open up a range of options as to the possible compromises. For a wide range of reasons, the choices made will differ across and even within countries. Some may lean toward centralized responsibilities and finance, some toward decentralization of both, others to decentralized responsibilities and centralized finance, and some even to centralized responsibilities and decentralized finance. The discussion of own revenues and transfers in this section indicate a range of options or tools that may be used to construct a workable fiscal structure for the provision of local government services. In some instances, some of the tools (e.g., certain types of taxes) or certain potential assignments may be rejected. If so, or if certain transfers are deemed unworkable, the range of possible arrangements becomes restricted. Indeed, it may be necessary to be pragmatic and admit that the functional allocation is constrained by the financing options (rather than the more ideal, finance follows function). In general, however, intergovernmental grants make a wide range of assignments workable.

Intergovernmental transfers, while offering an array of advantages, are unlikely to simplify local public service provision and its finance. As noted, grants, and notably conditional grants, are a mechanism for intergovernmental responsibility sharing. Walsh (1992) argues that transfers represent an important counterbalance to the potentially coercive power that can exist when only one level of government has responsibility for a particular function. Walsh also contends that the effective overlapping responsibilities stemming from the open-ended power to make grants is a design advantage and not a design flaw of intergovernmental relations. However, the underlying circumstance plus the opportunity for (healthy) competition among governments and between levels of government may necessitate arrangements that are not neat and tidy.

Concluding Observations

There are a few points to emphasize in closing this section. The revenue assignment is not independent of the expenditure assignment. Revenue options are conditioned or constrained by expenditure responsibilities.

Revenues should reflect the benefits that those paying receive from the local government. Benefits received is a sound criterion for local finance. This criterion emphasizes the importance of own-source revenues for funding local services; that is, user charges and local taxes. Local governments should have the ability to set the rates determining local own revenues and so determine the amount of revenue they raise and level of expenditures that they finance. The own-revenue sources (notably the tax bases) should prevent local authorities from exporting taxes/costs to nonresidents. If so, fiscal competition will be efficiency improving not predatory. The efficiency and equity roles of transfers are primarily to compensate for spillovers or for limitations of the revenue system and should be designed to address specific problems.

Conclusion

This chapter provides a conceptual overview of the principles of expenditure and revenue assignment to local governments. The rationale for decentralization of responsibilities to local government is that local government is more responsive to local interests, more accountable to local voter-taxpayers, and, in turn, welfare improving. The dominant role for local government is the provision of local (publicly provided) goods and services. Those providing local benefits (e.g., roads and streets, drainage, refuse collection, land use control) define a core of local government responsibilities found almost everywhere. A significant number of services provide important benefits to local residents, benefit from local input, but involve large spillovers or redistributional effects. Those services (largely social services such as schooling and basic health care) are considered non-core local responsibilities because they may be assigned to local or to other levels of government. The benefit criterion serves as a valuable guide to the financing of the services provided by local government and to the assignment of revenues. That beneficiaries should be expected to pay for the services obtained from their local governments gives importance to user charges and local taxes (i.e., local own revenues). Also critical is that local governments have the authority to set the rates of their charges and taxes so as to be able to effect significantly the levels of revenues and expenditures. Typically, local governments will rely to some degree upon transfers from other governments. The importance and the type of these transfers (and, indeed, even the local tax bases) will depend upon the responsibilities assigned. The revenue and expenditure assignments are not independent and usually the finance options depend upon the functions allocated.

References

Bahl, Roy, and Richard M. Bird. 2018. *Fiscal Decentralization and Local Finance in Developing Countries*. Northampton, MA: Edward Elgar Publishing.

Bahl, Roy W., and Johannes F. Linn. 1992. *Urban Public Finance in Developing Countries*. New York: Oxford University Press.

Besley, Timothy, and Stephen Coate. 2003. Centralized versus Decentralized Provision of Local Public Goods: A Political Economy Approach. *Journal of Public Economics* 87 (12): 2611–2637.

Bird, Richard M. 1993. Threading the Fiscal Labyrinth: Some Issues in Fiscal Decentralization. *National Tax Journal* 46 (2): 207–227.

———. 1999. *Rethinking Subnational Taxes: A New Look at Tax Assignment*. IMF Working Paper 165, International Monetary Fund, December.

———. 2000. *Intergovernmental Fiscal Relations: Universal Principles, Local Applications*. Working Paper 00-02, International Studies Program, School of Policy Studies, Georgia State University, April.

Bird, Richard M., and Michael Smart. 2002. Intergovernmental Fiscal Transfers: Some Lessons for International Experience. *World Development* 30 (6): 899–912.

Bird, Richard M., and Francois Vaillancourt, eds. 1998. *Fiscal Decentralization in Developing Countries*. Cambridge: Cambridge University Press.

Bird, Richard M., Robert D. Ebel, and Christine I. Wallich, eds. 1995. *Decentralization of the Socialist State: Intergovernmental Finance in Transition Countries*. Washington, DC: The World Bank.

Bjornskov, Christian, Axel Drehe, and Justina A.V. Fischer. 2008. On Decentralization and Life Satisfaction. *Economics Letters* 99 (1): 147–151.

Boadway, Robin, and Frank Flatters. 1982. Efficiency and Equalization Payments in a Federal System of Government: Synthesis and Extension of Recent Results. *Canadian Journal of Economics* 15 (4): 613–633.

Boadway, Robin, and Anwar Shah. 2009. *Fiscal Federalism: Principles and Practice of Multiorder Governance*. New York: Cambridge University Press.

Burki, Shahid Javed, Guillermo E. Perry, and William R. Dillinger. 1999. Beyond the Center: Decentralizing the State. In *World Bank Latin American and Caribbean Studies*. Washington, DC: The World Bank.

Byrnes, Joel, and Brian Dollery. 2002. Do Economies of Scale Exist in Australian Local Government? A Review of the Recent Evidence. *Urban Policy and Research* 20 (4): 391–414.

Council of Europe. 1985. *European Charter of Local Self-Government*. http://conventions.coe.int/treaty/en/Treaties/Html/122.htm.

Dahlby, Bev. 2001. *Taxing Choices: Issues in the Assignment of Taxes in Federations*. ISSJ 167/2001, UNESCO. Oxford: Blackwell Publishers.

Dethier, Jean-Jacques, ed. 2000. *Governance, Decentralization and Reform in China, India and Russia*. Dordrecht: Kluwer Academic Publishers.

Diaz-Serrano, Luis, and Andres Rodriquez-Pose. 2012. Decentralization, Subjective Well-Being, and the Perceptions of Institutions. *Kyklos* 65 (2): 179–193.

Dollery, Brian E., and Joe L. Wallis. 2001. *The Political Economy of Local Government*. Cheltenham: Edward Elgar.

Ebel, Robert D., and Serdar Yilmaz. 2001. *Concept of Fiscal Decentralization and Worldwide Overview*. Paper presented at the Symposium of the Quebec Commission on Fiscal Imbalance, Quebec City, Quebec, September 13–14.

Fisher, Ronald C. 1996. *State and Local Public Finance*. Chicago, IL: Richard D. Irwin.

Gao, Song, Xiangyi Meng, and Li Zhang. 2014. Fiscal Decentralization and Life Satisfaction: Evidence from Urban China. *Social Indicators Research* 119 (3): 1177–1194.

Gramlich, Edward M. 1977. Intergovernmental Grants: A Review of the Empirical Literature. In *The Political Economy of Fiscal Federalism*, ed. W.E. Oates, 219–239. Lexington, MA: Lexington Books.

Helliwell, John F., and Haifang Huang. 2008. How's Your Government? International Evidence Linking Good Government and Well-Being. *British Journal of Political Science* 38 (4): 595–619.

Helliwell, John F., Haifang Huang, Shawn Grover, and Shun Wang. 2018. Empirical Linkages Between Good Governance and National Well-Being. *Journal of Comparative Economics* 46 (4): 1332–1346.

Hooghe, Liesbet, and Gary Marks. 2016. *Community, Scale, and Regional Governance: A Postfunctionalist Theory of Governance*. Vol. II. Oxford: Oxford University Press.

Hooghe, Liesbet, Gary Marks, and Arjan H. Schakel. 2010. *The Rise of Regional Authority*. New York: Routledge.

Hooghe, Liesbet, Gary Marks, Arjan H. Schakel, Sandra Chapman Osterkatz, Sara Niedzwiecki, and Sarah Shair-Rosenfield. 2016. *Measuring Regional Authority: A Postfunctionalist Theory of Governance*. Vol. I. Oxford: Oxford University Press.

Ingram, Gregory K., and Yu-Hung Hong. 2008. *Fiscal Decentralization and Land Policies*. Cambridge, MA: Lincoln Institute of Land Policy.

Ivanyna, Maksym, and Anwar Shah. 2014. How Close Is Your Government to Its People? Worldwide Indicators on Localization and Decentralization. *Economics* 8: 1–61. https://doi.org/10.5018/economics-ejournal.ja.2014-3.

King, David. 1984. *Fiscal Tiers: The Economics of Multi-level Government*. London: George, Allen and Unwin.

Kitchen, Harry M., and Enid Slack. 1993. *Business Property Taxation*. Discussion Paper 93-24, Government and Competitiveness Series, Queen's University, Kingston, ON.

Litvack, Jennie, Junaid Ahmad, and Richard Bird. 1998. *Rethinking Decentralization in Developing Countries*, PREM Sector Studies Series. Washington, DC: World Bank.

Manor, James. 1999. *The Political Economy of Democratic Decentralization.* Washington, DC: The World Bank.

Martinez-Vazquez, Jorge, and Bob Searle, eds. 2007. *Fiscal Equalization: Challenges in the Design of Intergovernmental Transfers.* New York: Springer.

McLure, Charles E., ed. 1983. *Tax Assignments in Federal Countries.* Canberra: Australian National University Press.

———. 1999. *The Assignment Problem: Conceptual and Administrative Considerations in Achieving Subnational Fiscal Autonomy.* Washington, DC: The World Bank.

McMillan, Melville L. 1976. Criteria for Jurisdictional Design: Issues in Defining the Scope and Structure of River Basin Authorities and Other Public Decision Making Bodies. *Journal of Environmental Economics and Management* 3 (1): 46–68.

———. 1989. On Measuring Congestion of Local Public Goods. *Journal of Urban Economics* 26 (2): 131–137.

McMillan, Melville L., W.R. Wilson, and L.M. Arthur. 1981. The Publicness of Local Public Goods: Evidence from Ontario Municipalities. *Canadian Journal of Economics* 14 (4): 596–608.

Musgrave, Richard A. 1959. *The Theory of Public Finance.* New York: McGraw-Hill.

———. 1983. Who Should Tax, Where and What? In *Tax Assignments in Federal Countries,* ed. C.E. McLure, 2–19. Canberra: Australian National University Press.

Oates, Wallace E. 1972. *Fiscal Federalism.* New York: Harcourt, Brace Jovanovich.

———. 1993. Fiscal Decentralization and Economic Development. *National Tax Journal* 46 (2, June): 237–243.

———. 1999. An Essay on Fiscal Federalism. *Journal of Economic Literature* 27 (3): 1120–1149.

———. 2005. Towards a Second-Generation Theory of Fiscal Federalism. *International Tax and Public Finance* 12 (4, August): 349–373.

———. 2008. The Evolution of Fiscal Federalism: Theory and Institutions. *National Tax Journal* 61 (2, June): 313–334.

OECD (Organization for Economic Co-operation and Development). 1987. *Managing and Financing Urban Services Growth.* Paris: OECD.

———. 1997. *Managing Across Levels of Government.* Paris: PUMA.

———. 1999. *Taxing Powers of State and Local Government.* OECD Tax Policy Studies, No. 1, Paris.

———. 2013. *Fiscal Federalism 2014: Making Decentralization Work.* Paris: OECD Publishing.

———. 2016. *Fiscal Federalism 2016: Making Decentralization Work.* Paris: OECD Publishing.

———. 2018. *Assigning Responsibilities Across Levels of Government*. OECD Working Papers on Fiscal Federalism, September. https://www.oecd-ilibrary.org/docserver/f0944eae-en.pdf?expires=1551479356&id=id&accname=guest&checksum=3046DD4B5D67CBCB4DCBCDC89D5ECC8D.

Owens, Jeffrey, and John Norregaard. 1991. The Role of Lower Levels of Government: The Experience of Selected OECD Countries. In *Local Government: An International Perspective*, ed. Jeffrey Owens and Giorgio Panella, 3–54. Amsterdam: North-Holland.

Rondinelli, Dennis. 1999. What is Decentralization. In *Decentralization Briefing Notes*, ed. J. Litvack and J. Seddon, 2–5. Washington, DC: World Bank Institute.

Shah, Anwar. 1991. *The New Federalism in Brazil*. The World Bank Discussion Paper #124, Washington, DC.

———. 1994. *The Reform of Intergovernmental Fiscal Relations in Developing and Emerging Market Economies, Policy and Research Series, 23*. Washington, DC: The World Bank.

———. 1999. Intergovernmental Transfers and Grants. In *Decentralization Briefing Notes*, ed. J. Litvack and J. Seddon, 27–31. Washington, DC: World Bank Institute.

———. 2004. *Fiscal Decentralization in Developing and Transition Economies: Progress, Problems and the Promise*. World Bank Policy Research Working Paper 3282, The World Bank, Washington DC, April.

———. 2006. A Comparative Institutional Framework for Responsive, Responsible and Accountable Local Governance. In *Local Governance in Industrialized Countries*, ed. Anwar Shah, 1–40. Washington, DC: The World Bank.

———. 2014. Responsibility with Accountability: A FAIR governance framework for performance accountability of local governments. *Zbornik Radova Ekonomskog Fakulteta u Rijeci* 32 (2): 343–377.

Shah, Anwar, and Theresa Thompson. 2004. *Implementing Decentralized Local Governance: A Treacherous Road with Potholes, Detours and Road Closures*. World Bank Policy Research Paper 3353, The World Bank, Washington DC, June.

Stigler, George. 1957. Tenable Range of Functions of Local Government. In *Federal Expenditure Policy for Economic Growth and Stability*, ed. Joint Economic Committee, Subcommittee on Fiscal Policy, 213–219. Washington, DC.

Ter-Minassian, Teresa, ed. 1997. *Fiscal Federalism in Theory and Practice*. Washington, DC: International Monetary Fund.

Tiebout, Charles. 1956. A Pure Theory of Public Expenditures. *Journal of Political Economy* 64 (5): 416–424.

Tomaney, J., A. Pike, G. Torrisi, V. Tselios, and A. Rodríguez-Pose. 2011. *Decentralisation Outcomes: A Review of Evidence and Analysis of International Data*. Department for Communities and Local Government. https://blogs.ncl.ac.uk/curds/files/2013/02/DecentralisationReport.pdf.

Tresch, Richard W. 2015. *Public Finance: A Normative Theory*. 3rd ed. Waltham, MA: Academic Press.

Walsh, Cliff. 1992. *Fiscal Federalism: An Overview of Issues and a Discussion of Their Relevance to the European Community*. Canberra: Federalism Research Centre Discussion Paper No. 2, The Australian National University.

Wiesner, Eduardo. 2003. *Fiscal Federalism in Latin America: From Entitlements to Markets*. New York: Inter-American Development Bank.

World Bank. 1994. *World Development Report, 1994: Infrastructure for Development*. Washington, DC: The World Bank and Oxford University Press.

CHAPTER 3

Expenditure and Revenue Assignment: Practices

Introduction

Diverse developments in various parts of the world have increased interest in the potential of local government. Notably, countries among the transitional economies and countries in the developing world often look to the experience of the industrial countries in their efforts to redesign and restructure government—particularly government at the local level. Also, local government in industrial countries is not static, because such countries, if not continually at least sporadically, are reassessing and experimenting with local authorities in search of improvement (see, e.g., Danish Ministry of the Interior and Health 2005). The varying patterns, organizations, and intergovernmental relations found among industrial countries and the transitions that have occurred there offer many alternatives and potential insights for those seeking ways to structure, enhance, or reform local government.

The purpose of this study is to survey the fiscal structure of local government across the major industrial countries and to draw lessons from their practices and experience. The approach is not to duplicate the many country-by-country studies (see Batley and Stoker 1991; Hesse 1991;

Other than for minor editorial changes, this chapter is a reprint/reproduction of Melville L. McMillan, 2008, "A Local Perspective on Fiscal Federalism: Practices, Experiences and Lessons from Industrialized Countries," Chapter 7 in Anwar Shah (ed.) *Macro Federalism and Local Finance*, Washington DC: The World Bank, 245–289.

H. Kitchen et al., *Local Public Finance and Economics*,
https://doi.org/10.1007/978-3-030-21986-4_3

and Shah 2006b, among numerous others). In fact, the data used here, while affording valuable broad comparisons, fails to provide important details available only from the more intensive country analyses. Nevertheless, occasionally drawing from that literature is useful to illustrate notable practices and experiences relating to major features of local government, particularly the assignment of responsibilities and the funding of those activities. Many important nonfiscal features (e.g., organization and structure) are not covered here.[1]

The chapter consists of two major components. One examines the expenditure side of the budget and the other looks at the revenue side. Expenditures are considered from several perspectives. In particular, a distinction is made between core activities and social programs. Also, capital expenditures deserve special attention, and regulatory responsibilities need mentioning. The examination of revenues pays attention to alternative tax sources, nontax own-source revenue, and intergovernmental transfers. A summary with conclusions and lessons completes the chapter.

Expenditure Responsibilities of Local Government

What do local governments in industrial countries do? In particular, to what functions do local governments allocate their budgets, and in what proportions and in what amounts? The activities that are found in a broad selection of industrial countries are sketched herein, and the similarities and differences are highlighted.[2] The focus is almost entirely on the financial aspects—that is, the expenditures of local governments. The section begins by listing expenditure areas and by noting that their importance varies considerably among countries. The analysis continues with the consideration of expenditures in different contexts and from different perspectives.

Expenditure by Function

Examining the share of expenditures in common functional categories is a helpful start toward appreciating the expenditure responsibilities of local governments. Table 3.1 shows the distribution of local government expenditures across 10 major expenditure categories for 20 industrial

[1] This chapter is a (slightly edited) reprint of McMillan (2008) which, in turn, was an updated but much abbreviated version of an earlier paper with the same title (McMillan 1996). Dated but potentially valuable details and extensions are available in the 1996 paper.

[2] The group of industrial countries is based on those so identified in the International Monetary Fund's *Government Finance Statistics Yearbook* (IMF 2005).

Table 3.1 Local government expenditures by function (%), 2003

Country	*General public services*	*Public order and safety*	*Economic affairs*			*Environ-mental protection*	*Housing and community amenities*	*Recreation culture and religious affairs*	*Education*	*Health*	*Social protection*	*Other (defense)*	*Total*[a]
			Transpor-tation[b]	*Other*	*Total*								
Federal countries													
Australia	21.1	2.4	24.9	5.3	30.1	8.4	14.9	15.3	0.4	1.6	5.7	–	100.0
Austria	17.1	2.3	–	–	14.5	2.7	3.4	7.4	17.2	17.1	18.2	–	100.0
Belgium	23.5	11.9	–	–	11.2	5.0	1.8	8.6	19.9	2.0	16.1	–	100.0
Canada	8.7	9.3	11.3	1.7	12.9	5.5	7.1	7.4	41.4	1.6	6.2	–	100.0
Germany	14.9	4.5	–	–	11.8	5.9	6.8	6.6	16.5	2.0	31.0	–	100.0
Switzerland (2002)	15.7	4.6	7.1	1.6	8.7	5.9	2.5	5.4	23.0	19.2	14.4	0.5	100.0
United States (2000)	5.8	10.8	6.1	1.1	7.1	–	2.1	3.4	44.2	8.7	7.5	10.5	100.0
Average	15.3	6.5			13.8	4.8	5.5	7.7	23.2	7.4	14.2	1.6	100.0
Unitary countries													
Denmark	4.2	0.3	2.7	2.1	4.8	0.9	0.7	2.8	13.7	20.8	51.8	0.1	100.0
Finland	12.2	1.6	–	–	7.4	0.8	0.9	4.9	21.4	27.5	23.3	–	100.0
France (2002)	35.7	2.6	–	–	11.1	11.1	7.0	5.2	16.2	0.6	10.4	–	100.0
Iceland (2002)	12.0	2.1	12.8	2.0	14.8	...	6.9	14.2	29.7	1.0	19.8	–	100.0
Italy	12.6	1.6	–	–	15.4	5.1	5.4	3.5	10.3	41.5	4.4	–	100.0
Luxembourg (2002)	18.5	1.7	–	–	20.5	11.2	7.2	13.1	22.5	0.3	4.5	–	100.0
Netherlands	16.9	5.8	–	–	16.6	4.3	6.2	7.2	25.2	1.7	16.2	–	100.0
New Zealand	18.9	–	28.8	0.3	29.1	23.8	9.2	20.6	...	...	0.1	0.6	100.0
Norway	11.2	1.0	4.5	0.7	5.2	3.6	5.0	5.2	28.7	16.7	23.9	–	100.0
Portugal (2002)	26.1	1.4	–	–	24.1	7.8	12.3	11.7	8.7	5.4	2.4	–	100.0
Spain (2001)	35.1	9.5	8.4	3.9	12.3	9.6	12.5	9.8	2.9	1.8	6.3	–	100.0
Sweden	10.7	1.1	–	–	5.3	0.7	2.8	3.2	21.5	27.3	27.3	–	100.0

(*continued*)

Table 3.1 (continued)

Country	*General public services*	*Public order and safety*	*Economic affairs*			*Environmental protection*	*Housing and community amenities*	*Recreation culture and religious affairs*	*Education*	*Health*	*Social protection*	*Other (defense)*	*Total*[a]
			Transportation[b]	*Other*	*Total*								
United Kingdom (1998)	4.0	12.3	4.9	1.2	6.0	–	5.4	3.1	28.7	–	32.5	8.0	100.0
Average	16.8	3.1			13.3	6.1	6.3	8.0	16.1	11.1	17.2	0.7	100.0
Overall Average	16.2	4.3			13.5	5.6	6.0	7.9	18.6	9.8	16.1	1.0	100.0
Range													
Minimum	3.9	0.3			4.8	0.0	0.9	2.8	0.0	0.0	0.0	0.0	
Maximum	35.7	12.3			30.1	23.8	14.9	20.6	44.1	41.5	51.8	8.0	

Data are for 2003 unless otherwise indicated. There was a revision of classification as of 2001. Environmental Protection was added as a separate category; Social Security and Welfare changed to Social Protection and Other was deleted. Other Economic Affairs includes Fuel and Energy; Agriculture, Forestry, Fishing, and Hunting; and Mining, Construction, and Manufacturing. Other includes Defense (for the United Kingdom and Denmark) and Other Expenditures

In addition to those countries reported here, Greece, Ireland, and Japan are classified as industrialized by the International Monetary Fund. There are, however, no data available for those countries for this period

Source: Author's calculations from data in IMF *Government Finance Statistics Yearbook*, 2002, 2004, and 2005

Notes: '–' indicates not available; '...' indicates insignificant

[a]Totals may not sum to 100.0 due to rounding and statistical discrepancies

[b]Of those reporting transportation expenditures separately, 84.4 percent of Economic Affairs expenditures were for transportation

countries. The average percentage shares over the 20 countries show that the major expenditure categories are education (18.6 percent), general public services (16.2 percent), social protection (16.1 percent), and economic affairs, predominantly transportation (13.5 percent). Each takes more than 10 percent of the average budget, and together they account for almost two-thirds of local outlays. Ignoring a residual "other" category, the remaining categories require from 4.3 percent (public order and safety) to 9.8 percent (health).

The countries analyzed are categorized as federal or unitary. This division was included because the existence of a middle tier of government in the federal countries might affect the pattern of expenditures. In fact, inspection of the averages of the two groups suggests modest differences. Although the ranking varies, education, general public services, social protection, and economic affairs are the major expenditure categories and account for over 60 percent of outlays for both groups. However, some differences are observed. Expenditures for public order and safety are relatively higher in federal countries (6.5 percent vs. 3.1 percent of expenditures), and the share allotted for education is also larger. Meanwhile, local outlays for health and for social protection are somewhat larger in the unitary countries on average. However, the intercountry variation in these categories is large within both the unitary and federal groups.

The striking feature of Table 3.1 is that the distribution of expenditures among functional areas across the countries is so uneven. The ranges in these percentage shares are shown at the bottom of the table. On average, the range across the categories is from a low of 1.3 percent to a high of 28.3 percent. Aside from the other category, the minimum absolute difference is 12 percentage points (that for public order and safety). The portion of local expenditures devoted to public order and safety, for example, is high in the United Kingdom and the United States, where local governments bear a large share of or even full responsibility for local policing but is small (even nil in New Zealand) where policing is a provincial, state, or central responsibility as, for example, in Australia, Denmark, and France. Even the economic affairs category, which mostly comprises local road and transport services, varies from 4.8 percent in Denmark (figures are similarly low in Norway and Sweden) to 30.1 percent in Australia (with a similarly high percentage in New Zealand).[3] Most of the variation in the expenditure

[3] In the case of environmental services (largely solid waste and wastewater services), the zero values reported for the United Kingdom and the United States are odd because local governments in both countries are responsible for such services and report expenditures on them (see, e.g., King 2006; Schroeder 2006).

shares arises from differing local responsibilities for social programs—that is, for education (schooling), health, and social protection. These programs may account for essentially no local expenditures to 41.5 percent for health (Italy), 44.2 percent for education (the United States), and 51.8 percent for social protection (Denmark). In a few countries (Australia, New Zealand, and Spain), local governments spend little on social programs, whereas in others—notably the Scandinavian countries—those programs represent the vast majority of local budgets.

This diverse array of expenditure allocations can seem confusing and can cause one to wonder whether any rationale exists for the underlying responsibility assignment or whether any lessons can be drawn from the experience of these countries. In fact, both an underlying logic and lessons do exist. The variation, however, demonstrates the range of possibilities and the need for appropriate fiscal design. To begin sorting out the problem, the chapter considers first the allocation of responsibilities among levels of governments.

Expenditures by Level of Government

The role of local government in the public sector and in the economy differs among countries. This situation is made explicit in Table 3.2, which shows the share of government expenditures made by each level of government. Here, expenditures are attributed to the government that finally spends the public funds for goods and services regardless of whether those funds came from own-source revenues or from intergovernmental transfers.

Local government expenditures tend to be relatively more important in unitary countries than in federal countries. As might be expected, the presence of state or provincial governments diminishes the role of both central and local governments to some degree.[4] Across the federal countries, local government expenditures account for 17.8 percent of general government spending on average, while they undertake 29.9 percent on average in

[4] Government spending tends to be more decentralized in federal countries. About half of government spending is made by central governments in federal countries compared with an average of about 70 percent in unitary countries. Note that with central government expenditures amounting to about 40 percent or less of total government outlays, Canada and Switzerland are quite decentralized. In contrast, France, Luxembourg, New Zealand, and Portugal are quite centralized with over 80 percent of expenditures made by the central government, and the United Kingdom, at 73.9 percent, is not far behind. Denmark stands out as an exceptionally decentralized unitary country, with the central government accounting for only 40.5 percent of government outlays.

Table 3.2 Relative government expenditures for selected countries

Country	*Expenditure by level (%)*			*Government expenditure as % of GDP*	*Local government expenditure as % of GDP*
	Central	*State/provincial*	*Local*		
Federal countries					
Australia	53.8	39.4	6.8	35.5	2.4
Austria	68.3	16.2	15.5	50.5	8.0
Belgium[a]	–	–	–	–	6.7
Canada	37.2	44.7	18.1	41.0	7.5
Germany	63.4	22.1	14.5	48.4	7.3
Switzerland (2002)	40.1	34.1	25.8	37.4	9.8
United States (2000)	51.0	22.7	26.2	32.6	8.8
Average[b]	52.3	29.9	17.8	40.9	7.2
Unitary countries					
Denmark (2002)	40.6	–	59.5	55.7	33.1
Finland	61.1	–	38.9	50.9	19.5
France (2002)	81.4	–	18.6	53.7	10.2
Iceland (2002)	70.8	–	29.2	44.7	13.0
Italy	68.9	–	31.1	49.1	15.4
Luxembourg (2002)	86.0	–	14.0	41.8	5.9
Netherlands	64.8	–	35.2	49.2	17.4
New Zealand	90.5	–	9.5	36.4	3.4
Norway	69.1	–	31.1	48.8	15.2
Portugal (2002)	85.7	–	14.3	46.6	6.6
Spain (2001)	63.9	–	36.1[c]	36.9	6.5
Sweden	55.5	–	44.5	58.7	26.0
United Kingdom (1998)	73.9	–	26.1	39.6	10.4
Average	70.1		29.9	47.1	14.0

Data are for 2003 unless otherwise indicated
Expenditures are net of transfers to other governments

Sources: Author's calculations from data in IMF *Government Finance Statistics Yearbook*, 2002, 2004, and 2005

Notes: '–' indicates not available
[a]Not all values calculated due to large statistical discrepancy
[b]Average of number reporting
[c]Regional government in Spain accounts for 19.0 of the 36.1

unitary countries. Still, there is considerable variation in the local role in both types of countries. Among the federal countries, local government accounts for only 6.8 percent of government expenditure in Australia but 25.8 percent in Switzerland and 26.2 percent in the United States. At about one-fourth of government expenditure, the levels in Switzerland and the

United States equal or exceed the percentage represented by local government in 5 of the 13 unitary countries, where the local percentage ranges from 9.5 percent in New Zealand to 59.5 percent in Denmark. The overall range of 6.8–59.5 percent is huge, and though local governments in most countries fall into a 15–35 percent range, even that variation is large.

The size of local government relative to the economy also varies. Local government expenditure as a percentage of gross domestic product (GDP) is included in Table 3.2. In the federal countries, local government spending amounts to 7.2 percent of GDP, but, at 14.0 percent, the amount is almost twice as large in the unitary countries. These differences (as do those among individual countries) depend on both the intergovernmental division of responsibilities and the role of government in the economy. Government in the unitary countries is somewhat larger than government in the federal countries, 47.1 percent compared with 40.9 percent of GDP. Local government expenditures in countries like Australia and New Zealand are small relative to GDP (2.4 and 3.4 percent, respectively) both because their assigned expenditure responsibilities are modest and because total government in those countries is relatively small (35.5 and 36.4 percent of GDP). In contrast, local government expenditure in Denmark amounts to an extraordinarily large 33.1 percent of GDP, partly because total government spending there is large at 55.7 percent of GDP. Australia is exceptional even among federal countries because local expenditures in the other federal countries range from 6.7 to 9.8 percent of GDP. In the unitary countries, the range is larger, from 3.4 to 33.1 percent, and the percentages are more widely dispersed.

Social Programs and Local Government Finance

Responsibilities for social programs substantially affect local government budgets. As noted, those responsibilities are a major reason for the differences in the distribution of expenditures by function, and they affect the relative importance of local government in the public sector. The implications of the responsibilities for social programs (education, health, and social protection) are demonstrated in Table 3.3. In that table, countries are grouped by local government expenditure as a percentage of GDP. Australia and New Zealand constitute the low group, with an average of 2.9 percent. Denmark and Sweden constitute the high group, with an average of 29.5 percent. The middle group is subdivided into countries with upper-medium and lower-medium budget shares. The upper-medium group is made up of

Table 3.3 Social programs in local government finance, 2003

Country	*Local government expenditure as a percentage of GDP*	*Local government as a percentage of total government*	*Local social program expenditure*			*Local government nonsocial program expenditures as a percentage of GDP*	*Percentage of local government budget transfer financed*
			Percentage of local budgets	*Percentage of GDP*	*Percentage of national public social expenditures*		
Low budget share							
Australia	2.4	6.7	6.7	0.16	0.9	2.2	14.5
New Zealand (2004)	3.4	9.5	0.1	0.003	0.5	3.4	9.3
Average	2.9	8.1	3.4	0.08	0.7	2.8	11.9
Lower-medium budget share							
Austria	8.0	15.5	52.5	4.20	12.5	3.8	21.0
Belgium	6.7	n/a	38.0	2.55	6.7	4.3	49.1
Canada	7.5	18.4	49.2	3.69	14.2	3.8	39.0
France (2002)	10.2	18.6	27.3	2.78	7.7	7.4	41.7
Germany	7.3	14.5	49.5	3.61	10.4	3.7	32.5
Luxembourg	5.9	14.0	27.6	1.62	4.4	4.3	40.4
Portugal (2002)	6.6	14.3	16.5	1.09	3.7	5.5	44.0
Spain (2001)[a]	6.5	17.1	11.0	0.71	2.9	5.8	38.4
Switzerland (2002)	9.5	25.8	56.6	5.38	24.0	4.1	17.1
United Kingdom (1998)	10.4	26.1	61.2	6.36	na	4.0	70.0
United States (2000)	8.9	26.2	60.3	5.37	na	3.5	39.4
Average[b]	7.9	19.1	40.9	3.40	9.6	4.6	39.3

(*continued*)

Table 3.3 (continued)

Country	*Local government expenditure as a percentage of GDP*	*Local government as a percentage of total government*	*Local social program expenditure*			*Local government nonsocial program expenditures as a percentage of GDP*	*Percentage of local government budget transfer financed*
			Percentage of local budgets	*Percentage of GDP*	*Percentage of national public social expenditures*		
Upper-medium share							
Finland	19.5	38.9	72.2	14.08	40.5	5.4	26.4
Iceland (2002)	13.0	29.2	50.5	6.57	26.4	6.4	9.3
Italy	15.4	31.1	56.2	8.65	29.6	6.7	41.2
Netherlands	17.3	35.2	43.1	7.46	26.3	9.8	61.1
Norway	15.2	31.1	69.3	10.53	31.3	4.7	34.6
Average	16.1	33.1	58.3	9.46	30.8	6.6	34.5
High budget share							
Denmark	33.1	59.5	86.3	28.57	47.3	4.5	37.1
Sweden	26.0	44.5	76.1	19.79	49.9	6.2	19.4
Average	29.5	52.0	81.2	24.18	48.6	5.3	28.3

Data are for 2003 unless otherwise indicated
Social program expenditures are those for education, health, and social protection

Source: Author's calculations from data in IMF *Government Finance Statistics Yearbook*, 2002, 2004, and 2005

[a]Spain's regional governments are not included
[b]Average of observations with data

5 countries, with local expenditures as a percentage of GDP ranging from 13.0 to 19.5 percent and averaging 16.1 percent. The lower-medium group is the largest with 11 countries that have local expenditures ranging from 5.9 to 10.4 percent of GDP and an average of 7.9 percent. Local government as a percentage of total government parallels this classification, with averages across the groups (from low to high) of 8.1, 19.1, 33.1, and 52.0 percent. The absolute and relative size of local government corresponds to—and is essentially determined by—local responsibilities for social programs. Local government expenditures on social programs as a percentage of GDP across the groups average 0.08, 3.40, 9.46, and 24.18 percent. In contrast, the relative magnitude of nonsocial spending is much more homogeneous, with averages as a percentage of GDP of 2.8, 4.6, 6.6, and 5.3 percent.

Consider further the social expenditures by local government. First, because social programs are costly, they have a large effect on local budgets where local governments bear responsibility for such spending. Aside from the group with low budget shares (with an average of 3.4 percent), social spending averages 40.9, 58.3, and 81.2 percent of local government total expenditures. Among those three groups, the social expenditure share ranges from 11.0 in Spain to 86.3 percent in Denmark. Spain's share is low partly because its regional governments (which undertake 84 percent of spending on education) are not included with local government. Local government may or may not be responsible for a significant share of the national social expenditure. The striking feature here is that local governments with upper-medium and high budget shares account for one-fourth to one-half of national social spending (with averages of 30.8 and 48.6 percent of the total for the two groups). Among the countries in the other two groups, only Switzerland (where local government social spending represents 24 percent of total government social expenditure) approaches such levels. Elsewhere, local expenditures range from 0.5 to 14.2 percent and average 5.8 percent. Thus, in 40 percent of the countries examined (and those are predominantly Scandinavian), local government has a major responsibility for social programs, but in the other 60 percent, the local responsibility is typically quite small.

Because social programs usually involve significant redistribution and thus are not usually recommended as a local government financing responsibility, one might expect transfers to become more important as social expenditure represents an increasing share of the budget. Such is not the case. Although transfers from senior governments cover only 11.9 percent of expenditures in the group with low budget shares, transfers as a percentage of expenditures actually decline as the social expenditure share and level increases across the other three budget groups. Transfers average 39.3, 34.5, and 28.3 for the groups with lower-medium, upper-medium, and high budget shares, respectively. Differences in access to tax sources largely explain this situation, and further explanation must await that discussion.

Social expenditure responsibilities explain most of the large differences in the roles of local government among countries. Differences in the magnitudes of nonsocial expenditures are much smaller. As a percentage of GDP, nonsocial expenditures range from 2.2 percent in Australia to 9.8 percent in the Netherlands, but 17 of the 20 lie in the 3.5–7.4 percent range. Among those 17, the local governments in federal countries (where responsibilities are also shared with state or provincial governments) represent the lower end of that group, with values from 3.5 percent (the United States) to 4.3 percent (Belgium). Thus, there appears to be a core set of responsibilities for local governments that is relatively common among countries. Details of these local core activities and of local social programs are pursued in the next section.

Local Expenditures by Function as a Percentage of GDP

Further insight into and detail about local government expenditures are provided in Table 3.4, which reports expenditure by function as a percentage of GDP. Again, analyzing social and nonsocial spending separately is useful. Beginning with social programs, Australia and New Zealand, which have low budget shares, stand out because local governments spend very little individually or collectively on education, health, and social protection (less than 0.2 percent of GDP in Australia and effectively nothing in New Zealand). In the group with lower-medium budget shares, education is the major social expenditure category.

Education is largest of the three social programs in 7 (possibly 8) of the 11 countries and has the highest average at 1.8 percent of GDP. Education outlays are particularly large in the United Kingdom and the United States, where local government is fully responsible for schooling expenditure. Finance, however, can be quite different. In the United States, local school authorities finance about half of school spending from own sources, with the other half from (primarily) state transfers. In the United Kingdom, schooling is entirely funded by central transfers. In contrast, local authorities in France provide only the school infrastructure, and in Germany, the state governments provide the teachers. In Spain, education is the responsibility of the regional governments.

Table 3.4 Local government expenditures by function as a percentage of GDP, 2003[a]

Country	*General public services*	*Public order and safety*	*Economic affairs*			*Environmental protection*	*Housing and community annuities*	*Recreation, culture, and religious affairs*	*Education*	*Health*	*Social protection*	*Other*	*Total*
			Transportation	*Other*	*Total*								
Low budget share													
Australia	0.51	0.06	0.6	0.13	0.73	0.20	0.36	0.37	0.01	0.04	0.14	–	2.6
New Zealand	0.64	–	0.98	0.01	0.99	0.81	0.31	0.70	–	–	0.003	0.02	3.4
Average	0.57	0.03	–	–	0.86	0.51	0.33	0.53	0.005	0.02	0.07	0.01	2.9
Medium budget share													
Lower medium													
Austria	1.37	0.18	–	–	1.16	0.22	0.27	0.59	1.38	1.37	1.46	–	8.0
Belgium	1.57	0.80	–	–	0.75	0.33	0.12	0.58	1.33	0.13	1.08	–	6.7
Canada	0.65	0.69	0.84	0.12	0.96	0.41	0.53	0.55	3.09	0.12	0.46	–	8.4
France	3.63	0.27	–	–	1.13	1.13	0.71	0.52	1.65	0.06	1.06	–	10.2
Germany	1.09	0.33	–	–	0.87	0.43	0.50	0.48	1.21	0.14	2.27	–	7.3
Luxembourg	1.09	0.10	–	–	1.21	0.66	0.42	0.77	1.33	0.02	0.27	–	5.9
Portugal (2002)	1.72	0.09	–	–	1.59	0.51	0.81	0.77	0.57	0.36	0.16	–	6.6
Spain (2001)	2.28	0.62	0.55	0.25	0.80	0.62	0.81	0.64	0.19	0.12	0.41	–	6.5
Switzerland	1.54	0.45	0.69	0.16	0.85	0.58	0.25	0.53	2.25	1.88	1.41	0.05	10.6
United Kingdom	0.41	1.27	0.50	0.12	0.62	–	0.56	0.31	2.97	–	3.37	0.83	10.4
United States	0.51	0.95	0.53	0.09	0.62	–	0.18	0.29	3.87	0.76	0.66	0.92	9.4
Average	1.44	0.52	–	–	0.96	0.44	0.47	0.55	1.80	0.45	1.15	0.16	7.8

(continued)

Table 3.4 (continued)

Country	*General public services*	*Public order and safety*	*Economic affairs*			*Environmental protection*	*Housing and community annuities*	*Recreation, culture, and religious affairs*	*Education*	*Health*	*Social protection*	*Other*	*Total*
			Transportation	*Other*	*Total*								
Upper medium													
Finland	2.38	0.31	–	–	1.44	0.16	0.17	0.95	4.17	5.36	4.54	–	19.5
Iceland (2002)	1.56	0.27	1.66	0.26	2.92	–	0.90	1.85	3.86	0.13	2.57	–	13.0
Italy	1.94	0.25	–	–	2.37	0.79	0.83	0.54	1.59	6.39	0.68	–	15.4
Netherlands	2.94	1.00	–	–	2.87	0.74	1.08	1.24	4.37	0.29	2.81	–	17.3
Norway	1.70	0.15	0.68	0.11	0.79	0.55	0.76	0.79	4.36	2.54	3.63	–	15.2
Average	2.10	0.40	–	–	1.87	0.45	0.75	1.07	3.71	2.94	2.85	0.00	16.1
High budget share													
Denmark	1.40	0.10	0.88	0.69	1.57	0.30	0.23	0.92	4.53	6.89	17.15	0.02	33.1
Sweden	2.78	0.29	–	–	1.38	0.18	0.73	0.83	5.59	7.10	7.10	–	26.0
Average	2.09	0.19	–	–	1.47	0.24	0.48	0.87	5.06	6.99	12.12	0.10	29.5
Overall average	1.59	0.41	–	–	1.23	0.43	0.53	0.71	2.48	1.69	2.56	0.09	11.70

Sources: Author's calculations from data in IMF *Government Finance Statistics Yearbook*, 2002, 2004, and 2005

Notes: '–' indicates not available

[a]Data are for 2003 unless otherwise indicated

Within this budget group, local expenditure responsibilities for health care are small except for Austria and Switzerland, where they are in the 1–2 percent of GDP range. In the United Kingdom, health care is entirely a central responsibility and almost so in France and Luxembourg. Local spending on social protection actually averages 1.15 percent of GDP for this group, but the average is greatly affected by the high levels in Germany and the United Kingdom. The large percentage reported for the United Kingdom (3.37 percent) is not understood and is at odds with country reports (e.g., King 2006). Social protection there is primarily housing assistance for various disadvantaged groups and is largely directed and funded by the central government. In Germany, local social assistance and housing allowances are determined and paid for by the federal government.

Thus, where local governments in this budget group become involved in spending for social programs, it is primarily for schooling. Even there—and more so for health and social protection—programs are directed or supervised by senior governments that commonly provide most of the funding if the level of expenditure is notable.

Local social program spending is broadly based in those countries in the groups with upper-medium and high budget shares. For the upper-medium group, education, health, and social protection expenditures average 3.71, 2.94, and 2.85 percent of GDP, respectively, while for the high group, the averages are 5.06, 6.99, and 12.12 percent. Still, there are some notable variations among countries. Local expenditures for health care are high (over 5 percent) in Denmark, Finland, Italy, and Sweden but very low (under 0.3 percent) in Iceland and the Netherlands. In Italy, health could be considered the only major area of local social spending. At 17.15 percent of GDP, expenditures for social protection are remarkably large in Denmark. Denmark's local governments are responsible for a broad range of social protection programs (including old-age pensions, child allowances, and welfare and employment programs) that are more commonly the responsibilities of senior governments. However, old-age pensions and child allowances are funded entirely by the central government, and the costs of welfare and employment programs are shared on a 50:50 basis. Growth in the size of local government relates directly to expansion in the size and breadth of social program responsibilities. That expansion is, however, typically accompanied by senior government direction and support.

Local spending in the nonsocial program areas is relatively uniform overall. As shown in Table 3.4, the group averages of the levels of spending on general services, public order and safety, economic affairs (predominantly transportation), environmental protection, housing and community amenities, and recreation and cultural services are much more uniform than is the case for social programs. Still, the intercountry variations can be considerable. For example, spending on general public services, at 3.63 percent of GDP, is exceptionally high in France; spending on economic affairs is large in Iceland, Italy, and the Netherlands; expenditures for recreation and culture are relatively high in Iceland; and reported spending for environmental protection is low in the United Kingdom and the United States (but contrast with that indicated in country studies). The variation in expenditures for public order and safety relate to the assignment of policing responsibilities between local and senior governments. However, spending on environmental protection, housing and community amenities, and recreation and culture tend to be relatively consistent.

One country, the Netherlands, stands out. It consistently ranks first or second in the level of spending across the nonsocial functions and, for this expenditure class, has the distinctly highest level of spending at 9.8 percent of GDP (see Table 3.3). Local government in the Netherlands has unique water management issues to address, which may explain the higher expenditures on economic affairs, but not the higher spending across the board. Toonen (1991) characterizes the situation in the Netherlands as the central government being too reliant on local government to carry out state affairs. That local government there generated only 31 percent of its revenues from own sources and still generates only 39 percent may support that argument. Stoker (1991, p. 18) summarizes the situation of Dutch local governments with the comment that they are both "over-ambitious and overburdened." Although anomalies exist, these data lend support to the existence of a relatively consistent set of core activities for which local governments are responsible in most countries.

In summary, the fiscal role of local governments varies widely among countries. The differences depend primarily on the expenditure responsibilities of local governments for social programs (schooling, health care, and social protection). Although local governments commonly have some responsibility for schooling, their responsibilities for health and social protection are more diverse. Responsibilities for and expenditures on the non-social program functions tend to be more uniform and, as such, they form a set of core responsibilities typical of and more common to local governments.

Regulation: Completing the Concept of Core Services

The preceding discussion of core services focused on expenditures. Attention concentrated on the significant budget demands of major services, such as transportation (e.g., roadways and public transit); protection (e.g., policing, fire, and emergency services); water and sewerage and drainage; waste collection and disposal; economic development; recreation and cultural facilities and services; and general administration (e.g., council and tax assessment and collection). These largely physical services, sometimes referred to as *housekeeping activities*, are important for making a community functional and pleasant. Also essential is a second group of core services, which are largely regulatory. These services are the locally determined rules that promote safety (e.g., traffic regulation, fire regulation, and building codes); promote the enjoyment of property (e.g., regulation of development and land use, noise, and waste); manage business (e.g., business licenses and taxi permits); and generally control potential nuisances. These activities are not normally large within the local government budget and are only elements within the expenditure categories noted, so they are easily overlooked. Still, regulatory activities are important for creating a pleasant and safer local environment and so deserve recognition as part of the core activities of local governments.

Capital Expenditures

Local government is responsible for a disproportionate share of government capital—almost half the total. The International Monetary Fund's *Government Finance Statistics Yearbook* (IMF 2005) does not provide information on capital expenditures themselves, but it does provide estimates of the consumption of government-owned fixed capital, assuming normal use and obsolescence. Capital consumed must be replaced, so this measure of consumption reflects required replacement investment. Table 3.5 offers insight into local government's role in the consumption of this fixed capital. The table reports the consumption of total government capital by country for federal and unitary countries as a percentage of GDP. The overall average is 1.86 percent. The share of that from consumption of local government capital averages 47 percent. The average percentage is essentially equal for local government in both federal and unitary countries. Aside from Greece, where the local share is only 3.7 percent, the local shares range from 25 percent in Spain (but 48 percent if Spain's regional governments were included) to 65.8 percent in Portugal. On average, fixed-capital consumption is the equivalent of 13.6 percent of local government expenditure. The range here is broad, but the share tends to be larger where total local outlays are small (e.g., Australia and New Zealand, at 21.1 and 20.3 percent, respectively) and smaller where local expenditures are large (e.g., Denmark and Sweden, at 3.4 and 5.1 percent, respectively). Capital requirements are more closely associated with core services than social programs.

Table 3.5 Local government consumption of fixed capital and debt

Country	*Total general government consumption of fixed capital as a percentage of GDP*	*Local government*			
		Share (%) of total consumption of fixed capital	*Fixed-capital consumption as a percentage of expenditure by economic type*	*Net lending/ borrowing as a percentage of revenues*[c]	*Liabilities as a percentage of total revenue*
Federal countries					
Australia	1.45	31.6	21.1	+0.9	46.2
Austria (2003)	1.29	46.4	7.5	+2.2	32.1
Belgium (2003)	1.57	47.9	11.2	−7.1	78.9
Canada	–	–	–	−3.3	71.1
Germany	1.59	58.4	12.5	−2.5	–
Switzerland	–	–	–	+2.6	–
United States	1.29	–	–	–	–
Average[b]	1.44	46.1	13.1	−1.2	57.1
Unitary Countries					
Denmark	1.92	60.0	3.4	−2.2	23.7
Finland	2.38	55.0	6.8	−3.3	48.4
France	2.45	63.5	15.5	−1.1	70.8
Greece (2000)	–	3.7	0.1	+1.8	–
Iceland (2002)	2.08	30.2	5.3	−4.4	47.8
Italy (2003)	1.33	62.1	5.8	−1.6	–
Japan (2003)	2.76	–	–	–	–
Luxemburg	1.95	43.8	17.5	−2.5	40.4
Netherlands	2.49	64.6	10.1	−2.7	67.4
New Zealand	1.88	32.2	20.3	+5.0	64.4
Norway	1.96	50.6	7.2	−3.0	64.5[a]
Portugal (2002)	2.13	65.8	25.3	−7.8	–
Spain (2001)	1.43	25.0	7.0	−3.0	–
Sweden (2003)	2.39	57.2	5.1	−1.0	45.1
United Kingdom	0.93	47.3	3.6	+1.0	–
Average[b]	2.01	47.2	9.5	−1.8	52.5
Overall Average[b]	1.86	47.0	13.6	−1.6	53.9

Data are for 2004 unless otherwise indicated

Source: Author's calculations from data in IMF *Government Finance Statistics Yearbook*, 2005

Notes: '–' indicates not available

[a]Specific value is for 2003

[b]Averages are for those reporting values

[c]If unavailable, the cash surplus/deficit was used

Local governments finance capital expenditures from a variety of sources. These sources may include own reserves (accumulated from taxes and user charges, for example); developer contributions or charges; capital grants; and debt. Senior governments usually control borrowing by local government tightly. Normally, borrowing to finance capital expenditures is permitted, subject to controls, but borrowing to cover operating deficits is not allowed (except under very strict conditions). Hence, almost all borrowing is for capital purposes. Because borrowing to fund a portion of capital expenditures is common, local governments often run overall deficits. Net lending/borrowing as a percentage of revenues is reported in Table 3.5. Only 6 of the 20 countries for which there are data were net lenders. The average net borrowing position was 1.8 percent of revenue. This finding means that local governments may accumulate debt. Total local government liabilities as a percentage of total revenue are also reported in Table 3.5. Liabilities range from 23.7 percent to 78.9 percent of total revenue. Sources of funds vary among countries. In some (e.g., the United States), local governments may borrow in private markets and even from foreign investors, although foreign borrowing is unusual and is typically relatively small. In other countries (e.g., Australia and the United Kingdom), local governments may borrow only from senior governments. In many cases (most provinces in Canada), senior governments facilitate local borrowing and monitor it through special authorities.

Local Government Revenue

Local government revenues come from two main sources: own-source revenues and intergovernmental transfers. Own-source revenues are made up of taxes and nontax revenues. Nontax revenues come mostly from charges for services and privileges and from property and investment income. Although considerable variation exists among countries, on average taxes provide about 40 percent of local government revenue, nontax sources about 20 percent, and transfers about 40 percent. Before considering the distributions of these revenues among countries, one should examine taxes and tax sources.

Local Government Taxes

Local governments around the world use a variety of taxes. The spectrum of the main taxes used in federal and unitary countries is the main information reported in Table 3.6.[5] Taxes on income and profits, on property, and

[5] The table reports on 24 countries. At the local government level, tax information is more common than expenditure information.

Table 3.6 Main taxes and selected other own revenues of local governments as a percentage of GDP in OECD member countries, 2003

Country	*Income & profits taxes*	*Property taxes*	*General consumption taxes*	*Taxes on specific goods & services*	*Taxes on use*	*Other*[a]	*Total taxes*	*Nontax own-source revenue*[e,f]	*Total own-source revenue*	*Total expenditures*[g]
Federal countries										
Australia	...	0.9	...	...	...	...	0.9	1.2	2.1	2.4
Austria[b,d]	1.4	0.4	0.9	0.2	0.1	1.0	4.0	1.6	5.6	8.0
Belgium[b,d]	2.1	...	0.1	0.2	0.1	...	2.5	1.6	4.1	6.7
Canada	...	2.7	...	...	0.1	0.1	2.9	1.3	4.2	7.5
Germany[b,d]	1.8	0.4	0.1	...	...	...	2.3	1.8	4.1	7.3
Switzerland	4.0	0.8	...	...	...	...	4.8	3.2	8.0	9.8
United States	0.2	2.7	0.4	0.2	0.2	...	3.7	1.8	5.5	8.8
Average[c]	1.36	1.13	0.21	0.09	0.07	0.16	3.01	1.78	4.8	7.2
Unitary countries										
Denmark[b,d]	16.0	1.2	...	...	...	...	17.2	4.0	21.2	33.1
Finland[b,d]	9.0	0.5	...	...	...	...	9.5	4.3	13.8	19.5
France[b,d]	...	2.4	...	0.3	0.1	1.6	4.4	2.0	6.4	10.2
Greece[b,d]	...	0.2	...	0.1	...	...	0.3	1.1	1.4	2.7
Iceland	7.7	1.3	0.9				9.9	1.9	11.8	13.0
Ireland[b,d]	...	0.6	...	...	...	...	0.6	–	–	–
Italy[b,d]	1.6	1.1	0.2	0.9	0.5	2.9	7.2	2.1	9.3	15.4
Japan	2.9	2.1	0.5	0.6	0.4	0.1	6.6	–	–	–
Luxembourg[b,d]	2.3	0.1	...	...	...	...	2.4	1.3	3.7	5.9
Netherlands[b,d]	...	0.8	...	...	0.6	...	1.4	2.9	4.3	17.3
New Zealand	...	1.8	...	...	0.2	...	2.0	0.9	2.9	3.4
Norway	5.7	0.6	...	...	0.1	...	6.4	3.2	9.6	15.2
Portugal[b,d]	0.5	0.5	0.4	0.6	...	0.1	2.1	1.5	3.6	6.6

Spain[b,d]	2.4	2.6	2.4	1.8	0.7	0.1	10.0	0.7	20.7	6.5
Sweden[b,d]	16.5	…	…	…	…	…	16.5	3.7	20.2	26.0
Turkey	0.6	0.4	0.6	0.1	…	0.1	1.8	–	–	–
United Kingdom[b,d]	…	1.7	…	…	…	…	1.7	2.4	4.1	10.4
Average	3.83	1.05	0.29	0.26	0.15	0.29	5.88	2.29[f]	8.79[f]	13.2
Overall average[c]										
All	3.11	1.07	0.27	0.20	0.13	0.25	5.04	2.12	6.94	9.8
All > 0	4.66	1.17	0.64	0.51	0.27	0.76	5.04	2.45[f]	7.93[f]	11.2

Source: Author's calculations from data in *Revenue Statistics of OECD Member Countries, 1965–2004* (OECD 2005)

Notes: '–' indicates not available; '…' indicates insignificant

[a]For federal countries, other includes social security contributions attributable to local governments (Austria), and some residual taxes, mainly on business (Austria and Canada). Also, in Austria, it includes payroll taxes (0.8 percent). For unitary countries, this column includes taxes at death (Portugal) and some residual taxes, mainly business (France and Italy)

[b]Payments to the EU are excluded from these comparisons

[c]Averages are unweighted averages of those countries in the table with values greater than zero if (>0) and for all countries for which there is data whether zero or more otherwise

[d]EU countries are those that are members as of January 1, 2003. These countries are Austria, Belgium, Denmark, Finland, France, Germany, Greece, Ireland, Italy, Luxembourg, Netherlands, Portugal, Spain, Sweden, and the United Kingdom

[e]Includes property income, sales, fines, and miscellaneous

[f]Average of those reporting data

[g]From Table 3.2

on commodities and services (general sales, specific goods and services, and use) are the main sources of tax revenue. Most countries use more than one of these types of taxes. The figures in Table 3.6 show the amount of local tax revenue from each source as a percentage of GDP. Total taxes, like expenditures, vary widely as a percentage of GDP: from levels as low as 0.6 percent in Ireland and 0.9 percent in Australia to levels as high as 16.5 percent in Sweden and 17.2 percent in Denmark.[6]

Property taxes and income taxes are the most popular local taxes. Property taxes are a source of revenue in 22 of the 24 countries included in the table, and they generate revenues amounting to about 1.1 percent of GDP. When used, property taxes may generate relatively little revenue (e.g., 0.1 percent of GDP in Luxembourg), or they may be a major revenue generator (as is the case in Canada, Spain, and the United States, where property taxes represent from 2.6 to 2.7 percent of GDP). Local taxes on income and profits, reported in 16 of the 24 countries, are somewhat less common but generate more revenue (about 3.1 percent of GDP overall and 4.7 percent of GDP where used). Especially in the case of income taxes, these attributions require caution because, in some cases, the local authorities may have little (even no) discretion over the funds generated from the source. For example, revenue-sharing arrangements in which local governments automatically get a share of central income taxes qualify as "local" income taxes (OECD 2005, pp. 303–304). Austria, Germany, and Spain are examples of countries with such arrangements. In contrast, local governments in Denmark and Sweden, for example, set their own income tax rates. The magnitude of local income taxes also varies considerably (from 0.2 percent of GDP in the United States to 16.5 percent in Sweden). The degree of local discretion in taxing is examined later.

Local taxes on commodities and services (represented in the columns on general consumption taxes, taxes on specific goods and services, and taxes on use) appear in some form in 16 of the 24 countries. Any one type of those taxes, however, is used in only 10 or 11 countries, and the revenue from each is more modest, averaging from about 0.3 to 0.8 percent

[6] For reference, Table 3.6 also reports nontax own-source revenue and total own-source revenue. Nontax own-source revenue averages almost 2 percent of GDP, and total own-source revenue 7 percent (somewhat less, 4.8 percent, in federal countries and somewhat more, 7.8 percent, in unitary countries). To allow ready comparison and to reflect the importance of intergovernmental transfers, the table also includes total expenditures.

of GDP when used. Taxes on general consumption are particularly important in Spain, where they amount to 2.4 percent of GDP in contrast to less than 1.0 percent elsewhere.

Other taxes encompass a mixture of less common taxes (see footnote a of Table 3.6). They are typically minor sources of revenue, except in Austria (mainly social security contributions) and in France and Italy (mainly taxes on business).

Most countries rely primarily on a single major tax. For some, it is the property tax; for others, it is the income tax. Only a few countries use a more diverse mix of taxes. This pattern is demonstrated in Table 3.7. It reports the tax composition for countries grouped into three classes: those that are highly property tax reliant, those that are highly income tax reliant, and those using mixed-tax sources. Local governments in nine countries collect the majority of their tax revenue from property taxes. That percentage ranges from just over 50 percent in France and the Netherlands to 100 percent in Australia, Ireland, and the United Kingdom. For this group as a whole, property taxes represent almost 80 percent of local tax revenue. Note from Table 3.6 that property tax revenues do not amount to more than 2.7 percent of GDP. Most of these countries also use some other taxes to generate revenue, and most choose some form of tax on commodities or services. Among this group of countries, only in the United States do local governments also raise revenue from income taxes. In France, the *taxe professionnelle* is levied on business (an "other" tax), and it generates just over one-third of local tax revenues.

Nine countries compose the group that is highly income tax reliant. For them, income tax revenues provide 88 percent of local tax revenue on average, with the share ranging from 74.7 percent in Germany to 100 percent in Sweden.[7] Personal income taxes dominate, except in Luxembourg, where all the local income tax comes from corporations. Taxes on corporations are nil or essentially nil in four countries. Elsewhere, they account for about 8 percent (Finland) to 27 (Germany) percent of the local income tax collections. Within this group, property taxes are the next most common tax, and overall, they generate the next largest amount of revenue (8 percent on average). Taxes on commodities and services amount to more than 10 percent of revenues in only one country, Belgium.

[7] Recall the need to be cautious about the attribution of shared tax revenues to local governments.

Table 3.7 Composition of local government tax revenue in OECD countries, 2003

Country	*Income and profits*		*Property taxes*	*General consumption taxes*	*Taxes on specific goods & services*	*Taxes on use*	*Other*
	Total	*From Corporations*[a]					
High-property tax reliance							
Australia	...	...	100.0	...	...	...	...
Canada	...	...	93.8	0.2	0.2	1.8	4.1
United States	4.8	(0.8)	73.0	11.0	4.9	6.2	...
France	...	...	54.1	...	7.6	3.1	35.2
Greece	...	...	66.9	4.1	26.0	3.0	0.0
Ireland	...	...	100.0	...	...	...	...
Netherlands	...	...	56.6	...	1.5	41.9	...
New Zealand	...	...	90.4	...	1.1	8.5	...
United Kingdom	...	...	100.0	...	...	...	...
Average	0.53	(0.09)	81.64	1.70	4.59	7.17	4.37
High-income tax reliance							
Belgium	86.5	(17.7)	–	2.2	6.9	4.1	...
Germany	74.7	(20.1)	18.6	5.5	0.5	0.5	0.3
Switzerland	83.3	(10.2)	16.4	...	0.2	0.1	...
Denmark	93.0	(1.9)	6.9	...	0.1	...	0.2
Finland	94.9	(7.4)	4.9	...	...	...	...
Iceland	78.1	...	13.0	8.9	...	...	...
Luxembourg	93.5	(93.5)	5.0	...	1.0	0.2	0.3
Norway	89.2	...	8.7	...	...	2.1	...
Sweden	100.0	...		...	...	...	...
Average	88.13	16.75	8.17	1.84	0.97	0.78	0.89
Mixed-tax sources							
Austria[b]	35.7	(6.1)	10.5	22.0	4.0	1.7	25.0
Italy	22.1	(2.2)	15.1	3.0	12.5	7.3	39.9
Japan	45.2	(19.7)	32.2	7.3	8.5	5.8	1.0
Portugal	22.5	(14.8)	25.3	18.1	26.0	1.5	4.5
Spain	24.3	(1.7)	26.0	23.9	17.8	6.7	1.3
Turkey	32.5	(10.9)	18.8	34.1	6.9	1.8	6.0
Average	30.38	(6.15)	21.32	18.07	12.62	4.13	12.95
Overall average	40.84	(7.85)	39.01	5.85	5.24	3.99	5.21

May not sum to 100.0 percent due to rounding

Source: Author's calculations from data in *Revenue Statistics of OECD Member Countries, 1965–2004* (OECD 2005)

Notes: '–' indicates not available; '...' indicates insignificant

[a]Percentage of total local tax revenue attributed to income taxes from corporations is shown in parentheses

[b]For Austria, other includes payroll tax (20.9 percent) and social security contributions (4.1 percent)

Six countries are considered to have a mixed set of tax sources. Within this group, no single tax accounts for more than 45.2 percent of local tax revenue (the income tax in Japan). Income and property taxes are used in all these countries and, overall, represent about 30 percent and 21 percent of total tax revenue, respectively. Taxes on commodities and services are exceptionally popular with this group and raise about 35 percent of local tax revenue. Other forms of taxation are also more common with this group of countries although they are only major revenue sources in Austria and Italy. Other taxes in Austria are largely payroll taxes, and those in Italy are taxes on business.

One might note a geographic or cultural pattern to the tax grouping in Table 3.7. The property tax group is dominated by countries having a British heritage. This situation was especially true a decade ago, before France and Greece, with expanded reliance on the property tax, moved into this group from the mixed-tax group. The mixed-tax group tended then to be predominantly southern European (with France and Greece and without Japan, which shifted to the mixed group with a decrease in the importance of local income taxes). The group that relies on income tax tends to be more northern European and especially includes the Nordic countries.

Property Taxes

Property taxes can include taxes on a wide range of property. Of the countries most reliant on property taxes, these taxes are almost exclusively on immovable property (i.e., land and structures). Where property is taxed elsewhere, taxes on immovable property are an important source of property taxes. In Norway and Switzerland, however, taxes on net wealth generate the bulk of property tax revenues for their local governments. Among the mixed-tax countries, taxes on financial and capital transactions (notably property transfers) account for significant shares of the property taxes in some countries (e.g., Austria, Spain, and Turkey).

Taxation of immovable property is often recommended for local government. Reasons for its attractiveness include the following (Owens and Panella 1991):

- Immobility of the tax base hampers evasion and permits interjurisdictional variation in tax rates.
- Tax on immovable property is linked to benefits received because many municipal services benefit property.

- It is visible.
- The yield is predictable.
- It is relatively easy to administer.

These reasons relate closely to Bird's (1993) characteristics of a good local tax: immobile base, adequate source of revenue, stable and predictable yield, fair, easily administered, not exportable, and visible.

Property taxes are not without problems. Assessments must be kept current with capital or rental values. Also, assessments must be fair, which is widely interpreted as being uniform. Assessment relative to market value is often noted to vary by type of property—low for agricultural and residential property and high for commercial and industrial property. In addition, where tax rates can vary, they, too, are often lower on agricultural and residential property. Clearly, there is a tendency to shift taxes to business property to at least obscure the incidence of the property tax if not shift or export the property tax burden. Wide variations in (especially) the industrial tax base can create large fiscal disparities among local governments. Although property taxes may relate to certain benefits from local government, they may not relate as well to benefits from social services like schooling (or others with a more redistributive role). In addition, property taxes are often criticized as not relating well to current ability to pay. Hence, although attractive in many ways, property taxes may be inadequate in a number of situations.

Local Income Taxes

Local income taxes are a widely used and effective means of generating tax revenue. Income tax is really only a local tax if the local government gets to determine the tax revenue it can generate by setting the tax rate. Where rates are set centrally, are closely constrained, or are limited to a range where all jurisdictions essentially use the same rate (as in Norway and in the state of Maryland in the United States), the system becomes more a tax-sharing or tax-transfer system. Also, local income taxes operate best if they tax personal rather than business (i.e., corporate) income. Japan's local governments can and do tax corporate income, but normally it is not permitted. The Scandinavian countries, after experimenting with local corporate income taxation and faced with a combination of equity and efficiency problems, abandoned their local corporate income taxes or (as in Denmark and Norway) replaced them with corporate income tax sharing. Piggybacking the local income tax on the central government's personal income tax minimizes administration and compliance costs. The central government defines the base and administers and collects the tax for the local authorities. Local governments commonly set a single low tax rate. Progressive rate structures are rare but exist (e.g., in Japan). Commuters present a possible issue. In some places, they are not taxed, while in others they may be partially or even fully taxed. Local payroll taxes collected from employers are somewhat of an alternative to or variation on local personal income taxes. Often with payroll taxes—and many times intentionally—no distinction is made between residents and nonresidents. In addition, especially as demonstrated in many states within the United States, local income taxes can operate in environments where the tax mix is not uniform—that is, alongside other local taxes, such as property and sales taxes.

Local personal income taxes have a number of potential strengths. Among the advantages are the following:

- They can be a flexible and autonomous source of local tax revenue that is very visible to taxpayers.
- Administration and compliance costs can be low.
- Tax exporting can be minimal.
- The tax base is relatively immobile in that taxpayers must (as with the property tax) change their residence to avoid the local tax.
- More so than with property taxes, personal income tax revenue grows automatically with economic activity.

Major considerations are that they can generate relatively large amounts of revenue and that they can be seen as fair. Countries that are above average in terms of local tax revenues as a percentage of GDP predominantly are highly income tax reliant (and do not include those that are property tax reliant). They also tend to have high levels of expenditure responsibilities, with major responsibilities for social programs. In part, this arrangement works because, unlike other major local taxes, the local income tax results in a progressive distribution of the tax burden that is consistent with attitudes about fairness in financing social programs.[8] Hence, local income taxes enable an assignment of responsibilities that other taxes

[8] Hall and Smith (1995) demonstrate the potentially quite different distributional burdens of local income, property, and sales taxes. In their reasonable cases, the local income tax is progressive, the property tax largely regressive, and a local sales tax proportional.

would not likely support. Their acceptance and success in such situations rely heavily on effective equalization to offset disparities in fiscal capacities among jurisdictions and to ensure relative uniformity in access to and levels of services across jurisdictions.

Local Sales Taxes

Local governments in most countries of the Organisation for Economic Co-operation and Development (OECD) levy some form of sales tax, but they are a major source of revenue in relatively few countries (notably those in the mixed-tax group). Japan, Spain, and the United States provide illustrations. Japanese municipalities and the regional prefectures levy a wide range of specific taxes, including taxes on products, ownership or use of light motor vehicles, automobile acquisition, tobacco, mineral products, light oil delivery, landholding, property acquisition, fixed assets, meals and hotels, golf links, spas, business offices, city planning, water utility and land profits, and hunting. The central government requires and administers some of these taxes. Individually, few generate significant revenue. Spain's municipalities and regional authorities also have an extensive list of taxes on items and activities. Again, some involve arrangements with the central government, so their local nature is questionable. In the United States, about 6500 local authorities in 32 states levy local sales taxes. The tax is entirely a local option in 28 states. Local sales taxes are often piggybacked on the state general sales tax. In some states, special districts (e.g., school and transit) as well as general-purpose local governments can levy a sales tax. A wide variety of local specific or selective sales taxes is also found throughout the country.

Local sales taxes can generate significant amounts of revenue and may be popular (as in the United States), but they have some drawbacks. One of the complications is that the tax base is typically very uneven across local governments. Hence, the revenue-generating potential varies greatly, making sales taxes less than a viable revenue source for all local governments. Also, depending on the concentration of retail activity, for example, interjurisdictional tax shifting may result. Nonresident contributions to local taxes are not a problem if local costs correspond to the tax, but if significant tax exporting occurs, equity and efficiency questions emerge. Border problems are of greater concern. Consumers are mobile, and shopping patterns near borders can be sensitive to differences in sales tax rates, thereby leading to inefficiencies in firm location and consumer shopping behavior. Various operating complications exist as well. Local sales taxes paid on business inputs are usually not or are only imperfectly deducted; hence, they augment costs and double taxation occurs when the outputs are sold. Goods are more commonly taxed than services, thus distorting relative prices. Relative to revenues, the costs of collecting some sales taxes (e.g., some selective taxes) may be high. These various complications may contribute to the more limited reliance on sales taxes among OECD countries. They also contribute to making such taxes candidates for revenue sharing.

Business Taxes

In a few countries, major local taxes are levied on businesses beyond the conventional property taxes or local income taxes. These taxes are notable in Canada, France, Germany, and Japan.

In France, the *taxe professionnelle*, a tax on incorporated and unincorporated businesses, generates about one-third of total local tax revenues. Since 1999, the base is the rental value of a firm's fixed assets only. Removal of the wage component was compensated for by a central subsidy. Even before that, the central government was estimated to be paying 30 percent of the tax because it contributed any amount of a firm's *taxe professionnelle* beyond 4 percent of value added. Local rates are restricted by the central government. In addition, an estimated 80 percent of the tax is exported beyond the taxing jurisdiction.

German local governments impose a trade tax that is based on corporate profits. The highest local rates are about twice the lowest. This tax generates about one-third of tax revenue and 15 percent of total revenue in the western portion of the country.

In Japan, local governments obtain about 20 percent of their tax revenues from corporations. The prefecture governments collect an enterprise tax, which is based (primarily) on corporate net income. Enterprise taxes provide about 26 percent of their tax revenue. The municipal governments get about 9 percent of their tax revenue from taxes on corporate income. The central government sets standard rates and allows very little variation. Corporations with operations in several jurisdictions allocate their taxes according to measures of business activity in each jurisdiction.

In Canada, special local taxes on business are permitted in most provinces. Those taxes once amounted to one-tenth of local taxes, but that figure is reported to have declined to only about 2.1 percent over the past decade.

Extensive use of additional business taxes appears to be part of a politically attractive effort to shift a larger share of the local tax burden to non-resident taxpayers and beyond the local community. Shifting and exporting taxes in this way masks the cost of local services and promotes excessive expenditures because local taxes do not properly signal costs.

Nontax Revenues

Nontax revenue refers to revenue from government sales of goods and services; property and investment income (e.g., rentals, interest, and returns from enterprises); and income from fines and penalties. Generating an average of 21 percent of revenue overall, nontax revenues are a significant source of revenue for local governments. Because local governments provide numerous goods and services for which prices or charges can be levied (e.g., water and sewerage, public transit, refuse disposal, recreational facilities, and supplementary improvements such as lane lighting specific to select properties), many nontax revenues also have an important allocative efficiency role. Charges and fees for such services link benefits and costs and serve as a signal both to users and to the supplying local authorities. Well-designed charges can improve the decisions of consumers and of governments alike. Bird (1993), for example, argues that local governments should pursue benefit-related finance, and the first step should be to levy user charges (and specific benefit taxes) where possible.

The contributions of taxes, nontax sources, and intergovernmental grants are reported in Table 3.8. Across the countries reported there, nontax revenues of local governments average 2.04 percent of GDP and provide 21.55 percent of total revenue. With taxes accounting for about 42 percent of revenue, nontax sources generate half as much revenue as taxes do and are fully one-third of own-source revenues. The importance of nontax revenue varies considerably among countries. As a percentage of GDP, it is lowest in Spain at 0.70 percent and highest in Finland at 4.45 percent. Also, as a percentage of GDP, nontax revenue tends to be more important in the countries that are most reliant on income tax, where such revenues average 2.57 percent. However, as a percentage of total revenue, nontax revenues are more important for countries that are highly reliant on property tax (averaging 27.34 percent). They are also a relatively larger share of own-source revenues in those countries (about 46 percent on average). For some countries in this group, nontax revenues actually exceed tax revenues (i.e., Australia, Greece, the Netherlands, and the United Kingdom).

Table 3.8 Tax, nontax, and grant revenue of local governments as percentages of GDP and total revenue, 2003

Country	*Percentage of GDP*			*Total*	*Percentage of revenue*		
	Taxes	*Nontax*	*Grants*		*Taxes*	*Nontax*	*Grants*
High-property tax reliance							
Australia	0.98	1.20	0.36	2.54	38.6	47.2	14.2
Canada	2.93	1.33	2.81	7.07	41.4	18.8	39.7
United States	3.74	1.79	3.67	9.20	40.7	19.5	39.9
France	4.48	2.00	4.15	10.63	42.1	18.8	39.0
Greece (2000 IMF)	0.32	–	–	–	12.0	47.8	40.1
Ireland	0.62	–	–	–	–	–	–
Netherlands	1.49	2.95	11.66	16.10	9.3	18.3	72.4
New Zealand (1995)	1.99	0.95	0.37	3.31	60.1	28.7	11.2
United Kingdom	1.68	2.42	8.26	12.36	13.6	19.6	66.8
Average[a]	2.03	1.81	4.47	8.74	32.23	27.34	40.41
High-income tax reliance							
Belgium	2.35	0.95	3.27	6.93	33.9	13.8	47.2
Germany	2.60	1.87	2.38	6.95	39.2	25.8	32.7
Switzerland (2002)	4.89	3.47	1.67	10.03	48.7	34.6	16.7
Denmark	17.23	2.79	12.41	32.95	52.3	8.5	37.7
Finland	9.43	4.45	5.15	19.04	49.5	23.3	27.0
Iceland	9.83	1.91	1.27	13.00	75.6	14.6	9.7
Luxembourg	2.12	1.30	2.78	6.18	33.8	21.0	44.9
Norway	6.37	2.71	5.26	14.34	44.4	18.9	33.7
Sweden	16.52	3.73	5.04	25.73	64.2	14.5	19.6
Average	7.93	2.57	4.36	15.02	49.07	19.44	29.91
Mixed-tax sources							
Austria	4.50	1.58	1.68	8.15	55.2	19.4	20.5
Italy	6.87	1.83	6.57	15.14	45.4	12.1	41.9
Japan	6.56	–	–	–	–	–	–
Portugal (2002)[b]	2.22	0.92	2.91	6.12	36.3	15.0	47.5
Spain	2.77	0.70	2.23	5.73	48.3	12.3	38.9
Turkey	1.59	–	–	–	–	–	–
Average	4.09	1.26	3.35	8.79	46.30	14.70	37.20
Overall average	4.76	2.04	4.20	11.58	42.13	21.55	35.30

Percentages may not add up to the total reported because of the omission of capital revenue and social security contributions

Sources: Author's calculations from data in IMF *Government Finance Statistics Yearbook* (IMF 2005), and *Revenue Statistics of OECD Member Countries, 1965–2004* (OECD 2005)

Notes: '–' indicates not available

[a]Averages are of those for which data are available

[b]IMF and OECD figures differ

Table 3.9 Sources of nontax own revenue, 2003

Country category	*Average percentage of total nontax own revenue*			
	Property income	*Sales of goods and services*	*Fines, penalties, and forfeits*	*Miscellaneous*
High-property tax reliant countries	25.3	64.0	3.4	7.2
High-income tax reliant countries	19.9	68.8	1.0	10.3
Mixed-tax countries	10.7	62.0	0.2	27.1
All countries	19.2	65.5	1.5	13.8
Range	2.1–40.2	42.5–88.2	0–16.5	0–41.9

Source: Author's calculations from data in *Revenue Statistics of OECD Member Countries, 1965–2004* (OECD 2005)

The relative importance of the various sources of nontax revenues is shown in Table 3.9. Only the averages and the range are reported. Sales of goods and services account for about two-thirds of nontax revenues, with a range from 42.5 to 88.2 percent. Property income (e.g., rents for government-owned property) is next most important, averaging 19.2 percent. Fines, penalties, and forfeits are a minor source, with an average of only 1.5 percent; most countries report no such income. Miscellaneous nontax income provides 13.8 percent. Miscellaneous income is relatively more important in the mixed-tax countries, and property income relatively more important in the countries that are reliant on property taxes.

Intergovernmental Transfers

Intergovernmental transfers are an important source of revenue for local governments in essentially all industrial countries. Transfers have a role when local own-source revenue is considered to be inadequate or inappropriate for funding the expenditure responsibilities of local governments. For the countries in Table 3.8, grants average 35.3 percent of local government revenue. The averages are slightly larger (about 40 percent) for countries that are highly reliant on property taxes and somewhat lower (about 30 percent) for those countries that rely on income tax. In the federal countries, transfers average a seemingly low 30.1 percent, but the range (from 14.2 to 47.2 percent) is still large. Beyond that, patterns are not obvious. The contribution of transfers varies widely among individual countries. At the low end are Iceland, New Zealand, and Australia (9.7, 11.2, and 14.2 percent of revenue, respectively). At the high end are the Netherlands (72.4 percent) and the United Kingdom (66.8 percent), but the next largest is Portugal at 47.5 percent. Obviously, a broad distribution exists, and countries are relatively evenly dispersed over all but the highest levels of the range.

Tax-sharing arrangements can complicate the distinction between grants and taxes. International Monetary Fund and OECD criteria for designating shared tax revenues rely on having authority to impose the tax; having some ability to determine the revenue (e.g., set the rate); and having control over use of the funds raised (IMF 2001, p. 50; OECD 2005, p. 303). An OECD tax policy study (OECD 1999) analyzes the taxing authority of subnational governments. It also reports the share of tax revenue generated from various taxes, including shared taxes. That information for local governments is the basis of Table 3.10. One can see there that the OECD attributes the majority of local tax revenue in most countries to tax sources over which local governments have control of the tax rate, the tax base, or both (i.e., they set the tax). Shared tax arrangements over which local authorities have limited (or no) control but that generate large amounts of tax revenue exist in only 4 of 15 countries: Norway, Austria, Germany, and Portugal (94, 81, 47, and 37 percent, respectively).[9] Still, some caution is necessary because some difference of opinion may exist over these attributions. In the case of Japan, for example, the OECD designates 94 percent of tax revenues as coming from taxes set by local governments, but Mochida (2006, p. 164) argues that the failure of local governments to deviate from the nationally set standard tax rates implies that those taxes effectively approximate tax revenue sharing. Hence, to feel fully comfortable with the assignment between own-source revenues and transfers, one may need to assess for oneself the arrangements within individual countries.

Two sections follow. One reviews the purposes of transfers and provides illustrations. The second reviews the role of grants in the overall fiscal arrangements.

[9] Some general information has been added for countries examined here but not in the OECD study. In those countries, too, local determination of local tax revenue is predominant. See OECD (2002) and Darby and others (2003) as supplementary references.

Table 3.10 Local government tax autonomy, 1995 (percentage of revenue by type of tax)

Country	*Local government controls tax base or rates*		*Local government receives shared tax revenue*			*Central government sets tax base and rate*
	Local government sets tax base and rate	*Local government sets tax rate only*	*Revenue split requires local government consent*	*Revenue split fixed by national legislation*	*Revenue split part of central government annual budget*	
Highly property tax reliant						
Australia	Predominant					
Canada[a]	Predominant		Minimal			
United States	Predominant		Some			
France	Predominant					
Netherlands	...	100	...	...	...	...
New Zealand	98	...	...	...	...	2
United Kingdom	...	100	...	...	...	...
Highly income tax reliant						
Belgium	13	84	...	2	1	...
Germany	1	52	47	...	...	...
Switzerland	...	97	...	3	...	...
Denmark	...	96	...	...	4	...
Finland	...	89	...	11	...	...
Iceland	8	92	...	...	...	...
Norway	...	5	...	1	94	...
Sweden	4	96	...	...	...	...
Mixed tax						
Austria	9	11	81	...	...	...
Japan	...	94	...	...	...	6
Portugal	49	14	...	...	...	37
Spain	33	51	16	...	...	...

Source: OECD 1999

Note: '...' indicates insignificant

[a]Characterizes general-purpose (municipal) government. Local school authorities in most provinces have little or no independent tax powers

The Purposes and Types of Grants

Intergovernmental transfers exist for both economic and political reasons. The economic reasons are (a) to close (vertical) fiscal gaps arising from local authorities' expenditure requirements exceeding their revenue-generating capacities, (b) to reduce (horizontal) fiscal disparities among local governments in their abilities to deliver public services, and (c) to correct for misallocations resulting from interjurisdictional spillovers (externalities).[10] In practice, grants typically do not fit neatly into these categories. Grants are normally categorized as *conditional* and *unconditional*—that is, grants that are designed or earmarked to be used for specific purposes and transfers that the recipient government is free to use as it sees fit. Transfers aimed at gap closing and equalization normally fall into the unconditional category, whereas those oriented toward correcting spillovers are classed as conditional. A cross-country comparison of grants by type has been made available only recently (Bergvall et al. 2006). The analysis of Bergvall and others for local governments in most of the countries under examination here is reported in Table 3.11.[11] Across the 15 countries in Table 3.11, conditional and unconditional grants are equally important on average, with each accounting for half of total transfers to local governments. Again, however, wide differences exist among the countries. Conditional funding ranges from as little as 9.1 percent of total transfers to as much as 96.0 percent (and unconditional grants are just the opposite). No relationship exists between the level of conditional or unconditional funding and the importance of transfers in local government budgets.

Further detail is provided on both conditional and unconditional transfers. Grants can be divided into those that are provided entirely at the discretion of the granting government and those that are based on formal agreements (usually legislation and sometimes constitutions). As seen in Table 3.11, discretionary grants are normally a small portion of total transfers, 13.5 percent on average. Italy, at 75.5 percent, is clearly an exception. Transfers for capital purposes make up half the discretionary transfers in these countries and the vast majority of all transfers for capital. The formal arrangements provide transparency and some certainty for as long as the arrangements last. Formal arrangements for conditional grants can require some portion of matching local funds, or they may be nonmatching but still require certain criteria to be satisfied to obtain the grant (e.g., meeting certain service standards or other criteria besides spending on specified functions). Matching grants are a more important source of

[10] Bergvall and others (2006) refer to these purposes as financing services, equalization, and subsidization.

[11] The terms *conditional* and *unconditional* are substituted here for Bergvall and others' *earmarked* and *nonearmarked* grants. Also, *formal* here replaces *mandatory* in their article.

Table 3.11 Type of grants received by local governments

Country	*Conditional*				*Unconditional*				*Total grants as a percentage of revenue*
	Formal		*Discretionary (%)*	*Total (%)*	*Formal*		*Discretionary (%)*	*Total (%)*	
	Matching (%)	*Nonmatching (%)*			*General purpose (%)*	*Block (%)*			
High-property tax reliance									
Australia	...	...	17.2	17.2	82.8	...	...	82.8	14.2
Canada	...	95.7	...	95.7	4.3	...	...	4.3	39.7
France	6.5	0.1	5.1	11.7	81.9	6.4	...	88.3	39.0
New Zealand	70.0	...	...	70.0	30.0	...	...	30.0	11.2
High-income tax reliance									
Belgium	71.6	0.1	24.3	96.0	4.0	...	...	4.0	47.2
Switzerland	80.4	...	...	80.4	19.6	...	...	19.6	16.7
Denmark	66.6	0.5	2.6	69.7	30.2	...	...	30.2	37.7
Finland	5.7	...	3.4	9.1	16.3	74.0	0.6	90.9	27.0
Iceland	3.0	8.4	9.6	21.0	79.0	...	...	79.0	9.7
Norway	12.2	9.4	23.3	44.9	...	55.1	...	55.1	33.7
Sweden	...	...	28.8	28.8	71.3	...	...	71.3	19.6
Mixed-tax sources									
Austria	42.8	42.2	1.2	86.2	13.7	0.1	...	13.8	20.5
Italy	...	...	75.5	75.5	24.5	...	...	24.5	41.9
Portugal	...	...	11.4	11.4	85.0	...	3.6	88.6	47.5
Spain	30.7	3.1		33.8	66.2	...	...	66.2	38.9
Average	26.0	10.6	13.5	50.1	40.6	9.0	0.3	49.9	29.6

Source: Bergvall et al. (2006)

Notes: '...' indicates insignificant. Data are for either 2002 or 2003

revenue than nonmatching grants, 26.0 versus 10.6 percent on average. However, both types display a tremendous range (from 0 to 80.4 and 95.7 percent for matching and nonmatching, respectively).

Unconditional transfers are dominated by formal arrangements providing general-purpose funding. Such grants account for over 80 percent of unconditional grants and 40.6 percent of total transfers in the countries Table 3.11 reports on, but the differences among countries are huge. Bergvall et al. (2006) include block grants with unconditional grants. However, because block grants are for broadly specified purposes (e.g., education, social programs) and do not change relative prices to the recipient, they might equally well be considered nonmatching conditional grants. Norway, one of the only four countries shown with this type of grant revenue, might be an example. Nevertheless, considerable flexibility exists in the actual use of those funds.

Illustrations of Unconditional and Conditional Transfers

Unconditional Transfers

Unconditional transfers are intended to close fiscal gaps or to provide equalization, and they typically embody elements of both objectives. Hence, identifying such grants with solely one purpose or the other is usually difficult. Revenue sharing and equalization grants illustrate. Revenue sharing can be viewed as a transfer primarily oriented toward closing a fiscal gap but normally allocated on an equalizing basis, whereas equalization grants are primarily aimed at equalization—although not uncommonly all or almost all local governments receive funds through the equalization program.

Revenue sharing—normally tax sharing—exists when senior governments assign a specific share of certain revenues to local governments. Several countries have such transfers. Some major cases serve to illustrate. In Austria, most of the major taxes are shared among federal, *Länder* (or state), and local governments. The sharing arrangements are renegotiated regularly. Shared income taxes provide Germany's local governments with over 40 percent of their tax revenues; about 5 percent comes from a share of the value-added tax. Since 1990, Italy has experimented with a variety of dedicated or shared taxes to fund (primarily) health services through its regional governments. Since 2000, the regional authorities have shared 38.55 percent of the national value-added tax and get the revenue from a

0.9 percent personal income tax surcharge. Japan's central government shares its revenues from personal and corporate income taxes, national consumption tax, and alcohol and tobacco taxes with its local governments. With local income tax rates at the maximum, the local personal income tax system in Norway is effectively a tax-sharing arrangement. The federal government in the United States had a revenue-sharing arrangement with local governments from 1972 to 1986. In Canada, some provinces share selected tax revenues with some or all localities, but the amounts are relatively small.

Although local governments overall may lack sufficient revenue capacity, individual authorities' requirements vary. Hence, shared revenues are normally allocated by formulas that take into account individual fiscal capacities and fiscal needs. The indicators vary depending on responsibilities and own-source revenues. Thus, the allocation of shared revenues is usually done on an equalizing basis.

Equalization grants are far more common than revenue sharing. Equalization transfers are directed to reducing fiscal disparities that arise among local authorities because of differences in revenue-generating capacity or expenditure needs. Ideally, good estimates of both fiscal capacity and expenditure requirements can be made, and the differences can be offset by the equalization grants. Examples of countries using such a method are Denmark, Japan, Sweden, and the United Kingdom. Equalization may be fraternal (i.e., from rich to poor localities, as occurs in Denmark and Sweden) or, more commonly, paternal, with the equalizing transfer coming from a senior government. Often, equalization grants are funded from a pool of resources (not necessarily determined by capacities and needs) that is simply shared among local governments according to some formula. The factors in the sharing formula include population and other elements deemed to reflect fiscal capacity (e.g., per capita tax bases) and need (e.g., population, road length, area, or number of students). Examples of this type occur in Canada, the Netherlands, Portugal, and Spain. In some cases, the pool of funds for equalization may not be sufficient to meet fiscal deficiencies (if calculated), while in other instances it may be more than adequate. In some cases, Australia for example, all local governments may receive a basic or a minimum per capita amount from the equalization pool. In such instances, the program clearly goes beyond pure equalization and incorporates an element of fiscal gap-closing transfer.

Conditional Transfers
Transfers to correct for spillovers can be important if public services provided by one local government afford significant benefits to residents of other jurisdictions. Transportation, schooling, recreational and cultural facilities, policing, and certain health services are examples. The failure to match well those paying with those benefiting can cause distortions (with the concern normally being undersupply). Grants can be designed to reduce such distortions. Usually, such grants are conditional (i.e., for a specific purpose), and often they require some matching local contributions (reflecting local benefits at the margin).

Specific-purpose (conditional) grants dominate transfer programs in many countries. Canada illustrates this situation. In only one of ten provinces do general-purpose transfers exceed the amount of specific-purpose transfers. As in many other countries, specific-purpose transfers tend to be concentrated on schooling and other social services and often represent a large share of their costs. Among core services, transportation is a major beneficiary of transfers. Transfers to fund capital projects are popular, but care must be taken in designing them to avoid distorting the allocation between capital and operating expenditures. Also, differing matching rates (not justified by differing spillovers) can distort expenditure choices among functions. This distortion was a reason for France's amalgamation of its capital grants into a single fund. A related problem is that conditional grants can proliferate and lead to a large and confusing array. In many countries, a multitude of specific-purpose grants have been considered unnecessary. For example, during the 1980s, Norway collapsed more than 200 specific-purpose grant programs into four block grants, each targeted to a specific broad function and with somewhat different distribution and performance criteria. In many cases, block grants have successfully simplified grant arrangements without sacrificing results.

An extreme version of conditional grants exists when the granting government provides essentially all the funding and dictates the grant's use. In such cases, local autonomy is essentially nonexistent, and the local government is really an agent of the senior authority hired to perform an activity. Such "transfers" are often hard to distinguish from payments or reimbursements for contracted services. The Danish arrangements for old-age security and selected other social services illustrate the local authority acting as agent.[12] Similar arrangements exist, but are more explicitly recognized as such, in Germany.

[12] Under local government reform to be implemented in 2007, grants will replace certain reimbursements (Danish Ministry of Interior and Health 2005).

Summary, Conclusions, and Lessons

Local government may have a relatively small or a very large role in the government and the economy of a country. For example, among industrial countries, local government expenditures range from 2.4 to 33.1 percent of GDP. Four groups of countries appear: (a) 2 countries with low budget shares have expenditures averaging 2.9 percent, (b) 11 countries with lower-medium budget shares have expenditures averaging 7.9 percent, (c) 5 countries with upper-medium budget shares have expenditures averaging 16.1 percent, and (d) 2 countries with large budget shares have expenditures averaging 29.5 percent.

The magnitude of local government is explained primarily by its involvement in the delivery of social programs (i.e., schooling, health, and social protection). Local governments almost uniformly undertake a set of core activities that include providing local roadways and walkways, fire (and often some police) protection, recreational and cultural facilities and programs, water and sewerage services, waste removal and disposal, and regulation of local activities (largely to enhance safety and enjoyment of property, to control nuisances, and to regulate business). Those programs typically require 3.5–7.4 percent of GDP. Spending on social programs, however, ranges from essentially 0 to 28.6 percent of GDP. Among social programs, some significant local expenditure responsibility for schooling is most common, with substantial involvement in health and social protection being more erratic. Local expenditures on schooling average 2.5 percent of GDP, and local authorities spend half of that or more in all but four countries.

Local governments must fund their expenditures from taxes, other own-source revenues, and intergovernmental transfers. On average, these sources account for about 42, 22, and 35 percent of revenues, respectively, but there is wide variation in the relative shares. Although a smaller share, the other nontax own-source revenues are important. Charges are a recommended source of funding where possible, and about two-thirds of this other revenue comes from sales of goods and services, with another one-fifth coming from property rentals and investment income.

Local governments commonly have access to property taxes, income taxes, and taxes on sales or use of commodities. Local governments in most countries rely primarily on one major type of tax, either property tax or income tax. The nine countries that rely heavily on property taxes obtain (on average) almost 82 percent of their tax revenue from property taxes. The nine countries that rely heavily on income taxes obtain (on average) about 88 percent of their tax revenues from income taxes. Sales taxes encompass a variety of taxes on sales and use, and in no country are these taxes the dominant revenue source. Countries that use sales taxes heavily also rely heavily on both property and income taxes and can be considered mixed-tax countries. Property taxes are levied on immobile land and structures, relate well to the benefits from core services, are widely recommended for local government use, and are used to some extent in almost all industrial countries (and have gained importance in some, notably France and Italy). Local taxes on personal income are widely accepted, can be applied easily when piggybacked on the personal income tax systems of senior governments, and have substantial (particularly relative to the property tax) revenue-generating power. Both property taxes and personal income taxes benefit from the relative immobility of residents. Taxes on corporate income and sales are more subject to exporting and reduced accountability and so are less conceptually appealing as local taxes. These problems contribute to their less widespread use and the wider appeal to intergovernmental revenue sharing of both (and especially corporate income taxes). Local taxes on business income are diminishing in importance. Local governments in the industrial countries have extensive tax autonomy. Local governments in about three-fourths of the countries get the vast majority of their tax revenues from tax sources that they control, usually by being able to set the tax rates.

At about 35 percent of revenues, intergovernmental transfers are important to local governments. Unconditional and conditional transfers are the two main types. Unconditional transfers address problems of fiscal gap (when expenditure responsibilities exceed reasonable expectations of revenue-generating capacities) and fiscal equalization (often without a clear distinction between the two objectives). Conditional transfers are better suited to correcting for spillovers (but, in practice, they sometimes embody aspects of gap closing and equalization). Across the industrial countries, grants are about half unconditional and half conditional. Conditional funding often involves matching contributions, whereas unconditional grants are nonmatching. Major conditional grants are often associated with the funding of social expenditures. Even then, they may be block grants without excessive strings attached. In cases where local authorities have little effective control in tax sharing, distinguishing between unconditional grants and tax sharing is often difficult. Formal agreements govern the vast majority of transfer arrangements. Although agreements do not ensure the stability of grants, agreements do make grants transparent so that their purposes and distribution are more apparent. Only about 14 percent of transfers are discretionary, and those transfers are mostly for capital funding purposes.

Capital expenditures and their financing deserve special mention. Local governments account for a disproportionate share of infrastructure—about half. Usually, the largest part of that amount is concentrated in the core local services, such as streets and roadways, public transit, water and sewerage systems, drainage, and recreational and cultural facilities. Infrastructure spending represents about 14 percent of expenditures. Capital expenditures are financed from operating revenues, reserves, and borrowing. Borrowing for capital purposes is almost the only borrowing that local governments are permitted to undertake. Even then, that borrowing is closely regulated and monitored, but senior governments typically assist or facilitate such debt.

In conclusion, the major observations and potential lessons for anyone interested in the fiscal design of local governments are highlighted:

- Effective performance by local government is not determined by size but by design. There is no single overriding assignment of responsibilities to recommend. Local governments may be small, undertaking only the essentially local core responsibilities, or large, depending on their roles in delivering social services. Social programs can benefit from local decision-making, but they involve spillovers and redistribution calling for central engagement. As a result, responsibilities are often shared between senior and local authorities. Responsibility sharing can be done in many ways. On behalf of their citizens, senior governments have a legitimate interest in realizing at least minimum standards, if not uniformity, of schooling, health, and social protection programs. If local governments are responsible for delivering those programs, senior governments can ensure minimum standards by regulation and funding (providing grants or more adequate tax bases and grants). Experience indicates that there is considerable flexibility in the range of local tax and intergovernmental grant combinations that are workable for the local delivery and funding of social programs.
- Property taxes and user charges go far toward being adequate for the financing of core activities. For governments limited to core programs, grants for correcting for spillovers (e.g., transportation) and for affording horizontal equity can be expected but are likely to be relatively minor in the overall local budget. Social programs have

high costs, and the evidence indicates that property taxes are not sufficient for funding them. For those governments limited to property taxes but responsible for significant social programs, transfers (usually designated specifically for the program) will be a substantial source of funds. Access to local income taxes greatly enhances local governments' abilities to finance programs—especially social programs. That source of funding, however, does not necessarily reduce the use or importance of transfers. Although tax revenues and social expenditures are typically larger (as a percentage of GDP) in countries with local governments having access to local income taxes, the choice between using local income taxes and using intergovernmental transfers seems somewhat arbitrary (often historically determined), and the mix is quite varied. Local access to income taxes does, however, provide the option of lower transfers when responsibilities are major. It does not, however, eliminate the need for grants. At a minimum, effective equalization is needed to ensure the capacity to provide comparable programs (especially social programs) across local authorities. The varied blends of property-related services and social services provided by local governments demonstrate how finance follows function. Designing a mix of taxes and transfers to provide those combinations efficiently and equitably is essential. Although the potential combinations are large, selecting the successful mix can be challenging.

- Local own-source finances should fund the local services for which residents are willing to pay. Such finances need to be visible, have a close benefit-cost linkage, and be determined by local government. User charges are an initial choice. When benefits are generally available, however, taxes are necessary. Property taxes and local personal income taxes meet these and other requirements relatively well, and one or the other is the dominant local tax source in most industrial countries. Taxes on sales or use are less prevalent and, in all but a few countries, serve only as a supplement to other taxes. The potential for shifting or exporting sales taxes and corporate income taxes or special business taxes—and the exceptionally uneven distribution of their bases—make them conceptually less appealing as local taxes and more suitable for revenue sharing (i.e., transfers rather than taxes). Regardless of the type and the range of taxes, a high degree of local tax autonomy is generally found in industrial countries.

- Transfers are almost entirely provided through formal arrangements; that is, they are not at the discretion of the grantor. In addition, fully half the transfers are unconditional (primarily for meeting fiscal gaps and for equalization). Even many of the conditional programs (largely for addressing spillover correction) have modest restrictions (e.g., block grants). Thus, while ensuring adequate services generating spillover benefits, local governments still enjoy a relatively high degree of fiscal autonomy. Transfers have a variety of important roles to play—especially when local governments have considerable responsibilities for social programs. In fact, they make the sharing of responsibilities for social programs workable. The appropriate design of transfers is vital.
- Local governments have disproportionately large responsibilities for infrastructure. Financing infrastructure involves borrowing. Borrowing for capital expenditure purposes is usually the only permitted borrowing that local governments can do. Such borrowing is often closely regulated and monitored by senior governments but is commonly also assisted in one form or another. Important to note is that local debt is funded largely on a commercial basis whether through public or private agencies.
- Although not specifically addressed here, essential to note is that the democratic nature of local governments in the industrial countries is their dominant and critical underlying characteristic (see Shah 2006a). This feature makes local authorities accountable ultimately to their electorate and, to greater or lesser extents, affords relatively substantial degrees of autonomy to what they do and how they accomplish it. The accountability and autonomy that accompany democratic institutions are central to successful local government.

References

Batley, Richard, and Gerry Stoker, eds. 1991. *Local Government in Europe: Trends and Developments.* New York: St. Martin's Press.

Bergvall, Daniel, Claire Charbit, Dirk-Jan Kraan, and Olaf Merk. 2006. Intergovernmental Transfers and Decentralised Public Spending. *OECD Journal on Budgeting* 5 (4): 114–162.

Bird, Richard M. 1993. Threading the Fiscal Labyrinth: Some Issues in Fiscal Federalism. *National Tax Journal* 46 (2): 207–227.

Danish Ministry of the Interior and Health. 2005. *The Local Government Reform: In Brief.* Copenhagen: Ministry of the Interior and Health.

Darby, Julia, Anton Muscatelli, and Graeme Roy. 2003. *Fiscal Decentralization in Europe: A Review of Recent Evidence.* Scotland: Department of Economics, University of Glasgow.

Hall, John, and Stephen Smith. 1995. *Local Sales Taxation: An Assessment of the Feasibility and Likely Effects of Sales Taxation at the Local Level in the U.K.* London: Institute for Fiscal Studies.

Hesse, Joachim Jens, ed. 1991. *Local Government and Urban Affairs in International Perspective.* Baden-Baden: Nomos Verlagsgesellschaft.

IMF (International Monetary Fund). 2001. *Government Finance Statistics Manual.* Washington, DC: IMF.

———. 2002. *Government Finance Statistics Yearbook.* Washington, DC: IMF.

———. 2004. *Government Finance Statistics Yearbook.* Washington, DC: IMF.

———. 2005. *Government Finance Statistics Yearbook.* Washington, DC: IMF.

King, David. 2006. Local Government Organization and Finance: United Kingdom. In *Local Governance in Industrial Countries*, ed. Anwar Shah, 265–312. Washington, DC: World Bank.

McMillan, Melville L. 1996, Revised in 2001. *A Local Perspective on Fiscal Federalism: Practices, Experiences, and Lessons from Developed Countries.* Washington, DC: World Bank.

———. 2008. A Local Perspective on Fiscal Federalism: Practices, Experiences and Lessons from Industrialized Countries. Chap. 7 in *Macro Federalism and Local Finance*, ed. Anwar Shah, 245–289. Washington, DC: The World Bank.

Mochida, Nobuki. 2006. Local Government Organization and Finance: Japan. In *Local Governance in Industrial Countries*, ed. Anwar Shah, 149–188. Washington, DC: World Bank.

OECD (Organisation for Economic Development and Co-operation). 1999. *Taxing Powers of State and Local Governments.* Paris: OECD.

———. 2002. *Fiscal Decentralization in EU Applicant States and Selected EU Member States.* Paris: OECD Centre for Tax Policy Administration.

———. 2005. *Revenue Statistics of OECD Member Countries, 1965–2004.* Paris: OECD.

Owens, Jeffrey, and Giorgio Panella. 1991. *Local Government: An International Perspective.* Amsterdam: North-Holland.

Schroeder, Larry. 2006. Local Government Organization and Finance: United States. In *Local Governance in Industrial Countries*, ed. Anwar Shah, 313–358. Washington, DC: World Bank.

Shah, Anwar, ed. 2006a. A Comparative Institutional Framework for Responsive, Responsible, and Accountable Local Government. In *Local Governance in Industrial Countries*, 1–40. Washington, DC: World Bank.

———, ed. 2006b. *Local Governance in Industrial Countries.* Washington, DC: World Bank.

Stoker, Gerry. 1991. Introduction: Trends in Western European Local Government. In *Local Government in Europe: Trends and Developments*, ed. Richard Batley and Gerry Stoker, 1–20. New York: St. Martin's Press.

Toonen, Theo A.J. 1991. Change in Continuity: Local Government and Urban Affairs in the Netherlands. In *Local Government and Urban Affairs in International Perspective*, ed. Joachim Jens Hesse, 291–332. Baden-Baden: Nomos Verlagsgesellschaft.

CHAPTER 4

Structural Design

Introduction

The recent trend where the municipal sector in most developed and developing countries has increased its reliance on own-source funding and reduced its reliance on grants has been accompanied by a renewed interest in municipal structure and organization. This includes interest in municipal consolidations, amalgamations, and reliance on voluntary arrangements including intermunicipal agreements and/or service boards to improve the overall efficiency of the municipal sector.

Municipal amalgamations, consolidations, and restructuring generally occur in response to the rapid increase in urbanization, a need to provide additional services passed down from senior levels of government, the desire of senior levels of government to deal with fewer municipalities, and the necessity of getting access to a local tax base that encompasses a wide geographical area. In almost every instance, major municipal consolidations and amalgamations have been initiated (driven) by senior levels of government with the major rationale generally being that of cost savings and improved efficiency. Many of these initiatives have been accompanied by offers of financial rewards for the restructured municipalities and nothing if restructuring does not take place; for example, withdrawing grants by a senior level of government if municipalities do not restructure or merge such as in Ontario, Canada (Kitchen 2002), or offering grants (subsidies) to those municipalities who do merge such as in France (Prud'home 2005). Not surprisingly, a senior government initiative of this sort is often

H. Kitchen et al., *Local Public Finance and Economics*,
https://doi.org/10.1007/978-3-030-21986-4_4

the subject of considerable discussion, debate, and frequent dispute. Most locally driven initiatives, on the other hand, have involved the creation or extension of some kind of voluntary association, generally through the use of intermunicipal agreements or local service boards. These, however, are not free of problems and difficulties, as is noted later in this chapter.

The governing structure for a municipality is particularly important. It can affect the quantity and quality of services provided, the efficiency with which services are delivered, and the funding of local services; that is, whether service costs are shared throughout the region, area, or district in a fair, accountable, transparent, and effective manner. All of this has a significant impact on a city or city-region's ability to deliver services that will make the city or city-region competitive on an international scale (Slack et al. 2003). Given the importance of municipal structure and organization, then, the rest of the chapter is separated into three sections.

Section "Structures and Responsibilities in Selected Countries" briefly describes the structure of municipal government in a few countries along with major service responsibilities. Section "Options" describes the criteria that should be met to create efficient, transparent, and accountable municipal government. Section "Municipal Structures" uses these criteria to evaluate possible options. This includes a two-tier system; a large single-tier option; and voluntary cooperation through the use of intermunicipal agreements or special-purpose bodies or service boards. In some form or other, most of these arrangements exist in most countries, although in many instances these structures fall short of satisfying the criteria for an optimal municipal structure. Finally, section "Summary" summarizes the chapter.

Structures and Responsibilities in Selected Countries

This section highlights municipal governing structures, organizations, and major spending responsibilities in a few countries.[1] These were chosen on the basis of geography, availability of information, and an attempt to illustrate a range of governing options and spending responsibilities. From the information, readers will note both similarities and differences in structure and service responsibilities.

[1] Data and information were collected from websites for each country and from the OECD.

Canada

Canada is a federation with three levels of government—1 federal, 13 provincial/territorial, and more than 4000 municipal governments. Municipalities, under the Canadian constitution, are creatures of the province. The province has the power to create or eliminate municipalities, to determine where they can spend their money, and what revenue sources they can use to meet their spending obligations.

In general, municipal government structures consist of a mix of single-tier and two-tier incorporated municipalities. Under a single-tier structure, each municipality is responsible for all services. Frequently, however, these municipalities rely on intermunicipal agreements or special-purpose bodies for sharing some services with neighboring jurisdictions.

The most common type of municipal structure in Canada is the two-tier system. This is made up of a number of lower tiers or area municipalities—cities, towns, villages, and townships—and an upper tier that is called a county, region, or district. Here, the lower tier assumes responsibility for certain services, although this varies across provinces and quite often across regions/counties/districts within a province. For some services, lower tiers rely on intermunicipal agreements (fire and roads being the most common). The upper tier is responsible for the remaining services and generally, because of its geographic area, is more self-sufficient and much less dependent on intermunicipal agreements.

Specific services that are generally, but not exclusively, the responsibility of the upper tier include water and sewer, solid waste disposal and sometimes collection, arterial roads, public transit, police, social services and social housing where these are partially (shared with the province) a local responsibility, public health and land ambulance where these are partially a local responsibility, regional land use planning, and economic development. Lower tiers are generally responsible for local roads and streets, fire protection, street lighting, sidewalks, local land use planning, local libraries, parks, and recreation. Where there is only a single tier of local government, it is responsible for all municipal services.

Japan

Japan is a unitary country (central and local governments) with a two-tiered local government system everywhere. At the local level, there are 47 prefectures (upper tier). Within these prefectures, there are hundreds of municipalities (lower tier). This includes 790 cities, 745 towns, and 183 villages and a number of local public entities that have been established for providing specific services. There are no notable differences between cities, towns, and villages when it comes to service responsibility.

Prefectures oversee services that encompass a wide area including development plans, forest conservation, and flood control. They also serve as a conduit for communicating and coordinating policies between the central government and municipalities, and for advising and guiding municipalities on matters of organization and management including the formulation of amalgamation plans for municipalities. Prefectures are also responsible for establishing and operating senior high schools and universities.

Municipalities—here there are no essential differences between cities, towns, and villages—are responsible for public safety (firefighting, crime prevention, disaster prevention), health (establishing and operating hospitals), and environmental conservation (pollution control and garbage disposal). They are also responsible for local development (planning, roads, and agricultural development), establishing and maintaining various municipal facilities (public halls, nurseries, elementary and junior high schools, libraries, and welfare facilities), and providing welfare services.

United Kingdom

The United Kingdom is a union of four countries—England, Scotland, Wales, and Northern Ireland. Each of these has a local government act. In England, the local government structure is a mix of two-tier and single-tier systems. There are 33 two-tier systems with the upper tier being the county[2] and the lower tier being the district, of which there are 201 units. The county is responsible for the majority of public services including education, secondary and tertiary roads, social services, libraries, waste disposal, fire, police, and strategic planning. The district is responsible for housing, leisure and recreation, environmental health, waste collection, planning applications, and local tax collection. There are also 87 single-tier structures that are responsible for all local services. These are in place in some cities, large towns, and small counties. In many parts of England, an additional level of local government called a parish or town council exists. There are literally hundreds of these and each has minimal responsibility, mainly for village halls, cemeteries, leisure facilities, and war memorials.

[2] In London, the upper tier is called the Greater London Authority (instead of a county) and the lower tiers are referred to as boroughs (instead of districts) except for the City of London which is called a city.

In Scotland and Wales, the single-tier system is responsible for all local services. There are 32 local governments in Scotland and 22 in Wales. In Northern Ireland where there are 11 unitary systems, each is responsible for a limited range of services including environmental matters, sanitation, and recreation. The remaining services are the responsibility of the Northern Ireland government.

South Africa

South Africa is a federal country with 278 municipalities. This includes eight single-tier metropolitan governments that are responsible for all local public functions and services. The remaining municipalities are organized in a two-tier system. This includes 44 upper-tier districts and 226 lower-tier municipalities. District governments have no authority over the lower-tier municipalities but they share several responsibilities with the local municipalities within their jurisdiction. The district governments were created to provide those services that benefit from economies of scale; to provide coordinated planning across a large geographical area; and to handle those services that are primarily income redistributional in nature.

Differences in service responsibility vary somewhat across the country and it has continuously evolved since the two-tier system came into existence in 2000. The general pattern, however, is that districts are responsible for environmental health, arterial roads, and water supply and sanitation. Electricity is the responsibility of the lower tier as is parks, sports and recreation, local roads, street lighting, traffic control, and bylaw monitoring and enforcement. Some municipal services are a shared responsibility with provincial governments.

Chile

Chile is a unitary country with two levels of local government—345 municipalities and 15 regions. Regional governments are mainly responsible for carrying out a variety of tasks prescribed by the central government. Their responsibilities are limited—they include regional development, social and cultural development, the promotion of productive activities, municipal advice, rural roads, land management, and so on. As a result of an ongoing decentralization process started in 2013, plans are in place to modernize and strengthen municipal functions and to transfer to regions, responsibility for economic development, infrastructure, and housing.

Municipalities have 6 exclusive (sole responsibility) and 13 non-exclusive functions (shared with other levels of government). Own-level responsibility includes municipal zoning plans, local development, regulation of local transport, hygiene services, urbanism, and construction norms. Shared service responsibilities include public health, primary and secondary education, culture, training and economic development, tourism, traffic regulations, social housing, sanitary infrastructure, and citizen safety.

Poland

Poland is a unitary country with three levels of local government—almost 2500 municipalities, 379 counties plus 65 cities with county status, and 16 regions. The municipal level, however, is the only one protected by the constitution. The other two levels are not named in the constitution and their existence depends on laws adopted by the parliament.

Municipalities are largely responsible for spatial planning, infrastructure development including local roads, street lighting, bridges and public transport, utilities (water supply and sewerage, waste collection and disposal. energy), municipal housing, social services (including family benefits), pre- and primary education, environmental protection, basic health care, recreation, and culture.

Counties are responsible for local issues not ascribed to municipalities and have a more limited role and influence. Their responsibilities include secondary education, public health services (general hospitals), social welfare (beyond municipal territorial boundaries), economic activity, and job creation (employment offices).

Regions are responsible for issues of regional importance as determined by law. They play a relatively limited role in providing public services. Their main responsibilities are regional economic development, regional roads, and public transport including railways, higher education, health (regional hospitals), social welfare, labor market, environmental protection, and so on.

France

France is a unitary country with a central government and three levels of local government. At the local level, mainland France has there are 13 regions, 101 departments, and nearly 36,000 communes.

Spending responsibilities of the local governments are not always clearly and formally defined, but in general, regions and departments are responsible for regional economic development (innovation, internationalization), territorial planning, environmental protection, regional transport, high schools and vocational training, social solidarity, and territorial cohesion for the departments (social welfare for families, elderly, disabled, insertion, secondary schools, support to rural municipalities).

Communal responsibilities generally include primary education, town planning, local roads, urban public transport, social support for families and youth, local police, housing, drinking water and sanitation, waste, culture, sports, and so on.

Germany

Germany has a federal system of government that is based on the principle of cooperative federalism. The local level is a combination of two tier and single tier. In the two-tier structure, there are 295 districts and 11,092 municipalities. There are also 107 single-tier cities.[3]

Local government functions vary considerably from one area to another. However, they usually include both mandatory and optional functions. Mandatory district functions include secondary roads, public transport, spatial planning, fire protection, nature and landscape, hospitals, education (secondary schools), and so on. For municipalities, they include local roads, town planning, housing, sewerage, waterways, education (primary schools), recreational areas, and social and youth welfare. Optional functions include cultural activities, economic development, tourism, local public transport, sports and leisure, and so on.

Denmark

Denmark is a unitary country with a central level of government and two levels of local government. There are 5 regions (upper tier) and 98 municipalities (lower tier). Local governments in Denmark have substantial responsibilities; in fact, it is the most decentralized country in the OECD.

Regions are primarily responsible for health care (hospitals, health insurance, and outpatient medicine), regional development, regional transport, and regional environment. Municipalities are responsible for

[3] Overall, the number of German municipalities has decreased by one-third since 1990.

social welfare, education including pre-school, primary, lower secondary and specialized education, health care (preventive medicine, dental care, home care, etc.), social welfare (child, elderly), support services (unemployment insurance, early retirement benefits, cash benefits, and sickness benefits), sports and culture, spatial planning, nature and local environment, job centers, integration of immigrants, local roads, and so on.

United States

The United States is a federal country. According to the US Census Bureaus of 2012, there were 87,576 local governments. This included 3034 counties, 19,429 municipalities (cities, towns, and villages), 16,364 townships, 13,506 single-purpose school districts, and 35,052 other special-purpose districts that are typically designed to provide one or two services (conservation, fire protection, water and sewerage, public transportation, public libraries, public parks, and forests are examples). Over the past two decades or so, the number of special-purpose districts has grown, largely because of attempts to deal with cross-boundary issues (spillovers), a desire to take advantage of economies of scale, and because of their low public visibility (lack of accountability, in all likelihood) when compared with other levels of local government and school districts. Special-purpose districts are often governed by appointed officials while the other levels of local government are governed by elected officials.

Most states have at least two levels of general purpose local government. There are a number of metropolitan governments in highly urbanized areas with metro being the upper tier and cities being the lower tier. In more rural and less populated areas, counties are generally the upper tier[4] with towns, villages, boroughs, and townships constituting the lower tier. In rural areas where there is no level of local government below the county level, the county is the sole governing unit. In some other areas, there are consolidated county-city governing structures. Clearly, the variety of structures is wide ranging.

General purpose local governments are responsible for a broad range of services including transportation (roads and public transit), public health services (often, especially counties, including hospitals), social welfare

[4] County government has been eliminated in Rhode Island, Connecticut, and parts of Massachusetts. In addition, a number of independent cities and consolidated city-counties operate under municipal governments that serve the functions of both city and county.

(often administration and sometimes, significant financing), police and fire protection, recreation and culture, and land use planning and local business regulation. Local governments may also operate public utilities but often these are provided through special districts or as public enterprises. School districts are responsible for elementary and secondary schooling. The upper tier is generally responsible for area-wide services that benefit from economies of scale, are income redistributional in nature, and would generate spillovers if provided by each of the lower tiers.

Summary

The range and diversity of municipal government spending responsibilities around the world tends to be greater than the range and diversity of municipal governing structures. In some countries, municipal governments have little if any spending responsibilities for social services, education, hospitals, and health. In other countries, these services are an important local government responsibility. In some countries, police protection is a local responsibility, whereas in others, it is the responsibility of a more senior level of government. In general, municipal governments everywhere are responsible for the more traditional municipal services including fire protection, local roads and streets, public transit, street lighting, sidewalks, water, sewerage, solid waste collection and disposal, local planning, parks and recreation, and local libraries.

Municipal structures may be classified as single tier or two tier (sometimes multi-tier if special districts are included) with the former showing very little variation from country to country and the latter showing some variation. Most countries have some kind of mix of single-tier and two-tier systems.

In a single-tier structure, each municipality is responsible for all services although there may be some intermunicipal cooperation for services that cross municipal boundaries. In a two-tier system, the upper tier may be referred to as a county, region, district, or metropolitan level of government with responsibility for a set of services and the lower tier called a city, town, township, municipality responsible for another set of services. In a few cases, some service responsibilities may be shared between both tiers of local government. Finally, some countries rely on special service districts to provide a few services with these districts transcending municipal boundaries.

Options

In discussing municipal government structure, emphasis should be on a system that is responsible for setting policy and determining funding. It should not be on delivery (Osborne and Gaebler 1992; World Bank 1994; Batley 2001). Services may be delivered in a variety of ways as is described in Chaps. 5, 6, and 7. Furthermore it must be mentioned that a desirable structure for one municipality or a group of municipalities (Slack and Bird 2013) may differ. For example, the governance structure for a large metropolitan area or an area where there is a mix of contiguous rural and urban areas very likely will differ from the structure for noncontiguous, sparsely populated, municipalities in remote areas (Bird and Slack 2004; Kitchen and Slack 2006). Even the governing structure for one type of government such as a metropolitan area may differ from country to country (Bahl and Linn 2014; Slack and Chattopadhyay 2013), especially if demographic patterns diverge, and expenditure responsibilities and/or revenue sources differ across countries.

Governing structures come in different forms. Probably, the most common municipal structure is the two-tier system. This is made up of a number of lower tiers or area municipalities—cities, towns, villages, and townships—and an upper tier often referred to as metropolitan, county, region or district level of government. Here, each tier assumes responsibility for specific services although the range of responsibilities often differs from country to country and quite often across regions/counties/districts within a country. The upper tier, because of its geographic area, is generally more self-sufficient and much less dependent on intermunicipal cooperation. Finally, both the upper and lower tier may share responsibility for a small number of services.

A second structure that is common is a consolidated large single tier, often emerging out of municipal amalgamations, annexations, or restructuring. Here, all local service responsibilities are under one governing unit.

A third option used in many countries for selective services exists in conjunction with either the two-tier or single-tier model, although it seems to be more common in smaller contiguous and sometimes noncontiguous municipalities. It may take the form of intermunicipal agreements or special-purpose bodies, often referred to as service boards. These are primarily used for providing and funding services that spill across municipal boundaries. As well, they are often preferred by officials of smaller municipalities who are resisting becoming part of a larger municipal unit. Finally, they are frequently used for services that would otherwise be the responsibility of the upper tier in a two-tier system.

Deciding on which of these options would be most desirable for a specific geographic area often depends on a number of factors, not the least of which is the capacity for the model or structure to satisfy a number of criteria for an efficient, fair, and effective governance model. These criteria are described next.

Criteria

A municipal governing structure should be designed so that it is efficient, accountable, fair, transparent, and easy to administer. If these objectives are achieved, an effective municipal governing structure should ensue. To achieve this, several criteria may be used (Slack and Bird 2013) in designing such a structure. At the outset, however, it should be mentioned that it will not likely be possible to satisfy all criteria simultaneously and it may not be possible to secure agreement on whether one structure or another best meets certain criteria. For example, some individuals might argue that a specific model adequately controls spillovers while others might argue that it does not. Similar disagreements may exist for the other criteria. Finally, depending on local characteristics and features of the area, criteria that are deemed to be most important in one municipality or part of the country may not be deemed to be important in another municipality or part of the country.

Controlling spillovers or externalities: A spillover or externality exists when a policy of one level of government generates benefits or costs that are incurred by residents in other municipalities without the latter having any control over the policy decision of the originating municipality. The existence of spillovers or externalities can impede efficient and effective governing structures and create unwanted consequences if not properly accounted for or controlled.

There are at least three ways in which spillovers from municipal services may be controlled. First, the affected municipalities may be combined (amalgamated) into a single-tier municipality that is large enough to include all benefits from public services within its governing jurisdiction and large enough to ensure that all costs of government activity are funded by the residents within the jurisdiction. Second, services generating spillovers could become the responsibility of the upper-tier level of government in a two-tier municipal structure. Either option should ensure that the proper level of service is provided and that all costs and benefits are taken into consideration in reaching decisions on service quantity and quality. Third, spillovers may be controlled or internalized through grants from senior levels of government or from other benefiting local governments, or coordination among the affected municipalities. In reality, neither of these latter two possibilities is likely to be as effective. Intergovernmental grants are declining in most countries and where they are used, they are generally ineffective in capturing spillovers (see Chaps. 12, 13, and 14 for a more detailed discussion of this). Fourth, spillovers may be internalized through the use of intermunicipal agreements (Spicer 2015), special-purpose bodies, or service boards (Slack and Bird 2013). These are seldom "first best" solutions, however, because they have the potential for being unaccountable, inefficient, and ineffective over the long run.

Economies of scale: Economies of scale exist when per unit costs of delivering services decline as the population served increases. As with services generating spillovers, there are two ways in which economies may be realized; either through the creation of a large single-tier structure or through upper-tier responsibility in a two-tier system. Using economies of scale as a criterion for creating a large single-tier government, it has been suggested, creates problems because different services achieve the lowest per unit cost at different scales of operation. Single-tier responsibility means that some services may be beyond the most efficient size (diseconomies set in) of municipal structure. For example, the optimal size of government may be different for fire services than for police or waste management (Found 2012; Allers and Geertsema 2016).

In a two-tier structure, economies of scale may be achieved by assigning services displaying large economies of scale to the upper tier and the remainder to the lower tier. Service boards or intermunicipal agreements may also handle these services where there is a series of smaller (non-metropolitan) single-tier municipalities. Examples where economies of scale are found generally include water, sewerage, major transportation routes, and solid waste management (most of these services have large infrastructure costs).

Ensuring a uniform quantity and quality of service: Provision of a uniform quantity and quality of service (regardless of whether it is mandated by a senior level of government or because it is desired by local residents) across a large geographical area could be the responsibility of a large single-tier municipality, or it could be the responsibility of the upper tier in a two-tier governing structure, or it could be provided through some type of intermunicipal agreement or special service body. Examples include arterial roads, water and sewers, and policing. Failure to provide these services at uniform levels in some municipalities may lead to harmful and costly externalities for other municipalities within the same geographical area.

Local preferences: This supports small-scale, fragmented local governments because they maintain a quasi-market. It results in competition and provides an incentive for efficient, accountable, and effective service responsibility because neighboring municipalities may benchmark service costs with each other. The benefits of competition cannot be disputed. In a two-tier system and when everything else is equal, services that differ because of local preferences should be the responsibility of the lower tier. In a large consolidated single-tier system, similar preferences could be captured through the creation of delivery zones and by benchmarking with other municipalities and the private sector where applicable.

Income redistribution: Income redistributional issues are also important in designing local government structure. Within the local sector, there are almost always rich communities and poor communities. Richer communities will have a relatively large tax base from which to fund services and a relatively low demand for some services (fire and police protection). Poorer communities, on the other hand, may have higher demands for services and a small revenue base for funding these services. One solution would be to consolidate these municipalities into one jurisdiction, in effect taxing the rich municipalities and using some of the proceeds to subsidize the poor municipalities just as is currently done in any municipality where there are both rich neighborhoods and poor neighborhoods.

Alternatively, the upper tier in a two-tier structure could have some taxing power that could tax richer areas to help fund services in poorer areas within any jurisdictional setting. This is akin to the funding of central governments where taxes imposed on taxpayers in some areas of the country are taxed to finance projects or services in other areas. After all, an inherent characteristic of a "public" service is that it has some income redistributional consequences; that is, why these services are the responsibility of government and not the private sector.

Accessibility: This criterion suggests that citizens should have access to local government so that they can influence government policy. This is done through public meetings, hearings, elections, and direct contacts with officials. Smaller government units, it is often suggested, can provide the average citizen with greater "access" to local politicians, better representation, and better decisions.

This may also be tied in with the subsidiarity principle where it is argued that a service should be provided by the level of government that is closest to the people subject to satisfying the above-noted criteria.

Summary: The optimal design of government structure may depend on which criteria are to be satisfied. Four criteria (benefiting from economies of scale, controlling externalities, providing services at a uniform quantity and quality, and redistribution of taxes) lend themselves to large government units over a large geographical area; or to provision by the upper-tier level of government in a two-tier governing structure; or to the use of intermunicipal cooperative arrangements across a number of municipalities. Other criteria (local preferences and access) point toward smaller government units or a role for lower-tier municipalities in a two-tier governing system.

Municipal Structures

By and large, all developed countries and a number of developing countries have engaged in some type of municipal restructuring over the past 20–30 years. Municipal boundaries that were established many decades ago have, in many cases, outgrown their purpose and have become outdated and out of touch.

The continuing migration of people from rural and remote areas to cities and highly concentrated urban areas (Bahl and Linn 2014) is changing the importance and relevance of many local government structures. The growing percentage of a country's economic activity that is generated in cities has changed the dynamics between urban and rural areas. Population growth and its subsequent sprawl have melded what were noticeably distinct municipalities into larger, more integrated and cohesive communities with far fewer differences than previously existed. A growing tendency for people to live in one jurisdiction and work in neighboring jurisdictions has effectively removed most intermunicipal differences attributed to local preferences and produced a leveling out of citizen expectations for both the quantity and quality of public services provided across all municipalities. Requirements of senior levels of government that municipalities meet specific service standards (social services, social housing; fire prevention, training, and education; building and fire inspections, and bylaw enforcement; and so on) have removed the opportunity for municipalities to provide many services with different standards.

Arguments that rural and tourist areas should be excluded from urban areas in any governing structure may also be unrealistic and impractical.

Urban areas are the focal point for most economic, recreational, and social activity across a large geographical area. Consequently, the governance of urban centers revolves around the need to maintain a coherent balance among policies for the entire area. Urban growth can enhance or restrict the area's economy. Transportation issues impact on the rural area as much as the urban area. Provision of social services and social housing for the rural and urban areas alike must be shared across the entire region to prevent the migration of recipients to the urban centers leaving them with the task of paying the entire bill. Region- or area-wide land use planning is important if the rural and tourist communities are to retain some of their identity and resist the temptation to urbanize in order to capture increased property assessment and more property tax revenue. Area-wide environmental protection practices are essential if some municipalities are to prevent their neighbors from ignoring their environmental responsibilities. Rural areas around an urban centered jurisdiction generally have better arterial roads, more recreation programs, enhanced library services, and better fire protection and safety standards, to name only a few, when compared with municipalities that are not part of an urban/rural governing structure.

Returning to an earlier comment that "no one size fits all," it is appropriate to evaluate the major options for governing municipalities that were identified in section "Options".

Pros and Cons of a Two-Tier Structure

The two-tier structure consists of an upper-tier governing body (usually region, county, district, or metropolitan area) encompassing a fairly large geographic area and a number of lower-tier municipalities (including incorporated cities, towns, villages, townships, and possibly unincorporated areas).[5] Greater London and Greater Manchester in the United Kingdom are examples of a two-tier model as is Barcelona in Spain. In designing a two-tier structure, two major issues are important; first, service responsibility and funding; and second, governance.

Within this two-tier structure, the upper tier should be responsible for services that generate spillovers (benefits or costs), that benefit from economies of scale, that are income distributional in nature, and where uniform standards are important across the entire area. Table 4.1 takes these

[5] For a more detailed discussion especially as they exist in Metropolitan areas, see Slack and Bird 2013; Bahl and Linn 2014; Slack and Chattopadhyay 2013; and Steylter 2009.

Table 4.1 Allocation of expenditure responsibilities in a two-tier system

Function	*Upper tier*	*Lower tier*	*Justification*
Social services			
Welfare assistance	X		Income redistribution; externalities
Child care services	X		Income redistribution; externalities
Social housing	X		Income redistribution; economies of scale; externalities
Public health	X		Income redistribution; economies of scale; externalities
Land ambulance	X		Economies of scale; externalities
Roads and bridges	X	X	Local versus regional roads
Public transit	X		Externalities; economies of scale
Street lighting		X	No externalities
Sidewalks		X	No externalities
Water system	X		Economies of scale
Sewer system	X		Economies of scale
Garbage collection	X		Economies of scale; externalities
Garbage disposal	X		Economies of scale; externalities
Police protection	X		Externalities; economies of scale
Fire suppression		X	Local responsiveness; scale economies for specialized services
Fire prevention/ training	X		Economies of scale
Local land use planning		X	Local access, responsiveness
Regional land use planning	X		Externalities
Economic development	X		Externalities
Parks and recreation		X	Local responsiveness
Libraries		X	Local responsiveness

Source: Bird, Richard M. and Enid Slack, 2004, "Fiscal Aspects of Metropolitan Governance" International Tax Program Paper 0401 (Toronto: Joseph L. Rotman School of Management, University of Toronto), p. 69

criteria and uses them in assigning local public services to either the upper or the lower tier (Bird and Slack 2004, p. 69). As the reader will observe, most of the responsibilities rest with the upper tier.

On the tax side, tax rates for upper-tier services would generally be levied at uniform rates across the region/district/area and the contribution of each lower-tier municipality to the upper-tier municipality would depend on the size of its tax base. The larger the tax base in any one municipality, the larger is its contribution to the upper-tier government. The result of a uniform property tax at the upper-tier level and region, district, or area-wide spending is a redistribution of resources from relatively large tax-base municipalities to relatively small tax-base municipalities. Of course, user fees should be used for services where beneficiaries can be identified.

Lower-tier responsibility should include services that do not have the above characteristics and whose benefits are confined primarily to the local community where residents have a choice over both quantity and quality. Tax rates may vary from municipality to municipality to reflect differences in standards and tax bases. Here, as with the upper tier, user fees should be used where consumers of specific services can be identified (Slack and Bird 2013).

A two-tier structure also requires an accountable and efficient governing structure. At the outset, it must be noted that the upper tier should be an agency of the electorate and should exist to provide individual residents of the county, region, district, or metropolitan area with a range of services. It should not be an agent of the lower-tier municipalities and it should not be a contract agency delivering services on behalf of the lower tiers. Lines of communication and accountability between the upper-tier council and individual residents should be direct and not filtered through local councils.

The objective in creating an effective upper-tier governing structure is to disentangle the lines of accountability from the upper-tier council to the electorate on the one hand and local councils to the electorate on the other. Upper-tier councilors should represent people, not other governments, and should be responsible for their actions to the electorate, not to other politicians. By clearly differentiating the political structures of the two tiers of municipal government, voters may exercise their judgment of and communicate their needs to the upper-tier council independently of any expressions they may wish to make to their local councilors. A clearer demarcation between the two tiers is intended in part to clear up the confusion among voters about responsibilities between the upper-tier and lower-tier municipalities, an important prerequisite for increased accountability and effectiveness. Local municipalities may protest that the importance of the upper-tier council's decisions to their communities requires that they be represented as municipalities on the upper-tier council. That logic, of course, would also require that representatives of local municipalities sit on the governing body of senior levels of government. To be sure, the two tiers must work in a cooperative manner, coordinating their efforts so as to achieve effectiveness and efficiency in service delivery.

This is an argument for administrative coordination, however, not for political intermarriage. In short, supporters of a two-tier structure argue that it permits a division of service responsibility that leads to an efficient, effective, and accountable governing structure.

Critics of the two-tier model, on the other hand, argue that costs are higher because of waste and duplication. Furthermore, they continue, two-tier levels of government are less transparent and more confusing to taxpayers who cannot figure out who is responsible for what services (Slack 2018). Finally, two municipal councils (upper tier and lower tier) are said to lead to considerable wrangling, inefficiency in decision-making and frequent stalling or postponement of the implementation of policies that would benefit taxpayers across the entire local government jurisdiction (Kitchen 2002, p. 312).

While the usefulness of this structure depends on the objectives to be achieved, the breadth of service responsibility, the size, and similarity or diversity of the area considered, it is an option that may be appropriate where there are a number of contiguous urban centers, and in metropolitan areas (Slack 2018; Bahl and Linn 2014; Bird and Slack 2004).

In remote areas where municipalities are isolated from each other, distances are such that benefits or costs of services provided by one municipality are unlikely to spill over into adjacent municipalities. Similarly, distance between municipalities and their isolation from each other prevent them from benefiting from economies of scale. Hence, the rationale for a two-tier structure at the municipal level in remote areas may be less compelling than it is for larger metropolitan areas or areas where municipalities are contiguous with each other (Kitchen and Slack 2006).

Pros and Cons of a Large Single-Tier Structure

Large single-tier governments in most countries have been created by merging (through amalgamations or annexations) a number of smaller lower-tier municipalities within an existing county, region, district, or metropolitan area into one consolidated municipality or by amalgamating a number of separate contiguous single-tier municipalities into one large consolidated municipality. Two often discussed examples include Cape Town, South Africa, and Toronto, Canada. Since there is only one level of municipal government across the entire geographical area, all municipal services become the responsibility of this newly created municipality and it is responsible for all municipal taxes and user fees. As well, there is only one political body responsible for making all policy decisions.

Supporters of large single-tier municipalities have argued that improvements in economic efficiency (cost savings because of fewer politicians, more efficient service delivery, less bureaucracy) arise from the removal of administrative duplication; pooling of insurance; lower input prices associated with greater purchasing power; and greater scope for using sophisticated and specialized technical equipment. Second, all spillovers or externalities would be internalized (Slack and Bird 2013). Third, clearer lines of responsibility may lead to more accountability because there is only one level of municipal government and taxpayers know who is responsible for the vast array of local services. Fourth, better service coordination and more streamlined decision-making could emerge because there is only one municipal council instead of two. Fifth, funding fairness in the provision of municipal services occurs because there is a wider revenue base (taxes, user fees, and borrowing capacity) for sharing the cost of services benefiting taxpayers across the entire area. Because of this, it can be more financially self-sufficient than smaller government units (Slack 2018). Finally, the larger taxable capacity of a one-tier government increases its ability to borrow and recover capital and operating costs from user fees (Bahl and Linn 1992, p. 415).

Beyond expenditure responsibilities and funding arrangements, a single tier[6] may be more effective at providing an environment in which the business community and residents are able to meet and adapt to the challenges of the new economy and to compete effectively at the regional, national, and international level (Meloche and Vaillancourt 2013). In particular, a single-tier municipality can more efficiently and effectively work toward a uniform and improved physical (highways and roads, road, water, sewer, and electricity) and social or recreational (parks, recreation, libraries) infrastructure. It will eliminate the inefficient and wasteful competition that frequently exists when one municipality competes with others to attract economic development away from neighboring jurisdictions without recognizing that it matters not where the new development locates or expands because everyone in the wider area benefits. A single-tier region-wide level of government could have the financial strength (base) to accept new responsibilities and to implement cost-sharing equity for those services that benefit all residents of the area. As well, a single-tier municipality may more effectively initiate policies that avoid social decay and environmental

[6]These advantages also extend to the upper-tier responsibility in a clearly defined two-tier system of local government.

degradation that frequently surfaces in an area fractured by a number of separate governing units.

Critics of a large single tier argue that this structure reduces competition between municipalities, leading to higher costs because there is less incentive to be efficient and responsive to local needs. Second, it is claimed that the least costly and most efficient size of government may differ for different services; that is, efficiency and cost savings may be different for roads than for fire or police or recreation. In other words, some services will benefit from economies of scale if assigned to larger units of government while others will incur diseconomies of scale. Third, for services whose benefits are entirely local in nature, local preferences may not be reflected in the quantity and quality of service provided. For example, services provided to rural and tourist areas should not be included in the same governing structure as urban areas because the range and level of services may be different. Fourth, the area is too large and citizens are removed from their local politicians leading to a reduction in access and accountability (Dafflon 2012).

Concerns such as these are important, but defenders of a large single-tier structure have suggested that these are concerns with the cost of delivering services and not specifically with the governance structure. For example, competition can be secured through greater use of alternative service delivery vehicles such as "contracting out" and creating delivery zones within a municipality. Further improvements could be secured through effective monitoring including performance measures and benchmarking.

In reply to the criticism that the opportunity to differentiate service levels to reflect local preferences will not be possible, single-tier responsibility does not mean that all services need to be provided with uniform standards and service levels across the entire area. Differentials in both service levels and funding could exist to reflect differences in the range and level of services—urban versus rural, neighborhood versus neighborhood. Differential service levels should be funded through area rates, special charges, and user fees (see Chaps. 9 and 11). It might even be argued that service level differentials could be captured more easily in a large municipality than in the pre-amalgamated municipalities as long as the former is able to establish seamless service areas that are not restricted by previous municipal boundaries.

Furthermore, designing a municipal structure to capture variations in local preferences in many countries (particularly for municipalities around a major urban center or a series of smaller urban areas adjacent to each other) may be, as was noted in the introduction to this section, less relevant today than it was at one time.

The claim that larger governing units are likely to be less accountable and more costly (less efficient) has created many hotly contested discussions and disputes. In terms of accountability, it has been suggested that large-scale, one-tier governments reduce access and accountability because the jurisdiction is too large and bureaucratic. To alleviate this concern, satellite offices and community committees have sometimes been established to address neighborhood issues. If properly structured, residents can pay local tax bills, apply for building permits, and so on at these offices (Slack 2018). The success of these, however, is uncertain—they may increase accessibility, but it is not clear how they impact on accountability. Furthermore, they could remove potential cost savings that might result from a larger government unit.

As for cost savings, many critics have argued that costs rise after an amalgamation. They may or they may not. The evidence on this is mixed (Allers and Geertsema 2016). On the one hand, costs will not likely fall if the newly elected council decides to retain all former employees and if it continues to "do business" as in the past. Similarly, if the amalgamation brings together municipal employees that previously received differing levels of compensation, the tendency to level up may negate any cost savings from restructuring. If, on the other hand, politicians are innovative and willing to change and "do business" in different and innovative ways, and if they are resistant to leveling up, costs could fall and average tax rates could decline.

Where studies have shown cost increases, many of these should be treated with caution. For example, the before and after cost comparisons often fail to take into consideration other factors changing at the same time. In Ontario, Canada, amalgamations occurred at a time when the province was off-loading increased spending responsibilities to municipalities. As well, many of these studies failed to extrapolate the increased costs associated with higher service levels provided in parts of the newly amalgamated municipality. Finally, these intertemporal cost studies ignore changes that simply evolve over time (e.g. due to increased population and housing density, changing work patterns, tastes, and preferences); changes that can affect both expenditure needs and revenue requirements that are not necessarily related to amalgamation.

While large single-tier municipalities currently exist and are an option in highly urbanized areas and in areas that are a mix of rural and urban, they are only ever created when the pre-amalgamated municipalities are adjacent to or contiguous with each other. They do not exist and would not be appropriate in remote areas.

Pros and Cons of Intermunicipal Cooperative Arrangements

Regardless of whether a municipality operates as single tier or two tier, many of them engage in some form of intermunicipal cooperation in the provision and funding of some local services. These arrangements may be in the form of intermunicipal agreements or special-purpose bodies or service boards. They take the form of consortia, communities of communes, urban communities (France), joint intermunicipal authorities (Spain and Belgium), public bodies, joint agencies, and core cities (the Netherlands and United States) (Bird and Slack 2004, p. 14; Hermann et al. 1999). These agreements or bodies provide services across a wider geographical area without engaging in amalgamations or annexations. Let us consider each of these options.

Intermunicipal Agreements

Intermunicipal agreements represent a form of voluntary cooperation between municipalities (Spicer 2015). They are formal or informal agreements designed to provide specific services, usually with no official area-wide body to oversee their arrangement. An example of such an intermunicipal agreement is the contract services plan in Los Angeles, under which Los Angeles County provides some services on a contract basis on behalf of municipalities in the Los Angeles metropolitan area. Similar city-county links occur in other US jurisdictions (Sharpe 1995).

Municipalities usually enter into these agreements to reduce costs and many have been successful, especially for services that can be contracted out and where outputs can be clearly identified. This includes bulk purchasing, issuing debentures, firefighting and emergency dispatch, and the maintenance of boundary roads.

In many instances, however, these agreements have created problems. At some point, difficulties generally emerge and problems almost always surface with these arrangements. The municipality buying the service generally becomes upset with the cost and suspects that it is being overcharged, particularly with respect to overhead. The municipality selling the service frequently develops concerns because it does not feel that it is fairly compensated (Kitchen 2002, pp. 317–318). Discontent with these agreements tends to be greater than it should be and often leads to increased intermunicipal litigation and conflicts (GTA Task Force 1996). These agreements do not foster region-wide coordination and they do not provide any clear public accountability, except through the contract or agreement. If a problem occurs, citizens seldom know whether to complain to their local government or to the local government that has been contracted to provide the service (Slack and Bird 2013, p. 17). In reality, intermunicipal agreements are all too frequently a "second best" solution for they lead to a jungle of "ad hoc" and complex arrangements that even the most conscientious municipal voter has trouble understanding (Sancton 1993, pp. 33–34). They can reduce local accountability and lead to inefficiency and ineffectiveness in service responsibility.

Service Board or Special-Purpose Body

Another suggestion for handling area-wide services involves the creation of a service board or special-purpose body. As reported in section "United States", these are very common in the United States. A service board is like a two-tier system of municipal government. In many ways, however, it is often perceived to be inferior to the type of two-tier governing structure discussed above. While advocates (most of whom are municipal administrators and politicians from municipalities in a two-tier structure or small single tiers who do not want to be amalgamated) of the service board concept are generally uniform in their view that the service board's role is to provide and sell services to area municipalities, this is where uniformity and consistency over their responsibility and operation stops. For example, views differ on the services for which these boards should be responsible (social services, arterial roads, police, public transit, water and sewer, waste management, major roads and highways, planning and economic development, and so on); whether or not they should be structured as a special-purpose body or bodies or whether they should continue as local governing units; how they should be governed (appointed or elected officials, and if elected, should they be directly elected or indirectly elected); how they should be financed (taxing authority or not); and whether or not the purchase of services by the area municipalities from the service board should be voluntary or compulsory. The following illustrates the kinds of problems they pose.

Service responsibility: To satisfy the criteria for optimum service responsibility in a two-tier structure, there is no conceptual basis for assigning services to the service board in a different fashion than one would use to assign service responsibility to the upper tier in a two-tier model. These include services benefiting from economies of scale, services generating spillovers, those that are primarily income redistributional, and those where area-wide uniform standards are required (see Table 4.1).

Special-purpose body or municipal government: Once the board has been assigned specific service responsibilities, should it be structured as a special-purpose body or should it operate like a municipal government? If the latter, it is like the current upper-tier structure in most two-tier systems. If it is set up as a special-purpose body, there is a strong possibility that it will take on its own powers and be less efficient and accountable than an all-purpose municipal governing structure because special interest groups will have an easier time gaining influence and favors from special-purpose governance institutions. The result is often cost increases that benefit certain parties, rather than cost savings or service delivery efficiencies (Berry 2009) benefiting everyone.

Should the board be governed by appointed or elected officials? It has been argued that the governing structure for service boards should be made up of appointed officials because, it is alleged, appointees could be technical experts in a particular field(s) and therefore, more professional and efficient because they are removed from political decision-making when compared with local politicians (Bahl 2013). The case against appointed officials is fairly strong because it is undemocratic to have appointed officials making policy decisions on expenditures funded by tax dollars and user fees. Accountability is likely to be missing if taxpayers do not have the opportunity to vote for the individuals who make public policy decisions. Without accountability, there may be no incentive to be economically efficient (even though they are technically efficient) if services are not delivered to the right people in the right quantities and qualities.[7] Finally, appointed officials may create an environment where the special-purpose governing structure becomes autonomous and independent from local councils.

[7] Professionals may be more technically efficient in delivering services but not more economically efficient in making decisions. Economic efficiency is more than technical efficiency—the latter is a necessary but not sufficient condition for economic efficiency. Technical efficiency exists when a producing unit (firm, government, agency) operates in a way such that it is not possible to secure any additional output given the available inputs (labor, material, and capital) and level of technology. Economic or allocative efficiency is achieved when society gets the greatest net benefits from the allocation of its scarce resources.

If members are elected, should they be directly elected or double directly elected? While arguments in favor of elected officials are stronger than arguments in favor of appointees, there is disagreement over whether the elected members of the service board should be directly elected (only to the service board) or double directly elected (to the council of the area municipality and the service board simultaneously).

Double directly elected decision makers provide for strong communication between the service board and the area municipalities because the same individuals are on both governing bodies. This may be appropriate if the service board is regarded as an agency or instrument of the area municipalities.

On the other hand, in a double directly elected system, accountability may become entangled because citizens/voters are unable to separate their vote for local issues from their vote for service board issues. For example, suppose a taxpayer is happy with a councilor at the local level but not as a member of the service board, for whom is he or she voting at election time—is it the individual as a local councilor or as a member of the service board? A further criticism of double directly elected councilors is that the service board could become the instrument or agency of local councils. This electoral system has the potential for parochialism in decision-making and may not be directly accountable to taxpayers/voters.

Directly elected members of the service board are generally preferred because accountability is enhanced when each member represents only area-wide issues. Those charged with the responsibility for directing area-wide operations will have an opportunity to present their ideas about area-wide issues directly to the public and to hear clearly their responses during election periods, without confusing the issues with matters of concern for the area municipalities. Elected members on the service board can be judged by the electorate on the basis of their performance on the service board and will be less likely to face conflict between service board and local interests. Members of the service board will be able to focus their energies entirely on region-wide issues and the less onerous workload may allow for an expanded pool of candidates for council/service board issues. The potential for parochialism will be reduced and the electoral process will be greatly simplified with separate slates of candidates for each level or unit of municipal government.

The case against directly elected members on the service board is that lines of communication between the service board and area municipalities may be weaker if elected members only serve on one level of local government. This concern, however, may be alleviated through administrative arrangements.

Financing of a special-purpose body or service board: Some supporters of a service board have suggested that it should not have taxing authority. Instead, they argue it should sell services to area municipalities with the latter assuming responsibility for raising the necessary funds (from its taxpayers). This role for a service board may be appropriate where the board is responsible for providing services such as solid waste collection and disposal, and water provision and sewage treatment where specific beneficiaries can be identified and user fees or charges imposed.

If, however, a service board is responsible for services where specific beneficiaries cannot be identified and specific charges not imposed such as for land ambulance, social services, social housing and police, it is difficult to see how the service board could finance these services without fairly and equitably raising the money through local taxation on taxpayers across the entire area. This basis for covering costs, of course, is identical to that which is currently in place or ought to be in place for financing services in either a single-tier system or a two-tier system. To do it in any other way would almost certainly be more inequitable, less accountable, and more inefficient.

Voluntary or compulsory purchasing from the special-purpose body or service board: This is not an issue if the board deals directly with taxpayers—in this instance, the role and structure of the board are similar, perhaps identical, to that of a region, county, district, or metropolitan area. It is an issue, however, if local municipalities buy services from the service board and, in turn, fund them from taxes and fees collected from their taxpayers. Compulsory purchasing may be a problem if each area municipality has the opportunity to determine its level and standard of purchased services that benefit from economies of scale, generate spillovers, and are redistributional in nature. If, on the other hand, area municipalities have no choice over the level and standard (such as where a senior level of government sets the standards—social services, land ambulance, for example), purchase of service by the area municipalities from the regional service board seems like an unnecessary, wasteful, and inefficient step.

Voluntary purchasing may also create problems if area municipalities can "opt in and opt out" as they wish. First, if some municipalities refuse to participate, this could prevent the service board from benefiting from economies of scale—a major reason for creating them, in the first place. Second and possibly more important, area municipalities in an attempt to gain control over all services provided to citizens in their municipalities (sometimes referred to as "empire building") may simply refuse to buy from the service board and, in turn, provide the service themselves even when this is more costly. As well, provision of services by each area municipality creates further problems if spillovers are generated or if the services are income redistributional in nature (Walisser et al. 2013).

Summary: There is no consensus on a number of critical issues around the concept of a service board or special-purpose body. Indeed, when these concerns have been raised with many proponents of this structure, the conclusion generally leads to an operational structure with service responsibilities and funding that are virtually identical to the upper tier in a two-tier structure of municipal government.

Summary

Municipal government structures around the world consist of a mix of single-tier and two-tier municipalities. In a single-tier system, each municipality is responsible for all services and each has a directly elected governing council. In a two-tier structure, each level of local government is responsible for specific services although some of these may be shared between both levels of local government. The upper tier in this structure is sometimes referred to as a county, region, district, or metropolitan level of government. In other cases, the upper tier may be an elected or appointed special-purpose body, agency, or commission with responsibility for providing specific services over a geographical area that is beyond the borders of any single lower-tier jurisdiction. In still other cases, region- or area-wide services may be provided through joint-use or intermunicipal agreements.

In designing a municipal government structure, the emphasis should be on a system that is responsible for setting policy and determining funding, not on delivery, for this may be handled in a variety of ways. Recent initiatives in consolidating or amalgamating municipalities in a number of countries have generally concentrated on two options: a two-tier structure and a large single-tier government. As well, there has been considerable interest in intermunicipal cooperation, including reliance on intermunicipal agreements and the creation of some kind of special-purpose body with responsibility for services that transcend existing municipal boundaries.

When each option is examined in terms of its ability or capacity to meet the following criteria: capacity for benefiting from economies of scale, controlling externalities, providing services at uniform standards, redistributing taxes, capturing local preferences, and being accessible, the optimal design may depend on which of the criteria is given the highest priority. The first four support larger governing units and the last two support smaller units. As well, the ideal structure may vary depending on whether one is considering a large metropolitan area, an area where there is a mix of contiguous rural and urban areas, or municipalities in noncontiguous, sparsely populated, and isolated communities in remote areas.

Although the municipal government system does not, in itself, determine the success or failure of local economies and social policies, it plays an important role in the financial and economic viability of municipalities, especially those that are urban centered because they are critical for the growth and vitality of an economy. These municipalities are frequently referred to as city-regions. City-regions are economically and socially becoming more and more important as recent trends—urbanization, social instability, and migration—focus on major urban centers. Not only are city-regions critical to the success of any country in the new global economy, they face serious problems with the cost of urban sprawl and higher demands for social service expenditures to accommodate the homeless and economically deprived. Resolving these problems is a major concern and is likely best handled under either a two-tier structure or large single tier. In some cases, intermunicipal cooperation arrangements may be necessary but these must be introduced carefully and judiciously.

References

Allers, Maarten A., and J. Bieuwe Geertsema. 2016. The Effects of Local Government Amalgamations on Public Spending, Taxation, and Service Levels: Evidence from 15 Years of Municipal Consolidation. *Journal of Regional Science* 56 (4): 659–682.

Bahl, Roy. 2013. The Decentralization of Governance in Metropolitan Areas. In *Financing Metropolitan Governments in Developing Countries*, ed. Roy Bahl, Johannes Linn, and Deborah Wetzel, 85–105. Cambridge, MA: Lincoln Institute of Land Policy.

Bahl, Roy, and Johannes Linn. 1992. *Urban Public Finance in Developing Countries*. New York: Oxford University Press.

Bahl, Roy W., and Johannes F. Linn. 2014. *Governing and Financing Cities in the Developing World*. Cambridge, MA: Lincoln Institute of Land Policy.

Batley, Richard. 2001. Public-Private Partnerships for Urban Services. In *The Challenge of Urban Government: Policies and Practices*, ed. Mila Freire and Richard Stren, 199–214. Washington, DC: The World Bank.

Berry, Christopher R. 2009. *Imperfect Union: Representation and Taxation in Multilevel Governments*. New York: Cambridge University Press.

Bird, Richard M., and Enid Slack. 2004. *"Fiscal Aspects of Metropolitan Governance" International Tax Program Paper 0401*. Toronto: Joseph L. Rotman School of Management, University of Toronto.

Dafflon, Bernard. 2012. *Voluntary Amalgamation of Local Governments: The Swiss Debate in the European Context*. Working Paper. Atlanta: International Center for Public Policy, Andrew Young School of Public Policy, Georgia State University.

Found, Adam. 2012. *Economies of Scale in Fire and Police Services in Ontario*. IMFG Papers on Municipal Finance and Governance Series, University of Toronto, No 12. http://munkschool.utoronto.ca/imfg/resources/.

GTA Task Force. 1996. *Greater Toronto*. Toronto: The Queen's Printer.

Hermann, Zoltan, M. Tamas Horvath, Gabor Peteri, and Gabor Ungvari. 1999. *Allocation of Local Government Functions: Criteria and Conditions—Analysis and Policy Proposals for Hungary*. Washington, DC: The fiscal Decentralization Initiative for Central and Eastern Europe.

Kitchen, Harry. 2002. *Municipal Revenue and Expenditure Issues in Canada*. Toronto: Canadian Tax Foundation.

Kitchen, Harry and Enid Slack. 2006. Providing Public Services in Remote Areas. Chap. 7 in *Perspectives on Fiscal Federalism*, ed. Richard M. Bird and Francois Vaillancourt, 123–140. Washington, DC: World Bank Institute.

Meloche, Jean-Philippe, and Francois Vaillancourt. 2013. *Public Finance in Montreal: In Search of Equity and Efficiency*. IMFG Paper No. 15. Toronto: Institute on Municipal Finance and Governance, University of Toronto.

Osborne, David, and Ted Gaebler. 1992. *Reinventing Government—How the Entrepreneurial Spirit is Transferring the Public Sector*. Reading, MA: Addison Wesley Publishing Co. Inc.

Prud'home, Remy. 2005. Local Government Organization and Finance in France. A Chapter in *Local Government Organization and Finance: Comparative International Practices*, ed. Anwar Shah. Washington, DC: World Bank Institute.

Sancton, Andrew. 1993. *Local Government Reorganization in Canada Since 1975*. Toronto: Intergovernmental Committee on Urban and Regional Research.

Sharpe, L.J. 1995. The Future of Metropolitan Government. In *The Government of World Cities: The Future of the Metro Model*, ed. L.J. Sharpe. Chichester: John Wiley & Sons Ltd.

Slack, End. 2018. *Options for Metropolitan Governance in Greater Kampala*. IGC (International Growth Centre), Working Paper Reference Number C-43425-UGA-1.

Slack, Enid and Richard Bird. 2013. *Merging Municipalities: Is Bigger Better?* IMFG Paper No. 14. Toronto: Institute on Municipal Finance and Governance, University of Toronto.

Slack, Enid, and Rupak Chattopadhyay. 2013. *Finance and Governance of Metropolitan Areas in Federal Systems.* Toronto: Oxford University Press.
Slack, Enid, Larry Bourne, and Meric Gertler. 2003. Small, Rural and Remote Communities: The Anatomy of Risk. Research Paper 18 Prepared for the Panel on the Role of Government in Ontario. http://www.law-lib.utoronto.ca/investing/index.htm. Accessed 20 July 2004.
Spicer, Zachary. 2015. *Cooperation and Capacity: Inter-Municipal Agreements in Canada.* In IMFG Papers on Municipal Finance and Governance Series, University of Toronto, No 19. http://munkschool.utoronto.ca/imfg/resources/.
Steylter, Nico, ed. 2009. *Local Government and Metropolitan Regions in Federal Systems.* A Global Dialogue on Federalism for the Forum of Federations, McGill-Queen's University Press, Montreal, QC, Canada.
Walisser, Brian, Gary Paget, and Michelle Dann. 2013. New Pathways to Effective Regional Governance: Canadian Reflections. In *New Century Local Government: Commonwealth Perspectives*, ed. Graham Sansom and Peter McKinley. London: Commonwealth Secretariat.
World Bank. 1994. *World Development Report: Infrastructure for Development.* New York: Oxford University Press for the World Bank.

CHAPTER 5

Expenditures and Service Delivery: Core Services and Regulation

Introduction

There are a set of services that local governments are responsible for in almost all countries. Those services include local streets and roadways, fire protection, parks and playgrounds, recreation and cultural facilities and programs, waste collection and (sometimes) disposal, water and sanitation services, drainage, land use planning and control, and local nuisance and safety regulation. These are the core responsibilities or core services of local governments. How large these core services are in local governments' budgets depends upon what noncore responsibilities local governments are assigned. Those noncore responsibilities include schooling, health care, and social assistance; that is, they are social programs. As demonstrated in Chap. 3, (a) local responsibility for these social programs varies widely across countries and (b) those programs are expensive and, where local governments are responsible for one or more of them, they are typically large items in the local budget. For example, the addition of schooling to core responsibilities often almost doubles local expenditures. Hence, the financial magnitude of local government is largely determined by what, if any, responsibilities it has for social programs. While it is important to understand the role of social program responsibilities upon the structure and financing of local government, it is equally important to appreciate the host of core

H. Kitchen et al., *Local Public Finance and Economics*,
https://doi.org/10.1007/978-3-030-21986-4_5

programs for which local governments are responsible.[1] That is the objective of this chapter.

There are two major forms of core services. One is that set of services that involve substantial expenditures to provide. Those include the construction and maintenance of transportation systems (e.g., roadway and public transit), public order and safety services (police, fire, and emergency services), water and sewerage and drainage, environmental (largely waste collection and disposal), economic development (e.g., promotion of business and tourism), and general administration (e.g., council, tax assessment, and collection). These activities provide the physical services, sometimes referred to as the housekeeping activities, that make a community functional and pleasant. The second form of core services is essentially regulation. These are the locally determined rules that normally promote safety (e.g., fire regulations, traffic rules, building regulations, food services inspection), promote enjoyment of property (e.g., regulation of land use, noise, waste), manage business (e.g., business licenses, taxi permits), and generally control potential nuisances. While usually not large items in the overall local government budget, regulatory activities are important for facilitating a pleasant and safer environment and also quality services without infringement on individuals. The discussion below follows this pattern by addressing the more budgetary important services first and then looking at the regulatory activities of local governments.

Core Expenditures

Transportation

Transportation is important for economic, social, and even political reasons. Transportation systems can be readily categorized into those components that are of predominately national, regional, and local importance. Hence, responsibilities for transportation services in many countries follow those geographic lines. Among alternative transportation modes, government responsibility for air and railroads is more centralized while that for road transport more decentralized. Because it is more decentralized and because it is so important for the movement of commodities and people, road transport is the focus of attention here. Naturally, the assignment of

[1] For insight into functional responsibilities among a wide range of countries, see Shah (2006a, b). Also see Boadway and Shah (2009). Those interested particularly in urban services may also refer, for example, to Bahl and Linn (1992), Dillinger (1994) and Freire and Stren (2001) and to Chap. 14.

responsibilities for regional systems depends upon the existence and role of regional governments. Where regional government is important, as in federal countries, state and provincial governments normally have a major role in transportation services but, where they do not, the national government has a greater responsibility.[2]

The local role in transportation services was illustrated in Table 3.1 of Chap. 3. In the more advanced industrialized countries represented there, local governments' share of total government transportation expenditures ranged from about one-quarter to one-half. In the federal countries (Australia, Canada, and Germany), the local share is smaller because state or provincial governments also have an important role. In the unitary countries (Denmark, France, and the United Kingdom), the local share is larger. Among the transition countries, although unitary, the local shares are less consistent. In Bulgaria and Estonia, the local shares are a relatively small 26.7 and 13.5 percent, respectively, while, in the Czech Republic, its 43.3 percent share is similar to other European unitary countries. For the three developing countries (Bolivia, Paraguay, and Kenya), the local shares are very small as they range from 0 to 15.9 percent. Low real incomes definitely influence the demand for and capacity to provide local roads in these developing countries, but, in addition, the small local share also reflects the high degree of government centralization there.

While local transportation services benefit local residents, regional and central governments often have some interest in transportation systems at the local level. For example, the local networks feed into the regional and central systems and they also provide the network for regional and central agencies to serve the local and often outlying areas. In addition, a particular project may meet the objectives of both local and of central or regional governments. Also, regional and central networks will want to ensure good linkages and connections with local systems. As a result, upper-level governments often provide grants specifically to support local transportation. Interestingly, among the countries just examined, such grants are almost unique to the federal countries. There, conditional transfers for transportation financed between 16.3 and 38.5 percent of local transportation expenditures. Among the advanced European countries, grants there did not account for more than 4.5 percent and there were none in the developing countries. Among the transition countries, the contributions of transfers (if any) are not known. Interestingly, grants for transportation can vary widely even within a country. In Canada, where local

[2] See McMillan (2002) for some discussion and illustration.

governments are responsible for about one-quarter of total government transportation outlays, the transfers specifically for transportation from the provinces to the local authorities range from less than 1 percent to over 43 percent of local expenditures.[3] This degree of variation is unexpected where local responsibilities are similar among provinces, and if one expected that, such transfers would largely reflect spillovers.

Transportation is one of the major core expenditure areas. It typically ranks as the first, second, or third largest core expenditure area with levels ranging between 12 and 30 percent of core expenditures. Although the specific activities can vary, roads and streets dominate.

Roadways and Streets

When speaking of local government transportation expenditures, it is primarily roads and streets that are being considered. Roads and streets itself encompasses a variety of areas. Associated structures such as bridges and tunnels are involved. Construction, maintenance, cleaning, clearing, and restoration are obviously included. In addition, it will include lighting, signage, signals, sidewalks, other walkways, planning, and engineering and may include parking. Thus, when speaking of roads and streets, a wide variety of related facilities and services are encompassed.

Local governments are well positioned to make good decisions about the transportation needs and priorities of their communities. Also, the complexity of construction, maintenance, and care of transportation systems often parallels the size of the community and so corresponds to the local capacity. In addition, there are usually many consulting firms with the expertise to provide planning and engineering services where needed and to undertake construction and maintenance. Many local governments provide the required transportation services internally through municipal departments and employees while others rely heavily upon private suppliers and still others contract with units of neighboring (or, in some cases, senior) governments. These service delivery alternatives are discussed elsewhere. The main point here is that, for roads and streets, an efficient scale of service is sufficiently modest that local authorities typically have a range of options to select from in providing the services.

Local networks provide local benefits for the most part. A major benefit is that streets and roads provide or improve access to property and, so, make that property more valuable. Hence, a property tax is a very reasonable tax

[3] Transfers from the federal government are small in aggregate and those for transportation are typically less than 1 percent of municipal transportation expenditures.

for generating the funds to support a local transport network. Regardless of the tax system used, street and road systems provide general or widespread benefits and are largely financed out of general tax revenues. In some cases, the beneficiaries are more clearly identifiable. For example, development levies are a reasonable means of providing streets in new developments. The system also provides benefits specific to users and so user charges are a financing option as well. That makes local licenses, perhaps local fuel taxes (or tax-sharing arrangements), and tolls appealing. User demand varies as is evidenced by rush-hour traffic. It is these peak flows that place the greatest demands on roadway infrastructure. Hence, local congestion charges are logical (and, with technological improvements, are becoming more common but by no means widespread). Thus, there are a range of local financing mechanisms that may be utilized to fund streets and roadways providing local benefits.

Public Transit

Bus transportation is the most common form of public transit. There are two major questions about bus services for local government. One is the issue of whether or not local government will be involved in the provision of the service—that is, whether or not there will be publicly operated busses. The other is the issue of what involvement local government will have in the pricing of those services.

Public ownership and operation of local bus service is common. However, public ownership is not necessary. Private companies provide bus service in many cities and smaller municipalities where public service does not exist or provides only partial coverage. Many private operators may emerge and result in a system that seems unorganized and even chaotic in comparison, for example, to a single public operation. However, private systems operate efficiently and develop where there is sufficient demand to meet costs. Public systems, or heavily regulated private systems, may lack competitive pressures and, for better or worse, be expected to meet other objectives.

Public transit is often subsidized. The underlying logic for this varies but typically includes that it serves the poor (i.e., those unable to afford automobiles) and that public transit reduces congestion by reducing automobile traffic and speeding up the transportation system for the benefit of all. Low fares, however, benefit all users (not just those with low incomes) and they are likely not to be the most effective way to aid low-income earners. Also, because automobiles are the primary source of congestion and congestion charges on them are becoming more feasible, it is more logical to impose congestion charges on automobiles than to subsidize public transit to address the congestion problem.

In major population areas, mass transit is more likely to include subway and rail transit for commuting. Such systems are usually large and so will often encompass many local governments. Therefore, it is not uncommon that they will be operated by a regional authority representing many local governments in the region or, as in Melbourne, the state government.

Airports

Air transport involves long distances and, by its nature, is not local. Hence, airports have often been operated by national governments or agencies. Still, airports are important for the services that they provide to the businesses and people in the neighboring communities. Airports are considered important to the economic development of their service area. As a result, the local communities and their governments have interests in the services that airports provide and may seek a voice in their operations. In some cases, responsibilities for airports and their operations have been decentralized to regional airport authorities comprised of representatives of the nearby local governments. Those authorities are expected to operate and manage the airport and fund it from the landing fees, passenger charges, and business operations of the airport. Airports are also sometimes operated by a single local government. In many cases, but not necessarily, those are small-scale operations catering to light or small aircraft.

Water, Sewerage, and Drainage

Water and Sewerage

Water and sewerage services are one of the major core service expenditure categories of local governments. There is, however, a wide variation in the magnitude of this category among local governments. The major reason for the variation is that the demands or necessity of these services varies across jurisdictions. In sparsely settled rural municipalities, individual households provide these services for themselves and the government role is minimal. On the other hand, in urban or more urbanized areas, public water and sewerage systems are both economically feasible and attractive (even essential) for health reasons. Significant economies of scale are available to water and sewerage systems. As a result, it is often attractive to operate regional systems rather than numerous individual municipal systems. Regional water and sewerage authorities may be formed from amalgamations of local authorities, may be organized through a regional level of local government (e.g., counties as opposed to the municipalities within them), or may be operated by a single local government that contracts with surrounding municipalities as well as serving its own residents.[4] Private ownership is also possible but less common. Because of the monopoly nature of water and sewerage services, private ownership entails government regulation to protect customers and ensure fair and reasonable rates of return to the owners. Private management of public systems is also an option. The attractiveness of this alternative depends upon the effectiveness of the public sector management and that of the private alternative. In many places, public operations are highly efficient. But where they are not, private management (or even ownership) may be an improvement. The experience with private management has been mixed. It has made marked improvements in some cases but failed to live up to expectations in others. Part of the problem is that the culture and institutions that generate poor public management are not necessarily replaced or circumvented with contracting to the private sector. Whether public or private, there is a strong case for water and sewerage utilities to meet their full operating and capital costs from their sales and services to customers. A wide range of charges are practical and include development levies, hookup fees, fixed monthly charges, and monthly usage charges (that may vary depending upon volume, type, and timing). Also, services and service costs to different parts of the system may differ significantly because of distance and geography. Costs to the customers in those different areas should reflect the costs in each.

Drainage

The need for drainage services depends upon precipitation, climate, geography, the extent and type of built-up areas, and so on. The major objective is to avoid flooding and water damage. Those who avoid the adverse effects of excessive water are beneficiaries but those whose structures cause the run-off also have responsibilities. Thus, both parties have obligations to pay for proper drainage. Those contributing to run-off and the need for drainage should bear those costs, and those that benefit from reduced natural water damage should pay for that. Appropriate charges should be levied on both.[5] Different parts of the municipality may be designated according to their drainage characteristics and the costs of supplying ade-

[4] In some cases, utilities, including water and sewerage services, are operated by state/provincial or central governments. Brazil is an example.

[5] It is to be recognized that in some, likely most, areas the residents may both contribute to the need for drainage plus benefit from the drainage system reducing water damage.

quate service then be charged. In particular, where good drainage systems reduce or eliminate water damage, property values will increase so charges based on resulting improvements in property values would distribute costs in relation to benefits realized. Drainage and sewerage systems have often used the same network of pipes. More recently, however, concern for the treatment of all sewerage and not polluting water sources has led increasingly to the separation of the two systems.

Waste Collection and Disposal

A standard responsibility of local governments is solid waste collection and disposal. This activity may range from as little as provision of a "dump" for public use to a sophisticated system of collection, disposal, and recycling (including perhaps even the collection of methane from landfill sites). Collection may be supplied by a local government department, but it is often contracted out to private operations. Also, it is not uncommon for household and nonresidential services to be handled in different ways. Waste collection from households is organized and often supplied by government, but business and industry (and often large residential units like apartments and condominiums) are required to arrange for the collection of their own solid waste through private operators. The cost of household collection may be paid for through property taxes (or other general revenues) or by fees that may even be on a per bag or can basis. Business and other users contracting for collection services cover the costs through the fees charged. Fees will include any charges for delivery to disposal sites and disposal fees but do not necessarily cover the full cost of the collection and disposal system. Depending upon local concerns and/or environmental regulations, disposal sites may be simple to sophisticated facilities. Hazardous wastes, especially from industry, may be subject to special regulations and handled in specialized facilities. Recycling is being more widely adopted as both a means to reduce the demands on landfills and because many components have value and can be profitably separated. Of course, informal systems of recycling exist in many countries.

Recreation and Culture

The provision of recreational and cultural services is usually one of the larger core expenditure areas of local government. It also is a responsibility for which spending tends to be concentrated at the local government level. Local facilities and programs focus on serving the community generally (children, families, and individuals) and rely heavily upon volunteers for much of their operations. Recreational and cultural undertakings of the senior governments are oriented to providing training and facilities for more accomplished participants representing the province or nation.

Recreation encompasses the provision of parks, playgrounds, playing fields, sports facilities, and related programs. These are called for, used by, and benefit the local community so it is natural that local government be engaged. The public role results in large part from the public nature of the facilities. Local parks, open spaces, playgrounds, and so on are open access in that they are free for use at the user's will. It is not practical to charge for them even if there was some will to do so. Sometimes modest charges are imposed, especially for playing fields and picnic areas, but they are normally only to reserve a space for a specific group at particular time. Much of the use of these spaces is organized (to the extent that it is organized) by the community and relies upon volunteers. Parents organizing and coaching children's sports are examples. Also, many of these activities are coordinated to make better use of public school fields and sports facilities. A consequence is that this sort of recreational facilities and programs are financed through general taxes. Superior access to such facilities and views of open spaces in urban areas are often shown to enhance property values and so property tax payers make some differential contribution for those benefits.

Local governments are also involved in the provision of recreational facilities such as pools, arenas, playing courts, and courses where the general public participates in sports. Activities in these facilities are customarily organized and access can be restricted and participants are usually required to pay something toward the cost of these more expensive and higher quality facilities and programs. Very often, the charges may meet only operating costs, if that, without making any contribution toward capital costs. Hence, the local government (and sometimes senior governments and volunteer organizations) subsidize these activities. Also, private (non-profit and for profit) operations may supply some of these same, similar, or substitute facilities and directly or indirectly compete with the public services. The voter-taxpayers of these communities have to decide their willingness to subsidize what often could be provided otherwise independently of government. This issue is raised another level when it comes to public provision or subsidy to professional sports teams with highly paid players and wealthy owners. Many communities have been willing to provide (often generous) public support presumably because of the attention and (perhaps) honor that such teams bring to the community and the team's broad public support.

Cultural activities and programs are a complementary area of local government programs. These activities can include museums and historic societies, preservation, and promotion of ethnic cultures, theater, dance, music, libraries, and so on. As with sports, there tends to be broad public participation across cultural programs and a heavy reliance on the contributions of volunteers in many instances. Public support may include building space and building operations and maintenance, support for basic professional input, travel expenses, special exhibits and performances, and the like. Such groups rarely generate funds sufficient to meet most of their costs and the subsidies come from general government revenues. In exchange, such groups are expected to contribute to the public good. Sometimes, the local government decision makers may have problems distinguishing between a potential deserving group and what might almost be a private club. Especially in larger centers, the magnitude and quality of services require professional input and specialized facilities. Concert orchestras, public libraries, major museums are illustrations. While admission fees and charges (and financial donations) are likely to be more successful at generating funds for such organizations, local government support is still important.

Public Order and Safety

Public order and safety refers to fire and police protection and emergency services. This too is often a major expenditure category of local government, but it is one for which the importance of varies to a considerable degree. Each of these main areas is considered in turn.

Fire Protection

Fire protection is at the heart of public order and safety services at the local government level. While there is some history of fire protection being privately provided, the non-uniformity of service and the dangers that imposed on neighboring property and persons led to public provision. Because the adverse effects of fire are very localized, response times require nearby stations, and economies are achieved at a modest scale, the responsibilities for fire protection have come to local governments. A variety of organizational structures are found. Sometimes, special fire protection districts are formed and, also, smaller departments will normally have cooperative arrangements with neighboring departments for backup in case of emergencies. Small and isolated local governments often rely on volunteers to provide their service. As community size, fire frequency, and fire complexity increase, communities turn more and more to full-time professional fire services. While governments provide the service, not all deliver it themselves. Some contract with other governments for service and some contract with private fire protection firms. Particularly in urban areas, property taxes based on property market value are a natural base for financing fire protection. In some places (e.g., Melbourne, Australia), fire protection costs are based on and collected through property insurance premiums. That method has the cost to property owners related to fire risk as well as property value.

Police Protection
Local government responsibility for police services actually varies considerably from country to country. Policing definitely provides local benefits but it also provides regional and national benefits. Hence, the assignment of responsibility differs from country to county.

It is not uncommon that police services are the responsibility of the central government (e.g., Denmark) or of state or provincial governments (e.g., Australia). In such cases, public order and safety is not a large component of (even core) local protection expenditures because policing normally dominates this class of outlays. Where policing is a local responsibility, public order and safety, and policing specifically, is a large item in local budgets. Public order and safety accounts for about 10 percent of local government budgets in Canada, the United Kingdom, and the United States and it amounts to about 18–25 percent of their core expenditures.[6] Policing costs represent the majority of those expenditures in Canada and the United States and about 80 percent of those costs in the United Kingdom.

Although local governments may be responsible for police services, they need not bear all the cost. In the United Kingdom, specific purpose grants meet almost half of the local expenditures for policing and policing costs are also factored into the general purpose grant. While local governments are responsible for policing, the actual authority rests with a joint police board that consists of representatives of the local councils serviced by the police board (the majority of the board members), selected magis-

[6] See Table 3.1 of Chap. 3 or McMillan (2008).

trates, and independent representatives appointed by the central government. The joint board oversees the budget, assesses strategies, and appoints senior officers including the chief constable. Even so, the chief constable has considerable operational independence. The joint board structure and operation is intended to reflect the special nature of police services and to provide independence from political influence.[7]

While local government has policing responsibilities in most provinces in Canada, transfers to support policing are small. Transfers for protective services (essentially police and fire) average only 1 percent of protective expenditures.[8] However, assistance may come in other ways, at least to some municipalities. In the province of Alberta, for example, the provincial government pays for the policing of all rural municipalities and that for urban centers with populations under 5000 persons (recently increased from 2500). Other municipalities receive a small per capita grant. While the larger municipalities tend to have their own police forces, most municipalities contract with the federal Royal Canadian Mounted Police (RCMP) for local service. The province, in turn, has contracted with the RCMP for provincial policing. Some provinces (e.g., Ontario and Quebec) have their own provincial police forces. While the arrangements vary across the provinces, Canadian municipalities overall are responsible for an exceptionally large share of policing costs.[9]

Policing is a service for which the responsibility assignments are diverse. It is one of those services for which there are advantages to both centralization and decentralization. People are concerned about the protection and the control of criminal activity in their communities and wish to have some local control over that. On the other hand, criminals and criminal activities cross borders create interjurisdictional spillovers and there are potential advantages to communication, coordination, and training from a more centralized police force. The issue is to strike a balance. Where policing is centralized, there is merit on permitting the local governments to negotiate some flexibility. Where policing is quite decentralized, as in Canada, there needs to be policies to ensure coordination and cooperation. In addition, one would expect that specific purpose transfers would play an important role in funding police services in the decentralized situation; more so than is the case in Canada.

[7] See King in Shah (2006b).

[8] See McMillan in Shah (2006b).

[9] In the United States, the situation is much the same. Local governments there account for about 85 percent of state and local policing expenditures. See Schroeder in Shah (2006b).

Ambulance and Emergency Services

Emergency services cover a range of services that are not specifically police, fire, or medical. Often they include planning and coordination of protective and other services required for disasters for relief in case of floods, hurricanes, major explosions, and so on. Emergency services also include services designed for small emergencies, often related to traffic accidents. These latter units are often integrated with fire and/or ambulance services.

Ambulance or, more generally, emergency medical services are to deal with emergency medical situations. Often, but not necessarily, they are called because of injuries related to fires or accidents to which the fire and police services also respond. The nature of the service allows costs to be covered to a large extent by user fees. Hence, ambulance services may or may not be provided by government. Where government has not become involved, private services usually are available although they may be more limited in availability and capacity. Also, local government may or may not be involved. In some cases, ambulance/emergency medical services may be part of a senior government's public health-care system.

Economic Development and Tourism

Local governments, like other levels of government, are interested in improving the local economy. Usually this interest results in two strategies. One is to encourage business to move to (or stay in) the community. The other is encouraging people to visit the community. At a basic level, both of these involve advertising the local jurisdiction so that potential firms and tourists are aware of it as an alternative. In other cases, more aggressive strategies are pursued. For example, to attract tourists, the local government may invest in convention centers or sponsor major sporting events. The economics of these pursuits is often debated. To attract business and jobs, some local governments offer economic incentives such as tax concessions, land at reduced prices, and other inducements. Again, the economics of such incentive programs is debated. Reflecting that debate, some senior governments prohibit their local governments from offering economic incentives to firms. The promotion of economic development and tourism is a relatively small part of the budgets of local governments but expands if the more aggressive strategies are followed.

Local governments occasionally actually engage in business or business-like ventures. Utilities are an example although those often were initiated as a result of the lack of private suppliers at the time (e.g., electricity, telephone, natural gas) or the reluctance of private suppliers to undertake those ventures (e.g., water and sewerage). An example of business ventures more akin to economic development efforts is public markets which are common. The markets attract suppliers and customers to the local community and the local government usually rents space to the sellers. Some local governments also engage in land assembly and servicing in preparation for sale to small builders to facilitate the availability of land for new homes or businesses. These ventures are expected to at least cover their costs. The need for such land development efforts depends upon the extent of private interests in land development and may be more common in smaller centers. Cities interested in land development often have to do with redevelopment in old and run-down areas. The task of reconstruction and turning an area around to restore its economic viability often exceeds the capacity of single developers. Hence, a local government may get involved in land assembly and incentives for new development in area revitalization efforts. Some novel initiatives and financing tools have emerged to aid pursuit of these objectives (Chapman 1998; Ingram and Hong 2010). Of course, in countries such as China, where local government is actively involved in business, this local government activity can be much more extensive, varied, and important.

General Government

The broad expenditure category, general government or general government services, is usually a relatively significant part of local government core expenditures. Having it amount to 10 percent of core expenditures is not uncommon. Obviously, this category includes a variety of activities that are essential for the functioning of local government but are not associated with any particular activity or expenditure area. Among those functions are council and its operation, elections, information and communication with constituents and taxpayers, and, among others, the finance department that does assessment and taxation. While individually these activities are small in budgetary terms, collectively they amount to a sum comparable to major and well-recognized activities. Also, they are important to successful operation of local government.

Regulation

In addition to granting powers to raise revenues and to spend on particular programs, the legislation governing local governments also grants local governments powers to pass bylaws to regulate certain activities. A number of such regulations readily come to mind—land use controls, traffic regulations, building codes, and constraints on waste disposal. The establishment and enforcement of these bylaws are not obvious, nor particularly large, items in the municipal budgets and so this dimension of local government may be overlooked (especially when concentrating on the financial perspective). However, the rules and regulations governing much of individuals' and businesses' behaviors in the local environment are vital to the smooth functioning of the community and the general enjoyment of living and working there.[10]

The need for regulatory powers emerges from a number of situations common to public economics. Having bylaws governing behavior in a community parallels having laws and a justice system for the country. Everyone benefits from the protection afforded and the protection provided for one person does not diminish the protection available to another. That is, the regulatory system of a local government can be characterized as a local public good. Land use planning and controls provides a more specific example. Knowledge as to how land will be used, where and what roads will be built, to where services will be extended, enable individuals to make better decisions. Regulations are to avoid adverse externalities. Zoning, for example, helps decision makers avoid undesirable or incompatible locations and, alternatively, helps them take advantage of agglomerations. For example, households can avoid high traffic areas near what will become concentrated commercial developments and noisy industry. Commercial enterprises, on the other hand, can congregate in anticipation of establishing a shopping node. Similarly, traffic regulations are intended to minimize the adverse spillovers among vehicles and between vehicles and pedestrians. Regulations also help offset problems of asymmetric information; that is, when sellers and buyers have different amounts of information about the product. Building codes are an illustration. When building codes are in place and enforced, buyers of new structures have assurance that the building meets certain standards. Otherwise, it is difficult to judge construction quality after completion. Thus, local government bylaws arise from the presence of certain market failures. Their presence affords greater security of persons and their property for improvement of individual and community welfare.

[10] Discussion including the regulatory powers of local governments can be found for Canada in Scancton and Young (2009). A survey of regulation in European countries, including regulation at the local level, is found in a series of OECD papers entitled *Better Regulation in Europe.*

Local regulations are not necessarily essential to avoid the more serious adverse effects of the limitations of the local market.[11] Local governments in different places and in different countries do not have the same regulatory powers nor, even if available, do not necessarily use them to the same extent. Where local bylaws do not exist to govern particular activities, the community and the private sector create substitutes. Customs and conventions may be sufficient. In other cases, individuals will rely more on private contracts and, if necessary, courts to protect their interests. Thus, the extent of reliance upon local regulations is a choice. It is a matter of weighing the cost and benefits of the alternatives. In addition, the need for and extent of local regulations will depend upon the extent of the laws and regulations of senior governments. For example, an extensive product and building code at the senior government level reduces the need for or the extent of local codes. Thus, there are options to local regulation and the degree of local regulation will depend, in part, upon them.

Illustrations of Local Regulation

Land Use Regulation

Land use regulation by local governments exists presumably, as other regulation, because local voters consider that the nature of land use that results under regulation is superior to that resulting under an unregulated land market. The objective of the controls may be directed primarily at controlling the pattern of land use within the jurisdiction and to maintain and enhance the community's character. Controlling the pattern of land use focuses on zoning to separate incompatible land uses.[12] That is, particularly separating residential, commercial, industrial activities. Critical in doing so is that these designations are made in advance of development to enable land users to make informed choices. In the case of developed areas in transition, rezoning should allow existing and new owners to plan and to avoid negative externalities resulting from the changes.

Zoning for preserving and enhancing the community's character is a more recent dimension of land use controls. This aspect encompasses a variety of directions that can include ensuring greater homogeneity within neighborhoods or subdivisions and possibility limiting diversity in the

[11] For an early discussion of the alternatives, see Coase (1960).

[12] Fischel (2015) provides an extensive examination of zoning and land use regulation.

municipality altogether. That is, perhaps to maintain the character of the community, perhaps to improve property values, perhaps to realize fiscal benefits for the local government and taxpayers, zoning is used to make the municipality more attractive to certain groups and activities and less attractive or accessible to others. Minimum lot size, construction codes, density restrictions, limitations on commercial space, and so on are examples of the methods. In part, the community may be attempting to attract residents and businesses that have low service costs and a high ability to pay taxes so as to provide the municipality a fiscal advantage. According to Ladd (1998), this objective of land use controls has become more important in the United States and in cases clearly becomes exclusionary. She notes that the courts have been reluctant to reject zoning based on economic factors (e.g., as opposed to racial). Ladd notes that land use controls evolve reflecting the pressures of property developers, current residents, and, to some degree, potential residents. At this point, current residents seem to have the greater influence.

Land use controls and zoning in the United States increased sharply after a watershed legal case in 1926 and subsequent template legislation advanced by the federal government (Ladd 1998). Thereafter the use, the scope, and the objectives expanded with the objective of enhancing the community's character developing a greater presence. Despite the growth of land use controls, not all jurisdictions have adopted them. A notable exception is Houston, Texas, which does not have conventional municipal zoning but relies upon private agreements created through land developers. The use of land use controls varies widely among countries.

Regulations for Health and Safety

Local governments often make many regulations designed to protect health and promote safety. These include those governing traffic and transportation, building standards and conditions, fire safety, food services, and disposal of remains. These are addressed briefly below.

Traffic and Transportation

Addressing the infrastructure needs of motor vehicle traffic is one of the major responsibilities of local governments. Also important are the rules and regulations that enable the effective and safe use of the transportation system by drivers and pedestrians. Regulations governing traffic flows (e.g., one- and two-way streets) and speed limits are standard. Parking regulations are important as well. Regulations extend to pedestrian traffic and non-motor vehicle traffic as well. In environments where snow and ice is a problem, property owners may be required to clear sidewalks to facilitate pedestrian traffic.

Building Standards

Local regulations covering buildings are to benefit two groups—buyers, particularly of new structures, and users of buildings (i.e., residents, workers, visitors). Building codes are in place to (try to) ensure that all building built (or renovated) in the municipality meet at least minimum standards. Normally those standards cover the basic structure plus internal services such as electricity, heating, cooling, ventilation, plumbing, and lighting. Conditions related to fire safety are also normal. In addition, local conditions may pose special hazards that must be accounted for in construction codes. For example, cities in areas prone to earthquakes often have special provisions to reduce damage should an earthquake occur. Severe weather (winds, rain, snowfall, temperatures) or unusual geological conditions (soil, slopes) can call for special requirements. The existence and enforcement of building codes can improve the safety of buildings. These standards provide assurance to buyers of structures (especially if they were not involved in their design or construction) and assurance to those living, working, or visiting buildings in the municipality that certain standards have been met.

While local standards have advantages, if these vary widely among localities within an economic area (e.g., many municipalities within a metro region), the differences can make construction more complex and impose higher costs without real improvements in safety. Coordination providing a common acceptable code can be an advantage. Having local differences that matter is valuable, but local differences that do not matter, but may develop haphazardly, are a burden.

Local governments also commonly have regulations governing the conditions that buildings must meet in order to be occupied or be used for specific purposes. Rental properties and work sites, in particular, are customarily expected to meet minimal space and hygienic standards or be closed down. Particular attention may be assigned to homes for the elderly, schools, and daycare facilities. Business serving the public—for example, theaters, clubs, stores, markets—are expected to meet safety standards and are subject to periodic inspections (especially in regard to fire safety).

Fire Risk and Hazardous Products
Protection from fire, fire prevention, and safety in the event of fire are important concerns. In addition to firefighting, fire departments are usually responsible for inspecting buildings to check for fire hazards, to check that exits are adequate and accessible, and to see that protection equipment is present and functional. Closely related is the regulation of hazardous products. That regulation can involve places and conditions of use, storage, transport, and so on.

Food Services
Business selling food to the public is commonly subject to local regulations. There is concern that the products are safe for consumption. Local inspection can cover food production and transportation facilities and those sites involved in the preparation and sale of the products to the public. This oversight reduces the danger of adverse consequences resulting from improper handling or preparation of food products that could affect many people. It provides assurance to consumers who, for the most part, are unable to make assessments themselves of the safety of the services provided.

Disposal of Remains
Especially in urban or relatively densely populated rural areas, the proper disposal of dead animals is important for health reasons. Hence, regulations (and perhaps facilities) addressing their disposal are in place.

Appropriate disposal of human remains is also an issue of some local responsibility. In addition to regulations covering proper disposal, local governments often provide cemeteries or crematoriums and may be responsible for supervision of those operated by religious or private organizations.

Nuisances
The daily activities or choices of some people often have negative consequences for others. Especially when the actions and their effects are of a small scale and very local in nature (essentially nuisances), local governments have been called upon to create regulations to protect people from undue adverse effects and to avoid conflicts. The basic rationale is that the regulations are there so that individuals can be assured reasonable enjoyment of their activities and their property.

Nuisances come in many forms. Some of the more common types are noted here for illustration. Improper disposal of waste is a common complaint. This may take the form of littering to dumping garbage in public places or on the property of others and extends to the accumulation of garbage or the collection of items on an individual's own property that interferes with others (notably neighbors). Local governments often have regulations against these activities and penalties to enforce them. Draining or diverting water onto some else's property is another example. The issue might be as modest as the flow of water from downspouts. Large bodies of water and special areas (e.g., wetlands) normally involve senior governments. Small sources of air pollution present another case. Smoke from burning rubbish could be the cause and rubbish burning is commonly regulated by local authorities. Excessive noise, especially during evening hours, is another example of an activity subject to local bylaws. Control of animals including pets—presence, restraint, noise from, disposal of their waste are examples—is another popular area of local regulation. Trees overhanging another's property also present an area of regulation. Weed control is a final example and one that is of particular importance for rural municipalities. Adverse spillovers that can result from relatively common daily activities is the common issue. Regulation by local government provides a reasonable avenue to avoid those negative effects.

Regulation of Business

Local businesses can be subject to a variety of regulations imposed by their local governments. Land use controls have been discussed. Licensing is standard. Licensing provides a (usually small) source of revenue, information about business activity, and an avenue for control. Licensing and zoning together can work to exclude undesirable business or to relegate them to well-defined areas where the negative spillovers will be kept to a minimum. Business hours are often regulated, presumably to avoid excessive hours or inconvenient shifts being expected of workers (and owners). The type and extent of business activity that can take place out of a residence is also subject to control. Controls on business activities operated in public spaces and on itinerant business are common. Privately operated public utilities can be a particular focus of attention. In particular, local governments often regulate public transportation. Sometimes that has the effect of limiting competition, that is, although possibly intended to ensure orderly service. Limitations on the number of taxis that can operate is a good example. Another reason is to ensure that the equipment and staff (particularly drivers) are safe for public service.

Behavior in Public

A final major category of public regulation covers people's behavior, activities, and things in public places or in places open to the public. Such regulations may cover appropriate dress, exposure, bodily functions, consumption of alcoholic beverages, begging, aggression, signage (e.g., political, business and other), and so on. The objective is to constrain the behavior of persons that infringes on acceptable standards, endangers the person engaged or others, or unduly detracts from people's enjoyment of their activities or property.

Conclusion

This chapter has focused on the core activities of local government. Core activities refer to that set of responsibilities that are almost universally assigned to local government. These activities are of two types. They include a set of core services (sometimes characterized as housekeeping services) and a set of regulations. Core services include local roads and transportation, water and sewerage and drainage, waste collection and disposal, protection and safety, economic development, and general government. This set of services contrasts with local government engagement in social services. As noted in Chap. 3, local responsibility for social services differs greatly across countries; from nil to full responsibility. Core services are almost uniquely local. The one service that stands out as a potential exception is policing. In some countries policing is a local responsibility and in some it is the responsibility of a senior government. Otherwise, the exceptions usually relate to ambulance and emergency services that are sometimes part of a national health service and regional mass transit that is sometimes centrally operated.

Regulation is also an important function of local government. Because it is not usually an obvious budgetary item, its role is sometimes overlooked. Regulation is directed at a variety of activities of primarily local importance. The scope of local regulations usually covers land use, traffic and transportation, various local conditions relating to reducing risk and improving health and safety, coping with nuisances, business operations, and activities in public places. As with public services, local regulations emerge because they are seen as an effective way of dealing with certain limitations of the market.

Although distinctly local, core services are not entirely separated from senior government. On the services side, senior governments may require that certain standards of local services be provided and they often provide conditional grants to promote certain activities (some of which may reflect spillover benefits). On the regulatory side, senior governments also make laws and regulations and the spheres of influence may overlap. Normally, senior governments' laws take precedence. The extent and scope of senior government regulations will affect the extent and scope of local government regulation. However, senior government can work with local governments to provide template regulations that minimize complicating ad hoc differences among local governments while permitting local variations where important.

References

Bahl, Roy W., and Johannes F. Linn. 1992. *Urban Public Finance in Developing Countries*. Published for the World Bank. Oxford: Oxford University Press.

Boadway, Robin, and Anwar Shah. 2009. *Fiscal Federalism: Principles and Practice of Multiorder Governance*. New York, NY: Cambridge University Press.

Chapman, Jeffrey I. 1998. Tax Increment Financing as a Tool of Redevelopment. In *Local Government Tax and Land Use Policies in the United States: Understanding the Links*, ed. Helen F. Ladd, 182–198. Cambridge, MA and Cheltenham: Lincoln Institute of Land Policy and Edward Elgar Publishing.

Coase, Ronald H. 1960. The Problem of Social Cost. *Journal of Law and Economics* 3 (1): 1–44.

Dillinger, William. 1994. *Decentralization and Its Implications for Urban Service Delivery*. Urban Management Program. Washington, DC: The World Bank.

Fischel, William A. 2015. *Zoning Rules!* Cambridge, MA: Lincoln Institute of Land Policy.

Freire, Mila, and Richard Stren, eds. 2001. *The Challenge of Urban Government*. Washington, DC: The World Bank.

Ingram, Gregory K., and Yu-Hung Hong. 2010. *Municipal Revenues and Land Policies*. Cambridge, MA: Lincoln Institute of Land Policy.

Ladd, Helen F. 1998. Introduction. In *Local Government Tax and Land Use Policies in the United States: Understanding the Links*, ed. Helen F. Ladd, 1–21. Cambridge, MA and Cheltenham: Lincoln Institute of Land Policy and Edward Elgar Publishing.

McMillan, Melville L. 1997. Taxation and Expenditure Patterns in Major City-Regions: An International Perspective and Lessons for Canada. In *Urban Governance and Finance: A Question of Who Does What?* ed. Paul Hobson and France St. Hilaire, 1–56. Montreal, Ottawa: The Institute for Research on Public Policy, Renouf Publishing.

———. 2002. *Financial Relationships Between Regional and Municipal Authorities: Insights from the Examination of Five OECD Countries.* Working Paper 2004(3), Institute of Inter-Governmental Relations, Queen's University.
———. 2008. A Local Perspective on Fiscal Federalism: Practices, Experiences and Lessons from Industrialized Countries. In *Macro Federalism and Local Finance*, ed. Anwar Shah, 245–289. Washington, DC: The World Bank.
Organization for Economic Cooperation and Development. Various Years. *Better Regulation in Europe.* Paris. https://www.oecd-ilibrary.org/governance/better-regulation-in-europe_20790368.
Scancton, Andrew, and Robert Young, eds. 2009. *Municipal Government in Canada's Provinces.* Toronto: University of Toronto Press.
Shah, Anwar, ed. 2006a. *Local Governance in Developing Countries.* Washington, DC: The World Bank.
———, ed. 2006b. *Local Governance in Industrialized Countries.* Washington, DC: The World Bank.

CHAPTER 6

Expenditures and Service Delivery: Social Services

Introduction

During the second half of the last century, there was dramatic growth in government, especially in the industrialized countries. Across 17 industrialized countries, Tanzi and Schuknecht (1995) report that the ratio of government expenditures (G) to GDP increased from 27.9 percent to 47.2 percent between 1960 and 1994. Growth in social spending was the main driver of that growth in government. For that group and time, social expenditures increased from 10.1 to 21.7 percent of GDP and those for subsidies and transfers rose from 8.3 to 23 percent. More recently, the G/GDP ratio has not only stabilized but has declined slightly, to where G is an average of 43.9 percent of GDP, in part due to declining interest rates and debt-servicing costs (Schuknecht and Tanzi 2004).[1]

Governments have typically had a role in providing social programs and, clearly, that role has increased. Governments' role in providing assistance for the needy has resulted because the care available from religious and volunteer groups has usually been considered insufficient (and vice versa). Also, over time, a social safety net has come to be recognized as supporting market specialization, labor mobility, and risk taking; benefits that take on more relevance as trade and international trade expands. Governments have usually played a particularly prominent role in schooling

[1] Afonso and Furceri (2010) report parallel results across 28 OECD and European Union countries to 2005.

H. Kitchen et al., *Local Public Finance and Economics*,
https://doi.org/10.1007/978-3-030-21986-4_6

and education. The increasing importance of education and skills in the labor market has pushed the public role further as secondary education became the norm and post-secondary (vocational and academic) education is increasingly expected by employers. Advances in health services have expanded the benefits from quality medical and hospital care. While the benefits increased, so have the costs. Public health insurance has been widely adopted as a means to ensure general access at reasonable cost. Public health programs have usually included public delivery of significant components of the system, especially hospitals. Overall, public social programs have grown substantially largely because they afforded a popular means of sharing risk and of realizing growing benefits.

Has the growth in public social programs had implications for local government? It was demonstrated in Chap. 3 that the size of local government depends largely upon what responsibility local government has for social programs. In some (indeed many) countries, those responsibilities have been major so the growth of social (or particular social) programs has had an obvious impact. In other countries, local governments have almost no role in social programs. Yet, in these cases, it is too simple to assume that social program growth has not affected them. Not infrequently, responsibilities for (at least some) social programs have been reassigned or assumed to varying degrees by senior governments because, in part, of their growth.

The purpose of this chapter is to look closely at the delivery of social services by local government so as to better understand the differences that exist among countries, the range of delivery options, and factors affecting their success. The initial section examines the fundamental question of decentralization of delivery versus decentralization of funding and the alternative approaches that emerge. Subsequent sections look at the major specific social services: schooling, health care, and social assistance. A conclusion completes the chapter.

The Social Service Quandary

Local Delivery Versus Local Funding

A fundamental difficulty often encountered when assigning responsibilities for social programs is that the government that is the right size for delivery is the wrong size for funding. That is, there can be a delivery-funding mismatch. Schooling presents a good example. Schools serve a distinctly local community (those in its catchment area), and the schooling provided is of special interest to those sending their children to the school. Hence, the delivery of schooling is very localized.[2] The benefits of schooling, however, are more dispersed. Clearly the children, their parents, and the local community reap large benefits, but the social benefits extend much further as they encompass the benefits of educated citizens and a more productive workforce. In particular, graduates are mobile and the resulting social and economic (e.g., taxes) gains are very likely to be realized elsewhere. These externalities call for sharing the cost of local schools with a broader community and result in the larger community having a voice in the quantity and quality of local education. In parallel, local residents are willing to contribute to ensure quality schooling elsewhere because of spill-in benefits. Thus, while the delivery of schooling is very much oriented to local units, funding is usually not constrained to local sources. The authority best suited for delivering schooling is not the authority best suited for financing the service. The disconnect between the two may be broadened if the local authority has a tax base that is felt to poorly match benefits received and ability to pay for the schooling.

Similar situations exist for health care and social assistance. The services of hospitals, clinics, and health professionals serve a local clientele. The ideal group among which to share health risks, however, is likely larger than most local jurisdictions, especially for the more serious health problems. Hence, again, the jurisdiction that is best for delivery may not be the one best for financing. Social assistance is widely recognized as a responsibility not well suited for local governments. Under provision can be expected because generous benefits will attract clientele and burden local taxpayers while meager benefits will shed clientele and reduce the local taxpayers' burden. In addition, local governments often do not have taxes well suited to financing social assistance. The conventional recommendation is that social assistance be a central responsibility because then (a) neither clients nor taxpayers have an appealing migration option and (b) central governments have a broader range financing alternatives. The issue with central delivery is that local decision makers may be better positioned to identify the needy and their needs plus take into account local conditions (e.g., living standards and costs).[3]

[2] Even school services provided by a broader school district are still quite local.

[3] For a comprehensive discussion of the assignment of responsibility and funding for social services, refer to Boadway and Shah (2009) and Litvack and Seddon (1999).

Alternative Approaches

When faced with a situation in which the local authority is best for delivery but not for funding, what options are available? Viewed from the perspective that the local government is the one now delivering and financing the service, five options are discussed below. They are: do nothing, centralize, contract with the local government, introduce transfers, and introduce alternative taxes.

Maintain the Status Quo

This is the do nothing option. Assuming that the local government is the one now both delivering and financing the service, let things continue that way. This arrangement may be less than ideal but it may be the most practical alternative. That is, although it has its faults, any feasible alternative has more serious problems or the potential improvements do not warrant the costs of undertaking the change. An existing less than perfect arrangement might be the best that can be accomplished. While it should not be an excuse for inaction, the status quo option should not be ignored.

Centralize

The opposing alternative is to centralize both delivery and finance. Here, the central government takes over both responsibilities.[4] It is assumed that the central authority is able to internalize the benefits and has suitable taxing powers to match, better than the local government, the benefits received and/or ability to pay criteria appropriate for the service. In this case, however, the central government takes over delivery. This is where problems are usually expected to arise. Centralized services are commonly characterized by a uniformity that overlooks local preferences and conditions resulting in reduced satisfaction and production inefficiencies. Thus, while centralization may offer benefits on one side (internalizing externalities and providing greater financing options), it may result in losses on the other (local satisfaction and production efficiency).

Contract with Local Government

If central financing provides major benefits while local delivery produces important gains, the central government may find that contracting with local

[4] The "central" authority need not be the central government but could be a higher government (e.g., a province) that suitably internalizes the benefits and has suitable financing options.

authorities to deliver the service is an attractive alternative. Here, the central government can define (national) standards for the service (such as access, coverage, and quality) and pay the local authority to deliver as specified. In this case, the local government is the agent of the central government. Often, to help promote local economy in delivery, central compensation is slightly less than (e.g., 95 percent of) local outlays for the service.

Transfers

One of the more common mechanisms for addressing the delivery-funding mismatch problem is intergovernmental transfers. The central government can offer to share part of the cost of the service with a grant or transfer of funds. The portion of the cost that the grant would represent should correspond to the spillover of benefits beyond the supplying local government. Grants can be designed to approximate the external interest; for example, a fixed amount per unit produced, open-ended matching, or closed-ended matching. Thus, the central authority shares part of the cost and it promotes local provision of the externality generating commodity. In addition, the granting government may impose other conditions designed to ensure that the commodity meets the broader social interests and promotes cost-effective provision. Local governments are left to deliver the service. In addition, they may vary the service somewhat to meet better local preferences and circumstances.

A different local provision problem arises if under provision results only because some localities have low fiscal capacity. That is, municipalities having adequate fiscal capacity produce sufficient output (e.g., schooling) so that the central authority is satisfied but low fiscal capacity municipalities produce less and their output is considered to be insufficient by the central authority. In this case, an option is to give grants that equalized fiscal capacity to the fiscally disadvantaged local authorities (e.g., municipalities or school boards). If the funding goes to a multi-purpose local government, the granting government will need to assess carefully whether an equalization grant will accomplish the objective better than a targeted specific categorical grant. Also, it is possible that all the local authorities lack the fiscal capacity to provide the particular service at appropriate levels. If so, then a fiscal gap exists between the levels of government. In this case, all local authorities would need a gap-filling transfer to ensure them the capacity to provide the services at levels considered adequate. Again, in these cases, local fiscal capacities will vary and not all local governments should get identical funding, that is, the gap-filling gaps would be equalizing as well.

It is very likely that a service involves both externalities and fiscal disparities. In that case, (probably separate) grants to address the two problems will be required.[5]

Introduce Alternative Local Taxes or Charges

Even if services provide purely local benefits, local governments may encounter difficulties providing the desired level of public services because their funding options do not correspond well with local attitudes about a fair allocation of costs. Such a situation could arise when charges for services are controlled or restricted by central authorities. Residents may be prepared to pay higher user charges in order to get better services, but instead, if better services are to be realized in the existing restricted situation, the additional cost must come from some local tax that may be seen as imposing the extra burden in an unfair fashion. Similarly, local governments limited to a property tax may be unwilling to provide social services to the same level that they would if they had access to a broader range of taxes, for example, a local income tax. Such situations may be improved by reducing controls on local fees or tax rates and even by allowing the introduction of new alternatives. In addition, if spillovers, significant disparities, or fiscal gaps exist or persist, transfers may still be required.

Schooling

For both OECD countries and ten developing countries, over three-quarters of students at the primary and secondary levels are enrolled in public schools and their operations typically require 3 to 4 percent of GDP (Mitch 2004). Thus, public schools are responsible for the provision of most schooling, and the necessary resources are considerable and command a large share of government budgets. The interest here is in how the public sector funds schools and, in particular, the role of local authorities in their finance and operations. The format will follow the financing alternatives discussed in the previous section with arrangements in selected countries illustrating each method. However, given the broad concern for youth getting a fair educational opportunity and the diverse abilities of local governments to provide that, it is rare to find schooling entirely a

[5] For a comprehensive discussion of grants (intergovernmental transfers), refer to Chaps. 12, 13, and 14.

local responsibility. However, there are instances (e.g., El Salvador until recently) where remote rural schools relied entirely upon local resources. Hence, the local option is skipped to proceed directly to consider the central provision or at least participation in school finance.

Central Financing and Delivery

In some countries, schooling is provided by central authorities and local governments have nothing, or very little, to do with schooling. Australia is such a case. There, the states are responsible for schooling. New Zealand is another example. New Zealand, however, decentralizes important aspects of school decision-making by funding schools through a combination of block and per pupil grants plus providing students the option of attending the school of their choice. As a result, schools compete for students and funding. Criticisms of the system are that central funding can be insufficient (and there are no real alternative sources) and that disadvantaged students become isolated (Mitch 2004).

France provides a variation on the centralized theme. There, schooling is the responsibility of the central government and it provides and pays the teachers (determines curriculum, etc.) but the school buildings are a local responsibility (Prud'homme in Shah 2006b). The communes (the lowest level of local government) are responsible for the primary school buildings, the departments (the next level) for the junior high schools, and the regions (the upper tier) for the lycées (high schools).

The school system in India is also highly centralized. While authority is nominally decentralized to the local level, resistance by the teachers' organizations and the schooling bureaucracy has effectively made the states responsible for schooling. In contrast to those centralized systems already noted, the school system in most of India is unsuccessful. Teacher absenteeism and deteriorated schools are noted problems stemming from a lack of adequate state supervision and no local authority (Dethier 2000).

Central Government Contracting with Local Governments

Since 1980, Chile has had a "voucher" system for funding schooling. The system is based on a per student grant paid monthly for students attending the school. The per student grant is effectively a "voucher" in that the student can chose to attend a municipally operated public school or a (publicly supported) private school.[6] Thus, the system funds (at least subsidizes) students' schooling and it expands school choice to include private schools. About 55 percent of the per student transfers go to municipal schools and 45 percent to private schools. The per student grant depends upon numerous factors including grade level, type (scholastic or academic), location (urban or rural), and hours of instruction. Due to capacity constraints, most government schools operate two half-day classes. For public schools, the per student grant meets school expenses. However, public schools, like the private ones, can charge fees but, if they do, the grant is adjusted downward as the level of the fees increase. Also, municipalities may supplement schools' grant revenues. A modest portion (10–15 percent) of the national government's school funding is dedicated to special programs designed to support expanded access, improving quality, and supporting particular groups or reducing particular problems. A major initial impact of the voucher system was to increase substantially the number of students in private subsidized schools (from 14 percent in 1980 to 34 percent in 1990). Municipal reforms during the 1990s providing greater local voice and autonomy and reducing the gap between responsibility and authority is seen as having contributed to convergence of performance indicators both among public schools and between the municipal and the private schools.[7]

The basic funding for schools in the province of Alberta, Canada, is a provincial per pupil instructional grant paid per student in attendance. That payment varies by level of schooling but is uniform across the province. Other needs-based grants are provided to address transportation costs, students with special needs, other special programs, special circumstances (e.g., isolation), and the capital requirements notably for school buildings. Provincial funds cover essentially all of the costs of public schools. School fees are kept to a minimum (e.g., for excursions, sports shoes, sundry supplies, extra supervision) and, while there is a provision for school authorities to levy a supplementary tax (not to exceed 3 percent of budget) if approved by referendum, it has not been used. Voluntary fund raising at the school level exists but provides very small amounts. The approximately 60 school divisions in the province are the local authorities responsible for schooling. They are independent from the general-purpose

[6] There are also non-publicly supported private schools.

[7] See di Gropello (2004, 2005) and Letelier in Shah (2006a). See Angrist et al. (2002) for results of a school voucher experiment in Colombia. Letelier and Ormeno C (2018) point out that the recent government in Chile is undertaking a program to centralizing the administration of schools.

local governments, the municipalities, and they have their own elected councils (school boards). Although elected, because the school authorities can effectively only decide on how provincial funds are allocated for school purposes and (effectively) cannot tax and so affect the level of school finance within their jurisdiction, it is debatable whether they can really be considered a true local government. School authorities are more local authorities contracting with the provincial government to provide schooling with the funds provided to them for that purpose and according to provincial criteria concerning curriculum, standards, teacher qualifications, and so on. The school divisions are responsible for hiring (and firing) teachers and other staff and they negotiate salaries.[8]

Private schools are minor players in the Alberta (indeed, even in the Canadian) schooling system. Only 4 percent of kindergarten to grade 12 students attend private schools. Those schools usually have a religious or alternative academic focus. Essentially all of those students attend schools accredited by the Alberta Ministry of Education. Accredited private schools receive support from the provincial government at 60 percent of the level provided to public schools.

The province has done much to promote decentralized decision-making. Part of that effort was to expand the flexibility of budgeting at the individual school level and to promote parent councils at the schools. Following the pioneering and successful lead of the capital city's school board, the province introduced an open boundary policy. Students can choose to attend any public school and the funds follow the student. The Edmonton Public School Board has had a highly successful internal open boundary policy under which students could select any school within its jurisdiction. The only restriction is that the school must take neighborhood children first and then accommodate others as space permits. The result has been that schools compete for students and teachers and, in some cases, design their programs to appeal to particular interests (e.g., sports, the arts). This program has proven successful and popular and has attracted considerable, including international, attention. Open boundaries are most effective in larger urban areas having many schools in close proximity to one another, but it has broadened options for students in rural areas as well.

[8] Information on schooling in Alberta can be obtained from the Ministry's website www.alberta.ca/ministry-education.aspx. An overview of schooling in Canada can be found in Rosen et al. (2008), Kitchen (2002) and Lawton (1996).

Alberta only adopted full provincial school funding in the mid-1990s. Before that, the province provided transfers to the school boards to assist local school financing. The magnitude of the grants varied considerably over time depending upon the province's fiscal condition but amounted to over 50 percent of school budgets province wide. The school boards taxed local property owners for the remainder of the funds that they and their electorate felt was required.[9] The share met by grants and so the portion of budgets generated locally depended upon local tax capacity. The local tax and transfer model was typical of school funding for most Canadian provinces until the late 1990s. Today, only two of the ten provinces follow that model and provincial support there has increased. The others have essentially full provincial funding. While full provincial funding equalizes finances, an issue is that total funding can be sensitive to the province's financial condition without local authorities and their residents having any recourse to alternative sources if they consider the provincial funding insufficient.

Intergovernmental Transfers

The typical arrangement in the United States has local school authorities responsible for providing schooling to the children in their jurisdiction.[10] The school districts are usually separate single-purpose local governments with elected boards. The local school districts operate under the authority and supervision of the state government's ministry of education. The state sets curriculum, teacher qualification, performance standards, and, increasingly, funding. Schools have relied heavily (initially almost entirely) upon local funding, typically from local property taxes, but state support gradually increased.[11] State support has expanded, particularly beginning in the 1970s, as a result of a series of court cases ruling that the states had a responsibility to moderate the disparities in per student school expenditures across local districts, that is, equalize funding (at least more than had been the case). In 1960, local funds accounted for about 57 percent of school

[9] When the provincial government assumed full responsibility for funding schooling, it introduced a provincial property tax that replaced the local school property taxes and raised a similar amount of revenue.

[10] Only in Hawaii is schooling a state responsibility. Further information on schooling in the United States can be found in Mitch (2004), Schroeder in Shah (2006b), and the Urban Institute (www.urban.org/).

[11] School districts in a few states have access to a local income tax.

finances but, in 2015, local funds represented 45 percent. The average state contribution is 47 percent. The contribution of state funds varies widely across the states, for example, from about 20 percent to about 90 percent in 2013–2014.

The usual methods for equalizing local school funding are foundation programs or power equalizing programs. The foundation program is designed to provide a minimum standard or foundation level of funding per student in all districts. The state sets the level of per student expenditure to be provided and a standard tax rate to be applied to the local (e.g., property) tax base. To the extent that the local base is insufficient to generate the funds required to meet the foundation level of expenditure, the state grants the difference. Thus, taxation at a standard rate (plus grants as needed) ensures the foundation level of expenditures in all districts. The program may limit all jurisdictions to the foundation level or it may allow districts to spend above the minimum but any extra would be funded entirely from local sources. The power equalization approach equalizes the per pupil revenue-generating capacity of tax rates among jurisdictions. That is, regardless of the per pupil tax base, a given local tax rate will generate, from local and state sources combined, the same amount of tax revenue per pupil. Under power equalization, rich districts might be expected to contribute to equalization (recapturing), but, normally, transfers are only made to districts with a per pupil tax base less than some standard base set by the state. The larger that base, the more districts will receive grants and the larger those grants will be.

Local government in the England is also responsible for schooling but the arrangements are quite different from those in the United States. In England, the general local council (upper tier if two tiered) is responsible for schooling.[12] There are not independent school boards. Schooling represents almost one-third of council expenditures and funding is determined by the council. Local governments in England rely heavily upon grants for financing. Grants provide two-thirds of total revenues. Also, the only tax that local councils have at their disposal, the council property tax, generates only 13.5 percent of total revenues. Grants specifically for schooling meet about 10 percent of school expenditures. Beyond that, funds come from council funds. The Revenue Support Grant (RSG) is an unconditional support grant and provides one-quarter of the funds for general services (which includes schooling). Expenditures deemed necessary for schooling are large

[12] See King in Shah (2006b) for information on local governments in the United Kingdom.

(43 percent) in the financial needs calculations that underlie the RSG. Because the RSG also takes into account other payments from the government and the potential revenue from the council tax, the importance of the RSG to any council varies considerably. Thus, councils have resources—generally modest amounts from own sources and significant amounts from the central government—with which to provide the full range of local services. Schooling must compete directly for those resources in the council decision-making process.

In many ways, the funding of schooling in Poland parallels that in England. Local governments are responsible for providing schooling, municipal governments for primary schooling, and county governments for secondary schooling. Education is the major expenditure item for both. In 2002, schooling took 45 percent of municipal budgets and 40 percent of county budgets. Grants and shared taxes provide about two-thirds of the municipal revenues and about 90 percent of the county revenues. The general-purpose grant has an education component (about 75 percent of the total) that, overall, provides about 25 percent of municipal revenues and 37 percent of county revenues. The education designation comes only from the factors that are taken into account in determining the distribution among local governments.[13] The funds need not be used to finance schooling but are general-purpose funds and can be used as the councils see as appropriate. Generally, local authorities see the education component as inadequate and direct additional funding to schooling. However, there is evidence that a small portion of the councils spent less on schooling than the funds calculated as the education component of the general grant.[14] Local governments in Poland are required to subsidize students in non-public schools at the same level as students in public schools.[15]

Local governments in Uganda are responsible for the delivery of schooling and that accounts for 45–50 percent of local governments' budgets. Local governments fund schooling entirely or almost entirely from conditional transfers from the central government. Those grants cover teacher salaries, instructional materials, and facilities. Primary schooling dominates enrolments and budgets. Primary students account for 87 percent of school

[13] The education component of the grant consisted of 12.8 percent of state budget revenue, but, as of 2004, the funding was no longer tied to state revenue and is instead determined annually in the state budget. Also, the allocation formula was modified.

[14] See Swianiewicz in Shah (2006a) for information on Polish local government.

[15] While there are few purely private schools, there are a significant number of not-for-profit schools operated by parent organizations and a smaller number by religious organizations.

enrolments. A policy of universal secondary education has only been in place since 2006. An analysis focused on primary schooling in the districts (i.e., the rural local governments in which 85 percent of the Ugandan population lives) revealed wide disparities in school services. For example, pupil-teacher ratios ranged from 32 to 100 and per capita funding in the best funded districts was four times that in the poorest funded districts. Performance also differed widely. The analysis suggested that per student central funding would be equalizing. A further finding was that real per capita funding declined in the decade preceding the 2011/2012 fiscal year.[16,17]

Expanding the Local Tax Base

It is unusual for local governments to be entirely responsible for the delivery and financing of schooling. Several Nordic countries, notably Denmark and Sweden, are exceptions to the norm and, interestingly, they are an exception that works well.[18] Municipal governments there are responsible for primary education, while the county governments are responsible for the secondary levels of schooling. At both levels the local governments are responsible for the entire cost of their schools. There are no transfers from the central government directed in support of school expenditures. Why does this unusual arrangement work? There are two important contributing factors. One reason is that local personal income taxes account for about 90 percent of local government revenues. Personal income and so local income

[16] Discussion and analysis of school finance in Uganda is found in World Bank (2013).

[17] The earlier organization of school finance in Uganda is described by Steffensen in Shah (2006a). Central government support provided only about 40 percent of expenditures with the remaining coming from local parent-teacher associations (PTAs). The central government paid teachers directly, although that was supplemented by about 50 percent by PTAs. A central capitation grant amounting to about 23 percent of the total transfers for primary education (and intended for instructional materials and other non-wage operating costs) went to the district local governments for distribution to local schools. A study of those grants from 1991 to 1996 found that only 13 percent were received by schools and 87 percent was diverted to other uses or (mostly) into private hands (Reinikka and Svensson 2004). Few people, notably parents, were aware of the capitation grant. Those findings prompted a strong response from the central government to publicize information on the grants which appeared to have led to better outcomes. The considerable unevenness in the allocation of school funding suggests that difficulties, although not necessarily the same problems, remain. Transfers are a valuable mechanism for achieving public objectives, but transparency and accountability are essential to ensure that those objectives are being met.

[18] See Lotz in Shah (2006b).

taxes relate closely to the economic benefits of education. In countries where local governments obtain transfers to finance schooling, the senior governments providing those transfers typically generate an important share of their funds from income taxes, while the local authorities are constrained to rely upon less equitable sources (for school finance) such as the property tax.[19] The second important reason is that there is an equalization system in each of these countries that is very effective in removing fiscal disparities among the local authorities. Sweden equalizes 95 percent of differences and Denmark only somewhat less. Thus, differences in own fiscal capacities does not translate into uneven school services. The equalization systems give considerable weight to school populations and related factors. The combination of access to local income taxes plus substantial equalization enables local governments on their own to deliver and finance an important social service such as schooling.

Overview

A range of approaches to financing public schooling exist and may operate effectively in their respective environments. They range from financing and delivery by the central (or state) government, central government finance but delivery provided by local authorities, provision by local governments with the financial assistance from central government, to both financing and delivery provided by local authorities. Typically, central finances are the only or are a major source of funds for most local governments providing schooling. Where local governments effectively fully finance schooling are unusual if not exceptional cases. They typically have access to tax sources not typical of those available to most local governments and, even then, disparities in fiscal capacity call for fiscal capacity equalizing transfers from (or arranged through) the central government.

Health Care

Government involvement in health care is less uniform than its role in schooling. A survey of 36 governments in the industrialized countries found that on average they spend 6.5 percent of GDP on health care and that finances almost three-quarters of national spending on health care.[20]

[19] In Norway, where the tax rates of local governments are restricted, the central government funds 50 percent of local school expenditures.

[20] The data are for 2015 and are direct government expenditures or that on state-based compulsory insurance. The data come from the OECD Health Statistics database at https://stats.

In other countries, government health expenditures average 3 percent of GDP and finance almost half of national health-care expenditures.[21] In higher-income countries, national programs providing high levels of hospital and medical care are much more common and extensive. Where government is involved in health care, responsibilities tend to be relatively centralized.[22] Features of the need for and delivery of health services—for example, the risk of illness, the insurance nature of health programs, the training and specialization of staff, assurance of qualifications and practices, the need for an integrated referral system—make extensive decentralization difficult.[23] Hence, the role of local government in health-care delivery is often, though not necessarily, minor. In the following sections, the role of local governments in the delivery and financing of health services is addressed. The approach is to examine situations where the role is minimal, then where it is moderate and, finally, where the local role is major.

A Minimal Local Government Role

In many countries, local governments have little if any responsibilities for health care. The United Kingdom, France, Australia, and Canada are examples. In each of these countries, there are nation-wide public programs that through government (sometimes employing private options) provide health care to all citizens. Those programs are operated by the senior governments and local authorities have a very limited or no role in provision. Local governments in the United Kingdom report no responsibilities and no expenditures for health and in France almost none. In Australia and Canada, local

oecd.org/BrandedView.aspx?oecd_bv_id=health-data-en&doi=data-00349-en. The 6.5 percent represents 73 percent of total spending on health care. That percentage ranged from 51 to 85 percent across the countries. Also see OECD (2015).

[21] Calculated from the Global Health Observatory data repository of the World Health Organization, http://apps.who.int/gho/data/node.main.HEALTHFINANCING.

[22] See, for example, Hulbert and Vammalle (2015) and Mossialos et al. (2017). When discussing the degree of decentralization, and especially so when interested in the role of local government, care must be taken in distinguishing local from subnational governments. Subnational governments (state and provincial) in federal countries often play a large fiscal role but they have their own local governments. The importance of local governments in those countries in services such as health care is quite different than those of subnational governments. In Canada, for example, the provincial expenditures amount to 93 percent of total government health expenditures and those of local governments to about 1.5 percent. From the local perspective, health is centralized, albeit at the provincial level.

[23] For discussion, see Boadway and Shah (2009, Chapter 11).

general-purpose governments do report expenditures on health but they are small, amounting to 1.6 percent of local government expenditures (Chap. 3; McMillan 2008). The province of Ontario in Canada reports the largest health expenditures of the Canadian provinces and there it represents only 3.5 percent of municipal outlays.[24]

The local role in the provision of health care has diminished in some countries.[25] Poland is an example. There, counties had health-care responsibilities but those were reduced with the establishment of 16 independent regional health authorities (sickness funds) under the central government in 1999. A further re-centralization of the financing of the public health system occurred in 2003 when the sickness funds were eliminated in favor of a single national fund. The national fund continues to operate with the regional branches.[26] Of the municipal, county, and regional governments, the counties have the major responsibilities as they have (as before) responsibility for the buildings (e.g., for general hospitals and clinics) and participate in their management. Local governments together account for about 4 percent of total health expenditures. About half of that is for hospitals (largely for capital) and 20 percent for health insurance contributions on behalf of those not subject to compulsory insurance. The local governments are responsible for any deficits of their health services.

Latvia is another case. Following Latvia's independence in 1990, health-care delivery and financing was initially assigned as a responsibility, indeed the major responsibility, of the rajon (a county level of local government). Local governments owned most of the hospitals and operated sickness funds. The system did not operate well. In response, the sickness funds went through consolidations but, in 2011, a single state level National Health Service was created and made responsible for financing and implementing health policy. Local governments still own most of the basic hospitals and are responsible for any deficits that they might incur. Thus, while local authorities were initially made responsible for health care, that responsibility has been centralized.[27]

[24] McMillan in Shah (2006b).

[25] Saltman (2008) and Hulbert and Vammalle (2015).

[26] See European Observatory on Health Systems and Policies (2011) for further information.

[27] See European Observatory on Health Systems and Policies (2012).

A Moderate Role for Local Government

In various countries, local governments have a modest role to play in the delivery of health services. Some examples are considered here.

Municipal governments in Chile have been responsible for the administration of primary health services since 1980. The local governments' role is primarily to manage the resources, not to fund the primary health-care programs. Chile's system has been characterized as one that municipalizes production but centralizes finances (Burki et al. 1999). The municipalities receive funds specifically to finance the delegated services of primary health and schooling.[28] The funds for primary health care are about 10 percent of the transfers for both health and schooling. The delegated funds for health amount to about 14 percent of the country's government spending for health. The delegated funds are based on the estimated cost of a basic package of primary health services that is adjusted by a factor to account for rural and urban conditions and poor and non-poor municipalities. In addition, there are a number of complementary transfers administered by the Ministry of Health that supplement the basic grants. Data are not available to determine how much the total transfers for primary health care are or whether that revenue covers fully local expenditures for that service. Municipalities may augment (or possibly divert) central funding and this results sometimes in considerable variation in the level of local health services among local governments. However, the overall assessment is that while local government is responsible for delivery of primary health care, the central government essentially finances those services.

Health care is a shared responsibility in Brazil.[29] Central, state, and local governments all have some responsibility. Since 2000, state governments have been required to spend 12 percent and municipal governments 15 percent of their budgets on health.[30] The central government operates the national health system that provides coverage to about three-quarters of the population (although private insurance grew in popularity until the 2014 recession). The national system reimburses service providers (public and private) for services delivered. Most public health-care facilities are

[28] See Letelier in Shah (2006a).

[29] Afonso and Araujo in Shah (2006a) and Massauda et al. (2018) provide good insight.

[30] The percentages are of taxes plus constitutional transfers from the federal government. A decade later, it was estimated that 98 percent of municipalities met the 15 percent requirement but only about half of the states met their 12 percent requirement. Some municipalities spend more than 30 percent of their budgets on health.

municipal operations. If municipalities do not provide health facilities and services, the state must. Usually, municipalities will, at least, be involved in the delivery of primary health services. In addition to payment from the national health system, municipal governments receive transfers specifically to support health-care operations. Those transfers amount to only 7.5 percent of municipal revenues and are equivalent to only 0.5 percent of GDP. Municipal health expenditures grew from 25.5 percent to 32.2 percent of government health spending between 2003 and 2016 (and almost doubled in real per capita terms), while the federal share fell from 50 percent to 40.8 percent. Total health expenditures have grown from 7.0 percent to 8.3 percent of GDP between 2000 and 2014. Brazil's health-care system is a web spanning all levels of government and the private sector. Local government play a significant role in delivery but the financing of those local services primarily comes from the central government.

In the United States, local governments often make an important contribution to public health services, particularly by providing hospitals.[31] Overall, local government expenditures account for 10.4 percent of the country's (8.1 percent of GDP) government health spending. Health expenditures amounts to 8.6 percent of local government expenditures but that amounts to 13.5 percent of local government expenditures net of school authority outlays. As such, health is the largest expenditure category of what may be considered to be general-purpose government.[32] The funding of health services provided by local government comes from various sources. Charges for services are important especially for hospital services which represent about two-thirds of local health expenditures. Charges, paid by (private or public) health insurers or patients, cover 84 percent of hospital outlays. The remainder comes from transfers or local governments' own revenues. Insurance meets three-quarters of national health expenditures and 55 percent of that is public. Medicaid, a federal

[31] See Schroeder in Shah (2006b).

[32] Values are calculated from 2016 data in the Statistical Abstract of the United States. Data in Hartman et al. (2018) report state and local governments' expenditures on health as amounting to 16.9 percent of total national expenditures which, since local government accounts for 56 percent of the state and local total, implies a local contribution of about 9.5 percent (1.6 percent of GDP). Since government expenditures amount to 45 percent of total expenditures on health in the United States, the 9.5 percent figure from Hartman et al. is about twice the share reported in the Statistical Abstract data (0.8 percent of GDP). The difference appears to result mostly from the Hartman et al. data including government employer contributions to public and private health insurance plans.

insurance program to meet the medical costs of low income persons and families and which covers almost 20 percent of residents, illustrates the financing and cost-sharing arrangements that exist. Medicaid is operated by the state governments with financial assistance provided by the federal government. The federal contribution (through an open-ended matching program) to the costs of each state varies between 50 and 74 percent depending upon state per capita income. The states determine the state-local cost-sharing arrangements (usually at the county level). County governments may be required to contribute up to 60 percent of the non-federal funded costs and counties contribute in 26 states. Arrangement vary considerably but, overall in the United States, local governments play a significant role in the provision of health services and fund a substantial share from own revenues.

German local governments have a significant role to play in the German health-care system. While German local government expenditures on health are small (at least in general government budgets), local governments own about half of all the hospital beds.[33,34] Although hospitals are a *Land* (state) responsibility, hospitals are often provided by local authorities. Their operating costs, however, are largely met from insurance payments (the statutory insurance/sickness funds or private insurance) or, to a minor amount, out of patients' pockets. The *Land* governments regulate the capital investments in hospitals and fund those that conform to their plans (independent of ownership). The portion of local health expenditures met by transfers is very small. Local governments also provide some long-term care. The introduction of long-term care insurance in the 1990s reduced by half the share of health-care costs financed from government general revenue. Local governments were the major beneficiary of the switch to payment from insurance funds. Local governments reimburse sickness funds for services provided to social assistance recipients. They also finance emergency services.

[33] Current health-care expenditures in the OECD:Stat and post-2002 IMF Government Finance Statistics report small amounts. Those data contrast with pre-2003 data in the IMF Government Finance Statistics which indicate the local government health outlays amounted to 15 percent of national public health expenditures which represented 1 percent of GDP and that accounted for 14.5 percent of local governments' budgets. While the German health system has not changed materially, the accounting system has.

[34] See McMillan (2004), European Observatory on Health Systems and Policies (2014) and Blumel and Busse (2016).

Where Local Government Has a Large Role

In very few countries providing comprehensive public health care do local governments have a major role in providing that service. The Scandinavian countries, particularly Denmark and Sweden, illustrate this case.

In the Scandinavian countries, local governments are responsible for providing a broad range of social services. Health care is one of those services. County governments (or regional authorities) in those countries are responsible for the management and financing of hospitals and the bulk of health services.[35] Only in Norway is this no longer the case. There, since 2002, the central government, now as the owner of four regional health authorities, has recently taken over health services from its counties but left primary care with the municipalities. In Denmark and Sweden, county/regional governments remain responsible for the vast majority of health care.[36] In those two countries, the major municipal responsibilities for health care are care of the elderly, the disabled, and school children. Sweden illustrates the considerable responsibilities of local governments in this field. There, in 2014, 83 percent of health expenditures are government financed with county governments meeting 57 percent of the 83 and municipal governments 25 percent.[37] Health care represents about one-quarter of local government expenditures (and 90 percent of county expenditures). In Sweden, county and municipal taxes (largely proportional income taxes) are the major source of local government finances. Those funded 69 percent of county expenditures in 2015. Hence, in Sweden, local taxes finance the bulk of health expenditures. In contrast, the regions in Denmark received 83 percent of their revenues from the central government and the remainder as contributions from municipal governments—both still heavily reliant on income taxes. Thus, local and especially regional governments in Denmark and Sweden have major responsibility for health

[35] For further information see Lotz in Shah (2006b) and the relevant sections of the European Observatory on Health Systems and Policy http://www.euro.who.int/en/about-us/partners/observatory/publications/health-system-reviews-hits/full-list-of-country-hits and International Profiles on Health Care Systems https://www.commonwealthfund.org/sites/default/files/documents/___media_files_publications_fund_report_2017_may_mossialos_intl_profiles_v5.pdf.

[36] Denmark also consolidated its county governments, from 14 counties to 5 regions in 2007, but the regions remain responsible for hospital and outpatient services.

[37] In all three Scandinavian countries, government financing covers about 85 percent of health expenditures and private sources about 15 percent (typically related to dental, optical, and prescription drugs).

care (although the reliance on local finance differs). Although regional health authorities in Norway are now a central responsibility, local government (especially with primary care a municipal function) accounts for over one-quarter of government health-care expenditures and, so, local government continues to bear a considerable responsibility for health services there as well. In all three countries, fiscal disparities among counties are largely overcome by a strong equalization system. This combination of income tax plus equalization is fundamental for the success of the assignment that makes local governments responsible for the financing as well as the delivery of health services.

Social Assistance[38]

Social assistance is not a function that is recommended for local governments.[39] Typically, the broader social benefits of the redistribution and the local financial burdens are inconsistent and call for social assistance (among other social services) to be the responsibility of senior governments. While local governments usually do provide some social assistance services, they are normally not a major part of their budgets and, even then, are often supported by central or state governments. In turn, local government expenditure on social protection is customarily a small component of the total national social protection outlays. Across the countries for which the OECD provides data, local government expenditures on social protection average 13.5 percent of national social protection expenditures by general governments and, in the majority of countries, the level is less than 10 percent.[40] Local governments in Canada and Spain, at about 3.4 percent, are among the lowest contributors.

Local governments in the Nordic countries account for relative large shares of the national outlays for social assistance.[41] Even among those countries, Denmark stands out. Expenditures for social protection programs by local governments in Denmark have averaged 83 percent of the

[38] Social assistance is also widely referred to as social protection or social welfare. Here, that includes care for the elderly, family and child services, care for the sick outside the health-care system, services for the disabled and unemployed, and public housing among others.

[39] See Chap. 2, Boadway and Shah (2009) and Shah and Shah (Chapter 1) in Shah (2006a).

[40] See Government Expenditure by Function in OECD:Stat at https://stats.oecd.org/.

[41] Social protection expenditures of local governments in Japan and Korea also represent a relatively large portion of the total government outlay for that purpose.

total government spending on that function in recent years.[42] Municipal governments in Denmark are responsible for a wide variety of social services beyond schooling and health care. Most notable are day care for children five and under, after school care or organizations, elder care (e.g., nursing homes, home care), rehabilitation outside hospitals, and support services (unemployment insurance, family and sickness benefits, disability benefits).[43] For certain services, the municipality receives (at least some) reimbursement in the form of co-payments (e.g., day care, stays in long-term facilities) and payments from the central government. These represent major financial responsibilities but the municipalities are assisted by transfers and reimbursements from the central government amounting to about 40 percent of expenditures. The municipalities' own revenues come almost entirely from taxes on income which, in 2014, were at an average rate of 24.9 percent. Fiscal disparities among the municipalities are largely offset by equalizing block grants. The Danish system for addressing social protection is unique but has worked well due to the social and economic structure of the country, national standards, the progressive tax system funding local governments, central government support, and, in particular, the commitment to substantial fiscal equalization among municipalities.

Conclusion

Social services are an important component and have become an increasingly important component of government. The role of local government in providing such services—be it schooling, health care, or social protection—differs considerably among countries. The reason for the differences is that social services involve redistribution and, if provided at the local level, generate important externalities or spillovers. While those characteristics argue for central (or, at least, senior) government provision or involvement, local participation is likely to be valuable in order to accommodate local preferences and may facilitate efficient delivery. The result is that those services are usually, but not necessarily, provided through some senior-local government collaborative system. Normally, the senior government will have both regulatory and financing roles. Given careful design, workable arrangements can vary considerably with local governments' responsibilities ranging from small to

[42] The other Nordic countries shares range from one-quarter to one-third.

[43] For a broad range of services, the central government defines standards of service and payments to clients.

large. The arrangement selected and the arrangements among the set of social services are major in determining the magnitude of local government itself and in the national framework. The survey and numerous illustrations provided demonstrate the scope and variety of arrangements.

Schooling is a social program in which local residents, especially parents, have a major interest. Probably for this reason, and the fact that schools have distinctly local service areas, schooling normally involves a considerable degree of local participation. Even where financing is centralized, efforts are usually made to provide a degree of local governance. Where local government participates in financing, central support is important and includes mechanisms to equalize fiscal capacities among local school authorities.

Local governments are less engaged in the provision of health care than schooling. This may be a product of health care being more insurance based and interest being primarily in accesses to quality service when needed. Very centralized systems are not uncommon. In addition, there are cases where decentralized systems are being converted to more centralized systems with important responsibilities shifted to central or regional governments. Still, in other instances, local governments have a notable role. Often that role is concentrated on primary care and non-hospital services. It is rare to find local governments responsible for the majority of a nation's public health expenditures.

Social protection is also a function for which local governments typically have limited financial responsibility. The substantial redistributive role undoubtedly contributes to this pattern of assignment. As is the case with social spending by local governments generally, it is the Nordic countries where local social protection responsibilities are relatively large. Besides history and social attitudes, the local tax systems and the strong fiscal equalization systems in place facilitate local government in those countries carrying an unusually large role in providing and funding social programs.

References

Afonso, Antonio, and Davide Furceri. 2010. Government Size, Composition, Volatility and Economic Growth. *European Journal of Political Economy* 26 (4): 517–532.

Angrist, Joshua, Eric Bettinger, Erik Bloom, Elizabeth King, and Michael Kremer. 2002. Vouchers for Private Schooling in Colombia: Evidence from a Natural Experiment. *American Economic Review* 92 (5): 1535–1558.

Blumel, Miriam, and Reinhard Busse. 2016. The German Health Care System, 2015. In *2015 International Profiles of Health Care Systems*, ed. Elias Mossialos and Martin Wenzl, 69–76. New York, NY: The Commonwealth Fund.

Boadway, Robin, and Anwar Shah. 2009. *Fiscal Federalism: Principles and Practice of Multiorder Governance*. New York, NY: Cambridge University Press.

Burki, Shahid Javed, Guilllermo Perry, William Dillinger, et al. 1999. *Beyond the Center: Decentralizing the State*. Washington, DC: The World Bank.

Dethier, Jean-Jacques, ed. 2000. *Governance, Decentralization and Reform in China, India and Russia*. Dordrecht: Kluwer Academic Publishers.

di Gropello, Emanuela. 2004. *Education Decentralization and Accountability Relationships in Latin America*. Policy Research Working Paper 3453. Washington, DC: The World Bank, November.

———. 2005. A Comparative Analysis of School-Based Management in Central America. *en breve*, June, No. 72. Washington DC: The World Bank.

European Observatory on Health Systems and Policies. 2012. *Health Systems in Transition: Latvia Health System Review* 14 (8): 1–219.

———. 2014. *Health Systems in Transition: Germany Health Systems Review* 16 (2): 1–296.

Hartman, Micah, Anne B. Martin, Nathan Espinosa, Aaron Catlin, and the National Health Expenditure Team. 2018. National Health Care Spending in 2016: Spending and Enrollment Growth Slow after initial Coverage Expansions. *Health Affairs* 37 (1): 150–160.

Hulbert, Claudia, and Camila Vammalle. 2015. Decentralization of Health Financing and Expenditure. In *Fiscal Sustainability of Health Systems: Bridging Health and Finance Perspectives*, 115–127. Paris: OECD Publishing.

Kitchen, Harry M. 2002. *Local Government Finance in Canada*. Toronto: Canadian Tax Foundation.

Lawton, Stephen B. 1996. *Financing Canadian Education*. Toronto: Canadian Education Association.

Letelier, Leonardo S., and Hector Ormeno C. 2018. Education and Fiscal Decentralization: The Case of Municipal Education in Chile. *Environment and Planning C: Politics and Space* 36 (8): 1499–1531.

Litvack, Jennie and Jessica Seddon. 1999. *Decentralization Briefing Notes*. WBI Working Papers. Washington, DC: The World Bank Institute.

Massauda, Adriano, Thomas Hone, Fernando Antonio Gomes Leles, Marcia C. de Castro, and Rifat Atun. 2018. The Brazilian Health Systems at Crossroads: Progress, Crisis and Resilience. *BMJ Global Health* 3 (4): e000829. https://doi.org/10.1136/bmjgh-2018-000829.

McMillan, Melville L. 2004. *Financial Relationships between Regional and Municipal Authorities: Insights from the Examination of Five OECD Countries*. Working Paper 2004(3). Canada: Institute of Inter-Governmental Relations, Queen's University.

———. 2008. A Local Perspective on Fiscal Federalism: Practices, Experiences and Lessons from Industrial Countries. In *Macro Federalism and Local Finance*, ed. Anwar Shah, 245–289. Washington, DC: The World Bank.

Mitch, David. 2004. School Finance. In *International Handbook on the Economics of Education*, ed. Geraint Johnes and Jill Johnes, 260–297. Cheltenham: Edward Elgar Publishing.

Mossialos, Elias, Ana Djordjevic, Robin Osborn, and Dana Sarnak. 2017. *International Profiles on Health Care Systems, 2017*. New York: The Commonwealth Fund.

OECD. 2015. *Health at a Glance 2015: OECD Indicators*. Paris: OECD Publishing.

Rosen, Harvey S., Jean-Francois Wen, and Tracy Snodden. 2008. *Public Finance in Canada*. 2nd ed. Toronto: McGraw-Hill Ryerson.

Reinikka, Ritva, and Jakob Svensson. 2004. Local Capture: Evidence from a Central Government Transfer Program in Uganda. *Quarterly Journal of Economics* 119 (2, May): 679–705.

Saltman, Richard B. 2008. Decentralization, Re-centralization and Future European Health Policy. *European Journal of Public Health* 18 (2): 104–106.

Schuknecht, Ludger, and Vito Tanzi. 2004. *Reforming Public Expenditure in Industrialized Countries: Are There Trade-Offs?* Preliminary Draft (October) of a Paper for the Workshop on Fiscal Policy in EMU Organized by the European Commission's Directorate General for Economic and Financial Affairs, November 12.

Shah, Anwar, ed. 2006a. *Local Governance in Developing Countries*. Washington, DC: The World Bank.

———, ed. 2006b. *Local Governance in Industrial Countries*. Washington, DC: The World Bank.

Tanzi, Vito, and Ludger Schuknecht. 1995. *The Growth of Government and the Reform of the State in Industrialized Countries*. Working Paper 95/130. Washington, DC: International Monetary Fund.

World Bank. 2013. *Republic of Uganda: Service Delivery with More Districts in Uganda—Fiscal Challenges and Opportunities for Reforms*. Public Expenditure Review, AFTPS Africa, June.

CHAPTER 7

Provision and Finance of Infrastructure

Introduction

Local governments are responsible for providing a large share of countries' public infrastructure. That infrastructure makes important contributions to national productivity and well-being. Yet, municipal officials everywhere have become increasingly concerned with the deteriorating state of their infrastructure, its impact on economic productivity, and consequent environmental impacts. Crumbling, over-congested roads, antiquated water and sewage systems, inadequate public transit, and so on have moved from council agendas to newspaper headlines to coffee shop conversations and sometimes in reverse order. As municipalities expand and age, it has become apparent that resources must be devoted to expanding, rehabilitating, or replacing local capital stock. Water, sewage and waste facilities, cultural and recreational complexes, and transportation and transit need updating and expanding. Brownfield remediation must be addressed and "blighted" areas of cities revitalized and redeveloped. These are the types of infrastructure that must be financed.

This chapter is organized in the following parts. Section "Capital Expenditures by Local Government" demonstrates the magnitudes, uses, and types of local government capital, and Sect. "Infrastructure's Contribution to Economic Growth" highlights the contribution of infrastructure investment to growth. Section "Municipal Infrastructure" identifies what is referred to as municipal infrastructure; comments on the often heard "municipal infrastructure deficit" and the importance of correctly

H. Kitchen et al., *Local Public Finance and Economics*,
https://doi.org/10.1007/978-3-030-21986-4_7

pricing or taxing the services provided by it; offers a decision rule for infrastructure spending; and discusses the importance of capital budgets. Section "Financing Instruments" discusses and evaluates both internal and external financing instruments used by municipalities in financing local infrastructure. This discussion focuses on the relevance of each instrument, when each should be used or what type of infrastructure should be financed by it, and changes that should be made in both the structure and use of each instrument if the criteria for efficient, accountable, and fair financing are to be met. Section "Summary" summarizes the chapter.

Capital Expenditures by Local Government

Capital expenditures are an important part of local governments' budgets. Across the OECD countries for which there are data, capital expenditures average 15 percent of expenditures (Table 7.1). The range, however, is large in the data reported: from a low of 4.1 percent in Denmark to high of 38.5 percent in Australia. No particular pattern is evident in this data except that the share of expenditures for capital tends to increase as the share that local government expenditures is of GDP diminishes, and decrease as the share of GDP increases. This occurs because many of the fundamentally local services are of the infrastructure type—that is, water, sewerage, roads, and streets—while, when the role of local governments is expanded, the extended responsibilities usually are of the personal services kind which involves relatively less capital investment.[1]

Local governments account for a disproportionately large share of total government capital expenditures. On average, local governments make almost 40 percent of the capital investments by all governments while representing only 25 percent of general government total expenditures. Only in the Baltic countries and Sweden does the local share of capital outlays approximate the local share of total government expenditures. At over 70 percent, the local share of capital expenditures in Japan is exceptionally large.

Evidence from selected countries illustrates the programs in which local governments make capital expenditures. The distribution of net capital expenditures across nine functional categories of government activities is reported in Table 7.2 for ten countries. Looking at the averages, economic

[1] Also, for example, there is no particular difference in the averages between federal and unitary countries.

Table 7.1 Local government capital expenditures

Country (2015 unless otherwise indicated)	*GDP (billions of domestic currency)*	*Local government expenditure*		*Net capital expenditure as % of GDP*		*Percent of total government net capital expenditure by local government*
		Total expenditure as % of GDP	*Net capital expenditure as % of local government expenditure*	*Total general government*	*Local government*	
Australia	1634.0	2.1	38.5	3.1	0.8	26.3
Austria	339.9	8.7	10.1	3.0	0.9	29.0
Belgium	410.2	7.2	9.8	2.3	0.7	30.4
Canada (2008)	1652.9	7.4	19.5	3.9	1.5	36.9
Czech Republic	4596.0	11.3	12.0	5.1	1.4	26.3
Denmark	2007.0	35.3	4.1	3.5	1.4	41.2
Estonia	17.9	10.7	13.6	6.0	1.5	24.1
Finland	209.6	23.2	9.2	3.8	2.1	56.1
France	2194.0	11.4	17.6	3.5	2.0	57.1
Germany	3044.0	7.8	8.6	2.1	0.7	31.6
Hungary	28,661.0	9.4	29.8	7.9	2.8	35.5
Ireland	261.6	2.2	15.8	1.8	0.4	19.7
Israel	1162.5	5.4	20.2	2.0	1.1	53.8
Italy	1645.0	14.6	9.1	2.2	1.3	60.0
Japan	530,157.0	15.6	16.9	3.7	2.6	71.9
Korea	1,564,000	13.7	16.9	4.2	2.3	54.5
Latvia	24.4	9.3	14.4	4.7	1.3	28.3
Lithuania	37.3	7.9	13.8	3.7	1.1	29.4
Netherlands	683.5	14.1	12.8	3.3	1.8	54.4
Norway	3117.0	16.0	11.9	4.8	1.9	39.8

(continued)

Table 7.1 (continued)

Country (2015 unless otherwise indicated)	*GDP (billions of domestic currency)*	*Local government expenditure*		*Net capital expenditure as % of GDP*		*Percent of total government net capital expenditure by local government*
		Total expenditure as % of GDP	*Net capital expenditure as % of local government expenditure*	*Total general government*	*Local government*	
Poland	1799.3	12.9	16.1	4.3	2.1	48.0
Portugal	179.5	5.9	17.1	2.4	1.0	42.7
Slovak Republic	78.7	7.5	20.1	6.4	1.5	23.3
Slovenia	38.8	8.9	22.6	4.8	2.0	42.6
Spain	1076.0	6.1	10.2	2.6	0.6	24.0
Sweden	4181.0	24.7	8.6	4.3	2.1	50.1
Switzerland	653.6	7.4	13.1	3.1	1.0	31.4
United Kingdom	1873.0	10.6	8.2	2.6	0.9	33.7
United States	18,131.0	8.8	15.6	3.4	1.4	40.1
Average		11.2	15.0	3.7	1.5	39.4

Source: Calculations made from OECD: Stat national account statistics but for Canada and the United States for which domestic statistical sources were used as data for those two countries were not included in the OECD data

Table 7.2 Distribution of net capital expenditures by local governments in selected countries, 2015 (%)

	General government	*Public order and safety*	*Economic affairs*	*Environment*	*Housing and community amenities*	*Recreation and culture*	*Education*	*Health*	*Social protection*
Australia	20.7	0.7	43.3	13.2	2.0	18.8	0.2	0.2	0.8
Canada (2008)	6.8	4.7	39.7	29.7	4.3	13.1	23.7	1.1	0.4
Germany	4.7	6.0	34.9	7.9	8.0	10.8	22.9	0.3	4.5
France	15.1	2.1	30.4	10.6	12.7	12.3	14.0	0.4	2.3
Sweden	19.2	1.8	15.9	0.8	12.8	6.8	15.7	22.5	4.4
United Kingdom	6.5	3.9	37.6	3.6	23.7	1.5	22.1	0.0	1.2
Japan	5.8	5.0	46.3	16.3	10.2	4.0	9.2	0.6	2.6
Hungary	23.8	0.2	12.0	34.7	15.1	6.5	5.1	1.1	1.6
Latvia	2.4	0.7	17.2	4.5	19.6	18.0	24.9	7.0	5.8
Poland	8.6	2.3	46.1	11.2	4.2	12.0	6.9	7.8	0.9
Average	11.4	2.7	32.3	13.3	11.3	10.4	14.5	4.1	2.5

Source: Calculated from national accounts data of OECD. Stat expect for Canada for which Statistics Canada data (for 2008) are used. Net expenditures are gross less disposals

affairs (which includes roadways and transit) is the dominant category at almost one-third of capital expenditures. Beyond that, those functions that can be considered the conventional or core local activities combine to account for the bulk of capital outlays, that is, those for general government, environment (notably solid waste and wastewater services), housing and community amenities (which includes water supply), and recreation and cultural services. On average, those each represent from about 10 to 13 percent of capital outlays. The other relatively large category is education. Across these countries, education (essentially schooling) takes 14.5 percent of capital spending. Only small percentages of the capital budgets are allocated to the other two areas of social expenditures, health, and social protection. That reflects that major responsibilities for those services are not normally assigned to local governments and also that those services (especially social protection) are not capital intensive.

Looking across countries for any function, Table 7.2 reveals considerable variation in the importance of capital expenditures in local government budgets. That variation reflects both the assignment of functional responsibilities among governments including those for both operating and capital expenditures (which may be different). For example, Australian local governments have very little responsibility for social services so their capital outlays are concentrated in the core local services. On the other hand, Swedish local governments are directly responsible for general hospitals and spending for health accounts for 22.5 percent of their capital outlays in 2015 (in contrast to an average of 4.1 percent). A wide variation also exists for education where four countries spend nearly one-quarter of their capital budgets while the share in the others is much less. Considerable diversity can also be found within the core services. Even within economic affairs, the range goes from 12 to 46 percent.[2] Similar variations are found across the other functions. Hence, the type of capital expenditures of local governments can differ considerably among countries. Regardless of that variation, local governments are responsible for providing large part of the national public sector infrastructure.

Table 7.3 provides an illustration of the actual capital assets of local governments. The data are for general purpose municipal governments and the local school authorities in the Province of Alberta, Canada. Of the

[2] The comparisons here are complicated by the varying importance of local government across the countries. However, even when comparisons are made with a more standard base, percentage of GDP, there is still substantial variation in the relative importance of local government capital expenditures by function among the countries.

Table 7.3 Distribution of local government tangible assets, Alberta, Canada, 2016

	Percent of municipal	*Percent of school*	*Percent of total local*
General municipal government			
Transportation			28.0
Roadways	27.3		24.7
Light rail	3.7		3.4
Water services			23.7
Water supply	8.9		8.0
Waste water	9.5		8.6
Storm and drainage	7.8		7.1
Electricity and gas utilities	0.9		0.8
Construction	6.4		5.8
Buildings	13.3		12.0
Machinery and equipment	2.9		2.6
Fiber optic systems	0.1		0.1
Vehicles	2.7		2.4
Land and land improvements	16.3		14.9
Total general government	100.0		90.3
School authorities			
Buildings		78.5	7.6
Construction		14.5	1.4
Equipment		3.5	0.3
Vehicles		1.2	0.1
Land		1.4	0.1
Other		0.9	0.1
Total school authorities		100.0	9.7
Total local government			100.0

Sources: Municipal Financial and Statistical Data of Alberta Municipal Affairs and K to 12 Education Financial Statements (combined) of Alberta Education. Sums may not equal their aggregates due to rounding

total tangible assets there, 90.3 percent are municipal and 9.7 percent are school. The transportation assets of the municipal governments are the largest category at 28 percent of the total local assets with one-quarter of the total dedicated to road infrastructure and the remainder of that category to light rail transit. Water services is the next largest category with assets divided almost equally among those for supplying water, disposing of wastewater and drainage and stormwater systems. Electricity and gas utilities appear negligible here but these accounts understate the municipal role because those utilities, where owned by municipalities (which is quite common in Alberta), are typically held as independent companies owned by the municipal government (i.e., appear in the accounts as financial assets). Municipal buildings account for 12 percent of local government tangible assets. Land and improvements to land amount to 14.9 percent. Capital assets under construction appear separately and amount to 5.8 percent of the total. Other assets—machinery and equipment, vehicles, and especially fiber optic systems—are a much smaller portion representing just over 5 percent in total.

The tangible assets of the school system are only about 10 percent of the value of the total local government tangible assets.[3] Buildings, and those under construction, represent the vast majority of the school-related assets at about 90 percent.[4] Buildings, municipal and school combined, are almost one-quarter of local tangible assets and, so, of a similar magnitude as each of the transportation and water-related assets. If one includes land, those three types of assets and land account for 90 percent of total value of local government tangible assets.

Overall, capital expenditures by local governments are a significant share of local government budgets and represent a disproportionately large share of total government capital expenditures. Those investments are primarily to support the core functions of local government and to support education. The specific types of capital (or tangible assets) are primarily for transportation (notably roadways), water-related systems, and buildings (with school buildings being a major part of the buildings). The importance of capital expenditures and assets differs substantially among countries depending upon the allocation of public sector responsibilities. This is demonstrated also by the variation in net capital expenditures as a percentage of GDP. Across the 29 countries reported in Table 7.1, that percentage ranges from 0.4 in Ireland to 2.8 in Hungary and around an average of 1.5 percent. A declining trend and now low levels of public investment relative to GDP are common and are a lingering concern.[5] The magnitudes and trends in local government investment make capital financing an important topic.

[3] This 10 percent in Alberta is a smaller share of assets than the education share of net investment (23.7 percent in Table 7.2) in Canada.

[4] Schooling, including school buildings, is totally funded by the Alberta government. While the local school authorities have substantial flexibility in allocating their operating budgets, the province decides on school construction.

[5] For example, see OECD Regional Outlook reports since 2011 and especially the 2019 report.

Infrastructure's Contribution to Economic Growth

The importance of capital investment and the availability and quality of services provided by municipal infrastructure—water, sewers, solid waste facilities, public transit and transportation systems, recreation and cultural facilities—are critical factors in improving quality of life, productivity and economic growth, international competitiveness (The Institute 2005, p. 17; OECD 2009). In particular, a number of studies have illustrated the extent to which spending on infrastructure is very much an investment, not just an expense. One survey that reviewed more than 200 studies on the role of public infrastructure investment (Holden and Vander Ploeg 2013) concluded that there is a strong link between public infrastructure investment and long-term economic growth. In addition, the Conference Board of Canada has suggested that infrastructure spending produces a $1.11 increase in gross provincial product for every infrastructure dollar invested. Further, it has accounted for fully 12 percent of provincial labor productivity gains in Canada during the 1980–2008 period (Antunes et al. 2010; Brodhead et al. 2014). A more recent study (Smetanin et al. 2014) using an alternative economic modeling technique (agent-based) made the case that investing in infrastructure pays net fiscal dividends that are much higher than reported in previously completed studies. The short lesson from all of these studies is that investing in infrastructure can be socially and economically beneficial and productive.

Financing this investment, then, must not be treated lightly. The choice of financing instrument and the way it is employed impacts on both the level of services provided by infrastructure and the size and range of the infrastructure itself. Furthermore, and perhaps of greater importance, is the way in which services provided by this infrastructure are financed. Correctly designed user fees and local taxes (see Chaps. 9, 10, and 11) act as a mechanism for revealing the true demand for—and, therefore, indicating the efficient supply of local public infrastructure. Incorrect or inadequate user fees and taxes result in usage that is far from efficient or optimal and, subsequently, a level of infrastructure that has led to too much public capital in some sectors and too little in other sectors. Indeed, there is evidence of this kind of mis-investment in Canada throughout the latter part of the twentieth century (Gillen 2001).

Municipal Infrastructure

Municipal infrastructure or capital expenditures differ from municipal operating expenditures in two important respects. First, infrastructure or capital expenditures tend to be lumpy in nature. Large expenditures in one year generally preclude similar expenditures in subsequent years with little, if any, consistent trend or pattern. Second, financing of capital expenditures frequently differs from that for financing operating expenditures. The latter are generally financed from locally raised revenues and grants from senior governments, while the former may be financed from these sources in addition to monies generated from special assessments, development charges, reserves, and borrowing.

The way in which the term capital is interpreted and applied at the municipal or local level may also vary from country to country and from municipality to municipality, within a country. Although there may be varying definitions of capital expenditures, it is generally agreed that they include the following: acquisition and construction of new buildings, structures, facilities, equipment, rolling stock, furnishings, studies, development and purchase of land, and all associated items to bring the foregoing into operation—or major rehabilitation of the above—and normally have a useful life of more than one year.

Municipal infrastructure in this chapter is interpreted to include physical infrastructure. This differs from social and community infrastructure. The former generally refers to bridges, roads, highways, sidewalks, public transit, water supply and distribution, sewage collection and treatment, storm sewers, solid and hazardous waste recovery and disposal, public libraries, and recreational facilities, for example. The latter often includes public health, public education, children's services, public shelters, environmental protection initiatives, and hospitals.

As for physical, social, and community infrastructure, the vast majority of it in virtually every country is located in cities and municipalities.

"Municipal Infrastructure Deficits"

Over the past decade or two in most developed economics and some developing countries, much has been written about the size of the "municipal infrastructure deficit or gap" and the importance of closing it. This shortfall, it has been argued, has led to less economic activity and a poorer quality of life than is otherwise desirable. Further, it has often been followed by a plea from municipal officials for more financial assistance, generally in the form of grants, from senior governments to help in closing this deficit or gap.

While it is generally conceded that a gap exists, disagreement has often surfaced over its size and the way it is measured. Correctly estimating the deficit is important if municipalities are to avoid over- or underinvesting in infrastructure. The following comments on the weaknesses of many measures of the deficit and highlights the importance of setting efficient prices and taxes for financing the services provided by the infrastructure.

There are at least four reasons why one should be cautious in relying on the estimates of the deficit. First, most are based on information collected from surveys that are administered by associations—water and wastewater operators, public transit systems, municipal engineers—whose respondents have an incentive to include their "wish list" as being equivalent to needs, especially if they perceive or believe that the larger the list and the larger the deficit, the greater the likelihood of provincial and federal grant assistance.

As well, even where a benchmark or standard has been set for determining needs, it is often set by the association representing the asset or assets, once again creating an incentive to set high standards or benchmarks if there is a possibility that it could lead to increased grants and investment. Furthermore, these standards or benchmarks are almost always based on engineering standards and do not include serious economic reasoning or assessment based on economic performance. This distinction is important because engineering standards rely on technical measures of conditions and needs for development and spending, and not on economic performance that should include an analysis of why the need came about or what caused it. It is important to assess whether the deficit is due to an asset management problem, a pricing problem, or something else.

A second weakness in infrastructure deficit estimates is that views and estimates often differ on the amount of upgrading or rehabilitating that is required to bring the quality of the asset up to a certain standard, regardless of how the standard is set. Although technical in their approach, assessments of engineering needs have subjective elements when they determine current quality and what is required to rehabilitate or repair an asset to meet specific standards.

Third, there is no consistency or clarity in how infrastructure needs, and their resulting impacts on deficits, are estimated. In some cases, it has been left to individual respondents to determine their needs without referring to a generally accepted provincial or national standardized benchmark. In other cases, respondents have determined their needs by comparing their existing infrastructure with what it would be if it met national or provincial standards or benchmarks. Furthermore, where shortfalls have been identified, they have been based on an assumption that existing taxation/pricing policies for the services provided by the assets will continue rather than on an estimate of what the need would be if more effective demand management and conservation-based pricing policies were implemented.

Fourth, studies that take some past infrastructure spending measure (capital stock per capita or per thousand dollars of GDP or something else), perhaps 25 or 30 years ago, as the base for deriving the current infrastructure deficit must also be treated with caution. These studies and reports estimate the current infrastructure gap as the difference between today's current stock of public infrastructure and what it would have been if the measure from 25 or 30 years ago had increased at the rate of population growth, or inflation, or GDP or some combination of these. In other words, the size of the gap depends on the starting point (year).

While it may not be possible to derive solid estimates about the size of the infrastructure deficit across countries, it is critical that investment decisions not be undertaken until the following is met. First, services provided by this infrastructure must be priced efficiently (see Chaps. 9, 10, and 11). Second, all costs must be reported and included in pricing/taxation structures. And third, asset management programs need to be clearly articulated and implemented.

A Decision-Making Rule for Infrastructure Investment

Local policy makers should decide what capital expenditures to undertake before they consider the capital budgeting process and the various means of capital financing available to them. The determination of justifiable capital projects is, in principle, straightforward. A project is desirable if the net present value (NPV) arising from its implementation is greater than zero, that is, if the discounted value of the stream of current and future benefits exceeds the discounted value of the stream of current and future costs. More specifically, the present value of the benefits and costs of a capital project in any year is calculated by multiplying each respective benefit or cost by the discount factor which is $1/(1+r)^i$ where r is the rate of discount and i denotes the year. The discounted values of benefits and costs for all years are then totaled to yield the present value of benefits and costs as follows. The present value of benefits where $B_0, B_1, \ldots B_n$ reflect the benefits in each year is obtained from the following expression:

$$B_0 / (1+r)^0 + B_1 / (1+r)^1 + B_2 / (1+r)^2 \ldots\ B_n / (1+r)^n = \Sigma(B_i / (1+r)^i$$

The present value of costs, where $C_0, C_1, \ldots C_n$ reflect the costs in each year is calculated in the following manner:

$$C_0 / (1+r)^0 + C_1 / (1+r)^1 + C_2 / (1+r)^2 \ \ \ldots\ C_n / (1+r)^n = \Sigma(C_i / (1+r)^i$$

Finally the net present value (NPV) of a capital project is obtained by subtracting the sum of the discounted costs from the sum of the discounted benefits.

$$\text{NPV} = \Sigma(B_i / (1+r)^i - \Sigma(C_i / (1+r)^i$$

A positive net present value means that the project will generate benefits that exceed the cost of the project. If there is a budget constraint and not all projects with a positive net benefit can be initiated, those generating the highest net present value subject to the constraint should be selected.

Although simple in theory, capital expenditure decisions are not as simple in practice, since it is frequently difficult to identify and quantify all relevant benefits and costs. In the public sector, for instance, many benefits are of an intangible nature and not amenable to easy or obvious quantification. How does one evaluate the benefits to users of a facility (football fields, community parks, streets, or bridges) when the users are not required to pay a fee or price each time the facility is used? Further difficulties are encountered in attempting to place a value on spillovers (benefits accruing to those who do not directly use the facility) from a project or facility. Additional problems can arise if the information or data included in the cost/benefit analysis is incorrect or incomplete. In spite of measurement problems such as these, attempts should be made to estimate all benefits of a capital project and to identify all non-quantifiable benefits along with any perceived or potential weakness in the information or data used in the benefit analysis.

The most difficult issue around a cost/benefit analysis is the estimation of benefits. Where similar facilities exist in the private sector (e.g., recreational facilities), calculation of benefits to direct users could be based on the amount that users pay for the services in the private sector. Where similar services do not exist in the private sector or where spillover benefits are prevalent, calculation of benefits will be more complex and require the use of more sophisticated estimation techniques. Fortunately, the past decade has witnessed the emergence of a variety of techniques for estimating benefits of a more indirect nature.

Calculation of projected costs may also be problematic and may not always be complete. All current and future construction costs as well as future maintenance and operating costs must be included. Any costs that a project imposes on third parties (spillovers or externalities) should be included. In reality, there is a tendency to ignore third-party costs as well as future projected construction costs and annual operating and maintenance costs.

Improvements in capital expenditure decision-making require a careful and thorough benefit-cost analysis prior to the initiation of a capital project. This should prevent questionable projects, for example, those promised by local politicians in the enthusiastic environment of a political campaign or those for which grant support is available from a senior level of government.

Capital Budgets and Their Importance

A capital budget should be a multi-year (generally five or ten years) financial plan that lays out the construction or acquisition timing for capital projects. At the same time, this plan should indicate how all capital expenditures are to be financed (own-source revenues, borrowing, grants, and so on). The capital budget is distinguished from the annual operating budget in that the latter provides for ongoing expenditures such as salaries, wages, benefits, heat, hydro, maintenance of buildings and infrastructure, and so on, whereas, the former lists the costs associated with the acquisition or rehabilitation of capital assets.

While it is generally recognized that separate capital and operating budgets (Bird 2005) are important if capital financing decisions are to be made in an efficient, transparent, and accountable manner, many small municipalities and some not so small often do not have separate budgets for capital and operating purposes. Not only does this create problems, but municipalities with more sophisticated capital budgeting techniques often face a range of problems as well. These, by the way, are not restricted to a particular country or municipality—they tend to be worldwide. First, future annual operating and maintenance costs are often ignored in making decisions on whether or not to spend on capital projects. This happens most frequently when capital expenditures are made in response to the availability of grants from senior governments or when decisions are made without the aid of a carefully developed and detailed capital budget.

Second, municipalities almost never consider opportunity costs (the value of forgone alternatives if a municipality chooses this project) in their capital budget, although many now take into consideration debt costs.

Third, municipalities all too frequently ignore depreciation or asset replacement costs in determining annual operating costs. This is especially important for those projects that are funded from user fees (water, sewers, etc.) and whose fee should include all costs (including those to replace the asset or facility) associated with the operation of the facility.

Fourth, capital programs are often not integrated with growth management objectives. For example, capital programs and budgets are often drawn up or altered without the consent or involvement of all local departments or officials. Lack of coordination between local departments and local government enterprises and special-purpose bodies such as utility commissions creates situations where capital maintenance or construction of a specific project may not be coordinated with other capital projects. This is often observed where roads, streets, and sidewalks are torn up shortly after rehabilitation or construction so that water and sewer mains may be replaced or rehabilitated. Uncoordinated efforts of this sort prove to be costly and a waste of public sector resources.

Fifth, problems abound if capital projects represent political compromise and compliance with legal approval dates (calendar) rather than well thought-out plans for community improvement. The notion that capital projects flow smoothly from well-organized community plans to implementation is often not borne out. Among the reasons for this is the likelihood that a number of development or management decisions are made in a public forum (e.g., public meetings) or influenced by public input from special interest groups. These forums or the public input, however, seldom consider all aspects of community planning such as the maintenance, renewal, and construction of new projects. Even though municipal government may include an integrated approach to capital programs and growth management objectives, this objective is often paid only lip-service. The sheer numbers of people involved and their interest in only selected aspects of the overall plan place constraints on the actual achievement of this objective.

Sixth, the largest proportion of capital spending tends to be devoted to short-term rehabilitation and renewal projects even though longer-term projects may generate greater net gains for society. Emphasis on short-term projects as opposed to longer-term projects arises for two reasons. First, the relatively short term of office for municipal politicians means that they are generally more interested in short-term projects because they coincide with their term of office and provide visible signs of political initiatives. Second, municipal decision makers are reluctant to become locked into long-term projects without guarantees of future funding and concern about the impact of future annual interest and debt repayment charges on local budgets.

Financing Instruments

Municipalities pay for capital expenditures from both internal and external revenue sources. Internal revenue sources include current operating revenues, reserves, and a variety of special charges. External sources include tax incremental financing, grants from senior governments, borrowing, and public-private partnerships.

The specific choice of a revenue source for financing capital projects is dictated by a variety of factors. It depends on a number of things including the location and size of the municipality or the province-/state-/region-wide agency that may borrow on behalf of all municipalities; their credit rating or creditworthiness; their fiscal capacity for meeting capital expenditures out of current revenues; their anticipated future expenditures, restrictions, controls, and constraints of senior levels of government; availability of financial markets for borrowing; and so on.[6]

Each instrument and its applicability for financing municipal infrastructure are evaluated within the framework of the benefits-based model of municipal finance. The underlying principles of this model have been discussed in Chap. 8 and will not be repeated here, other than to state that each instrument is addressed in terms of its ability to meet the criteria of efficiency, accountability, transparency, fairness, and ease of administration.

[6] For a more detailed discussion of financing in developing countries, see Bahl and Bird 2018, ch. 4.

Internal Sources

Internal revenue sources consist of general operating revenues from local taxes and user fees, earmarked taxes, reserves, and special charges.

General Operating Revenues

Local taxes and user fees when compared with borrowing generally fund proportionately more of all capital spending in rural municipalities, towns, and smaller cities. This is so, because in part, capital markets view smaller municipalities as being a higher risk when compared with larger cities and city-regions, hence making it more costly for the former to borrow. In addition, the relative importance of grants and greater reliance on pay-as-you-go financing for capital projects tends to be more predominant in small municipalities.

Under the benefits-based model of municipal finance, the use of annual operating revenues to finance capital spending is desirable to the extent that the benefits accrue to current users. Municipalities often use current operating revenues for assets with a short life expectancy (such as police cars and sometimes fire engines) or recurrent expenditures (such as the maintenance and upgrading of sidewalks, roads, street lighting, and parks). For non-recurrent expenditures (such as expenditures for libraries, museums, buildings, and other large fixed assets) or assets with a long life expectancy (such as sewer lines and water works), annual operating revenues are inappropriate because current taxpayers will fund projects that benefit future users—a violation of intergenerational equity.

Sometimes, municipalities generate revenues for capital projects through a "capital levy." This is generally done by assigning revenue from a few percentage points (two, three, or four) of the local tax rate (generally where there is a property tax) to a capital fund. The capital fund is called a reserve or reserve fund.

Earmarking

An earmarked tax or user fee, which is benefit based, is one whose revenue is dedicated to a specific expenditure or project; for example, revenues from a municipal fuel tax or road charges could be earmarked for road construction and public transit (Kitchen and Lindsey 2013), water and sewer rates for water and wastewater infrastructure (Kitchen 2017a; Fenn and Kitchen 2016), solid waste fees for collection and disposal, and so on.

Earmarking is generally supported, however, where there is a close link between the cost of a good or service provided by a capital asset and the revenue for funding it including its capital cost (Slack and Tassonyi 2017a). This permits a citizen to associate more closely the benefits received as reflected in the price paid with the costs of providing the good or service and decide for himself or herself whether the good or service is worth the tax or fee. This, in turn, leads to a greater likelihood that efficiency and accountability in local service responsibility will be achieved. In addition, more optimal and efficient investment decisions will likely ensue if the tax or charge is based on marginal cost pricing or multi-part pricing as may be the case (see Chap. 11). Earmarking can, however, be a disaster if it channels funds into services and activities where there is no clear link between those who use a service and those who pay for it.

Reserves

Financing capital projects through reserves (funds that are set aside in a separate fund for capital spending) is essentially the reverse of financing through borrowing. Instead of borrowing to finance capital expenditures and repaying this debt in the future, reserves or reserve funds reverse that timetable. A portion of current revenue is set aside annually in a special account(s) and allowed to accumulate until it is eventually withdrawn and used to finance or partially finance a specific capital project or projects. These reserves, while they are accumulating, are deposited in interest earning accounts.

Reserve funds may be either obligatory or discretionary. An obligatory reserve fund is created whenever a statute requires that monies be segregated from the general revenues of the municipality. In Canada, examples include revenues received under provisions of the *Development Charges Act*, *Planning Act*, or *Municipal Act*. Similar legislation exists in many countries. A municipal council may also establish discretionary reserve funds to earmark revenues for specific projects in the future.

Capital reserves are created for future acquisitions. As well, in most developed countries, municipalities have moved toward greater reliance on reserves for replacing assets such as buildings, facilities, vehicles, and equipment. While the use of reserves is growing, they tend to violate the principle of intergenerational equity because current users and taxpayers pay for capital expenditures that will be used by future generations.

Special Charges
In some countries, there are a number of special charges that may be imposed on properties to pay for local infrastructure. These include special assessments and local improvement charges which can be characterized as property-related specific benefit levies, development charges or lot levies which are prepayments for growth-related capital requirements, and other exactions that include density bonusing, linkage fees, value capture levies, and parkland dedication.

Assessments and Local Improvement Charges
A special assessment or local improvement charge (sometimes referred to as a betterment levy) is a specific levy added to the existing property tax on residential and/or commercial/industrial properties to pay for additional or improved capital facilities that border on these properties. The value of the charge is based on a specific capital expenditure in a particular year, but the costs may be spread over a number of years. Examples of capital projects often financed in this way include the construction or reconstruction of sidewalks, the initial paving or repaving of streets, and the installment or replacement of water mains, sanitary sewers, or storm sewers. In each instance, the abutting property is presumed to benefit from the local improvement and expected to bear a portion or all of the capital costs.

Special assessments do not generally contribute large sums of revenue to local budgets; they are, nevertheless, an important means of financing local improvement projects. Their structure may be designed so that project costs are allocated according to some measure of benefits received.

Municipalities use several types of special assessments, and the appropriate apportionment depends upon the base for assessment. The most common base, foot frontage of each benefiting property, is appropriate for projects whose cost per property increases with the width of the lot—sidewalks and roads, for example (Slack and Tassonyi 2017b). For projects such as neighborhood parks, whose benefits accrue to particular areas or blocks within a community, the best approach may be zone assessment, under which all properties in the serviced area pay the same share (Kitchen 2017b). Lot size has been suggested as a proxy for the depth of the lot in cases where the distance of the house from the street affects the cost of the service. Lot size, however, is neither a close proxy for lot depth nor does it necessarily bear a close relationship to the actual costs of constructing or replacing local services as they pass through or by abutting properties. A combination of foot-frontage charges and connection fees would more accurately reflect the capital costs of service provision in this situation (Kitchen and Tassonyi 2012).

Where local governments rely on property taxes, the criteria for responsible infrastructure financing would be satisfied if the charge on each property equaled the value of benefits that each property received from a local improvement project. In practice, however, calculating the increase in property values attributed to this project alone might require extensive checking and record keeping. In fact, this calculation could be extremely difficult, perhaps impossible.

Accurate apportionment of costs is especially difficult in the case where improvements are shared between an abutting property and the public at large. For example, a common approach in Canada to financing the capital costs of sidewalk construction or replacement is to charge the bordering properties between 40 percent and 60 percent of the total construction costs, leaving the municipality with the responsibility for raising the balance. Similar policies exist for other local improvement projects. Whether the percentage assigned to abutting properties truly measures the benefit of the project to those properties is a matter of conjecture. The important point, however, is that municipal governments are operating on the right principles when they assign some of the costs of most local improvements to abutting properties.

Development Charges

Development charges (sometimes referred to as lot levies, development cost charges, or off-site levies) are widely used by municipalities in Canada and the United States. The development charge is an important financing instrument for capital projects required to accommodate growth. The charge is a fixed dollar value per lot (or per hectare or acre) and is imposed on the developer to finance the off-site, growth-related capital costs[7] of new development. Historically, charges have been levied to finance the so-called hard services such as water supply systems, sewage treatment plants, stormwater systems, trunk mains, roads, and highways. More recently, coverage has expanded to include soft services such as libraries, recreational and cultural facilities, and schools.

[7] In Canada, on-site services such as local roads, sidewalks, street lighting, sewers, and water are the responsibility of the developer in most municipalities and are funded in subdivision approval plans that must be submitted, by developers, to municipal governments for approval prior to development.

A development charge corresponds best to the benefits received principle when the costs and benefits of the infrastructure for each property can be determined.

An efficient development charge must cover the full cost of delivering the service: a capacity component which covers the capital cost of constructing the facility, plus a location or distance/density charge that reflects the capital cost of extending the service to properties or neighborhoods (Kitchen and Tassonyi 2012). In fact, it has been argued that development charges are the fairest and most efficient way of paying for growth-related capital costs (Found 2019).

The most efficient development charges are those that vary by type of property (residential, commercial, or industrial), neighborhood, and distance from source of supply, so that each charge captures the extra cost of the infrastructure required to service the new growth. Many municipalities, however, do not use variable charges. Instead, they impose identical charges on all properties of a particular type, regardless of location. While administratively convenient, this practice levies the same charge on residential dwellings in low-density neighborhoods as it does on residential dwellings in high-density neighborhoods. This occurs even though the marginal cost per property of infrastructure projects in low-density areas is higher, which can lead to urban sprawl (Slack 2002). Likewise, levying similar charges on properties that absorb different amounts of resources, due to factors such as terrain or soil type, will encourage development in the wrong places. While it may be naive to expect municipal officials to calculate the infrastructure cost for each new property, costs could and should be calculated for each new development area or neighborhood, to discourage inefficient patterns of development (Slack and Tassonyi 2017a; Kitchen 2013; Kitchen and Tassonyi 2012).

One study on water and sewer pricing has taken a contrasting view on using development charges for new growth (Clayton 2014). In particular, it argued that development charges for these services should be terminated and replaced by user fees that are high enough to cover the costs of new infrastructure (which could be financed initially by borrowing). The argument continues that development charges are not used for other similar monopolistic-type community utility businesses such as natural gas. This change, the study continued, would lead to increased efficiency and conservation because each liter consumed would be priced more efficiently. At the moment, the development charge is a lumpsum up-front payment and, as such, there is no reason to recover this cost through annual water prices. Consequently, prices are lower than they would be if they captured all annualized costs on a per unit basis. Lower prices, it must be noted, lead to overconsumption and over-investment in infrastructure. As well, the report continues, it would be fairer because new users, through existing water rates, often pay a share of the costs of providing water to existing customers while new customers are not being supported likewise by existing users. It could also increase housing affordability, it maintains.

Other Exactions

Exactions consist of money, land, or construction projects provided to a municipal jurisdiction by a developer. Examples include value capture levies, density bonusing, linkage fees, and parkland dedication.

Value capture levies: Municipal spending on public infrastructure and subsequent zoning decisions may increase the commercial value of holdings of private landowners. Value capture levies permit the municipality to capture some of these economic rents.

The impact of value capture levies is similar to special assessments or betterment charges discussed above, so the various ways in which the value may be captured and the impact of each will not be repeated here. We have, however, included them as a separate topic because of their widespread use in a number of countries especially in Latin America (Smolka 2013).

Under this scheme, value added is captured by having the developer provide various facilities and infrastructure, or cash, in return for permission to undertake the development that the new municipal infrastructure makes possible. Value added may be captured through the taxation of commercial revenues generated from property that abuts the infrastructure or more likely, the municipality levies a special annual tax on the property that has acquired value added.

Value capture levies are often touted for mega-projects such as subway (underground) or rapid transit expansion. There are, however, a number of questions that any proposal to use value capture levies must address. For example, who are the real beneficiaries of the capital asset or infrastructure project? Are the beneficiaries of the project taxed twice—once through the charge on value added and the other, through higher annual property taxes because market value has risen (Youngman 2016)? What disincentive effects will the use of value capture levies create for private development? Answers to these questions are seldom clear-cut; yet the response is critical because of the ultimate impact on both the provision of public services and the incentives or disincentives to contribute to local economic activity.

Density Bonusing: These schemes have been used in large cities in North America since the 1960s and more recently in a number of cities outside of North America. Density for benefit agreements allows municipalities to secure from developers cash contributions or amenities in the form of subsidized housing, daycare centers, restoration of historic buildings, and so on, in return for permission to exceed currently prevailing height and density restrictions. While municipalities often use these as vehicles for acquiring additional services and infrastructure, they are far from problem free and without controversy.

Legislation controlling the use of bonusing schemes is often vague and subject to different interpretations, leading to decisions that are often made on an "ad hoc" basis with different outcomes at different times and for different people (Moore 2013). Planning principles that were used in establishing zoning legislation to restrict height and density are presumably designed to control urban development, servicing, and transportation. If these height and density restrictions are exchanged for "facilities, services or matters," one may very well ask why zoning legislation was enacted in the first instance. If a municipal statement with regard to maximum densities is defensible by a sound planning rationale, why should the need for a local day care center, additional subsidized housing, and restoration of historic facades alter that rationale? Trade-offs of this sort throw planning principles into question and may lead to abuse.

Indeed, the ad hoc nature of many negotiations along with the lack of transparency over how things are being handled has led to problems with a number of density bonusing schemes. Questions over the determination of benefits is often a subject of dispute, as is the allocation of public services provided by these schemes—should they be confined to the local area or pooled across the entire city (Friendly 2017; Moore 2013)? Determining the value of economic rent or the contribution that increased density makes to economic rent is difficult and often leads to people being suspicious of these schemes. Further, should developers be asked to pay what amounts to a "density tax" which in all likelihood will be passed on, at least in part, to future occupants?

Concerns such as these raise the issue of whether density bonusing schemes should be abolished or replaced. To answer this, one need to look at the rationale for their use. If they are needed to cover the cost of infrastructure to service the development, they are justifiable. If the benefits or amenities financed by the bonus are provided to local residents to compensate them for the negative consequences (externalities) created by the increased density (e.g., causing congestion), the scheme is justifiable. The reality is, however, that the amenities rarely benefit local residents (Moore 2013). If, on the other hand, they are used to achieve broader planning objectives, one might very well ask why these have not been included in the overall city plan in the first place. In reality, their current use in many cities may be a "cash grab" (much like the land transfer tax discussed in Chap. 9) for funding municipal services that benefit a much wider segment of the local population. For this reason, it is unlikely that their replacement or abolition will be seriously contemplated.

Linkage Fees: Linkage fees are used in a number of cities in the United States, but they are not permitted in many other countries (e.g., Canada). Linkage fees are charged to commercial developments with revenues used to assist in the funding of affordable housing. They are sometimes used where there is a presumed link between the growth in commercial space and the impact on the supply and demand for affordable housing. For example, it has been argued that the construction of commercial space reduces the supply of housing either through the demolition of existing housing or indirectly through higher land prices created by this development and the subsequent difficulty or inability of developers to provide affordable housing. On the demand side, low wage service jobs created by the commercial development will result in increased demand for affordable housing.

In some cases, the linkage fee is a mandatory requirement for project approval; in others, it applies only to extra density that a developer requests through an application for a zoning amendment. Linkage fees resemble development charges in being a charge on a developer to cover municipal costs created by the new development. In this case, however, the developer on whom the fee is levied neither creates the need for the service in question nor enjoys the benefits from that service. Hence the rationale that links these fees with low-cost housing is questionable. A more plausible rationale is one based on the economic rents that arise from public investment in infrastructure or public approval of increased density. According to this rationale, the investment generates windfall profits to the developer, and the municipality can appropriately tax away some of these profits without generating any inefficiency in the allocation of resources. Determining the size of these rents as has been noted earlier, however, is very difficult.

Parkland dedication. In some countries, developers may be required to set aside land within a development or elsewhere, for parks. For example, the *Provincial Planning Act* in the province of Ontario, Canada, permits (but does not require) municipalities to enact local legislation requiring developers to set aside up to 5 percent of the area of land for new residential development and up to 2 percent of the area of land in the case of new commercial/industrial development. In the province of Alberta, Canada, dedicated parkland amounts to 10 percent of the land area for new development. In lieu of this land requirement, however, the developer and municipality may agree to a cash payment equal to the market value of the stipulated amount of land. These funds, however, may be spent in whatever fashion the municipality chooses. In the province of British Columbia, Canada, land must be dedicated for elementary and secondary schools, as well.

Since parkland dedication is a charge on developers to pay for the costs of growth-related capital projects, its equity and efficiency effects are similar to those of development charges.

External Sources

The discussion here concentrates on tax incremental financing, grants from senior levels of government, borrowing, and public-private partnerships.

Tax Incremental Financing

Tax increment financing (TIF) is an economic development tool that was originally intended to encourage private investment in urban cores by stimulating downtown revitalization and encouraging brownfield remediation. This, it was argued, would make it easier for the core to compete with suburban and exurban areas, and it would lead to an improved urban quality of life and future tax revenues (Merk et al. 2012).

TIFs are widely used in the United States although California dissolved the legislation permitting them in 2011, primarily because of problems and abuses. In other countries, they tend to be used sparingly if at all (Merk et al. 2012). In Canada, for example, cities are permitted to use them in the province of Manitoba but none currently do so. Legislation in Alberta permits municipalities to use a form of TIF known as the "community revitalization levy." This permits municipalities to impose a property tax on the incremental assessed value of property in a community revitalization area. This revenue is then used to pay for infrastructure and other costs associated with the redevelopment of property in the community revitalization area. Municipalities can issue debentures to cover the costs of redevelopment and use the taxes collected on the increased assessed value to repay the debenture. Ontario municipalities may use tax increment equivalent grants (TIEGs). Under this program, municipalities can designate an area or the entire municipality as a community improvement project area. They can then implement a community improvement plan (CIP) with grants and/or loans which can, if the municipality chooses, be calculated on a tax increment basis. In other words, the municipality can offer developers a grant or loan that is based on the higher property tax that is generated from development (Kitchen and Tassonyi 2012). American-style TIFs, however, are far from common in Canada; in fact, they have only ever been used for two projects.

TIFs work in the following way. For a specific period of time (long enough to recover all costs of public funds used to redevelop the property), it divides property tax revenue from the designated area into two categories. Taxes based on pre-developed assessed property values are retained by the municipality for general use. Taxes on increased assessed values arising from redevelopment are deposited in a special increment fund with revenue from this fund used to repay municipal bonds that have been issued to finance public improvements in the redeveloped area. In other words, increases in property tax revenue from the redevelopment of an area are dedicated to financing public improvements in that area.

Supporters argue that there is no transfer of funds from a local government to subsidize a business, nor any transfer of tax dollars from one business to another, because development is financed from increases in the tax revenue that it generates. Unlike bonuses or tax abatements where taxes are reduced or forgiven on a particular property, property owners in a tax increment district (TID) incur the same local tax rate as property owners outside the district. Preferential treatment is granted only in that taxes from the increased assessment base of the TID are dedicated to financing local improvements. Dedicated tax dollars reduce the risk and uncertainty facing the private sector. If used to stimulate downtown development (infilling) or brownfield remediation, TIFs could discourage urban sprawl.

In recent years, TIFs have incurred a considerable amount of criticism (Youngman 2016). They were originally intended for "blighted" areas in urban cores where the development would not take place "but for" the incentive. In recent years, however, the requirement that the area be "blighted" has often been ignored, and TIFs have been used in more affluent neighborhoods and open spaces including farmlands where there is greater potential for property value increases and higher tax revenues (Youngman 2011). The "but for" test has also been compromised because many developments would have occurred anyway (Youngman 2011, 2016). Finally, TIFs target funds to a designated area and this targeting may be at the expense of areas on the periphery of the TIF district or at the expense of overall municipal growth.

TIFs' success as a financing instrument is mixed. While a number of studies found a positive impact in that property values in the TID areas increased faster than in the non-TID areas, a number of other studies found the opposite. Furthermore, in many cases, TIF revenue fell short of the forecasted amount, generally because of market conditions. In other words, when the economy is growing and times are good, TIFs have the capacity to service the debt. However, when times are bad and growth is stagnant, they fall short of being able to service the debt (Haider and Donaldson 2016).

Grants

Grant assistance from senior levels of government for capital infrastructure may be economically sound if the projects for which funds are provided generate spillovers or if they are projects in which donor governments have a specific interest or need. Here, conditional grants could be justified for partial or full funding with the funding rate set to match the proportion of benefits deemed to be in the form of spillovers or the rate could be set to match the proportionate interest of the donor government (Slack and Tassonyi 2017a).

One of the strongest arguments in support of grants from a senior level of government is for support of productivity-enhancing infrastructure (e.g., roads, bridges, transit, and educational facilities) that generate nation-wide benefits as opposed to infrastructure that improves the local quality of life (Dahlby and Jackson 2015). Even if this infrastructure does not generate spillover benefits to individuals in other communities, federal funding can be justified because the increase in federal tax revenues from the productivity improvement benefits citizens across the country through reduced tax rates or increased expenditures. As well, there are two other justifications; first, when fiscal stimulus is needed during a recession, such measures are more effective when instituted at the federal level. Second, federal infrastructure investment is justified where it fulfills international trade or environmental agreements (Dahlby and Jackson 2015).

If grants are used to fund more than this, they often create problems as the following notes. First, transfers can distort local decision-making. Conditional transfers require municipalities to spend the funds they receive according to the guidelines of senior governments. As well, they often require matching funds on the part of the recipient municipality even though some of them may not have the ability to meet this condition. A matching transfer, by lowering the price of some services, encourages municipalities to spend more on these services. This may mean that municipalities are spending in areas that may not be a priority for them.

Second, funding from senior governments can also lead to inefficient local revenue decisions. In particular, there is no incentive to use proper pricing policies for services provided where grants cover a large proportion of capital costs. Large grants for capital projects such as water and sewage treatment plants, for example, may remove all incentives to use volumetric pricing to reduce the demand for water. As well, they have removed the incentive to set up carefully thought-out asset management and asset cost-recovery programs. In other words, intergovernmental transfers may be working against any objective designed to set correct prices for delivering local services in an efficient and accountable manner (Kitchen 2017a).

Third, transfers may encourage people to stay in communities at risk. Capital grants may prop up communities that simply cannot survive on their own. Some small, rural, and remote communities, for example, may be unable to provide adequate levels of service at reasonable tax rates (Slack et al. 2003) or at reasonable user fees. On the expenditure side, low population density leads to high per capita expenditures because these communities cannot take advantage of economies of scale in service provision. As well, expenditures on roads, water, and sewer infrastructure may be higher because of harsh climatic conditions and terrain. On the revenue side, small rural and remote areas may not have sufficient capacity to finance local expenditures. The tax base is limited relative to local needs. The high cost of services means that user fees and local taxes are less likely to cover the full cost of service provision. Under these circumstances, senior levels of government often provide capital grant assistance so these municipalities can deliver services provided by local infrastructure. If service provision is considerably more expensive and higher levels of financial assistance are required, there is a question about the use of senior government resources to artificially support remote communities.[8] An important issue is whether communities that cannot survive in the absence of disproportionate senior government funding (when compared to other urban areas) should exist at all.

[8] The issue is not whether taxpayers in remote communities should be excluded from paying for municipal services. Clearly, they should pay at least some of the costs of services if accountability, fairness, and efficiency are to be achieved.

The argument against subsidizing remote areas is based on efficiency. Reliance on grant funding reduces the incentive for residents of these municipalities to leave and move to areas where there are greater employment and educational opportunities. Politics sometimes leads to a different conclusion, however, because people form emotional attachments to communities and politicians are reluctant to move them even though the long-term costs of not moving them are high.

Fourth, more generally, transfers reduce accountability. When two or more levels of government fund the same service, accountability problems arise. When users or taxpayers want to complain about the service, they are not sure which level of government is responsible for the problem. When the level of government making spending decisions (municipalities) is not the same as the level of government that raises the revenues to pay for them (a more senior level of government), the accountability is blurred. There is little incentive to be efficient when someone else is responsible for funding (Slack and Tassonyi 2017a). International experience tells us that governments are more likely to carry out their operating and capital expenditure responsibilities in a responsible, efficient, transparent, and accountable manner if they are also responsible for raising their own revenues to pay for these services (Bird 2001).

Economic arguments in support of capital grants are often not strong. Their use, where they are prevalent, should be conditional on recipient governments setting efficient user fees, prices, and local taxes for services provided by the funded or partially funded physical infrastructure (see discussion in section on proper pricing practices). This should include the proper use of asset management programs and the inclusion of asset replacement costs in the charge or price for services provided (Boadway and Kitchen 2018). Indeed, this should be compulsory regardless of whether or not the asset is financed by grants. The practice of fully expensing capital expenses in the year of acquisition and subsequent failure to depreciate the value of capital assets and to include this as cost to be recovered leads to underpricing of services provided and over-investment in the size of the capital asset or local infrastructure.

Borrowing

In many countries, long-term municipal borrowing is only permitted for capital projects. In some countries, however, local governments may borrow for both operating and capital purposes, although they may face constraints and restrictions on what they can borrow and for what purpose.

Borrowing for capital projects can be justified as long as the benefits from the project fall on future users. This matches the financing term with the asset's life span. Here, the project is financed by borrowed funds with annual principal and interest charges repaid out of future operating revenues.

Borrowing plays an important role in financing local government capital projects even where local government access to capital markets is controlled by senior governments. Indeed, local access to capital markets is often heavily restricted in both developing (Rodden et al. 2003) and developed countries (Bird and Slack 2004; Slack and Tassonyi 2017a). These controls are in place because the latter do not want to be responsible for unlimited municipal borrowing and possible "bailouts" or repayment of municipal debt. As well, unrestricted municipal access to capital markets may in some circumstances crowd out private-sector borrowing.

To illustrate, the following methods are often used to control municipal borrowing. First, borrowing is only permitted for capital projects approved by a senior level of government—the province, state, region, and so on. Second, prior approval by local taxpayers (through a referendum) is required for borrowing above a specific limit. Third, the amount of debt financing cannot exceed a specified percentage of municipal revenues. Fourth, annual debt-servicing costs (interest and principal repayment) are restricted to an upper limit such as a set percentage of annual budgetary revenue.

The vehicle through which long-term municipal debt (borrowing for capital projects) is conducted varies across countries and even within countries. In some, municipalities borrow on their own; in others, they borrow through an agency or department of a senior level of government. In still others they may borrow through a municipal finance agency specifically charged with the task of collecting requests from all municipalities within a country/state/province or region and issuing bonds on a pooled basis.

Issuing debt through a centralized agency generates significant benefits when compared with municipalities issuing their own debt. These agencies permit municipalities to pool their debt under a single umbrella, thus lowering interest costs. One Canadian study (Gilbert and Pike 1998) compared the cost of municipal borrowing for pooled versus stand-alone issues using data for municipalities in the province of Ontario. The findings indicated that pooled financing through a hypothetical municipal financing corporation or authority lowered costs significantly to municipal borrowers compared to the actual cost of capital for municipal issues in that province. The authors concluded that the benefits of participating in a municipal finance authority that issues ten-year debentures through investment dealers varied inversely with population size and credit rating. Issue size was not a factor.

Province-wide authorities often issue bonds on a regular basis; some only for municipalities but others issue bonds for schools, hospitals, utilities, and other municipal bodies. Administrative costs are funded in a variety of ways—by a senior level of government, by earnings on reserve funds, by participants, or by a combination of these. Loans are sometimes guaranteed by a senior level of government, thus lowering interest rates. Borrowing costs may also be lowered by adding credit enhancements at the provincial/state/regional level and by the ability to issue debt in national and international markets. The lower borrowing cost reflects the reduced cost of capital but also lower administration costs to issue debt. A centralized finance authority substitutes one contract with an underwriter for separate contracts between each borrower and debt issuer. As such, it economizes on transaction costs because it issues bonds more frequently than individual municipal borrowers and it operates in volatile capital markets that are subject to uncertainty. Finally, it can exercise a greater degree of flexibility over issue terms and costs to municipal clients.

The Decision to Borrow

Borrowing is generally favored when current revenues (local taxes and user fees, primarily) are insufficient to fund large expenditures on a "pay-as-you-go basis." Because capital expenditures are lumpy, a municipality may need millions of dollars to finance an infrastructure project in one year and nothing for a number of years. In addition, all infrastructure or capital spending must be completed before any benefits are derived. Borrowing smooths out the repayment of debt and permits municipalities to synchronize the costs and benefits of infrastructure over time. A project built today may provide benefits for the next 25 years. If funds are borrowed, the project is paid for over the next 25 years through annual repayment of principal and interest. This means that those who benefit from the facility (the users over the next 25 years) pay for the costs of the project. These charges are generally paid out of revenues from local taxes and user fees. Here, borrowing is more equitable and efficient because those who benefit from the infrastructure or project pay for it. Finally, since inflation reduces the cost of borrowing, it may be favored because debt repayment is made with funds that are worth less than the value of the funds initially borrowed.

Where municipal governments have access to bond markets and have well-developed municipal finance systems (proper budgetary and accounting systems, and reasonable autonomy in setting local taxes and user fees), arguments against borrowing and in support of "pay as you go" financing include savings in interest costs (available for spending on other projects), creation of debt capacity for more important future projects, and avoiding situations where future users have no say in the issuance of to-days debt yet they must pay for projects approved by today's policy makers.

Where municipal governments do not have ready access to bond markets or where municipal finance systems are not well developed, arguments against borrowing are much more basic. They are based on arguments such as inadequate municipal budgetary and accounting systems and therefore problems in qualifying for loans, approval procedures that are extensive and restrictive, lack of financial markets for issuing municipal bonds, and a general lack of municipal government creditworthiness.

Types of Bonds

There are a variety of borrowing instruments that are used in different countries. These include general obligation bonds (often called debentures), revenue bonds, and tax-exempt bonds. Within these categories, municipalities in some countries have issued bonds (sometimes called green bonds, or environmental impact bonds, or catastrophe bonds) that are restricted to financing infrastructure specifically designed to mitigate the impact of climate change. These bonds, however, are generally deemed to be riskier and less financially attractive to investors when compared with general obligation bonds that are backed by the overall revenue base of the local government (Carvalho 2018).

General Obligation Bonds

In Canada (except for the city of Toronto which can issue revenue bonds), municipalities may only issue general obligation bonds—often called serial or sinking-fund debentures. In Italy, by comparison, municipalities are not permitted to use general obligation bonds. In the United States, municipalities may use these bonds as well as other bonds.

Serial debentures are issued for a fixed number of years with a certain number reaching maturity and being redeemed by the municipality or provincial agency each year. Serial debentures may take different forms including annuity serials, straight serials, and irregular serials.

Annuity serials are similar to a home mortgage in that the total interest and principal repayment is roughly the same throughout the life of the security. In the early years, the interest portion of the payment is higher and in later years the principal portion is higher. Straight serials require annual principal payments of approximately equal amounts. Interest payments are higher in the early years and decline as the securities approach maturity. Irregular serials involve a "balloon maturity" date, that is, a significant portion of the principal is postponed until the full term of the issue is reached.

In choosing a particular type of serial debenture, a number of considerations must be weighed. Annuity serials may be favored in instances where capital projects must be built with a capacity large enough to service additional users in the future. Examples of municipal projects that may be financed in this way include water and sewage plants, fire stations, and police stations, all of which are constructed on the basis of meeting a current and potentially expanding population base. Under this financial arrangement, a municipality is able to avoid heavy debt service charges in the early years of the project and to redistribute the costs in a more equitable and manageable way.

Straight serial debentures carry heavier debt charges in earlier years than in later years (see Table 7.4 for a comparison of debt charges on straight versus annuity serials). As far as the municipality is concerned, this has the advantage of lowering interest charges and freeing up the municipality for future borrowing without increasing annual debt-servicing costs. For most capital projects, however, this method of financing violates the rationale of equating those who receive the benefits from the capital project with those who bear the cost. Indeed, acceptance of this criterion provides a stronger basis for utilizing annuity rather than straight serials for most capital projects. Unfortunately, financing to equate future beneficiaries with those who pay the costs is seldom part of the decision-making once a municipality has decided to borrow through serial debentures. Instead, simplicity and ease of marketing along with minimizing the debt-servicing charge are of prime importance. To meet these objectives, straight serial debentures have a simpler maturity schedule, are easier to understand, and quicker to market than annuity serials. As well, the nature of the money market may dictate the issuance of straight serials rather than annuity serials if debt service charges are to be minimized. For example, the interest rate on straight serials may vary with their maturity dates. If longer-term interest rates are noticeably lower than shorter-term interest

Table 7.4 A comparison of debt service charges on $1 million over ten years using straight and annuity serial debenture financing

Payable at end of year	*Straight serial debentures*				*Annuity serial debentures*			
	Outstanding principal	*Principal repayment*	*Interest payment*[a]	*Annual debt charges*	*Outstanding principal*	*Principal repayment*	*Interest payment*[a]	*Annual debt charges*[b]
	$	$	$	$	$	$	$	$
1	1,000,000	100,000	100,000	200,000	1,000,000	62,745	100,000	162,745
2	900,000	100,000	90,000	190,000	937,155	69,020	93,726	162,745
3	800,000	100,000	80,000	180,000	868,236	75,921	86,824	162,745
4	700,000	100,000	70,000	170,000	792,314	83,514	79,231	162,745
5	600,000	100,000	60,000	160,000	708,800	91,865	70,880	162,745
6	500,000	100,000	50,000	150,000	616,936	101,051	61,694	162,745
7	400,000	100,000	40,000	140,000	515,884	111,157	51,588	162,745
8	300,000	100,000	30,000	130,000	404,727	122,272	40,473	162,745
9	200,000	100,000	20,000	120,000	282,455	134,499	28,246	162,745
10	100,000	100,000	10,000	110,000	147,956	147,949	14,796	162,745
Total	–	1,000,000	550,000	1,550,000	–	1,000,000	627,456	1,550,000

Source: Calculations completed by authors

[a] 10 percent of outstanding principal

[b] Total debt charges = Principal * $[i(1 + i)^n]/[1 + i)^n - 1]$ where i = interest rate and n = number of years

rates, then the issuance of straight serial debentures provides a means of lowering interest charges by bringing a larger proportion of the principal under the lower interest rate. On the other hand, if the demand for short-term money is abnormally high, there is little advantage in competing for it, unless of course, the municipality assumes that interest rates are going to rise in the future in which case it may wish to finance through borrowing now rather than later.

Irregular serials, known as "balloon issues," are used occasionally where there is uncertainty as to future requirements for servicing the debt after construction costs have been met. When combined with the creation of reserve funds, these serials can be justified as an adequate basis for funding certain local capital projects.

By comparison, sinking-fund debentures are issued to mature at a fixed future date. Each year the municipality pays an agreed sum of money to a trustee who, in turn, invests the portion that is not immediately applied toward paying the debt or discharging the obligation.

Where these debentures are permitted, municipalities or their borrowing agencies generally place greater reliance on serial rather than sinking-fund debentures. Sinking funds are more expensive and more difficult to administer because they require expert advice on the investment of funds along with frequent actuarial computations to ensure that adequate funds are available to cover the principal repayment at maturity. As well, types of securities that can be held in sinking funds are often closely restricted by senior government regulations and they frequently generate less revenue than can be earned on other safe securities. The inflexible maturity dates of sinking-fund debentures seem to create more difficulties in marketing these securities when compared with serial debentures.

Sinking funds, however, provide at least one benefit and that is the opportunity for municipalities or their debt-issuing agencies to sell their own securities to the sinking fund. This is especially advantageous when market conditions do not favor the public issuance of new debentures; however, it appears that this advantage may not be sufficient to outweigh the substantial administrative costs associated with the operation of sinking funds.

Revenue Bonds

Revenue bonds are permitted in the United States but not in Canada except for the city of Toronto. They are the only type of bond that Italian municipalities are permitted to use. They finance infrastructure that generates a revenue stream and where the beneficiaries (consumers of the service provided by the asset) can be identified such as in water and sewer consumption. These bonds are backed by future revenue (e.g., raised by user fees) generated by the funded project. To be marketable, revenue bonds are secured by revenue streams that are adequate, predictable, and spread over the project's life. Their credit quality depends on the financial strength of the underlying capital asset. Where revenue bonds are secured by specific revenue sources and not by the local governments' unlimited taxing power, their credit quality is sometimes viewed as lower than that of similarly rated general government bonds and hence, higher interest rates are needed. To eliminate possible interest rate differentials on revenue and general government bonds, municipal governments may guarantee them. Within the benefits-based model for financing local capital infrastructure, revenue bonds are an important instrument. They are fair, efficient, and accountable because those who benefit from the service pay for it.

Tax-Exempt Bonds

Many municipalities in the United States issue tax-exempt bonds. Tax-exempt bonds pay interest income and the recipient of this income is not subject to income taxation. For the issuing municipality or agency, bonds carry interest rates that are below market rates. For example, a potential bond buyer in a 40 percent marginal tax bracket (personal income tax) may be indifferent between buying a taxable bond paying interest at the rate of 7.5 percent and a tax-exempt bond paying interest at the rate of 4.5 percent assuming that both bonds are equally risky or riskless. If, however, the interest rate affixed to the tax-exempt bond were above 4.5 percent, the municipal bond would be more attractive to the investor when compared with the alternatives.

Tax-exempt bonds have been criticized, however, because they are inequitable; that is, they provide more income tax relief to higher-income taxpayers than they do to lower-income taxpayers, and because they distort capital markets.

Infrastructure Banks

The growing need for a reliable base for financing infrastructure in some countries has led to a growing interest in the establishment of infrastructure banks or iBanks. Much of this interest is driven by their emergence and use in the United Kingdom and the United States.

Infrastructure banks are capitalized by a combination of funds provided by senior levels of government and the private sector. Once established, funds are provided through loans for a range of eligible public sector infrastructure projects. These banks, depending on their design, have been touted to have a couple of advantages. First, they could offer loans at interest rates that are below market rates. Second, they could provide technical assistance and expertise to municipalities and other public sector agencies that do not have the capacity to deal with projects themselves (Siemiatycki 2016).

Whether or not an infrastructure bank is needed in a country or region of a country may depend on existing agencies. If a public or private agency or corporation already exists with a mandate to finance and manage large infrastructure projects, the creation of an infrastructure bank could simply be a duplication of what already exists. In fact, this kind of duplication is a distinct possibility in the province of Ontario, Canada, where the federal government recently initiated legislation to set up a federal infrastructure bank when the province already has a crown corporation (Infrastructure Ontario) with a mandate that is basically the same as the federal mandate. The provincial corporation already has a solid record in offering short-term and long-term loans for eligible public sector infrastructure projects at affordable rates. It provides access to capital market financing without fees or commissions. The length of the loan may be structured to match the life of the asset; hence, there is no need to refinance over the life of the loan. Loans may be available for any depreciable asset. Finally, the provincial body offers technical expertise and assistance for municipalities about to engage in infrastructure investment (Kitchen and Lindsey 2013, p. 31).

Public-Private Partnerships[9]

Public-private partnerships (PPPs or P3s) are often viewed by politicians as a way to raise money for cash-strapped governments. Such enthusiasm, however, must be tempered with the reality that P3s are not a source of free money since the private partner must be repaid for any financing it provides. The following quote illustrates this point:

> Smart governments have come to realize that to rely on a P3 for purely financial reasons is a bad reason. As a method to raise funds, P3s can run into the trap of so-called asset monetization, whereby a government off-

[9] Public-private partnerships are also discussed in Chap. 2 on service delivery in *Local Public, Fiscal and Financial Governance: An International Perspective.*

> loads onto a private partner the operation and maintenance of an … asset simply in order to raise cash for immediate use or balance sheet embellishment. (Gómez-Ibáñez 2011, p. 30)

A P3 is a contractual arrangement between the public sector and a private provider. The public sector's role should be to facilitate, regulate, and guarantee provision of an asset, and the private sector's role should be to do one or more of the following with the public sector picking up whatever the private sector does not do—design, finance, build, operate, and maintain the infrastructure in a formalized partnership agreement (Siemiatycki 2017).

P3s vary widely in structure, but the most common models or variations include the following. First, the "Design-Build-Finance-Maintain-Operate" (DBFMO) model. Here, the private sector looks after everything including design, building, financing, and provision of management services and operations under a long-term agreement. This arrangement has the potential for transferring significant project risks to the private-sector partner including construction cost overruns, the risk that the asset may not operate as expected (because of breakdowns in service provision) once it is completed, and the possibility that the demand for the service may not meet expectations thus leading to lower revenue than anticipated. At the end of the agreement, the facility is transferred to the local government who either contracts out service delivery or provides it directly.

Second, the "Design-Build-Finance-Maintain" (DBFM) model leaves the public sector with more responsibility than the above model. Here, the private sector looks after the design, build, finance, and maintenance of the asset or facility under a long-term agreement while the public sector controls the provision of the service. This is commonly used for large urban rail transit projects.

Third, there is the "Design-Build-Finance" (DBF) model. The private sector designs, builds, and finances the infrastructure for a fixed fee and transfers it to the public sector. The risk of cost overruns is borne by the private sector. In this model, the private-sector investor is paid for the costs of design and construction following substantial completion of the build. The municipality is then responsible for providing the service.

Policy makers and practitioners generally acknowledge that P3s can generate significant efficiencies, better cost controls, stronger operational knowledge, and greater operational flexibility when used to deliver projects that have passed a rigorous and thorough value for money (VfM) assessment (Vining and Boardman 2008; Siemiatycki and Farooqi 2012). A VfM compares the net present value (NPV) of the P3 option with the NPV of a comparable project delivered through conventional procurement methods. While not a straightforward or easy task, the VfM is intended to capture all quantitative and qualitative factors affecting both costs and benefits. A critical issue in this calculation is the way in which risks are assigned to the public and private operators.

Two survey papers examined the success of a number of P3s in Canada. Vining and Boardman (2008) included ten case studies of P3s across Canada. It concluded that "Canadian governments have sometimes found it difficult to effectively reduce either their total costs (that is, the sum of production and transaction costs) or their budgetary risk exposure (by transferring revenue risk) through the use of P3s" (p. 11). This led the authors to conclude that P3s are not socially desirable for all public infrastructure projects, but may work well under certain circumstances; for example, where governments have not attempted to transfer revenue risk (uncertainty over future revenue streams) to the private sector, where projects have required specialized knowledge that the public sector lacks, and where governments have been able to transfer construction risks (e.g., cost overruns and construction delays) at something close to a fixed price. These projects are close to design-build or build contracts, thus suggesting that governments should limit their P3 initiatives to infrastructure projects of this type or else do a much better job of reducing transactions costs in contract design.

A second and more recent study by Siemiatycki and Farooqi (2012) conducted a VfM assessment for 28 provincially approved P3 projects in Ontario from 2007 to 2010. This study noted that the base cost of P3s was, on average, 16 percent higher than conventional tendered contracts. The higher cost was attributed to higher interest rates paid by private borrowers and a premium for taking on greater project risks arising from potential cost overruns, construction delays, and so on. Transaction costs for lawyers and consultants added another 3 percent to private-sector costs.

Conventional government procurement practices also face a number of risks. As with P3s, these include cost overruns, construction delays, design flaws, and fluctuating revenues. To account for these risks and to attempt to establish a level playing field for comparative purposes, a risk premium that averaged 49 percent of base costs was added to the more conventional alternatives. It was this risk premium that drove the VfM in favor of a P3 for each of the 28 projects. A major concern here is that there is no empirical evidence to support such a large risk premium. Siemiatycki and Farooqi emphasized this concern and it was also highlighted by Ontario's Auditor General (McKenna 2012). Hence, no one really knows whether Ontario's taxpayers have been and are getting the best value for their money under a P3.

Based on international experience, city infrastructure projects that may be suitable for a P3 include roads and public transit, water and wastewater treatment systems, and solid waste disposal as long as they pass a rigorous and carefully constructed VfM assessment. A P3 may be most appropriate when outputs can be clearly defined (Grimsey and Lewis 2004) where risks are correctly assigned to each party (Ugate et al. 2012), where proper incentives can be introduced for encouraging private partners to get better value and if there is clear communication and accountability between the private and public partners. Where P3 contracts are properly structured and based on performance measures, they can lead to improved local governance including increased accountability, transparency, and value for money.

Because P3s are monopolistic in nature, there is a role for government in monitoring their behavior. Governments should set the terms and conditions for service delivery, funding, and quality of service and establish performance standards or measures. Government could even provide the pricing structure to be used for services provided by the infrastructure (volumetric pricing for water and sewers, tolls and other charges for roads and public transit, user fees for solid waste disposal) or set up a price regulation or monitoring system. Determining optimal prices for services, however, is particularly tricky for road and public transit networks when some links cannot be priced efficiently, or if control of the network is divided among multiple governments or institutions (Lindsey 2012).

Letting a private partner operate a P3 can raise transactions costs because of the need to monitor service quality. However, it has the potential advantage that user fees are more politically acceptable because the public expects private-sector services to be priced (Vining and Boardman 2008). Prices should be regulated, however, in such a way that they do not prevent flexible or innovative pricing structures.

Summary

Growing concern over the state of local government infrastructure in both developing and developed countries has highlighted the importance of capital expenditures and the way in which they are financed. As municipalities expand and grow older, resources must be devoted to the expansion or replacement of their capital stock. Water plants and sewage treatment facilities, cultural and recreational facilities, transportation, and communication facilities—all must be updated and expanded. Brownfield remediation must be addressed, and "blighted" areas of cities revitalized and redeveloped. Capital spending on these facilities, however, should not be initiated by a local or municipal council until it has carefully and thoroughly articulated a multi-year capital budget that lays out current and future capital expenditure requirements and the way in which these expenditures are to be financed.

Infrastructure funds may be drawn from a variety of internal sources including operating revenues (local taxes and user fees), earmarked taxes, reserves, special charges consisting of specific assessments, development charges, and other exactions made up of value capture levies, density bonusing, linkage fees, and parkland dedication. External capital funding may come from tax incremental financing, grants, long-term borrowing in the form of general obligation bonds, revenue bonds, tax-exempt bonds, and public-private partnerships.

Evaluation of these instruments has been completed by reference to the benefits received model of public finance. Whenever a direct link is made between the users of a service and its funding, one observes a more efficient use of resources, better accountability, increased transparency, and improved fairness. The choice of financing instrument and the way it is employed has an impact on both the level of services provided by infrastructure and the size and range of the infrastructure itself. Incorrect or inadequate prices (user fees) and taxes result in a use of services that is far from efficient or optimal and, subsequently, a level of infrastructure that is too large or too small.

As for the range of financing instruments, operating revenues are appropriate for assets that are short lived; special property charges or exactions are useful for assets that benefit specific areas of a municipality; reserves are often used but they generally violate the principle of intergenerational equity because current users and taxpayers pay for capital expenditures that will be used by future generations; development charges with variable rates are good for growth-related infrastructure; tax incremental financing can assist in the remediation of brownfields and blighted areas; borrowing is preferred for infrastructure that benefits future generations; grants may have merit for local infrastructure that generates positive externalities and for projects in which the donor government has an interest; and public-private partnerships may be preferred for large infrastructure projects.

References

Antunes, Pedro, Kip Beckman, and Jacqueline Johnson. 2010. *The Economic Impact of Public Infrastructure in Ontario*. Conference Board of Canada. Ottawa: Canada. http://www.conferenceboard.ca/e-library/abstract.aspx?did=3492. Accessed 20 July 2018.

Bahl, Roy, and Richard M. Bird. 2018. *Fiscal Decentralization and Local Finance in Developing Countries*. Northampton, MA: Studies in Fiscal Federalism and State-Local Finance, Edward Elgar Publishing.

Bird, Richard M. 2001. *Subnational Revenues: Realities and Prospects*. Washington, DC: World Bank Institute.

———. 2005. *Evaluating Public Expenditures: Does It Matter How They Are Financed?* International Tax Paper 0506. Toronto: Institute for International Business, Rotman School of Management, University of Toronto.

Bird, Richard M., and Enid Slack. 2004. *Fiscal Aspects of Metropolitan Governance*. International Tax Paper 0401. Toronto: Institute for International Business, Rotman School of Management, University of Toronto.

Boadway, Robin, and Harry Kitchen. 2018. A Fiscal Federalism Framework for Financing Infrastructure. Chap. 5 in *Canadian Federalism and Infrastructure*, ed. John R. Allan, David L.A. Gordon, Kyle Hanniman, Andre Juneau and Robert A. Young. Montreal: McGill-Queen's University Press.

Brodhead, John, Jesse Darling, and Sean Mullin. 2014. *Crisis and Opportunity: Time for a National Infrastructure Plan for Canada*. Canada 2020 Foundation, Ottawa. http://canada2020.ca/crisis-opportunity-time-national-infrastructure-plan-canada/. Accessed 20 Sept 2018.

Carvalho, Gustavo. 2018. *Climate Finance for Canadian Cities: Is Debt Financing a Viable Alternative?* IMFG Papers on Municipal Finance and Governance Series, No. 37, University of Toronto. http://munkschool.utoronto.ca/imfg/resources/.

Clayton, Frank. 2014. *A New Direction for Funding Growth-Related Water and Wastewater Infrastructure in the Greater Toronto Area and Hamilton*. Toronto: Centre for Urban Research and Land Development (CUR), Ryerson University.

Dahlby, Bev, and Emily Jackson. 2015. *Striking the Right Balance: Federal Infrastructure Transfer Programs, 2002–2015*. SPP Research Papers 8(36). Calgary: School of Public Policy, University of Calgary.

Fenn, Michael, and Harry Kitchen. 2016. *Bringing Sustainability to Ontario's Water Systems: A Quarter-Century of Progress, with Much Left to Do*. A Study for the Ontario Sewer and Watermain Construction Association. www.OSWCA.org.

Found, Adam. 2019. *Development Charges in Ontario: Is Growth Paying for Growth?* IMFG Papers on Municipal Finance and Governance Series, No. 41, University of Toronto. http://munkschool.utoronto.ca/imfg/resources/.

Friendly, Abigail. 2017. *Land Value Capture and Social Benefits: Toronto and Sao Paulo Compared*. IMFG Papers on Municipal Finance and Governance Series, No. 33, University of Toronto. http://munkschool.utoronto.ca/imfg/resources/.

Gilbert, M., and R. Pike. 1998. Financing Local Government Debt in Canada: Pooled Versus Stand-Alone Issues—An Empirical Study. *Canadian Public Administration* 42: 529–552.

Gillen, David. 2001. Public Capital, Productivity, and the Linkages to the Economy: Transportation Infrastructure. In *Building the Future: Issues in Public Infrastructure in Canada*, ed. Aidan R. Vining and John Richards, 36–72. Toronto: C.D. Howe Institute. Policy Paper 34.

Gómez-Ibáñez, José A. 2011. Quoted in "Public-Private Pragmatism, Motion Magazine". International Transport Forum, Issue 1, p. 30.

Grimsey, Darrin, and Mervyn K. Lewis. 2004. *Public Private Partnerships*. Northampton, MA: Edward Elgar.

Haider, Murtaza, and Liam Donaldson. 2016. *Can Tax Increment Financing Support Transportation Infrastructure Investment?* IMFG Papers on Municipal Finance and Governance Series, No. 25, University of Toronto. http://munkschool.utoronto.ca/imfg/resources/.

Holden, Michael, and Casey Vander Ploeg. 2013. *At the Intersection: The Case for Sustained and Strategic Public Infrastructure Investment*. Calgary: Canada West Foundation.

Kitchen, Harry. 2013. Property Tax: A Situation Analysis and Overview. Chap. 1 in *A Primer on Property Tax Administration and Policy*, ed. William J. McCluskey, Gary C. Cornia and Lawrence C. Walters, 1st ed. John Wiley & Sons Ltd.

———. 2017a. Paying for Water in Ontario Cities: Where Have We Come From And Where Do We Go? Chap. 3 in *Financing Infrastructure: Who Should Pay?*, ed. Richard M. Bird and Enid Slack, 53–86. Montreal: McGill-Queens University Press. Published for the Institute on Municipal Finance and Governance at the Munk School of Global Affairs.

———. 2017b. *Financing City Parks in Canada: What Might Be Done?* A Paper Prepared for Park People, Toronto, March. https://parkpeople.ca/park-people-reports.

Kitchen, Harry, and Robin Lindsey. 2013. *Financing Roads and Public Transit in the Greater Toronto and Hamilton Area*. Residential and Civil Construction Alliance of Ontario. www.rccao.com.

Kitchen, Harry, and Almos Tassonyi. 2012. Municipal Taxes and User Fees. Chap. 9 in *Tax Policy in Canada*, ed. Heather Kerr, Ken McKenzie and Jack Mintz. Toronto: Canadian Tax Foundation.

Lindsey, Robin. 2012. Road Pricing and Investment. *Economics of Transportation* 1 (1–2): 49–63.

McKenna, Barrie. 2012. The Hidden Price of Public-Private Partnerships. *The Globe and Mail*, October 15, p. B-1. Accessed 10 Aug 2018.

Merk, Olaf, Stéphane Saussier, Carine Starapoli, Enid Slack, and Jay-Hyung Kim. 2012. *Financing Green Urban Infrastructure*. OECD Regional Development Working Papers 2012/10, OECD Publishing. http://dc.doi.org/10.1787/5k92p0c6j6r0-en. Accessed 20 April 2014.

Moore, Aaron. 2013. *Trading Density for Benefits: Toronto and Vancouver Compared*. IMFG Papers on Municipal Finance and Governance Series, No. 13, University of Toronto. http://munkschool.utoronto.ca/imfg/resources/.

OECD Territorial Reviews. 2009. *Toronto Canada, Preliminary Version*. Paris: Organization for Economic Co-Operation and Development.

Rodden, Jonathan, Jennie Litvack, and Gunnar Eskeland, eds. 2003. *Fiscal Decentralization and Hard Budget Constraints*. Cambridge, MA: MIT Press.

Siemiatycki, Matti. 2016. *Implementing a Canadian Infrastructure Investment Agency*. Residential and Civil Construction Alliance of Ontario. www.rccao.com.

———. 2017. The Role of User Fees in Urban Public-Private Partnerships: Canada in a Global Perspective. Chap. 8 in *Financing Infrastructure: Who Should Pay?*, ed. Richard M. Bird and Enid Slack. Montreal: McGill-Queens University Press.

Siemiatycki, Matti, and Naeem Farooqi. 2012. Value for Money and risk in Public-Private Partnerships. *Journal of the American Planning Association* 78 (3): 286–299.

Slack, Enid. 2002. *Municipal Finance and the Pattern of Urban Growth*. Commentary. Toronto: C.D. Howe Institute.

Slack, Enid, and Almos Tassonyi. 2017a. Financing Urban Infrastructure in Canada: Overview, Trends and Issues. Chap. 2 in *Financing Infrastructure: Who Should Pay?*, ed. Richard M. Bird and Enid Slack. Montreal: McGill-Queens University Press.

———. 2017b. *Financing Urban Infrastructure in Canada: Who Should Pay?* IMFG Papers on Municipal Finance and Governance Series, No. 34, University of Toronto. http://munkschool.utoronto.ca/imfg/resources/.

Slack, Enid, Larry Bourne, and Meric Gertler. 2003. *Small, Rural and Remote Communities: The Anatomy of Risk*. Research Paper 18 Prepared for the Panel on the Role of Government in Ontario. http://www.law-lib.utoronto.ca/investing/index.htm. Accessed 20 July 2004.

Smetanin, Paul, et al. 2014. *Ontario Infrastructure Investment: Federal and Provincial Risks & Rewards*. Commissioned by Residential and Civil Construction Alliance. http://www.rccao.com/news/files/RCCAO_Ontario-Infrastructure-Investment_July2014-WEB.pdf. Accessed 10 Sept 2016.

Smolka, Martin O. 2013. *Implementing Value Capture in Latin America: Policies and Tools for Urban Development*. Cambridge, MA: Lincoln Institute of Land Policy.

The Institute for Competitiveness and Prosperity. 2005. *Taxing Smarter for Prosperity*. Working Paper 7. Toronto: The Institute.

Ugate, Carlos, Gabriel Gutierrez, and Nick Phillips. 2012. *A Roadmap to Funding Infrastructure Development*. Discussion Paper 2102-09. Prepared for the Roundtable on: Public Private Partnerships for Funding Transport Infrastructure. https://www.oecd-ilibrary.org/.../a-roadmap-to-funding-infrastructure-development. Accessed 8 June 2018.

Vining, Aidan R., and Anthony E. Boardman. 2008. Public-Private Partnerships in Canada: Theory and Evidence. *Canadian Public Administration* 51 (1): 9–44.

Youngman, Joan. 2011. *TIF at a Turning Point: Defining Debt Down*. Cambridge, MA: Lincoln Institute on Land Policy.

———. 2016. *A Good Tax: Legal and Policy Issues for the Property Tax in the United States*. Cambridge, MA: Lincoln Institute of Land Policy.

CHAPTER 8

Local Taxation

Introduction

Over the past few decades, local governments in almost every developed country and many developing countries have faced a similar pattern—declining grants from senior governments, devolution of additional funding responsibilities, and a limited tax base that may not be sufficient to meet future fiscal challenges and objectives. This, in turn, raises a number of issues around local taxation, many of which are discussed in this chapter.

The section "Local Taxation: An International Comparison" provides an international comparison of local taxes. In particular, it reviews the pattern of local taxation in OECD (Organisation for Economic Co-operation and Development) countries and comments on the fiscal autonomy that local governments have in making their tax decisions.

The section "Financing Model for Local Government" outlines a financing model that is used to evaluate a number of issues around local taxation. Using this model, the section "Issues in Local Taxation" evaluates the following: which local tax or taxes should be used—is one tax preferred over another? Who should set local tax rates? Should these rates be uniform or differentiated across a taxing jurisdiction? Should local tax rates be regulated? Should local government tax businesses? Could local and metropolitan governments rely on different taxes? The section "Summary" summarizes the chapter.

H. Kitchen et al., *Local Public Finance and Economics*,
https://doi.org/10.1007/978-3-030-21986-4_8

Local Taxation: An International Comparison

Since most locally generated revenues come from local taxes (user fees and charges, discussed in Chap. 11, are the other major source of locally generated revenue), the following two sections provide data on a number of features of local taxation in 8 federal countries (a multi-order governance structure with all orders of government having some independent as well as shared decision-making responsibilities), 1 regional country (quasi-federal), and 25 unitary (a single or multi-tiered government in which effective control of government functions rests with the central government) OECD countries.

Patterns of Local Taxation

Table 8.1 illustrates the relative importance of a range of local taxes in OECD countries in 2014 (the last year for which data were available at time of writing). From this table, the following may be noted. First, income taxes (corporate and personal) are the most important source of local tax revenue in 12 countries (column 2). In Denmark, Finland, Norway, Sweden, Luxembourg, Iceland, and Switzerland, income taxes account for more than 80 percent of local tax revenue. In 15 countries, by comparison, local governments do not have direct access to income tax revenue of any sort.

Second, local sales taxes (in various forms but referring generally to taxes on goods and services that are sold) are the most important source of tax revenue in three countries (Chile, Hungary, and Turkey). They generate between 25 percent and 75 percent of total local tax revenue in eight countries (column 3). At the other extreme, local sales taxes are nonexistent in 7 countries and produce less than 10 percent of local revenue in another 13 countries.

Third, property taxes are the most important source of local tax revenue in 18 countries (column 4). They account for more than 90 percent of all local tax revenue in seven countries (Australia, Canada, Ireland, New Zealand, the United Kingdom, Greece, and Israel). While local governments in every country get at least a little money from property taxes, there are only three (Finland, Sweden, and Luxembourg) where property taxes account for less than 10 percent of all local taxes.

Fourth, local governments in France, Italy, Mexico, Korea, and Slovak Republic get more than 10 percent of all tax revenue from other local taxes (column 5), mainly on businesses. None of the other countries come close to this.

Table 8.1 Relative importance of local taxes in OECD countries, 2014

Countries	*Tax sources as a % of total local tax revenues*				*Local taxes as a % of GDP*	*Local taxes as a % of all taxes*[e]
(1)	*Income*[a] *(2)*	*Sales*[b] *(3)*	*Property*[c] *(4)*	*Other*[d] *(5)*	*(6)*	*(7)*
Federal						
Australia	0	0	100	0	1	3.5
Austria	73.7	9.6	14.6	2.7	1.3	3.2
Belgium	31.2	8.2	60.6	0	2.1	4.6
Canada	0	1.7	97.2	1.2	3.2	10.3
Germany	79.4	6	14.5	0.2	2.9	8.2
Mexico	0	3	83.5	13.6	0.2	1.6
Switzerland	82.8	0.4	14.7	2.1	4.1	15.3
United States	6.1	21.2	70.1	0	3.7	14.1
Unweighted average	*34.2*	*6.3*	*56.9*	*2.5*	*2.3*	*7.6*
Regional country						
Spain	17.9	34.2	42.9	5	3.6	10
Unitary						
Chile	0	58.6	41.3	0	1.4	7.6
Czech Republic	0	45	55	0	0.4	1.2
Denmark	88.7	0	11.3	0	12.4	25
Estonia	0	14.9	85.1	0	0.3	1.1
Finland	92.8	0	7.1	0.1	10.3	23.5
France	0	23.6	51.8	24.7	6	13
Greece	0	6.4	93.6	0	1.1	3
Hungary	0	80.5	19.5	0	2.1	5.7
Iceland	82.3	0.8	17	0	9.6	24.5
Ireland	0	0	91.5	8.5	0.8	2.8
Israel	0	5	95	0	2.5	8
Italy	24.7	20.4	20.2	35	7.3	16.5
Japan	51.5	19.2	28.6	1.1	7.5	23.5
Korea	16	27.2	45.3	11.5	4.3	16.9
Luxembourg	87.4	1.5	9.1	0.2	1.2	3.3
Netherlands	0	48.2	51.8	0	1.4	3.8
New Zealand	0	9.6	90.3	0	2.2	6.7
Norway	87.5	1.3	11.2	0	5.4	13.9
Poland	56.7	5.3	32.4	5.6	4.2	13.4
Portugal	27.1	26	45.2	1.7	2.5	7.2
Slovak Republic	0	25.5	51.3	23.2	0.8	2.7
Slovenia	77.9	6.4	15.8	0	4.1	10.6

(*continued*)

Table 8.1 (continued)

Countries	*Tax sources as a % of total local tax revenues*				*Local taxes as a % of GDP*	*Local taxes as a % of all taxes*[e]
(1)	*Income*[a] *(2)*	*Sales*[b] *(3)*	*Property*[c] *(4)*	*Other*[d] *(5)*	*(6)*	*(7)*
Sweden	97.5	0	2.5	0	15.8	36.9
Turkey	26	50.2	14.8	9.1	2.8	9.4
United Kingdom	0	0	100	0	1.6	5
Unweighted Average	*32.6*	*19*	*43.5*	*4.8*	*4.3*	*11.4*

Source: Calculated from Tables 5.1, 5.2, 5.8, 5.10, 5.11, and 5.12 in OECD, *Revenue Statistics 1965–2015* (Paris: OECD 2016)
[a]Includes individual, corporate, and payroll tax
[b]Includes general consumption taxes, value-added taxes, specific taxes on goods and services (fuel taxes, hotel and motel occupancy), and taxes on use of goods or on permission to use goods or perform activities
[c]Taxes on property, including recurring taxes on net wealth
[d]Includes a miscellaneous collection of local taxes
[e]Total includes central government, state government, local government, and social security funds

Fifth, column 6 of Table 8.1 provides information on the relative importance of local taxes by calculating them as a percent of gross domestic product (GDP) which is a measure of the level of economic activity in each country. In federal countries, local government taxes varied from a low of 0.2 percent of GDP in Mexico to a high of 4.1 percent in Switzerland with the unweighted average for these countries being 2.3 percent. For unitary countries, local government's tax share of GDP ranged from a low of 0.3 percent in Estonia to a high of 15.8 percent in Sweden and 12.4 percent in Denmark with the unweighted average being 4.3 percent.

Sixth, column 7 looks at the relative importance of local taxes in the entire tax system in each country. When local taxes are calculated as a percent of total taxes (central, state, provincial, cantonal, local government, and social security funds), they range widely in relative importance. For example, in federal countries, local taxes ranged from a low of 1.6 percent of all taxes in Mexico to a high of 15.3 percent in Switzerland with the unweighted average being 7.6 percent. For unitary countries, the range extends from a low of 1.1 percent in Estonia and 1.2 percent in the Czech Republic to a high of 35.6 percent in Sweden, 25 percent in Denmark, 24.5 percent in Iceland, 23.5 percent in Finland, and Japan with the unweighted average being 11.4 percent.

Finally, local governments in non-OECD countries, while not reported in Table 8.1 because of a lack of comparable data, show similar variation in the extent to which local governments rely on a variety of taxes. Local governments in Brazil use a property tax, sales tax, and a tax on property transfers. Municipalities in Russia have access to property and land taxes. Property taxes are widely used in African countries, although they vary considerably in their capacity as a revenue generator for municipalities (Franzsen and McCluskey 2017). The most widely used local tax in India is the property tax, although some of the large cities generate more revenue from an entry (octroi) tax that is applied to all goods entering the city. As well, there are a wide range of smaller taxes on specific services or transactions. Local governments in China, unlike most other countries, have a major reliance on land leasing fees but also have access to a share of central taxes such as business and value-added taxes (70 percent share), enterprise (20 percent share), and personal income taxes (24 percent share) and a wide range of local taxes that include, in order of relative importance, land appreciation tax, city maintenance and construction tax, urban land use tax, house property tax, farmland occupation tax, and stamp tax (see Shah 2015). In many African, East European, and South American countries with a functioning real estate market and good administrative apparatus for managing property taxes, they are the most dominant local tax, often supplemented by a variety of other local charges and taxes.

Observations

The above pattern leads to a number of observations. Obviously, the importance of local taxation is primarily driven by expenditure responsibilities—those municipalities with a lot of funding responsibilities have a greater need to rely on the local tax base.

The relative importance of local taxes in a country's tax system is generally less in federal countries than in unitary countries—federal countries have a middle (state, province, canton) level of government that assumes some spending responsibilities often left for local governments in unitary countries. As such, the province, state, or canton has access to taxes that are often the domain of local governments in unitary countries.

Local property taxes play a more important revenue role at the local level in federal countries where almost 57 percent of all local tax revenue, on average, comes from the property tax, than in unitary countries where almost 44 percent of total local taxes, on average, are generated by the property tax. These percentages are higher than they were in 1998 when they accounted for almost 45 percent, on average, of all property taxes in federal countries and almost 33 percent, on average, in unitary countries.[1] This pattern illustrates the growing dependence on property taxes in many countries over the past two decades. At the same time, for countries not reported in Table 8.1, almost all of them now have a property tax of one form or another and like the OECD countries, most have increased their reliance on property taxes over the past two decades.

Local income taxes, on average, are equally important in both unitary and federal countries—around 33–34 percent of all tax revenues. This is a notable decrease from 1998 where they accounted for almost 45 percent, on average, in federal countries and almost 41 percent, on average, in unitary countries.

Local sales taxes are relatively less important in federal countries—accounting for slightly more than 6 percent, on average, of all local tax revenue compared with unitary countries where they account for 19 percent, on average, of local tax revenue. This difference in relative importance between these two groupings of countries largely exists because the state, provincial, cantonal level of government collects considerable sales tax revenue in federal systems, whereas this source of revenue is more likely to be available to local governments in unitary countries. In 1998, by comparison, local sales taxes accounted for more than 10 percent of all local tax revenue, on average, in federal countries and more than 16 percent in unitary countries.

Local income taxes as a percent of all taxes increased in some federal countries and decreased in others, but, on average, they accounted for about 7.6 percent of all tax revenue in both years. Similar variation is noted across unitary countries, but overall, local taxes, on average, fell from 12.7 percent of all revenues in 1998 to 11.4 percent in 2014.

As a percent of GDP, local taxes fell from 3.3 percent in 1998 to 2.3 percent in 2014 in federal countries and from 5.1 percent in 1998 to 4.3 percent in 2014 in unitary countries. This is, by and large, a reflection of a faster increase in GDP over the past two decades than in local tax revenues.

More specifically, at the local government level, there is heavy reliance on income taxes in the Nordic countries whereas heavy reliance is placed on property taxes in countries that, in the past, were part of the British Commonwealth or significantly influenced by it.

[1] For an illustration of the pattern of local tax systems in 1998, see Kitchen and Slack 2003, p. 2228.

Where local taxes are a comparatively higher percentage of total tax revenue and GDP, local governments tend to rely more heavily on local income taxes. Local governments in some countries only have access to one tax (property or income) whereas local governments in many countries have access to two or more local taxes.

Where local taxes account for more than 10 percent of all tax revenue, there is no common pattern. Local governments in some of these countries have access to a wide range of taxes (Austria, some states in the United States, Italy, Iceland, Japan, Korea, Spain, and Turkey). In other countries where local government taxes are equally important (Nordic countries and the Czech Republic), local governments are restricted to only one tax of any significance.

From the information provided above, there are no definitive conclusions that can be drawn about the appropriateness of one tax over another tax. There is nothing in the data to suggest that local government is more or less efficient, effective, and accountable if it has access to a range of taxes as opposed to only one major tax. Local government access to a specific tax or taxes is dependent on a number of things including the local government's capacity to administer the tax, the types of expenditures that local government must fund, the willingness of a senior level of government to assign taxes to local government, constitutional and legislative requirements, and a variety of other factors.

Fiscal Autonomy and Local Taxation

International experience tells us that an essential ingredient in creating a good local public sector is a responsive and responsible local government. A necessary condition for this is that local governments possesses the fiscal capacity to provide required and desired levels of public infrastructure and services (Rodden et al. 2003). In other words, local governments carrying out their expenditure responsibilities are likely to be more efficient, responsible, and accountable if they are required to set their own tax rates and raise the revenue that they spend (Bird 2011; Slack 2017).

Furthermore, this is dependent on the fiscal autonomy or fiscal discretion that local governments have in determining their tax base and setting their tax rates. Fiscal autonomy, in theory, is greatest when local governments are free to determine both the tax base and tax rates without senior governments imposing limits on either of these. Fiscal autonomy is least when both the tax base and tax rate are set or controlled by senior levels of government (Blochliger and Nettley 2015).

In reality, local governments in every country have no or very little control over their tax base. In countries with a property tax, the base is determined by standards and practices set and implemented by a senior level of government.[2] In countries with income and sales taxes, the base is also set and controlled by a higher level of government.[3] Control over the tax base while it may limit a local government's autonomy has some advantages. A common base is less expensive to administer than a diversity of local tax bases within a large jurisdictional area. Furthermore, if the tax can be "piggybacked" onto the tax base of a senior level of government, administrative costs will certainly be less than if each local government set up and administered its own tax. More importantly, however, is the capacity to avoid potential distortions and inefficiencies that might surface if local governments were to tamper with the tax base to satisfy some constituency or other.

A common practice and one that gives local government considerable autonomy is a requirement that each sets its own tax rate. This is the practice in developed and many developing economies. Responsibility for setting local tax rates is particularly important because it means that those who set the tax rate will face the political consequences of levying taxes that are necessary to fund the cost of services they provide (Mikesell 2013). Sometimes, however, limits are placed on these rates to deter local decision makers from using them to create potential distortions and inefficiencies that could lead to negative or harmful consequences for neighboring municipalities and other levels of government.

Tax-sharing arrangements also exist in a few countries (Chile, Denmark, Estonia, Finland, France, Germany, Hungary, Poland, Portugal, Slovenia, Spain, and Turkey). Here, a local tax is shared with a more senior level of government. Tax sharing takes a variety of forms. Nowhere is the split determined by local governments. In Germany and Spain, the split is by mutual consent between the two parties. In the remaining countries, the sharing formula is determined by the senior government, sometimes annually, but more frequently for a longer period of time (Blochliger and Nettley 2015). Here, then, the degree of autonomy is not high because local governments are not responsible for setting their share of the tax (OECD 1999).

[2] See Chap. 9 for more detail.
[3] See Chap. 10 for more detail.

Three Examples of Diversity in Municipal Taxes

Local governments in every developed and developing country rely on property taxation in one form or another. In some countries, it is the major source of revenue; in other countries, it is superseded by income or sales taxes revenue. At the same time, every local government collects revenue from an ever expanding range of relatively small taxes and charges, many of which are imposed on businesses. Everyone uses a range of permits, licenses, fees, concessions, and so on to extract further revenue from the local revenue base with almost all of these having no direct relation to the cost of any public service that local governments provide. By and large, they generate revenue which, in the overall picture, is not large, but, at the margin, is helpful in financing services.

Given the importance of property, income, and sales taxes at the local level, this section briefly describes the system in one country (Canada) where local governments have direct access to only one tax (property), four countries (Nordic) that rely almost solely on the personal income tax, and one country (United States) where local governments may have access to as many as three local taxes.

Canada[4]: Local governments are creatures of the province and, as such, are permitted to use only one tax—the property tax.[5] Although free to set their general property tax rate, municipal governments face a significant number of provincial rules and regulations with respect to their tax base and rates. While some of these restrictions and constraints may be necessary to satisfy a variety of broader social and economic objectives, the point is they do restrict municipal fiscal autonomy. Examples of these restrictions and controls are described here.

In all ten provinces and the three territories, real property is the tax base. Its principal components include land, buildings, and structures and, in some provinces, machinery and equipment. Provincial government's legislation/regulations exempt certain properties from property taxation, however. These include colleges and universities, churches and cemeteries, public hospitals, charitable organizations, and so on. Under the constitution, provincial- and federal-owned properties are also exempt from property taxation. For federal and provincial properties including colleges, universities, penal institutions and public hospitals, grants-in-lieu of taxes (based on

[4] For more detail see Dahlby and McMillan 2019; Kitchen and Tassonyi 2012.

[5] In all provinces but one, the provincial government also levies a property tax.

number of students or number of beds in some provinces and on assessed value of the property in other provinces) are paid to the municipality. As well, provincial legislation/regulations require special treatment for other types of property—agricultural land and managed forest properties receive favorable property tax treatment in every province. Favorable treatment takes the form of exemptions, lower property tax rates, or assessment on the basis of the land's current use rather than its market value.

For all taxable properties, every province has legislation that calls for the assessment of real property at some value. In some provinces, this is called "real and true value," "current value," or "fair value." In practice, these terms refer to market value. To avoid unintended variation in provincial assessment practices and to achieve intended variation, every province has established a central assessment authority and has moved recently to more updated and frequent reassessments.

Although municipal governments are responsible for setting their general property tax rate without restriction, provincial rules and regulations control the rate structure across all properties. For example, some provinces permit municipalities to apply a single general tax rate to all classes of property; others permit the application of different rates to different property classes with lower rates assigned to residential and farm properties and higher rates to commercial and industrial properties. In one province, property tax rates are lower for residents of the province than for nonresidents of the province.

In summary, municipal governments are free to set their general tax rate. Their tax base and rate structure (across property types), however, are frequently controlled or restricted by provincial legislation, rules, and regulations.

Nordic countries[6]: The best known examples of local income taxes are in these countries (Sweden, Norway, Finland, Denmark) where it is the only local tax of any significance (Table 8.1) for local governments. In general, local income taxes apply to personal income only including capital income in the Nordic dual income tax system.[7] Local taxes are "piggybacked" onto the national income tax. They are levied at a flat, locally established rate on the same tax base as the national income tax. The progressive part of the rate structure is created by the central government's

[6] For more detail, see Lotz 2012.

[7] The Nordic income tax system is a dual income tax system that levies a proportional tax rate on all net income (capital, wage, and pension income less deductions) along with progressive tax rates on gross labor and pension income.

rate structure. Variation in tax rates across municipalities has decreased over time and it now stands at around five percentage points in Denmark, Norway, and Sweden and around one percentage point in Finland. Norway has a cap on the local income tax rate and all municipalities currently apply the maximum rate. A similar situation exists in Iceland where local governments are also highly dependent on local income taxes.

The income tax is collected by local authorities in Norway who keep their share and then transfer the rest to the central government. In the other countries, taxes are collected by the central government and remitted to each local jurisdiction according to place of residency rather than place of employment.

There are a number of features of the Nordic system of local income taxes that warrant emphasis. One is that the taxes are levied by local governments on their residents and the revenues go to the jurisdiction of residence. Part of the logic for this is that the taxes largely finance social services and those are more closely associated with residence than place of employment. Sharing between locality of residence and employment has been attempted but was abandoned. The systems are supported by strong equalization programs. The importance of equalization is understandable given the importance of social programs in local budgets and the importance of local income taxes as a source of revenue. The fiscal significance of local government and its reliance on local income taxes has made macro control or stability a concern of central authorities in Norway and Sweden particularly, but also in Denmark. Much of that issue stems from the growing cost of social and especially of health services (an issue that is a concern in many countries independent of the particular level of government responsible for those services).

United States[8]: In some states, there is considerable variation in a municipality's access to local taxation. For example, the property tax is used everywhere, and in some states it is the only tax that is permitted. Many states permit local sales taxes and some states permit local income taxes. Many cities have a local fuel tax. Regardless of the tax or taxes permitted, state approval or permission has either been legislated or granted.

Fourteen states and the District of Columbia allow one or more of their cities, counties, school districts, and municipalities to levy their own individual income taxes. For the states, coverage varies from 1 city in Alabama (Birmingham) and Delaware (Wilmington), 2 cities in Missouri (Kansas

[8] For more detail, see Mikesell 2010, Mikesell 2013, and St. Louis 2017.

City and St. Louis) and New York (Yonkers and New York City), all 92 counties in Indiana, all 666 school districts in Iowa, 235 cities and 331 villages in Ohio, and most municipalities in Pennsylvania. Not every jurisdiction in states where local income taxes are in play has chosen to levy or is permitted to levy a local income tax. In fact, municipalities in Arkansas and Georgia are permitted to levy a local income tax but none of them have chosen to do so.

In some municipalities, the tax is on personal and corporate income, but in most, it is only on the former. For administrative simplicity and cost savings, taxes are sometimes imposed at a flat percentage rate "piggybacked" onto the state income tax. Many jurisdictions, however, have chosen to set up their own tax structure and administer their own tax system because it gives them more local autonomy, control, and flexibility in determining the tax base even though it is more expensive to implement and administer.

Tax rates vary across municipalities and often rates vary across municipalities within a state. The authority to set tax rates is sometimes constrained by the state or by voter approval. Some cities levy local income taxes on earnings; some levy on earnings and business net profits; and some levy on personal income. Local income taxes may be residence based or employment based (payroll tax). When residence based, tax rates are generally not differentiated. If it is earnings (payroll) based, differential rates may be used with lower rates applying to commuters.

The income tax is an important revenue generator in many places. For example, in Detroit, income tax revenue is 1.12 times the property tax revenue; in Columbus, it is 10 times the property tax revenue; and in Philadelphia, it is 2.8 times the property tax revenue.

Local sales taxes are permitted in 36 states where they are used in roughly 10,000 jurisdictions including more than 6500 cities and over 3500 towns, counties, boroughs, special districts, school districts, and transit authorities to name the most obvious. In some states, it is universal; in others, it is voluntary. General sales taxes are levied on retail purchases at "ad valorem" (fixed percent of selling price) rather than per unit rates. Most municipalities are allowed to choose their own tax rate subject to an upper limit. They are almost always "piggybacked" onto the state sales tax. They are sometimes shared across a range of jurisdictions—state, county city, and so on.

Sometimes, the tax revenue goes into general funds, but in some cases, all or a portion of it is earmarked for a specific service or infrastructure project. Like the income tax, it is also an important revenue generator; for example, in Phoenix, sales tax revenue is 4.5 times the property tax revenue; in Denver, it is 2.8 times the property tax revenue; and in New York City, sales and income tax revenue combined are 1.66 times the property tax revenue.

All municipalities levy a property tax, one that is similar to the system in many other countries. Property taxes are administered and collected at the local level. Local governments are free to set their rates but the tax base is essentially controlled by state policy (legislation) and practice. The many other nuances and features of the property tax are similar to those described for Canada (above) and will not be repeated here.

Financing Model for Local Government

A major observation from the international experience is that there is no consistent or uniform approach to local government taxation. Some rely on one major tax only while others rely on more than one major tax. Regardless of the practice, however, it is widely agreed that local governments should operate within a framework that constitutes the "benefits received model" for financing local governments. This is examined below.

"Benefits-Based Model" in Principle

Let us turn to the constitutional place of local governments in virtually every country. Local governments are generally "creatures of the state/province" in federal countries and established by central direction/legislation in unitary countries. Their spending responsibilities and revenue options are controlled by a senior level of government. Because of this, it is best to examine local fiscal roles and responsibilities within the principal-agent model (Bird and Chen 1998) of state-local fiscal arrangements. In this model, local governments are the agents while the state is the principal. The latter has the power to alter jurisdictional boundaries, to change revenue and expenditure responsibilities of the agent, and to change intergovernmental fiscal arrangements to overcome differing objectives between the principal and the agent. Within this context, the role of the agent is to provide and fund services that benefit local constituents; hence, financing of each service is best completed within the benefits-based model of public finance (Bird 1993).

Criteria

The underlying principle of the benefits received model[9] of local finance is straightforward (Duff 2004): those who benefit from local public services are those who should pay for them. This model satisfies the following principles or criteria.

Economic (or allocative) efficiency[10] is achieved when the tax or user fee per unit equals the extra cost of the last unit consumed. This is the well-known price equals marginal cost pricing principle. The tax or fee, by definition, indicates what consumers are willing to pay for a service, and marginal cost, by definition, measures the cost of resources used up in producing that service. Perhaps this can be illustrated by reference to a simple example. Suppose the extra (marginal) cost of producing the last liter of water is 10 cents and customers are willing to pay 15 cents for it. This is not an efficient level of output because the value that customers place on this liter is greater than the cost of producing it. In other words society is the beneficiary of a net gain of 5 cents for this unit. Collectively, society would be better off if water consumption increased as long as the price paid for each additional unit exceeded the cost of producing that unit, that is, for each of these units, marginal benefit would exceed marginal cost—a net gain.

If, on the other hand and more likely the case, the marginal cost of producing the last liter is 10 cents and customers are only willing to pay 5 cents, this is not an efficient level of output either. The benefit that customers get from this unit is less than the cost of the resources used up in producing it and society is worse off—worse off by 5 cents for this unit. As long as the extra cost of producing the unit is less than its price, society is

[9] An alternative approach would be to argue for taxation on the basis of ability to pay. This is appropriate for governments that have access to income taxes (federal and provincial) and where services funded by these taxes benefit all of society as opposed to specific beneficiaries, either individually or as a group that can be identified.

[10] Economic efficiency is more than technical efficiency—the latter is a necessary but not sufficient condition for economic efficiency. Technical efficiency exists when a producing unit (firm, government, commission) operates in a way such that it is not possible to secure any additional output given the available inputs (labor, material, and capital) and level of technology. In other words, technical efficiency is achieved when the output per unit of input is maximized or the cost per unit of output is minimized. This, it should be noted, is not concerned with whether one good or service generates more or fewer net benefits than another good or service. It simply concentrates on the efficient employment of inputs in the production of a specific good or service. Finally, as the level of technology advances, a technically efficient production process leads to increased output with the same inputs.

devoting too many resources to its production. It follows, then, that resource efficiency is achieved where marginal cost equals price because this is the point where society secures the greatest net gain from the consumption of this service.

It should be apparent, then, that the main economic reason for imposing correctly designed taxes or fees on beneficiaries (individuals or businesses) of public services is to provide the public sector with incentives for using resources in the most efficient manner possible. The goal of maximizing efficiency in a government's provision of services is not an objective dreamed up by some economist. It is simply common sense. Surely any society should allocate its scarce resources to those services that provide its people with as large a bundle as possible of services that they want. That is all that is meant by efficient resource use (Bird 2011).

Accountability is enhanced when the purpose for a tax or user fee is clear to taxpayers. The more direct the relationship between those who benefit from a government service and those who pay for it, the greater the accountability. The principle advantage of linking expenditures to user fees is that the cost of a service may be seen clearly by beneficiaries. Citizen/taxpayer demand for a local government service will thus be based on some knowledge of service costs and a realization of what must be paid for its consumption. People know what they are getting for the tax or fee charged and better able to judge whether the expenditure is appropriate. As such, taxes and user fees are of considerable assistance to municipal managers in determining efficient or optimum service levels—whenever a tax, price, or charge for a unit of service is linked to its per unit cost of provision, consumers have enough information to determine desired levels and hence, managers are able to provide these levels (Bird and Slack 2019).

Transparency is an extension of the accountability argument. It is improved when citizens/taxpayers have access to information and decision-making forums so that the general public is familiar with the way in which local tax rates, charges, and user fees are set. Emphasis on transparency is intended to mitigate the risk of corruption by making information available and by ensuring that all public policy decisions are made in an open and transparent manner (IMF 2001).

Fairness or equity within the benefits model is achieved when those who use public services pay for them, just as someone who benefits from a private good pays for it. Concerns about the tax burden on low-income individuals should be addressed through lower rates for these people, or better still, through income transfers from senior levels of government and social assistance programs targeted to individuals in need. It is far more equitable and efficient to handle income distribution issues through income transfers or targeting specific users (Boadway and Kitchen 1999, chapters 8 and 9) than to tamper with uniform charging mechanisms to accommodate these concerns.

Ease of administration. Local taxes and user fees should be relatively easy to administer and easy for taxpayers to understand.

Applying the Criteria

The benefits-based model is best achieved when there is a close if not direct link between taxation and spending (Bird and Slack 2019, 2017). In such a system, expenditure responsibilities should be matched with revenue resources, revenue capacities matched with political accountability, and benefit areas matched with financing areas. The services provided by the public sector are then (so to speak) sold to those who receive them and the revenues yielded by such sales are sufficient to pay for the cost of providing the service. In effect, this approach treats local governments as essentially "firms" that produce and sell services to their customers.

Depending on the services provided, then, different financing tools could be used. For services with private good characteristics (such as water, sewers, garbage collection and disposal, transit, and recreation), user fees are appropriate to fund at least some portion of the costs.[11] In general, user fees are appropriate where there is a clear relationship between the fees charged and the benefits received, the taxpayer has the choice about the extent to which he or she uses the service, it is possible to collect the charge at a reasonable cost, and equity concerns can be addressed (e.g., by lowering or waiving fees for low-income users).

Services with public good characteristics (e.g., police and fire protection, neighborhood parks, local streets, and street lighting) have collective benefits that are enjoyed by local residents but which cannot easily be assigned to individual beneficiaries. These services are more difficult to charge for and require some form of local benefit-based taxation such as the property tax or in some instances income and sales taxes. The local tax allows individuals to express their demand for services where benefits are consumed collectively. In this respect, local taxes may be considered to be generalized, or non-specific, user charges.

[11] See Chap. 11 for more detail.

There are also services where the benefits (or costs) spill over municipal boundaries but where local provision is still desirable. Positive spillovers (externalities) occur if residents of neighboring jurisdictions receive a service for free or at less than the cost of providing the service. For example, major roads constructed in one jurisdiction may be used by residents of another jurisdiction without any charge to them. The result will be an under-allocation of resources to that service because the municipality providing the service would base its expenditure decisions only on the benefits captured within its jurisdiction. It would not take account of the benefits to those outside the jurisdiction. One way to provide an incentive to the municipality to allocate more resources to the service generating the externality is through a transfer from a senior level of government.

Services that redistribute income (e.g., social services, social housing, schooling),[12] it is widely conceded, should not be the responsibility of local governments. These are more appropriately handled by a senior level of government because it has access to a wide range of taxes, most of which are more progressive in their impact on taxpayers when compared with local government taxes.

Grants from senior levels of government may also have a role in funding local services.[13] Specifically, conditional grants could be used for partial or full funding of services generating spillovers and for services in which the state has an interest (e.g., to ensure uniform or minimum standards). Unconditional grants play a role in filling the fiscal gap (mismatch in local own-source revenues and expenditure responsibilities) and in supporting municipalities in their attempts to provide comparable levels of service for comparable tax rates (equalization).

In summary, within the "benefits-based model" of local finance, there is a role for local taxes, just as there is a role for user fees, and grants. Local governments, however, should not have to fund programs specifically directed toward the redistribution of income among individuals (e.g., social services, social housing) and they should also not cross-subsidize services to residences versus services to business nor should they be responsible for funding services that are national or statewide in their impact and scope (education and health, to name two). These functions are more appropriately the responsibility of central and state/provincial/regional/cantonal governments and should be funded by them.

[12]While some elements of income redistribution are inherent in almost all public services, income redistributional services include welfare payments, children's aid, social housing, and income transfers to name the most obvious.

[13]For more detail, see Chaps. 12, 13, and 14.

Issues in Local Taxation

The current fiscal environment in which municipalities in almost every country face increased spending responsibilities, reduced grants from senior levels of government, and a restricted local tax base raises a number of issues around local taxation, issues that are discussed next.

Which Tax or Taxes?

Within this model, there is a clear role for local taxes, but what is not so clear is which local tax or taxes. Here, the strongest economic and fiscal arguments for assigning a tax or taxes to local governments come from the literature on fiscal federalism where there is widespread agreement on general principles that should be followed. In short, this theory prescribes a limited tax base for local governments (McClure 2001). The best municipal/local taxes are those that have the following characteristics (Bird and Slack 2004; Bird and Bahl 2008; Inman 2005). They are based on an immobile tax base and, therefore, borne primarily by local residents (not exported). They do not create problems with harmonization or harmful competition between local governments and more senior levels of government. They generate sufficient, stable, and predictable revenues. They are visible to ensure accountability and transparency. They are perceived to be fair. They are easy to administer locally.

Property Tax

The real property tax (discussed in Chap. 9) which is widely used meets these criteria better than any other tax. Its base is largely immobile. Revenue is generally predictable and stable. The residential portion of the tax is unlikely to be exported.[14] It is highly visible which enhances accountability because it makes local governments responsible for their spending decisions. It is fair on the basis of benefits received. One criticism that has been levied at the property tax is that it may be more expensive to administer than other local taxes (e.g., income and sales) that could be "piggybacked" onto existing taxes of a senior level of government. This claim has elicited a couple of responses. First, it is a small price to pay if local governments are to have autonomy and flexibility in setting tax policy—important

[14] The same cannot be said for the nonresidential property tax because some of it may be exported to other jurisdictions through higher prices of goods and services (see Chap. 9).

ingredients of responsible, efficient, and accountable local governments (Bird 2011; Bird and Bahl 2008). Second, it has been argued that if all costs (administration plus compliance) associated with a property tax system are considered, they differ very little from the costs of collecting a sales or income tax (Almy 2001).

Income and Sales Tax

Other significant taxes have also been defended at the local level, even though they are generally less effective at satisfying the above identified criteria. These include an income tax on individuals[15] and a general sales tax.[16] The only local tax currently used, by itself, in place of the property tax is a local income tax. Support for it is generally based on the following arguments.

It is more progressive than the property tax in its distributional impact on local taxpayers. Its use would permit local governments to cast a wider net in capturing revenues from those who benefit from municipal services—residents, commuters, and visitors—and as such, would be preferable for metropolitan areas rather than for smaller municipalities. As noted above, a key tenet of the benefits model of local government finance is that those who enjoy the benefits of local services should pay for them. Some US evidence suggests that the cost of inner city services used by people who live in the suburbs and commute to work (in the city center) exceeds, sometimes substantially, the taxes they pay for inner city services (Chernick and Tkacheva 2002; Chernick 2002). For these services, an income tax and/or a sales taxes could be more effective at linking the costs and benefits of services than the property tax. Third, it is more revenue elastic than the property tax—a useful feature for local governments faced with increasing costs of local services. Fourth, it could be less costly to operate and easily administered if local governments "piggybacked" onto the tax base of a senior level of government. Local sales taxes, while not as progressive in their impact on taxpayers could achieve many of these objectives as well.

[15] A municipal corporate income tax is not suggested because corporate capital is highly mobile and a municipal tax could lead to capital mobility, a violation of criteria for a good local tax.

[16] See Chap. 10 for a more detailed discussion. Other taxes or what may be more appropriately referred to as charges or fees include road pricing and parking levies. These have been on occasion referred to as environmental taxes or charges. They are discussed in Chap. 11.

Environmental Taxes

Many activities and products cause damage to the environment. Some of these such as the discharge of effluents are rarely taxed, whereas others such as gasoline and fuel are either under-taxed or subsidized. Corrective taxes on activities or substances with negative externalities (effluents, pollution, noise, congestion, etc.) can expand the tax base and at the same time restrict such activities. If the tax succeeds in inducing environment-friendly practices among producers and consumers, it will not generate much revenue but will be efficient in protecting the environment. If, however, producers and consumers continue to follow environmentally damaging practices, the tax will generate revenue that can be used either to lower other distortionary taxes or to fund cleanup programs or abatement technologies.

There are a range of taxes or charges that municipalities could adopt to internalize the costs of negative externalities. Some of these could be piggybacked onto taxes/charges of a senior level of government while others could be implemented at the local level. Regardless of how they are implemented, however, their capacity for internalizing environmental costs and minimizing potential distortions and inefficiencies is likely to be minimized if they are implemented at a regional or metropolitan area level as opposed to the town or city level.

As for specific taxes and charges (discussed in more detail in Chaps. 10 and 11), road pricing and motor fuel taxes or a carbon tax could be designed to include environmental costs (congestion and pollution) created by road users. Stormwater management fees could be adopted and designed to minimize the harmful impact of excess water run-off caused by sudden and violent storms that are appearing more frequently in many places. Better use of user fees for solid waste management and recycling would reduce the negative consequences of too much garbage. This could include environmental charges on consumer products that are non-biodegradable such as plastic bags and containers. Given recent improvements in technology, better use could be made of effluent charges on sewerage and industrial liquid waste. Permits (user fee) are now required for tree removal (with a required replacement) in many urban areas and could be expanded to many more areas. This is intended to protect the urban canopy and minimize harmful climate impacts created by unnecessary tree removal and clear-cutting.

A Mix of Taxes

Municipal governments currently fund a range of services: a range that varies from country to country but one that almost everywhere has grown over the past few years as cities and metropolitan areas have struggled to keep up with increasing demands driven by rapidly growing urbanization, increased densification, potentially harmful congestion, reduced grants, and continued off-loading of additional responsibilities onto the local tax base. Included in this list are a number of tax-funded services that provide considerable benefits for real property (sidewalks, local streets, police and fire, land use planning to name a few) while others primarily benefit people (social services, education, social housing, health and drug prevention, neighborhood parks, etc.). This distinction is important because it raises the question of whether one local tax is preferable to other local taxes for funding the wide array of local services. In general, the answer is probably no.

The property tax which is the mainstay of local finance in the majority of countries has served this purpose well, especially at a time when most local services were primarily associated with property. Increased urbanization, densification, and congestion over the past few decades have expanded the services now demanded from municipal governments. Many of these needs are more closely associated with people than with property, thus throwing into question whether the property tax is still the ideal or only tax that municipalities should use. At the same time, relying primarily on the income tax as local governments in the Nordic countries do has similar potential downfalls in that some of the services provided may be more appropriately funded from local property taxes because of their closer association with property than with people.

Many local governments rely on more than one tax and there are strong arguments for doing so especially for large cities and metropolitan areas. A mix of taxes would give cities more flexibility in responding to local expenditure needs. For example, local politicians might choose to levy sales taxes for services enjoyed by commuters and visitors. An employee-based personal income tax (often referred to as a payroll tax) would tax commuters. Property taxes might be chosen where there is a need for a more stable revenue source. Environmental taxes could be used to internalize the cost of negative externalities as well as managing the demand for local services and improving overall economic efficiency in the provision of local services.

A portfolio of taxes would allow cities and metropolitan areas to increase or stabilize revenue while maintaining fairness (Bahl 2010; Slack 2011). Reliance on a range of taxes would allow city politicians to set a lower-tax rate for any particular tax. Since the excess burden of a tax increases with its tax rate (i.e., the distortions increase as the tax rate increases), a more diversified system should yield a given amount of revenue more efficiently with a smaller negative impact on the overall tax base (Chernick et al. 2010).

Access to new taxes would permit cities to reduce their dependence on property taxes. When compared with excise taxes, licenses, permits, and fees, general sales and income taxes are less likely to create inefficiencies, distortions, and relatively large administrative costs (Mikesell 2011). Additional taxes could address two concerns that are growing in importance in a number of countries. First, it would assist homeowners who are asset rich (high property values) but income poor and facing increasing difficulty in meeting their property tax obligations. Second, it could be an important tax source for local governments facing increasing service demands while at the same time facing limits or restrictions imposed by senior levels of government on the amount of revenue they can generate from the property tax.

Third, it could reduce some of the burden of business property taxes. This is a real problem with the property tax in many countries, especially where local decision makers have increased the tax burden on the nonresidential tax base rather than the residential base even though there is evidence to suggest that the latter receives more benefits than the former.[17] In particular, a recent study for Canada estimated that city business property and land transfer taxes represent about two-thirds of the total investment tax burden faced by the nonresidential sector (Found and Tomlinson 2017). When a tax burden like this is not offset by associated benefits from local public services as some studies have suggested (Mintz and Roberts 2006; Kitchen and Tassonyi 2012), over-taxation ensues and the level of investment can fall hindering economic growth.

In general, arguments for more than one tax at the local level are particularly strong especially for large cities and city-regions, particularly when tax rates are set locally. In addition to the advantages noted above, these are large revenue generators. In one Canadian study, it has been estimated that a relatively small surtax (between 7 and 16 percent depending on the city) on the provincial income tax could yield the equivalent of

[17] See Chap. 9.

20 percent of property tax revenue. Likewise, the yield from a one percentage point increase in the provincial sales tax and, depending on the city, could generate revenues ranging from 9 percent to 25 percent of property taxes (Kitchen and Slack 2016). The increase in these taxes, it should be noted, could be offset by lower property taxes although the income distributional impact would change.

Who Should Set Local Tax Rates?

International experience tells us that local governments are more responsible, efficient, and accountable if they are required to fund their expenditures from locally generated revenues. This includes setting local tax rates (Slack 2017). Additional autonomy could also be achieved if local governments were free to establish and determine their local tax base; however, high administrative costs of doing so generally argue against it. For income and consumption-based taxes, it is far less expensive to "piggyback" onto an existing state tax with local governments setting the local tax rate. For property taxation where a senior level of government is not involved, local administration will be necessary.

For single-tier local governments, local tax rates should be set by the governing council of the jurisdiction responsible for spending the money. For two-tier local governments where the lower tier is responsible for a range of services and the upper tier or metropolitan area (encompasses a number of lower tiers) is responsible for services that spill over the lower-tier boundaries (Slack 2011), the lower tier should set its own tax rates and the upper tier should set its tax rates. This follows the principle that those who spend the money should be responsible for raising it.

The practice of having each tier of local government in a two-tier structure set its own property tax rate on the same property tax base is common in Canada (Kitchen and Tassonyi 2012). Setting local income tax rates and applying them to the same income tax base as is used by the central/state government is the practice in the Nordic countries (Lotz 2012) and in many states in the United States. Similarly many municipalities in the United States set their own local sales tax rate and "piggyback" it onto the state sales tax base (Mikesell 2013). These examples suggest that it is not uncommon for different levels of government to impose different tax rates on the same tax base. Nor does it follow that the level of government that sets the tax rate need collect the tax revenue. Returning to the Canadian experience, let us consider the province of Ontario. Here, all regional and county governments (upper tier) set their own taxes independently of the tax rates set by the local municipalities (lower tier). The local municipalities then send out combined tax bills and collect both upper-tier taxes and lower-tier taxes. This practice has been around for years and has been fiercely defended in the presence of a number of proposals to migrate billing and collection to the upper tier where cost savings could be achieved because of distinct economies of scale that are present in this operation. Billing and collection is an administrative function and has nothing to do with policy setting or decision-making; hence, there is no reason why billing and collection needs to rest with the taxing jurisdiction that sets the tax rate.

Should Local Tax Rates Be Uniform or Differentiated Across a Municipality?

Given that municipal governments should be responsible for setting their own tax rates, there is the question of whether or not these rates should be uniform throughout the entire jurisdiction or whether they should be differentiated across property types and geographical areas within the jurisdiction. Whether a tax should be differentiated or not could also depend on the type of tax or the way it is administered.

Under benefits-based taxation, individuals and businesses that benefit from local public services should pay for them. Where these benefits vary by individual, by property type, or by area of the municipality, a case exists for charging differential taxes to the extent that it is possible. For property taxes, this is possible through the use of variable rates.[18]

For a personal income tax, split rates are only possible if the tax is payroll based. Split rates are justified on benefit grounds. Those who work and live in the same city benefit from city services and should pay for them. Those who work in one city and live in another community still benefit from some of the former city's services—local roads and streets, sidewalks, police and fire protection, and so on. For this, under benefits-based taxation, they should also pay a tax although at a lower rate than the tax on residents. In cities where split rates are used, the practice is to impose a lower rate of income tax on commuters (those who work in the taxing jurisdiction but live elsewhere) and a higher rate on residents. Here, it should be noted that New York City in 1999 dropped its income tax on commuters in spite of solid analytical and empirical support for continuing with it (Chernick and Tkacheva 2002).

[18] Discussed in Chap. 9.

For consumption-based taxes, however, differentiated tax rates are not administratively possible. A local sales, fuel, or hotel and motel occupancy tax, for example, is collected by the vendor. The vendor could not be expected to charge different rates to different customers on the basis of residency or some other characteristic of the customer.

Should Local Tax Rates Be Regulated?

Regulation of local tax rates may depend on the type of tax used and the role it plays within a country. If local governments use taxes that are only in their domain (property tax, for instance) and if their tax rates are set to generate required revenues for funding local services, there are no solid economic or political arguments for regulating the general tax rate. In democratically elected local councils where all decision-making responsibilities rest with local councils, citizens/taxpayers have the ultimate control or power over council's tax decisions—the opportunity to vote the politicians out of office at the next election.

If, however, local governments share the tax base with a senior level of government, yet have the power to set their own rates (which they should, as was argued earlier), there may be a case for regulation if the rate setting action of local government creates spillover or externality problems for senior governments. For example, if state or central and local governments have access to the same income tax or sales tax system and if the senior level of government lowers tax rates to achieve important state or national goals (e.g., to foster economic growth or to enhance competitiveness), they may wish to regulate what local governments do to prevent the latter from increasing its tax rates to take up the vacated tax room. While regulation here would be justified, significant funding problems may still exist for local governments that need tax revenue to meet expenditure needs.

A further externality argument for regulation arises in instances where local governments tax businesses. If the local tax on business is set to recover the cost of services used, it is efficient, fair, and accountable. The practice in many countries, however, is for local taxation to overtax business, thus creating potentially serious economic problems for the entire state or country. To prevent harmful and serious consequences, there may be a case for some state regulation to prevent municipalities from overtaxing businesses. This is discussed in more detail below under the taxation of businesses.

Regulation has also been defended as a way of controlling local government service costs. Cost efficiency in service provision, however, is more effectively achieved through the introduction of competitive elements in the production and delivery of each public good and service, not through regulating tax rates.

Should Local Government Tax Business?

A common tendency in virtually every country is for local governments to tax businesses. In general, this includes a property tax on commercial and industrial properties, a tax on capital, a corporate income tax, and a range of other industry and commerce taxes (Bird and Slack 2004). The strongest economic argument for local taxation of commercial and industrial properties is to tax them in order to recover the cost of local public services that they use. Where specific beneficiaries of these services can be identified, user charges are preferred. Where user charges are not possible, some general tax levy may be appropriate as long as is on a relatively immobile tax base with limited opportunities to export the tax to other jurisdictions.[19]

As for a local corporate income tax or local capital tax, there is no sound economic justification. Capital is highly mobile and the tax is almost certain to be exported, thus making it an unsatisfactory tax for local governments. In fact, concerns over capital mobility were instrumental in the Nordic countries decision to prevent municipalities from having access to a corporate income tax (Lotz 2012).

Could Local and Metropolitan Governments Use Different Taxes?

In principle and practice, local and metropolitan governments could have access to the same tax or they could have access to different taxes. It depends on the types of services for which each of these governing units is responsible. If local governments provide services that benefit their own residents, do not generate spillovers or externalities, that are non-income redistributional in nature, the property tax is probably the best tax although it could be supplemented by another tax or taxes. It is on local people and pays for local services. Indeed, the same may be said for metropolitan governments if their services have the same characteristics.

[19] A fuller discussion of the inefficiencies and distortions of local government's taxation of commercial and industrial property is completed in Chap. 9.

In reality, metropolitan governments are closer to those of provinces and states in terms of the services they provide and, as such, are better candidates for a wider range of taxes when compared with local governments (Kitchen and Slack 2016; Kitchen 2019). They are often called on to address poverty, crime, social housing and social assistance, land use planning, regional transportation, and other region-wide needs. Here, an income tax would appear to be an appropriate revenue source either by itself or as a supplement to the property tax.

An additional justification for income taxes for metropolitan areas has been made on benefit grounds. Since large metropolitan areas have a more heterogeneous population, it has been suggested that income is more highly correlated with consumption of public services than it is with property values (Bird and Slack 2004). In this case, a local income tax may be a better benefit tax than a property tax. On the other hand, this argument does not apply if there is a strong relationship between income and property values, which may be the case in large cities in many developed countries (Bird and Slack 2004, p. 34).

Finally, if either local or metropolitan governments provide services that are used by nonresidents, a case exists for giving these governments access to one or more consumption-based taxes or charges.

Should Local Taxes Be Earmarked?

Earmarking refers to a situation where the revenue generated by a local tax is dedicated or assigned to funding a specific service. It does not go into general revenue of the taxing jurisdiction.

The case for earmarking is largely based on the benefits received principle, especially when there is a close link between the tax revenue generated and its use in financing a specific local public service(s). In this context, it makes economic sense for the revenue from a selective sales (or excise) tax such as one that is levied on motor fuel to be dedicated to funding local roads. Here there is a link between the user of the road and the price paid (though the fuel tax) for its use. As well, a dedicated tax has a further advantage—it facilitates long-term planning and is more likely to prevent political abuse of the funds collected.

Earmarking, in general, of a portion of the property tax, personal income tax, or general sales tax is not recommended unless there is a pressing need for ensuring that a municipality has sufficient funds to develop and maintain an increasingly important local service that would otherwise not be maintained. For example, dedicated funds might be necessary to ensure that neighborhood parks are developed and maintained in highly urbanized and densely populated cities. Here, parks are becoming more and more important as exercise, recreation, and social gathering places; this is a service that is particularly vulnerable to local funding cuts especially during budgetary debates (Kitchen 2017).

Other than the occasional service such as the one identified in the preceding paragraph, revenue from local property, income, and general sales taxes should not be earmarked or dedicated to specific services. These revenues should be used to fund a range of local services that provide collective benefits to the local community.

Summary

There are no definitive conclusions that can be drawn about patterns of local taxation across countries nor can anything be concluded about whether one tax is always superior to other taxes. Municipal governments in some countries rely on property taxes; in other countries, they rely on income taxes; and in still other countries, they rely on a mix of local taxes—property, sales, and income. Reliance on a specific tax or taxes is dependent on a number of things including the traditional or historical pattern of taxation in that country, the local government's capacity to administer its own taxes, the types of expenditures that local government must fund, the willingness of state or central governments to assign taxes to local government, the constitutional and legislative requirements within which local governments operate, and a variety of other factors.

What we do know from international experience is that local governments carrying out their expenditure responsibilities are likely to be more efficient, responsible, accountable, and transparent if they are required to raise the revenue that they spend. Local governments in most countries have considerable autonomy in setting local tax rates but almost no control over their tax base.

Within the benefits-based model of local finance, the best taxes are those that are based on an immobile tax base and, therefore, borne primarily by local residents (not exported), that do not create problems with harmonization or harmful competition between local governments or local governments and more senior levels of government, and that are easy to administer locally. Here, there is a strong case for using a property tax, but personal income and sales taxes have also been defended at the local level, even though they are generally less effective at satisfying the criteria for a good local tax.

There are also arguments in support of a mix of local taxes, especially for large cities and metropolitan areas. This would make the overall local tax structure more flexible, thus permitting local governments to choose taxes that fit local conditions and circumstances. Additional tax sources would increase the revenue elasticity of the local tax base and allow it to adapt more easily to rising costs and service demands.

Regardless of the taxes in place, there is a general consensus that local taxes should only fund those services that benefit the local community; that there is no single tax that is ideal or preferred everywhere—indeed, a mix of taxes may be desirable especially for large urban or metropolitan areas; that the governing unit that spends tax dollars should be responsible for raising it including setting local tax rates; wherever possible, differential tax rates should be used to capture differences in the cost of delivering local services; that local tax rates, in general, should not be regulated; that local governments should not tax businesses to subsidize residential services as they do in virtually every country; and that local and metropolitan governments could use different taxes.

References

Almy, R. 2001. *A Survey of Property Tax Systems for Europe*. A Report Prepared for the Department of Taxes and Customs, Ministry of Finance, Republic of Slovenia.

Bahl, Roy. 2010. Financing metropolitan cities. In *United Cities and Local Governments, Local Government Finance: The Challenges of the 21st Century*. Second Global Report on Decentralization and Democracy. Barcelona: UCLG.

Bird, Richard M. 1993. Threading the Fiscal Labyrinth: Some Issues in Fiscal Decentralization. *National Tax Journal* XLVI (2): 207–227.

———. 2011. *Are There Trends in Local Finance? A Cautionary Note on Comparative Studies and Normative Models of Local Government Finance*. In IMFG Papers on Municipal Finance and Governance Series, University of Toronto. http://munkschool.utoronto.ca/imfg/resources/. Accessed 20 April 2018.

Bird, Richard M., and Roy Bahl. 2008. *Subnational Taxes in Developing Countries: The Way Forward*. Institute for International Business Paper No. 16. Toronto: Joseph L. Rotman School of Management, University of Toronto.

Bird, Richard M., and Duan-jie Chen. 1998. Federal Finance and Fiscal Federalism: The Two Worlds of Canadian Public Finance. *Canadian Public Administration* 1 (Spring): 50–74.

Bird, Richard M., and Enid Slack, eds. 2004. *International Handbook of Land and Property Taxation*. Northampton, MA: Edward, Elgar Publishing Limited.

Bird, Richard, and Enid Slack, eds. 2017. *Financing Infrastructure: Who Should Pay?* Montreal: McGill-Queens University Press.

———. 2019. Municipal Taxation in a Federal System: Linking Taxes and Expenditures. In *Funding the Canadian City*, ed. Enid Slack, Lisa Philipps, Lindsay M. Tedds, and Heather L. Evans, 22–43. Toronto: Canadian Tax Foundation and Institute on Municipal Finance and Governance.

Blochliger, H., and M. Nettley. 2015. *Sub-Central Tax Autonomy: 2011 Update.* OECD Working Papers on Fiscal Federalism, No. 20, OECD Publishing.

Boadway, Robin W., and Harry Kitchen. 1999. *Canadian Tax Policy.* 3rd ed. Toronto: Canadian Tax Foundation.

Chernick, Howard. 2002. The Effect of Commuters on the Fiscal Costs of the District of Columbia. *Mimeograph*, p. 36.

Chernick, Howard, and Olesya Tkacheva. 2002. The Commuter Tax and the Fiscal Cost of Commuters in New York City. *State Tax Notes* 25 (6): 451–456.

Chernick, Howard, Adam Langley, and Andrew Reschovsky. 2010. *Revenue Diversification and the Financing of Large American Central Cities.* Working Paper. Cambridge, MA: Lincoln Institute of Land Policy.

Dahlby, Bev, and Melville McMillan. 2019. What is the Role of Property and Property-Related Taxes? An Assessment of Municipal Property Taxes, Land Transfer Taxes, and Tax Increment Financing. In *Funding the Canadian City*, ed. Enid Slack, Lisa Philipps, Lindsay M. Tedds, and Heather L. Evans, 45–73. Toronto: Canadian Tax Foundation and Institute on Municipal Finance and Governance.

Duff, David G. 2004. Benefit Taxes and User Fees in Theory and Practice. *University of Toronto Law Journal* 54: 391–447.

Found, Adam, and Peter Tomlinson. 2017. *Business Tax Burdens in Canada's Major Cities: The 2017 Report Card.* E-Brief, C.D. Howe Institute, December 6.

Franzsen, Riel, and William McCluskey, eds. 2017. *Property Tax in Africa: Status, Challenges, and Prospects.* Lincoln Institute of Land Policy. Cambridge: Massachusetts.

Inman, Robert P. 2005. *Financing Cities.* Working Paper 11203. Cambridge, MA: National Bureau of Economic Research. http://www.nber.org/papers/w11203. Accessed 25 May 2018.

International Monetary Fund. 2001. *Code of Good Practices on Fiscal Transparency.* Washington, DC.

Kitchen, Harry. 2017. *Financing City Parks in Canada: What Might Be Done?* A Monograph Prepared for Park People, Toronto. March. https://parkpeople.ca/park-people-reports. Accessed 11 April 2018.

———. 2019. Beyond the Property Tax: What Taxes for Large Cities? In *Funding the Canadian City*, ed. Enid Slack, Lisa Philipps, Lindsay M. Tedds, and Heather L. Evans, 75–95. Toronto: Canadian Tax Foundation and Institute on Municipal Finance and Governance.

Kitchen, Harry, and Enid Slack. 2003. Special Study: New Finance Options for Municipal Governments. *Canadian Tax Journal* 51 (6): 2215–2275.

———. 2016. *More Tax Sources for Canada's Largest Cities: Why, What, and How?* IMFG Papers on Municipal Finance and Governance Series, No. 27, University of Toronto. http://munkschool.utoronto.ca/imfg/resources/. Accessed 16 April 2018.

Kitchen, Harry, and Almos Tassonyi. 2012. Municipal Taxes and User Fees. Chap. 9 in *Tax Policy in Canada*, ed. Heather Kerr, Ken McKenzie, and Jack Mintz. Toronto: Canadian Tax Foundation.

Lotz, Jorgen. 2012. *You Get What You Pay For: How Nordic Cities Are Financed.* In IMFG Papers on Municipal Finance and Governance Series, University of Toronto, No. 7. http://munkschool.utoronto.ca/imfg/resources/. Accessed 15 April 2018.

McClure, Charles E., Jr. 2001. The Tax Assignment Problem: Ruminations on How Theory and Practice Depend on History. *National Tax Journal* LIV (2): 339–363.

Mikesell, John L. 2010. The Contribution of Local Sales and Income Taxes to Fiscal Autonomy. Chap. 6 in *Municipal Revenues and Land Policies*, ed. G.K. Ingram and Y.-H. Yang. Cambridge, MA: Lincoln Institute of Land Policy.

———. 2011. Consumption and Income Taxes. Chap. 10 in *Greenbook.* International City Managers Association.

Mikesell, John. 2013. Administration of Local Taxes: An International Review of Practices and Issues for Enhancing Fiscal Autonomy. Chap. 4 in *A Primer on Property Tax Administration and Policy*, ed. William J. McCluskey, Gary C. Cornia, and Lawrence C. Walters, 1st ed. Hoboken, NJ: John Wiley & Sons Ltd.

Mintz, Jack M., and Tom Roberts. 2006. *Running on Empty: A Proposal to Improve City Finances.* Commentary No. 226. Toronto: C.D. Howe Institute.

OECD. 1999. *Taxes Powers of State and Local Government.* OECD Tax Policy Studies No. 1. Paris: OECD.

OECD. 2016. *Revenue Statistics 1965–2015.* Paris.

Rodden, Jonathan A., Gunnar Eskeland, and Jennie Litvack, eds. 2003. *Fiscal Decentralization and the Challenge of Hard Budget Constraints.* Cambridge: MIT Press.

Shah, Anwar. 2015. Taxing Choices for Economic Growth with Social Justice and Environmental Protection in the People's Republic of China. *Public Finance and Management* 15 (4): 326–357.

Slack, Enid. 2011. *Financing Large Cities and Metropolitan Areas.* IMFG Paper on Municipal Finance and Governance, No. 3, IMFG Perspectives Series, University of Toronto. http://munkschool.utoronto.ca/imfg/resources/. Accessed 18 April 2018.

———. 2017. *How Much Local Fiscal Autonomy Do Cities Have? A Comparison of Eight Cities Around the World.* MFG Perspectives Series, University of Toronto. http://munkschool.utoronto.ca/imfg/resources/. Accessed 18 April 2018.

ST LOUIS. 2017. *U.S. Cities That Levy Income (Earnings) Taxes.* www.stlouis-mo.gov. Accessed 18 April 2018.

CHAPTER 9

Property Taxation: Principles

Introduction

For many decades now, property taxation has been the backbone of municipal finance in many developed countries. More recently, it has played an increasingly important role in financing local government services in developing and transitional economies. As municipal spending responsibilities have increased, its relative importance as a revenue generator has increased. In particular, as a percentage of all local taxes, on average, its relative importance in OECD countries rose by 10–12 percentage points from 1998 to 2014 (Chap. 8).

The vast majority of countries tax immobile property only (land and buildings), but a few include movable property (personal property such as yachts, boats, and aircraft) in the tax base.[1] In many countries, property-related taxes used to fund operating expenditures include a tax on real property, special assessments (benefiting area taxes), payments-in-lieu of taxes, land transfer taxes, and a host of smaller charges affixed to property.[2] While the general tax on property is common across countries, other charges are less common.

As a tax for financing local services, the literature is very clear—it is a good tax! The perception that the taxpaying public have of this tax is often quite different, however. Its high visibility and the public's general lack of

[1] The country of Georgia and some states in the United States, for example.

[2] There are additional property-related charges for financing infrastructure—see Chap. 7.

H. Kitchen et al., *Local Public Finance and Economics*,
https://doi.org/10.1007/978-3-030-21986-4_9

or misunderstanding as to what is funded by the tax frequently lead to an inordinate amount of criticism. Some of these may be legitimate but many are not.

Legitimate criticism and concerns about the property tax range from those associated with its implementation and administration to a range of distortions or incentives that often emerge when the property tax is not implemented in an efficient, accountable, transparent, and fair manner.

At the outset, it must be mentioned that this chapter does not engage in a discussion of property taxes as they are applied in many countries for this has been covered extensively in books, articles, monographs, and reports extolling the structure, virtue, and problems of property taxes.[3] Instead, this chapter concentrates on a discussion of the major issues that should be addressed if the tax is to be fair in its impact on taxpayers (based on the benefits received model for local finance), nondistortionary (i.e., efficient) unless there are very good policy reasons for creating the distortion, and transparent. When this is achieved, local accountability is enhanced and criticism minimized, although the property tax because of its visibility will always be ripe for criticism (Slack 2013).

The section "Importance of Property Taxes" highlights the relative importance of property taxes as a generator of local revenue in OECD countries. Since there are two main components to the property tax—the tax base and the tax rate—the remainder of the chapter concentrates on each of these. In particular, the section "Assessment Base" describes the assessment base. The section "Issues in Assessment" looks at issues in assessment. The section "Issues Affected by Tax Rates" evaluates a number of efficient and fairness concerns that may be affected by property taxes. "Summary" summarizes the chapter.

Importance of Property Taxes

The role for local property taxation was laid out in Chap. 8. It is to fund services that provide collective benefits to the local community (Dahlby and McMillan 2019; Cornia 2013; Kitchen and Tassonyi 2012). Today, municipal or local governments in almost every country rely on some form of property tax for this purpose. Their relative importance, of course, varies from country to country (Bahl and Bird 2018, ch. 6). Not only does it

[3] See Bird and Slack 2004; McCluskey et al. 2013; Youngman 2016; and Franzsen and McCluskey 2017; Bahl and Bird 2018.

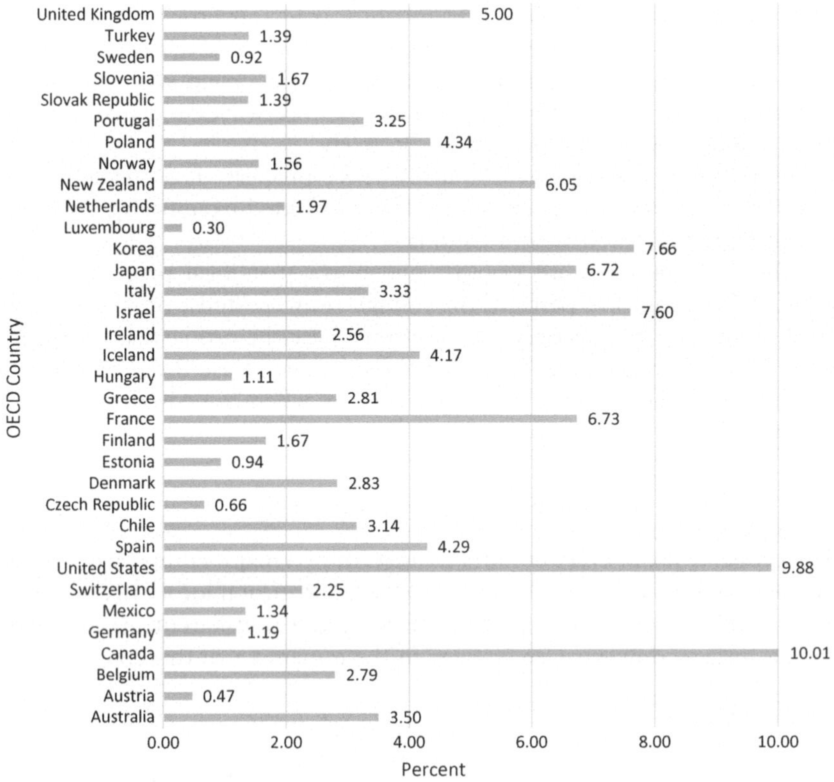

Fig. 9.1 Property tax as a percentage of all taxes: OECD countries, 2014. Source: Calculated from data in OECD, *Revenue Statistics 1965–2015* (Paris: OECD 2016)

depend on the extent to which other local taxes are used by municipal governments, it also depends on the division of tax-funded spending responsibilities between local and senior levels of government—the fewer tax-funded responsibilities that local governments have vis-à-vis senior levels, the less important local taxes will be in the country's overall tax system.

Figure 9.1 illustrates[4] the relative importance of property taxes in 34 OECD countries by measuring municipal property taxes as a percentage

[4] The data in this figure measure property taxes as a percent of all taxes, whereas the data in Table 8.1 in Chap. 8 measured property taxes as a percent of all local taxes.

of all taxes collected. At one extreme are Canada and the United States where property taxes account for roughly 10 percent of all tax revenue in the country. This is notably higher than the next group which includes Korea and Israel followed by France, Japan, and New Zealand at about 7.6 percent and more than 6 percent, respectively.

At the other extreme are countries where property taxes account for less than 1 percent of all tax revenue. These include Luxembourg, Austria, Czech Republic, Sweden, and Estonia.

When all countries are pooled, one notes that local property taxes account for about 3.4 percent, on average (unweighted), of all tax revenues. Furthermore, it is only 12 countries where the property tax actually exceeds the average, suggesting that these countries use the property tax much more extensively for tax-funded services when compared with those countries below the average.

Property Tax Structure

The property tax in every country consists of two major components—the tax (assessment) base and the tax rate. Each is critical if local governments are to utilize these taxes in a fair, efficient, and transparent manner and each is discussed in separate sections in the remainder of this chapter.

Assessment Base

The first major issue in property taxation is selecting the tax or assessment base. The choice depends on a number of factors including the history or tradition of taxation in the country, its capacity to implement an efficient and cost-effective administrative system, and most importantly as practice shows, whether there is an active, formal, and transparent property market transaction system. Where the latter is widely prevalent, countries largely rely on value-based assessment. This includes two possibilities—market value assessment and site value assessment. Where real estate markets are weak as in developing and transitional economies, the tendency is to rely on area or unit-based assessment systems. The more salient features[5] of each of these systems are discussed here.

[5] For a more detailed discussions, see Franzsen and McCluskey 2017, ch. 1; Youngman 2016, ch. 3; and Bahl and Bird, ch. 6.

Market Value

Market value is the clearest example of a value-based assessment system. Market value is the price that is determined between a willing buyer and a willing seller in an arms-length transaction. Three principal methods are used to value properties: sales method, income method, and cost method and all three may be used in any taxing jurisdiction. Property values under the sales method are based on the selling price of comparable properties. For similar or comparable properties, sales are recorded and assessed values are based on observed market transactions with adjustments to reflect differences (location, size, condition, etc.) between the subject property and observed sales. This method is common for single-family residences, condominiums, and other property types that have similar characteristics and for which a ready real estate market exists.

Where there is a scarcity of observed sales, the depreciated cost approach may be used. This is most appropriate for properties that are relatively new, and for which there are no comparable sales, and where improvements are relatively unique. Here, the property value is determined by assigning a value to the land as if it were vacant and then the cost of replacing buildings and other improvements are added. This approach is often used for assessing industrial properties.

For rental properties (multi-residential and commercial properties), a capitalized income approach may be used. Here, the annual net rental income (gross annual rental income minus annual operating expenses) is estimated with this annual net income subsequently converted to a capitalized property value (market value) using a capitalization factor. To illustrate, if net annual rental income from a specific property is $10,000 and if the current interest rate is 5 percent (e.g., current rate of return on a bond), the capitalized value of the property would be $200,000 (net rent divided by interest rate or $10,000/0.05). This is also the market value because an individual would be willing to pay $200,000 for a property that generates an annual net rent of $10,000—a 5 percent return which is identical to the return on bonds.

Either the comparative sales or depreciated cost approach appears to be superior to net rental income (gross rental income minus expenses) in determining market value. For properties such as vacant land and those subject to rent controls, there may not be a reliable measure of net rental income at market rates. Second, rental income may be difficult, perhaps impossible, to estimate for unique commercial and industrial properties including steel mills, mining operations, and so on. Third, during economic downturns when tourist traffic and hotel occupancy is down, estimates of future cash flows will be difficult to determine. Fourth, assessors may not have access to rental income information because this information is not publicly available in the same way as are sales prices (Bird and Slack 2004b, pp. 28–30).

Site Value Assessment

In its purest form, site value assessment[6] (SVA) is a special case of market value assessment where only land is assessed.[7] All capital improvements (e.g., buildings) are excluded from the assessment base. A form of site value assessment is used in a range of countries including Australia, New Zealand, Kenya, Jamaica, and sometimes used in cities even when another system is predominant elsewhere in the country (Franzen and McCluskey 2013).

An advantage of this system is that it is relatively inexpensive to administer because the physical attributes of land remain fairly constant. Difficulties emerge, however, in separating the value of land from the value of buildings and their components, especially in heavily built-up areas (Bahl 1998; McCluskey and Franzen 2004). In addition, this narrower tax base leads to higher nominal tax rates, a consequence which often elicits political resistance (Bahl 1998; Bahl and Wallace 2010). Finally, it excludes a significant amount of wealth that is tied up in buildings and it does not fit in with the tax base for property or land transfer taxes because these are based on total property values (Bahl and Wallace 2010).

Some countries have a split rate system. Here, different rates may apply to land and buildings or the same rate may be used for both. Often, however, a higher rate is applied to land to encourage its development. A major problem with a split rate system, however, is the costly valuations that are required to separate out land from buildings (Bahl and Wallace 2010; Bourassa 2009). Further, the inclusion of both land and buildings in the tax base tends to be more politically palatable because the base is broader and the nominal tax rate is lower.

[6] Sometimes referred to as unimproved land value assessment.

[7] In a few countries where land cannot be privately owned (e.g., Ghana and Tanzania), the property tax is levied only on buildings and improvements.

Area-Based Assessment

Under area or unit value assessment, the tax base is a combination of building area and lot area. For each property, assessed value is the sum of lot area times an assessment rate per square meter (foot) of lot area plus building area times an assessment rate per square meter (foot) of building area. The assessment rate may be the same for both building and area or it may differ, as it often does, with a lower rate applied to buildings to encourage development.

In its purest form, unit assessment does not take into consideration any variation in the assessment base to reflect location, market conditions, or quality of structures. In less than pure form, unit assessment may introduce variation to reflect location, zoning, use of property and other factors deemed appropriate.

Area-based systems are often used in countries (e.g., Czech Republic, India, and Slovenia) which do not have active, developed, and transparent real estate markets or where there is a resistance to move to a value-based assessment system.

Self-Assessment

This system is seldom used. Where it exists, property owners place an assessed value on their own property. Ireland is an example. Here, taxpayers value their property and assign it to a band for taxation purposes. As long as taxpayers are honest, this can be easy to administer and requires little administrative capacity. The problem, of course, is that property owners frequently underestimate the value of their property with more expensive properties being undervalued by a greater amount than lower-valued properties, leading to a regressive tax impact (Slack and Bird 2015). Because the amount of underestimation can be high, governments have difficulty enforcing a fair and efficient tax system and need, therefore, to hire a number of assessors and set up more sophisticated administrative capacity which, in the end, often proves to be quite costly. In essence, self-assessment systems are generally perceived as being inferior to either value-based assessment or area-based assessment. A comparison of some of the implications of the latter two comes next.

Which Is Preferred?

While the choice is often driven by whether there is an active, formal, and transparent real estate market, there are a number of distinct advantages that market value offers; for example, it is able to capture the amenities of the neighborhood through market prices, amenities that are often created by local government policies (e.g., zoning legislation). Area-based assessment in its truest form will not capture these amenities (McCluskey and Franzen 2013). To illustrate, assume two properties of identical size (i.e., identical in building size and land area) and age but located in different parts of a community. One is adjacent to a greenbelt while the other is next to an abattoir. Under area or unit assessment, both would be assessed in an identical fashion, whereas the two would be assessed differently under market value assessment. It is unlikely that many would argue that unit assessment would be fair in such an instance.

In addition, benefits from local public services are more closely reflected in property values than in the size of the property (Slack and Bird 2015). Properties close to parks and public transit systems benefit more from public services than do properties located some distance away. Furthermore, these benefits are reflected in higher property values for neighboring properties. Market value assessment captures these benefits, whereas area-based assessment does not.

Area-based assessment also results in relatively greater tax burdens on low-income households compared to high-income households because a comparable property in a high-income area pays the same tax as a comparable property in a low-income area. Similarly, older houses in need of substantial repairs, but with a large floor area, pay relatively high taxes (Bird and Slack 2004b). If property location has no effect on property taxes, land markets become distorted. For example, land located in high priced areas will not be recognized as such, potentially leading to a type of development that would not exist if the full value of land were considered in the location decision (Brzeski 1999).

In spite of arguments in support of value-based assessment, there are times when it will not work and area-based assessment will be needed. For example, it is the only reasonable choice in countries or areas of countries where fully functioning and transparent real estate markets do not exist (Slack and Bird 2015; Youngman and Malme 2000). This includes parts of countries (e.g., Canada and Russia) where there are isolated hamlets and no clearly functional market for property values because the government owns most of the housing and rents it to occupants. In some countries, it is the basis for taxing agricultural land with the unit value per square meter or hectare varying with location (distance from markets, region of country) and fertility (type of land, climate, and so on) and sometimes with the crops grown (Bird and Slack 2004b, p. 27).

Issues in Assessment

The success of any assessment system depends on the way in which the tax base is structured and administered. Here, there are two issues that are critical: first, the composition of the tax base, and second, the administration of the tax.

Composition of the Tax Base

To achieve the above-mentioned objectives, the tax base should be uniform in its treatment of all properties; that is, they should all be assessed in the same way—residential, commercial, industrial, farm, government, properties of charitable organizations and not-for-profit agencies, and so on. In most countries, however, there are a number of deviations from this practice, deviations that challenge the fairness of the system and lead to a number of unforeseen or unwanted outcomes. The following is a discussion of the major deviations.

Exemptions

Exemptions come in a variety of forms. First, some are dictated by the constitution or other policies and practices of senior levels of government. Here, municipalities are prevented from levying property taxes on property owned by these upper levels of government. There are two possible consequences of this. One is that local governments are simply unable to collect any revenue from these properties even though they benefit from local public services. The other is where the senior level of government (as in Canada) provides grants or payments-in-lieu (PILs) of property taxes to local governments.

Second, there is a group that includes places of worship (e.g., churches, temples, mosques) and cemeteries. A third group includes public or quasi-public organizations such as hospitals, educational institutions, libraries, nursing homes, non-profits organizations, and so on. Fourth, public parks, roads, schools, public libraries, foreign embassies, and property owned by international organizations also tend to be exempt from property taxes. Finally, some exemptions, such as for machinery and equipment, are given to encourage economic development. For each of these categories, property taxes or PILs are not paid. In many cases, properties which are exempt are not assessed; in other cases, properties are assessed although they are not taxed.

Exemptions have been criticized on a number of grounds (Youngman 2016, ch. 10; Slack and Bird 2015; Kitchen and Tassonyi 2012; Kitchen 2013). On the basis of fairness, they are difficult to justify unless, of course, payments-in-lieu equal what the property tax would have generated. In reality, however, PILs are criticized because they have not kept up with the property taxes that would have otherwise been paid (Kitchen and Vaillancourt 1990).

Another exemption available in a number of states in the United States is the "homestead exemption." While the limit and rules vary from state to state, the practice is to exempt the first few thousand dollars of assessment from property tax liability. This provides relatively more tax relief for lower-valued properties than higher-valued properties. In some states, the exemption is only available for residents; nonresidents including seasonal property owners cannot use it. In other words, two identical properties using the same local public services face different tax bills if one owner is a resident of the state and the other owner is not. A similar outcome, although not as a result of an exemption, is achieved in at least one province in Canada (Prince Edward Island) where all properties are assessed in the same way but nonresidents (generally seasonal) face a higher property tax rate than residents. Each of these situations is subject to the same criticisms directed at exemptions more generally.

Exempt properties use municipal services like other properties that occupy space and, hence, should be taxed (Bahl and Linn 1992). Second, exemptions narrow the tax base resulting in increased taxes (higher than they would be otherwise) on nonexempt properties or a reduction in service levels. Third, differential treatment may affect location decisions, choices about what activities to undertake, and other economic decisions (Kitchen and Vaillancourt 1990). Fourth, if there is a sound public policy reason or rationale for the exemption, it should be made explicit. The best way to determine this would be to assess all exempt properties in the same way as nonexempt properties. The property tax rate, then, could be applied to the assessment base to calculate the value of forgone tax revenue. In this way, local government officials and the taxpaying public would be better aware of the real cost of the exemptions and better able to judge whether they are acceptable and fair. If it turns out that there is no solid public policy rationale, the exemption should be terminated and the property should be subject to the tax rate levied on nonexempt properties.

Finally, since the proportion of tax-exempt properties varies by municipality, disproportionate tax burdens may be created across communities. This is especially troublesome when a senior level of government is able to determine what is exempt from local property taxation and what is not (Slack and Bird 2015).

Capping, Freezing, or Restricting Residential Assessment Increases

Capping, freezing, or limiting residential assessment increases is almost always a response to rapid increases in property values. In recent decades, these have been used in a variety of places. In Canada, they have been or are in place in three provinces (Prince Edward Island, Nova Scotia, and New Brunswick) where annual assessment increases have either been frozen for a short period of time or restricted to the increase in the Consumer Price Index until the property was or is sold at which time it is reassessed at market value.

Similar restrictions are in place in a number of US states (Youngman 2016, ch. 11). For example, in California, properties can only be assessed or reassessed at time of sale or resale. Between sales, annual assessment values may only increase by 2 percent or the rate of inflation whichever is less. In Michigan, reassessment increases are restricted to the lesser of 5 percent or the inflation rate. Some states have limited the increase in both property tax rates and assessed values (O'Sullivan 2001).

The problem with capping or freezing assessments is not so much a reduction in local tax revenue that municipalities get because they could, in many cases, increase their local tax rate to collect the same amount of revenue; the problem is the inequities that result when properties of similar market values face very different property tax liabilities. Furthermore, the frozen assessment creates a much larger benefit (in terms of taxes saved) for those who are benefitting from rapidly increasing property values at the expense of those whose property values are rising slowly or not at all (Youngman 2016, p. 211; Kitchen and Slack 2014).

Tax administration is complicated by capping, which creates confusion among taxpayers because the taxes paid are no longer calculated simply as a tax rate multiplied by the tax base. Moreover, there is no incentive to review one's assessment. If one of the reasons for the volatility has to do with assessment errors, these errors will never be corrected.

In addition, assessment limits such as freezing have resulted in "phantom tax relief"—the appearance of property tax relief where none actually exists (Haveman and Sexton 2008). This arises because an increase in the tax rate that is required to raise revenues when the size of the tax base has been reduced (by limiting assessment) can offset relatively small reductions in assessed value. The result is that, for some properties, a reduction in market value assessment actually results in higher property taxes (Youngman 2016, p. 210).

Further, freezing assessment until the property is sold reduces the incentive to move and may distort economic decision-making. For example, homeowners may not move if their job location changes because their property taxes would rise even if they move to a house of equal value. Freezing also creates a disincentive for skilled labor to move because new homeowners would pay the full property tax (not capped). It could also discourage new construction which is never included under a freeze and this can lead to a lower level of economic activity than might otherwise exist.

Another way in which volatility has been addressed is through land averaging over a period of years—three or four years or whatever time period is established by local tax authorities. Here, property values are averaged if the property tax increase exceeds a threshold amount. The cost of the program is recovered through a higher tax rate on all properties in the affected tax classes. Averaging maintains a commitment to full market valuations but slows the speed at which any individual taxpayer's property taxes can change. Averaging means that properties in the same class with the same pre-averaged market values do not pay the same amount of tax. In other words, averaging results in horizontal inequities. Land averaging works in both directions: as land values increase, the averaging slows the rate of increase; as land values decrease, averaging slows the rate of decrease. Not surprisingly, those who do not see immediate reductions when property values are falling tend not to be as supportive of averaging as those whose property values are increasing.

Averaging is inequitable because those taxpayers whose market value assessment goes down subsidize those taxpayers whose assessments have increased. In a period of generally rising land values, land averaging reduces the total assessed value for a class of property from what it would be in the absence of averaging. Therefore, to raise the same tax revenue from a class of property, the tax rate applied to the averaged values will be higher than for the un-averaged values. The higher the tax rate, the greater is the distortion on economic decisions.

As with capping, averaging weakens the link between current assessment and taxation. It attempts to increase predictability and provide greater stability for property owners but at the expense of equity—properties of equal value do not pay equal taxes—and transparency—taxpayers have trouble understanding how their taxes were calculated.

Finally, it is difficult to remove a scheme such as a freeze and land averaging and go back to a straight market value system if it has been in place for a long time and often, it would be politically suicidal to do so (Slack 2013).

Single Residential Versus Multi-residential Properties

The practice in many assessment jurisdictions is to assess multi-residential properties at higher values than single-unit residential properties. Given that the same residential tax rate is levied on both types of property, this leads to higher effective tax rates on the former. Since both single-unit and multi-unit residential properties have access to the same set of municipal services, it is neither fair nor economically efficient to overtax multi-residential properties vis-à-vis single-unit residential properties.

Administration of the Assessment System

Even if a country has a fair and efficient assessment base, it still needs a skilled, competent, and professional administrative structure to ensure that fairness, efficiency, transparency, and revenue generation are prevalent (Kelly 2013). This involves some key steps: identification of taxable properties; responsibility for assessment; frequency of assessment; appeals procedure; billing and collection; and assessment technique.

Property Identification

All taxable properties must be identified and described on the assessment roll with each property assigned a roll number. This number is important because it links assessment information with tax billing and property transfer records. The assessment roll or fiscal cadastre should include the address of the property, its owner, building and lot size in square meters (feet) or hectares (acres), a definition of property boundaries (using cadastral maps), the age of the building and information on renovations or improvements. Furthermore, this information should be updated whenever changes occur.

Responsibility for Assessment

Uniformity in assessment across a taxing jurisdiction is most easily achieved when the assessment function is centralized at the regional/state/provincial level if not at the central or federal level because it is able to benefit from economies of scale that might not be available to each municipality if each were to carry out their own assessment (Sjoquist and Walker 1999) and it creates more power for tax authorities in disputes with powerful taxpayers (Mikesell 2013). As well, uniformity in assessment has a greater chance of being achieved if it is centralized across a larger taxing area.

Staff competency requires all assessors to operate from a standard assessment manual where details of assessment practices and procedures are spelled out. Assessors should be required to attend training courses and pass clearly defined educational standards before becoming property assessors. This is the current practice in many countries, Canada included, where there are fully developed property assessment systems.

Frequency of Assessment

Periodic valuations and revaluations should be undertaken to ensure that assessment is kept up to date. In value-based systems, a shorter time frame for reassessment is preferred because this helps in maintaining the legitimacy of the tax base and it reduces the risk of sudden and dramatic changes in tax burdens that often arise when reassessments are conducted sporadically and infrequently (Bird and Slack 2004b).

Indexing the assessment base (between infrequent reassessments) to keep up with inflation, as is done in some countries, is not as equitable as conducting frequent property reassessments. Indexing all properties by the same factor (consumer price index or some other index) fails to capture the differential rates at which individual properties change in value. On the other hand, giving up some fairness may be a small price to pay if there are insufficient resources to conduct reassessments on a fairly regular basis. Furthermore, indexing that captures relative price changes by location and type of property could minimize some of the large assessment changes that might otherwise occur at the time when properties are actually reassessed (Slack and Bird 2015).

Appeals

An important component of a well-run assessment system is an effective appeals mechanism; that is, taxpayers should have an avenue for appealing their assessment if they feel it has been incorrectly determined (Slack and Bird 2015). In most cases, this starts with a reassessment by the assessment authority to correct factual errors and resolve minor differences of opinion over the value of the property. If differences cannot be resolved, the taxpayer should be able to proceed to a higher authority, generally made up of valuation experts. In some countries, there may be a further stage whereby the appeal could go to a specialized tax court.

Tax Billing and Collection

Before property taxes may be collected, each taxing jurisdiction is generally responsible for making sure that the tax role is prepared, tax liability is established (the tax bill), and ensuring that the tax bills are distributed to all property owners. In some countries, all of these functions are handled by the jurisdiction that sets the tax rate. In other countries, municipalities set their own tax rates with the remainder of the activities handled by another level of government (regional or state) or a private-sector institution (e.g., banks).

Tax billing and collection can benefit from economies of scale; hence, these two functions could be handled by a private-sector institution or by a larger unit of government. In the province of Ontario, Canada, for example, all regional and county governments (upper tier) set their own taxes independently of the tax rates set by the local municipalities (lower tier). The local municipalities then send out combined tax bills and collect both upper-tier taxes and lower-tier taxes. This practice has been around for years and has been fiercely defended in the face of proposals to migrate billing and collection to the upper tier in order to take advantage of economies of scale. Furthermore, billing and collection is an administrative function and has nothing to do with policy setting or decision-making.

Tax collection is usually, but not always, a local government function. If the property tax is not paid by a specific due date, interest charges and a late penalty are generally charged. If payment is not forthcoming after a considerable period of time, the property may be seized and sold to pay delinquent taxes and penalties. Such sales are rare, however. A more effective enforcement mechanism, especially in countries with well-defined legal systems for property ownership and transfers, involves preventing the transfer of legal title to the property (either through a sale or through a gift) until all past property taxes and penalties have been paid.

Tax arrears are a serious problem for countries if they lower the revenues generated by the property tax by a notable amount. The larger the uncollected taxes, the lower the effectiveness of the property tax system in generating revenue to fund local public services. Large tax arrears create higher taxes on those properties that pay their taxes and/or lead to fewer local public services than should otherwise be the case. Hence, the importance of enforcing tax collection.

Assessment Techniques

Even when reassessments are done frequently (yearly, every second year, or even every third year), it is not possible for property assessors to reassess each piece of residential property on such a frequent basis. This would require too many assessors and it would be too expensive. This shortfall, however, has been overcome with the use of computer-assisted mass appraisal (CAMA) techniques for residential properties. This relies on computers and mathematical formulas to establish a relationship between property characteristics and selling price, thus facilitating an estimate of market value for properties that have not sold recently (McCluskey and Franzen 2013).

Mass appraisal makes use of multiple regression analysis. This predicts the market value of properties from known values of other variables associated with these properties (such as living area, lot size, location, availability of garage, age of building, number of bathrooms, and so on). More recently, there has been a move to integrate geographical information systems (GIS), which include the impact of location on selling prices, into CAMA models (McIlhatton et al. 2013). These techniques examine properties that have actually sold and they identify the statistical relationship between a number of features of these properties and their selling price. This statistical relationship is used to estimate the price for properties that have not sold recently.

These approaches do not eliminate the need for traditional property assessors and assessment practices. Indeed, property assessors are necessary for examining a certain number or properties yearly and for assisting in developing and improving CAMA and GIS models that identify property features affecting price. Property assessors are also needed for assessing properties that display anomalies from the regular pattern and for handling property assessment appeals. What mass appraisal does do is to permit more frequent assessment updates without a physical inspection of all properties.

In many countries, assessment agencies now use software packages for these mass appraisals. Here, local assessors can quickly analyze thousands of sales and use this information to estimate market values for properties that have not recently sold. This has definitely improved the quality and frequency of reassessment and permitted municipalities to have much more up-to-date assessment rolls.

Issues Affected by Tax Rates

Setting the local tax rate is an integral and critical component of any property tax system. How it is set and how it is applied can have major consequences for revenue generation, fairness, transparency, accountability, and for incentives (efficiency) to affect taxpayer behavior. In general, there are three steps followed by countries that set their own tax rates. First, local governments determine their expenditure requirements or needs. Second, they deduct all nonproperty tax revenues (grants, user fees, charges, permits, etc.) from spending requirements leaving the amount that is to be funded from the tax base. Third, they divide the needed property tax revenues by the property tax base to get the tax rate. This rate, while easy to calculate, is seldom free from controversy, especially in the way in which it is applied in the vast majority of countries. Issues of importance for local taxes generally were discussed in Chap. 8. This section will concentrate on issues as they relate to property taxes more specifically.

Who Should Set Property Tax Rates?
In many countries, tax rates are set locally. However, in some of these countries, limits on what can be set are imposed by a senior level of government. In other countries, the property tax rates are set by senior levels of government (Bird and Slack 2004a, pp. 34–35).

Following on the established theme that the most transparent, efficient, and accountable local government is one that is responsible for raising its own revenue, it follows that local governments should be responsible for setting their own tax rates. Failure to permit and require this means that the close link between decisions over revenue generation and expenditure decisions is lost. An inability to set the tax rate, for instance, impedes local governments from controlling the level and composition of their revenues. If tax rates are centrally determined, accountability and transparency is almost certain to be reduced because local officials are unlikely to have much, if any, influence over rate setting (Zorn 2013). However, if tax rates are set locally but within limits (section “Should Limits Be Imposed on Property Tax Rates?”), imposed by a senior level of government, accountability and transparency will be, at least, partially achieved. Finally, in those countries where the tax base is determined by an independent assessment authority or where it is the responsibility of a senior level of government, responsibility for local rate setting is particularly important because this is the only means by which local governments can exert any autonomy over their tax system (Slack and Bird 2015).

In many countries, local governments function within a two-tier governing structure, sometimes referred to as an upper tier and a lower tier. The upper tier is generally referred to as a county, a region, a district, or a metropolitan level of government. It encompasses a number of lower-tier levels of government that are referred to as cities, towns, townships, villages, hamlets, and so on. Each level is responsible for funding a distinct set of local services, although there may be some overlap, and each has its own set of revenue tools including the property tax. Where the tax base is shared, each should set its tax rate independently of the other. For each level of government, the tax rate should be sufficient to generate the revenues needed to cover the cost of local tax funded public services that each level provides.

Should Limits Be Imposed on Property Tax Rates?
The practice of imposing tax limits on municipal governments by a senior level of government is more prominent in some countries than in others. In the United States, for example, the majority of the states now impose limits on tax rates for local government. In Canada, provincial governments have not placed limits on the general municipal tax rate, although some provinces have legislated the amount by which commercial/industrial tax rates may differ from the residential rate.

Limits are intended to control and restrict the growth in municipal government spending and hence, property taxation (Kitchen 2013). Research on the success of these limits has addressed three main questions. First, did property tax limits reduce property tax revenues? Based on the evidence, the answer is yes. Property tax revenues declined in constant dollars if not in current dollars. In California, proposition 13 led to an immediate decrease of about 45 percent. In Massachusetts, the initial impact was a decrease of 18 percent (Clemens et al. 2003, pp. 189–190). Overall in the United States, one calculation from a few years ago estimated that local property taxes per capita fell by 3 percent after tax limits were imposed (Shadbegian 1999).

Second, were reductions in property tax revenues offset by increases in other local revenues? The evidence here is not as compelling but it does indicate that other local revenue sources were generally substituted for property tax decreases (O'Sullivan 2001, pp. 189–191; Brunori 2007). Greater reliance was placed on local user fees, permits, licenses, and so on. This pattern, by the way, is also happening in countries that do not have limits on property tax increases.

Third, did property tax limits affect input choices (administrative staff vs. service providers such as police officers and fire fighters) and quantities of output produced by local governments? The evidence here was mixed. Some studies found that local governments responded to tax limits by cutting proportionately more of their administrative costs while others found that local governments responded by cutting proportionately more of their service costs. Similar variations in results were noted for output. Some studies found that municipalities produced roughly the same quantity of services with less revenue while other studies noted that private-sector provision replaced public provision of local services (O'Sullivan 2001, pp. 191–196).

Property tax limits also have another major impact. They curtail the decision-making power of municipal governments if they reduce the municipal sector's flexibility and capacity to raise its own revenue. This is particularly worrisome if it means that local governments cannot provide sufficient revenues to provide local public services that are desired or wanted by local residents.

Analytical arguments supporting property tax limits for local governments are generally weak unless, of course, they are necessary to prevent tax exporting (section "Is the Nonresidential Property Tax Exported?"). This arises when richer local governments levy higher taxes on industries believing that the ultimate tax burden will be borne by nonresidents (Boadway and Kitchen 1999, p. 373). As well, a minimum tax rate may be needed to prevent richer municipalities from tampering with the tax rate to retain and attract new businesses, an approach that could initiate a "race to the bottom" and ultimately, to a number of unfair and inefficient location decisions (Slack and Bird 2015).

In general, however, locally elected councils should be responsible for setting local property tax rates. They are in the best position to determine what citizens want and need. Furthermore, if these councils are unresponsive to local wishes, they are likely to be voted out of office at the next municipal election. As well, the comparatively large number of municipalities in every country means that local tax rates will be set in a competitive environment; that is, every municipality is aware of its neighboring jurisdiction's tax rates and unwilling to have its rate differ noticeably from its neighbors for fear of losing businesses and people. The literature tells us that property tax differentials play a role in intra-regional location decisions (section "Do Property Tax Incentives Stimulate Economic Development?"); hence, the reason why municipal governments compete with their neighbors to restrict property taxes. This tax competition works to control tax rates and it permits the municipality to make its own spending and taxation decisions without the restrictive controls of a senior level of government.

Should Municipalities Use Variable Tax Rates or Uniform Rates?
The issue here is whether a local taxing jurisdiction should apply a single uniform property tax rate to all properties within its taxing jurisdiction or whether different (variable) tax rates should be used; that is, tax rates that vary with the cost of servicing different properties by type or by location within a municipality or rates that may vary for other reasons. Many countries have one tax rate for all properties. Others have tax rates that differ by property class, or that differ by assessment practices, or that differ because of tax relief for specific classes of property (Bird and Slack 2004a). In most cases where variable rates are used, properties are assessed at a uniform percentage of market value (100 percent, or 80 percent, or some other fixed percentage) and differential rates are applied to the assessed values. In a few countries, differentiation is achieved by applying a uniform tax rate to properties that are assessed at different percentages of value.

Variable rates are fair on the basis of benefits received as long as the variation in the rate captures the variation in the differential cost of servicing different property types or property locations. Second, they are efficient if designed to cover the cost of local public services consumed—no incentive exists for a household or firm to alter its behavior or location to avoid the tax as long as it matches the cost of services used. Third, they are efficient as long as higher tax rates apply to tax bases that are more inelastic (highly insensitive to changes in tax rates) in supply. Since residential property is an inelastic tax base when compared with commercial and industrial property (the latter can move to other municipalities and to other countries), this calls for higher tax rates on residential properties than on commercial and industrial properties, a practice that is almost never followed as is noted later (section "Should Municipalities Levy Higher Tax Rates on Nonresidential Properties Vis-à-Vis Residential Properties?"). Fourth, variable tax rates have a further advantage in that they could be used to distort decisions deliberately to achieve certain municipal land use objectives. For example, if higher tax rates slow development and lower-tax rates speed up development, a deliberate policy to develop certain neighborhoods instead of others might be achieved through different tax rates for different locations (Slack and Bird 2015; Kitchen and Tassonyi 2012).

Should Municipalities Set Progressive Property Tax Rates?

Progressive property tax rates increase progressively as the value of the property tax base increases. Support for this approach comes from those who want to extract progressively more property tax dollars out of more expensive residential properties. In essence, this is a form of income redistribution where these properties pay proportionately more so that less expensive properties pay proportionately less.

Analytically, support for this approach is difficult to find. Asking municipalities to use the property tax base to engage in income redistribution in this way is a bad idea. Leaving income redistribution to the local level creates the following scenario. As long as people are mobile between the two jurisdictions, high-income people will move out of the progressive tax rate jurisdiction and low-income people will move in, other things being equal. Redistribution, then, breaks down unless it is carried out on a broader scale, such as the state/provincial/cantonal level (Youngman 2016).

Under the benefits-based model for local public finance, taxpayers pay for those services that provide collective benefits to the local community. For residential properties, all of which have access to the same set of services, this suggests that the tax rate should be the same. Since there is no evidence to suggest that the benefits received from local public services increase progressively with property values, there is no justification for charging higher tax rates on more expensive properties.

As well, a progressive property tax could exacerbate liquidity problems for those who are asset rich but income poor—an increasing concern in some cities where there is a heavy reliance on property taxes. For example, seniors on fixed incomes who purchased their properties many years ago face high property taxes because their assessed property values have increased but their incomes are low. A better way of handling concerns over a taxpayers' ability to pay is through the use of tax relief or concessions for low-income taxpayers (section "Why Tax Relief and What Form Should It Take?").

Lastly, from an administrative point of view, a uniform tax rate has the advantage of being simple, transparent, and predictable in terms of the amount of revenue that will be collected (Zorn 2013). Taxpayers find one tax rate easier to understand and it is less complicated for tax officials to administer a uniform tax rate than progressive tax rates. Moreover, where property values are divided into different classes by property value, there will be an incentive for those taxpayers at the bottom of a value class to appeal an assessment to move into a lower class. Hence, the number of appeals would surely increase.

Should Municipalities Levy Higher Tax Rates on Nonresidential Properties Vis-à-Vis Residential Properties?

Taxation of nonresidential properties (commercial and industrial) at higher tax rates than residential properties is a common practice across countries (Bird and Slack 2004a, b). Not only is this a consequence of higher property tax rates on these properties, it is often a result, as well, of other property-related charges that have no relationship to services received or to property value.

Higher taxes on commercial and industrial properties are generally the outcome of assessing these properties at higher values than residential properties and levying the same tax rate on both property types or through the simple application of higher tax rates on business properties (Bird et al. 2012).

There is very little economic rationale for higher taxation of business properties. Differentially higher tax rates that are not offset by higher levels or quality of public services distort land use decisions and favor residential over nonresidential properties (Maurer and Paugam 2000). Overtaxation of a factor of production such as real property also distorts productive efficiency because it changes the relative prices of factors of production (Slack and Bird 2015). A recent study on business taxation in Canada estimated that business property and land transfer taxes (section "Should Municipalities Adopt a Land or Property Transfer Tax?") represent about two-thirds of the total investment tax burden faced by the nonresidential sector (Found and Tomlinson 2017). When a tax burden like this is not offset by associated benefits from local public services as many have suggested (e.g., Mintz and Roberts 2006; and Kitchen and Tassonyi 2012), overtaxation ensues and the level of investment can fall hindering economic growth. Higher tax rates on the nonresidential sector also lead to the potential for the tax to be exported (section "Is the Nonresidential Property Tax Exported?") onto people in other communities, a violation of one of the principles for a good local tax.

Efficiency in municipal service levels will not be achieved if revenues collected from property taxes on business properties are used to subsidize services consumed by the residential sector and there is considerable evidence that this is the case.[8] Since service levels in any municipality are driven primarily by the demands of the residential sector (they vote), their subsidization means that the residential tax rate will be less than it would

[8] For a review of some of these studies, see Kitchen and Tassonyi 2012.

be in the absence of the subsidy and an oversupply of municipal services could ensue. Equity is not achieved either if those benefiting from the services are not paying full costs.

Further concerns with the overtaxation of the commercial/industrial sector arise because this tax represents a fixed charge that must be paid. The tax is fixed in the sense that it is unrelated to the value of municipal services used or profits earned. As long as the tax rate is more than necessary to cover the marginal cost of municipal services consumed or if there are no economic rents for it to capture, resources will be allocated inefficiently. This overtaxation of the nonresidential sector can lead to less economic activity, lower output, fewer jobs, and a less competitive business environment.

One defense of the overtaxation of business properties is often provided by municipal officials and some taxpayers and it is as follows. Since businesses can deduct all expenses incurred in earning income (including business taxes) for their corporate income tax base and since owner-occupiers of residential dwellings are not allowed similar deductions, it has been suggested that an extra tax on business is legitimate in that it attempts to even out the disparities in taxes that would otherwise exist on these two different categories of taxable property. While it is true that owner-occupiers are not able to deduct property taxes, it is also the case that owner-occupiers are not required to include in taxable income either imputed income from their owner-occupied dwellings or capital gains earned on the disposal of their principal residences (Boadway and Kitchen 1999). Such exclusion is similar to a deduction from income for tax purposes (as in the case of the tax on businesses) in that both reduce the taxable economic income of the taxpaying unit. On this basis, it is difficult to make a case for a higher tax rate on commercial and industrial properties.

Concern over the kinds of distortions noted above with the property tax on commercial and industrial properties has prompted at least one suggestion for reform in Canada (Bird and Mintz 2000; Bird and Wilson 2003). Specifically, it has been argued that revenues from a portion of the nonresidential property tax should be replaced with revenues from a new business value tax (BVT). This BVT would be a value-added tax. It would be levied on business income. It would be on production and not consumption. This would make it an origin, not destination-based tax; hence, it would tax exports and not imports. Further, it is suggested that it be a senior government's tax with municipalities having the opportunity to set local rates that are "piggybacked" onto the senior government rate. The latter could even impose limits on local surcharges to prevent unwanted locational distortions. Because the BVT is a value-added tax (essentially sales less cost of goods purchased), it would eliminate a number of the distortions created by the current overtaxation of business property. This type of local business tax is used in Germany and Japan.

Do Property Tax Incentives Stimulate Economic Development?

There is no general agreement about the importance of property taxes on location decisions. The available evidence, most of which is drawn from the United States, suggests that property tax differentials are relatively unimportant in intermunicipal or interregional location decisions but do play a role in intra-municipal or intra-regional location decisions. These results are not surprising. In terms of intermetropolitan location decisions, business activity is mostly influenced by market conditions, the availability and cost of a skilled labor force, access to transportation, the presence of necessary production materials, and proximity to markets. Since property taxes account for a relatively small proportion of the total costs for most businesses, it is unlikely to be large enough to initiate a relocation decision or encourage significant business activity.

Intra-metropolitan location decisions, on the other hand, may be affected by property tax differentials. The smaller the area over which the business is choosing to locate, the more similar are the nontax factors. Within a large urban or metropolitan area, for example, market conditions and cost variables (such as labor, transportation, and energy costs) tend to be reasonably uniform. In this context, fiscal factors take on more significance: lower property taxes in one community will generate lower costs at the margin and higher profits for businesses located in that particular community (Bartik 1991). The review of intra-metropolitan studies suggests an average elasticity of −2.0 for taxes with respect to business activity. This estimate means that a reduction in taxes of 10 percent will increase business activity by 20 percent. The elasticity within metropolitan areas is about four times the elasticity between metropolitan areas.

The influence of taxes on business location, even within metropolitan areas, varies for different types of business activities because industries differ in terms of their responsiveness to fiscal variables. For example, tax-sensitive firms are more likely to locate in a low-tax jurisdiction. According to studies that have been undertaken on different industries, manufacturing location decisions tend to be more sensitive to taxes than nonmanufacturing location decisions. The reason is that the manufacturers are more oriented to national and international markets. Local costs will have a greater effect on their profits because it will be more difficult to pass these costs on to consumers. Moreover, manufacturers tend to be more capital intensive and local property taxes are taxes on capital (Bartik 1991). Empirical studies confirm that capital-intensive industries are more sensitive to taxes on capital than are other industries.

Where there are advantages to locating near-similar activities (agglomeration economies), the tax will have a less significant impact. For example, businesses in the financial district may enjoy significant advantages from being in that particular location. In this case, the property tax may be less important in the business location decision than in those cases where business is fairly mobile.

Do Property Taxes Affect Competitiveness?

The few studies on nonresidential property taxes and economic competitiveness suggest that the impact of property taxes depends on a number of factors—the nature of the business decision (investment in new facilities, ongoing operations, etc.), the business in question (pulp and paper, forestry, mining, etc.), plus several other factors. One study on industrial property taxes in the province of British Columbia (Davies et al. 2011) analyzed the impact of property taxes on business decisions of major industrial facilities in that province: investment in new facilities, ongoing operations and temporary closures, reinvestment in existing plants, and economic obsolescence and plant closure.[9] In their analysis, they found that under typical operating conditions, property taxes are not a major issue for competition. The reason is that property taxes represent a relatively small portion of overall costs and, as long as industries are operating profitably, the tax has little impact on business operating decisions.

In terms of investment in major capital projects, property taxes are not a significant factor either because they are small relative to total costs and relative to the potential revenue from the new investment. These investments tend to be undertaken when commodity prices are high and investors see a potential for extraordinary profits.

When it comes to reinvestment in existing facilities, however, property taxes do have an impact. These investments tend to be undertaken when commodity prices are low in order to maintain production capacity or reduce operating costs.

[9] Their case studies included: pulp and paper, sawmills, mining, aluminum and smelting, shipbuilding and repair, and marine terminals and grain elevators.

Property taxes have a larger impact on firms with facilities in many different locations. These firms will optimize the allocation of capital to those projects which have the highest return. Other things being equal, firms will thus have an incentive to invest in those jurisdictions that have lower industrial tax rates. Finally, for firms in financial distress, property taxes are a major factor because they may account for a large portion of the firm's fixed costs.

Is the Nonresidential Property Tax Exported?

An important principle underlying a good local tax is that it be borne by taxpayers in the taxing jurisdiction and not exported beyond this jurisdiction. When the tax is exported, it has the potential for misallocating resources and lowering municipal accountability.

Tax exporting refers to situations in which some portion of the local tax burden is borne by people who live elsewhere either through a change in relative commodity prices or in a change in the net return to nonlocally owned factors of production (inputs in the production process). For example, if higher effective tax rates on commercial and industrial properties lead to relatively higher prices charged on the sale of that community's exports to other communities, the taxing jurisdiction will have effectively shifted part of its tax burden onto residents of other communities. If the commercial/industrial property tax in every jurisdiction is exported to some extent, those jurisdictions exporting relatively more of the tax will be better off than those jurisdictions exporting relatively less. In particular, if the burden of this tax is shifted from residents of high-income jurisdictions to those of low-income jurisdictions, the distribution of income among jurisdictions is worsened. Furthermore, this runs counter to equalization schemes of senior levels of government, where they exist, that are aimed at redistributing resources (income) from relatively high-income jurisdictions to relatively low-income jurisdictions.

There is limited evidence on tax exportation. One Canadian study on a sample of large municipalities in Ontario is dated by now (Thirsk 1982) but it is illustrative of a problem that almost certainly still exists. It concluded that the degree of exportation ranged from a low of 16 percent of the commercial/industrial tax burden to a high of 106 percent. More than this, relatively rich municipalities had relatively high exporting rates whereas relatively poor municipalities had relatively low-tax exporting rates. This led to an implicit transfer from relatively low-income municipalities to relatively high-income municipalities.

Finally, when the commercial/industrial sector exports its tax burden, municipal government accountability is weakened because the direct link between the government responsible for the service and the ultimate person/agency/body paying the tax for it is missing.

Is There a Role for Property Tax Incentives?

There is a significant literature on the pros and cons of nonresidential property tax incentives in the United States. In large part, this is due to the proliferation of tax incentives in that country[10] where it has been estimated that they cost state and local governments between $5 and $10 billion per year (Kenyon et al. 2012b). Property tax abatements are used to discourage existing businesses from leaving a city, to steer businesses to a particular location within the city, or to change the form of the property (Wassmer 2014). The idea behind reducing the property tax is to compensate a business for pursuing an economic activity that is in the public interest but which may not necessarily be in its private interest (Wassmer 2014).

Those who favor property tax incentives argue that recipient firms provide benefits to the community that exceed the costs to the municipality for business services and environmental degradation caused by the businesses (Glaeser 2002). When incentives succeed in attracting new business to a city, they can increase income and employment, expand the property tax base, and revitalize distressed areas (Kenyon et al. 2012a; Wagaman 2017). If the revenue generated by the business exceeds the cost of services provided to it, then the business generates a fiscal surplus for the city (Wassmer 2014). In the best of all cases, attracting a large facility can increase worker productivity and attract other firms to the area, creating agglomeration economies (benefits from firms locating in close proximity) (Glaeser 2002). Finally, tax incentives are an indication that the municipality is pro-business (Brunori 2007).

Critics of property tax incentives argue that property tax incentives have a poor record in promoting economic development. A quick review of the evidence should illustrate these concerns. Higher taxes that are matched by better public services will not discourage firms from locating in a municipality because public services also influence economic development. Expansion of public services may reduce the prices paid for those services

[10] A study of stand-alone property tax abatements in the United States indicates that 35 states allowed for these abatements in 2004 (Dalehite et al. 2005). In 2007, there were at least seven other states that allowed municipalities to offer a reduction in property taxes but only in conjunction with a larger economic development program (Wassmer 2007).

by business (e.g., education expenditures may reduce the quality-adjusted prices of labor by increasing the supply of workers of a given quality). Firms prefer to locate in communities with extensive business-related services because without local government provision of these services, the firms would likely have to provide them on their own.

Finally, if one jurisdiction lowers its property tax rate on businesses and neighboring jurisdictions keep their taxes the same, the expected impact on business activity in that jurisdiction is likely to be much greater than if all jurisdictions in the metropolitan area lower their business tax rates simultaneously (Wassmer 2007). Property tax incentives are effective for the first jurisdiction that implements them but once they proliferate across the metropolitan region, they lose their effectiveness in promoting economic growth (Kenyon et al. 2012b). Moreover, and more likely, they lead to destructive bidding wars.

In making a decision about whether or not to grant a tax incentive, information is needed on the cost to the firm of doing business in the city compared to other locations as well as the costs and benefits to the city of having the firm located there. Accurate information is not always available, however, because firms face the moral hazard of only offering information that supports their request for the tax incentive (Wassmer 2014). Once the firm has made its location decision, it is difficult to know what would have happened if the tax break had not been offered.

In short, opposition to tax incentives focuses on the zero-sum aspects of tax competition: development at one location will be at the expense of development at another location. Tax incentives are often wasted on firms that would have located there anyway. Lower taxes are offered to new businesses locating in the municipality at the expense of existing businesses. Tax incentives can lead to unfair competition among businesses and can lead to a situation where no major investments occur without them. Tax cuts need to be financed in some way and, if they are financed by cutting public services that businesses want, the net effect on economic development could be negative. Indeed, the extensive US evidence suggests that such incentives often lead to a deterioration of the tax base and lower levels of public services.

How Should Special Properties Be Taxed?

While the list of special properties and their tax treatment may vary from country to country, some tend to be common everywhere. These include the tax treatment of machinery and equipment, linear properties, farmland, forest land, and mines and mineral resources.

Machinery and Equipment

Local taxing jurisdictions vary in the property tax treatment of machinery and equipment (M&E): some tax it as long as it is affixed to real property; others tax it if it provides services to the building; and still others partially or entirely exclude it from the tax base. It may be an open debate as to whether or not excluding one component of the manufacturing sector (M&E) from the property tax base while taxing other components (buildings and land) is the fairest and most effective way to assist the manufacturing sector. A simple example may illustrate this. Suppose we have two neighboring industrial properties assessed at $2 million each, but with different proportions of M&E versus land/buildings. In this scenario, the property with the higher percent of M&E pays proportionately less in property taxes compared to the property with the lower percent of M&E (assuming that M&E is tax exempt). This situation, it could be argued, is not fair because one property pays less property tax than the other, even though each benefits from the same level of public services. Moreover, a policy of exempting taxes on one factor of production creates an incentive for companies, wherever possible, to use more of the nontaxable factor (M&E) and less of the taxable factors (land/buildings), thus distorting their economic decisions and also reducing the local assessment base.

On the other hand, if one were to draw an analogy to the property tax treatment of residential properties, personal property (furnishings, appliances, motor vehicles, and so on) is often not taxed while furnaces, air conditioners, and plumbing fixtures that are affixed to property and provide services to the property are factored into property values and hence, are taxed. Taxation of these fixtures is similar to the taxation of M&E that provides services to buildings. Excluding personal property may be similar to excluding M&E that does not provide services to the building.

In any case, exempting machinery and equipment to assist the manufacturing and processing sector is likely a second-best solution. A fairer and less distorting way of helping the manufacturing and industrial sector would be to lower the property tax burden on the entire sector as opposed to exempting or partially exempting one factor of production.

Linear Properties

Linear properties include railway rights of way, pipelines, telecommunications and cable properties, gas and oil wells, and electric power property (including generation, transmission, and distribution). Often, these properties cross municipal boundaries, thus complicating the levying of the property tax.

To illustrate the variation in property tax treatment across municipalities, let us turn to the Canadian experience (Kitchen 2007). In Ontario, real estate (land and buildings) holdings for telephone, cable, municipal electric utilities, and gas companies are assessed and taxed as commercial or industrial properties. Crown agency utilities are assessed at full value, do not pay taxes, but make payments-in-lieu of taxes. Utility poles, transmission towers, wires, underground cables are not valued and taxed. Underground pipes for natural gas distribution are taxed on a per meter (length) basis. "Rights of ways" owned by utilities and railways are taxed at a fixed rate per acre—province sets the rate for nine geographic regions and indexes it to the average provincial commercial tax rate changes.

In Quebec, land, buildings, attached machinery, and equipment that are part of a gas distribution, telecommunication, or electric power system are taxed as follows (not on assessed value). For natural gas and electricity distribution systems, the tax is 3 percent of gross revenues. For cable television systems, the tax rates are 2 percent of revenue under $5 million, plus 3 percent of revenue over $5 million. For other telecommunications systems, the rates are 3 percent and 5 percent, with same threshold revenue level. Revenues are allocated to municipalities on basis of subscribers.

In Newfoundland, utilities do not pay a property tax. Instead, they pay a tax of 2.5 percent of revenues collected in the municipality. In British Columbia, electricity, oil, natural gas, and telecommunications pay a gross receipts tax (1 percent) instead of a property tax. Railway "rights of ways" are assessed on the basis of weighted average assessed values for an area as approximated by assessed values of abutting properties.

In Saskatchewan, railway "rights of way" and pipelines are taxed on 75 percent of assessed values. Assessed values are estimated from values of abutting properties. In Manitoba, pipelines and railways are valued as follows: railway roadways are assessed on the basis of gross tons of freight per kilometer; natural gas distribution systems are assessed at market values—based on values of abutting properties; and pipeline assessment is based on the outside diameter of the pipe.

In Alberta, the tax on a railway "right-of-way" is a fixed dollar per kilometer that varies with the annual tonnage transported on that "right-of-way." The assessment of linear property is based on the values of abutting properties—properties include oil and gas wells; pipelines to transport petroleum products; electric power systems (generation, transmission, and distribution); telecommunication systems and cable TV. In all cases, the tax rates are set by the province.

This variation in practice is not unlike that in many other countries with extensively developed property tax systems. Each method is intended to measure the value of the asset. In virtually every case, the chosen measure is the one that is most practical and easily administered.

Farmland

Farm properties are favored in the property tax system in many countries as part of a more general policy of protecting farmland. A common approach is to assess farms at their value in current use rather than market value (which reflects the highest and best use). The value of a farm is determined by its selling price if it were to continue to be used as a farm. Alternative uses of the farm, or its speculative value, are not considered in the determination of value. Other ways of favoring farm properties include providing exemptions for part or all of the farm property, lowering tax rates on farms, or providing farm tax rebates.

Taxing agricultural land on the basis of its value in current use was originally designed to reduce development pressure, reflecting the widespread perception that it is unfair to tax farmers for nonfarming uses such as real estate development. Although protecting family farms is the main justification for current use assessment, these provisions seldom differentiate between family farms, hobby farms, corporate farms, and land being prepared for subdivision: these tax breaks, in practice, often benefit land developers (Youngman 2005, 2016, ch. 8).

The extent to which development will be delayed depends on the difference between value in current use as a farm and the market value in its developed use and the property tax rate. The greater the difference between value in current use and market value, the greater the impact of delaying development. The higher the property tax rate, the more effective is value in current use at delaying development. Value in current use does not benefit farmers in truly rural areas, however, because where farming is the most profitable use of the land, the value in current use is the same as the value in highest and best use.

Even in areas where agricultural owners are free to sell their land for development at any time, current use assessment by itself will not ensure the long-term preservation of farmland. Theoretical research suggests that current use assessment can defer, but not permanently prevent, development of land on the urban fringe (England and Mohr 2002). Preferential property tax treatment is not sufficient to preserve farmland because the resulting tax differential is unlikely, given the generally low effective tax rates on land, to be large enough to compensate for the much higher prices that would be paid if the land were converted to urban use (Maurer and Paugam 2000).

Forest Land

Managed forest land is taxed in different ways across countries. In Ontario, Canada, for example, the tax rate on forest property is set at 25 percent of the residential property tax rate (as is farm property). In other places, it is a fixed tax per acre or hectare. Elsewhere, it is taxed on a per acre or hectare basis with upper limits set for the tax rate.

There are at least two problems with a fixed rate per acreage approach. First, the rates often remain fixed from year to year even when commercial and residential property tax rates on other taxable properties are increasing. Second, concerns arise over the increasing hectares of forest land on which these relatively low rates are applied when, in reality, the land is no longer used for forestry.

Mines and Mineral Resources

Mineral resources are usually taxed on the basis of profits, acreage, or assessment of mineral values. Some taxing authorities obtain large sums of revenue through the imposition of royalties. These types of taxes, however, tend to be levied by a senior level of government.

In many countries, surface land and office buildings that are not connected with mining operations are assessed while mines and minerals may be treated in different ways. To illustrate this variation, consider Canada where there is considerable interprovincial variation (Kitchen 2002, pp. 63–64). In the province of Ontario, assessed property includes mines along with underground improvements and minerals. This tax base is effectively reduced, however, by the exclusion of machinery and equipment used for mineral processing along with the exclusion of mine site improvements directly used in mining activities. In the province of Nova Scotia, mines and minerals are assessed and taxed. In Manitoba, mines and minerals are not taxed. In Saskatchewan, machinery and equipment used in mining operations are included in the tax base while minerals are excluded. In New Brunswick, underground improvements at mine sites and minerals are explicitly excluded from the property tax base. In Prince Edward Island and Quebec, underground mining operations and minerals are exempt. The province of Alberta exempts minerals from property taxation.

Similar variation may be noted in other countries, In short, there is no consistent or necessarily ideal way for levying property taxes on mines and resources.

Is the Property Tax Regressive?

Local council meetings, taxpayer discussions, and newspaper reports on local government revenue issues frequently focus on the incidence of the residential property tax and more specifically, on its so-called regressivity—a tax is regressive if it absorbs a greater percentage of the income of lower-income individuals or households than of higher-income individuals or households. Most municipal officials, taxpayers, and some analysts believe that the residential property tax is regressive, though a number of studies have disputed this (for a summary of studies, see Kitchen and Tassonyi 2012). Determining the incidence of the property tax, or of any tax for that matter, is an empirical matter, and any empirical study of the property tax must begin with assumptions about the tax's distributional impact on taxpayers. These assumptions can be derived, however, only after one has decided on the role for the property tax.[11] In general, there are three different views of the incidence of the tax and depending on which one is accepted, one gets a different picture of its regressivity. Some view it as an excise tax. Others view it as a capital tax. Still others view it as a user charge (see Youngman 2016, chapter 2; and Dahlby and McMillan 2019 for a more detailed discussion of these views).

If the property tax is viewed as an excise tax, its burden is regressive because it takes a higher percentage of a lower household's annual income than of a higher household's annual income. If it is a capital tax, its burden is likely to be progressive because higher-income households are likely to own a disproportionately large share of the stock of capital. If it is viewed as a user charge, it funds those services that provide collective benefits to the local community. According to this view and one that seems most relevant for funding local public services as discussed in this book, the property tax should be treated as a benefits-based tax. Benefit taxes, however, are not based on ability to pay, which is the commonly accepted base for measuring regressivity; rather, they should be based on the linkage, sometimes direct but often indirect, between the benefits one receives from local public services and the taxes paid for these services. Issues of

[11] See Dahlby 1985 for an excellent summary of the assumptions used in the tax incidence literature and how these assumptions affect the incidence pattern.

regressivity, however, should be handled through property tax relief schemes (section "Why Tax Relief and What Form Should It Take?") or, more generally through income-transfer programs that are targeted for the truly needy (Boadway and Kitchen 1999). Regressivity should not be a primary focus of the property tax. The main focus should be on the structure and administration of the property tax so that it operates in an efficient, accountable, and transparent manner.

Why Tax Relief and What Form Should It Take?

Although it is generally true that "better off people live in more expensive houses" (Mirrlees 2011, p. 388), property taxes create liquidity problems for some taxpayers. The tax is not a real cash flow but rather an imputed one that may not necessarily reflect the owner's current situation (Johannesson-Linden and Gayer 2012). The imperfect association between homeowner incomes and property tax liabilities, which is sometimes referred to as "asset rich and income poor," creates problems for some taxpayers. Fortunately, there are a variety of ways in which taxpayer relief may be provided. All of them reduce the property tax burden on specific individuals in specific circumstances and all are motivated by a perception that the property tax is regressive. This has produced a variety of programs; the more notable are discussed here.

Circuit breakers or property tax credits target assistance to low-income and elderly residents whose taxes exceed a certain percentage of their income. The credit is designed so that its value varies inversely with personal income tax liability; that is, as income tax liability increases, the value of the credit, which is subtracted from personal income taxes, declines. The threshold could be based on income only or combined with age or family requirements.[12]

Refundable tax credits mean that even those with no taxable income benefit from this program. Tax credits are progressive because they take into account the taxable income as well as property taxes paid. In many cases, renters are also eligible to receive tax credits because it is assumed that a portion of their rent covers property taxes. Tax credits introduce an important element of progressivity in the property tax system.

One administrative problem with a tax credit is that residents pay their property taxes during the year, yet they do not receive the tax credit until their income tax return has been filed early in the following year. This

[12] See Haveman and Sexton 2008; Bird and Slack 1978 for a more detailed discussion.

practice creates liquidity problems for income-poor taxpayers because of the relatively long wait between payment of property taxes and receipt of the tax credit. Another concern that has sometimes been raised is whether a property tax credit that is designed to provide more relief to those with more wealth (higher property values) generates the desired income redistributional result especially when it is considered as a component of the state income-transfer system.

Tax deferral programs permit the property owner to defer some or all of his/her property taxes on an annual basis. Depending on the program, the lost revenue will come from revenue provided by a senior level of government or from general revenues of the municipality itself. The amount of the tax deferred becomes a lien against the property and is payable when the property is transferred. As well, there is usually, but not always, an interest charge applied to the deferred taxes.

There are a number of implications arising from the use of tax deferral schemes. First, if one's ability to pay taxes is measured by a combination of income and wealth where the property tax is viewed as a proxy for a tax on wealth, then a taxpayer who is asset rich but income poor could use this scheme to reduce his/her tax burden. In fact, tax deferral schemes can be especially useful in alleviating cash flow problems for income-deficient taxpayers.

Second, and more critically, eligibility for most tax deferral programs is restricted by age (seniors) and sometimes, disability. While one may be critical of age or disability dependent eligibility requirements for any income-transfer scheme, it may be administratively practical to impose restrictions of this sort. Otherwise, expanding the program to include everyone could lead to a significant increase in the number of applicants with the ensuing result that loans (tax deferrals plus interest charges on them) would be outstanding for a much longer period of time.

Grants, designed to remove some of the property tax burden, are provided to eligible homeowner's and/or renters in some countries. The value of the grant usually varies inversely with income and/or is given according to whether or not potential recipients are elderly or in receipt of welfare assistance.

As a mechanism for transferring income, the grant should be evaluated in the same way as any other component of the overall provincial income-transfer scheme. By comparison with some property tax credit schemes, the disbursement of grants could be more directly linked with the payment of or reduction in property tax liability. As well, it is frequently easier to direct grants to specific individuals especially in smaller communities where hardship cases are more quickly identified, even though it may be more complex administratively to operate than the tax credit program.

Exemptions from property taxes as is done for certain taxpayers under specific circumstances in some places effectively removes the burden of funding local services from these taxpayers and shifts the costs on to other taxpayers. Where the exemption is available to people over a certain age only (e.g., senior citizens), these exemptions, as a tax relief measure, may be deficient because they fail to consider the ability of the recipient to pay taxes. Similar deficiencies may exist where the criteria for exempting property for owner-occupiers is based strictly on taxpayer's income and ignores property values.

Homestead exemptions are a special category of exemptions. They lower the assessed value of owner-occupied principal residences and can be fixed at a dollar amount or set as a percentage of assessed value. If they are applied to all properties and depending on their limit, they can eliminate the property tax liability on low-income taxpayers or significantly reduce it and thus, make the property tax more progressive in its overall impact.

If, however, they are only available to resident homeowners (e.g., nonresidents and seasonal owners excluded), a number of inequities and inefficiencies are created. They are unfair because they treat homeowners, who are otherwise identical except for the residency requirement, differently even though each of them benefits from the same set of public services. They are inefficient because nonresidents pay more than residents for the same set of public services, thus creating potential distortions in the demand for these services. In particular, there is an incentive for residents to demand more public services that they would otherwise demand because nonresidents will end up paying a disproportionately higher share of the costs for these services.

Reducing, canceling, or refunding property taxes is generally associated with special circumstances, usually with poverty or illness. These programs are for a short duration and taxpayers are required to apply for them annually. The lost revenues are absorbed out of general municipal revenues. These programs are used infrequently and appear to operate more appropriately in smaller municipalities where it is easier to identify worthy recipients.

Do Property Taxes Provide an Incentive for Urban Sprawl?

Since the tax is levied on property, any investment that increases the value of the property (such as any improvements including an increase in density) will subject it to a higher tax. For this reason, higher property taxes are expected to discourage density. If, on the other hand, higher property taxes reflect higher levels of service, it is unlikely that there would be any impact on location or land use. To the extent that the allocation of service costs is based on property values and not on the volume of services consumed, some taxpayers pay more or less for services than the benefits they receive.

An extensive literature in the United States suggests that spatial factors do affect the costs of development (Brueckner 2001). In particular, the density of development and its location with respect to existing services influences the costs of providing services. For example, "hard" services such as sidewalks, street lighting, and roads cost less to provide per property in denser neighborhoods. Take the maintenance of roads, for example, in high-density neighborhoods, there are more dwelling units per kilometer of road over which to spread the costs.

An efficient property tax would reflect the higher costs associated with providing services in less-dense developments. This would generally mean that property taxes based on services received should be higher in suburban municipalities than in the core. If property taxes are higher in the core and service provision less costly, the property tax creates an incentive to move to less-dense developments (Slack 2002).

Should Municipalities Adopt a Land or Property Transfer Tax?

A land transfer tax (LTT) or property transfer tax is levied at the time of sale of a property and is usually calculated as a percentage of the value of the property transferred. The tax, which must be paid before the transfer is registered, is similar to a sales tax payable by the purchaser and is calculated as a percentage of the purchase price. A number of variations on land transfer taxes exist. For example, the tax rate sometimes increases with the value of the property; in some cases, taxes are higher on nonresidents.

Land transfer taxes[13] are levied in a few Canadian cities, a number of cities in the United States, and cities in Germany, France, and Australia. Quite bluntly, the land transfer tax is not a good tax for local governments (Dahlby and Larsen 2019). It bears no relationship to the benefits received

[13] See Dahlby and McMillan 2019 for an extensive review and examination of these taxes.

for local services and is, therefore, highly unfair in its distributional impact. Nor is it related in any way to ability to pay because there is no direct relationship between homebuyers and their income or wealth (Clayton 2015, p. 6).

It imposes a burden on those who buy property while placing no burden on those who remain in their existing property. It provides an incentive for those who remain in their homes to demand municipal services knowing that they will be disproportionately paid for by those who are buyers (Clayton 2015; Dahlby and McMillan 2019).

What the tax does do, however, is provide a disincentive for people to move, thereby resulting in potential inflexibilities in the labor market and encouraging people to stay in properties of a size and location that they may not have otherwise chosen. A large number of empirical studies have concluded that the LTTs discourage residential property transactions and impose larger welfare losses per dollar of tax revenue than are associated with property taxes. They are also a more volatile source of revenue than property taxes and generally no more progressive than a property tax. In short, land or property transfer taxes are less equitable and more distortionary than property taxes (Dahlby and McMillan 2019). They should, therefore, be abolished with the loss in revenue made up by increasing the annual general property tax rate (Franzsen and McCluskey 2017, p. 563).

Should Local Property Taxes Be Shared with a Senior Level of Government?

Shared taxes between municipal governments and a senior level of government are common in many countries. For example, in federal countries, income and sales taxes including a range of excise taxes (motor fuel, alcohol, and tobacco) are often shared between the federal and provincial/state/cantonal level. In some unitary countries, income taxes are shared between the central and local governments. In nine of the ten provinces in Canada (Newfoundland and Labrador being the exception), the property tax is shared between municipalities and the province. The original and ongoing rationale for this practice in Canada was and is to use the provincial property tax as a means of funding a portion of public elementary and secondary schooling.[14] This practice has often been criticized, but more

[14] Even so, property taxes are not earmarked for schooling; they become part of provincial general revenue.

generally, it raises the issue of whether property taxes should be shared with a more senior level of government.

As noted earlier, the property tax is a good tax for funding services that generate collective benefits for the local community. By comparison, it is not a good tax for funding services that should be the responsibility of a senior level of government. Examples include services that are primarily income redistributional in nature and those that generate significant spill-overs. Elementary and secondary schooling qualifies on both counts (Auld and Kitchen 2006). So do social services and social housing, to name two that municipalities have partial funding responsibility in many countries. These kinds of services should not be funded by local property taxes; rather they should be funded by a senior level of government from taxes that are primarily income redistributional in nature or by another municipal tax, if it exists, such as a local income tax.

If senior levels of government were to vacate the property tax field, leaving it with municipalities only, it has been argued that local autonomy could be strengthened because competition for access to the property tax base would be removed (Mikesell 2013). An example of this problem exists in Canada. Here, municipal governments collect the property tax for both municipalities and the province. While provincial property taxes are itemized separately on the property tax bill, taxpayers tend to look at the bottom line and blame the municipality (the tax collector) for both the municipal and the provincial portion. If the province were to vacate the property tax field, it would increase transparency and accountability because the municipality would be solely responsible for the tax bill and taxpayers would be able to easily identify the services funded by their property taxes (Mikesell 2013). It would also provide municipalities with needed tax room, thus relieving some pressure on the municipal tax base (Dahlby and McMillan 2019).

Summary

Drawing from theory and practice, the property tax meets the principles or criteria for a good local tax. In most countries, the tax is based on value, but in some countries it is based on area. Of these, valued-based assessment systems based on market value are generally deemed to be superior to area-based systems in countries where there are fully operational property or real estate markets. Where property or real estate markets are not active, formal, and transparent, area-based assessment is viewed as being superior.

Regardless of the assessment base chosen, the success of any assessment system depends on a number of critical components—property identification; uniformity in assessment; responsibility for assessment and its frequency; having an effective appeals mechanism; and making use of ever-improving mass assessment techniques. A uniform assessment system is necessary if one is to establish a tax base that is fair, transparent, and accountable. Uniformity is more likely achieved if a few practices are followed. First, within a region, state, or province, all assessors work from a standard and uniform assessment manual that is updated frequently to reflect changing conditions. Second, assessors should be required to pass specific education and training programs on assessment practices and procedures. Third, although the evidence is sketchy, assessors working for centralized assessment agencies seem to be more successful (because they are more likely to work at arms-length) than those working for municipalities in achieving uniformity in assessment. Fourth, the more frequent are reassessments, the fairer the assessment system, leading to fewer surprises, fewer complaints, and fewer appeals. Fifth, there should be an effective appeals mechanism in place to correct for perceived inequities in the assessment system. Finally, wherever possible, mass appraisal techniques should be used to improve the quality of the assessment system and to minimize its impact on costs.

The second major component of the property tax system is the tax rate. Here, it is generally conceded that each level of government (e.g., metropolitan and local) should be responsible for setting its own property tax rate(s). Variable tax rates should be used when the cost of providing municipal services varies by property type and location. Variable rates, when compared with a uniform rate, are more likely to discourage urban sprawl and to minimize the extent to which the local property tax is exported to other jurisdictions. Progressive tax rates are not recommended because they distort the link between those who benefit from a service and those who pay for it.

Business properties (commercial and industrial) should not be overtaxed vis-à-vis residential properties. Limits (by a senior level of government) should not be imposed on tax rates set by local governments unless they are to prevent local taxing authorities from imposing unnecessarily high rates on commercial and industrial properties vis-à-vis residential properties or unless they are to protect the policy interests of a more senior level of government. The use of property tax incentives has not proven to be very successful in stimulating economic development. Often, they have ended up costing local government more in lost tax revenue than they gained. Differentials in commercial and industrial property tax rates have not had much impact on interregional relocation decisions but have had some impact in intra-regional location decisions. Finally, even though land transfer taxes generate significant sums of money for local governments, they are far less equitable and far more distortionary than property taxes.

Allegations that the property tax is regressive have been around for decades even though the theoretical literature has offered mixed views on this. Concerns over regressivity should not be the primary focus of the property tax. Its role should be to fund local government services that provide collective benefits to the local community. If this leads to an unfair tax burden on lower-income households, there are a variety of programs that could be used—tax credits, tax deferral programs, grants, exemptions, and reductions, cancelations, or refunds. Or better still, this should be treated in the same way that every other income distributional concern should be treated; that is, relief should come in the form of a comprehensive tax relief scheme administered by a senior level of government and not a property tax relief scheme directed at specific property owners and implemented by local governments.

References

Auld, Douglas, and Harry Kitchen. 2006. *Financing Education and Training in Canada*. 2nd ed. Toronto: Canadian Tax Foundation.

Bahl, Roy. 1998. Land Taxes versus Property Taxes in Developing and Transition Countries. In *Land Value Taxation—Can It And Will It Work Today!* ed. D. Netzer. Cambridge, MA: Lincoln Institute of Land Policy.

Bahl, Roy, and Richard M. Bird. 2018. *Fiscal Decentralization and Local Finance in Developing Countries*. Northampton, MA: Studies in Fiscal Federalism and State-Local Finance, Edward Elgar Publishing.

Bahl, R.W., and J.F. Linn. 1992. *Urban Public Finance in Developing Countries*. New York: Oxford University Press.

Bahl, Roy, and Sally Wallace. 2010. A New Paradigm for Property Taxation in Developing Countries. In *Challenging the Conventional Wisdom on the Property Tax*, ed. R. Bahl, J. Martinez-Vazquez, and J. Youngman. Cambridge, MA: Lincoln Institute of Land Policy.

Bartik, T.J. 1991. *Who Benefits from State and Local Economic Development Policies?* Kalamazoo, MI: W.E. Upjohn Institute.

Bird, Richard M., and Jack M. Mintz. 2000. Tax Assignment in Canada: A Modest Proposal. In *Canada: the State of the Federation 1999/2000*, ed. Harvey Lazar, 261–292. Kingston: Queen's University, Institute of Intergovernmental Relations.

Bird, Richard M., and Enid Slack. 1978. *Residential Property Tax Relief Measures in Ontario.* Toronto: University of Toronto Press for the Ontario Economic Council.

Bird, R.M., and E. Slack, eds. 2004a. *International Handbook of Land and Property Taxation.* Northampton, MA: Edward, Elgar Publishing Limited.

———. 2004b. Land and Property Taxation in 25 Countries: A Comparative Review. In *International Handbook of Land and Property Taxation*, ed. R.M. Bird and E. Slack, 19–56. Northampton, MA: Edward, Elgar Publishing Limited.

Bird, Richard M., and Thomas A. Wilson. 2003. *A Tax Strategy for Ontario.* Research Paper 32 Prepared for the Panel on the Role of Government in Ontario. http://www.law-lib.utoronto.ca/investing/index.htm. Accessed May 2018.

Bird, Richard M., Enid Slack, and Almos Tassonyi. 2012. *A Tale of Two Taxes: Property Tax Reform in Ontario.* Cambridge, MA: Lincoln Institute of Land Policy.

Boadway, R.W., and H.M. Kitchen. 1999. *Canadian Tax Policy.* 3rd ed. Toronto: Canadian Tax Foundation.

Bourassa, S.C. 2009. The U.S. Experience. In *Land Value Taxation*, ed. R.F. Dye and R.W. England. Cambridge, MA: Lincoln Institute of Land Policy.

Brueckner, J.K. 2001. Property Taxation and Urban Sprawl. In *Property Taxation and Local Government Finance*, ed. W.E. Oates, 153–175. Cambridge, MA: Lincoln Institute of Land Policy.

Brunori, D. 2007. *Local Tax Policy: A Federalist Perspective.* 2nd ed. Washington DC: The Urban Institute Press.

Brzeski, J. 1999. Real Property Taxation in Poland. In *Comparative Property Tax systems: An International Comparative Review*, ed. W.J. McCluskey, 411–418. Aldershot: Avebury Publishing Limited.

Clayton, Frank A. 2015. *City of Toronto's Land Transfer Tax—Good, Bad or Merely Tolerable?* Toronto: Centre for Urban Research and Land Development, Ryerson University.

Clemens, J., T. Fox, A. Karabegovic, S. LeRoy, and N. Veldhuis. 2003. *Tax and Expenditure Limitations: The Next Step in Fiscal Discipline.* Critical Issues Bulletin. Vancouver: The Fraser Institute.

Cornia, Gary C. 2013. Tax Criteria: The Design and Policy Advantages of a Property Tax. Chap. 9 in *A Primer on Property Tax Administration and Policy*, ed. William J. McCluskey, Gary C. Cornia, and Lawrence C. Walters, 1st ed. John Wiley & Sons Ltd.

Dahlby, G.B. 1985. The Incidence of Government Expenditures and Taxes in Canada: A Survey. In *Income Distribution and Economic Security in Canada*, Collected Research Studies of the Royal Commission on Economic Union and Development Prospects for Canada, ed. F. Vaillaincourt, vol. 1, 111–151. Toronto: University of Toronto Press.

Dahlby, Bev, and Braeden Larsen. 2019. *Should Alberta Adopt a Land Transfer Tax?* SPP Research Paper, The School of Public Policy Publications, University of Calgary, Volume 12:5.

Dahlby, Bev, and Melville McMillan. 2019. What is the Role of Property and Property-Related Taxes? An Assessment of Municipal Property Taxes, Land Transfer Taxes, and Tax Increment Financing. In *Funding the Canadian City*, ed. Enid Slack, Lisa Philipps, Lindsay M. Tedds, and Heather L. Evans, 45–73. Toronto: Canadian Tax Foundation and Institute on Municipal Finance and Governance.

Dalehite, E.G., J.L. Mikesell, and C.K. Zorn. 2005. Variations in Property Tax Abatement Programs among States. *Economic Development Quarterly* 19: 157–173.

Davies Transportation Consulting Inc, Wave Point Consulting Ltd., and Lane Property Advisors Inc. 2011. *Major Industrial Property Taxation Impacts.* A Report Prepared for the Union of British Columbia Municipalities and the BC Ministry of Community, Sport and Cultural Development.

England, R.W., and R.D. Mohr. 2002. *Property Taxation and Current Use Assessment: A Theoretical Note.* Working Paper. Cambridge, MA: Lincoln Institute of Land Policy.

Found, Adam, and Peter Tomlinson. 2017. *Business Tax Burdens in Canada's Major Cities: The 2017 Report Card.* E-Brief, C.D. Howe Institute, December 6.

Franzen, Riel, and William J. McCluskey. 2013. Value-Based Approaches to Property Taxation. Chap. 2 in *A Primer on Property Tax Administration and Policy*, ed. William J. McCluskey, Gary C. Cornia, and Lawrence C. Walters, 1st ed. John Wiley & Sons Ltd.

Franzsen, Riel, and William McCluskey, eds. 2017. *Property Tax in Africa: Status, Challenges, and Prospects.* Cambridge, MA: Lincoln Institute of Land Policy.

Glaeser, Edward. 2002. Comment on 'Tax Incentives and the City'. *Brookings-Wharton Papers on Urban Affairs*, 115–124.

Haveman, Mark, and Terri A. Sexton. 2008. *Property Tax Assessment Limits: Lessons from Thirty Years of Experience.* Cambridge, MA: Lincoln Institute of Land Policy.

Johannesson-Linden, Asa, and Christian Gayer. 2012. *Possible Reforms of Real Estate Taxation: Criteria for Successful Policies.* European Commission, Directorate-General for Economic and Financial Affairs, Occasional Papers 119.

Kelly, Roy. 2013. Property Tax Collection and Enforcement. Chap. 6 in *A Primer on Property Tax Administration and Policy*, ed. William J. McCluskey, Gary C. Cornia, and Lawrence C. Walters, 1st ed. John Wiley & Sons Ltd.

Kenyon, Daphne A., Adam H. Langley, and B.P. Paquin. 2012a. *Rethinking Property Tax Incentives for Business.* Cambridge, MA: Lincoln Institute of Land Policy.

Kenyon, Daphne A., Adam H. Langley, and B.B. Paquin. 2012b. Property Tax Incentive Pitfalls. *National Tax Journal* 65 (4): 1011–1021.

Kitchen, Harry. 2002. *Municipal Revenue and Expenditure Issues in Canada*. Toronto: Canadian Tax Foundation.

———. 2007. *Valuing and Taxing Utilities: The Canadian Experience*. A Presentation at a Conference on "Municipal Property Rates Act: Critical Issues", at the University of Pretoria, South Africa, September 12, Mimeograph.

———. 2013. Property Tax: A Situation Analysis and Overview. Chap. 1 in *A Primer on Property Tax Administration and Policy*, ed. William J. McCluskey, Gary C. Cornia, and Lawrence C. Walters, 1st ed. John Wiley & Sons Ltd.

Kitchen, Harry, and Enid Slack. 2014. *Municipal Property Taxation in Nova Scotia*. Prepared for the Property Valuation Services Corporation, the Union of Nova Scotia Municipalities and the Association of Municipal Administrators. www.pvsc.ca/en/home/partners/municipal-property-taxation-in-nova-scotia.aspx. Accessed 26 May 2018.

Kitchen, Harry, and Almos Tassonyi. 2012. Municipal Taxes and User Fees. Chap. 9 in *Tax Policy in Canada*, ed. Heather Kerr, Ken McKenzie and Jack Mintz. Toronto: Canadian Tax Foundation.

Kitchen, Harry, and Francois Vaillaincourt. 1990. The Federal Grants-in-Lieu Program: An Assessment. *Canadian Tax Journal* 38 (4): 928–936.

Maurer, R., and A. Paugam. 2000. *Reform Toward Ad Valorem Property Tax in Transition Economies: Fiscal and Land Use Benefits*. Washington, DC: Land and Real Estate Initiative, Background Series 13.

McCluskey, W.J., and R.C.D. Franzen. 2004. *The Basis of the Property Tax: A Case Study Analysis of New Zealand and South Africa*. Working Paper WP04WMI. Cambridge, MA: Lincoln Institute of Land Policy.

McCluskey, William J., and Riel Franzen. 2013. Non-Market Valuation and Hybrid Approaches to Property Taxation. Chap. 13 in *A Primer on Property Tax Administration and Policy*, ed. William J. McCluskey, Gary C. Cornia, and Lawrence C. Walters, 1st ed. John Wiley & Sons Ltd.

McCluskey, William J., Gary C. Cornia, and Lawrence C. Walters, eds. 2013. *A Primer on Property Tax Administration and Policy*. 1st ed. Hoboken, NJ: John Wiley & Sons Ltd.

McIlhatton, David, Michael McCord, Peadar Davis, and Martin Haran. 2013. Geographic Information Systems and the Importance of Location: Integrating Property and Place for Better Informed Decision Making. Chap. 15 in *A Primer on Property Tax Administration and Policy*, ed. William J. McCluskey, Gary C. Cornia, and Lawrence C. Walters, 1st ed. John Wiley & Sons Ltd.

Mikesell, John. 2013. Administration of Local Taxes: An International Review of Practices and Issues for Enhancing Fiscal Autonomy. Chap. 4 in *A Primer on Property Tax Administration and Policy*, ed. William J. McCluskey, Gary C. Cornia, and Lawrence C. Walters, 1st ed. John Wiley & Sons Ltd.

Mintz, Jack M., and Tom Roberts. 2006. Running on Empty: A Proposal to Improve City Finances. *Commentary* No. 226. Toronto: C.D. Howe Institute.

Mirrlees, James. 2011. *Tax by Design (the Mirrlees Review)*. Oxford: Oxford University Press.

OECD. 2016. *Revenue Statistics 1965–2015*. Paris.

O'Sullivan, Arthur. 2001. Limits on Local Property Taxation: The United States Experience. In *Property Taxation and Local Government Finance*, ed. Wallace E. Oates, 177–200. Cambridge, MA: Lincoln Institute of Land Policy.

Shadbegian, R.J. 1999. "The Effect of Tax and Expenditure Limitations on the Revenue Structure of Local Government", 1962–1987. *National Tax Journal* 52 (2): 221–238.

Sjoquist, D.L., and M.B. Walker. 1999. Economies of Scale in Property Tax Assessment. *National Tax Journal* 52 (2): 207–220.

Slack, E. 2002. Municipal Finance and the Pattern of Urban Growth. *Commentary*. Toronto: C.D. Howe Institute

Slack, Enid. 2013. The Politics of the Property Tax. Chap. 3 in *A Primer on Property Tax Administration and Policy*, ed. William J. McCluskey, Gary C. Cornia, and Lawrence C. Walters, 1st ed. John Wiley & Sons Ltd.

———. 2015. *How to Reform the Property Tax: Lessons from around the World*. IMFG Papers on Municipal Finance and Governance Series, University of Toronto, No 21, 2015. http://munkschool.utoronto.ca/imfg/resources/. Accessed 5 June 2018.

Thirsk, W.R. 1982. Political Sensitivity Versus Economic Sensibility: A Tale of Two Property Taxes. In *Tax Policy Options in the 1980s*, ed. W.R. Thirsk and J. Whalley, 384–440. Canadian Tax Paper no. 66. Toronto: Canadian Tax Foundation.

Wagaman, Andrew. 2017. GASB77: Revealing the Cost of Property Tax Incentives for Business. *Land Lines*, July. www.lincolninst.edu/publications/issues/land-lines-july-2017. Accessed 12 June 2018.

Wassmer, Robert. 2007. *The Increasing Use of Property Tax Abatement as a Means of Promoting Sub-National Economic Activity in the United States*. Sacramento, CA: California State University.

———. 2014. Property Tax Abatement as Tax Expenditure? *Public Finance and Management* 14 (2): 194–220.

Youngman, Joan. 2005. Taxing and Untaxing Land: Current Use Assessment of Farmland. *State Tax Notes* (10): 37, 727–738.

———. 2016. *A Good Tax: Legal and Policy Issues for the Property Tax in the United States*. Cambridge, MA: Lincoln Institute of Land Policy.

Youngman, Joan, and Jane Malme. 2000. *An International Survey of Taxes on Land and Buildings*. Deventer: Kluwer Law and Taxation Publishers.

Zorn, Kurt. 2013. Establishing a Tax Rate. Chap. 5 in *A Primer on Property Tax Administration and Policy*, ed. William J. McCluskey, Gary C. Cornia, and Lawrence C. Walters, 1st ed. John Wiley & Sons Ltd.

CHAPTER 10

Local Income, Sales, and Environmental Taxes

Introduction

As was noted in Chap. 9, property taxes are widely used but they are not the most important local tax in every country. Local income taxes, by comparison, are most important in 12 OECD countries and local taxes on the sale of goods and services are most important in 3 OECD countries. This chapter examines the main features of these taxes as they are generally applied and presents and briefly discusses some of the major issues surrounding them. It does not describe the many details of each tax as it is used in a specific country or countries, although reference is often made to their use in selected countries.

The section "Local Income Taxes" examines the relative importance of local income taxes and highlights the major characteristics of the tax as it is constituted in most countries where it is used. The section "Local Sales Taxes" performs the same task for both a general sales tax and a handful of selective sales (or excise) taxes. Both parts include material that is an extension of introductory material on these taxes as provided in Chap. 8. The section "Common Issues" discusses a number of issues that are common in considering their use. In particular, should they be locally administered or "piggybacked"? Should they be set up as local taxes or a form of tax sharing? Should there be limits on their rates? How might they affect taxpayer behavior? Should they be levied at the local or regional/metropolitan level? Does their use complicate intergovernmental arrangements? What about their revenue yield and volatility? What is their incidence on taxpayers?

H. Kitchen et al., *Local Public Finance and Economics*,
https://doi.org/10.1007/978-3-030-21986-4_10

Environmental taxes or taxes oriented to improving the environment are not yet a major source of revenue for any level of government including local governments but they are emerging. The section "Environmental Taxes" examines local government environmental taxes. The section "Summary" summarizes the chapter.

Local Income Taxes

Figure 10.1 illustrates[1] the relative importance of income taxes in 34 OECD countries by measuring municipal income tax revenue[2] as a percent of all tax revenue collected in the country. At the high end is Sweden where local income taxes account for 36 percent of all taxes in the country. This is followed by Denmark, Finland, and Iceland where more than 20 percent of all tax revenues are generated by local income taxes. The next highest grouping of countries accounts for slightly more than 12 percent of all tax revenue—this includes Switzerland, Norway, and Japan. At the bottom end are 15 countries where local income taxes are not used.

Since Chap. 8 highlighted the major features of local income taxation in the Nordic countries and in parts of the United States where it is used, this discussion will not be repeated. Nor will this chapter include a discussion of local income tax systems in other countries, primarily because they are similar in design and structure and generally face a similar set of issues. It is the latter that will be considered next.

Should Municipalities Levy an Income Tax on Businesses?

Local income taxes are typically levied on personal income and not business income. This is the case in the Nordic countries and most of the US jurisdictions where income taxes are in place. There are a number of solid reasons for excluding business income particularly if there are other taxes or charges that ensure that businesses cover the costs of local services that they use or from which they benefit. First, corporate income taxes have fallen in major trading countries (the most recent example being the United States) over the past decade, so there does not appear to be any justification for making it more costly for businesses to compete.

[1] The data in this figure measure local income taxes as a percent of all taxes in the country, whereas the data in Table 8.1 in Chap. 8 measured local income taxes as a percent of all local taxes.

[2] Income tax revenue comes from both a local tax (one where local authorities set tax rates) and income tax revenue sharing.

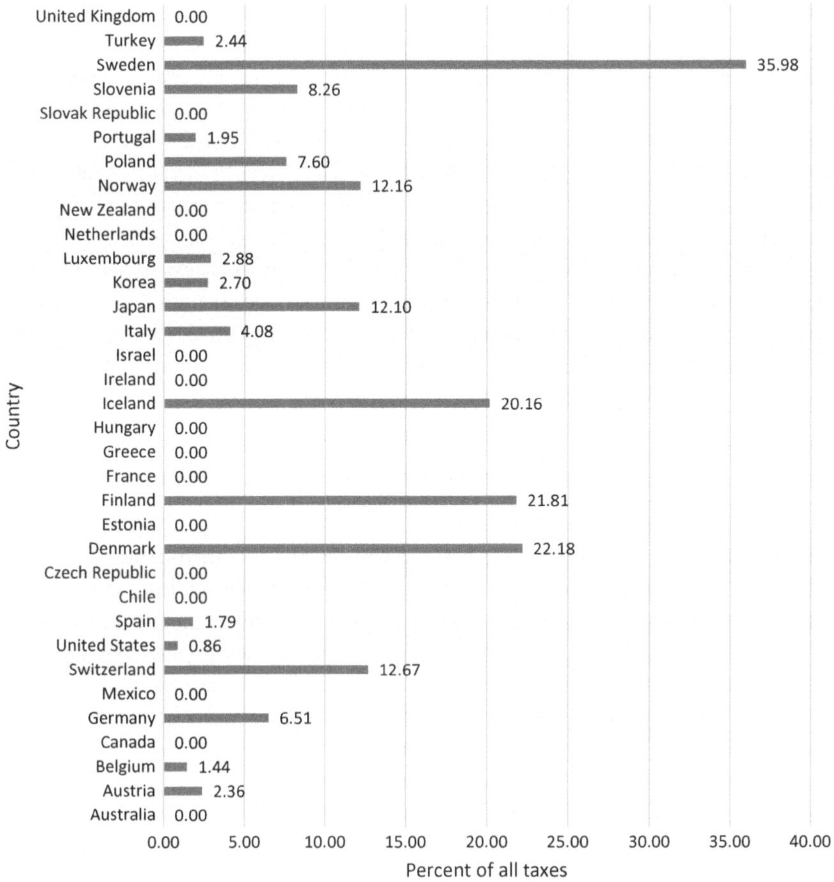

Fig. 10.1 Local income taxes as a percent of all taxes: OECD countries, 2014. Source: OECD, *Revenue Statistics 1965–2015* (Paris: OECD 2016)

Second, taxing mobile corporate capital and corporate profits encourages firms to shift their investments and profits to lower-taxed jurisdictions (Dahlby 2012); in other words, taxes based on a mobile tax base are not good candidates for local taxation. In fact, this was a major reason why central governments in the Nordic countries eliminated the local business income tax (Lotz 2012).

Third, property taxes on the commercial/industrial sector already overtax business (Chap. 9), and thus, there is no reason for an additional tax burden that bears no relationship to the cost of municipal services consumed.

Fourth, business income is very unevenly distributed among local governments and poorly related to the overall costs and benefits associated with the taxing jurisdiction, that is, those related to residential and non-residential inhabitants. Hence, fiscal disparities across municipalities would be larger and equalization more of an issue. Finally, business income taxes are prone to being exported beyond the local taxing jurisdiction, thus violating one criterion for a good local tax. The distortions created by exported taxes were discussed in Chap. 9.

Because of these concerns, a local income tax on business income is not the preferred choice. A local tax on personal income, however, is a different matter. It can be particularly useful for funding services that are primarily income redistributional in nature. Included here are social services, social housing, schooling, hospitals, health care, and so on.

Does a Personal Income Tax Satisfy the Criteria for a Good Local Tax?

Chapter 8 laid out the criteria for a good local tax—immobile tax base, adequate source of revenue, stable and predictable yields, fair, easily administered, not exportable, visible, and do not create harmful competition between levels of government. How well the local personal income tax meets these criteria is addressed in the next few paragraphs.

While analysts normally think of property as having the least mobile base, a personal income tax is also fairly immobile. Individuals or households can move more readily than their homes, but they must change their residence if they are to avoid a local income tax that is higher than neighboring jurisdictions. Changing houses and, even more so, communities, is not a minor choice or task.

Variations in neighboring income tax rates have the potential to lead to harmful interjurisdictional competition as municipalities compete to attract more people and more business, but this is not likely to be any different that the interjurisdictional competition that exists between inter-municipal property tax rates.

Like the residential property tax, a personal income tax on residents (unlike a local tax on business income) is essentially not exportable and, therefore, is not shifted onto people and businesses in other municipalities, thus contributing to the fairness of it as a tax.

Revenue yields can be very high as demonstrated in the Nordic countries and more progressive and fairer on ability to pay grounds in their impact on local taxpayers when compared with property taxes. Furthermore, a personal income tax is more appropriate and fairer as a basis for funding those local public services that are primarily income redistributional in nature (Kitchen 2019).

A further advantage of a local income tax relative to a property tax is that it makes the local tax burden more obvious to renters who are not exposed to property tax bills because they are usually hidden in monthly rent obligations.

Local income taxes can be easily administered especially if they are "piggybacked" onto existing income taxes of a senior level of government. If they are self-administered, their costs will be higher but not inordinately higher as demonstrated in many cities that administer their own income taxes in the United States. Like central income taxes, however, local taxes will fluctuate with the economic cycle although those changes may be predictable and various means can be used to stabilize the revenue.

Overall, local personal income taxes can meet the usual criteria for local taxes relatively well. In particular, Oates and Schwab (2004) analyze the relative merits of property and personal income taxes as sources of local taxes and conclude that both have their pros and cons but that both are workable and reasonably efficient.

Should the Tax Be Residence Based or Payroll Based?

In general, either of these options may be adopted for a local income tax. In most cases, a residence-based tax includes all forms of income—wages, salaries, investment income, rental income, and so on—but it need not. Usually, but not always, the base is identical to the income tax base of a senior level of government. If, however, the municipality sets up its own administrative structure (as a few jurisdictions have done), both the tax base and the tax rate may be left to the discretion of the taxing jurisdiction although limits, by a senior level of government, are often imposed on what can be done.

A payroll-based tax (the other option) only applies to wages and salaries and as such its base is smaller than the residence base. When payroll-based taxes are used, the treatment of commuters (those who work in one jurisdiction but live in another) must be explicitly addressed. Sometimes they are taxed at full rates, sometimes they are taxed at a reduced rate, and sometimes they are exempt from the tax. Depending on the treatment of commuters, the taxing authority has the power to set the tax rate so that it captures revenue from commuters who use city services and might not otherwise contribute to their cost.[3] Neither a payroll nor residence-based tax, however, applies directly to visitors.

Local Sales Taxes

Figure 10.2 illustrates[4] the relative importance of local taxes on the sale of goods and services in 34 OECD countries by measuring it as a percent of all tax revenue collected in the country. This includes revenue from a general sales tax plus revenue from sales taxes that may be applied to specific goods or services. Unlike property and income taxes, sales taxes are almost never the major source of local tax revenue (see Chap. 8). They are, however, much more widely used than local income taxes but not nearly as widely used or as important as local property taxes.

At the high end, sales taxes account for around 4.5 percent of all tax revenue in Turkey, Korea, Hungary, Japan, and Chile. The next grouping of four countries—Italy, Spain, France, and United States—get slightly more than 3 percent of all tax revenue from local sales taxes. At the bottom end where local sales taxes are nonexistent or where they contribute almost nothing to local tax revenues are the Nordic countries that rely almost entirely on income taxes and a number of countries that rely heavily on the property tax.

General Sales Tax

Local general sales taxes in the United States are widely used by municipalities, counties, townships, special districts, and school districts, often with more than one jurisdiction taxing a particular transaction. They are almost always similar to their state counterparts and state administration dominates. One exception is Alaska where there is no state sales tax, so local authorities are responsible for their administration (Mikesell 2011). They are also widely used in Brazil.

[3] See Chap. 8 for a discussion of the tax treatment of residents, visitors, and commuters under benefits-based taxation.

[4] The data in Fig. 10.2 measure local sales taxes on goods and services as a percent of all taxes in the country, whereas the data in Table 8.1 in Chap. 8 measured local sales taxes on goods and services as a percent of all local taxes.

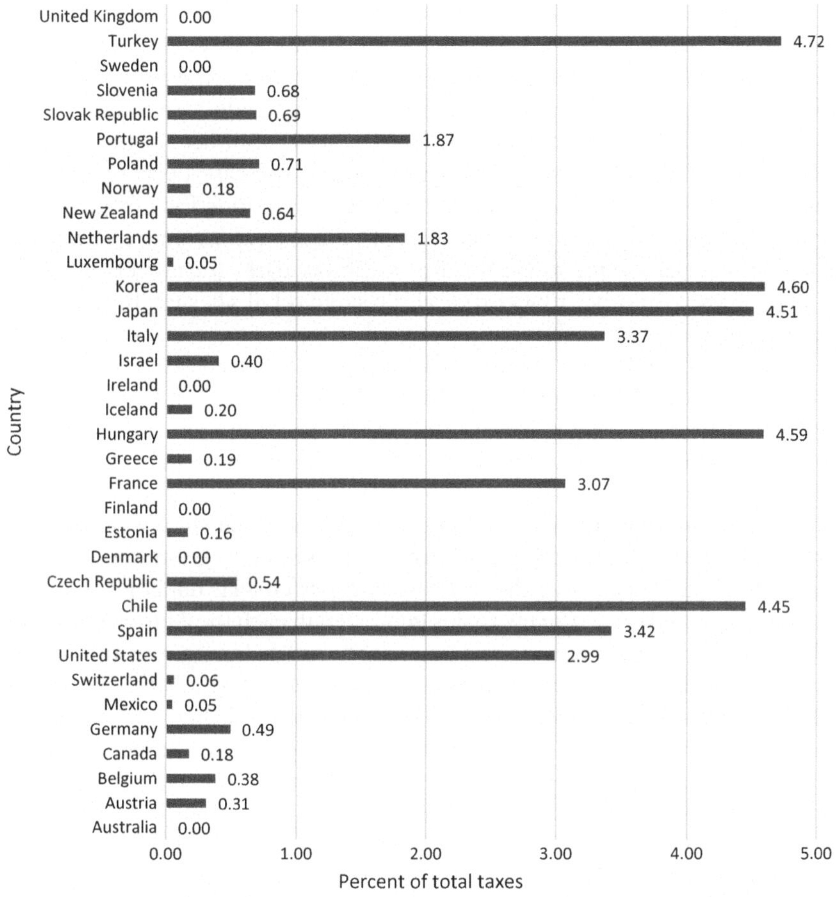

Fig. 10.2 Local sales taxes as a percent of all taxes: OECD countries, 2014. Source: OECD, *Revenue Statistics 1965–2015* (Paris: OECD 2016)

The most common general sales taxes are the retail sales tax and the value-added tax (VAT). The retail sales tax is applied at a single stage, when the product or service is sold at the retail level. The tax is paid by the purchaser, collected by the vendor who, in turn, sends the revenue to the collecting authority and if it is a senior level of government, the local share is periodically remitted to the taxing jurisdiction. Where these have been implemented, exemptions are often in place for purchases such as food and children's clothing, largely designed to alleviate some of the financial burden on those in difficult and stressful social or economic circumstances.

Most retail sales are to consumers (final stage) but some are to business as business inputs. Allowance may or may not be made for the latter. If it is, purchases are not double taxed as part of the purchasers output. If it is not, they are double taxed. This is more often the case because governments tend to overlook or make imperfect concessions for business purchases of taxed inputs either because of administration and compliance costs or because doing so would shrink the tax base. Ideally, both goods and services should be subject to a single stage retail sales tax but, characteristically, services are almost never taxed.

Value-added taxes are widespread throughout the world and, in some ways, value added is a logical base for local taxes. As a local tax, it is often rejected for administrative reasons. In the United Kingdom, it was rejected because of complexities in treating producers fairly where they export and import goods across localities (Hall and Smith 1995). Similar administrative complications exist in Canada. Neither the Canada Revenue Agency (responsible for administering the harmonized sales tax/goods and services tax [HST/GST]) nor any other statistical agency collects data on the value-added base and, hence, the tax that is generated in each local jurisdiction. All HST/GST revenues are collected annually by the federal government, and the entitlement for each province is calculated from a formula that estimates the consumption expenditure base in that province and then applies the tax rate for that province to its calculated share of the base. Revenues allocated to each HST/GST province are thus driven by the estimated taxable consumption base in that province. With very minor exceptions, how the revenue is allocated is completely unrelated to how the HST/GST actually functions (Bird 2012). The only way that a municipal levy could be imposed would be if the province increased its part of the tax rate and shared the revenues with all municipalities. This, however, would not be a local tax (discussed below). Rather, it would be akin to a provincial transfer (Kitchen and Slack 2016). In countries like the United States where a value-added tax does not exist, it cannot be used at the local level either.

Another type of general sales tax is the turnover tax as in Hungary. It is based on sales minus the cost of goods sold, materials, and subcontractors—a form of value added that makes no allowance for taxes paid on prior sales and, hence, its name as a turnover tax. This cascading effect becomes more and more noticeable when there is a sequence of sales. This is largely why a turnover tax has been rejected in a number of places (Hall and Smith 1995).

Selective Sales Tax

Sales taxes on selective products are popular with local governments in most countries although the revenues generated by them individually and even in aggregate may not be that large. Selective taxes commonly include local taxes on motor fuel, motor vehicle registration, temporary lodging (accommodation and room taxes), restaurant meals, beverages, entertainment, utility bills, land transfers, businesses, and so on. Often, the legislation allowing local governments to implement these taxes dictates the tax base and sometimes the rate.

Sometimes, these taxes/charges are referred to as excise taxes and sometimes as excise levies. One thing in common is that they are based on the selling price of a good or service. Not all of them are discussed here. Three have been chosen as being representative of a wide spectrum of local possibilities. These include a tax on motor fuel, a motor vehicle registration tax, and a temporary accommodation tax. Land transfer and property-related charges on businesses were discussed in Chap. 9. Utility pricing (water, sewer, electricity, etc.) is discussed in Chap. 11. Local taxes on restaurant meals, beverages, and entertainment establishments are not generally large revenue generators and are almost always added onto a similar tax of a senior level of government with characteristics similar to those discussed next.

A Local Fuel Tax

Although some US cities levy local fuel taxes, such is not the case in many other countries. A municipal gas and diesel fuel tax has a number of advantages. It is a benefit-based tax as long as revenues are earmarked for funding local roads and public transit. It can be an appropriate tool for internalizing the costs of greenhouse gas emissions because emissions increase as the amount of fuel burned increases. It can reduce the cumulative or total distance driven, thus also reducing unnecessary driving or engine idling. It provides an incentive for switching to more fuel-efficient cars and public transit. It contributes to reducing urban sprawl; specifically, one Canadian study found that a 1 percent increase at the pump in the 12 largest Canadian metropolitan areas between 1986 and 2006 resulted in a 0.32 percent increase in population living in inner cities and a 1.28 percent reduction in low-density housing units (Tanguay and Gingras 2011).

While a municipal fuel tax could have significant benefits in the short run, it is unlikely to be very effective in the long run. Fuel tax revenues are projected to decline because of a growing trend toward more fuel-efficient and hybrid vehicles as well as an increasing reliance on non-fossil-fuel vehicles such as electric cars; younger adults, especially those living in highly urbanized areas, are driving less; and retiring baby boomers are driving less than when they were younger. These factors suggest that other means of financing urban transit and roads will be required in the near future (Lindsey 2019; Kitchen and Lindsey 2013).

A fuel tax may be the easiest tax to administer at the local level. The tax rate should be set by the municipal council. It could be piggybacked onto the senior government's rate, with the latter collecting the tax and remitting the municipal portion. For those who argue that fuel taxes are regressive (i.e., they absorb a higher percentage of income for low-income individuals than for high-income individuals), this situation may not be the case in regions with good public transit because lower-income households generally use public transit for a larger fraction of trips than higher-income households.

A Motor Vehicle Registration Tax

Motor vehicle taxes (levies) include registration fees that are almost always levied annually in every country by a senior level of government. In some countries, they are also levied at the local level. Most time, they are fixed charges on ownership and do not vary with usage. They need not be, however. In fact, an efficiently designed tax would take into consideration the age and engine size (older and larger vehicles generally contribute more to pollution), or emissions with low-emission vehicles charged less than high-emission vehicles. Location could also be a factor (cars in highly urbanized areas add more to pollution and to congestion) or axle weight (heavier vehicles do more damage to roads and require more costly roads to be built) (Slack 2011). The fees are relatively easy to administer and generally perceived to be fair on the basis of benefits received.

There is little research on the impact of vehicle levies on vehicle ownership or usage.[5] A modest levy is unlikely to have any effect on ownership, and virtually none on usage. A tax based on fuel efficiency might have some influence on choice of vehicle type, but small fixed levies do not modify travel behavior because they are unrelated to usage.

[5] Litman (2012) briefly reviews studies that examined the effects on vehicle ownership of fuel taxes, income, population density, and access to other transport modes.

Vehicle levies are transparent because of a link between payment and ownership, but not mileage driven unless he latter is highly correlated with ownership. They are accountable if revenues are dedicated to transportation. A vehicle tax is a crude instrument for impacting traffic congestion, however, because it does not vary with time of use, traffic volume, distance traveled, or the area in which vehicles travel (central-city vs. intercity trips). On the other hand, it is a charge on those who use roads, at least in some capacity. It is also likely to have a greater impact on the rich than the poor, because the latter have a lower rate of car ownership. To minimize tax avoidance, registrants could be prevented from registering their vehicles in a jurisdiction (such as vacation locales) other than their principal place of residence (Kitchen and Lindsey 2013).

Temporary Accommodation Tax

An accommodation or room occupancy tax is a levy imposed on hotels, motels, and private dwellings (Vrbo, Airbnb, etc.). The tax is justified on the grounds that it compensates local governments for expanded services provided for tourists or visitors (e.g., the additional police and fire protection and highway and public transit capacity needed to meet weekend or peak convention and tourist demands). Whereas income and retail sales taxes may fall on both residents and nonresidents, an accommodation occupancy tax falls primarily on visitors.

Several cities around the world levy hotel or motel occupancy taxes (in addition to the sales tax of more senior levels of government), but fewer of them levy such a tax on room rentals in private accommodations. This, however, is changing; for example, recent legislation in British Columbia and Ontario (Canada) permit municipalities to tax these temporary accommodations in the same way as hotels and motels.

As with other taxes, cities could piggyback onto the existing sales tax on hotel and motel rooms through the addition of a few percentage points or they could self-administer. The extent to which the differential tax treatment of accommodation actually deters visitors from renting taxable rooms is uncertain. If demand is sensitive to price, then noticeable losses may occur. On that point, one might consider the impact on the convention business if a municipality were to impose a municipal hotel and motel tax that did not exist in other potential convention centers, since convention arrangements are often highly cost-sensitive.

Do Sales Taxes Satisfy the Criteria for a Good Local Tax?

The criteria for a good local tax have been spelled out in Chap. 8 in the section "Fiscal Autonomy and Local Taxation" this, so it will not be repeated here. A general sales tax is not likely to be as solid as a local personal income tax in satisfying most of the criteria and well behind that of a local property tax. Nevertheless, it has some positive benefits as a local tax.

On the down side, its base can be mobile which by itself does not meet one of the criterion of a good local tax—businesses and consumers may move to lower-taxed jurisdictions, thus leading to potentially harmful interjurisdictional competition. The tax has a greater likelihood of being exported onto residents of other jurisdictions when compared with the residential property tax and personal income tax. Further, the tax can be quite volatile, more so than the personal income tax, rising rapidly in good times and falling quickly in poor times. Certainly, it is much more volatile than the property tax.

On the other hand, a general sales tax can generate considerable revenue; in fact, it generates more revenue than the property tax in some US cities (see section "Three Examples of Diversity in Municipal Taxes" in Chap. 8). It, like the personal income tax if used in conjunction with the property tax, could take pressure off the property tax, thus aiding those who are asset rich but income poor as well as local businesses which tend to be overtaxed vis-à-vis the residential sector. An important advantage of a general sales tax is that it permits local taxing jurisdictions to capture revenue from visitors who use local public services but who otherwise would not pay for them through the local property tax or local personal income tax.

A selective sales tax, by comparison, is imposed on a good or service where specific beneficiaries can be identified. It satisfies the criteria of benefits received better than the other options as long as revenues are dedicated to funding the service for which the tax is levied. For the most part, revenues are predictable and stable and less likely to be exported than a general sales tax. All in all, both a general and selective sales taxes can be important contributors to a solid local revenue base.

Common Issues

There are a number of issues that need to be considered in discussions around the implementation and administration of both a personal income and sales taxes. Many are common to both taxes and are addressed next.

Locally Administered or "Piggybacked"?

Under local administration, taxing jurisdictions set up their own tax base and rate structure. The majority of local income taxes in the United States are administered locally. By comparison, almost all general and selective sales taxes are administered by the state. The tax base may be identical to that of a senior level of government or it may differ in a variety of ways. For a personal income tax, differences may be due to the definition of taxable income (e.g., earned vs. unearned) and/or through modifications to exemptions and deductions to broaden the definition of taxable income, and/or to bring more income earners into the tax net, and/or to set rates that would generate a given amount of revenue, and/or to change the progressivity of the overall income tax structure. For a general sales tax, it may differ by exempting certain goods and/or services.

Local administration gives local tax authorities considerable autonomy, control, and flexibility over local tax policy. As well, local tax jurisdictions do not have to wait for periodic remittances, which often happen when the tax is collected by a senior level of government. Finally, it has been argued that local administrators have a stronger incentive than senior government officials to enforce local tax policy and collections (Mikesell 2013).

One problem with local administration, however, is that there is likely to be little coordination across local jurisdictions unless effective limits are placed on what can be done (Mikesell 2010). Lack of coordination creates the potential for harmful and negative location effects (discussed later). As well, it is almost certain to be more expensive to administer and enforce than the option which is discussed next.

The other option is to "piggyback" on to the tax of a senior government. The local taxing jurisdiction adopts the tax base and rate schedule of the senior taxing authority. For a local personal income tax, the rate may be set in one of two ways, sometimes restricted by limits set by a senior level of government. It may be levied as a percentage of the senior government's personal income tax liability. This is the tax-on-tax method where the local tax has the characteristics of the central tax (deductions, exemptions, progressivity) and simply scales up that tax by the local rate. The other way is the tax-on-base method. Here, the local rate is set as a percentage of the taxable income (rather than the tax liability). If, as is usually the case, a single flat rate is adopted, the rate progressivity typical of central personal income tax schedule is forgone and the tax is closer to a proportional tax (but with exemptions and deductions).

For either the sales tax or selective sales taxes, the rate is a percent or percentage points added to the tax rate of a senior level of government.

Piggybacking is relatively inexpensive to administer, because the senior government collects the revenue and periodically remits the local share. One downside is that the local jurisdiction has no control over the tax base, no control over enforcement and collection, and may have to wait for tax remittances.

Local Taxes or Tax Sharing?

If local governments are to be accountable, transparent, and efficient in their spending and funding decisions, they must take responsibility for setting local tax rates, thus taking control of the revenue they raise and, subsequently, answering to their constituents for those decisions (Mikesell 2013). Local income and sales taxes could do this.

Responsibility for rate setting differs from tax sharing with a senior level of government which is what most local government officials would like because the latter will be criticized for the tax or tax increase while the former will escape such criticism. Responsibility for rate setting, the literature tells us, leads to greater accountability, enhanced transparency, and improved decision-making in the way in which municipalities spend their money (Slack and Bird 2015). Tax sharing, where the provincial government collects revenue from a tax and shares it with local governments, leads to little or no local autonomy because the local government has no control over the tax rate or tax base. They simply get a share of tax revenue collected by a senior level of government. Tax sharing, as such, is virtually synonymous with intergovernmental transfers (Bird 2011) and does not satisfy the criteria of autonomy, accountability, and transparency.

Limits or No Limits on Tax Rates?

As noted earlier, local autonomy, transparency, and accountability are best achieved when local authorities have the power to see tax rates without any restrictions by a senior level of government. The Nordic countries, for example, are free to set their own tax rates without limits. While there is some variation across local tax jurisdictions, differences do not appear to be large. In fact, it has been suggested that the similarity in rates across Finnish municipalities has been due to a tacit agreement not to use the income tax to compete for good taxpayers (Lotz 2012).

Restrictions or limits may be needed, however, to prevent local jurisdictions from setting tax rates in a way that inflicts harmful competition on other levels of government. The central governments in Norway and Iceland, some years ago, imposed a ceiling on local income tax rates to prevent municipalities from using their rate to generate excessive tax revenues. The result has been that all municipalities now use the capped rate. This constraint has basically converted the local tax into a tax-sharing program (Lotz 2012).

As well, limits on local taxes may be required if, at some limit, they account for a disproportionately higher share of the overall tax rate (local plus senior levels of government), thus creating impediments for senior levels of government who are responsible for overall macroeconomic management.

Limits are also placed on local income tax rates in some US taxing jurisdictions. As for general sales tax in the United States, most states have imposed upper limits on the local rates that may be set. These limits, by and large, have been introduced to prevent local tax authorities from encroaching on state taxes as well as preventing harmful intermunicipal tax competition.

Do Local Personal Income and General Sales Taxes Affect Behavior?

If local taxes have no impact on where people shop, work, and live, they are said to be neutral or economically efficient. If, as is almost always the case, the introduction of a new local tax or the increase in a local tax rate causes people to change their behavior, it may lead to distortions or inefficiencies. At the outset, it must be noted that distortionary (inefficient) taxes or tax increases are not always bad or undesirable, however. In fact, they may be necessary to remove or reduce a previous unwanted distortion or inefficiency. An illustration of this may be taken from road use in any large urbanized area. In almost all of these areas, motor vehicle drivers do not pay for the cost of congestion to which they contribute and the pollutants that they cause (Kitchen and Lindsey 2013; Lindsey 2019). Here, the introduction of road tolls or congestion charges provides an incentive for drivers to change their behavior through the use of public transit, or car pools, etc. This change while non-neutral is good for the economy because it corrects for a previous inefficiency where the costs of congestion and greenhouse gas emissions were not taken into consideration in driving decisions made by motor vehicle users.

Local personal income and sales taxes are not designed to correct for existing distortions or inefficiencies. They are primarily intended to generate much-needed revenue for funding local public services. Often, they do have an impact on location or cross-border decisions, especially with regard to living, shopping, and working. It is these effects that will be summarized in this section.

Most of the empirical work on local income and sales taxes has been on the latter, primarily because they are widely used across local jurisdictions in the United States, thus creating a large sample size for empirical studies.

Local sales tax. To the extent that differential tax rates across neighboring municipalities create an incentive for shoppers to shop in lower-tax jurisdictions, some tax avoidance could ensue. Studies in the United States suggest that local sales taxes have an impact on the local economy when they are adopted or when rate increases create a differential across municipalities. A 1 percent differential in the local sales tax reduces the local sales tax base by between 3 and 7 percent (see Mikesell 2010 for a summary of these studies).[6]

Evidence from the United States also suggests that distortions of this type are minimized if all municipalities within the state or region impose similar taxes (Mikesell 2010). One study that examined the employment impact in municipalities in the metropolitan Washington, DC, area concluded that a one percentage point increase in the local sales tax rate reduced annual employment growth by 2.17 percent (Mark et al. 2000). Finally, cross-border shopping effects tend to be greater when a sales tax is first introduced or immediately following a rate increase when compared with the impact over the longer-term duration of the tax (Mikesell 2010).

Similar results have been found in studies in the United Kingdom (Hall and Smith 1995). For example, after taking into consideration reasonable assumptions about purchases, tax differences, travel costs per mile, and jurisdiction size, it was found that between 5 and 27 percent of local residents cross-border shopped in response to local sales tax differentials. A similar analysis relating to large sales tax differences between Northern Ireland and the Republic of Ireland demonstrated a similar response, particularly for alcohol and petrol (Hall and Smith 1995).

There is an interesting example in western Canada where the city of Lloydminster is located in two provinces—part of the city is in Alberta

[6] The cross-border impact means that the tax base in neighboring municipalities expands, although there is no evidence on the amount by which it could expand.

which does not have a provincial sales tax and part is in Saskatchewan which has a provincial sales tax. Also, motor vehicle fuel taxes are higher in Saskatchewan. This city is an illustration of the sensitivity of consumers to sales tax differentials and the government's response. For city businesses on the Saskatchewan side to be competitive with those on the Alberta side, the Saskatchewan sales tax has been eliminated in Lloydminster but is gradually restored as distance from the border increases.

Local income tax. A residence-based income tax, depending on the rate, may cause people to move to areas that do not levy a similar tax. A payroll-based tax may cause employers to locate in areas where there is no such tax. The extent to which these distortions could surface is unclear. It will, in the end, depend on a taxpayers' responsiveness to municipal tax differentials.

Two empirical studies of the effect of local income taxes on location decisions suggest that a personal income tax may have a slight distorting impact but it is likely to be location specific and it is not possible to make any reliable general statements about its impact (Mikesell 2010). One study examined the income tax effects on employment and growth in the counties in the District of Columbia from 1960 to 1994 (Mark et al. 2000). The analysis found that a one percentage point increase in the residence-based personal income tax rate reduced annual population growth by 0.81 percentage points. A second study (Haughwout et al. 2004) found the elasticity of the New York City residence-based income tax to be around −0.5 with a somewhat smaller elasticity in Philadelphia.

Should These Taxes Be Levied at the Local Level or Metropolitan/Regional Level?

Because there is evidence that higher tax rates in one jurisdiction can lead to jobs relocating to neighboring jurisdictions, people moving to lower-taxed areas, and people shopping in neighboring municipalities, it has been suggested that one way of minimizing this problem, as the empirical literature tells us, is to implement these taxes in large cities and large metropolitan or regional areas making it more unattractive and costly for individuals to initiate activities to avoid the tax. More bluntly, the larger the taxing jurisdiction, the less likelihood there is of relocation in response to the tax. In addition, a tax at a metropolitan or region-wide level makes sense because of the extent to which the municipalities that are part of a regional area have become more integrated and unified over the past few decades.

Do These Taxes Complicate Intergovernmental Arrangement?

A potential complication of introducing local income or local sales taxes is that this can complicate the tax mix and, hence, intergovernmental relations. Central governments already occupy the personal income and often sales (excise) tax fields. In many federal countries, state or middle-level governments also levy income and sales taxes. Introducing a new local tax or any increase in rates, even if at low levels, adds a second and sometimes third player into these tax fields. Further, if these are piggybacked onto the tax rate of a senior level of government, taxpayers may be confused or at least not fully aware of which level of government is imposing the tax or responsible for increasing the rate. This may lead to a reduction in accountability and transparency.

While separation of tax sources, even if imperfect, has offsetting advantages in making the (local) public finance system more transparent and accountable, local income and sales taxes enable local governments to generate more own-source revenue; it permits them to take pressure off the property tax where it is used; and it could reduce the need for intergovernmental transfers which should help make the local revenue base more transparent and improve its accountability. As well, they are likely to be more appropriate than the property tax in contributing to the funding of many local non-related property tax services such as schooling, social services, social housing, and other services that are basically income redistributive in nature.

What About Revenue Yield and Volatility?

Evidence from the United States suggests that over the years, property taxes have grown the slowest, local sales taxes the fastest, and local income taxes in between. As for revenue stability, however, the ranking is different. Property taxes are the most stable or least volatile from year to year while sales taxes are the least stabile or most volatile (Mikesell 2010). Municipal spending responsibilities, on the other hand, are relatively steady and predictable. Volatility in tax revenues, in these circumstances, may create revenue problems for municipalities, thus requiring a responsive and effective intergovernmental transfer program. As a supplement to the property tax, however, local income and sales taxes could assist municipalities in meeting their expenditure needs.

As noted in Chap. 8, local sales and income taxes in a number of United States cities generate more revenue than the local property tax. Recent estimates for a number of large cities in Canada suggest that these taxes could be significant revenue generators as a supplement to the property tax.[7] For example, a surtax of between 7 and 16 percent on the residence-based provincial personal income tax could generate the equivalent of 20 percent of property tax revenue. A local sales tax rate of between 0.8 and 2.15 percent would yield the equivalent of 20 percent of property tax revenue. A tax of 10 cents per liter (roughly a 9 percent increase in price) on motor and diesel fuel tax would produce between 6 and 20 percent of current property taxes (Kitchen and Slack 2016). At the same time, some of the impact of these tax increases could be offset by lower property taxes.

Do Local Income and Sales Taxes Alter the Incidence of Local Taxes?

The distribution of the tax burden, or the incidence of the tax, will be quite different under these taxes when compared with the property tax. The property tax is generally deemed to be regressive in its impact on taxpayers; that is, it absorbs a higher percentage of a low-income earners income than of a high-income earners income. The income tax, by comparison, is generally deemed to be progressive because it takes proportionately more from high-income earners.

One study in England (Hall and Smith 1995), a number of years ago, compared the incidence on local taxpayers. After comparing the impact of a local general sales tax with the country's council tax (a property tax), former poll tax (community charge), and a potential local income tax, it concluded that the poll and property tax were regressive across all but the lowest income deciles, the income tax was quite progressive, and the sales tax essentially proportional. However, the latter results are at odds with some US estimates which show that sales tax are regressive. The degree of regressivity can vary, though, by permitting allowable exemptions (typically for necessities) and using tax credits.

This pattern suggests that by combining a local income tax with the property tax, one could more closely match taxes with services. For example, property taxes would be desirable for funding services closely

[7] The numbers vary from city to city; see Kitchen and Slack 2016.

associated with property (streets, fire protection as an example) while income taxes would be appropriate for services that are mainly income redistributional (schooling and social services). This, in turn, would improve the overall progressivity, or lessen the regressivity, of the local tax system.

Environmental Taxes

Environmental issues, notably greenhouse gases, are a prominent concern and governments should enact policies to reduce the problems. Local governments, and particularly cities, have important roles to play on the environmental file. On the one hand, as home to over half of the world's population, consumers of two-thirds of the energy used, and generators of over 70 percent of global emissions, cities are environmental hot spots. On the other, local governments face many of the consequences and burdens of environmental problems—damage to infrastructure, new mitigation efforts, and the direct expense of expanded central government regulations and environmental taxes. Environmental problems require a multilevel government approach and governments at all levels look, in part, to economic incentives (e.g., green taxes) to address those problems. Here, attention is focused on experience with local emissions markets and then on expanded and improved local levies for road services and for water and waste management utilities.

Local Environmental Taxes and Markets

Taxes to reduce greenhouse gases are normally levied by national governments. A notable exception is the city of Boulder, Colorado. Motivated by a strong interest in the environment and environmental concerns, city residents voted in 2006 (with a 60 percent approval rate) to implement a local tax on electricity consumption to finance its Climate Action Plan (CAP). The tax can be considered a carbon tax in that it taxes electricity not generated by solar or wind power (i.e., that largely coal generated). The tax generates about US $1.8 million annually. The tax amounts to about $21 per household, $94 per commercial establishment, and $9600 per industrial operation. The city's Climate Action Plan encompasses a suite of programs aimed at reducing local greenhouse gas emissions and at mitigating climate change. CAP programs are directed to outreach, promotion of renewables, and improving building efficiency. The program is credited with helping the community reduce greenhouse gas emissions by 16 percent from 2006 levels. Since it began, the tax rate has been increased and the program extended to 2023.[8]

The Boulder initiative has been implemented without there being any federal or state carbon taxation.[9] Thus, the local tax may be seen as an environmentally conscious community's action toward constraining greenhouse gases. Also, as a source of funds for its CAP programs, the tax finances a variety of climate-friendly programs that otherwise would be funded from other city revenues or not funded or not as well funded as they are with the tax on electricity use. Since the tax is a relatively small cost to most consumers, it is unclear how effective the tax has been at discouraging electricity use and emissions relative to the effects of the CAP programs and the awareness that those create. As a local tax and program with benefits that largely spill beyond the community, the city must consider the potential impacts on the city's attractiveness in a competitive interjurisdictional environment, a fact that may constrain the levels chosen.

Tokyo provides another example of a local market-based initiative to reduce greenhouse gases. In 2010, the Tokyo Metropolitan Government launched its mandatory cap and trade program to reduce CO_2 and other greenhouse gas emissions—a first for a local government. With a metropolitan population of 38 million in 2014, Tokyo's emissions amounted to 69.6 million tons of CO_2 equivalents or about 5.2 percent of Japan's total. Large industrial and commercial enterprises, of which there were 1255 in 2010, were required to participate in the cap and trade system—a system that got widespread approval from the business community. The trading system covers 40 percent of the total industrial and commercial sectors' emissions amounting to 20 percent of Tokyo's CO_2 emissions.[10] Over three five-year compliance/trading periods, emitters are expected to reduce in stages aggregate emissions by 25 percent from 2000 levels by 2020. Allowances, summing to a reduced aggregate level, are distributed free of charge at the beginning of each compliance period. Firms are to comply by reducing emissions or by purchasing offset credits in the market. The costs

[8] For further information see Koehn (2009), OECD (2010, p. 232), and the City of Boulder website, https://bouldercolorado.gov/climate/climate-action-plan-cap-tax.

[9] While a carbon tax has not appealed to voters in the State of Colorado, the State does have a carbon offset plan operating through the Colorado Carbon Fund.

[10] The three major greenhouse gases sources are the commercial, residential, and transportation sectors with contributions of 37.4, 30, and 17 percent, respectively.

or values of the credits stimulate finding least cost means of compliance. Performance is monitored and offenders are penalized. The price of the offsets has been declining, to about US $50 per ton in 2014, a level considered relatively high.[11] Substantial majorities of those covered have been successful in meeting their emission targets ahead of schedule.[12] Despite these successes, there is some question as to the contribution of the trading system (at least in its initial five years) to the realized emissions reductions (Wakabayashi and Kimura 2018).

The Tokyo cap and trade initiative is a part of wider programs of the Tokyo Metropolitan Government and the Government of Japan. A national emissions market was rejected but Japan's Global Warming Law permits its local and regional governments to pursue climate change policies. Tokyo began a climate change program in 2000 and announced emission reduction targets in 2006 well in advance of establishing its emission trading program. Tokyo also has programs aimed at reducing carbon emissions in the transportation and residential sectors.

Although not common, local emission trading programs are better suited for pollutants such as nitrogen and sulfur oxides and particulate matter which create more local or regional problems than CO_2. Widely noted are those in the metropolitan regions of Los Angeles and Chicago and the city of Santiago in Chile (OECD 2010). These programs cap the aggregate level of pollution, allocate emission permits, and allow trade among permit holders so as to facilitate lower cost solutions than command and control methods. The programs aim to control the bulk of the emissions which, at least in some cases, involves engaging small- and medium-sized sources as well as the large emitters. While the Chicago and Los Angeles programs are "local," they encompass the metropolitan regions. Also, those programs were initiated through regional air quality districts established by state governments to meet federal government air quality standards. Likewise, the emissions reduction program in Santiago is metropolitan focused and is in response to national government directives. The trading system, however, covers only total suspended particulate matter and it covers only the city of Santiago. In all three cases, air quality has improved but the extent of the contribution of the trading programs has been debated. In fact, RECLAIM (Regional Clean Air Incentive

[11] Information on government revenues from the program is not yet available.

[12] Additional information on the Tokyo program can be found, for example, in Confee-Morlot et al. (2010, p 91), Environmental Defense Fund (2015), and International Carbon Action Partnership (2019).

Market), the trading system in Los Angeles, is being phased out (SCAQMD 2018a). Also to be noted is that the trading program is not a revenue generator for local government. In 2017–2018, 56 percent of the South Coast Air Quality Management District's revenues came from (primarily state and federal) grants and 38 percent came from a variety of fees and charges (e.g., permit evaluation, permit operating, and emission fees and penalties). Over 80 percent of its funds went to emission reduction programs, ensuring compliance, review of permits, and monitoring (SCAQMD 2018b). Nonetheless, given the costs required to manage air quality, those are not falling directly on local governments and their taxpayers.

These local tax and market emission reduction programs (both for CO_2 reduction and for air quality improvement) are notable. The CO_2 initiatives have taken place where no national programs exist. If there were properly designed and implemented national programs, local efforts might impose minor distortions on those efforts. In the absence of national programs, however, local efforts are plagued by the limitations of locally large and uncompensated benefit spillovers.[13] In the presence of local or regional air pollution and national standards, local/regional initiatives may provide benefits more attuned to local preferences. Although market deficiencies have been recognized and the extent of their contributions to emission reductions have been questioned, these initiatives have contributed to improvements and in realizing them in a more cost-effective manner. As a mechanism for generating revenues for local governments, however, these environmental taxes and markets have (thus far) been relatively ineffective tools. At best, the returns seem to have limited to generating revenues to help offset the costs of other environmental initiatives.

Opportunities for Improved Taxes, Pricing, and Charges with Environmental Benefits

Opportunities exist for local governments in every country to introduce or expand the use of levies to improve the local environment. Traffic congestion is a widespread problem. Also, water and waste management utilities have environmental implications often not adequately managed by their existing charging systems. These are considered in this section.[14]

[13] An alternative approach for local governments to pursue reductions of local carbon emissions is to commit to using only electricity (and/or heat) from renewable sources. While such commitments are increasingly common, both San Francisco and New York City are introducing similar requirements on commercial properties.

[14] See Chap. 11, Sect. "For What Services?" for further discussion.

Road Pricing

Charging for road usage is becoming more common and is receiving more consideration. In urban areas, congestion charges levied on travel in congested central areas are appearing. London, Stockholm, and Singapore are frequently noted examples of where these are operating.[15] Cordon charges, that is, a fee for entry to the restricted zone, are most common. In addition, to reducing road traffic and congestion (in part by shifting some travel to alternative modes), these pricing systems are credited with reducing pollution and carbon emissions (e.g., OECD 2010, pp. 237–238). Linear versions of congestion pricing exist in the form of tolls for (often only) high occupancy vehicles to use designated lanes on highways. Often, some part of the revenues from congestion tolls are devoted to improving public transit which receives much of the diverted traffic. The cordon method is lacking in that charging for distance traveled in the zone and the level of congestion when traveling would increase the effectiveness of the pricing systems. Technology is now making such sophisticated charging systems possible. Along those lines, global positioning system (GPS) satellite tracking is now used in many European countries to toll truck traffic (e.g., Belgium, Germany, Slovakia, and the state of Oregon in the United States). Such systems (or others able to identify specific vehicles) could be used to monitor and toll travel based on distance/congestion/time of travel for passenger vehicles and light trucks on urban (or even regional or national) roadways.

At the local government level, vehicles are typically not charged for the use of roadways. That is, use of the road is "free"—at least to the extent that there is no charge for actual use (even when travel imposes externalities or congestion costs on others). National and state/provincial governments normally extract some revenues from road users in the form or fuel taxes and vehicle registration fees (and occasionally tolls). Whether earmarked for transportation or not, such levies do contribute toward the costs of the roadway systems. Some local governments also impose similar taxes (and parking charges) but the revenues from those are typically modest compared to local expenditures for the transportation systems. Particularly at

[15] New York City is planning to introduce such a congestion tax in 2021. While other cities have given consideration to the possibilities, NYC will be the first city in the United States to do so. See https://www.nytimes.com/2019/03/26/nyregion/what-is-congestion-pricing.html. Montreal, Canada, has also been considering a similar move. Also see section "Selective Sales Tax" above for discussion of alternatives.

the local level, these situations result in a significant deviation from the beneficiary pay principle applicable to many locally provided services. Also, divergence between the distribution of local taxes and the benefits of roadway use raise equity issues. A well-designed road tolling system (i.e., one that tolls use for distance and time of travel) would improve road services, enhance equity among local residents, and address significant interjurisdictional spillovers.[16] Furthermore, a tolling system that sought to meet both fixed and variable roadway costs would generate sufficient revenue to have a noticeable impact if substituted for local taxes.[17] While roadway pricing has yet to gain widespread public acceptance, charging for vehicle use of roadways offers considerable social benefits and is also a potential revenue generator for urban local governments.[18]

Water and Waste Utility Charges

Supplying water, handling wastewater, and managing solid waste are functions that are conventionally municipal government responsibilities. Data in Chap. 3 suggest that they amount to about one-sixth of the core expenditures of local governments. Data for Denmark indicate that expenditures for these three services represent 90 percent of the environmental expenditures of Danish municipal governments (OECD 2007). Of the expenditures for the three, waste management accounts for almost half, wastewater handling about one-third, and water supply almost one-fifth.[19] Given the importance of these services in local budgets and for the environment and health, their pricing is important. In Denmark and the Netherlands, these services are

[16] An example of a comprehensive study of a possible regional tolling system is Puget Sound Regional Council (2008). It reports large benefits to users, large benefits relative to costs and substantial potential revenues. The Netherlands examined nation-wide road pricing but has not (as yet) implemented such a system—a foregone opportunity in the view of OECD (2015).

[17] For example, analysis of data for a Canadian city indicated that roadway costs amounted to over 20 percent of the city's expenditures (i.e., of municipal government costs and excluding schooling, the only significant social expenditure of local governments in that province). If a significant portion of the roadway costs (e.g., one-half) were met through local vehicle registration charges and operating tolls, city property taxes could be reduced by one-half.

[18] Although likely less effective, a congestion-related charge and tax system on parking spaces may serve as a partial substitute for tolls (OECD 2015).

[19] See OECD (2007, p. 140). Water supply is not included in the calculations there, but its costs have been estimated from data elsewhere in that report. The distribution presented is consistent with data in the Netherlands and may well represent the situation in many other countries.

essentially covered by charges and reflect efforts to green the public finance system. While this discussion is a very brief review, these countries provide useful illustrations.

Water supply. Water supply in Denmark and the Netherlands is based on user pay and cost recovery from charges. Local governments (and/or regional water authorities in the Netherlands) are responsible for provision. There is a uniform water tax in Denmark (although that is rebated to industry) but the tax is only imposed on tap water in the Netherlands. In Denmark, the tax amounts to about one-third the total cost of water to users. These taxes are to discourage consumption and reflect the scarcity of water. Per capita water consumption in Denmark has declined as the cost of water has increased. In the Netherlands, water tax rates are indexed for inflation. Also there, the provincial governments levy taxes on groundwater abstractions. Relative to most other European countries, the cost to users of water is high.

Wastewater. The cost of wastewater services is essentially met on a full-cost-recovery basis from user charges and levies. Regional water authorities or municipal governments in the Netherlands and local governments in Demark typically operate the water systems and treatment plants. Both Denmark and the Netherlands set high standards for service and sewerage treatment. Charges, taxes or pollution levies are imposed on effluents—notably on nitrogen, phosphorous, and organic matter. The levies are set by the national governments, but the local fee component varies considerably among districts. Local tariffs are based on water consumption which is metered. In the Netherlands, in particular, wastewater service costs have escalated rapidly.

Solid waste. Dealing with solid waste is a difficult and costly problem for local governments. Recycling is often difficult and landfills have problems. Both Denmark and the Netherlands have greatly reduced landfilling (it is virtually eliminated in the Netherlands). Incineration has been the most important alternative with the heat generated used to produce electricity or for heating residential and business buildings. The widespread use of district heating systems facilitates the heating option. For example, 60 percent of Denmark's population obtains heat through district heating systems. Incineration is credited with actually reducing greenhouse gas emissions in the Netherlands. In addition, landfill emissions of methane are gathered and used for fuel. Regulations and taxes have helped divert waste from landfills. Taxes, charges, and returns have enabled the solid waste system to operate largely on a cost-recovery basis. Taxes are imposed on a variety of products (e.g., electronics, packaging, batteries, tires, vehicles) to promote safe disposal and cost recovery and to put responsibility on producers for the end-of-life costs of their products. Deposit and refund systems apply to bottles. Economic incentives are important in the management of the solid waste systems.[20]

Charges for water and waste utility services often do not cover their full costs. The result is that the local taxpayer bears some of the burden. Denmark and the Netherlands illustrate the potential for charges and environmental levies to meet the cost of those services and signal (or better signal) to users the full costs of their activities. Those signals are incentives to modifying behavior toward less socially costly options.

Environmental Regulations

Regulations are certainly not taxes but they are an important avenue of environment control. Hence, simply as a reminder of that, a few are noted here. Urban planning or land use planning (and the accompanying regulations) is probably one of the most important regulatory measures having environmental impacts. Density of development, for example, impacts the size and shape of the city and building standards such as energy efficiency standards affect energy consumption. A more direct fiscal impact comes from imposing development charges or requirements on developers to cover or provide (e.g., in their subdivisions) the infrastructure supporting their projects. Closely related is infrastructure design, especially for the roadway system and for public transportation. This influences mobility, energy use, and air quality. Prohibiting or taxing the use of disposable/plastic bags has become quite common. These are but a few of the many regulatory measures that impact local environments.

Closing Observations on Environmental Taxes

Measures of environmentally related taxes, fees, and charges typically show that taxes on fuels, motor vehicles, and transport services account for almost the entire total across countries.[21] Senior levels of government, as opposed to local governments, have been the major beneficiaries of these revenue

[20] Chapter 5 of OECD (2015) provides a particularly comprehensive discussion of solid waste management.

[21] For example, see the OECD environmental reviews.

sources. Typically these taxes/fees/charges were implemented before the environment was a serious concern or even considered—usually they were seen as a convenient way of generating revenue, especially for financing roads and public transit. The environmentally motivated portion of those taxes is modest. Still, the tax bases can have substantial environmental impacts and because the impacts cover many jurisdictions, decision-making should primarily be with senior levels of government (if not international in some cases). While recognizing that problems and possible solutions are multilevel and that environmental taxation deserves multi-jurisdictional coordination, this situation leaves limited room or scope for local governments in many instances—as with carbon taxes. Nevertheless, local governments currently provide important services that have local environmental impacts. Designing fiscal systems to signal the full social costs to the beneficiaries of those services, then, can enhance the local (and even the broader) environments. In particular, charging the full cost of utility services stands out as a valuable approach in terms of sending the right signals and in reducing the burden on less efficient and less equitable revenue sources. Although yet to find wide acceptance, road user charges appear to be an environment-friendly route to reducing congestion, improving infrastructure efficiency, and even generating significant revenues for local governments (more on these fees and charges in Chap. 11).

Summary

Personal income and sales taxes are important generators of local government revenues in a number of countries. In the Nordic countries, for example, the dominance of a local personal income tax reflects both historical developments and the funding of heavy social responsibilities that local governments carry. In the United States, income and sales taxes are widely used in combination with the property tax.

Local income and sales taxes represent the major local taxes in a handful of countries. In the majority of countries, however, they are used to supplement property taxes. Their desirability often depends on the services to be funded, availability of own-source revenues, and other circumstances. While not as solid as the property tax in meeting the criteria for a solid local tax, they have enough positive features to meet some of the criteria.

Municipalities fund a wide range of services extending from those that are primarily related to property and those that are more income redistributional in nature. For the former, the property tax is particularly useful. For the latter, income taxes have a number of redeeming features.

There are a number of issues to consider in discussions around the implementation and administration of both a personal income and sales taxes. First, there are contrasting views on whether it should be administered locally or piggybacked onto the tax of a senior level of government. Piggybacking is less costly, but local administration enhances autonomy, accountability, and transparency. Second, taking responsibility for setting local tax rates rather than entering into a tax-sharing arrangement with a senior level of government improves autonomy, accountability, and transparency. Third, in general, limits should not be imposed on tax rates, but they may be necessary to prevent harmful competition between levels of government or to prevent local decision makers from setting rates that go against a country's macroeconomic policy. Fourth, if a local tax jurisdiction implements one or other of these taxes or increases their rate when neighboring jurisdictions do not, some taxpayers will respond by changing their location, shopping, and working patterns. Fifth, to minimize these cross-border effects, it is generally argued that an income or sales tax or increase in their rates be the responsibility of the metropolitan or regional level of government rather than a town or city or any other local jurisdiction that is part of the larger metropolitan or regional area. Sixth, whenever local taxes, such as income and sales taxes, are shared with a senior level of government, there is always the potential of complicating intergovernmental relations. Seventh, both local income and sales taxes have the potential to generate significant sums of revenue, but they are much more volatile and less predictable than the property tax. Eighth, supplementing the local property tax with the addition of a local income and/or sales tax could improve the overall progressivity of the local tax system.

Though still a relatively minor contributor to local government revenues, environmental taxes deserve recognition and consideration. Many local government services have environmental impacts and some of those may not be adequately recognized and addressed by senior governments. Designing local charges/fees so that they cover the full costs of service provision including environmental impacts is both efficient and fair. As an example and still underappreciated and underutilized, road pricing is an environmental tax that offers many benefits including the potential to be a significant source of revenue.

References

Bird, Richard M. 2011. Subnational Taxation in Developing Countries: A Review of the Literature. *Journal of International Commerce, Economics, and Policy* 2 (1): 139–161.

———. 2012. *The GST/HST: Creating an Integrated Sales Tax in a Federal Country*. University of Calgary, School of Public Policy, SSP Research Papers, 5(12).

Confee-Morlot, Jan, Lamia Kamal-Chaoui, Michael G. Donovan, Ian Cochran, Alexis Robert, and Pierre-Jonathan Teasdale. 2010. *Cities, Climate Change and Multilevel Government*. OECD Environmental Working Paper No. 14.

Dahlby, Bev. 2012. *Reforming the Tax Mix in Canada*. University of Calgary, School of Public Policy Research Papers 5(14), April.

Environmental Defence Fund. 2015. *Tokyo: An Emissions Trading Case Study*, May. https://www.ieta.org/resources/Resources/Case_Studies_Worlds_Carbon_Markets/2015/tokyo_case_study_may2015.pdf.

Hall, John, and Stephen Smith. 1995. *Local Sales Taxation: An Assessment of the Feasibility and Likely Effects of Sales Taxation at the Local Level in the UK*. London: Institute for Fiscal Studies.

Haughwout, Andrew, Robert Inman, Stephen Craig, and Thomas Luce. 2004. Local revenue hills: Evidence from four US cities. *Review of Economics and Statistics* 86 (2): 570–585.

International Carbon Action Partnership. 2019. *Japan-Tokyo Cap-and-Trade Program*, April. https://icapcarbonaction.com/en/?option=com_etsmap&task=export&format=pdf&layout=list&systems[]=51.

Kitchen, Harry. 2019. Beyond the Property Tax: What Taxes for Large Cities? In *Funding the Canadian City*, ed. Enid Slack, Lisa Philipps, Lindsay M. Tedds, and Heather L. Evans, 75–95. Toronto: Canadian Tax Foundation and Institute on Municipal Finance and Governance.

Kitchen, Harry, and Robin Lindsey. 2013. *Financing Roads and Public Transit in the Greater Toronto and Hamilton Area*. Residential and Civil Construction Alliance of Ontario. www.rccao.com.

Kitchen, Harry, and Enid Slack. 2016. *More Tax Sources for Canada's Largest Cities: Why, What, and How?* IMFG Papers on Municipal Finance and Governance Series, No. 27, University of Toronto. http://munkschool.utoronto.ca/imfg/resources/. Accessed 16 June 2018.

Koehn, Jonathan. 2009. A Community Takes Charge: The Evolution of Boulder's Carbon Tax. In *Green Cities: New Approaches to Confronting Climate Change*, 195–206. OECD Workshop Proceedings, June.

Lindsey, Robin. 2019. User Fees for Transportation: Road Tolls and Congestion Pricing. In *Funding the Canadian City*, ed. Enid Slack, Lisa Philipps, Lindsay M. Tedds, and Heather L. Evans, 123–156. Toronto: Canadian Tax Foundation and Institute on Municipal Finance and Governance.

Litman, Todd. 2012. Road Pricing: Congestion Pricing, Value Pricing, Toll Roads and HOT Lanes. http://www.vtpi.org/tdm/tdm35.htm.

Lotz, Jorgen. 2012. *You Get What You Pay For: How Nordic Cities Are Financed.* In IMFG Papers on Municipal Finance and Governance Series, University of Toronto, No. 7. http://munkschool.utoronto.ca/imfg/resources/.

Mark, Stephen T., Therese J. McGuire, and Leslie E. Papke. 2000. The Influence of Taxes on Employment and Population Growth: Evidence from the Metropolitan Washington D.C. Area. *National Tax Journal* 53 (1): 105–123.

Mikesell, John L. 2010. The Contribution of Local Sales and Income Taxes to Fiscal Autonomy. Chap. 6 in *Municipal Revenues and Land Policies*, ed. G.K. Ingram and Y.-H. Yang. Cambridge, MA: Lincoln Institute of Land Policy.

———. 2011. Consumption and Income Taxes. Chap. 10 in *Greenbook.* International City Managers Association.

Mikesell, John. 2013. Administration of Local Taxes: An International Review of Practices and Issues for Enhancing Fiscal Autonomy. Chap. 4 in *A Primer on Property Tax Administration and Policy*, ed. William J. McCluskey, Gary C. Cornia, and Lawrence C. Walters, 1st ed. John Wiley & Sons Ltd.

Oates, Wallace E., and Robert M. Schwab. 2004. What Should Local Governments Tax: Income or Property? In *City Taxes, City Spending: Essays in Honor of Dick Netzer*, ed. Amy Ellen Schwartz, 7–41. Northampton, MA: Edward Elgar.

OECD. 2007. *OECD Environmental Performance Reviews: Denmark.* Paris: OECD Publishing.

———. 2010. *Cities and Climate Change.* Paris: OECD Publishing.

———. 2015. *OECD Environmental Performance Reviews: The Netherlands.* Paris: OECD Publishing.

———. 2016. *Revenue Statistics 1965–2015.* Paris.

Puget Sound Regional Council. 2008. *Traffic Choices Study: Final Report.* April. https://www.psrc.org/sites/default/files/traffic-choices.pdf.

SCAQMD (South Coast Air Quality Management District). 2018a. 2017 Annual Report.

———. 2018b. *Popular Annual Financial Report for the Year Ended*, June 30.

Slack, Enid. 2011. *Financing Large Cities and Metropolitan Areas.* IMFG Paper on Municipal Finance and Governance, No. 3. Toronto: Institute on Municipal Finance and Governance.

Slack, Enid, and Richard M. Bird. 2015. *How to Reform the Property Tax: Lessons from around the World.* IMFG Papers on Municipal Finance and Governance Series, University of Toronto, No 21, 2015. http://munkschool.utoronto.ca/imfg/resources/.

Tanguay, Georges A., and Ian Gingras. 2011. *Gas Prices Variations and Urban Sprawl: An Empirical Analysis of the 12 Largest Canadian Metropolitan Areas.* CIRANO—Scientific Publication No. 2011s-3. http://ssrn.com/abstract=1919003.

Wakabayashi, Masayo, and Osamu Kimura. 2018. The Impact of the Tokyo Metropolitan Emissions Trading Scheme on Reducing Greenhouse Gas Emissions: Findings from a Facility-Based Study. *Climate Policy* 18 (8): 1028–1043.

CHAPTER 11

Charges and User Fees

Introduction

Charges and user fees are like local taxes in that they generate revenue for municipal services. At one extreme, they include charges such as permits, licenses, concessions, penalties, fines, and so on. In most countries, these contribute very little revenue to municipal coffers, although at the margin, they may be important for covering the cost of certain facilities or activities. In some countries, for example, licenses, permits, and concessions may be required for using a park with revenues offsetting some or all park maintenance costs. As well, local planning regulations everywhere require a range of charges for land and property development and redevelopment. In countries without a fully effective local tax system, permits, licenses, or concessions may be required to open a retail shop in a commercial part of the city with funds dedicated to the cost of services such as local sidewalks and streetlights. None of these charges, however, are based on volume of use; rather they are charges that permit the use of a facility or access to it. As such, they are not really a user fee or user charge as discussed in this chapter. At the same time, municipal governments everywhere impose penalties and fines to prevent or control socially undesirable activities and, failing this, to penalize those who chose to ignore or violate these restrictions. These are not user fees either.

User fees or user charges that are based on the volume or amount of use an individual gets from a local public service differ from local taxes in one very important way. If correctly designed, user fees provide valuable

H. Kitchen et al., *Local Public Finance and Economics*,
https://doi.org/10.1007/978-3-030-21986-4_11

information on the municipal services that should be produced, their optimum quantity and quality, and for whom. Local taxes do not do this. This is an important difference and one that should not be treated lightly for it has important consequences for achieving an efficient, accountable, and equitable allocation of resources. This issue of efficient resource allocation, it should be noted, is the main rationale for user fees as is explained in the section "When Should User Fees Be Implemented?". The section "How Should User Fees Be Set?" discusses how user fees should be designed and applied when economies of scale are prevalent, when capacity constraints exist, when peak period demand differs from off-peak demand, when distance from source of supply affects costs, when second-best conditions surface, and when externalities abound.

Recent trends where senior governments have passed additional service responsibilities onto municipal governments, has reduced the relative importance of grants, and placed increased reliance on local revenue sources. This has changed the fiscal environment in which local governments in many countries now operate. In particular, this has led to an increased reliance on user fees, especially since local politicians are reluctant to raise local taxes. With user fees potentially taking on greater importance as a municipal revenue source, the section "For What Services?" of this chapter discusses and evaluates a number of local services that could be fully or partially funded by user charges. These services include water and sewers, stormwater, electricity, solid waste, public transit and roads, public recreation, public libraries, police, and fire.

The section "Issues with User Fees" discusses a range of issues around user fees: Who should set them? Should they be regulated? Should they be used to subsidize other services? Are they fair? And should they vary be discounted? The section "Summary" concludes the chapter.

When Should User Fees Be Implemented?

The short answer is that they should be adopted whenever and wherever possible (Tedds 2019; Althaus and Tedds 2016). Why are they important? It is primarily due to their capacity, if properly structured, to satisfy a number of important principles in local government finance: efficiency, accountability, transparency, fairness, and ease of administration (see Chap. 8).

A major problem with the current application of many user fees is that they are not set in a manner that satisfies these principles. As such, we see a demand for services and often a demand for physical infrastructure that is not allocatively efficient or optimal (Kitchen and Slack 2016; Bird and Slack 2017). Inefficiently set user fees often lead to over-investment and larger facilities than would be justified if more efficient pricing practices were adopted. At the same time, failure to price properly has resulted in considerable unplanned and implicit income redistribution, much of which would be unacceptable if it were made explicit (Bird 1976, p. 104; Fenn and Kitchen 2016, p. 29). Clearly, income distribution considerations are very important but they should be handled through transfer programs that target the poor (or through special concessions such as lifeline rates for water) rather than changing or distorting prices where the rich frequently benefit more than the poor.

User fees, then, are ideal for funding those services where specific beneficiaries can be identified and non-payers excluded. They should not be employed for services with "public goods" characteristics, that is, where the service is non-excludable (it is difficult or very costly to exclude someone from using the service) and non-rival in consumption (the additional resource cost of another person using the good is zero). Examples include local streets and roads and neighborhood parks. Nor should they be used for services where specific beneficiaries cannot be identified and where the services are primarily income redistributional in nature (social services, social housing, and public education). For these services, reliance on grants from senior levels of government and local taxes are much more appropriate as a funding instrument (see Chaps. 9, 10, 12, 13, and 14).

How Should User Fees Be Set?

Designing user fees is relatively straightforward in theory, yet often difficult to implement. Opposition arises because they are alleged to be regressive (i.e., they absorb a higher percent of lower-income individuals or households' income when compared with higher-income individuals or households). In some cases, they are resisted because municipal cost data are not collected and recorded in a way that permits an estimation of marginal costs. This is generally a problem with fixed costs or where there are joint costs with other services such as in assigning general government expenses to individual services. There is often political and, sometimes, administrative reluctance to introduce user fees for services that were previously not funded by these fees and to alter user fee structures that have been around for a long time. Although our analytical tools give us no guidance on overcoming political resistance to user fees, they do permit us to design efficient user fees under a variety of circumstances—when economies of scale are present, when capacity constraints exist, when demand differs in peak and non-peak periods, when second-best considerations are prevalent, and when externalities exist. Each of these is addressed following a discussion of marginal and average cost pricing, the two most commonly discussed basis for setting user fees.

Marginal Cost Pricing

Figure 11.1 illustrates the application of the marginal cost pricing principle to a municipal service bearing in mind that the existence of only one delivery agent exists in each municipality. In effect, this means that each municipal system operates as a monopolist. In Fig. 11.1, economies of

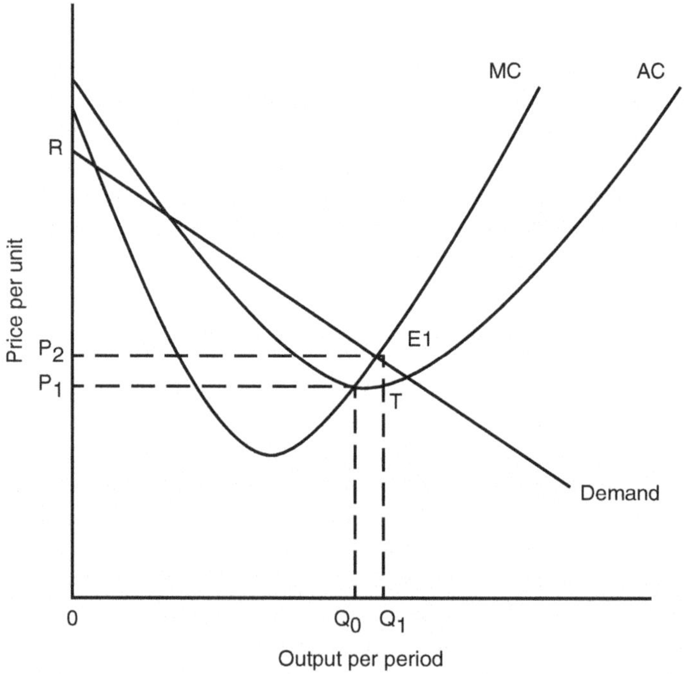

Fig. 11.1 Application of marginal cost pricing when a profit is generated. Source: Kitchen, Harry, 2002. *Municipal Revenues and Expenditure Issues in Canada* (Toronto: Canadian Tax Foundation), at 125

scale (decreasing costs per unit of output as the output increases) exist over levels of output up to the minimum point of the average cost (AC) curve (at output level Q_0) and diseconomies of scale (increasing costs per unit of output as the output increases) over higher levels of output. This is represented by the U-shaped average cost curve. At the same time, the marginal cost (MC) must be below the average cost when the average cost is declining and above the average cost when it is increasing. In Fig. 11.1, total consumer benefit as measured by willingness to pay equals the area under the demand curve for OQ_1 units (ORE_1Q_1). Total production costs equal the area under the marginal cost curve for OQ_1 units or the average cost per unit (OP_1) times the number of units (OQ_1) which is the area represented by OP_1TQ_1—either of these measures yields the same total cost. At the point where price equals marginal cost (E_1), total revenue (price times quantity) as measured by $OP_2E_1Q_1$ exceeds total cost as measured by OP_1TQ_1. While the municipal service illustrated in Fig. 11.1 generates a profit, this merely reflects the fact that consumers value the service as being important enough to pay the price that generates this profit. Furthermore, if the municipality wishes to return the profit or surplus to its customers, the most efficient way would be through a dividend or money transfer. Returning this profit through a per unit subsidy either to the producer (this would artificially shift the MC down) or the consumer which effectively lowers the price per unit (this would artificially shift the demand curve to the right) is inefficient and wasteful because it leads to a level of consumption that exceeds the allocatively efficient level.

Instead of the AC curve in Fig. 11.1, suppose the municipality faced a higher average cost curve such as AC_1 in Fig. 11.2 (the demand and marginal cost curves are the same as in Fig. 11.1). Here, the municipality would be losing money if it continued to provide it at the most efficient level (E_1). This loss is illustrated by the area $P_1P_3JE_1$—total revenue of $OP_1E_1Q_1$ minus total cost of OP_3JQ_1. Furthermore, this loss would have to be funded from other revenues and it is the funding of this loss that has prompted modifications to the strict marginal cost pricing principle. These are discussed next.

Average Cost Pricing

One solution to avoiding the loss that might exist under marginal cost pricing is to set the price where average cost (AC) equals price. This is at point F in Fig. 11.2. Here total revenue (OP_4FQ_2) equals total cost

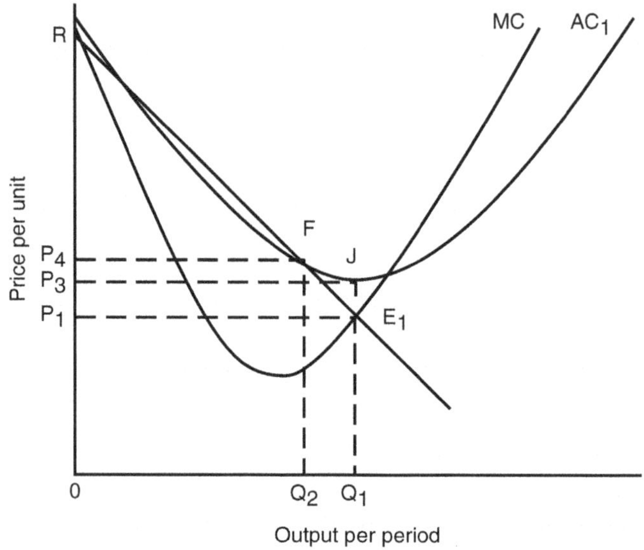

Fig. 11.2 Application of marginal cost pricing when a loss ensues. Source: Kitchen, Harry, 2002. *Municipal Revenues and Expenditure Issues in Canada* (Toronto: Canadian Tax Foundation), at 126

(OP_4FQ_2). Average cost pricing simply takes the total cost and divides it by the number of units currently produced to obtain the price. A positive feature of this approach is that prices are easier to calculate especially if only financial costs are considered as is usually the case.

Average cost pricing produces some important differences when compared with marginal cost pricing. If average cost is declining as at point F in Fig. 11.2, too little of the good is provided and the price is too high. If average cost is rising, too much of the output is produced and the price is too low. In either case, an inefficient level of output will result. Only if marginal and average costs are constant (the same regardless of the level of output) will average cost generate the efficient level of output. In spite of potential efficiency losses, average cost pricing is the most common structure for funding many municipal services that rely on user fees.

Average incremental cost pricing is a variant of average cost pricing (Bird 2001, p. 176). It attempts to calculate the cost incurred as a result of an additional user—like marginal cost pricing—but it does so in a way that is computationally easier for public managers to estimate. Briefly, it includes all additional costs of providing an increased level of service. This cost is then divided by the anticipated number of additional users. Each user is charged the average of the incremental total costs. This does not amount to marginal cost pricing in the strict sense, which refers to the additional cost for each user, but for many services, it may be as close as one can get in practice.

Pricing for Economies of Scale

For services where marginal cost pricing generates a loss such as illustrated in Fig. 11.2 or where they have the characteristics of a natural monopolist,[1] an efficient pricing policy involves more than simply setting price equal to marginal cost. Equating price to marginal cost results in an annual operating loss that must be subsidized from another local revenue source, a solution that is highly improbable for political reasons and almost certain to be allocatively inefficient because the subsidy will almost certainly come from taxes that create distortions elsewhere. Setting price equal to average cost or some variant of it is also inefficient as was illustrated in the preceding section.

An economically efficient and politically acceptable solution in this case frequently involves the use of a multi-part tariff or price. In its simplest form, this includes a variable charge equal to the marginal cost of the last unit consumed and a fixed charge for the privilege of using or gaining access to the service. The variable charge, if correctly set, would ensure that the right amount is consumed so that allocative efficiency is achieved and the fixed charge could provide enough revenue to cover the fixed costs. More complicated versions may include more than two pricing variables. This multi-part pricing policy is particularly appropriate for local utility services because they have substantial fixed production costs and a declining average and marginal cost structure.

Pricing with Capacity Constraints

Capacity constraints arise when the service provided by a given infrastructure is limited. If capacity is uneven and can be expanded only in discrete amounts, marginal cost pricing will typically lead to under or overprovision relative to the efficient level. When consumption presses on capacity,

[1] A natural monopolist is often depicted by local utility type services (water, sewers, natural gas where it is a municipal responsibility). Their predominant characteristic for analytical purposes here is that they exhibit decreasing per unit costs over the entire range of output (economies of scale).

then, the price should be raised to allocate the limited supply efficiently. This approach justifies a price above short-run marginal cost whenever consumption is at or close to capacity. Peak-load pricing (see next topic), time-of-use pricing, and seasonal pricing are mechanisms to implement this approach and to provide enough revenue to help cover fixed costs.

Although generally more difficult to implement, there is another approach to setting prices above marginal cost to fund fixed costs. Since prices will be too high, consumption will be less than its desirable level. The lost satisfaction from reduced consumption can be minimized if there are several classes of consumers, by raising the price the most for those whose demand is most inelastic, meaning that they will not reduce their consumption much in response to high prices. This is known as the Ramsey pricing rule (Church and Ware 2000, ch. 25).

Pricing in Peak Periods

A further issue in user fee pricing is the pricing of services in peak and off-peak periods of demand (seasonal and time of day are examples). Efficient pricing may call for higher charges in peak periods and lower charges in off-peak periods. This arises because peak demand strains capacity and only lasts for a fraction of the demand cycle. Marginal benefit to peak users only occurs over a portion of the demand cycle, whereas the marginal cost of capacity expansion is incurred over the entire demand cycle which means that the marginal benefit to peak users exceeds their marginal costs. In addition, since off-peak users gain no additional benefit from capacity expansion, the additional capacity costs should be shouldered entirely by peak users. In other words, the off-peak price should be set equal to marginal operating costs, while the peak price should be set equal to the sum of marginal capacity and operating costs.

Pricing and Distance from Source of Supply

For a number of services, distance from source of supply affects marginal cost. If the unit price or user fee is not differentiated to reflect this, users with lower marginal costs subsidize users with higher marginal costs. If this subsidy is capitalized into land values, the properties that are farthest from the source will be priced higher than would otherwise be the case. One way of handling this is to impose zone charges or differential fees on customers in areas where the costs of servicing are higher because of distance from source.

Pricing and Second-Best Considerations

Second-best considerations arise if prices elsewhere in the system are inefficient—that is, different from the marginal social cost. This situation occurs for instance, when a municipality imposes a user fee for a particular service, such as public transit, but does not apply a specific charge to a substitute for that service, such as road or expressway use. Road and expressway users pay nothing to the municipality for each trip taken, whereas public transit users are charged for each trip. In this instance, the municipality may be able to improve efficiency by setting the price in the controllable sector, public transit, below the marginal cost, in the hope of stimulating an increase in the use of transit services and a concomitant decrease in the use of roads and expressways (the uncontrollable sector). This pricing strategy is known as a "second-best" solution—a solution that one adopts when the price equals marginal social cost solution is impractical (Boadway 1997).

Pricing and Externalities

Finally, subsidizing certain services may be warranted if externalities or spillover benefits accrue to nonresidents. Much of the capital and social infrastructure in a municipality benefits both residents and nonresidents and user fees or charges collected from local citizens may be less than the full marginal social cost. While user charges can be imposed on nonresidents as well, these may not capture capacity costs appropriately. In such circumstances, it may be preferable to provide a subsidy in the form of a provincial grant rather than shift the associated costs to local residents. The standard recommendation here is that costs of provision could be subsidized from provincial revenue sources or revenues collected from beyond the local community. The subsidy rate should equal the share of benefits accruing to nonresidents.

For What Services?

The traditional model of local and metropolitan government finance within a unitary or federal system argues that services benefitting the local community should be funded, as closely as possible, by revenues generated in the local community. Within this model, it is further argued that local services with "public goods" characteristics should be funded from local taxes. Services with "private goods" characteristics, on the other hand, should be funded by user fees or charges on those who benefit from the service. In general, then, it makes considerable economic sense to apply user fees to water and sewer systems, stormwater management, solid waste collection and disposal, public transit, major highways and arterial roads, parking, public recreation, and public libraries to name the most obvious. A brief description of their application to local services is described below. For all services, the arguments are the same for local responsibility as they are for metropolitan responsibility.

Water

Water is becoming an increasingly scarce resource, much like oil a few decades ago. The difference is that the world cannot survive without water, but in the long run it will, in all likelihood, be able to survive without oil. The impacts of climate change, population growth, and increasing stress on natural ecosystems along with more frequent and prolonged periods of drought such as in California and South Africa are posing increasing pressure on the sustainability of many country's water supply. When combined with increasing urbanization and densification, deteriorating infrastructure, leaky pipes, and ever expanding contaminants in our supply chain, pressure has never been greater to efficiently and effectively manage the provision and use of water. This is where efficiently and fairly designed user fees are badly needed.

There are basically two general rate structures—flat rates that do not vary with consumption and a variety of volume-based charges. Each of these is discussed below with an emphasis placed on the incentives that each structure creates for improving efficiency and leading to conservation practices. Each rate structure can be accountable and transparent as long as revenues are deposited in accounts that are dedicated to funding capital and operating costs. All volume-based structures are fair as long as those who use the service are those who pay for the service.

Flat Rates for Water

Flat rates are the simplest rate structures to administer and understand. Flat rates are fixed payments per billing period, unrelated to volume consumed but they may vary by customer class (residential vs. commercial) and property type, such as the number and types of rooms, the size of the lot, the number of water-using fixtures, whether or not there is a swimming pool, and so on. Some indirect methods of charging for water are equivalent to a flat-rate charge. These are generally based on property values and the charge takes the form of an addition to the property bill, a frontage charge, or a special levy. This is the approach adopted for a large number of residential properties in the province of Quebec in Canada (Ecofiscal Commission 2017). This ongoing practice is surprising in today's political climate where municipalities are looking for ways to take some of the burden off the property tax and place it on those who can be identified as being specific beneficiaries of a service.

Because flat rates are unrelated to volume consumed and meters are not used, there is no incentive to economize on the use of water or to engage in conservation practices such as fixing leaking taps, turning off sprinkler systems during rainstorms, washing cars excessively, and so on. In Canadian municipalities where flat rates have been used over the past 25 years, average daily residential consumption per capita has been considerably higher than in municipalities where volume-based charges have been used. In fact, the average daily residential consumption per capita under flat-rate systems exceeded volume-based consumption by something between 37 percent and 133 percent, depending on the year. Regardless of the rate structure, however, water consumption per household in most Canadian cities has declined over the past two decades, largely because of two initiatives—higher water rates regardless of structure and a variety of non-price water-conservation initiatives (Kitchen 2017b).

Volume-Based Rates for Water

Volume-based rates link the amount paid for water to the amount of water consumed. They require the use of meters which are now largely universal in most countries. These rates take a variety of forms including constant unit charges, decreasing block rates, increasing block rates, or some combination of these.

A *constant unit rate* (CUR) is an equal charge per unit of consumption (e.g., cubic meter) and seldom varies across classes of customers. It may also include a fixed charge component that is unrelated to water consumption. It is an efficient pricing policy only if the marginal cost of water is constant (in which case, the average cost will be constant). We know, however, that the marginal cost is not constant—it either rises or falls with quantity consumed. Since price must equal marginal cost for efficient use, this pricing structure is inefficient and it is not very effective in encouraging water conservation.

A *declining block rate* (DBR) structure generally includes a basic or fixed service charge per period combined with a volumetric charge that decreases in blocks (discrete steps) as the volume consumed increases (the more you use, the less you pay per unit). Typically, one or two initial blocks cover residential and light commercial water use, with subsequent blocks levied on heavy commercial and industrial uses. The fixed component of the charge often varies with the size of the service connection. Minimum charges that correspond to a minimum amount of water consumption in each billing period are common in systems of this kind.

Traditionally, the municipality sets the consumption limit for the first block to represent the largest amount of water that a consumer in a single-family dwelling might use. The second block encompasses the consumption of most middle-sized commercial customers, and the third (and any subsequent) block encompasses larger industrial users. A typical declining block rate system has at least three blocks, but declining block volumetric charge structures with only two blocks are also used.

DBRs are efficient if the marginal cost of water provision is falling, such as may exist if economies of scale are present when servicing large-volume customers. Critics argue, however, that DBRs do not promote water conservation since the price of water declines as more water is used, hence there may be little incentive to economize on water use. On the other hand, a declining block rate system may be an appropriate tool for water conservation if it is the small customers who are responsible for inefficient water use. Charging them a higher price gives them a greater incentive to conserve.

An *increasing block rate* (IBR) works in the following way. The first block for a given class of customer is generally designed to cover the normal water use of an average customer in that class. The rate increases with each subsequent block—the more you use, the more you pay per unit.

IBRs may be appropriate for residential customers who as a customer class are the main cause of peak demand, and for industrial customers if limitations on the availability of water justify shifting the cost burden to the largest users. Here, it is these users that have the largest impact on water system planning and sizing since systems are built to meet the largest demands. Of particular interest to policymakers interested in promoting conservation, price differences from block to block could be set in a way that would give the customer a clear and strong incentive to conserve water.

A *humpback block rate* system combines increasing and decreasing block rates to produce the rate structure, shaped like an inverted "U." Under this approach, the municipality applies its highest rate to the consumption block that captures the peak seasonal demand of residential customers. The intention is to encourage water conservation by residential customers by encompassing residential use within increasing block rates while offering large industrial users block rates that decline as use increases and thereby benefit from the economies of scale associated with providing water to customers of this kind.

This structure is sometimes used in municipalities promoting economic development. Many municipalities are eager to leverage any competitive advantage that they may enjoy, with a view to retaining and attracting industries and jobs. Despite some implicit cross-subsidization among classes of users, the ready availability of clean water at a reasonable price can be a distinct advantage in sectors like food processing or beverage manufacturing.

Municipalities often use *variations or combinations of the pricing structures* described above. Two-part pricing schemes, for example, are fairly common in every pricing structure. They consist of a fixed charge designed to cover costs of meter reading, billing, customer accounting, and capital and maintenance costs of meters plus a constant commodity charge applied to all consumption. Another variant is the lifeline rate which is an artificially reduced price for a minimum amount of water that is deemed necessary for essential water consumption. It is intended to assist low-income households. Lifeline pricing is common in cities with a fixed charge as all customers must pay the fixed charge regardless of consumption. Other variants include vintage rates, which distinguish between new and existing customers, or seasonal or peak demand rates to reflect increased cost of delivery or a desire to reduce consumption during certain seasons or times of the day. A few municipalities have combined components of residential and commercial pricing systems into one schedule.

Efficiency Issues

Historically, water pricing has been viewed as an engineering issue rather than an economic issue. Local politicians and administrators, reluctant to use water prices to promote efficiency and conservation, have relied on technological improvements and non-price demand management tools such as restrictions on use—for example, forbidding lawn watering during periods of low rainfall or limiting residential construction until water/

sewer infrastructure capacity expands. These may be useful but they are not as effective as properly set prices and pricing structures in generating efficient outcomes and proper levels of infrastructure investment.

Clearly, meters should be adopted universally; for without them, there is no way in which volumetric prices could be introduced. In principle, water rates should be set so that the charge per liter equals the extra cost of supplying and treating the last unit; that is, price should equal marginal cost (OECD 2010; Kitchen and Tassonyi 2012); the marginal cost, of course and as noted above, will vary depending on such things as capacity constraints, distance from source, time of day and season of year to name the most obvious.

The efficiency advantages of marginal cost pricing are well documented as noted earlier in this chapter, but municipalities seldom implement marginal cost pricing as usually outlined by economists. One study on 77 water utilities in Ontario (Renzetti 1999) estimated that the marginal cost of supplying water exceeded the price for water in every municipality studied. Specifically, the average price for residential customers was calculated to be $0.32 per cubic meter, while the estimated marginal cost was $0.87 per cubic meter. By comparison, the average price for the nonresidential sector was $0.734 per cubic meter and the estimated marginal cost was $1.492 per cubic meter. At the same time, the average marginal cost of sewage treatment was $0.521 per cubic meter, while the average price was $0.128 per cubic meter. Another study estimated that Ontario municipalities recovered only 64 percent of the full costs of water and wastewater services from water revenues (Swain et al. 2005, p. 53). Failure to include all costs leads to overconsumption, over-investment, and larger facilities (and obviously more costs) than would exist if more efficient pricing practices were in place (Clayton 2014). While this is for one country, similar results are almost certain to exist in other countries.

Difficulties, however, generally emerge around the determination of costs. For example, marginal cost pricing is often perceived as being an unnecessarily complex approach that cannot guarantee the matching of revenues with anticipated costs and that could cause revenue instability. Municipalities cannot implement marginal cost pricing if they fail to collect sufficient cost information including calculations of the opportunity cost of using water or if they have this information but fail to compile it in a manner that permits the calculation of marginal costs.

A recent initiative that has surfaced in a number of countries or parts of countries is a legislative move to full-cost pricing; that is, all water and sewer costs must be fully funded from charges on water and sewer users.

This removes the cross-subsidization that existed previously when municipalities might cover any shortfall in water revenues from other revenues, such as the property tax.

While there is a growing consensus on the merit of imposing "full-cost pricing" for water and wastewater services, there is no consensus on what it means and what it should include. Many practitioners argue that full-cost pricing is achieved if revenues from water and wastewater systems cover all production and maintenance costs, regardless of pricing structure.

Others take a more expansive view of the costs, in part as a response to contemporary utility accounting practices. They recognize that replacement costs may be greater than anticipated, due to more demanding technical specifications, greater system resilience to deal with climate change, and enhanced environmental provisions, such as separating stormwater run-off from sanitary sewers. These calculations of "full cost" add full valuation of water-related assets and liabilities, the use of depreciation and provision for replacement, and life-cycle capital planning.

Still others argue that the current approach ignores additional costs that should be included. They suggest that the definition of annual operating and capital costs is too narrow, because it ignores the opportunity cost of water withdrawn from the natural environment including the commercial exploitation of aquifers and its potential impact on regional wells, the opportunity cost of land holdings, the opportunity cost of invested capital, and the harm caused by pollution (Renzetti 2009). Here, it must be noted, these costs are significant (Dupont et al. 2013).

From an economics perspective, opportunity costs are a complete and accurate way of measuring all costs. They capture the return that would be generated if the resources were put into their next best alternative. One study on one municipality in Ontario, Canada, in the late 1990s highlighted the magnitude of these costs. The study concluded that the wholesale price for water would have to increase by at least 15 percent and possibly by as much as 45 percent if all of these costs were to be recovered (Renzetti and Kushner 2001). On this basis, one may infer that most Ontario municipalities are far from full-cost pricing if all financial and social costs are to be included (Environment Canada 2011, p. 14).

Much of the opposition to the implementation of full-cost pricing has come, in part, from a desire to retain existing rate structures to preserve and possibly increase revenues. Many system operators and municipal officials have argued that moving to efficiency-based prices will discourage consumption, thereby reducing total revenues, making it difficult to cover costs. In response, there are at least two comments that should be made. First, it is suggested that the existing plant capacity may be too big and there is evidence that some municipalities, in the past, overbuilt largely because of grant assistance from senior levels of government and inefficiently set prices that led to overconsumption and hence, over-investment. Second, because the demand for water is inelastic, an increase in price will be accompanied by a much smaller percentage reduction in quantity, leading to an overall increase in total revenue, not a decrease.

Sewer

Sewage collection and treatment expenses are almost always recovered through surcharges on water bills, not on sewage discharge. This is largely for administrative simplicity. In most municipalities, the surcharge on residential properties is a percentage of the water bill, but in some municipalities, it is a fixed charge or a flat rate.

This is also true for small commercial and industrial users. In a few cities, however, large industrial and commercial users are metered with rates or prices varying by volume of discharge but often not by quality. In addition, some larger cities have sewer bylaws that limit the concentration of contaminants entering the sewer system. If actual levels of contamination exceed the permitted limit, over-strength fees or charges based on the difference between the actual level of concentration and the permitted limit come into effect with the fee varying by the differential. These additional fees are intended to cover the extra treatment costs (Elgie et al. 2016) or to provide an incentive for users to treat their own sewage or to minimize its impact on municipal treatment systems.

In practice, pricing schemes for sewage collection and treatment are far from optimal. Charges prorated on the basis of the water bill are inefficient because they fail to reflect accurately the marginal cost of sewage disposal. The assumption that residential water consumption is directly and positively correlated with sewage generation is often inaccurate. For example, a large component of water consumption may be attributed to lawn sprinkling, car washing, swimming pools, and many other household uses, almost all of which are unrelated to sewage generation; that is, the run-off generally goes into the stormwater system, not the sanitary system, unless the two sewers are combined, which is common in older, more densified areas of many cities.

Like the underpricing of water, the underpricing of sewage (collection and treatment) is allocatively inefficient because there is no incentive to restrict use. Underpricing has also led to investment in sewage treatment facilities that are larger than they would be under a more efficient pricing policy (Renzetti 1999). One empirical study on pricing of sewage by Norwegian local governments (Borge and Rattso 2003) showed that sound user-charge financing of sewer services significantly reduced the cost of providing sewer services. Finally, it has been observed that underpricing of both water supply and sewage treatment has discouraged the development of alternative water and sewage treatment technologies.

For commercial and industrial properties, efficiency objectives and conservation goals could be improved through the efficient use of meters with sewer rates based on both the volume and quality of the discharge (Elgie et al. 2016). Pricing based on quality is currently used in some cities, but much more could be done. In fact, it is quite possible that metering of sewage discharge would help in identifying unauthorized sewage discharges such as is observed when smaller, older industries like auto body shops, paint shops, and metal fabricators dump high levels of waste into both sanitary and storm systems.

Stormwater

There is a close interrelationship between stormwater run-off and water-related utilities. Surface water is a direct source of potable water for some water systems, and its impact on the recharging of aquifers affects the groundwater sources of many municipal and private drinking water systems. Many older waterworks systems are still working to separate stormwater and sanitary sewage carried in the same pipes, either routinely or during peak flows. These combined flows must, of course, be treated as sanitary sewage when they reach the end of the pipe, creating significantly higher demands on sewage treatment plants and overflow cisterns. While many municipal water departments and utility corporations do not have a separate charge, some of them have recently introduced or expressed an interest in introducing stormwater charges. As of 2016, 1600 municipalities in the United States and 21 cities in Canada had implemented stormwater fees (Campbell et al. 2016). For those that do not have a separate charge, stormwater is lumped in with the wastewater charge and calculated as a component of water consumption. Such aggregation, however, means that consumers do not know what they are paying for in stormwater management.

Over the past two or three decades where the world has witnessed the increasing impact of climate change (severe storms and flooding), design requirements have been introduced for the implementation of more robust and resilient systems. Increased funding has been provided for stormwater infrastructure (sewers, spillways, retention and detention ponds, etc.) and where they persist, for separation of sanitary sewers from storm sewers. These developments have given rise to a desire by some municipalities to convert stormwater facilities to a utility model, supported by "user" charges that are based on the estimated amount of water that leaves their property. User fees make considerable sense because benefiting properties are those that add run-off or are served by the provision of stormwater services and they can be identified. As such, fees paid by stormwater generators can be based on the estimated amount of water that leaves their property or in relation to the services that the property receives (Johns 2018). Those who live or have businesses on properties whose impervious area is large will pay higher user charges than owners of properties that do not burden the drainage system to the same degree. As long as user charges are based on the property's burden on the stormwater infrastructure, an incentive is provided for property owners to reduce that burden by reducing the amount of run-off discharged into the municipal system (Aquije 2016).

There are two cost components to fund stormwater—fixed costs that are related to the infrastructure itself and variable costs that come from the pressure placed on the infrastructure from water run-off. The fixed portion could vary; for example, infrastructure costs for properties in rural areas may differ from those for properties in urban areas. Variable costs are based on factors that affect storm water run-off; for example, slope, vegetation, buildings, paved surfaces, and so on (Tedds 2019).

Electricity

Depending on the country, electricity may or may not be the responsibility of municipal governments. In most countries where local governments are responsible for its provision, residential and small and medium enterprises pay the same uniform price during all hours of the day and across the entire municipality (Faruqui and George 2005, p. 3). This average price approach leads to a number of distortions and inefficiencies because it fails to take into consideration that delivery costs vary across the municipality and by time of day (e.g., peak vs. non-peak). Users in low-cost areas and/or non-peak periods subsidize users in high-cost areas and peak periods. The extent of the cross-subsidization from non-peak period users to peak period users has been quantified in one study done in New South Wales, Australia. Here, it has been estimated that peak period prices are understated by a factor of four and off-peak prices are overstated by about 40 percent (Faruqui and George 2005, p. 2). This kind of subsidization places a burden on lower-income groups, especially those without air conditioners who do not place any burden on peak-load demand. By the way, the same pricing arguments and conclusions could be made about any source of power, such as from gas.

Uniform pricing practices lead to overconsumption and more investment in power plants and transmission and distribution lines than is allocatively efficient. Problems with a uniform average price are further exacerbated if the price is regulated at a level that is below the marginal cost of provision as is the case in many places.

Countries, and municipalities within countries, that have avoided most of these distortions have done so by introducing time-varying prices. The latter include time-of-use (TOU) and critical-peak pricing (CPP). TOU features two or more pricing periods in a day—peak and off-peak in a two-period configuration and peak, shoulder, and off-peak in a three period configuration. There could also be additional periods. Prices are fixed ahead of time for each of the periods and are highest in the peak and lowest in the off-peak. The rates are generally designed to be revenue neutral when compared with the standard rate—average customers, therefore, generally do not see a change in their electricity bill. Where this pricing practice has been adopted, residential customers have reduced peak period consumption. In the state of Washington in the United States, for example, customers reduced their monthly consumption of electricity by 5 percent when the peak price was 30 percent higher than the off-peak price. Utilities in Australia introduced TOU for three-phase supply on residential and small and medium commercial and industrial customers to dampen peak-loads caused by heavy appliance uses such as central air conditioners and water heaters (Faruqui and George 2005).

Critical-peak pricing (CPP) is an extension of TOU pricing. CPP customers are billed at time-of-use prices for most hours of the day and, in addition, face a much higher price during the year's most expensive 60–100 hours or for so-many days a year. CPP is used for residential customers serviced by the utility with the longest history of time-varying prices—Électricité de France; by customers of Gulf Power, a utility in

Florida; by customers of Orion Energy in New Zealand; and by California's Statewide Pricing Pilot (SPP) project that tested a variety of pricing options including TOU rates and CPP rates. In all instances, these pricing options reduced peak demand, generally by cutting back on air conditioning and by shifting some activities such as laundry, dishwashing, and cooking to off-peak periods; lowered electricity bills; and resulted in less capital investment than would otherwise be the case.

Solid Waste

The funding choice here generally is between local tax revenues and user fees. Of these two possibilities, user fees in the form of a specific charge per bag/container are preferred on efficiency grounds for both collection and disposal. As in the case of water and electricity, users can be identified and per unit costs calculated. A charge that includes the full marginal social costs of collection and disposal is critical if one is to provide an incentive for discouraging waste and overuse.

In addition to covering all operating and capital costs for collection, the fee should cover a charge for the landfill site. This should be set with efficiency objectives in mind. If a municipality pays for disposal by a third party, the cost is clear—it is the cost per ton of the contract. If the municipality operates the landfill site, the cost of placing a cubic meter of waste in a landfill is not just the current operating cost of the landfill—it must include all amortized capital costs, including closure and post-closure costs, plus the opportunity cost of that space, plus the value of environmental harm caused by the waste and its disposal. The most difficult concept here is that of the opportunity cost of space (Dewees 2002). Suppose that the operating cost of a landfill site is $10 per cubic meter of waste disposed and that a new landfill will cost $50 per cubic meter. The opportunity cost of placing a cubic meter of waste in the existing landfill is not $10 but $10 plus an amount determined by the fact that each cubic meter so disposed hastens the time when the city will have to pay $50 per cubic meter. The socially efficient tipping fee at the existing landfill is not $10 but $50 discounted for the number of years until the new landfill will be required.

Unfortunately, government-operated landfills tend not to charge tipping fees that reflect future scarcity of landfill sites. Worse yet, many municipalities only charge per-ton fees to private haulers. The tipping fees for garbage brought in by municipal operators are almost always paid for by local taxes and not by tonnage charges. The efficient size of the disposal site will only be determined if all waste is paid for on the basis of a uniform per-ton tipping fee. Further inefficiencies exist because tipping fees rarely include the expected value of environmental harm, except where financial liability for that harm is anticipated and built into the cost of operation. Environmental harm includes the annoyance to neighbors of the landfill from smells, birds, blowing refuse, and truck traffic. It may also include contamination of the groundwater if leachate escapes from the landfill during its operation or even decades after it is closed. All of these costs should be included in the tipping fee if we are to get an efficient size of operation.

A number of studies have been done on the effects of user-pay systems in municipalities in Canada and the United States.[2] In most studies, free (local tax-supported) garbage pickup was compared with a fee per bag or a fee per container. All studies measured the impact on garbage collected and many measured the impact on diversion (recyclables and yard waste). The results were uniformly consistent although the magnitude of the impact varied depending on location and methodology behind the study. In every case, reductions were noticed for solid waste, recycling increased, the use of other options such as composting grew. Prices work!

Critics of user fees for garbage argue that their implementation will lead to illegal diversion (in the form of dumping on road sides, in school/commercial dumpsters, stomping, and burning) and that the impact of these fees will be regressive on users. They have also argued that administrative costs will rise because the system will be more complex and will require additional staff to police violators. The notion that user fees are regressive is really a non-issue as will be addressed later in this chapter. As for the remainder of these complaints, illegal dumping has not turned out to be a problem and the administrative concerns have by and large disappeared.

Public Transit

Municipal public transit systems are funded mainly by fare box revenue, municipal taxes, and grants from senior governments. In addition, some systems generate additional funds from charter/rental services, advertising, and miscellaneous income.

[2] See Kelleher et al. 2005 for a review of these studies.

Concern about operating deficits in transit systems often brings discussions over the level of fares and fare structure that ought to be charged to transit users. Local government officials may consider a number of social, economic, and political factors in setting fares. These include the availability of and access to substitute forms of transportation, the ability of local residents to pay for transit services, the attitudes of local politicians toward acceptable levels of fares, the portion of operating costs to be recovered from fare box revenue, and so on. The tendency, in many communities, is to set different fares for adults, children, students, and seniors and to offer discounts for monthly passes. Where variation exists, the highest fare is for adults, with lower fares for seniors, students, and children. Furthermore, in some municipalities, lower fares are available for special groups—the blind, the disabled, and the unemployed.

Transit fares have several virtues. Fares based on marginal cost pricing are accountable and transparent because they are tied to usage. Transit fare revenues are fairly stable and predictable in the short run. Revenues increase if service is expanded, although financing costs naturally increase, too. Fares are consistent with the user-pay principle and benefits-based approach to financing municipal services.

Their current application in many cities and metropolitan areas is far from efficient and fair, however. Failure to vary fares by distance traveled means that short-distance travelers overpay while long-distance travelers underpay. This creates an incentive for urban sprawl.

Second, fares should vary by time of day and day of week to minimize crowding and congestion costs. Failure to charge higher prices in peak hours creates an incentive to over-invest in public transit infrastructure and to provide greater capacity than can be justified on efficiency grounds. A lack of peak-load charges is often complicated by the availability of quantity discounts which are used primarily by rush-hour travelers. This practice effectively lowers the price per trip at peak times, precisely when fares should be higher rather than lower. As well, lower fares for seniors, children, and students are difficult to justify—especially at peak times. Subsidies granted on the basis of age or status rather than income are difficult to support on any grounds.

Third, several types of transit passes are often used by transit authorities. These economize on transactions costs but are generally inefficient with respect to both time of day and distance traveled because the marginal cost of using them is zero during their valid period.

Transit fare revenues never come close to financing all operating costs, nor should they on efficiency and fairness grounds. The shortfall is subsidized by other local revenues or by grants from senior levels of government. There are a number of arguments for subsidizing public transit. First, many lower-income households use transit heavily and may not have ready or affordable access to other motorized transportation modes. Second, public transportation has scale economies in route density and service frequency.[3] Marginal cost pricing then calls for setting fares below average cost. Third, setting affordable fares encourages people to use transit rather than driving thus alleviating traffic congestion and other externalities. While public transit vehicles create externalities and passengers crowd and delay each other, the costs are typically much lower per transit user than the equivalent cost per automobile driver. Since automobile drivers do not pay their marginal social cost per each trip, why should transit users pay their social marginal cost per trip (second-best argument). Quantifying these three reasons for subsidizing transit is not an easy task, thus it is difficult to say when transit fares are too high, too low, or "about right," given the lack of road pricing in the vast majority of cities and metropolitan areas. One study on public transit in Washington, DC, Los Angeles, and London, however, suggested that optimal transit fees would be less than 50 percent of average costs (Parry and Small 2009).

Roads

At the moment, city expressways, highways, and streets in the vast majority of cities and metropolitan areas around the world are funded almost entirely from general revenues. This creates significant pressure on local budgets, not to mention increasing congestion which is leading to growing social and environmental costs and ultimately lost productivity. When combined with the negative impact this has on quality of life, we are witnessing slower economic growth, than would otherwise be possible, and a barrier to international competitiveness (OECD 2009). The traditional response to increased congestion has been to expand road capacity, but this has not worked. In one study using US time series data, it was shown that vehicle kilometers (miles) traveled increased approximately in propor-

[3] Scale economies exist because if ridership increases it is economically worthwhile to add routes and increase service frequency which reduces average access and waiting times as well as uncertainty about waiting time and arrival time.

tion to roadway lane kilometers (miles); hence, the conclusion that road capacity expansion is not effective in addressing traffic congestion (Duranton and Turner 2011). Other supply-side policies such as improvements in traffic management can be expensive to implement, and to the extent that they make driving more attractive they also encourage more driving (Lindsey 2019). Something must be done to better manage the use of roads in large cities and metropolitan areas. Much of the analytical discussion (although often not by local policy practitioners) has concentrated on arguments for new charges and user fees that better manage the demand for roads with revenues specifically earmarked for local transit and transportation. Suggestions that revenue generated from road prices could be used to fund public transit are justified on the basis of the "theory of second best" (discussed above under public transit). The discussion here will concentrate on road pricing and parking charges.

Road Pricing

The most effective instrument for funding and managing congestion is through road prices.[4] Efficiently set road prices offer a number of advantages. They are widely recognized as an effective demand management tool to cover all operating and capital costs of roads as well as to internalize congestion, pollution, and other external costs of driving. More so than parking fees, they can influence all dimensions of travel choice: trip frequency, destination, travel mode, time of day or week, route, and so on. To the extent that traffic demand is managed, cost pressure on city budgets is lowered because traffic-related costs should be reduced and infrastructure demands lower. Furthermore, if revenues are dedicated to public transit and roads, they are more likely to gain public acceptance.

Tolls are the most common form of a road price. They can be imposed on *individual traffic lanes.* In the United States, tolling has been implemented on high occupancy toll (HOT) lanes which can be used without charge (or at a discounted rate) by vehicles that meet a minimum occupancy requirement—typically two people (HOV2) or three people (HOV3). HOT lanes run parallel to toll-free lanes on the same road. The toll-free lanes are typically slower during peak times. Drivers can choose on each trip whether to take the HOT lanes and pay for a quicker and more reliable passage. Tolls are varied by time of day in order to maintain high speeds on the HOT lanes. On some facilities tolls are varied hourly

[4] More detailed analysis appears in Kitchen and Lindsey 2013 and Lindsey 2019.

according to a schedule that is revised every few months. On other facilities the tolls are adjusted dynamically every few minutes on the basis of currently measured traffic flows.[5]

By far the most common form of road pricing is on *individual roads*. Most roads feature flat tolls that do not vary by time of day. But time-varying tolls are becoming more common. In the United States, the term "electronic toll lanes" is used when all lanes of a road are priced by time of day. Truck-only toll lanes are another potential form of pricing that has been studied in the United States, but not yet implemented.

Tolling all lanes at different rates is more efficient than tolling only some lanes because it allows better control over the total number of vehicles using the road as well as the distribution of traffic across lanes. A study by Small et al. (2006) demonstrated that differential pricing could achieve a favorable trade-off between efficiency and equity compared to HOT lanes.

Road pricing can be implemented within areas using *cordons or zones*. Cordon schemes comprise one or more toll cordons around a city center or other congested area. Vehicles are charged for crossing the cordon(s) in one or both directions. Single cordons have been used in Singapore since 1975, in several Norwegian cities since the 1980s, and in Stockholm since 2006. With a zonal scheme, a toll is levied for moving within the zone as well as for crossing the boundary. Just two zonal schemes are currently operating: the London Congestion Charge (since 2003) and Area C in Milan (since 2012).[6] Both schemes are aimed at reducing congestion. In Milan, Area C was preceded by the EcoPass system which operated from 2008 to 2011 and was designed mainly to reduce pollution rather than congestion (Kitchen and Lindsey 2013).

[5] On some facilities electric and hybrid vehicles have been allowed to use HOT lanes toll-free without meeting the normal occupancy requirement. But as these vehicles have proliferated, traffic volumes on HOT lanes have grown. To maintain high speeds on the HOT lanes, it has been necessary to raise tolls which reduce the number of toll-paying drivers willing to use them. To address this problem, hybrid vehicle exemptions are being reconsidered. An alternative to raising tolls is to tighten occupancy requirements from HOV2 to HOV3 or to require HOV2 vehicles to register as official carpool vehicles.

[6] On January 1, 2013, Gothenburg introduced a cordon similar in design to the Stockholm scheme.

Area-based schemes are sometimes referred to as "congestion pricing."[7] This terminology may have arisen because, as its name indicates, the London Congestion Charge is targeted at congestion. The term is misleading because the Norwegian toll cordons were established mainly for revenue generation rather than congestion relief, and the former Milan EcoPass zone was implemented to combat pollution. Moreover, cordons and zonal schemes are not ideal for congestion relief because of their crude spatial boundaries.

Each scheme is different because of goals, budgets, political constraints, city topography, state of technology at the time of implementation, and so on. Briefly and to repeat, the fiscal and economic case for road pricing is solid, yet road pricing is often rejected by politicians and the public at large. Efficiently set road prices offer a number of advantages. They are widely recognized as an effective travel demand management tool for reducing congestion, pollution, and other external costs of driving (Lindsey 2019). They can influence all dimensions of travel choice: trip frequency, destination, travel mode, time of day or week, route, and so on. To the extent that traffic demand is managed, cost pressures on a city's budget are lowered because traffic-related costs are reduced and infrastructure demands lessened. Furthermore, if revenues are dedicated to public transit and roads, there is almost certain to be more public acceptance for funding the service than if it were funded from general revenues (Kitchen and Lindsey 2013). Each of these is most effective when applied at a metropolitan or regional level where there is a greater likelihood of managing intermunicipal traffic and a greater opportunity to minimize distortions that often arise when charges are restricted to smaller geographic areas.

Parking Fees

Parking in large cities includes a mix of residential and nonresidential spaces on private land, the street (curbside), surface lots, and parking garages. Parking policies, in general, are in need of reform. At the moment, most are designed to encourage driving.

On-street parking in high-demand areas is often priced well below its scarcity value. As a consequence, drivers spend considerable time looking for a vacant spot. In the United States, for example, it has been estimated

[7] Seattle is currently considering a congestion levy.

that cruising for parking accounts for roughly 30 percent of traffic in some cities at certain times of day (Shoup 2006, 2007; Au 2007). Excessive cruising leads to traffic congestion, pollution, as well as inefficiencies and lost productivity (Grush 2013). Meanwhile, privately owned garage parking is overpriced, because operators benefit from a degree of monopoly power due to their unique locations. Overpricing of garage parking contributes further to the stock of cars cruising for parking (Arnott and Rowse 2009), thus increasing traffic-related costs.

Efficiently set dynamic parking levies could help reduce the volume of traffic, leading to less congestion, faster trips, fewer policing and traffic enforcement costs, and reduced demand for new and expanded roads and highways. It could also generate much-needed revenue for improving and expanding public transit. Indeed, it has been argued that "underpriced parking does more to promote automobile use than good transit does to discourage it" (Grush 2013). To achieve more efficient prices, the following options are available.

First is a *commercial parking sales tax*. This is a special tax imposed on parking transactions. It is usually imposed as an ad valorem (i.e., percentage) tax that increases with parking duration, but a flat tax that is independent of the parking fee paid is also possible. People who park for a longer time (such as commuters) have a greater incentive to change behavior than people who park for a shorter time (such as shoppers). The opposite is likely to be true for a flat tax because it accounts for a smaller fraction of the parking outlay for longer-term parking. If the tax is imposed in a limited geographical area, however, motorists may choose to avoid the tax by parking elsewhere, whereas if the tax covers a wide area, it is difficult to avoid.

Second, a *parking levy* is a special property tax that is applied to nonresidential parking spaces. Parking levies can be imposed as a fixed amount per space or based on the surface area. They can be applied to all parking, or limited to certain types such as surface parking, priced parking, unpriced parking, or parking in certain areas. Rates can be differentiated by the type of user. For example, lower rates can be applied on infrequently used spaces, or on spaces used by carpoolers, car-sharing vehicles, or disabled persons. Higher rates often apply to the central business district and higher rates often apply to indoor lots. Parking levies are increasingly common worldwide (Doolittle 2012).

Off-street parking charges are often set inefficiently; that is, they do not adhere closely to marginal cost pricing principles. Some parking lots and garages issue monthly parking passes which simplify transaction costs and provide a guaranteed parking space, but they encourage people to drive because the incremental parking cost is zero. Passes could be replaced by bulk purchases of a given number of parking hours that do not expire at a given date but rather diminish in value only when they are used (Grush 2012).

More severe deficiencies exist for *on-street parking*. Conventional, mechanical parking meters are simple to operate, but they are time-consuming to service and maintain, and the costs of collection and enforcement amount to a substantial fraction of the revenues. Conventional meters also lack the flexibility to vary fees efficiently by time of day, duration of stay, and demand conditions. Time limits (e.g., 1–2 hours) are often used to encourage parking turnover, but they encourage parking search and are less efficient than variable rates (Calthrop and Proost 2000). Time limits are also costly to enforce, and parkers incur inconvenience and stress to avoid parking tickets (Greentown Sustainable Land Use Group 2009).

Electronic meters are now used widely in major US cities. They allow hourly rates to vary by time of day and duration. To maintain high utilization rates of parking space while minimizing time spent on search, parking fees can be set to maintain a target average occupancy rate of parking spots within a defined area. To achieve this, parking fees can be either set dynamically (i.e., in real time) or adjusted periodically. Redwood City and Pasadena, California, were two of the first cities to successfully implement high occupancy-based pricing. The result was a dramatic reduction in cruising for parking without losses to businesses (Nelson\Nygaard Consulting Associates 2006; Greentown Sustainable Land Use Group 2009). Since then, several other cities have moved in this direction and are even testing larger-scale versions of occupancy-based pricing.

Public Recreation

Municipal parks and recreational facilities rely on user fees for a variety of facilities—arenas (skating admissions, hourly ice rentals and instruction), football and soccer fields, swimming (swimming admissions, memberships, and instruction), tennis (court fees, membership, and instruction), camps and camping (campground fees and day camp charges), and so on. Here, user fees may be defended on two grounds. First, it permits individuals to use recreational facilities that could not be afforded from comparable private-sector facilities. This type of subsidization, however, is neither efficient nor fair because municipalities ought not to be concerned with major income distribution questions. Furthermore, if income distribution were a local responsibility, it should be provided through relief based on income or some other measure of ability to pay and not by reducing prices for everyone.

Second, municipal recreational facilities and programs may generate positive externalities or spillovers. These externalities, it is suggested, may take the form of a more physically fit and healthier society and hence lower medical costs for everyone. In reality, this may be a questionable supposition for the externalities are unlikely to be significant. Indeed, they would probably be greater under an alternative and equally subsidized scheme of improved health and educational programs.

Since the largest portion of the benefits accrue directly to users, these services should be priced so as to extract sufficient revenues to cover a comparable portion of the costs. The public sector, however, has not adopted many aspects of private pricing for recreational services. Private suppliers, faced with the prospect of recovering all costs through their pricing structures, have recognized the advantages of such things as an annual fixed levy plus an admission charge for each use of the facility. Municipalities virtually never follow this approach and, as such, neither cover cost nor efficiently utilize their scarce resources.

With the exception of a few local public services such as arena rentals and municipal golf courses, access to municipally provided facilities is generally rationed by queuing rather than prices. Failure to adopt a peak-load pricing policy so as to even out the demand over a day and a week has led to over-investment in many recreational facilities. This has been aggravated further by reduced charges for children and students (lower rates for skating, swimming, etc.) at all times. Lower fares for specific groups might be justified if a further restriction, as is frequently the case for private facilities but not public facilities, limiting them to use of the facility in off-peak hours were imposed. Such a policy would approximate the use of a peak-load pricing structure.

Public Libraries

The current structure of user fees employed by many local public libraries may be in need of reorganization. Local public libraries collect money from rentals, overdue books, and nonresident fees (fixed charge), but seldom ever from local residents on a usage basis. Consequently, a high percentage of funding for local public libraries comes from general municipal revenues.

Support for this subsidization may be warranted if significant and positive externalities arise from the existence of public libraries. Clearly, positive externalities do exist, both in terms of easy accessibility to a vast collection of library resources and because a better and more educated society creates a better environment in which to live. Substantial private benefits, however, also accrue directly to the users of these services. As such, it is difficult to justify the degree of general funding currently provided. A better pricing policy would include a usage charge that approximated the marginal private cost of each visit plus a government subsidy (from a senior level of government) covering the spillover benefits that extend beyond the local community.

Failure to price local public library services on a usage basis may have unplanned and perhaps unwanted consequences. For example, failure to charge for local library usage means that both users and non-users share in the cost of the library system. If a higher proportion of users come from higher-income rather than lower-income households, the implicit redistribution of income from this type of funding would not likely be tolerated if it were known and made explicit.

Police

Municipal police services, which include numerous functions, are often financed from general local revenues. Frequently, the only services for which special charges are levied are those involving the policing of special events. In fact, in the occasional municipality, higher rates are charged at certain times of the year, such as national holidays.

As long as police services generate positive externalities (and indeed many police services do), a case can be made for general funding. To the extent that some police services have private-use characteristics, efficiency and equity suggests, however, greater emphasis could be placed on charges imposed on direct users. Evidence of the "privateness" of some police services does exist. For instance, protection services are or can be purchased from private agencies. As well, individuals may purchase security systems and guard dogs. The fact that these activities are priced in the private sector suggests that similar protection services provided by the public sector could also be priced. Indeed, such pricing might very well generate the revenue needed for more efficient use of police services.

For those police services with private good characteristics, the difficulty in approximating a "price equals marginal social cost" charge on an individual basis is such that these charges are unlikely to be implemented. It could be argued, however, that all individuals who benefit from a certain service ought to pay a price that is the same for all members of that group. For example, special vehicle or operator license fees levied at the local level, or a transfer to local governments of revenue collected by senior levels of government from road user taxes (e.g., gasoline) and traffic vehicle offenses. This could help cover part of the police costs associated with traffic control and safety.

In addition, fines or charges may be instituted for people who fail to lock their automobiles and residential, commercial, and industrial buildings. This would, in all likelihood, reduce the moral hazard problem that exists when people fail to look after themselves as carefully as they should because they know that the state is there to look after them if anything happens. Failure to protect private property adequately encourages criminal behavior and increases the cost of police protection. In fact, it has been suggested that special fees or charges ought to be imposed on all enterprises with a high incidence of crime, while reduced rates should be provided for those dwellings where the incidence of criminal behavior is substantially lower (Bird 1976, pp. 129–133; Bird and Tsiopoulos 1997). This would help to reduce the moral hazard problem.

As long as the administrative costs of imposing an expanded system of user charges for police services is not prohibitive, a strong case can be made for greater use of such charges in funding a portion of policing costs.

Fire

Fire protection is generally a municipal responsibility that is financed from local revenues. As well, some municipalities charge neighboring municipalities for fire protection, and many charge individuals or insurance companies for assisting with road vehicle accidents.

The issue here is whether general revenue funding for fire protection is fair and efficient. While the presence of positive externalities supports such funding, the externalities tend to be reciprocal; hence, one can defend charging every taxpayer full direct costs. In this system, general revenue funding is unnecessary; instead everyone should be required to buy fire protection (Bird 1976, p. 137).

Prices for fire protection, as distinct from police protection, already exist in many countries through the extensive use of insurance policies. Premiums for a property reflect its distance from fire halls and its fire insurance experience as well as the risks associated with various structural types including the use of fire-resistant building materials and the presence of sprinkler systems.

Factors affecting insurance risks also determine municipal expenditures for fire services. Failure to differentiate the municipal price charged for fire protection on the basis of risk almost certainly leads to an oversupply of firefighting equipment. For example, failure to impose differential prices provides little incentive for the owners of risky properties to undertake actions designed to minimize their demand for fire protection and, hence, generates a demand for more spending on fire protection than would otherwise be the case. Charging neighboring municipalities for fire assistance and individuals for emergency road vehicle accidents is an appropriate direction in which to move even though there is no indication that correct prices are currently used.

Because insurance premiums take property values, fire probability, and damage susceptibility into consideration, they could provide a basis for a municipal user fee. As long as the charge is differentiated to reflect varying risks, a more efficient level of service should ensue (Bird and Tsiopoulos 1997). Finally, where there is a private market for fire insurance premiums, the administrative costs of managing a municipal user fee system for fire protection should not be prohibitive.

Issues with User Fees

Regardless of the way in which user fees are designed and the services they fund, there are issues that often emerge. These are noted here.

Who Should Set User Fees?

Following on the established theme that the most transparent, efficient, accountable, and effective local government is one that is responsible for raising its own revenue, it follows that local governments should be responsible for establishing their own user fees. Failure to permit and require this means that the close link between decisions over revenue generation and expenditure decisions is lost. Here, there is no apparent role for a senior level of government as long as the user fee is designed to fund the operating and capital costs of a local service.

Should User Fees Be Regulated?

As with local tax rates, in general there may be no need to regulate user fees if all decision-making responsibilities rest with democratically elected local councils; that is, if the locally elected council sets both tax rates and user fees. Here, citizens/taxpayers have the ultimate control or power over council's tax decisions—the opportunity to vote the politicians out at the next election. There is, of course, the obvious need for setting performance measures and benchmarking.

If, however, the services for which user fees are applied are provided by a local government enterprise governed by an independent or quasi-independent elected or appointed council, some type of regulation may be required. Support for a price regulatory scheme is defended on the grounds that it is necessary to protect consumers/taxpayers from inefficient and unfair price increases when decisions over service responsibility and funding are made in an environment in which there is no competition. In general, there are two types: rate of return and price cap regulation (Szalai 2001).

Where rate of return is used, the regulator defines a fair and reasonable profit level and the provider has the opportunity to increase price to the point where its maximum profit level is reached. Price cap regulatory schemes concentrate on creating incentives for the provider to increase efficiency.

For other services that are the direct responsibility of local councils, there may also be an argument in defense of regulation. Take water and wastewater, as an example. For decades, these rates have been set by municipal councils or utility commissions in many countries. On the surface, this is how it should be. Water is a local service, users can be identified, production and delivery costs can be calculated, and rates can be set. Water rates like property taxes are highly visible and increases are often subject to severe criticism. Unfortunately, this has led to widespread reluctance to raise water rates in many municipalities. As such, it may be unrealistic in the current political environment to expect a governing body to make efficient decisions about the structure and level of water rates without guidelines and support from an established regulatory body. While there may be a desire to use reduced water rates for economic development purposes, for example, or to cushion the impact on the vulnerable, system sustainability considerations should be paramount. At a minimum, the regulatory framework could be developed and used by municipal councils to approve rates and financial plans that ensure that rates attain a level sufficient to sustain the water-related systems into the future. If compliance with such a framework cannot be achieved through voluntary cooperation, there may be a need to impose some form of administrative tribunal process on those unable or unwilling to comply (Kitchen 2017a).

Should User Fees Subsidize Other Services?

User fees are appropriate for funding municipal services with "private goods" characteristics—beneficiaries can be identified, service costs can be determined, and prices can be set. For services with "public good" characteristics, local taxes are the more appropriate funding instrument. In principle, these provide a solid base for assigning funding instruments to the range of services provided by municipalities. In practice, however, the approach is often more convoluted. For example, municipalities in many countries are reluctant to use local taxes and inclined to overcharge user fees, that is, to set user fees for specific services so that revenue generated exceeds the cost of the service provided with the excess revenue used to subsidize other locally provided services.

Reluctance to use local taxes and the incentives for relying on user fees arise for a number of reasons. In some countries, senior levels of government share in local tax revenues but do not share in user fee revenues, hence, an incentive for relying on user fees (Matinez-Vazquez and Boex 2001, p. 38). Second, in some countries, municipal governments face legislated requirements that restrict a municipality's ability to raise taxes, a further reason for employing user fees. Third, almost everywhere, there is a perception in the minds of many local politicians and a high percentage of the population that user fees bring about more efficiency and accountability in service provision because services funded in this manner are run more like a business—a product or service is sold, revenue is raised, and costs are recovered. Fourth, many local politicians and administrators prefer user fees over local taxes because there are fewer citizen complaints about revenues generated from fees than there are from revenues generated by local taxes. More bluntly, it seems to be more acceptable politically to rely on user fees than to rely on local taxes (Kitchen 2006).

Given the comparative ease with which user fees have or may replace local taxes as a source of revenue raises the question of whether or not this type of cross-subsidization is appropriate. The short answer is no! A user fee should cover only the operating and capital costs of the service for which it is set. It should not subsidize other services for this would lead to both efficiency and income distributional consequences that would otherwise not be desired. For example, using excess revenue from water rates to subsidize the operational and capital costs of a local zoo means that water users are paying for a zoo that they may never visit. At the same time, visitors to the zoo are not paying the full cost and therefore likely to overuse the facility. As well, high water rates mean that low-income water users are almost certainly subsidizing higher-income zoo visitors. This is only one example of cross-subsidization but many others could be cited.

Are User Fees Unfair?

User fees are frequently criticized and sometimes not used because they are alleged to be regressive (unfair) in their impact on the poor; that is, they take a higher percentage of a poor person's or poor family's income when compared with a rich person or rich family. The same argument, by the way, could be made about every tax except for the personal income tax—this is because all taxes except for the personal income tax are not based on income yet their regressivity is measured as percent of income.

In the benefit-based model of local finance, user fees that are carefully designed to cover the cost of services consumed are fair in their impact on users—those benefiting from a service pay for it. Issues of regressivity, while extremely important, should not be addressed by eliminating or lowering fees for services appropriately funded by user fees. Instead, concern about the financial burden on low-income individuals, in general, should be addressed through income transfers from a senior level of government and social assistance programs targeted to individuals in need. It is far more equitable to handle income distribution issues through income transfers or targeting than to tamper with fees to accommodate these concerns. One example of targeting that exists in many municipalities is for water and sewer where lifeline rates are in place for low-income users.

Should User Fees Be Discounted?

Municipalities should not discount fees based on the age of the user (such as seniors) for services such as public transit, recreation, and libraries. Any discount should be on the basis of income (ability to pay). The practice of subsidizing municipal services by levying lower fees started many decades ago when a large percentage of seniors were living in poverty. This is no longer true in most, if not all, developed countries. In virtually every country, the percentage of poor people in the seniors' age cohort is now lower than the percentage who are poor in younger age cohorts. Two potentially serious and costly problems emerge if individuals in one age cohort (for example, seniors) pay lower user fees than individuals in another age cohort (non-seniors, for instance) for the same service. First, this is unfair because it leads to an implicit subsidy or redistribution of income from those paying higher prices to those paying lower prices, irrespective of income. Second, wealthier users within the senior age cohort get the same subsidy as impoverished individuals in that same group (Kitchen 2015).

At the same time, the practice of discounting user fees is inefficient because the group paying the lower price will not be covering the same share of operating and capital costs as the group paying the higher price. For those paying a lower percentage of costs, an incentive exists for overuse and overconsumption. This, in turn, often leads to a demand for more services and/or higher service levels than is economically efficient and ultimately more infrastructure investment than would be the case if every user paid the same price for the same service. Similar arguments may be made about discounted fares for students and children that are based on age or status rather than on ability to pay.

Summary

User fees are fair, efficient, and accountable for financing those services where individual beneficiaries are identified, where non-users can be excluded and where the per unit cost of provision can be estimated. Current practice in setting user fees, however, often deviates from that which is fair, efficient, and accountable. Often they are set to generate revenue rather than to allocate resources into their most efficient use.

Ultimately, the objective in setting correct fees should be to establish a clear link between services received and fees paid. This is relatively easy for water and sewers, stormwater, electricity, public transit and transportation, public recreation, libraries, solid waste collection, and disposal where pricing structures could take into consideration cost differentials attributed to such things as distance from source, time of use, capacity constraints, second-best conditions, and so on. For services such as police and fire, setting user fees would be more complicated but not impossible; indeed, their use almost certainly would lead to improvements in the allocation of municipal resources.

While economic arguments in support of user fees are persuasive, they often do not receive much political support. Refusal to introduce efficiency considerations into the pricing structure of most user fees or to entertain in any serious fashion, suggestions for expanding their use has been defended on grounds that they are regressive. This claim, however, is about as relevant as the claim that milk prices and movie tickets are regressive. As to whether or not user fees will become more important in the future, the answer is far from clear. The probability of this happening, however, may be greater than it ever has been. Political resistance to raising local taxes, reduced reliance on grants from senior levels of government, and increased spending responsibilities have increased the emphasis that will likely be placed on correctly designing existing user fees and extending their use.

Regardless of the design of user fees and the services they fund, their rates should be determined by municipal councils without regulatory restrictions unless, of course, the regulations are necessary to enhance local efficiency and accountability or to achieve important objectives of other levels of government. At the same time, user fee revenues should not be used to subsidize other local services. Within the benefits-based model for financing local public services, user fees are not unfair as long as those who benefit from the services pay for them. Finally, a user fee for a specific service should not vary by type of user (poor vs. rich or residential vs. commercial and industrial).

References

Althaus, Catherine, and Lindsay M. Tedds. 2016. *User Fees in Canada: A Municipal Design and Implementation Guide*. Toronto: Canadian Tax Foundation.

Aquije, Daniela D. 2016. *Paying for Stormwater Management*. IMFG Perspectives 12. Toronto: Institute on Municipal Finance and Governance, University of Toronto.

Arnott, Richard, and John Rowse. 2009. Downtown Parking in Auto City. *Regional Science and Urban Economics* 39 (1): 1–14.

Au, Ceri. 2007. The New Science of Parking. *Time Magazine*, July 9. http://www.transalt.org/newsroom/media/1329. Accessed 5 July 2018.

Bird, Richard M. 1976. *Charging for Public Services: A New Look at an Old Idea*. Toronto: Canadian Tax Foundation.

———. 2001. User Charges in Local Government Finance. In *The Challenge of Urban Government: Policies and Practices*, ed. Mila Freire and Richard Stren, 171–182. Washington, DC: The World Bank.

Bird, Richard, and Enid Slack, eds. 2017. *Financing Infrastructure: Who Should Pay?* Montreal: McGill-Queens University Press.

Bird, Richard M., and Thomas Tsiopoulos. 1997. User Charges for Public Services: Potential and Problems. *Canadian Tax Journal* 45 (1): 35–37.

Boadway, Robin. 1997. The Role of Second Best Theory in Public Economics. In *Trade, Technology and Economics: Essays in Honour of Richard G. Lipsey*, ed. B.C. Eaton and R.G. Harris, 3–25. United Kingdom: Edward Elgar Publishers.

Borge, Lars-Erik, and Jorn Rattso. 2003. The *Relationship Between Costs and User Charges: The Case of a Norwegian Utility Service*. CESifo Working Paper No. 1033, Munich.

Calthrop, Edward, and Stef Proost. 2000. *Regulating Urban Parking Space: The Choice Between Meter Fees and Time Restrictions*. K.U. Leuven, Faculty of Economics and Applied Economics: Center for Economic Studies—Energy, transport & environment Working Paper 2000–6. https://lirias.kuleuven.be/handle/123456789/238239.

Campbell, C.W., et al. 2016. *Western Kentucky University Stormwater Utility Survey*. https://www.wku.edu/engineering/civil/fpm/swusurvey/swusurvey. Accessed 18 July 2018.

Church, Jeffrey, and Roger Ware. 2000. *Industrial Organization: A strategy Approach*. Boston: Irwin-McGraw Hill.

Clayton, Frank. 2014. *A New Direction for Funding Growth-Related Water and Wastewater Infrastructure in the Greater Toronto Area and Hamilton*. Toronto: Centre for Urban Research and Land Development (CUR), Ryerson University.

Dewees, Don. 2002. Pricing Municipal Services: The Economics of User Fees. *Canadian Tax Journal* 50 (2): 586–599.

Doolittle, Robyn. 2012. *Parking Tax? It's a Global Trend*, February 24. http://www.thestar.com/news/gta/transportation/article/1136436. Accessed 12 Sept 2016.

Dupont, Diane, Steven Renzetti, et al. 2013. *Liquid Assets: Assessing Water's Contribution to Niagara*. Niagara Region and Brock University, 80. https://www.niagararegion.ca/living/water/pdf/NR-Liquid-Assets-Paper-2013-FINAL.pdf.

Duranton, Gilles, and Matthew A. Turner. 2011. The Fundamental Law of Road Congestion: Evidence from US Cities. *American Economic Review* 101 (6): 2616–2652.

Ecofiscal Commission, Canada. 2017. *Only the Pipes Should Be Hidden: Best Practices for Pricing and Improving Municipal Water and Wastewater Services*. https://ecofiscal.ca/reports/. Accessed 16 July 2018.

Elgie, Stewart, Michelle Brownlee, Sarah Jane O'Neill, and Mercedes Marcano. 2016. *Pricing Works: How Pricing of Municipal Services and Infrastructure Can Lead to Healthier and More Efficient Cities*. Green Prosperity Papers, Metcalf Foundation. http://metcalffoundation.com/stories/publications/pricing-works/. Accessed 20 July 2018.

Environment Canada, Ottawa. 2011. *Municipal Water Pricing Report*. Ottawa.

Faruqui, Ahmad, and Stephen S. George. 2005. Preventing Electrical Shocks. In *Commentary*. Toronto: C.D. Howe Institute.

Fenn, Michael, and Harry Kitchen. 2016. *Bringing Sustainability to Ontario's Water Systems: A Quarter-Century of Progress, with Much Left to Do*. A Study for the Ontario Sewer and Watermain Construction Association. www.OSWCA.org.

Greentown Sustainable Land Use Group. 2009. *The New Science of Parking. Parking Management Strategies for Los Altos*. August 4. http://greentownlosaltos.org/wp-content/uploads/GreenTown_Parking_Management_Strategies_WP.pdf. Accessed 10 Aug 2018.

Grush, Bern. 2012. Parking Policy Can Boost Modality Choice. http://grush-hour.blogspot.ca/2012/06/parking-policy-can-boost-modality.html. Accessed 5 July 2018.

———. 2013. Reduce, Rethink, Reform. *Thinking Cities*, 132–137. http://paybysky.com/wp-content/uploads/2013/04/Reduce-Rethink-Reform-from-Thinking-Cities.pdf. Accessed 15 Aug 2018.

Johns, Carolyn M. 2018. *Green Infrastructure and Stormwater Management in Toronto Policy Context and Instruments*. Toronto: Centre for Urban Research and Development, Ryerson University.

Kelleher, Maria, Janet Robins, and John Dixie. 2005. Taking Out the Trash: How To Allocate the Costs Fairly. In *Commentary*. Toronto: C.D. Howe Institute.

Kitchen, Harry. 2006. Local Government Enterprises. In *Perspectives on Fiscal Federalism*, ed. Richard M. Bird and Francois Vaillancourt, 141–174. Washington, DC: World Bank Institute.

———. 2015. *No Seniors' Specials: Financing Municipal Services in Aging Communities*. Institute for Research on Public Policy (IRPP), Montreal, No. 51. www.irpp.org/research/faces-of-aging/. Accessed 5 Aug 2018.

———. 2017a. *Paying for Water in Ontario's Cities: Past, Present, and Future*. IMFG Papers on Municipal Finance and Governance Series, University of Toronto, November. http://munkschool.utoronto.ca/imfg/resources/.

———. 2017b. Paying for Water in Ontario Cities: Where Have We Come From And Where Do We Go? Chap. 3 in *Financing Infrastructure: Who Should Pay?*, ed. Richard M. Bird and Enid Slack, 53–86. McGill-Queens University Press. Published for the Institute on Municipal Finance and Governance at the Munk School of Global Affairs.

Kitchen, Harry, and Robin Lindsey. 2013. *Financing Roads and Public Transit in the Greater Toronto and Hamilton Area*. Residential and Civil Construction Alliance of Ontario. www.rccao.com.

Kitchen, Harry, and Enid Slack. 2016. *More Tax Sources for Canada's Largest Cities: Why, What, and How?* IMFG Papers on Municipal Finance and Governance Series, No. 27, University of Toronto. http://munkschool.utoronto.ca/imfg/resources/.

Kitchen, Harry, and Almos Tassonyi. 2012. Municipal Taxes and User Fees. Chap. 9 in *Tax Policy in Canada*, ed. Heather Kerr, Ken McKenzie, and Jack Mintz. Toronto: Canadian Tax Foundation.

Lindsey, Robin. 2019. User Fees for Transportation: Road Tolls and Congestion Pricing. In *Funding the Canadian City*, ed. Enid Slack, Lisa Philipps, Lindsay M. Tedds, and Heather L. Evans, 123–153. Toronto: Canadian Tax Foundation and Institute on Municipal Finance and Governance.

Matinez-Vazquez, Jorge, and Jameson Boex. 2001. *Russia's Transition to a New Federalism*. Washington, DC: World Bank.

Nelson\Nygaard Consulting Associates. 2006. *City of Pasadena*. Traffic Reduction Strategies Study. http://ww2.cityofpasadena.net/councilagendas/2007%20agendas/Feb_26_07/Pasadena%20Traffic%20Reduction%20Strategies%2011-20-06%20DRAFT.pdf. Accessed 10 Aug 2018.

OECD. 2010. *Pricing Water Resources and Water and Sanitation Services*. Paris: OECD.

OECD Territorial Reviews. 2009. *Toronto Canada, Preliminary Version*. Organization for Economic Co-Operation and Development.

Parry, Ian W.H., and Kenneth Small. 2009. Should Urban Transit Subsidies Be Reduced? *American Economic Review* 99 (3): 700–724.

Renzetti, Steven. 1999. Municipal Water Supply and Sewage Treatment: Costs, Prices and Distortions. *Canadian Journal of Economics* 32 (3): 688–704.

———. 2009. Wave of the Future: The Case for Smarter Water Policy. In *Commentary*. Toronto: C.D. Howe Institute.

Renzetti, Steven, and Joseph Kushner. 2001. *"The Under Pricing of Water Supply and Sewage Treatment" Mimeograph*. St. Catharines: Economics Department, Brock University.

Shoup, Donald C. 2006. Cruising for Parking. *Transport Policy* 13: 479–486.

———. 2007. Cruising for Parking. *Access* 30 (Spring), 6–22. http://shoup.bol.ucla.edu/CruisingForParkingAccess.pdf.

Small, Kenneth A., Clifford Winston, and Jia Yan. 2006. Differentiated Road Pricing, Express Lanes, and Carpools: Exploiting Heterogeneous Preferences in Policy Design. *Brookings-Wharton Papers on Urban Affairs*, 53–96.

Swain, Harry, Fred Lazar, and Jim Pine. 2005. *Watertight: The Case for Change in Ontario's Water and Wastewater Sector*. Report of the Water Strategy Expert

Panel, Queen's Printer for Ontario (Toronto), 96. http://www.probeinternational.org/EVfiles/Watertight-panel_report_EN.pdf. Accessed 20 June 2006.

Szalai, Akos. 2001. New Models of Privatizing Public Utilities: Highlights of Reform in Post-Soviet Countries. In *Local Government Brief: The Quarterly Journal of Local Government and Public Service Reform Initiative*, 18–24. Budapest, Hungary.

Tedds, Lindsay. 2019. Non-Tax Revenue for Funding Municipal Governments: User Fees—Adoptions, Constraints, and Emerging Opportunities. In *Funding the Canadian City*, ed. Enid Slack, Lisa Philipps, Lindsay M. Tedds, and Heather L. Evans, 97–121. Toronto: Canadian Tax Foundation and Institute on Municipal Finance and Governance.

CHAPTER 12

Intergovernmental Fiscal Transfers: Principles

The practice of intergovernmental fiscal transfers is the magical art of passing money from one government to another and seeing it vanish in thin air.
—Anonymous

Intergovernmental fiscal transfers finance about two-thirds of subnational expenditures in developing countries and transition economies and about one-fifth of such expenditures in OECD countries. Beyond the expenditures they finance, these transfers create incentives and accountability mechanisms that affect the fiscal management, efficiency, and equity of public service provision and government accountability to citizens.

This chapter reviews the principles of intergovernmental finance, with a view to drawing some general lessons of relevance to policymakers and practitioners in developing countries and transition economies.[1] It provides a taxonomy of grants, their possible impacts on local fiscal behavior, and the accountability of grant recipients to donor governments and citizens. The first section describes the instruments of intergovernmental finance. The section "Achieving Results-Based Accountability Through Performance-Oriented Transfers" discusses performance-oriented, or

[1] This chapter draws heavily upon Anwar Shah (2007). A Practitioner's Guide to Intergovernmental Fiscal Transfers. In *Intergovernmental Fiscal Transfers*, edited by Robin Boadway and Anwar Shah, 2007, chapter 1: 1–54. Washington, DC: World Bank.

H. Kitchen et al., *Local Public Finance and Economics*,
https://doi.org/10.1007/978-3-030-21986-4_12

output-based, transfers, an important tool for results-based accountability. The section "Designing Fiscal Transfers: Conceptual Guidance" offers conceptual guidance on the design of fiscal transfers. This is followed by brief concluding remarks.

Instruments of Intergovernmental Finance

Intergovernmental transfers or grants can be broadly classified into two categories: general-purpose (unconditional) and specific-purpose (conditional or earmarked) transfers.

General-Purpose Transfers

General-purpose transfers are provided as general budget support, with no strings attached. These transfers are typically mandated by law, but occasionally they may be of an ad hoc or discretionary nature. Such transfers are intended to preserve local autonomy and enhance interjurisdictional equity. That is why article 9 of the European Charter of Local Self Government advocates such transfers by stating: "As far as possible, grants to local authorities shall not be earmarked for the financing of specific projects. The provision of grants shall not remove the basic freedom of local authorities to exercise policy discretion within their own jurisdiction" (Barati and Szalai 2000, p. 21).

General-purpose transfers are termed bloc transfers when they are used to provide broad support in a general area of subnational expenditures (such as education) while allowing recipients' discretion in allocating the funds among specific uses. Block grants are a vaguely defined concept. They fall in the gray area between general-purpose and specific-purpose transfers, as they provide budget support with no strings attached in a broad but specific area of subnational expenditures.

General-purpose transfers simply augment the recipient's resources. They have only an income effect as indicated in Fig. 12.1 by the shift in the recipient's budget line AB upward and to the right throughout by the amount of the grant (AC = BD) and the new budget line becomes CD. Since the grant can be spent on any combination of public goods or services or used to provide tax relief to residents, general nonmatching assistance does not affect relative prices (no substitution effect). It is also the least stimulative of local spending, typically increasing such spending by less than $0.50 for each additional $1 of unconditional assistance. The

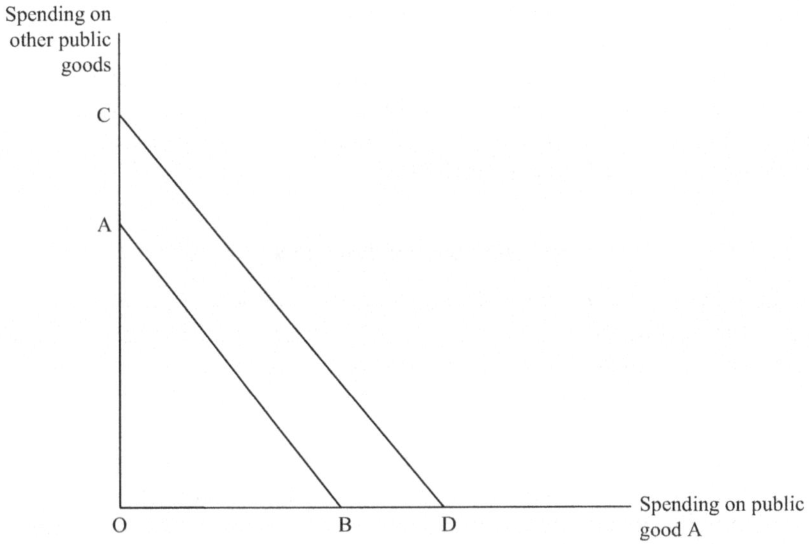

Fig. 12.1 Effect of unconditional nonmatching grant. Source: Shah (1994)

remaining funds are made available as tax relief to local residents to spend on private goods and services.

Conceptually a one-dollar increase in local residents' income should have exactly the same impact on local public spending as receipt of one dollar of general-purpose transfer. Both tend to shift the budget line outward identically. Contrary to this, all empirical studies show that a dollar received by the community in the form of general-purpose grant tends to have a greater increase in local public spending more than a dollar increase in residents' income, that is, the portion of grants retained for local spending tends to exceed the effective tax rate imposed by local governments on resident's incomes (Rosen 2005; Oates 1999, 2005; Gramlich 1977). Grant money tends to stick where it first lands, leaving a smaller than expected fraction available for tax relief, a phenomenon referred to as the "flypaper effect." The implication is that for political and bureaucratic reasons, grants to local governments tend to result in more local spending than they would have had the same transfers been made directly to local residents (McMillan et al. 1980). An explanation for this impact is provided by the hypothesis that bureaucrats seek to maximize the size of their budgets as it gives them greater power and influence in local community (Filimon et al. 1982).

Formula-based general-purpose transfers are very common. The federal and state transfers to municipalities in Brazil are examples of grants of this kind. Evidence suggests that such transfers induce municipalities to underutilize their own tax bases (Shah 1991).

Specific-Purpose Transfers

Specific-purpose, or conditional, transfers are intended to provide incentives for governments to undertake specific programs or activities. These grants may be regular or mandatory in nature or discretionary or ad hoc.

Conditional transfers typically specify the type of expenditures that can be financed (input-based conditionality). These may be capital expenditures, operating expenditures, or both. Conditional transfers may also require attainment of certain results in service delivery (output-based conditionality). Input-based conditionality is often intrusive and unproductive, whereas output-based conditionality can advance grantors' objectives while preserving local autonomy.

Conditional transfers may incorporate matching provisions—requiring grant recipients to finance a specified percentage of expenditures using their own resources. Matching requirements can be either open-ended, meaning that the grantor matches whatever level of resources the recipient provides, or closed-ended, meaning that the grantor matches recipient funds only up to a pre-specified limit.

Matching requirements encourage greater scrutiny and local ownership of grant-financed expenditures; closed-ended matching is helpful in ensuring that the grantor has some control over the costs of the transfer program. Matching requirements, however, represent a greater burden for a recipient jurisdiction with limited fiscal capacity. In view of this, it may be desirable to set matching rates in inverse proportion to the per capita fiscal capacity of the jurisdiction in order to allow poorer jurisdictions to participate in grant-financed programs.

Nonmatching Transfers

Conditional nonmatching transfers provide a given level of funds without local matching, as long as the funds are spent for a particular purpose. Following the grant (=AC), the budget line in Fig. 12.2 shifts from AB to ACD, where at least OE (=AC) of the assisted public good will be acquired.

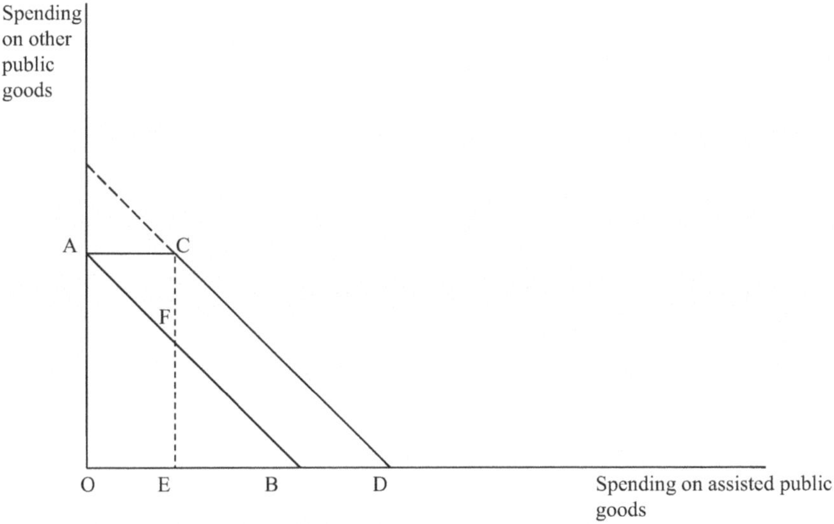

Fig. 12.2 Effect of conditional nonmatching grant. Source: Shah (1994)

Conditional nonmatching grants are best suited for subsidizing activities considered high priority by a higher-level government but low priority by local governments. This may be the case if a program generates a high degree of spillovers up to a given level of provision (OE), after which the external benefits terminate abruptly.

For a given level of available assistance, grant recipients prefer unconditional nonmatching transfers, which provide them with maximum flexibility to pursue their own objectives. Because such grants augment resources without influencing spending patterns, they allow recipients to maximize their own welfare. Grantors, however, may be prepared to sacrifice some recipient satisfaction to ensure that the funds are directed toward expenditures on which they place a priority. This is particularly so when federal objectives are implemented by line agencies or departments rather than through a central agency, such as the Ministry of Finance, with a broader mandate. Federal departments do not want local governments to shift their program funds toward other areas. In this situation, conditional (selective) nonmatching (bloc) grants can ensure that the funds are spent in a department's area of interest (e.g., health care) without distorting local priorities among alternative activities or inducing inefficient allocations in the targeted expenditure area.

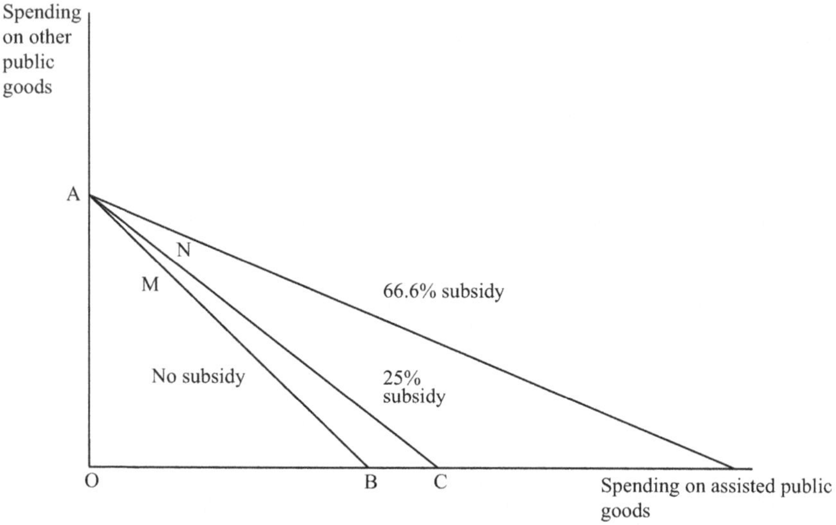

Fig. 12.3 Effect of open-ended matching grant. Source: Shah (1994) and McMillan et al. (1980)

Matching Transfers

Conditional matching grants, or cost-sharing programs, require that funds be spent for specific purposes and that the recipient match the funds to some degree. Figure 12.3 shows the effect on a local government budget of a 25 percent subsidy program for transportation. AB indicates the no subsidy line—the combination of transportation and other public goods and services a city can acquire with a budget of OA = OB. A federal subsidy of 25 percent of transportation expenditures (i.e., a grant of $1 for every $3 of local funds for spent on transportation) shifts the budget line of attainable combinations to AC. At any level of other goods and services, the community can obtain one-third more transportation services. If the community chooses combination M before the grant, it will likely select a combination such as N afterward. At N more transportation is acquired.

The subsidy has two effects: an income effect and a substitution effect. The subsidy gives the community more resources, some of which go to acquiring more transportation services (the income effect). Since the subsidy reduces the relative price of transportation services, the community acquires more transportation services from a given budget (the substitution effect). Both effects stimulate higher spending on transportation.

Although the grant is for transportation, more other public goods and services may also be acquired, even though they become relatively more expensive, as a result of the substitution effect. If the income effect is sufficiently large, it will dominate, and the grant will increase consumption of other goods and services. Most studies find that for grants of this kind, spending in the specified area increases by less than the amount of the grant, with the remainder going toward other public goods and services and tax relief. This is the so-called *fungibility effect* of grants. The fungibility of conditional grants depends on both the level of spending on the assisted public service and the relative priority of such spending. For example, if the recipient's own-financed expenditure on the assisted category exceeds the amount of the conditional grant, the conditionality of the grant may or may not have any impact on the recipient's spending behavior: all, some, or none of the grant funds could go to the assisted function. Shah (1985, 1988b, 1989) finds that while provincial assistance to cities in Alberta for public transit was partially diverted to finance other services, similar assistance for road transportation improvement was not.

Open-ended matching grants, in which no limit is placed on available assistance through matching provisions, are well suited for correcting inefficiencies in the provision of public goods arising from benefit spillovers, or externalities. Benefit spillovers occur when services provided and financed by a local government also benefit members of other local governments that do not contribute to their provision. Because the providing government bears all the costs but obtains only a portion of the benefits, it tends to underprovide the goods. If the affected communities cannot negotiate compensation, the situation can be corrected by a higher government subsidizing provision of the service, with the extent of the spillover determining the degree of subsidy or the matching ratio.

Matching grants can correct inefficiencies from spillovers, but they do not address uneven or inadequate fiscal capacities across state and local governments. Local governments with ample resources can afford to meet matching requirements and acquire a substantial amount of assistance. States with limited fiscal capacities may be unable to match federal funds and therefore fail to obtain as much assistance, even though their expenditure needs may be equal to or greater than those of wealthier states (Shah 1991). Other forms of assistance are needed to equalize fiscal capacities in such cases.

Grantors usually prefer closed-ended matching transfers, in which funds are provided to a certain limit, since such transfers permit them to retain control over their budgets. Figure 12.4 shows the effect of closed-ended

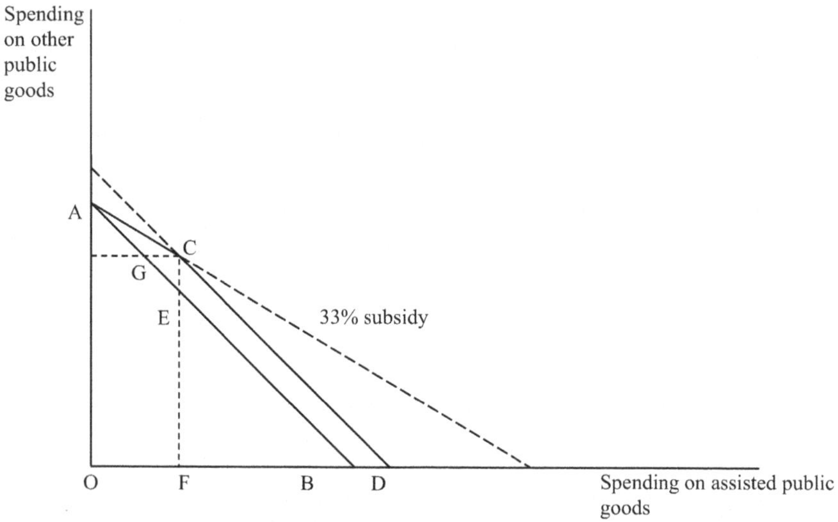

Fig. 12.4 Effect of closed-ended matching grant. Source: Shah (1994)

matching grants on the local budget. AB is the original budget line. When $1 of assistance is available for every $3 of local funds spent up to a pre-specified limit, the budget line becomes ACD. Initially, costs are shared on a one-third: two-thirds basis up to a level of OF, at which the subsidy limit of CG (=CE) is reached. Expenditures beyond OF receive no subsidy, so the slope of the budget line reverts back to 1:1 rather than 1:3 along the subsidized segment, AC.

Empirical studies typically find that closed-ended grants stimulate expenditures on the subsidized activity more than open-ended grants (Gramlich 1977; Shah 1994; Gamkhar and Shah 2007). The estimated response to an additional $1.00 of this kind of grant is typically $1.50. Institutional factors may explain this surprisingly large response.

Why are conditional closed-ended matching grants common in industrial countries when they seem ill designed to solve problems and inefficiencies in the provision of public goods? The answer seems to be that correcting for inefficiencies is not the sole or perhaps even the primary objective. Instead, grants are employed to help local governments financially while promoting spending on activities given priority by the grantor. The conditional (selective) aspects of or conditions on the spending are expected to ensure that the funds are directed toward an activity the grantor views as desirable. This, however, may be false comfort in view of the potential for fungibility of funds. The local matching or cost-sharing component affords the grantor a degree of control, requires a degree of financial accountability by the recipient, and makes the cost known to the granting government.

Conditional closed-ended matching grants have advantages and disadvantages from the grantor's perspective. While such grants may result in a significant transfer of resources, they may distort output and cause inefficiencies, since the aid is often available only for a few activities, causing overspending on these functions while other functions are underfinanced. If capital outlays are subsidized while operating costs are not, grants may induce spending on capital-intensive alternatives.

Conditional open-ended matching grants are the most suitable vehicles to induce lower-level governments to increase spending on the assisted function (Table 12.1). If the objective is simply to enhance the welfare of local residents, general-purpose nonmatching transfers are preferable, as they preserve local autonomy.

To ensure accountability for results, conditional nonmatching output-based transfers are preferable to other types of transfers. Output-based transfers respect local autonomy and budgetary flexibility while providing incentives and accountability mechanisms to improve service delivery performance. The design of such transfers is discussed in the next section.

Achieving Results-Based Accountability Through Performance-Oriented Transfers

Economic rationales for output-based grants (used interchangeably with performance-oriented transfers in this chapter) stem from the emphasis on contract-based management under the new public management framework and strengthening demand for good governance by lowering the transactions costs for citizens in obtaining public services under the new institutional economics approach. The new public management framework seeks to strengthen accountability for results by changing the management paradigm in the public sector from permanent appointments to contractual appointment and continuation of employment subject to fulfillment of service delivery contracts. It seeks to create a competitive service delivery environment by making financing available on similar conditions to all providers—government and nongovernment (see Shah 2007a, 2007b, 2010a, 2010b, 2012a, 2012b).

Table 12.1 Taxonomy of grants and their conceptual impacts

Type of grant	*Income effect*			*Price (substitution) effect*			*Total effect*			$\partial A/\partial G$	*Rank by objective function*		
	a_1	A	U	a_1	A	U	a_1	A	U		*Increases in expenditure*	*Accountability for results*	*Welfare*
Conditional (input-based) matching													
Open-ended	↑	↑	↑	↑	↑	↓	↑↑	↑↑	↑↓	>1	1	3 (none)	3
Closed-ended													
Binding constraint	↑	↑	↑	↑	↑	↓	↑↑	↑↑	↑↓	≥ 1	2 or 3	3 (none)	4
Nonbinding constraint	↑	↑	↑	n.a.	n.a.	n.a.	↑	↑	↑	≤ 1	3	3 (none)	2
Conditional nonmatching	↑	↑	↑	n.a.	n.a.	n.a.	↑	↑	↑	≤ 1	3	3 (none)	2
Conditional nonmatching output-based	↑	↑	↑	n.a.	n.a.	n.a.	↑	↑	↑	≤ 1	3	1 (high)	1
General nonmatching	n.a.	↑	↑	n.a.	n.a.	n.a.	n.a.	↑	↑	<1	3	3 (none)	1

Source: Adapted from Shah (1994)

Note: 1 = highest score, 4 = lowest score. ↑ = positive impact; ↓ = negative impact; a_1 = assisted sub function; A = assisted function; U = unassisted function; G = grant; n.a. = not applicable

The new institutional economics approach argues that dysfunctional governance in the public sector results from opportunistic behavior by public officials, as citizens are either not empowered to hold public officials accountable for their noncompliance with their mandates and/or for corrupt acts or face high transactions costs in doing so. In this framework, citizens are treated as the principals and public officials the agents. The principals have bounded rationality—they act rationally based on the incomplete information they have. Acquiring and processing information about public sector operations is costly. Agents (public officials) are better informed than principals. Their self-interest motivates them to withhold information from the public domain, as releasing such information helps principals hold them accountable. This asymmetry of information allows agents to indulge in opportunistic behavior which goes unchecked due to high transactions costs faced by the principals and a lack of or inadequacy of countervailing institutions to enforce accountable governance. Results-based accountability through output-based grants empowers citizens by increasing their information base and lowering their transactions costs in demanding action.

Output-based transfers link grant finance with service delivery performance. These transfers place conditions on the results to be achieved while providing full flexibility in the design of programs and associated spending levels to achieve those objectives. Such transfers help restore recipients' focus on the results-based chain (Fig. 12.5) and the alternate service delivery framework (competitive framework for public service delivery) to

Program Objectives →	Inputs →	Intermediate →	Outputs →	Outcomes →	Impact →	Reach →
Improve quantity, quality, and access to education services	Educational spending by age, sex, urban/rural; spending by grade level, teachers, staff, facilities, tools, books, regulations	Enrollments, student-teacher ratio, class size	Achievement scores, graduation rates, drop-out rates	Literacy rates, supply of skilled professionals	Informed citizenry, civic engagement, enhanced international competitiveness	Winners and losers from government programs

Fig. 12.5 Results chain with an application to education services. Source: Shah (2007a)

achieve those results. In order to achieve grant objectives, a public manager in the recipient government would examine the results-based chain to determine whether or not program activities are expected to yield the desired results. To do so, he or she needs to monitor program activities and inputs, including intermediate inputs (resources used to produce outputs), outputs (quantity and quality of public goods and services produced and access to such goods and services), outcomes (intermediate- to long-run consequences for consumers/taxpayers of public service provision or progress in achieving program objectives), impact (program goals or very long-term consequences of public service provision), and reach (people who benefit from or are hurt by a program). Such a managerial focus reinforces joint ownership and accountability of the principal and the agent in achieving shared goals by highlighting terms of mutual trust. Thus, internal and external reporting shifts from the traditional focus on inputs to a focus on outputs, reach, and outcomes—in particular, outputs that lead to results. Flexibility in project definition and implementation is achieved by shifting emphasis from strict monitoring of inputs to monitoring performance results and their measurements. Tracking progress toward expected results is done through indicators, which are negotiated between the provider and the financing agency. This joint goal setting and reporting helps ensure client satisfaction on an ongoing basis while building partnership and ownership into projects.

Output-based grants must have conditions on outputs as opposed to outcomes, as outcomes are subject to influence by factors beyond the control of a public manager. Public managers should be held accountable only for factors under their control. Outcome-based conditions diffuse enforcement of accountability for results. Since the grant conditions are concerned with service delivery performance in terms of quality of output and access, the manager is free to choose the program and inputs to deliver results. To achieve those results, he or she faces positive incentives by grant conditions that encourage alternate service delivery mechanisms by contracting out, outsourcing, or simply encouraging competition among government and nongovernment providers. This can be done by establishing a level playing field through at par financing, by offering franchises through competitive bidding, or by providing rewards for performance through benchmarking or yardstick competition. Such an incentive environment is expected to yield a management paradigm that emphasizes results-based accountability to clients with the following common elements:

- Contracts or work program agreements based on pre-specified outputs and performance targets and budgetary allocations.
- Replacement of lifelong rotating employment with contractual appointments with task specialization.
- Managerial flexibility but accountability for results.
- Redefinition of public sector role as purchaser but not necessarily provider of public services.
- Adoption of the subsidiarity principle—that is, public sector decisions made at the level of government closest to the people, unless a convincing case can be made not to do so.
- Incentives for cost efficiency.
- Incentives for transparency and competitive service provision.
- Accountability to taxpayers.

Under such an accountable governance framework, grant-financed budget allocations support contracts and work program agreements, which are based on pre-specified outputs and performance targets. The grant recipient's flexibility in input selection—including hiring and firing of personnel and implementation of programs—is fully respected, but there is strict accountability for achieving results. The incentive and accountability regime created by output-based transfers is expected to create responsive, responsible, and accountable governance without undermining local autonomy. In contrast, traditional conditional grants with input conditionality undermine local autonomy and budgetary flexibility while reinforcing a culture of opportunism and rent-seeking (Table 12.2).

Output-based grants create incentive regimes that promote a results-based accountability culture. Consider the case in which the national government aims to improve access to education by the poor and to enhance the quality of such education. A common approach is to provide grants to government schools through conditional grants. These grants specify the type of expenditures eligible for grant financing (books, computers, teacher aids, and so forth) as well as financial reporting and audit requirements. Such input conditionality undermines budgetary autonomy and flexibility without providing any assurance about the achievement of results. Moreover, in practice it is difficult to enforce, as there may be significant opportunities for fungibility of funds. Experience has shown that there is no one-to-one link between increases in public spending and improvements in service delivery performance (see Huther et al. 1997).

Table 12.2 Features of traditional and output-based conditional grants

Feature	*Traditional grant*	*Output-based grant*
Grant objectives	Spending levels	Quality and access to public services
Grant design and administration	Complex	Simple and transparent
Eligibility	Recipient government departments/agencies	Recipient government provides funds to all government and nongovernment providers
Conditions	Expenditures on authorized functions and objects	Outputs i.e. service delivery results
Allocation criteria	Program or project proposals approvals with expenditure details	Demographic data on potential clients
Compliance verification	Higher-level inspections and audits	Client feedback and redress, comparison of baseline and post-grant data on quality and access
Penalties	Audit observations on financial compliance	Public censure, competitive pressures, voice, and exit options for clients
Managerial flexibility	Little or none. No tolerance for risk and no accountability for failure	Absolute. Rewards for risks but penalties for persistent failure
Local government autonomy and budgetary flexibility	Little	Absolute
Transparency	Little	Absolute
Focus	Internal	External, competition, innovation, and benchmarking
Accountability	Hierarchical to higher-level government, controls on inputs and process with little or no concern for results	Results-based, bottom-up, client-driven

Source: Boadway and Shah (2009)

Output-based design of such grants can help achieve accountability for results. Under this approach, the national government allocates funds to local governments based on the size of the school-age population. Local governments in turn pass these funds on to both government and nongovernment providers based on school enrollments. Nongovernment providers are eligible to receive grant funds if they admit students based on merit and provide a tuition subsidy to students whose parents cannot afford the tuition. All providers are expected to improve or at the minimum maintain baseline achievement scores on standardized tests, increase graduation rates, and reduce dropout rates. Failure to do so will invite public censure and in the extreme case cause grant funds to be discontinued. In the meantime, reputation risks associated with poor performance may reduce enrollments, thereby reducing the grant funds received. Schools have full autonomy in the use of grant funds and are able to retain unused funds.

This kind of grant financing would create an incentive environment for both government and nongovernment schools to compete and excel to retain students and establish reputations for quality education, as parental choice determines grant financing to each school. Such an environment is particularly important for government schools, where staff has lifelong appointments and financing is ensured regardless of performance. Budgetary flexibility and retention of savings would encourage innovation to deliver quality education. Output-based grants thus preserve autonomy, encourage competition and innovation, and bring strict accountability for results to residents. This accountability regime is self-enforcing through consumer (parental choice in the current example) choice. Such a school financing regime is especially helpful in developing countries and poorer jurisdictions in industrial countries plagued with poor quality of teaching and worse teacher absenteeism or lack of access to education in rural areas. The incentive regime provided by results-based financing will create market mechanism to overcome these deficiencies over time.

A similar example of such a grant in health care would allocate funds to local governments based upon weighted population by age class with higher weights for senior citizens (65 years and over) and children (under 5 years). The distribution by local government to providers would be based upon patient use. Minimum standards of service and access to health care will be specified for the eligibility to receive such transfers.

Specific-purpose transfers can also be used to promote interjurisdictional competition or public-private partnership or other collaborative or competitive approaches to enhance public services delivery and access. To achieve these ends, grant payments can be made either on the basis of achieving pre-set benchmarks ("certification") or higher ranks in relative quantitatively measured performance ("tournaments") (see Zinnes 2009).

For metropolitan areas, output-based transfers are a useful candidate for financing operating expenditures for education, health, public transit, and infrastructure. Capital grants would be a useful financing tool for overcoming infrastructure deficiencies, or setting national minimum standards in quality and access of infrastructure. Tournament-based grants would be a useful tool to create a competition among metropolitan areas in improving slums or overcoming congestion and pollution.

Designing Fiscal Transfers: Conceptual Guidance

The design of fiscal transfers is critical to ensuring the efficiency and equity of local service provision and the fiscal health of subnational governments (for a comprehensive treatment of the economic rationale of intergovernmental fiscal transfers, see various chapters in Boadway and Shah 2007, 2009). A few simple considerations can be helpful in designing these transfers:

Guidelines for Grant Design

1. *Clarity in grant objectives.* Grant objectives should be clearly and precisely specified to guide grant design.
2. *Singular focus.* A single grant instrument may be used to achieve a single objective. Trying to achieve multiple objectives with a single grant program may lead to failure in achieving any objectives. For example, general revenue sharing with multiple factors that work at cross purposes, for example, inclusion of fiscal need and fiscal effort factors in the same formula.
3. *One size does not fit all.* Local governments of various classes, size, and urban and rural character have varying fiscal capacities and responsibilities for service delivery, having a single formula for all creates serious inequities.
4. *Autonomy.* Subnational governments should have complete independence and flexibility in setting priorities. They should not be constrained by the categorical structure of programs and uncertainty associated with decision-making at the center. Tax-base sharing—allowing subnational governments to introduce their own tax rates on central bases, formula-based revenue sharing, or Block grants—is consistent with this objective.
5. *Revenue adequacy.* Subnational governments should have adequate revenues to discharge designated responsibilities.

6. *Responsiveness.* The grant program should be flexible enough to accommodate unforeseen changes in the fiscal situation of the recipients.
7. *Equity (fairness).* Allocated funds should vary directly with fiscal need factors and inversely with the tax capacity of each jurisdiction.
8. *Predictability.* The grant mechanism should ensure predictability of subnational governments' shares by publishing five-year projections of funding availability. The grant formula should specify ceilings and floors for yearly fluctuations. Any major changes in the formula should be accompanied by hold harmless or grandfathering provisions.
9. *Transparency.* Both the formula and the allocations should be disseminated widely, in order to achieve as broad a consensus as possible on the objectives and operation of the program.
10. *Efficiency.* The grant design should be neutral with respect to subnational governments' choices of resource allocation to different sectors or types of activity.
11. *Simplicity.* Grant allocation should be based on objective factors over which individual units have little control. The formula should be easy to understand, in order not to reward gamesmanship.
12. *Incentive.* The design should provide incentives for sound fiscal management and discourage inefficient practices. Specific transfers to finance subnational government deficits should not be made.
13. *Reach.* All grant-financed programs create winners and losers. Consideration must be given to identifying beneficiaries and those who will be adversely affected to determine the overall usefulness and sustainability of the program.
14. *Safeguarding of grantor's objectives.* Grantor's objectives are best safeguarded by having grant conditions specify the results to be achieved (output-based grants) and by giving the recipient flexibility in the use of funds.
15. *Affordability.* The grant program must recognize donors' budget constraints. This suggests that matching programs should be closed-ended.
16. *Accountability for results.* The grantor must be accountable for the design and operation of the program. The recipient must be accountable to the grantor and its citizens for financial integrity and results—that is, improvements in service delivery performance. Citizens' voice and exit options in grant design can help advance bottom-up accountability objectives.

Some of these criteria may be in conflict with others. Grantors may therefore have to assign priorities to various factors in comparing design alternatives (Shah 1994, 2007, 2008; Canada 2006).

As noted earlier, for enhancing government accountability to voters, it is desirable to match revenue means (the ability to raise revenues from own sources) as closely as possible with expenditure needs at all levels of government. However, higher-level governments must be allowed greater access to revenues than needed to fulfill their own direct service responsibilities, so that they are able to use their spending power through fiscal transfers to fulfill national and state (regional) efficiency and equity objectives.

Principal Objectives of Transfers and Implications for Grant Design

Six broad objectives for state fiscal transfers to local governments can be identified. Each of these objectives may apply to varying degrees in different countries; each call for a specific design of fiscal transfers. Lack of attention in design to specific objectives leads to negative perceptions of these grants.

Bridging Vertical Fiscal Gaps

A vertical fiscal gap is defined as the revenue deficiency arising from a mismatch between revenue means and expenditure needs. In most countries local governments are faced with the largest fiscal gap.

Vertical fiscal gap may arise due to (a) inappropriate assignment of responsibilities; or (b) centralization of taxing powers at national and state levels; or (c) pursuit of beggar-thy-neighbor tax policies (wasteful tax competition) by local governments; and (d) lack of tax room at local levels due to heavier tax burdens imposed by the national and state governments. To deal with the vertical fiscal gap, it is important to deal with its sources through a combination of policies such as the reassignment of responsibilities, tax decentralization, or tax abatement by the state and tax-base sharing (by allowing subnational governments to levy supplementary rates on a national or state tax base). Only as a last resort should tax by tax yield sharing or general revenue sharing, or general-purpose (unconditional) formula-based transfers, all of which weaken accountability to local taxpayers, be considered to deal with this gap.

General Revenue Sharing to Deal with Vertical Fiscal Gap: Pros and Cons

General revenue sharing (commonly referred to as the "gap-filling" approach) to deal with vertical fiscal gap is almost universally practiced in developing countries. General revenue sharing represents a pragmatic yet unscientific approach as multiple factors with arbitrary weights are used to distribute an arbitrarily determined pool of resources. Factors typically used include: basic allocation (equal per jurisdiction component); population; population density; area—total, mountainous, arable; incidence of poverty; incidence of unemployment; backwardness index; infrastructure deficiency index; fiscal capacity indicators; tax effort indicators; and other need factors. General revenue sharing has some merits. It enables to reap efficiency gains of centralized tax administration. It represents a simple, objective, and transparent division of fiscal pie. It preserves local autonomy and it also offers potential to achieve grantor objectives by incorporating factors that create the right incentives or disincentives. These advantages of general revenue sharing typically pale against many drawbacks of this approach. General revenue sharing offer manna from heaven fiscal transfers that have the potential to weaken prudent fiscal management and accountability to local residents. It may lead to a lack of political and fiscal accountability if there is little local discretion in revenue raising at the margin. Revenue sharing with multiple factors that work at cross purposes introduces complexity and lack of clarity in impact. Tax effort provisions can introduce inequity. Equal per jurisdiction component, if significant, can create incentives for breakup of existing jurisdictions as happened in Brazil and Indonesia. Growth in local funding becomes dependent on state revenues and not on local own expenditure needs. Specific revenue sharing for individual taxes on narrow bases such as income and payroll taxes is even more undesirable due to perverse incentives for tax-collecting jurisdiction. General revenue sharing typically use a uniform grant formula for allocation to all local jurisdictions—metropolitan areas, large cities, small cities, towns, villages, rural municipalities, leading to injustice and inequity for all as these local governments vary in population, size, fiscal capacity, area served, types of services offered, and local priorities for various services. In view of this, it is advisable to classify local governments by population size, municipality type, and urban/rural character, creating separate formulas for each class of municipalities. Overall general revenue sharing while being transparent and objective may undermine fiscal equity, local accountability, and incentives for efficient provision of local public services.

Bridging the Fiscal Divide Through Fiscal Equalization Transfers

The purpose of equalization is to enable local levels of government to provide approximately comparable levels of public services at comparable tax burdens. In most countries, local governments have varying fiscal capacities and therefore varying ability to provide local public services. Rural local governments are particularly susceptible to weak fiscal capacities. This requires asymmetric assignment of responsibilities among local governments and states assuming varying degrees of public service delivery responsibilities in various local jurisdictions. If on the other hand such asymmetric division of powers were not possible then fiscal equalization transfers are advocated to deal with local fiscal equity concerns. These transfers would ensure that all residents of a state would have access to reasonably comparable level of local public services at reasonably comparable burdens of taxation. A suitable equalization system should have the following features:

- Be fair (have an explicit standard of equalization and the standard should determine the total pool and allocations from the pool),
- Be nonintrusive——preserve local autonomy,
- Be formula driven,
- Be relatively simple, transparent, and predictable (local governments should be able to calculate own grant entitlements for a defined period),
- Be based on readily measurable factors that are beyond the control of local governments,
- Be immune to strategic behavior,
- Be legislated for a fixed period, say, five years, and be subject to review and renewal at the end of the period.

Local fiscal equalization could be administered through a vertical state program (in federal countries) or central program (in unitary countries). It can also be administered through two types of horizontal programs (interlocal equalization) where rich local governments contribute to the pool and fiscally poor local governments receive a subsidy from this pool according to a defined equalization standard. Under a Robin Hood program state or

Table 12.3 Pros and cons of alternate local fiscal equalization programs

Program	*PROS*	*CONS*
Paternal (vertical)	• Easier to finance and administer • Supports state/national objectives in creating a common economic and social union • Glue holding the state/ country together	• Undermines local accountability to residents • Strategic behavior by recipients; complexity • Incentives for lobbying, inefficiencies, and disincentives for improving tax base and amalgamation • Nontransparent; • Central discretion; and • Lack of explicit national compact on equalization
Solidarity/ fraternal (horizontal)	• Ideal system. Simpler and transparent • Pool subject to discipline of an explicit compact and right balance in equalization	• Political bargain possible only in relatively homogeneous societies; and • Compact problematic for cost/ need equalization
Robin hood (horizontal)	• Transparent • But forced compact	• Excessive marginal tax rates; false prices for public goods; and • Disincentive for local economic development

Source: Authors' perspectives

the central government collects these monies from richer jurisdictions and distributes to the poorer jurisdictions. Under a solidarity program, the program is administered by local governments themselves. Table 12.3 lists the pros and cons of each type of local fiscal equalization programs.

The stated purpose of equalization can be reasonably achieved by combining revenue equalization and needs-based equalization into a single formula. Revenue equalization is particularly important where revenue raising is decentralized and can be achieved by the Representative Tax System (RTS) approach. Simply put, under RTS, a locality's revenue equalization per capita is determined by the amount of revenue that would be raised by applying state average local tax rates to state per capita base for each tax and comparing that with the amount that would be raised from applying the state average tax rates to each of the per capita local tax bases in a specific locality. The net aggregate difference, if positive, between the two multiplied by a locality's population is the local government's revenue equalization entitlement.

Expenditure needs equalization is necessarily more complicated because, unlike revenue which has a monetary value, expenditures provide heterogeneous public services whose quality is difficult to compare across local governments. The analog to the RTS would be a Representative Expenditure System (RES), which would require calculating a set of representative expenditures across localities by examining what a local government with average per capita fiscal capacity and average need factors would spend on a particular category of service and comparing it to what each local government would spend if it had state average per capita fiscal capacity but own need factors. The net aggregate difference if positive when taking into account all local public services would be the 'expenditure need' entitlement. Such calculations are data intensive and difficult to do (see Shah 1996 for a Canadian application). In practice, various second-best approaches are used to expenditure needs equalization, including:

1. Ignoring expenditure equalization and doing fiscal capacity equalization only, which would be equivalent to assuming that a dollar of expenditure buys the same amount of public services in each locality;
2. Cherry picking (ad hoc determination) of a few need or inherent cost disability factors as done, for example, in Germany: population size and population density; China: number of public employees; India: backwardness; Switzerland: demographics, area, unemployment, large cities, social assistance recipients, foreigners;
3. Imputation methods and/or econometric approaches that estimate empirically the determinants of expenditures by category based on different needs or cost disability factors (e.g., population, geography, demographic factors, socio-economic factors, ethnic factors), similar to that used in Netherlands, Indonesia, China, and Australia;
4. Costing the provision of major public services, as practiced in Sweden, Ethiopia, and as proposed in South Africa by the Financial and Fiscal Commission (the costed-norms approach);
5. Constructing relative needs/cost disability indexes across localities using needs factors as above under both determinants and costs-based approaches.

The first approach of ignoring needs differences is highly unsatisfactory when equalizing across local governments where needs can differ considerably. Needs are more often ignored in equalizing at the provincial/state/canton/länder level where heterogeneous needs of localities partially cancel out. Method (2) is completely subjective and highly controversial. Method (3) is very complicated, difficult to understand and not particularly reliable in the absence of very good data or for economies undergoing rapid transformation. It is also prone to causing disagreement among stakeholders and fails the transparency test. The costed-norms approach (Method 4) is also demanding empirically and cannot easily be applied to a broad set of expenditures. It embodies a straight-jacket paradigm of local governance and negates the essence of local governance, that is, competition and innovation in delivering better-quality services at lower costs. Method (5) is used in both the above approaches but begs the question of what the indexes should be and whether such indexes have the potential of perverse incentives, for example, infrastructure deficit indexes can create incentives to perpetuate infrastructure deficiencies and poverty and backwardness indexes would create perverse incentives for combating the incidence of poverty and/or backwardness.

Demand for Public Service Approach to Local Fiscal Need Equalization[2]

There is an alternate approach proposed by Boadway and Shah (2014)—*demand for public services approach (DPS)*—that is very simple and understandable, and that relies mainly on readily available data. It uses demand-side indicators for individual public services that are beyond the control of individual local governments. It is conceptually much sounder than the approaches listed above as it does not relate to a fixed public management paradigm of local governance and is neutral to how resources are used by various localities—a major drawback of RES type approaches. It approximates the RES approach in spirit by using the relative importance given to each public service by local government class as a whole but is much easier to apply. Like the RES, it relies on what local governments actually do in the aggregate. At the same time, it pays no attention to the supply side (activity costing and a fixed mode of delivery) emphasized by the RES type approaches but is simply based on demand-side factors over which individual local governments have no control. Undoubtedly, it is not 100 percent accurate, but no other method is either. Once such a method is in place, it can be further refined in the future as knowledge and data evolve. The DPS approach has yet to be applied in practice but has

[2] This section is based upon Boadway and Shah (2014).

been recommended and illustrated for Ethiopia and Indonesia to replace less satisfactory and complex systems of equalization (see Shah 2012, 2015; Shah et al. 2012). It is the system worthy of consideration for state (province) equalization transfers and its template is described next.

The method works as follows:

- Expenditure needs are determined by size, class, and urban/rural nature of local governments. In the first step, one would group urban local governments by population size and rural local governments by class or tier and then by area if wide differences in size (area) by each tier.
- Assign service weights based upon aggregate expenditure by size class. From major public services accounting for 90 percent of expenditures, for a recent year, calculate relative weights from aggregate expenditures for that class of local governments. Group smaller services accounting for remaining 10 percent of aggregate expenditures under "Other" services.
- Identify key demand-side factors (relating to target beneficiaries, i.e., service population) for each service category and allocate expenditure needs by these factors for each service based upon relative share of the service population by each local government. Table 12.2 presents illustrative calculations using this approach.

Equalization calculated in this way has some notable features.

1. The system provides a fair allocation as it groups local governments of comparable nature (type of public services provided, population and area size, and population density) together. It provides allocations based on demand-side factors beyond the control of individual local government units and thereby avoids perverse incentives provided by cost-based approaches.
2. Assuming the RTS is calculated for all revenue sources, the combination of revenue and needs equalization equalizes 100 percent of the differences among localities. In principle, total entitlements for high-income localities could be negative, in which case a "Robin Hood" type system would be required for full equalization. However, if the vertical gap is large enough (i.e., expenditure needs are high enough relative to revenue raising), full equalization can be achieved without requiring any negative equalization.

3. The absolute size of the equalization program as well as the entitlements of all localities is endogenous to the system. The entire program is formula-based rather than discretionary, which is a good thing.
4. The effective marginal equalization tax is 100 percent in the sense that increases in a locality's tax base reduces entitlements fully if the locality uses the national average tax rate, and changes in a locality's need index gives rise to offsetting changes in entitlements. As long as localities have limited ability to influence their need indexes or their tax bases, this should not be a big issue. To the extent that incentives are a problem, it is more pronounced on the revenue than on the expenditures equalization side. In principle, this could be addressed by equalizing revenue capacity less than fully.
5. The choice of classification of types of localities and the need indices are to some extent arbitrary and could be adjusted as time goes by.
6. Expenditure needs are equalized but costs are not. Whether costs should be equalized is a matter of dispute. Some have argued that costs are relevant where wage rates differ across localities. This could be addressed by adjusting entitlements by relative wage indices, although if a public sector wage index is used that could provide an incentive to increase wage rates. On the other hand, if costs differ across localities, there is an equity-efficiency trade-off in equalization: in a unitary state, one would not want to provide the same level of public services in high and low cost localities or in metropolitan areas versus remote rural municipalities
7. Annual equalization will have some volatility. To the extent that local governments cannot deal with risk as well as the national government, equalization can be smoothed over time using a moving average calculation of three to five years. This will also smooth over problems arising from time lags on obtaining accurate data. This could be further augmented by maximum and/or minimum bounds put on changes in equalization entitlements from year to year.

Table 12.4 illustrates how DPS needs calculation is done, separately for a large urban and a large rural local government.

Setting State Minimum Standards for Merit Public Services

Setting state minimum standards in local services are important for creating an internal common market so that factor mobility within the state is

Table 12.4 Illustrative calculations of expenditure needs using the "demand for public services" (DPS) approach

Public Service	*Expenditure need by large rural local government—LR1*			
	Need Factors	*Total expenditures by*	*Share of need factors*	*Expenditure need by*
		All large rural LGs	*Large rural LG LR1*	*Large rural LG LR1*
Education	School age population	1,000,000	0.15	150,000
Health	Weighted population with ages 0–4 (2.0) and ages 65+ (1.5)	2,000,000	0.2	400,000
Transportation paved road	Paved roads lane (kms)	500,000	0.3	150,000
Transportation graveled	Graveled road lane (kms)	200,000	0.1	20,000
Transport dirt roads	Dirt roads (kms)	100,000	0.2	20,000
Water	No. of households	700,000	0.25	175,000
Agri extent	No. of farm households	800,000	0.3	240,000
Vet services	No. of livestock	50,000	0.15	7500
GSA	Area	900,000	0.3	270,000
All other services	Area	400,000	0.3	120,000
ALL services		6,650,000		1,552,500
Public service	*Expenditure need by large urban local government—LU1*			
	Need factors	*Total exp by*	*Large urban LG LU1*	*Large urban LG LU1*
		All large urban LGs ($)	*Share of need factors*	*Expenditure needs ($)*
Education	School age pop (ages 5–17)	20,000,000	0.3	6,000,000
Health	Weighted population with 0–4 ages (2.0), 5–64 (1.0), and 65+ (1.5)	30,000,000	0.25	7,500,000
Transportation—roads	Paved roads lane (kms)	15,000,000	0.15	2,250,000

(*continued*)

Table 12.4 (continued)

Public service	*Expenditure need by large urban local government—LU1*			
	Need factors	*Total exp by*	*Large urban LG LU1*	*Large urban LG LU1*
		All large urban LGs ($)	*Share of need factors*	*Expenditure needs ($)*
Public transit	Population	20,000,000	0.25	5,000,000
Water & sewer	No of residential, comm., and ind. properties	5,000,000	0.1	500,000
Solid waste	Population	4,000,000	0.15	600,000
Police/security	Population (50%), property values (50%)	6,000,000	0.35	2,100,000
Snow clearing	Street lane (kms)	2,000,000	0.15	300,000
Street lighting/ cleaning	Street lane (kms)	3,000,000	0.15	450,000
Parks and rec	Park area	1,000,000	0.1	100,000
Public housing	Population below poverty line	9,000,000	0.2	1,800,000
General admin	Population	10,000,000	0.25	2,500,000
Other services	Population	7,000,000	0.25	1,750,000
All services		132,000,000		30,850,000

Source: Boadway and Shah (2014)

in response to economic considerations alone. This would also limit wasteful local tax competition and the resulting race toward bottom in local services. These standards are best achieved by instituting conditional nonmatching grants, in which the conditions reflect state efficiency and equity concerns and there is a financial penalty associated with failure to comply with any of the conditions. Conditions are thus imposed not on the specific use of grant funds but on attainment of standards in quality, access, and level of services—the so-called output conditionality. Such output-based grants for operating expenditures do not affect local government incentives for cost efficiency, but they do encourage compliance with state-specified standards for access and level of services (see Table 12.5 for an example of such a grant). Properly designed conditional nonmatching output-based transfers can create incentives for innovative and competitive

Table 12.5 Output-based grants to set minimum standards: an illustrative example for school finance

Allocation basis to state/local governments: school-age population—population aged 5–17
Conditions: Universal access to primary and secondary education. Nongovernment school access to poor on merit. Improvement in achievement scores and graduation rates from baseline. No conditions on the use of funds
Distribution basis for service providers: Equal per pupil to both government and nongovernment schools
Impact implications: Encourages competition, innovation, and accountability to citizens for improving quality and access. Automatic monitoring and enforcement provisions through parental choices of school enrollments
Incentives: Grant funds increase automatically as school attracts more students. Retention of savings for optional use from better management of resources
Penalties: Public censure, reduction of grant funds, and risk of termination with persistent noncompliance. Grant funds automatically decrease if parents pull out their children from nonperforming school

Source: Shah (2007), Boadway and Shah (2009, p. 320)

approaches to improved service delivery. Commonly used conditional grants in most countries that impose conditions on how the money is to be spent undermine local autonomy and flexibility and fail to create such an accountability environment.

State minimum standards may not be achievable if there are wide variations in infrastructure deficiencies across local governments. To overcome these infrastructure deficiencies, a state needs to establish state minimum standards for infrastructure and a planning view as to how these deficiencies would be overcome over a defined period taking into account availability of capital finance perspective. For example, a state may establish a standard that a school must be within 5 kilometers of a child's home and that they have the resources to achieve this standard over a period of ten years. State five-year plans would then present a staggered view on how this is to be achieved and identify various local jurisdictions eligible for a capital grant for school construction as done through INPRES grants in Indonesia in the 1990s. This planning view is then integrated with annual budgeting to ensure phased completion and availability of funds for upkeep upon completion. This suggests that capital grants to overcome major infrastructure deficiencies may not be formula-based grants available to all jurisdictions as in most developing countries but must embody a physical planning view and be available only to jurisdictions that do not meet minimum standards.

Compensating for Benefit Spillovers
Compensating for benefit spillovers is the traditional argument for providing matching conditional grants. For example, city transportation and library services may be used by nonresidents who do not pay city taxes and charges. Local governments will not face the proper incentives to provide the correct levels of services that yield spillover benefits to residents of other jurisdictions. A system of open-ended matching grants based on extra expenditures necessitated by spill outs of benefits or free riders will provide the incentive to increase expenditures. Because the extent of the spillover is usually difficult to measure, the matching rate will be somewhat arbitrary.

Influencing Local Priorities
In a decentralized fiscal system there is always some degree of conflict among priorities established by various orders of government. One way to induce lower-level governments to follow priorities established by the higher-level government is for the higher-level government to use its spending power by providing matching transfers. The higher-level government can provide open-ended matching transfers with a matching rate that varies inversely with the recipient's fiscal capacity in areas of high state priority but relatively lower local priority. Use of ad hoc grants or open-ended matching transfers is inadvisable. Ad hoc grants are unlikely to result in behavioral responses that are consistent with the grantor's objectives. Open-ended grants may create budgetary difficulties for the grantor.

Creating Macroeconomic Stability in Depressed Local Areas
Fiscal transfers can be used to serve state government objectives in local stabilization. Capital grants are appropriate for this purpose, provided funds for future upkeep of facilities are available. Capital grants are also justified to deal with infrastructure deficiencies in poorer jurisdictions in order to strengthen the common economic union.

Financing Local Services and the Role of Grant Finance

The role of grant financing is closely linked to the service delivery responsibilities of each local government as several local services are better financed through other tools as discussed below. For the purpose of our discussion, local services are grouped together either as people-oriented services or services to both people and property.

People-Oriented Services

Primary and secondary education and public health. These are merit services that are redistributive in nature and as a result higher-level grant financing would be important to ensure state/national minimum standards. Operating expenditures for these services are best financed by surcharges on personal income taxes and fees supplemented by output-based nonmatching grants. Capital expenditures could be financed by borrowing and/or matching capital grants.

Welfare assistance. This service, if a local responsibility, is again a strong candidate for grant finance due to the redistributive nature of this service. Local governments that provide a generous package of welfare assistance from own resources are likely to lose tax base as happened in the early 1970s in the New York City and more lately in St. Louis, Missouri (see Inman 2006).

Parks, recreation, and libraries. These services are weak candidates for grant finance but good candidates for finance through residential property taxes, surcharges on personal income taxes, and fees.

Museums, sports and fitness facilities, and concert halls. These facilities are poor candidates for grant finance and instead are better financed locally perhaps through reserves, revenue bonds, or other forms of capital finance which ultimately are funded by fees and surcharges on local real property taxes and personal income taxes. However, if some of these facilities are intended for preserving national/state heritage, holding global events (e.g. Olympics), and developing national caliber athletes and performers, then such facilities should receive at least some national/state funding.

Mixed People and Property-Oriented Services

Water, sewer, airports, and ports. Capital costs could be covered by borrowing financed by reserves, real property taxes, surcharges on personal and corporate income taxes, frontage taxes, matching grants, and public-private partnerships. Operating costs could be recovered by user fees and franchises.

Arterial roads and regional public transit. Higher-level grant assistance would be important to finance partially both capital and operating costs. Capital costs could be financed by matching capital grants, borrowing, frontage taxes, and reserves. Operating costs could be financed by fuel taxes, tolls, fines, general revenues, transit fees, congestion charges, and benefit spillover compensation by conditional matching grants.

Local streets, roads, public transit, street lighting, and parking. These are purely local services and not appropriate for grant finance.

Fire protection and ambulance. These services are best financed from general revenues.

Police, courts, and prisons. To the extent, these services may have some national or state externality; these could be partially financed by grants.

Garbage and solid waste disposal. These services are best financed by user charges/fees and franchises.

Local environmental protection, discouraging "sins" and "bads." These services are best financed by environmental charges, congestion tolls, and taxes on gambling, alcohol, and tobacco.

General services. Grant financing is not appropriate and instead these services should be financed by local general revenues.

The above paragraphs have highlighted the relevance of service delivery responsibilities in determining relevant grant structures. The following chapters on the international practice demonstrate that these considerations are completely absent in grant design in developing countries.

Institutional Arrangements for Fiscal Relations

Who should be responsible for designing the system of federal-state-local fiscal relations? There are various alternatives (see Shah 2007a for an evaluation framework and comparative reflections on alternate institutional arrangements). The first and most commonly used practice is for the federal/central government to decide on it alone The most obvious one is to make the federal government solely responsible, on the grounds that it is responsible for the national objectives that are to be delivered through the fiscal arrangements. In many countries, this is the norm and one or more central government agencies assume exclusive responsibility for the design and allocation of fiscal transfers. A potential problem with this approach is the natural tendency of the federal government to be overly involved with state decision-making and not to allow the full benefits of decentralization to occur. This biases the system toward a centralized outcome, despite the fact that the grants are intended to facilitate decentralized decision-making. To some extent, this problem can be overcome by imposing constitutional restrictions on the ability of the federal government to override state and local decisions. In China, central government agencies assume sole responsibility without having any legislative checks (Shah and Shen 2007). In India the federal government is solely responsible for Planning

Commission transfers and centrally sponsored schemes. These transfers have strong input conditionality with potential to undermine state and local autonomy. The 1988 Brazilian constitution provides strong safeguards against federal intrusion by enshrining the transfers' formula factors in the constitution. These safeguards represent an extreme step, as they undermine the flexibility of fiscal arrangements to respond to changing economic circumstances.

Alternatively, a separate body could be involved in the design and ongoing reform and enforcement of fiscal arrangements. This could be an impartial body, or a body made up of both federal and state representatives. It could have true decision-making authority or be purely advisory. Whatever body is responsible, to be effective, it needs to be able to coordinate decision-making by the two levels of government. Three commonly practiced options are (a) independent grants commission; (b) intergovernmental forum; and (c) intergovernmental-cum-civil-society forum.

Some countries set up a quasi-independent body, such as a grants commission, to design and reform the fiscal system. Such commissions can have a permanent presence, as in Australia or South Africa, or they can be brought into existence periodically to make recommendations for the next five years, as in India. India has also instituted independent grants commissions at the state level as advisory bodies for state-local fiscal transfers. These commissions have proven ineffective in some countries, largely because many of their recommendations have been ignored by the government and not implemented, as in South Africa. In other cases, the government may have accepted and implemented the commission's recommendations but been ineffective in reforming the system due to self-imposed constraints, as in India. In some cases, these commissions become too rigorous and academic in their approaches, contributing to the creation of an overly complex system of intergovernmental transfers. This has been the case with the Commonwealth Grants Commission in Australia (Shah 2017).

A few countries use intergovernmental forums or executive federalism or federal-provincial committees to negotiate the terms of the system, as Canada and Germany do. In Germany this system is enhanced by having state governments represented in the Bundesrat, the upper house of the parliament. This system allows for explicit political input from the jurisdictions involved and attempts to develop a common consensus. Typically, such forums opt for simplicity in design to make the system transparent and politically acceptable.

Finally, a variant of the above is to use an intergovernmental-cum-legislative-cum-civil-society committee with equal representation from all constituent units, chaired by the federal government to negotiate changes in existing federal-provincial fiscal arrangements. The Finance Commission in Pakistan is an example of this model, which is constituted periodically to determine allocations for the next five years. Pakistan also follows the same approach by having province-level finance commissions for designing and allocating provincial-local fiscal transfers. This approach has the advantage that all stakeholders—donors, recipients, civil society, and experts—are represented on the commission. Such an approach keeps the system simple and transparent. An important disadvantage of this approach is that due to the unanimity rule, such bodies may be permanently deadlocked, as has recently been witnessed at the federal level in Pakistan.

Conclusions

In conclusion, moving from a public sector governance culture of dividing the fiscal pie to an environment that enables responsive, responsible, equitable, and accountable governance is critical. Doing so requires exploring all feasible tax decentralization options, instituting output-based operating and planning-based capital fiscal transfers, establishing a formal fiscal equalization program with an explicit standard of equalization, and ensuring responsible access to borrowing to creditworthy local governments.

References

Barati, Izabella, and Akos Szalai. 2000. *Fiscal Decentralization in Hungary*. Budapest: Centre for Public Affairs Studies, Budapest University of Economic Sciences.

Boadway, Robin, and Anwar Shah. 2007. *Intergovernmental Fiscal Transfers: Theory and the Practice*. Washington, DC: The World Bank.

———. 2009. *Fiscal Federalism: Principles and Practice of Multi-order Governance*. New York and London: Cambridge University Press.

———. 2014. *A Simple and Transparent Approach to Expenditure Need Equalization*. A Short Note Prepared for the Ministry of Finance, Poland and the World Bank, Warsaw Office, December 23.

Canada, Government of. 2006. *Achieving a National Purpose: Putting Equalization Back on Track*. Expert Panel Report on Equalization and Territorial Formula Financing. Ottawa: Department of Finance, Government of Canada.

Filimon, R., T. Romer, and H. Rosenthal. 1982. Asymmetric Information and Agenda Control: The Bases of Monopoly Power and Public Spending. *Journal of Public Economics* 17: 51–70.
Gamkhar, Shama, and Anwar Shah. 2007. The Impact of Intergovernmental Fiscal Transfers: A Synthesis of the Conceptual and Empirical Literature. Chap. 8 in *Intergovernmental Fiscal Transfers: Principles and Practice*, ed. Robin Boadway, and Anwar Shah. Washington, DC: World Bank.
Gramlich, Edward. 1977. Intergovernmental Grants: A Review of the Empirical Literature. In *The Political Economy of Fiscal Federalism*, ed. Wallace Oates, 219–239. Lexington, MA: Heath.
Huther, Jeff, Sandra Roberts, and Anwar Shah. 1997. *Public Expenditure Reform Under Adjustment Lending: Lessons from World Bank Experiences.* Washington, DC: World Bank.
Inman, Robert. 2006. Financing Cities. In *A Companion to Urban Economics*, ed. Richard Arnott and Daniel McMillan, 311–332. Malden, MA: Blackwell.
McMillan, Melville, Anwar Shah, and David Gillen. 1980. *The Impact of Provincial-Municipal Transportation Subsidies.* Edmonton: Alberta Transportation.
Oates, Wallace E. 1999. An Essay on Fiscal Federalism. *Journal of Economic Literature* 37 (September): 1120–1149.
Oates, W.E. 2005. Towards a Second Generation Theory of Fiscal Federalism. *International Tax and Public Finance* 12 (4): 349–373.
Rosen, Harvey S. 2005. *Public Finance.* 7th ed. Boston, MA: McGraw-Hill/Irwin.
Shah, Anwar. 1985. Provincial Transportation Grants to Alberta Cities: Structure, Evaluation, and a Proposal for an Alternate Design. In *Quantity and Quality in Economic Research*, ed. Roy Chamberlain Brown, vol. 1, 59–108. New York: University Press of America.
———. 1988b. An Empirical Analysis of Public Transit Subsidies in Canada. In *Quantity and Quality in Economic Research*, ed. Roy Chamberlain Brown, vol. II, 15–26. New York: University Press of America.
———. 1989. A Linear Expenditure System Estimation of Local Response to Provincial Transportation Grants. *Kentucky Journal of Economics and Business* 2 (3): 150–168.
———. 1991. *The New Fiscal Federalism in Brazil.* Washington, DC: World Bank.
———. 1994. *The Reform of Intergovernmental Fiscal Relations in Developing and Emerging Market Economies, 1994.* Policy and Research Series 23. Washington, DC: World Bank.
———. 1996. A Fiscal Need Approach to Equalization. *Canadian Public Policy* 22 (2): 99–115.
———. 2007a. A Practitioner's Guide to Intergovernmental Fiscal Transfers. Chap. 1 in *Intergovernmental Fiscal Transfers*, ed. Robin Boadway and Anwar Shah, 1–54. Washington, DC: World Bank.

———. 2007b. Institutional Arrangements for Intergovernmental Fiscal Transfers and a Framework for Evaluation. Chap. 10 in *Intergovernmental Fiscal Transfers*, ed. Anwar Shah, 293–318. Washington, DC: World Bank.

———. 2008. Fiscal Needs Equalization: Is it Worth Doing? Chap. 1 in *General Grants Versus Earmarked Grants: Theory and Practice. The Copenhagen Workshop, 2007*, ed. Junghun Kim, and Jorgen Lotz, 35–60. Copenhagen: Schultz Grafisk a/s.

———. 2010a. *Sponsoring a Race to the Top: The Case for Results-Based Intergovernmental Finance for Merit Goods*. Policy Research Working Paper 5172. World Bank, Washington, DC.

———. 2010b. Autonomy with Accountability: The Case for Performance-Oriented Grants. Chap. 2 in *General Grants Versus Earmarked Grants: Theory and Practice. The Copenhagen Workshop, 2009*, ed. Junghun Kim, Jorgen Lotz, and Niels Jorgen Mau, 74–106. Copenhagen: Rosendahls- Schultz Grafisk a/s.

———. 2012a. *Public Services and Expenditure Need Equalization: Reflections on Principles and Worldwide Comparative Practices*. World Bank Policy Research Working Paper Series WPS# 6006, March, World Bank, Washington, DC.

———. 2012b. *Autonomy with Equity and Accountability: Towards a More Transparent, Objective, Predictable and Simpler (TOPS) System of Central Financing of Provincial-Local Expenditures in Indonesia*. World Bank Policy Research Working Paper Series WPS6004, March, World Bank, Washington, DC.

———. 2015. *Financing Subnational Governments in Ethiopia: Options to Enhance Fairness, Objectivity*. Transparency and Simplicity of Federal and Regional Fiscal Transfers. June 2015 Report, Governance Global Practice, World Bank, Washington, DC.

———. 2017. *Horizontal Fiscal Equalization in Australia: Peering Inside the Black Box*. Submitted to the Australian Productivity Commission, November.

Shah, Anwar, and Chunli Shen. 2007. Fine Tuning the Intergovernmental Transfer System to Create a Harmonious Society and a Level Playing Field for Regional Development (with Chunli Shen). In *Public Finance in China: Reform and Growth for a Harmonious Society*, ed. Jiwei Lou and Shuilin Wang, 129–154. Washington, DC: World Bank.

Shah, Anwar, Riatu Qibthiyyah, and Astrid Dita. 2012. *General Purpose Central-Provincial-Local Transfers (DAU) in Indonesia: From Gap Filling to Ensuring Fair Access to Essential Public Services for All*. Policy Research Working Paper No. 6075, World Bank, Washington, DC.

Zinnes, Clifford. 2009. *Tournament Approaches to Policy Reform. Making Development Assistance More Effective*. Washington, DC: Brookings Institution.

CHAPTER 13

Higher-Order Fiscal Transfers to Local Governments: An Overview of Worldwide Practices

Introduction

In the past several decades, a silent revolution has swept the globe. Hugely complex factors such as political transition in Eastern Europe, the end of colonialism, the globalization and the information revolution, assertion of basic rights of citizens by courts, divisive politics and citizens' dissatisfaction with governance, and their quest for responsive and accountable governance have contributed in gathering this storm. The main thrust of this revolution has been to move decision-making closer to the people to establish fair, accountable, incorruptible, and responsive (F.A.I.R.) governance. The revolution has achieved only modest success in governmental transformation across the globe due to inhibiting factors such as path dependency accentuated by powerful political, military, and bureaucratic elites. To overcome these impediments, recent literature has emphasized an enhanced, autonomous, and leadership role for local governments in improving economic and social outcomes for local residents. An expansive role of the local government is also deemed critical to international competitiveness in a globally connected world. This leadership role requires local governments to assume a catalyst's role in directing and coordinating governmental (including state and central government) and beyond government agencies, self-help groups, and networks in facilitating provision of local public services and creating an enabling environment for private sector-led local economic development. Local governments would be in a position to play this role if their responsibilities are determined by home

H. Kitchen et al., *Local Public Finance and Economics*,
https://doi.org/10.1007/978-3-030-21986-4_13

rule and community governance principles and they have adequate access to revenues from own sources or they can piggyback on central/state tax bases. In addition to strengthen their accountability to local residents, not only finance should follow function but also intergovernmental finance should be structured so as to strengthen local autonomy and flexibility while enhancing results-based accountability to local residents. This chapter is concerned with the practice of higher-order fiscal transfers to local governments with a view to deriving lessons of interest to countries contemplating fiscal system reforms.

The chapter is organized as follows. The section "Higher-Order Transfers to Local Governments: The Practice" presents an overview of the international practice in central/state fiscal transfers to local governments. The section "Lessons from International Practices in Intergovernmental Fiscal Transfers" draws both positive and negative lessons from the international practice and provides pathways to design such transfers for state governments contemplating reform of their fiscal transfers to local governments. A final section provides concluding remarks.

Higher-Order Transfers to Local Governments: The Practice

In this section, we review practices of central/state-local transfers in selected countries to draw lessons of interest for any country contemplating a reform of their state transfers to local governments.

Industrial Countries

Canada: In Canada local governments are creatures of the provinces and therefore most of the higher-order fiscal transfers to local governments flow from the provinces. Provincial grants finance 16 percent and 25 percent of municipal expenditures in all and rural municipalities, respectively. About 20 percent of provincial grants are given as unconditional (mostly fiscal capacity equalization) transfers and the rest as specific-purpose transfers. While the design of these fiscal capacity equalization transfers varies across provinces, most provinces equalize per capita fiscal capacity by each municipality. Specific-purpose transfers are mostly for road transportation and urban transit, social services, and environment. Specific-purpose transfers relate to provincial minimum standards for these services. Road grants are typically based upon kilometers of road length and police grants are based upon number of households. In addition, provinces also finance about 50 percent of school expenditures through grants to public and private (mostly religious or parochial) school boards based upon school enrollments. Most provinces have separate programs for urban and rural municipalities. The Province of New Brunswick has separate equalization for six classes of municipalities (see Shah 1994, Slack et al. 2007).

Nordic countries (Denmark, Finland, Norway, and Sweden). In Nordic countries, the role of intermediate order of government is almost nonexistent (Denmark, Finland, and Norway) or highly constrained (Sweden). Local governments are mostly self-financing but do receive central assistance for health, education, social welfare, and local fiscal equalization. In general, specific-purpose transfers relate directly to demand factors for local public services. Local fiscal capacity equalization programs use explicit standard of equalization that determine total pool and allocation among local governments (see Table 13.1). The programs are administered based upon either (a) solidarity principle (fiscally rich municipalities contribute to the pool and fiscally poorer municipalities

Table 13.1 Local fiscal equalization in Nordic counties: a summary view

Country	*Fiscal capacity equalization*	*Expenditure need equalization*
• Denmark	• Mixed central plus Robin Hood program with 85% tax rate if PCFC > 115%. Subsidy rate (SR) = 85% if PCFC < 90%; otherwise 45%	• Solidarity program
• Finland	• Solidarity RTS program with 37% tax rate for above national average PCFC; SR 100% if PCFC < 92%	• Central program of cost equalization for health, welfare, and education and rural/urban cost differences above 65% of national average
• Norway	• Robin Hood program covering major taxes except property tax with 60% rate fort above average PCFC. SR 95% for PCFC < 90%; otherwise 60%	• Solidarity program plus special central grants to smaller local governments, northern counties and faster growing local governments
• Sweden	• Same as in Denmark but 85% if PCFC < 115%	• Solidarity program of cost equalization for nine local services

Notations: PCFC: per capita fiscal capacity; SR: subsidy rate

Sources: Author's summary based upon individual country documents; Kim et al. (2010), Kim and Lotz (2008)

receive from the pool) or (b) Robin Hood principle where the central government taxes fiscally rich municipalities and uses the proceeds to provide subsidy to the fiscally poor jurisdictions or (c) a hybrid of the two with or without a central component. Finland uses the solidarity program for fiscal capacity equalization. In Denmark, Sweden, and Germany, mixed program using central component and Robin Hood components are in place. Norway uses Robin Hood principle in financing and allocation of these transfers. Expenditure need equalization is organized on solidarity principles in Denmark and Sweden. Norway uses solidarity plus central grants to smaller local governments and northern counties, and Finland uses central program of cost equalization (see Kim and Lotz 2008; Kim et al. 2010).

Developing and Transition Countries

Brazil: Brazil finances local governments through direct federal transfers to municipalities—the Municipal Participation Fund (FPM) and through state-municipal revenue-sharing programs. The FPM uses separate criteria for state capitals and metropolitan areas and for five classes of smaller and medium municipalities and for larger municipalities. State capitals and large metropolitan areas receive 18 percent of these funds and the remaining receive 82 percent. The distribution of all funds is by formulae that take into consideration population and per capita income of each municipality. The formulae allocate grant funds directly with the population and inversely with per capita income of each municipality. In addition to FPM, municipalities also receive 50 percent of revenues from centrally administered rural property tax, 100 percent of payroll deductions of income taxes of municipal employees; 70 percent of tax on gold; 2.3 percent of revenues from crude oil based on the value of production; and 50 percent of hydroelectricity and mineral taxes by the sales value of minerals by origin. A second important source of municipal revenues in Brazil is the constitutionally mandated state-municipal revenue-sharing arrangements which return 25 percent of state value-added tax to municipalities. The Federal Senate defines the allocation criteria for these transfers. The distribution criteria advised by the Federal Senate specifies that states must distribute at the minimum 75 percent of these funds from the state value-added tax by origin to each municipality. For the remaining 25 percent of the funds, each state has the discretion to include other objective factors. Typically states use share of population and share of state revenues raised in each municipality as additional factors (see Shah 1991). In addition, states return 50 percent of revenues from motor vehicle registration to municipalities by origin.

China. Central transfers to provincial and local governments are the dominant source of revenues of these governments. In 2012, they financed 43 percent of subnational expenditures. In minority provinces and other fiscally poorer jurisdictions, these transfers finance more than 75 percent of local expenditures. In the People's Republic of China (PRC), most of the service delivery responsibilities are assigned to subnational governments yet for reasons of efficiency in tax collection and administration and to finance programs of national importance the central government collects revenues far in excess of its direct spending needs. In 2012, it collected 48 percent of national revenues but accounted for only 15 percent of direct spending creating a spending power to advance national objectives of 33 percent of national revenues. Table 13.2 provides a view of vertical fiscal gap arising from a division of fiscal powers in 2011.

The existing structure of central-provincial transfers in the PRC. The fiscal system in China is based upon a layer cake model where there is strict vertical hierarchical relationship among different orders of government. Therefore, the central government only determines transfers to the

Table 13.2 Vertical fiscal gap in the People's Republic of China (PRC)—2011

Order of government	*Number of jurisdictions*	*Average 2011 population*	*Share of revenue collection*	*Share of direct expenditures*	*Fiscal gap surplus (+) or deficiency (−)*
Center	1	1.35 billion	49.4	15.1	+34.3
Provinces, municipalities, autonomous, and special administrative regions	23/4/5/2	52 mil. 22 mill. 21 mil. 4 mill.	11.3	18.9	−7.6
Prefectures	382	4 mil.	22.1	29.7	−7.6
Counties and townships	2853/40,466	470,000/33,000	17.2	36.3	−19.1
Total			100	100	0

Source: Shah (2014)

provincial-level governments[1] and there are no direct central grants to prefecture, county, or township governments. It is worth mentioning that county governments get transfers directly from provincial-level governments in provinces where "province managing county" model has been implemented. The sub-provincial transfer design is quite similar to that of central transfers to provincial governments, though the grant composition varies significantly across provinces due to the diversity of regional fiscal resources.

Central transfers in the PRC can be classified into two broad categories: general-purpose and specific-purpose transfers. The details of these transfers are presented below:

General-purpose transfers. The general-purpose transfers consist of (a) tax sharing from enterprise and personal income taxes and VAT rebates; (b) compensation for fuel and rural tax reforms; and (c) equalization transfers. In 2012, these transfers constituted 35 percent of total transfers with equalization grant alone accounting for 19 percent of general-purpose transfers (see Shah 2014).

Specific-purpose transfers. These transfers are intended for specific purposes, but conditionality varies by program and there may also be significant opportunities for fungibility of these funds so long as local government expenditures on the specific category of expenditures exceed the grant amounts. A number of so-called general-purpose transfers in the PRC are considered specific-purpose transfers in this analysis as they are intended to be used for specific expenditures. These include subsidies for basic pension, rural education, rural health insurance, and compensation for wage increases. In addition, there are 200 plus individual transfers by central line agencies requiring specific mandates to be fulfilled by local governments. Transfers for agriculture, forestry, irrigation, and housing account for nearly half of total specific-purpose transfers. In aggregate specific-purpose transfers accounted for 65 percent of total central transfers in 2012 (see Table 13.3).

The existing structure of provincial-local fiscal transfers. Most of the central transfers to provinces (more than 70 percent of total transfers) are intended for below province local governments. But depending upon provincial delegation, prefectures may have some discretion in designing pass-through mechanisms and allocation criteria. It therefore matters how

[1]The five separately planned cities, Dalian, Qingdao, Shenzhen, Xiamen, and Ningbo, are treated as provincial governments fiscally.

Table 13.3 Central-provincial transfers in the PRC—2012

Transfer type	*Percent of total transfers*
General-purpose transfers	35%
Tax-sharing transfers and tax rebates	11%
Compensation for fuel and rural tax reform	5%
Equalization transfers	19%
Specific-purpose transfers	65%
Basic pensions	8%
Rural education	4%
Rural health insurance	2%
Agriculture, forestry, and irrigation	22%
Transport	7%
Housing	5%
Others	17%
All transfers	100%

Source: PRC Central Government Budget Execution, 2012

provinces manage their relationships with lower orders of government. Currently these relationships are guided by two alternate models.

(a) "Prefecture Managing County" model. In this model, provincial governments only deal with prefecture governments on fiscal matters and prefecture governments in turn deal with county governments and design arrangements for pass through of central transfers.

(b) "Province Managing County" model. Some provincial government bypass the prefecture level and directly relate with county governments on fiscal matters. The fiscal connection between the prefecture and the county is entirely removed.

With the encouragement of the central government most provinces have also adopted a "county replacing township" model in which the township government no longer acts as an independent budget unit. It is hoped that government efficiency can be improved with less managerial layers.

The sub-provincial transfers mimic the grant structure for central-provincial transfers. Provinces and prefecture typically retain 20–30 percent of the transfers for own purpose and pass the rest to lower-order local governments (see Shah 2017 for details).

Ethiopia. State (regional) transfers to local governments (woredas) finance most of local government expenditures as local governments in most regions (with the exception of three regions) do not have any taxing powers. Regions provide general-purpose transfers with revenue equalization and cost-equalization components. Both operating and capital expenditure needs are combined in cost equalization. Regional approaches are surprisingly similar with some variations for factors and weights used for both components (see Shah 2015 for details). All local governments are treated alike, and formulae make no urban versus rural or large versus small distinctions. Fiscal capacity is generally not considered, and instead actual own revenues are used for revenue equalization. Almost all state governments use average unit cost approaches based upon historical expenditures in determining expenditure needs for various services. Capital expenditure needs are usually based upon various relative infrastructure deficiency indexes with only one state basing these on the state regional development plan. These needs are separately determined for general administration, education, health, water, agricultural natural resources and rural development, rural roads, micro and small-scale enterprises, works and urban development, and capital expenditures. Across states there are some variations in aggregation of various services and a few exceptions to the common estimation methods. Three states (Tigray, Southern Nations, Nationalities and People's (SNNP), and Benishangul-Gumuz) use regression analysis for estimating general services expenditures. One state (SNNP) uses Cobb-Douglas production function to estimate needs for agriculture and rural development.

India. Under the 1951 Constitution Act (article 246), local governments in India were the creatures of the state governments. The 73rd and 74th Amendments to the Constitution Act, 1992, accorded constitutional status to rural and urban local bodies (governments) respectively. These amendments classified 5151 (2006 figures) urban local bodies (ULB) into three categories: municipal corporation (35 in 2006) for a larger urban area, municipal council for a smaller urban area, and *nagar panchayat* for an area in transition from rural to urban area (see Mathur 2006). It also created three tiers of 248.968 (2006 figures) rural local bodies; 543 district (*zila*) panchayats having a population of 1.5–2 million; 6097 intermediate order (*taluk*) panchayats having a population size of 150,000–200,000, and 242,328 village (*gram*) panchayats with populations ranging from 1000 to 30,000 with an average size of 2500 people (Alok 2006). Schedule 11 of the 73rd Amendment advises states to consider transferring 29 functions to rural local bodies. Article 243 W of the 74th Amendment lists 18 types of functions that can be exercised by urban local bodies. These include planning related (2 functions), infrastructure and services (7 functions), environment (1 function), redistributive functions (3), and regulatory and miscellaneous functions (5) (see Mohanty 2015). On average urban and rural local governments' expenditures amount to less than US $15 and US $10 per capita in 2001/2002 (see Mathur 2006, Alok 2006, 2008). Urban local bodies finance 52 percent of expenditure from own-source revenues whereas rural municipalities finance only 7 percent of expenditures from own-source revenues. Among the three tiers of rural local bodies district (*zila*) and intermediate order (*taluk*) panchayats have no taxing powers and are fully financed by state transfers and only village (*gram*) panchayats finance a small percentage of expenditures from own revenues.

India has both federal (state pass-through) general-purpose transfers to local governments and direct state general-purpose transfers to local governments. The former transfers are advised by the Union Finance Commission which issues an award every five years (Table 13.4). The latter are designed by the State Commissions (see Table 13.5). The Indian Constitution mandates each state to establish independent Grant Commission to advice on the criteria for distribution of state general-purpose transfers to local governments. Total pool of these transfers is arbitrarily determined by the state finance ministers. The total pool is set as a share of total state revenues in three states, as a share of own revenues in seven states, as a share of non-loan gross own revenues in one state and as a share of state own tax revenues only in three states. These shares have wide variations (see Table 13.5). The state commission recommends share

Table 13.4 Criteria adopted by union (federal) finance commissions for distribution of grants to states for urban local bodies

Criteria	*Weight assigned by*			
	11th finance commission	*12th finance commission*	*13th finance commission*	*14th finance commission*
Population	40	40	50	90
Area	10	10	10	10
Distance from highest per capita income	20	20	20	–
Decentralization index	20	–	–	–
Devolution index	–	–	15	–
Revenue efforts	10	20	–	–
Deprivation index	–	10	–	–
Finance commission Urban Local Bodies grant utilization index	–	–	5	–

Source: Reports of the Finance Commission of India (various years)

Table 13.5 India: state finance commission's recommendations for state transfers to local governments

State	*%*	*Share of Panchayat Raj Institutions (PRI) and urban local bodies (ULB)*	*Basis of distribution*
Total revenue of state			Development criteria Population
Andhra Pradesh (I)	39.24	70% and 30%	Population, geographical area, performance
Assam (I)	2.0	Not mentioned	
Goa (I)	36.0	75% and 25%	
Own revenue of state			
Andhra Pradesh (II)			Development criteria
J & K (I)	10.39	65% and 35%	Not mentioned
Kerala (I)			Population
Madhya Pradesh (I)	13.5	67% and 33%	Population, area, tax efforts
Orissa (II)	1.0	Not mentioned	Population, density, number of holdings, revenue efforts
	11.579	25.13% and 74.87%	ULB does not exist in the state
Sikkim (I)	10.0	80% and 20%	Population, area, deprivation index, remoteness index, tax efforts
Uttarakhand (II)			Population (80%); area (20%)
	1.0	100% and 0%	Population and area
Uttar Pradesh (I)	10.0	60% and 40%	
Uttar Pradesh (II)	10.0	30% and 70%	
	12.5	40% and 60%	
Non-loan gross own revenue			For panchayats—population, area, index of decentralization and for ULBs population 67% and illiteracy rate 33% [Karnataka II has followed it]
Karnataka (I)			
Karnataka (II)	36.0	85% and 15%	
	40.0	80% and 20%	
State own taxes			
Assam (II)	3.5	Based on 1991 census	Population, area, net district domestic product
Kerala (II)	9.0	78.5% and 21.5%	Population
Kerala (III)	25.0	Not mentioned	Not mentioned
Madhya Pradesh (II)	4.0	77.33% and 26.67%	Population

(*continued*)

Table 13.5 (continued)

State	*%*	*Share of Panchayat Raj Institutions (PRI) and urban local bodies (ULB)*	*Basis of distribution*
Punjab (II)	4.0	67.50% and 32.50%	Population, per capita, revenue, SCs (population of scheduled castes)
Rajasthan (I)	2.18	77.3% and 22.7%	Population
Rajasthan (II)	2.25	76.6% and 23.4%	Population
Tamil Nadu (I)	8.0	60% and 40%	Population
Tamil Nadu (II)	10.0	58% and 42%	Population, SCs and STs (population of scheduled tribes), per capita own revenue, area, asset maintenance, resource gap Population, resource potential, needs
Tamil Nadu (III)	10.0	58% and 42%	Population and distance from rail head Population and % of SC/ST, nonliterates
Uttarakhand (I)	11.0	42.23 and 57.77	Population 50% and 7% to other variables, population density, SC/ST, nonliterates, Infant Mortality Rate, rural population per capita income
West Bengal (I)	16.0	Breakup as per population. District wise	
West Bengal (II)	16.0	Breakup as per population. District wise	

Source: Alok (2008)

of rural and urban local governments as well as distribution factors. A majority of states distribute these funds simply based upon population share of each municipality.

Besides general-purpose transfers, both rural and urban local bodies receive specific-purpose transfers from central (centrally sponsored schemes) as well as state governments. Some notable centrally sponsored schemes for urban local bodies in recent years include Jawaharlal Nehru Urban renewal scheme launched in 2005 to support infrastructure and basic services to the poor in cities contemplating 23 centrally specified reforms; Smart Cities and Atal Mission for Urban Rejuvenation and Transformation matching grant programs with 50 percent central matching launched in 2015. The

Table 13.6 Central-provincial/local transfers in Indonesia (2010)

Transfer	*Share of total transfer in 2010*	*Share of subnational expenditures in 2010*
Tax sharing	25%	20%
Gap filling (DAU)	56%	46%
Special Allocation Grant (DAK)	6%	5%
Other specific purpose	13%	10%
All	100%	90% (Provinces: 54%; cities: 86%; and districts: 93%)

Source: Ministry of Finance, Indonesia

latter program is aimed at improving fiscal management in recipient cities (see Mohanty 2015).

Indonesia. Central transfers are the most important source of revenues for subnational governments in Indonesia. These financed 90 percent of subnational governments, 54 percent of provincial, 86 percent of cities, and 93 percent of districts expenditures in 2010. Major transfers (balance grants or *Dana Perimbangan*) to finance provincial and local expenditures are provided in Table 13.6.

Tax by tax sharing (Dana Bagi Hasil—DBH). Central government collects taxes on personal income, property, and renewable and nonrenewable natural resources and returns by origin a pre-defined share of the revenues to the originating jurisdiction. These transfers accounted for 25 percent of total central transfers in 2010 and financed 20 percent of subnational expenditures.

Transfers to deal with vertical and horizontal fiscal gaps. Central government provides a basic allocation for wages and salaries and a fiscal gap transfer (*Dana Alokasi Umum* or DAU) if a jurisdiction's revenues fall short of calculated expenditure needs using macro indicators. These transfers accounted for 56 percent of total central transfers and financed 46 percent of subnational expenditures. The total pool for the fiscal gap transfer, DAU is set annually (at 26 percent of central revenues net of tax-sharing transfers in 2011). The 20 percent of the total pool is allocated to provinces and the remaining 80 percent to all cities and districts. The DAU provides a basic allocation to cover wages of provinces, cities, and districts. The remaining funds are allocated by formula that determines fiscal gap based upon the differences between fiscal needs and fiscal capacity. Formula factors for both provinces and cities are the same but receive differential weights due to the peculiar application to DAU allocation of the weighted coefficient of variation—the so-called Williamson's Index.

Fiscal capacity of a province is determined by summing up 50 percent of own-source revenues, 80 percent of nonresource tax sharing, and 95 percent of resource and mining tax sharing. Fiscal capacity of a city or district government on the other hand is based upon 93 percent of own-source revenues, 100 percent of nonresource tax revenue sharing, and 63 percent of resources and mining tax revenue sharing. The weights for individual revenue sources to determine fiscal capacity varies from year to year as weights are picked up to achieve a given numerical value for the Williamson's income inequality variation index for each year. Fiscal needs of provinces and cities/districts are determined separately for each of this group by developing a composite index based upon relative population, relative area, relative construction price index, inverse of human development index (HDI; comprising arbitrary weights for life expectancy, literacy rate, mean years of schooling, and purchasing power adjusted relative real GRDP per capita), and inverse of relative nominal per capita gross regional domestic product (GRDP). The weights for the above-mentioned factors vary for provinces and districts/cities and over time for each group based upon the specified value to be achieved for the Williamson's index. The resulting indexes are multiplied by the average aggregate spending for the past year to arrive at numerical values of the expenditure need component. DAU allocation for each jurisdiction is then determined as follows:

$$\text{DAU} = \text{Basic Allocation} + \text{Fiscal Gap}\left(\text{Fiscal needs minus Fiscal Capacity}\right)$$

The DAU is a gross program and compensates a jurisdiction for excess needs but does not tax regions with excess fiscal capacity. The jurisdictions displaying negative fiscal gap (surplus fiscal capacity), for example, Jakarta metropolitan region, receive only the basic allocation and the negative fiscal gap is ignored.

Specific-purpose grants. These grants include the Special Allocation Grant (*Dana Alokasi Khusus* or DAK). The primary objective of this grant is to finance, in selected regions, the infrastructure needs of basic public services that are of high national priority but are regional government responsibilities. Other stated objectives include providing special assistance to certain regions and to accelerate regional development and the achievement of national priorities. Local governments with lower than average fiscal capacity are expected to receive higher priority in financing their infrastructure deficiencies. The revised DAK program effective 2014 is divided into two sub-programs: physical and nonphysical. Nonphysical DAK is purely discretionary by the central government. Physical DAK has three components—each with its own objectives and process of approval.

(1) DAK regular: This component is intended to overcome infrastructure deficiencies. It is a proposal-based system where local governments can submit proposals to the central government directly through a web-based system called KRISNA. The district governments nevertheless complain that the provinces require clearance prior to their online submissions.
(2) DAK assignments: These allocations are based upon national priorities as determined by the central government.
(3) DAK affirmative: These are special allocations for local governments located in remote border regions.

Special Autonomy grants for Aceh, Papua and Papua Barat, Adjustment Fund compensation, and Special Incentives grants (*Dana Insentif Daerah* or DID), and *Hibah*. DAK is intended to influence local government spending on areas of national priority. It accounts for 6 percent of central transfers and finances 5 percent of subnational expenditures. Adjustment Fund compensation (*Dana Penyesuaian* or DP) provides special ad hoc assistance, for example, for school operational assistance (BOS), allowances for certified teachers, and so on. Special Autonomy grants (*Dana Otonomi Khusus* or DOK) are intended to provide special and preferential support to Aceh and Papua provinces. DID is a small grant program accounting for less than 1 percent of total transfers and are granted to better performing provinces and cities on public financial management, tax effort, having higher HDI relative to fiscal capacity, higher economic growth, higher reductions in poverty, unemployment, and inflation. *Hibah* transfers are primarily financed by external assistance and are intended to finance subnational infrastructure and social development expenditures. Specific-purpose transfers in total accounted for 19 percent of central transfers in 2010 and financed 15 percent of subnational expenditures (see Shah 2012, Shah et al. 2012).

Nigeria: In Nigeria, National Revenue Mobilization, Fiscal and Allocation Commission is entrusted with designing the allocation criteria for the division of the federation account among federal, state, and local governments. Federal, state, and local governments receive 52.7 percent, 26.7 percent, and 20.6 percent, respectively, of total pool. The pool is then distributed among local governments using the following factors and weights advised by the commission:

Equal per jurisdiction—40 percent
Land area and terrain—10 percent
Own revenues—10 percent
Population—30 percent
Social development factors (territorial spread—1.5 percent; rainfall—1.5 percent; primary/secondary enrollment—4 percent; hospital beds—3 percent)—10 percent

In addition, proceeds from value-added taxes collected by federal, state, local governments are distributed to federal, state, and local governments by 15 percent, 50 percent, and 35 percent, respectively. The pool available to each order is distributed among jurisdictions based upon the following criteria (see Adeyemi 2013):

Equal per jurisdiction—50 percent
Population—30 percent
By derivation (origin or point of collection)—20 percent

Pakistan: Pakistan also mandates establishment of a Provincial Finance Commission comprising representatives of provincial and local governments with access to advice from independent experts (Shah 2003). Table 13.7 summarizes the awards of these commissions for provincial-local transfers. The table shows that majority of funds are distributed by population followed by area and a backwardness index.

Russia. Major types of federal transfers to regions (oblasts) are equalization transfers, gap-filling subsidies, the compensation fund, co-financing of social programs, capital transfers, regional finance reform transfers, operating, transfers to special territories, ad hoc transfers, and transfers to "closed" (having military-industrial complex) cities. Equalization transfers account for about half of federal transfers. Twenty percent of these funds are set aside for the lowest six income regions and 80 percent are formula-based transfers to all regions that take into account relative fiscal capacity (regional GDP) and fiscal needs (differential cost of public service provision based upon expenditure need indexes that account for price, demographic, socio-economic geographic, climatic, and other factors) of each region. Gap-filling subsidies compensate regions for implementation of

Table 13.7 Pakistan: provincial operating grants to district governments

Total pool and the distribution criteria	*Punjab*	*Sindh*	*Khyber Pakhtunkhwa*	*Baluchistan*
Total pool: local share of provincial divisible pool	39.8%	40%	40%	31%
Formula factors and weights—total	100%	100%	100%	100%
Population	75%	50%	50%	50%
Backwardness	10%	17.5%	25%	
Tax effort	5%	7.5%		
Fiscal austerity	5%			
Area				50%
Development incentive for overcoming infrastructure deficiency	5%		25%	
Hold harmless/transitional assistance		25%		

Source: Shah (2003)

federal policies leading to regional revenue gaps and/or expenditure increases. The Compensation Fund compensates regions for carrying out tasks mandated by the federal government. Co-financing of social programs partially compensates regions for a number of social safety net entitlements. Capital transfers finance construction of schools, hospitals, information technology, and other infrastructure investments. Regional finance transfers are competitive grants to regions introducing public finance management reforms. Operating transfers to special territories are transfers to Chechnya and other region that suffered from radiation-related adverse consequences. Ad hoc transfers include special wards to cities for better performance or celebrating anniversaries. Transfers to closed cities are direct federal subsidies to military-industrial complex or R&D centers (Deryugin and Kurlyandskaya 2007).

Regional governments typically establish two funds for transfers to local governments: (a) the Fund for Financial Support to City and Municipal Districts. Through this fund, regions provide financial support to city and municipal districts. The municipal districts in turn execute transfers to villages; and (b) Fund for Financial Support to Settlements. This fund provides financial support to city districts and villages. Regional transfers to local governments predominantly come in the form of three types of grants: (1) equalization grants. These are formula-based unconditional grants that take into consideration fiscal capacity and fiscal needs and are separately constituted for settlements and for districts; (2) the compensation fund transfers to lower-order governments for carrying out regional tasks; and (3) mutual settlement grants. These are matching grants for municipal development or for priority social expenditures (Zulkarnay 2003).

South Africa: South Africa (a quasi-federal country) uses an equitable share formula to provide transfers from the central government to local governments. The size of the grant is determined as follows:

$$\text{Grant} = \left(BS + D + I - R\right) \pm C,$$

where *BS* is the basic services component, *D* is the development component, *I* is the institutional support component, *R* is the revenue-raising capacity correction, and C is a correction and stabilization factor.

Basic Services Component

The purpose of the basic services component is to enable municipalities to provide basic services (water, sanitation, electricity, refuse removal, and other basic services), including free basic services to households earning less than R800 (about US $111 a month). (As of April 1, 2006, environmental health-care services have been included as a basic service.) Since by its nature environmental health is delivered to everyone in a municipality, this subcomponent is calculated on all households, not only poor ones. For each subsidized basic service, there are two levels of support: a full subsidy for households that actually receive services from the municipality and a partial subsidy for unserved households currently set at one-third of the cost of the subsidy to serviced households. This component is calculated as follows:

$$\begin{aligned} BS = & \left[\text{water subsidy } 1 \times \text{poor with water} + \text{water subsidy } 2 \times \text{poor without water}\right] \\ & + \left[\text{sanitation subsidy } 1 \times \text{poor with sanitation} + \text{sanitation subsidy } 2 \times \text{poor without sanitation}\right] \\ & + \left[\text{refuse subsidy } 1 \times \text{poor with refuse} + \text{refuse subsidy } 2 \times \text{poor without refuse}\right] \\ & + \left[\text{electricity subsidy } 1 \times \text{poor with electricity} + \text{electricity subsidy } 2 \times \text{poor without electricity}\right] \\ & + \left[\text{environmental healthcare subsidy} \times \text{total number of households}\right]. \end{aligned}$$

Institutional Support Component

The institutional support component is particularly important for poor municipalities, which are often unable to raise sufficient revenue to fund the basic costs of administration and governance. Such funding gaps make it impossible for poor municipalities to provide basic services to all residents, clients, and businesses. This component supplements the funding of a municipality for administrative and governance costs. It does not fully fund all administration and governance costs of a municipality, which remain the primary responsibility of each municipality. The institutional component includes two elements: administrative capacity and local electoral accountability. The grant is determined as follows:

$$I = \text{base allocation} + [\text{admin support} \times \text{population}] + [\text{council support} \times \text{number of seats}]$$

where the values used in the formula are $I = \text{R}350,000 + [\text{R}1 \times \text{population}]$ + [R36,000 × councilors

The "base allocation" is the amount that goes to every municipal structure (except for a district management area). The second term of this formula recognizes that costs rise with population. The third term is a contribution to the cost of maintaining councilors for the legislative and oversight role. The number of "seats" that will be recognized for purposes of the formula is determined by the minister for provincial and local government.

The Development Component

The development component was set at zero when the current formula was introduced on April 1, 2005, pending an investigation of how best to capture the factor in the formula.

The Revenue-Raising Capacity Correction

The revenue-raising capacity correction raises additional resources to fund the cost of basic services and administrative infrastructure. The basic approach is to use the relationship between demonstrated revenue-raising capacity by municipalities that report information and objective municipal information from Statistics South Africa to proxy revenue-raising capacity for all municipalities. The revenue that should be available to a municipality is then "corrected" by imposing a "tax" rate of 5 percent. In the case of the Regional Service Councils levy replacement grant, the correction is based on the actual grant to each municipality (South Africa 2006; Boadway and Shah 2007, 2009).

Table 13.8 Sources of local authority revenues in Thailand (2010)

Local revenue source	*Share*
Total own-source revenues	16%
Total shared taxes	41%
Central government transfers	43%
General-purpose transfers	38%
(a) VAT tax transfer (formula based on population, area, expenditure needs)	69%
(b) General subsidy (65% equal per capita, 35% equal per jurisdiction to urban and smaller rural municipalities)	31%
Specific-purpose transfers	62%
(a) General subsidy with specific earmarking	32%
(b) Specific-purpose grants	68%
Total local authority revenues	100.00%

Source: Boothe et al. (2011)

Thailand. Central transfers finance 43 percent of subnational revenues (see Table 13.8). Formula-based general-purpose transfers constitute 38 percent of these transfers and the remaining 62 percent of these transfers are intended for specific purposes, that is, to finance expenditures in specified activities such as education, health, social services, water and environment, and general administration (Boothe et al. 2011).

General-Purpose Transfers

Two types of general-purpose transfers are currently in use under the Thai system:

(a) *The value-added tax transfer according to the Decentralization Act.* Under the 1999 Decentralization Act, local authorities are entitled to receive a share of not more than 30 percent of VAT collected by the central administration. The VAT transferred to local authorities constitutes about 18.5 percent of total local revenues in 2009 (10 percent for provinces, 35 percent for municipalities, and 49 percent for smaller rural municipalities), making it the second largest revenue source for local authorities. Allocation of this tax is undertaken by the National Decentralization Committee and is subject to amendment on an annual basis. As such, allocation changes from year to year, but the criteria typically used to determine allocation includes population, area, revenue, and/or budgetary needs.

(b) *The general subsidy.* The primary objective of the general-purpose subsidy is filling the financing gap and allowing local authorities to meet their mandated expenditure responsibilities. Total pool for this transfer is annually determined by the central government. Five percent of the total is set aside as deficit grants and allocated according to the difference between revenue and expenditure in basic public service provision of local governments. Of the remaining 95 percent, 90 percent is allocated to urban municipalities and smaller rural municipalities and the remaining 10 percent is allocated to the provinces.

Specific-Purpose Transfers

A significant portion of general subsidy is earmarked for central recurring mandates. In addition, there are currently 30 specific-purpose transfers. These are targeted toward meeting central mandates in social and environmental policies and/or the achievement of specific nationally set policy objectives. Specific-purpose subsidies targeting environmental programs are a matching transfer, where 90 percent is provided by the central administration and 10 percent is provided by local authorities. However, others such as the subsidy for the elderly are allocated strictly on a per capita registered elderly basis, 500 baht per registered recipient. Specific-purpose subsidies cover a wide range of different policy objectives, ranging from health and education to social welfare. Allocation of specific-purpose transfers follow a number of different rules, but most typically, these are allocated on a per capita basis. With a few exceptions such as disaster relief funds or environmental subsidies, special-purpose transfers are commonly used to subsidize specific central government priorities than to target specific areas or districts. While some of these subsidies are directed toward infrastructure investment, many are targeted toward social service and welfare provision. These transfers are attractive to the central administration because control remains firmly entrenched at the central level, allowing for central prioritization of different policy objectives.

Concluding Remarks on International Practices

A review of higher-order transfers to local governments suggests discernible differences in approaches by industrial and developing countries. Industrial country transfers have singular focus with design of each grant consistent with the objective. Further local governments are distinguished by size, class, urban, and rural characteristics with a separate formula for each type of jurisdiction. Developing countries, on the other hand, combine several objectives in one formula that applies to all local jurisdictions. The pool of funds and the formula factors and weights are all arbitrarily selected and often changed abruptly over time. While for the most part (with the exception of Ethiopia in case study countries), these formulae are simple and transparent, they may not satisfy the equity and efficiency criteria and in practice may fail to achieve any of the objectives sought. Further the grant formulae are simply focused on dividing an arbitrary pool and passing the funds like manna from heaven without any incentives for improved local service delivery performance and accountability to local residents. This approach strengthens local autonomy but may undermine local fiscal accountability as well as local government responsiveness to local preferences in view of overwhelming dependency on higher-level transfers in financing local expenditures at the margin.

Lessons from International Practices in Intergovernmental Fiscal Transfers

A review of international practices yields a set of practices to avoid and a set of practices to emulate (see also Boadway and Shah 2007, 2009). A number of important lessons also emerge (Table 13.9).

Negative Lessons: Types of Transfers to Avoid

Policymakers should avoid designing the following types of intergovernmental grants:

- Grants with vaguely specified objectives.
- General revenue-sharing programs with multiple factors with arbitrary weights that work at cross purposes and undermine accountability and do not advance fiscal efficiency or fiscal equity objectives. Tax decentralization or tax-base sharing offer better alternatives to a general revenue-sharing program, as they enhance accountability while preserving subnational autonomy.
- Grants to finance subnational deficits, which create incentives for running higher deficits in future.

Table 13.9 Principles and better practices in higher-order grants to local governments

Grant objective	*Grant design*	*Examples of better practices*	*Examples of practices to avoid*
To bridge vertical fiscal gaps	Reassignment of responsibilities, tax abatement, tax-base sharing. Only as a last resort general revenue sharing	Tax abatement and tax-base sharing (Norway, Sweden, Denmark, Finland, Thailand)	Deficit grants, wage grants (China, Indonesia), tax by tax sharing (China)
To reduce regional fiscal disparities	General nonmatching fiscal capacity equalization transfers	Fiscal capacity equalization with an explicit standard that determines total pool as well as allocation (Canada, Denmark, Germany, and Finland)	General revenue sharing with multiple factors (Brazil and India); fiscal equalization with a fixed pool (Australia, Indonesia, China)
	Demand for services approach (allocation by service population) to compensate for fiscal need differentials		Econometric or imputation or cost-based approaches to fiscal need compensation as in Australia, Netherlands, and Ethiopia
Compensate for benefit spillovers	Open-ended matching transfers with matching rate consistent with spill-out of benefits or interjurisdictional partnership agreements	Grant for teaching hospitals (South Africa)	Closed-ended matching grants
Set national minimum standards for merit public services	Conditional nonmatching output-based bloc transfers with conditions on standards of service and access	Road maintenance and primary education grants (Indonesia until 2000) Education transfers (Brazil, Chile, Colombia, Thailand) Health transfers (Brazil); roads, transit, school, and police grants (Canadian provinces)	Conditional transfers with conditions on spending alone (most countries), pork-barrel transfers (United States e.g., $200 million earmark in 2006 for a "bridge to nowhere" in Alaska), ad hoc grants
	Conditional capital grants with matching rate that varies inversely with local fiscal capacity to local governments that have infrastructure deficiencies based upon a planning view compared to national standards	Capital grant for school construction (Indonesia before 2000), highway construction state matching grants to local governments (United States)	Capital grants with no matching and no future upkeep requirements Formula-based capital grants to local governments as in Indonesia and Bhutan (ongoing)

Promoting competition among local governments	Project or output-based grants using pre-set benchmarks ("certification") or higher ranks in relative quantitatively measured performance ("tournaments")	Competitive grant program for local public investment in Albania and Russia (ongoing)	Subjective selection processes
Influence local priorities in areas of high state but low local priority	Open-ended matching transfers (preferably with matching rate varying inversely with fiscal capacity)	Matching transfers for transportation and public transit (Province of Alberta, Canada)	Ad hoc grants
Provide stabilization and overcome infrastructure deficiencies	Capital grants provided maintenance possible	Capital grants with matching rates that vary inversely with local fiscal capacity	Stabilization grants with no future upkeep requirements

Source: Shah (2007a) and Boadway and Shah (2009)

- Unconditional grants that include incentives for fiscal effort. Such incentives reward richer jurisdictions. Further, improving service delivery while lowering tax costs should be public sector objectives.
- Having a formal open, contestable, and deliberative process for municipal incorporation, amalgamation, and annexation should be a prerequisite for introducing an equal per municipality component in grant finance. The lack of such a process can create a perverse incentive for the breakup of existing jurisdictions to qualify for additional assistance, as demonstrated by the experiences in Brazil and Indonesia.
- Complex econometric expenditure needs calculations and costed-norms approaches to equalization grants lead to a lack of transparency and inequity in grant allocations.
- Input- (or process-) based or ad hoc conditional grant programs, which undermine local autonomy, flexibility, fiscal efficiency, and fiscal equity objectives.
- Capital grants without assurance of funds for future upkeep, which have the potential to create white elephants. Formula-based capital grants serve as Christmas tree approach and distribute small amounts of grants to all jurisdictions and are not helpful in overcoming infrastructure deficiencies.
- Negotiated or discretionary grants in a federal system, which may create dissention and disunity.
- One size fits all formula-based grants to all local governments (large and small, urban and rural), which create huge inequities.
- Capital grant funds to individual members of the state or national legislative branch for local economic development. Such grant funds undermine local governance and may create projects with no funds for future upkeep. Grants that involve abrupt year to year changes in the total pool and its allocation.

Positive Lessons: Principles and Practices to Ameliorate

Policymakers should strive to respect the following principles in designing and implementing intergovernmental transfers:

- Keep it simple. In the design of fiscal transfers, rough justice may be better than precise or full justice, if it achieves wider acceptability and sustainability.

- Focus on a single objective in a grant program and make the design consistent with that objective. Setting multiple objectives in a single grant program runs the risk of failing to achieve any of them.
- Introduce ceilings linked with macro indicators and floors, to ensure stability and predictability in grant funds.
- Introduce sunset clauses. It is desirable to have the grant program reviewed periodically—say, every five years—and renewed (if appropriate). In the intervening years, no changes to the program should be made, in order to provide certainty in budgetary programming for all governments.
- Equalize per capita fiscal capacity to a specified standard in order to achieve fiscal equalization separately among various local governments grouped together by size/class and urban/rural distinctions. Such a standard would determine the total pool and allocations among recipient units. Calculations required for fiscal capacity equalization using a representative tax system for major tax bases are doable for most countries. Fiscal need equalization is best achieved through demand for services approach that allocates funds by service population indicator for each service, for example, school-age population for school finance. Alternately fiscal need equalization can be achieved through output-based sectoral grants that also enhance results-based accountability. A national consensus on the standard of equalization is critically important for the sustainability of any equalization program. The equalization program must not be looked at in isolation from the broader fiscal system, especially conditional transfers. The equalization program must have a sunset clause and provision for formal review and renewal. For local fiscal equalization, one size does not fit all.
- In specific-purpose grant programs, impose conditionality on outputs or standards of access and quality of services rather than on inputs and processes. This allows grantors to achieve their objectives without undermining local choices on how best to deliver such services. Most countries need to establish national minimum standards of basic services across the nation in order to strengthen the internal common market and economic union.
- Recognize population size class, area served, and the urban/rural nature of services in making grants to local governments. Establish separate formula allocations for each type of municipal or local government.

- Establish hold harmless or grandfathering provisions that ensure that all recipient governments receive at least what they received as general-purpose transfers in the pre-reform period. Over time, as the economy grows, such a provision would not delay the phase-in of the full package of reforms.
- Make sure that all stakeholders are heard and that an appropriate political compact (agreement or consensus) on equalization principles and the standard of equalization is struck. Politics must be internalized in these institutional arrangements. Arms-length institutions, such as independent grant commissions, are not helpful, as they do not allow for political input and therefore tend to opt for complex and nontransparent solutions.

Concluding Remarks

This chapter has reviewed the practice of central/state-local fiscal transfers. Local governance works best when municipal services are self-financed and social services are mostly grant financed. The design of these transfers has important implications for F.A.I.R. governance. The chapter emphasized the critical importance of consistency of grant design with its objectives and having separate grant programs to achieve each objective and separately for each class/size or urban/rural character of local governments. A review of the international practice reveals that in industrial countries, the role of local government is expansive (nearly two-thirds of consolidated public expenditures in Nordic countries); local governments that enjoy significant fiscal autonomy are mostly self-financed for municipal services but are grant financed for social services (education, health, and social welfare). In addition, local fiscal equalization receives priority attention in grant structure and design. Further, overall higher-level grants finance a smaller proportion of local government expenditures, that is less than 20 percent in most OECD countries. In developing countries (with the sole exception of China where local governments account for two-thirds of consolidated public expenditures), role of local government in provision of public services is highly constrained (accounting for 1–10 percent of consolidated public expenditures), fiscal autonomy is also highly constrained, and local governments are treated as wards of the state. They typically self-finance less than 25 percent of their expenditures and receive manna from heaven formula-based one-size-fit-all transfers to meet most of their operating expenditures. These operating transfers mostly take the form of gap-filling revenue sharing through formula-based allocation. These transfers are objective and transparent but undermine incentives for better service delivery and accountability to local residents. Capital grants are in some cases formula based and use a Christmas tree approach to allocating capital finance distributing small amounts to every unit but not having enough funds to overcome local infrastructure deficiencies as done in Indonesia. Alternately as in most developing countries, capital grants are distributed on an ad hoc nontransparent and discretionary basis with highly intrusive grant conditions that undermine local autonomy and accountability. Members of legislature typically also receive individual grants for their own constituencies. These grants undermine integrity and autonomy of local governance and may create white elephants that may impose undue financing burdens on local governments for upkeep of these projects.

Economic growth, international competitiveness, local economic development concerns dictate an expansive role of local governments in public governance. This role implies that local governments should enjoy home rule and fiscal autonomy. Such fiscal autonomy could be achieved by expanding local government access to productive tax bases and user charges and allowing local governments piggybacking on central and state taxes. In addition, states should facilitate regulated access to capital market finance for infrastructure projects by creditworthy local governments. This would ensure that local governments would be able to finance own municipal expenditures. Grant financing instead should focus on financing state minimum standards of merit social services, overcoming interlocal infrastructure deficiencies from defined and affordable state/national minimum standards and ensuring interlocal fiscal equalization so that all the residents of the state could enjoy access to reasonably comparable levels of public services at reasonably comparable local tax burdens. This is an unfulfilled and ambitious reform agenda for most developing countries that have come a long distance in recent decades in moving from an opaque, negotiated system of fiscal transfers to an objective, transparent yet seriously flawed system that provides perverse incentives for citizen-based accountability for results and responsiveness to local preferences. Reform is eternal. We never fully succeed, but we owe it to billions of disempowered and impoverished citizens of the developing world to keep trying.

References

Adeyemi, Oluwatobi. 2013. Local Government and the Challenges of Service Delivery: The Nigerian Experience. *Journal of Sustainable development in Africa* 15 (7): 84–98.

Alok, V.N. 2006. Local Government Organization and Finance: Rural India. Chap. 6 in *Local Governance in Developing Countries*, ed. Anwar Shah, 205–230.

———. 2008. The Role of State Finance Commissions in Fiscal Decentralization in India. In *Fiscal Decentralization in India*. New Delhi: Cambridge University Press.

Boadway, Robin, and Anwar Shah. 2007. *Intergovernmental Fiscal Transfers: Theory and the Practice*. Washington, DC: The World Bank.

———. 2009. *Fiscal Federalism: Principles and Practice of Multi-order Governance*. New York and London: Cambridge University Press.

Boothe, Robert, Shabih Mohib, and Anwar Shah. 2011. *Central-Local Fiscal Relations in Thailand*. Bangkok: World Bank.

Deryugin, Alexander, and Galina Kurlyandskaya. 2007. Russian Federation. In ed. Shah. op.cit. 235–261.

Kim, Junghun, and Jorgen Lotz, eds. 2008. *General Grants Versus Earmarked Grants: Theory and Practice*. The Copenhagen Workshop, 2007. Chap. 1, 35–60. Copenhagen: Schultz Grafisk a/s.

Kim, Junghun, Jorgen Lotz, and Niels Jorgen Mau, eds. 2010. *General Grants Versus Earmarked Grants: Theory and Practice*. The Copenhagen Workshop, 2009. Chap. 2, 74–106. Copenhagen: Rosendahls- Schultz Grafisk a/s.

Mathur, Om Prakash. 2006. Local Government Organization and Finance: Urban India. Chap. 5 in *Local Governance in Developing Countries*, ed. Anwar Shah, 169–204.

Mohanty, P.K. 2015. *Intergovernmental Fiscal System in India*. Presentation at the International Seminar on Management of Intergovernmental Fiscal Relations, Thimphu, Bhutan, December 7.

Shah, Anwar. 1991. *The New Fiscal Federalism in Brazil*. Washington, DC: World Bank.

———. 1994. *The Reform of Intergovernmental Fiscal Relations in Developing and Emerging Market Economies, 1994*. Policy and Research Series 23. Washington, DC: World Bank.

———. 2003. *The Reform of Provincial-Local Fiscal Transfers in Pakistan*. Unpublished Report, Word Bank, Washington, DC.

———. 2007a. A Practitioner's Guide to Intergovernmental Fiscal Transfers. Chap. 1 in *Intergovernmental Fiscal Transfers*, ed. Robin Boadway, and Anwar Shah, 1–54. Washington, DC: World Bank.

———, ed. 2007b. *The Practice of Fiscal Federalism: Comparative Perspectives*. Montreal and London: McGill-Queen's University Press.

———. 2012. *Autonomy with Equity and Accountability: Towards a More Transparent, Objective, Predictable and Simpler (TOPS) System of Central Financing of Provincial-Local Expenditures in Indonesia*. World Bank Policy Research Working Paper Series WPS6004, March, World Bank, Washington, DC.

———. 2014. *The Reform of Fiscal System of the People's Republic of China (PRC): An External Perspective*. Unpublished Paper, Southwestern University of Finance and Economics, Chengdu and Wenjiang.

———. 2015. *Financing Subnational Governments in Ethiopia: Options to Enhance Fairness, Objectivity. Transparency and Simplicity of Federal and Regional Fiscal Transfers*. June 2015 Report, Governance Global Practice, World Bank, Washington, DC.

———. 2017. *Reforming Local Governments to Work Better, Cost Less, Facilitate Urbanization and Inclusive Economic Growth: An Emerging Success Story From Hubei 'Province-Managing County' Reforms*. Unpublished Paper, World Bank, Beijing Office.

Shah, Anwar, Riatu Qibthiyyah, and Astrid Dita. 2012. *General Purpose Central-provincial-local Transfers (DAU) in Indonesia: From Gap Filling to Ensuring Fair Access to Essential Public Services for All*. Policy Research Working Paper No. 6075, World Bank, Washington, DC.

Slack, Enid, Melville McMillan, Harry Kitchen, and Francois Vaillancourt. 2007. *Roles, Responsibilities, Resources and Relationships. Report to the Provincial*. Territorial and Municipal Associations. Toronto, June 15.

South Africa, Government of. 2006. *Budget, 29006: National Budget Review*. Pretoria: Government Printing Office.

Zulkarnay, Ildar. 2003. Fiscal Equalization in the Russian Federation. In *Dilemmas and Compromises: Fiscal Equalization in Transition Countries*, ed. Sergei Slukhai, 65–106. Budapest: Open Society Institute.

CHAPTER 14

Higher-Order Government Financing of Metropolitan Areas

Introduction

The allure of metropolitan areas is irresistible for a large majority of people. Metropolitan areas promise good jobs, good homes, a good life, a good time for the young and the young at heart, and sweet dreams of a prosperous future for all (see Inman 2005). In an information age with a borderless world economy where economic success is more closely tied to the competitive advantage as opposed to hackneyed notions of comparative advantage, metropolitan governments are at the core of the future prosperity of a nation. In an age of mistrust in governments, metropolitan governments serve as a tool to overcome a lack of trust and restore confidence in governments through their commitment to improve social and economic outcomes.

These great expectations however are critically linked with the fiscal health of metropolitan areas. Fiscal health is closely tied to the fiscal regimes available; in particular, the taxing powers and other financing options such as grant and bond financing. This chapter is concerned with

This chapter is a revised version of Anwar Shah (2013). "Grant Financing of Metropolitan Areas: A Review of Principles and Worldwide Practices." In Roy Bahl, Johannes Linn and Deborah Wetzel (2013). *Metropolitan Governance and Finance in Developing Countries*. Cambridge, Mass.: Lincoln Institute of Land Policy. The author is grateful to the editors and the Lincoln Institute for granting permission for republication.

H. Kitchen et al., *Local Public Finance and Economics*,
https://doi.org/10.1007/978-3-030-21986-4_14

a critical aspect of this financing—mainly higher-level fiscal transfers. While these transfers may not be the dominant source of revenues for a large number of metropolitan areas, they have a significant bearing on the incentives and accountabilities and associated impacts on fiscal health of metropolitan areas. The design of these transfers requires a careful thought on special features of metropolitan areas that distinguish them from smaller local government entities.

Most metropolitan areas have large populations, typically in excess of one million. Mumbai, India, has a population of 21 million and Istanbul, Turkey, has a population of 13 million. Metropolitan areas are larger and compact areas with higher population densities than the rest of the nation. This compactness facilitates agglomeration economies as well as making metropolitan areas centers of arts and culture and learning and sources of innovation, growth, and productivity. They also afford better transportation and communication facilities and overall a better quality of life. This leads to a larger concentration of specialized skills and wealth, and on the downside, higher incidence of crime and poverty. Metro areas have typically much broader responsibilities than smaller local governments. Beyond municipal services, these encompass health, welfare, and hub functions for national and international finance, trade, and economic links. Because of this in some countries metro areas are treated as provinces/ states. Examples include Canberra in Australia; Bangkok in Thailand; Beijing and Shanghai in China; Tokyo in Japan; Seoul and Busan in South Korea; Berlin, Bremen, and Hamburg in Germany; Helsinki in Finland; and others. Metro areas typically have multiple local jurisdictions and, in some cases, multiple tiers of local jurisdictions. Metropolitan areas also have a typically larger revenue base and greater tax autonomy and therefore greater potential for self-finance (Bird and Slack 2004, Chernick and Reschovsky 2006, Kubler and Rochat 2010).

In view of this, grant financing needs of metro areas are very different from other local governments. If taxing powers are adequately decentralized, there may in fact be no need for grant financing of operating expenditures of metro areas as demonstrated by Tokyo and Seoul. This, however, is not the case for most metropolitan areas. They lack autonomy in taxing powers. They have limited access to dynamic productive tax bases. Existing tax bases, especially property tax bases, are overtaxed to finance municipal and education services, for example, in the United States and Canada, leaving little room to grow. In the United States, this problem is compounded by limits on local revenues and unfunded mandates in environmental and social spending. In most developing countries metro governments lack administrative and fiscal autonomy and act as wards of the state and pied pipers of national and provincial governments. They are hamstring to play a leadership role in local economic development. In these circumstances grant financing can play an important role but grants must be tailored to specific circumstances of metro areas, especially their broader role in local, national, and international governance with an expanded array of responsibilities associated with serving as nodes of national and international connectivity and special needs of a knowledge-based local economy. Grant design also must incorporate incentives and accountability mechanisms to ensure responsible and accountable local governance. This chapter provides a synthesis on conceptual underpinnings of this literature as well as providing a brief overview of practices across the world based upon a review of 41 metropolitan areas. It must be noted at the outset that the assignment of responsibilities must underpin any design of grant program (see McMillan 2008). With appropriate assignments or reassignments, it is possible to minimize need for higher-level assistance for metropolitan areas. However, this chapter takes these assignments (or mis-assignments) in practice as given and examines options in grant design to facilitate better functioning of metropolitan governance. An overall theme of this chapter is that grants can be (and should be) properly designed in almost any institutional/organizational setting—even if the organizational setting may not seem to be ideal.

The rest of the chapter is organized as follows. The section "Grant Instruments, Rationale, and Relevance for Metropolitan Areas" provides a typology of grant instruments and discusses their rationale and relevance for metro areas. The section "Models of Metropolitan Governance and Implications for Higher-Level Fiscal Transfers" outlines stylized models of metropolitan governance and draws implications for the design of higher-level transfers. It also discusses implications of existing institutional arrangements for developing a grant strategy for metropolitan financing. The section "Grant Financing of Metropolitan Areas: The Practice" provides a review of worldwide practices in grant financing of metro areas. This is done (a) by type of metropolitan governance and (b) by type of country. The section "Conceptual Guidance Versus Practice: Notable Points of Departure" highlights the divergence of the practice in grant financing from theory. The section "Lessons from International Practices and an Agenda for Reform" draws lessons from grant financing of metropolitan areas and develops an agenda for reform.

Grant Instruments, Rationale, and Relevance for Metropolitan Areas

Grant Instruments

Instruments of intergovernmental finance have important bearings on efficiency, equity, and accountability in governance. These are discussed below.

Tax Base, Tax Yield, and Revenue-Sharing Mechanisms

Tax-base sharing (metropolitan areas levy supplementary taxes on national bases), tax yield sharing, and revenue-sharing mechanisms are customarily used to address fiscal gaps or mismatched revenue means and expenditure needs arising from constitutional assignment of taxes and expenditures to different levels of governments. Tax-base sharing means that two or more levels of government levy rates on a common base. Tax-base determination usually rests with the higher-level government with lower orders of government levying supplementary rates on the same base. Tax collection is by one level of government, generally the central government in most countries, with proceeds shared downward or upward depending on revenue collection arrangements. Metropolitan Bangkok levies a surcharge on central value-added taxes, excise taxes, business taxes, liquor, gambling, and horse racing licenses and taxes. Tax-base sharing is quite common in Eastern Europe and East Asia but almost nonexistent in most developing countries in Asia and Africa.

A second method of addressing vertical fiscal gap is tax yield sharing. Typically, central government collects shared taxes and apportions these on pre-specified shares on a tax by tax basis to jurisdictions of origin. Tax sharing contributes to collection efficiency but may introduce disincentives for the government collecting taxes to make relatively less effort on taxes it has to share with other governments. Tax by tax sharing is quite common in developing countries. Metropolitan Jakarta receives a fixed share of personal income, property taxes, and natural resource revenues collected by the central government in its jurisdiction.

A third method of addressing vertical fiscal gaps is revenue sharing, whereby one level of government has unconditional access to a specified share of revenues collected by another level. Typically, not all revenues of the higher-level government but only a specified set of revenue sources is subject to pooling for revenue sharing using a formula. Revenue-sharing agreements typically specify how revenues are to be shared among national and lower-level governments, with complex criteria for allocation among lower-level governments and sometimes imposing conditions for the eligibility and use of funds. The latter limitations if imposed run counter to the underlying rationale of unconditionality. Revenue-sharing mechanisms are quite common in developing countries. They often address multiple objectives, such as bridging fiscal gap, promoting fiscal equalization and regional development, and stimulating tax effort at lower levels. Metropolitan cities in India receive funds from both central and state revenue-sharing mechanisms. Metropolitan areas in Brazil receive transfers from state revenue-sharing mechanisms for municipal governments—the so-called Municipal Participation Funds.

Intergovernmental Grants
Chapter 12 provided a review of grants and their relevance for metropolitan areas (see also Boadway and Shah 2007, 2009). The role of grant financing is closely linked to the service delivery responsibilities of each metropolitan area and several of these services are not suitable for grant finance. A reader is invited to revisit the relevant sections for a discussion of these issues.

Grant Objectives and the Choice of Grant Instruments: A Stylized View
In concluding this section, it is useful to summarize the choice of grant instrument in meeting specific objectives. This taxonomy of grants by objective is not specific to grant financing of metropolitan areas but is broadly applicable.

Bridging vertical fiscal gaps. Reassignment of responsibilities, tax decentralization, tax abatement accompanied by tax-base sharing would be preferred instruments. Tax by tax sharing and deficit grants are less desirable alternatives.

Setting national minimum standards. Output-based grants with conditions on service standards would be desirable. Conditional input-based grants are less desirable.

Overcoming infrastructure deficiencies in establishing national minimum standards. Conditional capital grants based upon a planning view with matching rates that vary inversely with local fiscal capacity.

Compensating benefit spillovers. Matching grant with matching rate consistent with the spillover of benefits.

Influencing local priorities that are in conflict with national priorities. Open-ended matching grant desirable.

Promoting competition among local governments. Project or output-based grants using certification to meet pre-specified standards or tournament-based approach to reward top performers would be desirable.

Interlocal equalization. Fiscal capacity equalization with explicit standard using Robin Hood approach where richer jurisdictions contribute to the pool and poorer jurisdictions receive financing from the pool would be desirable.

Models of Metropolitan Governance and Implications for Higher-Level Fiscal Transfers

Metropolitan areas could be broadly grouped into six areas based upon the level of coordination or centralization of metropolitan governance.

I. *Unitary governance.* Under this model, the metropolitan area has single unified or uni-city or single-tier coordinated governance. Examples of this governance include Prague, Yogyakarta, Addis Ababa, Pretoria, Bern, London, Melbourne, and Toronto. Yogyakarta has a joint secretariat comprising heads of the municipality of Yogyakarta and the districts of Sleman and Bantul for harmonization of infrastructure development with special emphasis on solid waste and waste water management. Such governance arrangements offer the potential that metropolitan area will be largely self-financed if it is given adequate fiscal autonomy. Canberra, Australia, is unique in this group as it is a city-state with single-tier governance. It has an elected assembly based upon proportional party representation. The Assembly chooses the Chief Minister.

II. *Vertically coordinated metropolitan governance.* These are typically provincial (state) cities having both the status of a state or province as well as being a metropolitan city. Governance structure usually comprises two tiers with the lower tier either serving as a deconcentrated arm of the upper tier, although having a directly elected council to provide oversight on central administration at the district or ward level as in Bangkok, or having autonomy for some local/neighborhood services as in Beijing, Tokyo, and Madrid.

These jurisdictions by virtue of having city-state status have the potential to be largely self-financing. Also, intra-metropolitan spill-overs are internalized with such governance arrangements. Examples of metropolitan areas having city-state status include Istanbul, Tirana, Warsaw, Zagreb, Bangkok, Beijing, Shanghai, Berlin, Brussels, Busan, Madrid, Montreal, Seoul, and Tokyo. Istanbul has a two-tier unified structure. The metropolitan municipality has 73 lower-tier municipalities. The upper-tier municipality has the power to override or approve lower-tier decisions. Tirana, Albania, has two-tier coordinated governance with the upper tier governed by the Municipal Council and directly elected mayor and 11 sub-municipal units have directly elected councils and executive heads. Warsaw is treated as an urban county with 18 districts. Each district has a directly elected district council and district executive. Warsaw capital region is governed by a directly elected Warsaw Council and is responsible for metropolitan tasks. It coordinates these tasks through district offices. Zagreb, Croatia, has a two-tier governance structure with the top tier comprising a joint council of the city and the Zagreb County. Both the city and the county assembly elect two members each to joint council and the joint council is chaired on a rotating basis between the city mayor and the county governor. Bangkok, Thailand, is a single-tier provincial city covering the entire Bangkok metro area. The Bangkok Metropolitan Area Council comprises 57 councilors, one each for 100,000 people. The Bangkok Metropolitan Area (BMA) is divided into 18 districts each with its own directly elected council to supervise BMA offices. The BMA chief executive is elected at large for a four-year term. The Governor is assisted in executive functions by a centrally appointed civil servant—permanent secretary. Brussels Capital Region, Belgium, has a higher-tier region with an elected parliament and a centrally appointed government responsible for municipal laws and supervision and regional infrastructure, housing, and environment. The lower tier has directly elected councils responsible for education, health, police, and municipal services. Madrid, Spain, comprises the Community of Madrid (CM) that includes 179 municipalities including the City of Madrid. The CM is responsible for regional infrastructure, education, and health, and at the lower-tier Madrid City and municipalities have elected councils and mayors (with dual role as council chair and chief executive) responsible for all municipal services. Montreal, Canada, comprises metropolitan cities of Montreal, Longueil, and Laval and 63 municipalities. It has a two-tier governance structure with the upper tier—the so-called Montreal Metropolitan Community—responsible for coordination of a few selected services. Seoul metropolitan area has an upper tier—Seoul Metropolitan Government—with provincial status and 25 autonomous lower-tier municipalities. Tokyo Metropolitan Government has a prefecture or regional government status with 23 special wards, 26 cities, 5 towns, and 8 villages performing lower-tier functions.

III. *Horizontally coordinated mandatory two-tier metropolitan governance.* Under this structure both upper tier and lower tier have well-defined independent responsibilities. Examples include Belgrade, Serbia; Skopje, Macedonia; and Copenhagen, Denmark. Belgrade has a directly elected city mayor and assembly as the first/upper tier and 17 municipalities with a directly elected municipal assembly and municipal chair elected by each assembly as the second/lower tier. Skopje, Macedonia, has a similar governance structure with the city as the first/upper tier and ten municipalities as the second/lower tier. Copenhagen Metropolitan Region, Denmark, has a directly elected regional council as the first/upper tier responsible for intermunicipal coordination and health services and 45 municipalities delivering all local-municipal services including education at the second tier. Grant financing needs of such governments would be limited to mass transit, social services financing, benefit-spillover compensation, and intra-metropolitan equalization.

IV. *Horizontally coordinated voluntary two-tier metropolitan governance.* Under this governance structure metropolitan areas comprise multiple local jurisdictions which voluntarily cooperate with each other on selected metro-wide functions as well as deliver some services jointly through partnership agreements. Examples include Helsinki, Finland (24 municipalities), and Vancouver, Canada. In both cases, upper tier represents partnership arrangement among municipalities in the metropolitan area. Grant financing needs of such areas are primarily for mass transit and social services and intra-metropolitan equalization.

V. *Uncoordinated two-tier metropolitan governance.* Regional and local governments co-exist with little formal coordination mechanisms either horizontally or vertically. Examples include Bucharest in Romania and Chisinau in Moldova. Bucharest has a directly elected autonomous but uncoordinated two-tier system with the city having a council and a mayor serving as the top tier and six sectors (districts) serving as second-tier municipalities. Metropolitan Chisinau comprises the capital city of Chisinau and 18 territorial local government units with each having independent legislative and administrative organs. The upper-tier municipality has a directly elected Municipal Council and General Mayor. The municipality is responsible for metro-wide regulation of land and residential property, coordination of social and economic development, civil and social protection, public order and emergency regime, and response. All other local functions are performed by the city and municipalities. These governance arrangements require separate and substantive needs for intergovernmental finance including intra-metropolitan equalization.

VI. *Uncoordinated/fragmented single-tier metropolitan governance.* Several independent local jurisdictions sometimes belonging to different states and provinces deliver services in sub-areas with little coordination. Examples include Mexico City, Chennai, Delhi, Hyderabad, Jakarta, Kolkata, Mumbai, Poona, Abuja, Cape Town, Milan, and Washington DC metropolitan area. Mexico City Metropolitan Area comprises the Federal Capital district with 16 districts (delegaciones), 58 municipalities of the State of Mexico, and 1 municipality of the State of Hidalgo. These jurisdictions are uncoordinated, although a plethora of coordinating agencies/commissions and planning bodies exist. Chennai Metropolitan Area, India, comprises 1 municipal corporation (Chennai), 8 municipalities, 26 town panchayats, and 1 Cantonment Board. These 36 governments are uncoordinated. Similarly, Delhi, India, has three uncoordinated local governments—Municipal Corporation of Delhi, New Delhi Municipal Corporation, and Delhi Cantonment Board (Bandyopadhyay and Rao 2009, Sridhar et al. 2008b). Jakarta Metropolitan Area (JMA) comprises the City of Jakarta, three urban municipalities, and three rural municipalities (districts) belonging to three provinces, Jakarta, Banten, and West Java. Governance structure in JMA is a single tier uncoordinated, although an inter-governmental cooperation agency, Badan Kerja Sama Pembangunan—BKSP—has been established that brings together all heads of provincial and local governments to promote task coordination. Washington, DC Metropolitan Area includes Washington, DC, municipalities in Northern part of the State of Virginia, and parts of the State of Maryland. Milan represents a special case as according to the 1990 law it is supposed to have a two-tier structure with the higher tier—metropolitan city—having a provincial status performing regional functions and lower-tier municipalities within the metro region performing municipal functions. However, it still operates as a single-tier uncoordinated metropolitan area with multiple jurisdictions. There is little coordination among multiple local jurisdictions in the metro area. Such fragmented governance maximizes the need for higher-level financing.

Table 14.1 provides a stylized view of grant financing, taking into account the governance and finance model adopted for the metropolitan area. If the "finance follows functions" principle is adopted, then metropolitan areas should have significant taxing powers such that their revenue means would be largely consistent with their expenditure needs so that the needs for higher-level transfers to metropolitan areas will be minimized. They would still need transfers or other compensatory arrangements to compensate them for spillover of benefits to nonresidents for use of metro services. It would also be desirable to provide them with assistance in financing redistributive services as local financing of such services would lead to an erosion of their tax bases. For horizontally coordinated or fragmented metro governance, in addition, some grant mechanisms for intra-metropolitan equalization would also have to be examined.

In the event, taxing powers are not commensurate with metropolitan responsibilities and a large vertical gap persists, a menu of tax decentralization and grant financing options would have to be explored regardless of the governance structure. In addition, for horizontally coordinated or fragmented governance models, intra-metropolitan equalization alternatives would have to be examined. Competitive grants also are important for improving metro-wide performance through incentives for performance excellence (see Table 14.1).

So far, we have highlighted the implications of the metropolitan governance and finance models for grant design. These are critical elements for developing a grant strategy for metropolitan areas. Several additional issues in developing such a strategy also require discussion.

Table 14.1 Models of metropolitan governance and finance and implications for grant design

Governance model	*Revenue means match responsibilities or finance follows functions*	*In the presence of large vertical fiscal gap*
I. Fully integrated metropolitan governance Examples: uni-city model as in Toronto and most developing countries	Grants or partnership agreements for spillovers to nonmetro jurisdictions Grants for redistributive services, e.g., education, health, and social welfare	Tax-base sharing Grants for interjurisdictional spillovers Grants for redistributive services Equalization grants Capital grant
II. Provincial-city model with multiple tiers as in Beijing, Seoul, Tokyo, Bangkok	Grants or partnership agreements for spillovers to nonmetro jurisdictions Grants for redistributive services, e.g., education, health, and social welfare	Tax-base sharing Grants for interjurisdictional spillovers Grants for redistributive services Equalization grants Capital grant
III. Horizontally coordinated Mandatory two-tier metro governance with multiple jurisdictions as in Copenhagen	Grants or partnership agreements for spillovers to metro and nonmetro jurisdictions Grants for redistributive services, e.g., education, health, and social welfare Equalization grants (inter and intra) Capital grants Competitive grants	Tax-base sharing Grants for interjurisdictional spillovers Grants for redistributive services Equalization grants (inter and intra) Capital grants Competitive grants
IV. Horizontally coordinated voluntary two-tier metro governance with multiple jurisdictions as Vancouver and Helsinki	Grants or partnership agreements for spillovers to metro and nonmetro jurisdictions Grants for redistributive services, e.g., education, health, and social welfare Equalization grants (inter and intra) Capital grants Competitive grants	Tax-base sharing Grants for interjurisdictional spillovers Grants for redistributive services Equalization grants (inter and intra) Capital grants Competitive grants

(*continued*)

Table 14.1 (continued)

Governance model	*Revenue means match responsibilities or finance follows functions*	*In the presence of large vertical fiscal gap*
V. Two-tier uncoordinated as in Bucharest and Chisinau	Grants or partnership agreements for spill outs to metro and nonmetro jurisdictions Grants for redistributive services, e.g., education, health, and welfare Equalization grants (inter and intra) Capital grants Competitive grants	Tax-base sharing Grants for interjurisdictional spillovers Grants for redistributive services Equalization grants (inter and intra) Capital grants Competitive grants
VI. Uncoordinated/ fragmented single-tier metropolitan governance as in Washington Metro Area or Mexico City	Grants or partnership agreements for spill outs to metro and nonmetro jurisdictions Grants for redistributive services, e.g., education, health, and welfare Equalization grants (inter and intra) Capital grants Competitive grants	Tax-base sharing Grants for interjurisdictional spillovers Grants for redistributive services Equalization grants (inter and intra) Capital grants Competitive grants

Source: Authors' illustration

Additional Considerations in Developing a Grant Strategy for Metro Areas

Autonomous public agencies for service delivery. Some metro-wide services are delivered by autonomous public agencies run on commercial principles rather than by general government. Such practice is quite widespread for water, sanitation, gas, electricity, and toll roads. These arrangements should have no bearing on grant design as the case for grant finance should be based on the objectives and results sought and should not be linked to the management paradigm for such services.

Functional, overlapping, and competing jurisdictions. Under such arrangements jurisdictions are organized along functional lines but overlap geographically within the metropolitan areas. Individuals and communities express their preferences directly through initiatives and referenda (see Frey and Eichenberger 1995). The jurisdictions could have authority over their members and the power to raises taxes and fees to fulfill their tasks. The school communities of Zurich metropolitan areas and special districts and boards in North America follow this concept in practice. Output-based grants are a suitable tool to finance such jurisdictions.

Fragmentation of metropolitan governance through proliferation of single-purpose jurisdictions. Special-purpose jurisdictions with access to tax finance are quite common in metropolitan areas in industrial countries. Most common example of such jurisdictions is school boards with access to supplementary rates on residential property tax base. Proliferation of these agencies leaves municipal services with inadequate finance as existing tax bases especially property taxes are overtaxed with little or no room to grow. These problems are sometimes further compounded by limits on raising local revenues and unfunded higher-level mandates in environmental and social spending as has been the case for metropolitan areas of San Francisco and Los Angeles in the United States. Decline in general-purpose or equalization transfers exacerbate this problem. Matching conditions for specific-purpose transfers do not help either. In designing a metropolitan grant strategy, these considerations have to be kept in mind so as to ensure that metropolitan governments have adequate resources to deliver municipal services.

Contracting out metropolitan services. Metropolitan governments may choose to deliver some services through contractual arrangements or through concessions or franchises. For some services, they could use multiple providers to achieve more efficient provision outcomes. In such circumstances grant design must ensure that service quality and access to the poor are not compromised. Output-based grants are an ideal tool to have this assurance.

Grant Financing of Metropolitan Areas: The Practice

A review of international practices on grant financing of metropolitan areas is constrained by the scant details available even for metro areas in industrial countries. The data limitations restricted our sample to 41 metropolitan areas worldwide. To capture the diversity of experiences, the sample was organized using two alternative classifications—(b) by type of metropolitan governance and (b) by the use of four-tier typology of countries.

The Practice by Type of Metropolitan Governance

I. *Unitary governance (unified or uni-city metro or unified single-tier multi-jurisdiction governance).* Ten sample areas fall in this category. Contrary to expectations, grant financing is an important source of finance for most metro areas with the notable exception of Addis Ababa, Pretoria, and Melbourne, which are largely self-financed. Close behind these leaders are Toronto (Kitchen 2010) and Bern. London is an outlier receiving more than 80 percent of funds from central grant finance. Tax sharing is dominant for Prague only in this sample. Overall for the sample as a whole 9.4 percent of financing comes from tax sharing, 16.4 percent from general-purpose or equalization transfers, 13.7 percent from specific-purpose transfers, and the remaining 60.9 percent is self-financed (see Table 14.2). In this cluster, Prague relies significantly on revenue sharing from personal income and value-added taxes. Revenue sharing is by the number of inhabitants multiplied by the coefficient of the size category of municipality. Prague has a coefficient of 2.7611 (Kubatova and Pavel 2009). In this sample Prague is the only metropolitan area receiving special treatment due to its size class. All other metro areas are treated in similar manner to other municipalities. Metropolitan London is an outlier in view of its predominant reliance on central transfers and having the most constrained access to own finances. It receives 25.6 percent from revenue-sharing transfers (the so-called Revenue Support plus redistributed non-domestic rate grant) and 55 percent as specific-purpose transfers, of which the police grant amounts to 5.3 percent and the area-based grant contributes 2.4 percent to total amount of specific-purpose transfers (UK Government 2010).

II. *Unified two-tier governance—city-state metro areas.* Fourteen sample areas have this type of governance. However, there is a great diversity in central financing of these areas.

Metro Istanbul is treated just like another local government with revenue sharing based upon population and 5 percent of centrally collected revenues returned by origin (OECD 2008).

Tirana receives central general-purpose transfers based upon population (70 percent), area (15 percent), and urban services (15 percent for other local governments, 0 percent weight for Tirana). Corporate Income Tax Sharing is mandated by law but not implemented as 80 percent of national revenues are collected in Tirana. Thus, in general the general-purpose transfers discriminate against Tirana. It should be noted that Albania is among the handful of countries (Russia being another) that operates a competitive grant program. The program was initiated in 2006

Table 14.2 Grant financing of uni-city and city-state metro areas (percent of total revenues)

Metro Area	*Population (Million)*	*Tax Sharing*	*General Purpose Transfers (GPT)*	*Specific Purpose Transfers (SPT)*	*Total grants (TG)*	*Total Transfers (TT)*	*Own source revenues (OSR)*
I. Uni-city metro areas ($n = 9$)							
Addis Ababa	3.1				3.1	3.1	96.9
Pretoria	2.0				9.9	9.9	90.1
Melbourne	3.5				14.2	14.2	85.8
Toronto	5.1			24.0	24.0	24.0	76.0
Bern	0.3				24.4	24.4	75.6
Canberra	0.3		27.8	14.6	42.4	42.4	57.6
Prague	2.3	40.4	na	na	19.3	59.7	40.3
Yogyakarta	2.0		66.5	7.2	73.7	73.7	26.2
London	7.2		25.6	53.0	80.6	80.6	19.4
Average (I)	2.9	4.5	16.4	13.7	32.4	36.9	63.1
II. Unified two-tier governance—city-state metro areas ($n = 14$)							
Tokyo	13.0				5.7	5.7	94.3
Seoul	10.4	0.8			8.3	9.1	90.9
Busan	3.7	3.0	2.0	13.0	15.0	18.0	82.0
Montreal	3.4				24.0	24.0	76.0
Tirana	0.6		8.5	17.9	26.4	26.4	73.6
Brussels	1.0	36.0	3.0		3.0	39.0	61.0
Bangkok	2.5	24.0	7.0	20.0	27.0	51.0	49.0
Beijing	15.0	29.2	16.6	5.2	21.8	51.0	49.0
Warsaw	1.7	40.0	Na	na	14.0	54.0	46.0
Shanghai	17.4	32.9	24.7	1.5	26.2	59.1	40.9
Zagreb	0.8	67.7	0	0.1	0.1	67.8	32.2
Madrid	6.0	64.0		5.0	5.0	69.0	31.0
community (city)	(3.1)				(39.0)	(39.0)	(71.0)
Istanbul	13.4	65.0	10.0	0.0	10.0	75.0	25.0
Berlin	3.4	39.1	18.3	21.9	40.2	79.3	20.7
Average (II)	5.4	28.7	6.4	12.2	18.6	47.3	53.7

POP: Population in millions (most recent year); TS: tax sharing (may include tax-base sharing); GPT: general-purpose transfers; SPT: specific-purpose transfers; TG = total grants (=GPT + SPT); TT: total transfers (=TS + TG); OSR: own-source revenues

Source: Shah (2013, p. 226) For details on individual metro areas see OECD (2001, 2003a,b, 2004a,b,c, 2005a,b, 2006a,b, 2007, 2008a,b, 2009, 2010)

with a pool as large as the general-purpose transfers and finances local capacity investment in education, health, water supply, and general municipal infrastructure. The criteria for allocation includes expected impact on economic and social development and compliance with local/regional development priorities; impact on poverty reduction and improved access to basic services; projects promoting cooperation among local governments; projects with community participation and funding; funding for the local counterpart of foreign funding; and ongoing projects that have contractual obligations (Dhimitri et al. 2009).

In Warsaw, the most prominent central transfer is for financing the metro subway system (Jefremienko and Wolksa 2007).

Zagreb receives financing from a share of taxes on income (personal and corporate) and real estate transfers and specific-purpose grants. Income tax proceeds are allocated to local government using the following criteria: by origin municipality or town share: 52 percent; county share: 15 percent; share of decentralized functions: 12 percent share of decentralized function realignment. In addition, local government receives a supplementary allocation for decentralized functions: primary education: 3.1 percent; secondary education: 2.2 percent; social welfare centers 0.5 percent; nursing homes 1.7 percent; health care 3.2 percent; and fire protection: 1.3 percent. The metro region also receives 60 percent of the proceeds of the real estate transfer tax derived from the region. General-purpose transfers are available to local governments with below average fiscal capacity based on PIT. Zagreb is not eligible for these transfers. The decentralized functions are financed through specific grants based upon standard costs (Kopric et al. 2007).

In Bangkok Metropolitan Area (BMA) tax sharing, 5 percent of value-added tax and 40 percent of revenues from natural resources and fisheries and teak wood are shared with provinces. Hundred percent of BMA surcharges on central taxes such as VAT, specific business tax, liquor tax, excise tax, liquor and gambling licenses, and gambling tax on horse races are returned by origin. General-purpose transfers have two components: (a) VAT transfer according to the Decentralization Act, 1999. 18.5 percent of VAT revenues are allocated to local governments based upon a formula that includes population, area, revenue, and budget needs. BMA received 5.8 percent of total pool in 2008. (b) The General Duty Transfer: 5 percent of total pool is set aside as deficit/expenditure need grants. Of the remaining 95 percent, 10 percent is allocated to the provinces with 65 percent allocated on a per capita basis and the remaining 35 percent equal per jurisdiction basis. Specific-purpose transfers mostly fulfill central mandates for health, education, public transit, school lunch, support for elderly care, AIDS patients, and disabled persons, social services, and water and environmental services (Boothe et al. 2011).

The Brussels Metropolitan Region receives tax shares proportional to the yield of income taxes in the region. The region also receives equalization payments—under the National Solidarity Intervention (INS) program, when income tax receipts per capita are below national average (Van Wynsberghe 2009).

In Madrid Metro Region, two regimes exist for central transfers for small versus large municipalities. For large municipalities with population in excess of 75,000 the general grant consists of two parts: a tax share of central government taxes and a grant from the Complimentary Fund. Tax shares are 1.7 percent of PIT, 1.8 percent of VAT, and 2 percent of excise revenues. PIT is allocated among municipalities based upon taxes collected locally and VAT and excise shares are distributed by consumption and population shares (OECD 2007, p. 208).

Washington, DC, receives federal grant funds for Medicaid, community development, education, public welfare, and public safety (Gandhi et al. 2009).

For this sample, tax sharing is the most significant if not the predominant source of revenues for metros in European and East Asian countries. For the sample as a whole, tax sharing contributes 28.7 percent, general-purpose transfers 6.4 percent, specific-purpose transfers 12.2 percent to metro revenues, and 53.7 percent of financing is raised from own sources (see Table 14.2). Being provincial cities, most of the metros in this group benefit from greater access to self-finance, but given their greater responsibilities, only about half of their expenditures are self-financed. It is interesting that in the sample countries there is no special recognition of their metropolitan character. Only Spain accords limited recognition to this nature by grouping large urban municipalities together for grant financing. Competitive grant finance is practiced only in Tirana.

III. *Horizontally coordinated with mandatory two-tier governance.* Three sample jurisdictions fall into this category and they vary significantly in their dependence on grant finance.

For Belgrade, Serbia, tax sharing from personal income taxes by origin is the dominant source of revenue. In addition, it receives financing from formula-based general-purpose transfers. Equalization transfers are distributed to local governments with shared revenues per capita below the national average and of course Belgrade does not qualify (Gilorijevic et al. 2009).

Tax sharing from PIT and VAT is the dominant source of revenues for Skopje, Macedonia. Three percent of the revenues from PIT and VAT are transferred to municipalities. Of the PIT pool, the city and its municipalities get a share of 10 percent. Of the VAT pool for municipalities, 12 percent of revenues go to City of Skopje (40 percent share) and its ten municipalities (60 percent share) (Veljanovski 2009).

Copenhagen, Denmark, is primarily self-financed. Denmark has a separate horizontal equalization program for metropolitan areas requiring richer jurisdictions to contribute to the pool and poorer jurisdictions receive assistance from this pool.

For this sub-group, tax sharing is the predominant source of central transfers financing 30.5 percent of metro expenditures, general-purpose transfers finance 7.2 percent, specific-purpose transfers 4.6 percent, and 57.7 percent of financing is raised from local taxes and charges (see Table 14.3). Copenhagen is unique in this sub-group for its participation in horizontal equalization among metro areas.

IV. *Horizontally coordinated voluntary two-tier metro governance*. Of the sample metro areas, only Helsinki, Finland, falls into this category. Helsinki is primarily self-financed and just like Copenhagen, it contributes to a horizontal equalization program.

V. *Uncoordinated two-tier metro governance*. Of the sample jurisdictions, Bucharest, Romania, and Chisinau, Moldova, have uncoordinated two-tier governance structure. Of these Bucharest is primarily transfer financed whereas in Chisinau, own source of finance dominates.

In Bucharest, Romania, PIT and VAT are shared taxes. Metro districts receive 23.5 percent of PIT and General Council receives 47.5 percent and an additional 11 percent for district equalization. VAT sharing is discretionary (past allocation indexed by inflation) and given as lumpsum grants earmarked for salaries and social benefits. Specific-purpose grants are mostly capital grants for streets, rural infrastructure, and school rehabilitation (Ionita 2009).

Chisinau, Moldova, receives financing from personal income tax sharing and formula-based general-purpose transfers (Roscovan and Melnic 2009).

For the sub-group, two-thirds of financing are received from transfers mostly in the form of proceeds from shared taxes and one-third from own sources. There is no special treatment of metro areas in this group.

VI. *Uncoordinated or fragmented single-tier metro governance*. Twelve sample jurisdictions have fragmented single-tier metro jurisdiction, that is, several local governments operate in a metro area without any formal coordination arrangements. There is a wide variation in the role of

Table 14.3 Grant financing under horizontally coordinated or fragmented metro governance (% of total revenues)

Metro Area	*Population (Million)*	*Tax Sharing (TS)*	*General Purpose Transfers (GPT)*	*Specific purpose transfers (SPT)*	*Total grants (TG)*	*Total transfers (TT)*	*Own source revenues (OSR)*
III. Horizontally coordinated with mandatory two-tier governance (*n* = 3)							
Copenhagen	2.4		7.0	10.0	17.0	17.0	83.0
Belgrade	1.7	41.5	9.0	0.1	9.1	50.6	49.4
Skopje	0.5	50.0	5.5	3.7	9.2	59.2	40.8
Average III	1.5	30.5	7.2	4.6	11.8	42.3	57.7
IV. Horizontally coordinated with voluntary two-tier governance (*n* = 1)							
Helsinki	1.2				10.3	10.3	89.7
V. Uncoordinated two-tier governance (*n* = 2)							
Chisinau	0.7	24.0	15.0	5.0	20.0	44.0	56.0
Bucharest	2.0	60.0	7.6	15.4	23.0	83.0	17.0
Average (IV)	1.3	42.0	11.3	10.2	21.5	63.5	36.5
VI. Fragmented single-tier metro governance (*n* = 12)							
Pune	3.8				9.0	9.0	91.0
Cape Town	3.0		20.0		20.0	20.0	80.0
Mumbai	21.0				20.0	20.0	80.0
Washington	5.0		12.0	14.0	26.0	26.0	74.0
Delhi	13.9	17.9			9.0	26.9	73.1
Milan	7.4				33.0	33.0	67.0
Mexico	18.4		38.0	32.0	70.0	70.0	30.0
Chennai	6.3	24.0			10.0	34.0	66.0
Hyderabad	4.1	25.0			15.0	40.0	60.0
Jakarta	18.9	46.3			0.0	46.3	53.7
Kolkata	15.0				58.4	58.4	41.6
Abuja	1.4		60.0		60.0	60.0	40.0
Average (VI)	9.8	9.4			23.1	32.5	67.5

Source: Shah (2013, p. 230)

central/state transfers in financing metro expenditures with Mexico City Metropolitan Region having the highest dependency on these transfers and Pune, India, the least. It should be noted, however, that Mexico delivers a wider range of local services than Pune. Jakarta is noteworthy as it receives only financing from shared taxes.

In the Mexico City Metropolitan Region, there are wide variations in the sources of finance of various jurisdictions. Mexico Federal District finances 37 percent of expenditures from general-purpose transfers and an additional 19 percent from specific-purpose transfers and 45 percent of expenditures are self-financed. The municipality from the State of Hidalgo receives 27 percent of financing from general-purpose transfers, and 66.8 percent from specific-purpose and other transfers and financing 6.8 percent from own sources. The Mexico State municipality receives 39 percent of financing as general-purpose transfers and 35 percent as specific-purpose or other transfers and the remaining 26 percent raised from own sources (OECD 2004a).

Chennai, India, has access to state tax sharing from entertainment tax, motor vehicles tax, and stamp duty surcharge. In addition, it receives general-purpose transfers based upon formula allocation using population and deprivation index. It also receives specific-purpose transfers for education and road maintenance (Sridhar et al. 2008a).

Hyderabad, India, receives a state per capita grant that varies from Rs. 4 (10 cents) in Metropolitan City of Hyderabad to Rs. 202 (US $5) for Alwal (Sridhar et al. 2008c).

Jakarta, Indonesia, is a provincial city. It receives both the provincial and city share from central taxes. Provinces receive by origin 8 percent of PIT and 16 percent of property taxes, property transfer taxes, mining land rent, mining royalty, forestry license, and forestry royalty. Local governments receive by origin 12 percent of PIT, 64 percent of other taxes, and 32 percent of forestry royalty. Provinces receive by origin 3 percent of oil and 6 percent of natural gas revenues. Local governments receive by origin 6 percent of oil and 12 percent of natural gas revenues. It also receives compensation for public sector wages. Just like any other small or large local government, it is also eligible to receive financing of its fiscal gap based upon the difference in its revenues and fiscal needs using population, per capita GDP, Human Development index, and construction price index as need factors. However, Jakarta is considered to have a fiscal surplus and therefore receives no funds from the general-purpose gap-filling transfer. Local governments with below average fiscal capacity are also eligible to receive specific-purpose transfers to meet education, health, infrastructure, and agriculture development needs. Again, Jakarta does not qualify (Shah 2012c).

Abuja, Nigeria, receives revenues from formula-based revenue-sharing transfers from Federal Excess Crude Oil Account, value-added tax, and sale of government properties (Elaigwu 2009).

Cape Town, South Africa, receives general-purpose formula-based transfers that incorporate factors such as relatively poor households, infrastructure deficiencies, and needs for a limited range of services (OECD 2008b, p. 279).

Washington, DC, receives federal grant funds for Medicaid, community development, education, public welfare, and public safety (Gandhi et al. 2009).

There is no sample area receiving a special treatment for being a metropolitan area in this sub-group. For the sub-group as a whole, tax sharing finances about 10 percent of expenditures, grants 23 percent, and financing from remaining 67.5 percent of expenditures come from own sources.

All Metro Areas

There are significant across-group variations in own-source financing of metropolitan expenditures by type of metropolitan governance, with horizontally coordinated two-tier metro areas least dependent on higher-level transfers and metro areas with uncoordinated single-tier governance most dependent (see Fig. 14.1).

While this review has unearthed isolated examples of better practices in grant design (see Table 14.4), an overall conclusion is that almost all countries, industrial and developing alike, do not recognize the governance structure of metropolitan areas, their responsibilities, their unique

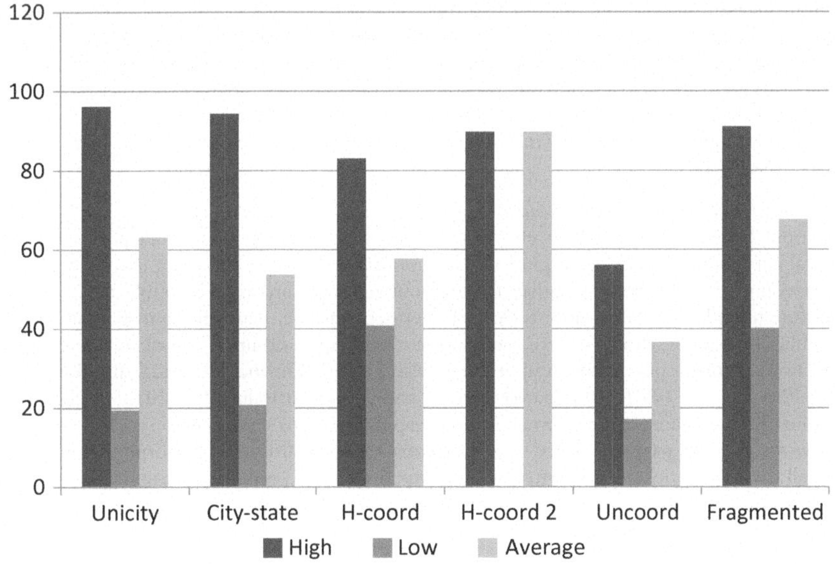

Fig. 14.1 Own-source financing of metropolitan expenditures by type of metro governance. Source: Shah (2013, p. 232)

Table 14.4 Better practices in grant financing of metropolitan areas

Better practices in grant financing of metropolitan areas are hard to find. A few exceptions are noted below
One size does not fit all One size fits all approaches to grant allocation lead to much complexity in allocation criteria and yield inequitable results, for example in Indonesia (Shah 2012a). Most countries adopt a one-size-fits-all approach in grant allocation to local governments. Prague, Czech Republic, is the only metropolitan area receiving special treatment due to its size class in a general-purpose transfer (revenue-sharing) program. The formula used for revenue sharing from PIT and VAT in the Czech Republic assigns a differential coefficient for redistribution depending upon the size class of the municipality with the highest weight assigned to Prague (Kunatova and Pavel 2007). Denmark, Sweden, and Finland represent even better examples as they adopt "one size does not fit all" principle in their central transfers to local governments and group local governments by size class and type of municipality in grant determination (Shah 2012b). Under such an allocation system, metropolitan areas receive more equitable access to central finances.
Grants to promote competition among local jurisdictions These grants create incentives for greater cost efficiency and access in public service provision through interjurisdictional competition. Only in two countries, Albania and Russia, do grant programs have incentive provisions for greater interjurisdictional competition. Albania provides capital grant for social and physical infrastructure to municipalities that can demonstrate that their proposed projects would have greater potential impact on economic and social development and poverty reduction with improved access to basic services. Projects with higher level of own or external financing and intermunicipal cooperation are given priority in grant allocation (Dhimitri et al. 2009). Russia through its Regional Fiscal Reform Fund established in 2007 provides competitive grants to local governments for achieving pre-specified reform objectives (see Zinnes 2009).
Output-based grant for school finance Output-based grants provide incentives for results-based accountability while preserving local autonomy. Output-based grants are not practiced anywhere but grant design in a few countries does create incentives for competitive service provision by public and private providers and albeit indirectly for better performance. Bangkok Metropolitan Area public and private schools receive central grant financing based upon school enrollments. Somewhat similar practices prevail in Brazil (also for health finance), Canada (also for health finance), Chile (through a voucher program), and Australia (Shah 2010a, b). In none of these countries are grant allocation directly linked to service delivery performance, yet parental choice on school enrollment reward better performing schools in all these countries thereby introducing competition and bottom-up accountability for results as schools experiencing higher enrollments receive higher grant financing

(*continued*)

Table 14.4 (continued)

Intermetropolitan and intra-metropolitan equalization
Interjurisdictional equalization serves to equalize per capita fiscal capacity and compensate for differential fiscal needs arising from inherent disabilities so that there is reasonably comparable access to public services at reasonably comparable tax burdens across local jurisdictions. For an equalization program based upon the solidarity principle, rich jurisdictions contribute to the pool and poorer jurisdictions receive financing from the pool. Only Denmark and Finland have such programs for metropolitan areas as a class (Shah 2010a, b).

Tax rebates by origin of collection
Tax rebates by origin provide incentives for local economic development. China returns 25 percent of VAT by origin to its local governments including Shanghai and Beijing (Shah and Shen 2007).

Source: Shah (2013, p. 233)

roles in national and global connectivity in designing transfers to finance metropolitan expenditures. The only exceptions are Denmark and Finland and the Czech Republic. While there are significant differences in the composition of metropolitan finance across different models of metropolitan governance, these differences could not be explained by the nature of the underlying governance structure.

The Practice by Typology of Countries

The sample of 42 metro areas was divided into four country groupings as discussed below and the results are reported in Table 14.5.

Metro Areas in Type I Countries

These are highly urbanized middle-income countries with low to medium rates of expansion of metropolitan areas in a context of slow to medium economic growth performance (mostly Latin America, Europe and Central Asia, and Middle East, and North Africa). A review of ten metro areas was conducted. These include Belgrade, Bucharest, Chisinau, Istanbul, Mexico City, Prague, Skopje, Tirana, Warsaw, and Zagreb. Population range for this sample is from 600,000 in Tirana to 18.4 million in Mexico City. Metro areas in this sample with the exception of Mexico City have extensive local and metropolitan service responsibilities. Tax by tax sharing especially for income and value-added taxes with pre-specified central-local shares dominates central-local transfers. General-purpose central transfers are formula based, transparent, and predictable. Typically,

Table 14.5 Summary statistics on grant financing of metropolitan areas—by typology of countries

Country grouping	*Sample metro areas*	*Range of LG responsibilities*	*Population range*	*Tax sharing % (TS)*	*General-purpose grants % (GPT)*	*Specific-purpose grants % (SPT)*	*Total grants % (TG)*	*Total transfers % (TT)*	*Own-source revenues % (OSR)*
Type I: Highly urbanized middle-income countries with low to medium metro and economic growth rates	10	Wide	600 K (Tirana)–18.4 m (Mexico city)	38.6	14.0	13.9	27.9	59.0	41.0
Type II: Low to medium urbanized middle-income countries with high metro and economic growth rates	12	Narrow to wider	2 m (Yogyakarta)–21 m (Mumbai)	25.2	19.7	9.7	29.4	43.2	56.8
Type III: Low to medium urbanized low-income countries with high metro but low to medium economic growth rates	4	Narrow	1.4 m (Abuja)–3.1 m (Addis Ababa)	0	NA	NA	23.2	23.2	76.8
Type IV: Industrial countries	15	Wider	340 K (Canberra)–13 m (Tokyo)	8.9	13.2	21.4	25.4	34.3	65.7
ALL	41		340 K (Canberra)–21 m (Mumbai)	18.2	15.6	15.0	26.5	39.9	60.1

Source: Shah (2013, p. 235)
Note: All transfers figures are simple averages of sample metro areas expressed in percentage of total revenues

these embody one size fits all formulae that do not recognize special needs of metropolitan areas. Metro areas are at a disadvantage for general-purpose transfers but are assured reasonable financing due to return of fixed proportion of tax yield from major taxes by origin. Overall central transfers inclusive of tax sharing finance 59 percent of metro expenditures (see Table 14.5).

Metro Areas in Type II Countries

These are low to medium urbanized middle-income countries with rapidly growing metropolises in the context of high economic growth (mostly Asia). A review of 12 sample metro areas was conducted. These include Bangkok, Beijing, Brazil metro areas as a group, Chennai, Delhi, Hyderabad, Jakarta, Kolkata, Mumbai, Pune, Shanghai, and Yogyakarta. This represents a diverse sample with Yogyakarta with 2 million people as the smallest metro area and Mumbai with a population of 21 million as the largest metro area. There is also a great diversity in the metropolitan service responsibilities with Beijing and Shanghai having the status of provincial governments and having responsibilities for a wide range of metropolitan services with Chennai, Delhi, Hyderabad, Kolkata, Mumbai, and Pune being responsible primarily for municipal services only with Bangkok (provincial status), Brazil metro areas, Jakarta, and Yogyakarta having intermediate range of metropolitan responsibilities. Tax sharing and tax-base sharing dominate for metro areas with wider powers such Shanghai and Beijing and also for intermediate range of powers such as Bangkok, Jakarta, and Yogyakarta. Specific-purpose transfers have greater prominence in financing Brazil metro areas that have intermediate range of local service responsibilities. Formula-based, one size fits all, general-purpose transfers dominate for metro areas with constrained powers such as Indian metro areas. On average transfers finance 43.2 percent of expenditures in sample metro areas.

Metro Areas in Type III Countries

This grouping of countries includes low to medium urbanized low-income countries with high rates of metropolitan growth but low to medium rates of economic growth (mostly Africa). Four metro areas of Abuja, Addis Ababa, Cape Town, and Pretoria/Tshwane are reviewed. Population range for sample areas is 1.4 million in Abuja to 3.1 million in Addis Ababa. These metro areas have a narrow range of metropolitan responsibilities. Formula based, with a uniform formula for all local governments, revenue-sharing general-purpose transfers dominate. These formulae work to the disadvantage of metro areas. Grants on average finance 23.2 percent of metro expenditures. While local taxes finance most of the expenditures, taxing powers of local governments are highly constrained.

Metro Areas in Type IV Countries
This grouping includes industrial countries. The sample includes 16 metro areas that include: Berlin, Bern, Brussels, Busan, Canberra, Copenhagen, Helsinki, London, Madrid, Melbourne, Milan, Montreal, Seoul, Toronto, Tokyo, and Washington. Population range for this sample is from a low of 340,000 in Canberra to 13 million in Tokyo. There is also wide diversity in the range of metropolitan responsibilities with Tokyo, Seoul, Busan, and Helsinki (all with provincial status) at the high end of the spectrum and Melbourne and London at the lower end and the rest of the sample in between these ranges. Metro areas at the upper end of the spectrum are largely self-financing and at the lower end primarily grant financed. An extreme example is London which had central transfers finance of 81 percent of its expenditures in 2008–2009. For the sample as a whole, specific-purpose transfers with input conditionality dominate higher-level financing. On average central and state transfers finance 34.3 percent of metro expenditures.

All Countries
For the sample as a whole there is a great diversity in the range of metropolitan responsibilities shared by the metro areas with Tokyo, Copenhagen, Helsinki, Seoul, Busan, Shanghai, and Beijing at the top of the totem pole and Melbourne and Indian metro areas such as Mumbai at the bottom end. For the sample average, tax sharing has a slight edge over general and specific-purpose transfers. Nearly 40 percent of metro finances are from central transfers. Eight well-known metropolitan areas in our sample finance two-thirds of their expenditures from higher-level transfers, with Berlin, Bucharest, and London receiving about 80 percent of financing from such transfers (see Fig. 14.2).

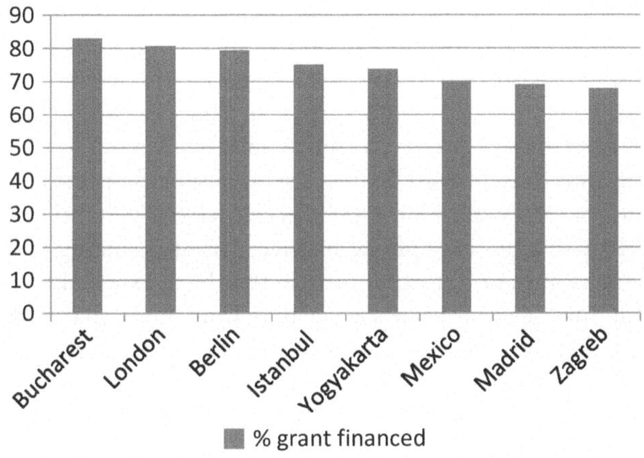

Fig. 14.2 Metro areas with greater than 66 percent grant financing. Source: Shah (2013, p. 237)

Conceptual Guidance Versus Practice: Notable Points of Departure

Earlier sections highlighted conceptual considerations in the use of grant instruments. This was followed by a review of worldwide practices in grant financing of metropolitan areas. This section distills main points of departure of practice from the conceptual guidance.

One size does not fit all. The practice contradicts this, and most countries treat metro governments in generic formula used for grant allocation to all local governments. But this introduces inequities and inefficiencies, as metro government fiscal needs are measured on a yardstick that includes small towns with widely divergent fiscal capacities and needs. This introduces injustice for metro areas as they have above average fiscal capacities as well as needs, but they are treated as if they have above average fiscal capacity and average need. Fair treatment of metro areas requires a metro grant strategy that considers governance, finance, and special needs of metro areas.

Nature of metropolitan services must be taken into consideration the design of grants and other instruments of finance. The practice provides no evidence of this. In fact, the practice even in industrial countries often contradicts this. For example, metropolitan areas in Canada, the United States, the United Kingdom, and a number of developing countries including India use property taxes and input-based conditional grants for school finance, whereas as noted earlier surcharges on personal income taxes and output-based grants are more suitable for school finance. The United Kingdom and United States also use specific-purpose grants for financing police protection in metro areas where general revenues are more suitable instruments of police finance. Grant financing is relevant for financing a fraction of police expenditures that have externality for national security. Matching capital grants with matching rates that vary inversely with fiscal capacity for financing school, health, and transportation facilities are rarely practiced. Museums, sports and fitness facilities, and concert halls are poor candidates for grant finance unless they serve national objectives yet grant financing of such facilities is widely practiced. Benefit spillovers compensation is rarely available to metro areas.

Model of metropolitan governance and finance matter for grant finance. In an earlier section, we highlighted how the models of metropolitan governance and finance matter for type and tools of grant financing. We did not discover any evidence that such considerations entered into designing grant financing of metro areas in practice. This neglect is unfortunate as a holistic view of metropolitan financing and required tools for grant financing is not possible without explicit consideration of governance and finance arrangements. For example, in horizontally coordinated and uncoordinated metro governance, there is a need for intra-metro equalization and use of competitive grants for enhancing competition—the two tools that are rarely practiced. Output-based grants could also be used to facilitate functional, overlapping, and competing single-purpose jurisdictions giving residents greater voice, choice, and exit options. If metro governance is fragmented due to monopoly single-purpose jurisdictions with preferred access to tax finance, then more funds have to be directed to municipal finance through equalization grants. Output-based grants would also serve important tools in ensuring equitable access in the event services are contracted out.

Keep it simple. This principle is frequently ignored in practice, especially in designing revenue sharing and equalization grants. Multiple factors that work at cross purposes are introduced leading to a sacrifice in transparency and equity and efficiency of allocations.

Singular focus. Most general-purpose grant programs have multiple objectives and as a result unlikely to achieve any of the specified objectives. Having each grant instrument focus on a single objective would enhance chances of success.

Input- (or process-) based or ad hoc conditional grant programs undermine metropolitan autonomy, flexibility, fiscal efficiency, and fiscal equity objectives. Specific-purpose transfers available to metro areas are mostly input control conditional grants. The only exceptions are school transfers available to metro areas in Brazil, Canada, Chile, Colombia, Finland, Sweden, Denmark, and Thailand and health transfers in Brazil, Denmark, Finland, and Canada.

Introduce results-based finance to incentivize excellence in service delivery performance. Output-based transfers are rarely practiced but hold great promise for improving metropolitan government performance and accountability while preserving local autonomy.

Introduce sunset clause and review provisions. This is not practiced anywhere in grants to metropolitan areas.

Lessons from International Practices and an Agenda for Reform

A review of worldwide practices leads to the following stylized view of grant financing of metro areas. Metro areas have large economic bases and therefore little a priori needs for grant financing, yet they have strong dependence on central transfers. This is because of the highly constrained fiscal autonomy given to these areas in most countries especially in the developing world with the notable exception of metro areas in China. Such a strong reliance on transfers undermines local autonomy and local accountability. Only Tokyo, Seoul, Busan, Melbourne, Helsinki, Copenhagen, Mumbai, Pune, and Cape Town stand out as being largely self-financed metro areas. The practice of tax-base sharing is practiced only in a few metro areas such as Tokyo, Seoul, and Bangkok. Tax by tax sharing is widely practiced. While such a practice is helpful in ensuring transparency and predictability of transfers, it creates disincentives for the central tax administration to make lesser effort on taxes it has to share with metro areas. General-purpose transfers are formula based, transparent, and predictable, yet they discriminate against metropolitan areas as they utilize a one size fits all (common formula) for all local governments—large or small. Such formula typically incorporates equal per jurisdiction components that discriminate against large metropolitan areas. Compactness is rarely rewarded and higher needs of metro areas for transportation, education, health, culture, and welfare go unrecognized. Specific-purpose transfers are typically ad hoc project-based transfers with input conditionality. Such transfers typically address higher-level mandates with inadequate financing. In general, specific-purpose transfers are intrusive, reward grantsmanship, and distort local priorities. Egregious examples of specific-purpose capital transfers can be seen in Bangkok where central financing for a section of above ground metro was withdrawn leaving poles that support no rails and in Jakarta where external financing of metro was blocked by the central government after local government had already initiated construction leaving an eyesore in its wake. Only a handful of examples of results-based intergovernmental finance and of tournament-based approaches to encourage interjurisdictional competition were discovered in grant financing of sample metropolitan areas. Grants to compensate metro areas for benefit spillovers are also not practiced. Overall emphasis in grant financing of metro areas remains in dealing with vertical fiscal gaps or project-based specific-purpose grants.

To assure that metropolitan areas can play their dual roles in improving economic and social outcomes for residents, it is important to strengthen their fiscal autonomy while at the same time also enhancing their accountability to local residents. This would be possible if metro areas have access to wide array of productive tax bases including income, sales, and environmental taxes and charges. Given the special needs of metro areas, it would be best to have a separate and distinct treatment of these areas in grant financing. Results-based grant financing of social and transportation services and tournament-based approaches to encourage interjurisdictional competition need to be given serious consideration to ensure metropolitan autonomy while strengthening their citizen-based accountability. Incidentally, these reforms have less demanding data requirements than needed for traditional input-based conditional grants.

Overall, the practice of grant financing of metropolitan areas is at variance with the conceptual guidance in both industrial and developing countries. Such divergences represent important opportunities to reform metropolitan finances to enhance quality and access of metro services as well as making metro governments more responsive and accountable to local residents in both developing and industrial countries.

References

Bahl, Roy, Johannes Linn, and Deborah Wetzel. 2013. *Metropolitan Governance and Finance in Developing Countries*. Cambridge, MA: Lincoln Institute of Land Policy.

Bandyopadhyay, Simanti, and M. Govinda Rao. 2009. *Fiscal Health of Selected Indian Cities*. NIPFP, New Delhi, World Bank Working Paper Series, Washington, DC.

Bird, Richard, and Slack, Enid. 2004. *Fiscal Aspects of Metropolitan Governance*. ITP Paper 0401 Rotman School, University of Toronto.

Boadway, Robin, and Anwar Shah, eds. 2007. *Intergovernmental Fiscal Transfers. Principles and the Practice*. Washington, DC: World Bank.

———. 2009. *Fiscal Federalism. Principles and Practice of Multi-order Governance*. London and New York: Cambridge University Press.

Boothe, Robert, Shabih Mohib, and Anwar Shah. 2011. *Central-Local Fiscal Relations in Thailand*. Bangkok: World Bank.

Chernick, Howard, and Andrew Reschovsky. 2006. Local Public Finance: Issues for Metropolitan Regions. In *Competitive Cities in the Global Economy*, ed. OECD, 417–432. Paris: OECD Territorial Reviews.

Dhimitri, Albana, Belinda Ikonomi, and Majlinda Dhuka. 2009. *Financing Metropolitan Government—Tirana City*. Budapest: Open Society Institute.

Elaigwu, J. Isawa. 2009. "Abuja, Nigeria". Chap. 8 in *Finance and Governance of Capital Cities in Federal Systems*, ed. Enid Slack and Rupak Chattopadhyay, 198–221. Montreal: McGill-Queen's University Press.

Frey, Bruno, and Reiner Eichenberger. 1995. Competition Among Jurisdictions: The Idea of FOCJ. In *Competition Among Jurisdictions*, ed. Luder Gerken, 209–229. London: Macmillan.

Gandhi, Natwar, et al. 2009. Washington, District of Columbia, United States of America. Chap. 11 in *Finance and Governance of Capital Cities in Federal Systems*, ed. Enid Slack and Rupak Chattopadhyay, 263–291. Montreal: McGill-Queen's University Press.

Gilorijevic, Žaklina, Miodrag Ferencak, Darko Savić, and Vesna Velović. 2009. *Financing Metropolitan Governments in Transitional Countries—The City of Belgrade*. Budapest: Open Society Institute.

Inman, Robert. 2005. *Financing Cities*. NBER Working Paper No. 11203. Cambridge, MA.

Ionita, Sorin. 2009. *Financing Metropolitan Government—Bucharest*. Budapest: Open Society Institute.

Jefremienko, Marek, and Halina Wolksa. 2007. *The City of Warsaw, Poland*. Budapest: Open Society Institute.

Kitchen, Harry. 2010. *Canada: Governance and Finance of the Greater Toronto Area and Metro Vancouver.* Unpublished paper.

Kopric, Ivan, Anamarija Musa, Tereza Rogic Lugaric, and Tijana Vukojicic. 2007. *The City of Zagreb.* Budapest: Open Society Institute.

Kubatova, Kveta, and Jan Pavel. 2009. *Financing Capital Governments in Transitional Countries—Czech Republic.* Budapest: Open Society Institute.

Kubler, D., and P. Rochat 2010. *Governance and Finance of Large Metropolitan Areas in Federal Systems.* Zurich.

McMillan, Melville. 2008. A Local Perspective on Fiscal Federalism: Practices, Experiences and Lessons from Industrial Countries. Chap. 7 in *Macro Federalism and Local Finance*, ed. Anwar Shah, 245–290. Washington, DC: World Bank.

OECD. 2001. *Competitive Cities in the Global Economy.* Territorial Review, 2006 and Cities for Citizens: Improving Metropolitan Governance.

———. 2003a. *Territorial Review Melbourne, Australia.* Paris: OECD.

———. 2003b. *Territorial Review Helsinki, Finland.* Paris: OECD.

———. 2004a. *Territorial Review, Mexico City, Mexico.* Paris: OECD.

———. 2004b. *Territorial Review Montreal, Canada.* Paris: OECD.

———. 2004c. *Territorial Review Athens Greece.* Paris: OECD.

———. 2005a. *Territorial Review Seoul, Korea.* Paris: OECD.

———. 2005b. *Territorial Review Busan, Korea.* Paris: OECD.

———. 2006a. *Territorial Review Stockholm, Sweden.* Paris: OECD.

———. 2006b. *Territorial Review Milan.* Italy: OECD.

———. 2007. *Territorial Review Madrid, Spain.* Paris: OECD.

———. 2008a. *Territorial Review Istanbul, Turkey.* Paris: OECD.

———. 2008b. *Territorial Review Cape Town, South Africa.* Paris: OECD.

———. 2009. *Territorial Review, Copenhagen, Denmark.* Paris: OECD.

———. 2010. *Territorial Review Toronto, Canada.* Paris: OECD.

Roscovan, Mihai, and Doina Melnic. 2009. *Financing Capital Governments in Transitional Countries: The Case of Chisinau.* Budapest: Open Society Institute.

Shah, Anwar. 2010a. *Sponsoring a Race to the Top: The Case for Results Based Intergovernmental Finance for Merit Goods.* Policy Research Working Paper No. 5172. Washington, DC: World Bank.

———. 2010b. Adapting to a Changing World. Reflections on the Reform of Local Governance for the Next Decade. In *Local Public Sector: A Nordic Perspective*, ed. Antti Moisio, 185–220. Helsinki: Office of the Prime Minister.

———. 2012a. Options for Financing Subnational Governments in Indonesia. In *Fiscal Decentralization in Indonesia: A Decade After the Big Bang*, ed. Ministry of Finance, 222–254. Jakarta: University of Indonesia Press.

———. 2012b. *Public Services and Expenditure Needs Equalization. Reflections on Principles and Worldwide Comparative Practices.* World Bank Policy Research Working Paper Series no. WPS6006, World Bank, Washington, DC.

———. 2012c. Autonomy with Equity and Accountability: Towards a More Transparent, Objective, Predictable and Simpler (TOPS) System of Central Financing of Provincial-Local Expenditures in Indonesia. World Bank Policy Research Working Paper Series WPS6004, March, World Bank, Washington, DC.

———. 2013. Grant Financing of Metropolitan Areas: A Review of Principles and Worldwide Practices. Chap. 9 in *Metropolitan Governance and Finance in Developing Countries*, ed. Roy Bahl, Johannes Linn, and Deborah Wetzel, 213–242. Cambridge, MA: Lincoln Institute of Land Policy.

Shah, Anwar, and Chunli Shen. 2007. Fine Tuning the Intergovernmental Transfer System to Create a Harmonious Society and a Level Playing Field for Regional Development. In *Public Finance in China*, ed. Jiwei Lou and Shuilin Wang. Washington, DC: World Bank.

Slack, Enid. 2006. Fiscal Aspects of Alternative Methods of Governing Large Metropolitan Areas. Chap. 6 in *Perspectives on Fiscal Federalism*, ed. Richard Bird and Francois Vaillancourt. Washington, DC: World Bank.

———. 2007. Grants to Large Cities and Metropolitan Areas. Chap. 6 in *Intergovernmental Fiscal Transfers. Principles and Practice*, ed. Robin Boadway and Anwar Shah, 453–482. Washington, DC: World Bank.

Sridhar, Kala, Simanti Bandyopadhyay, and Satadru Sikdar. 2008a. *Improving the Fiscal Health of Indian Cities: A Pilot Study of Chennai.* New Delhi: National Institute of Public Finance and Policy.

———. 2008b. *Improving the Fiscal Health of Indian Cities: A Pilot Study of Delhi.* New Delhi: National Institute of Public Finance and Policy.

———. 2008c. *Improving the Fiscal Health of Indian Cities: A Pilot Study of Hyderabad.* New Delhi: National Institute of Public Finance and Policy.

United Kingdom, Government of. 2010. *Local Government Financial Statistics England, No. 20.* London: Communities and Local Government Department.

Van Wynsberghe, Caroline. 2009. Brussels, Belgium. Chap. 2 in *Finance and Governance of Capital Cities in Federal Systems*, ed. Enid Slack and Rupak Chattopadhyay, 33–54. Montreal: McGill-Queen's University Press.

Veljanovski, Aleksandra M. 2009. *The City of Skopje.* Budapest: Open Society Institute.

Zinnes, Clifford. 2009. *Tournament Approaches to Policy Reform. Making Development Assistance More Effective.* Washington, DC: Brookings Institution Press.

Name Index[1]

[1] Note: Page numbers followed by 'n' refer to notes.

H. Kitchen et al., *Local Public Finance and Economics*,
https://doi.org/10.1007/978-3-030-21986-4

C

D

E

F

G

H

I

J

Subject Index[1]

[1] Note: Page numbers followed by 'n' refer to notes.

H. Kitchen et al., *Local Public Finance and Economics*,
https://doi.org/10.1007/978-3-030-21986-4

E

F

O

P

R

The manufacturer's authorised representative in the EU is Springer Nature Customer Service Centre GmbH, Europaplatz 3, 69115 Heidelberg, Germany. If you have any concerns regarding our products, please contact ProductSafety@springernature.com

Printed and bound by CPI Group (UK) Ltd, Croydon, CR0 4YY
05/10/2026
02228125-0019